Microsoft® Visual C#® .NET Programming:

From Problem Analysis to Program Design

Microsoft® Visual C#® .NET Programming:

From Problem Analysis to Program Design

Barbara Doyle

Australia • Canada • Mexico • Singapore • Spain • United Kingdom • United States

THOMSON
COURSE TECHNOLOGY

Microsoft® Visual C#® .NET Programming: From Problem Analysis to Program Design
by Barbara Doyle

Managing Editor:
Jennifer Muroff

Editorial Assistant:
Amanda Piantedosi

Cover Designer:
Steve Deschene

Senior Product Manager:
Tricia Boyle

Production Editor:
Philippa Lehar

Compositor:
Gex, Inc.

Development Editor:
Betsey Henkels

Product Marketing Manager:
Amy Yarnevich

Manufacturing Coordinator:
Laura Burns

Associate Product Manager:
Mirella Misiaszek

Disclaimer
Course Technology reserves the right to revise this publication and make changes from time to time in its content without notice. The programs in this book are for instructional purposes only. They have been tested with care but are not guaranteed for any particular intent beyond educational purposes. The author and the publisher do not offer any warranties or representations, nor do they accept any liabilities with respect to the programs.

ISBN-13: 978-0-619-15997-9
ISBN-10: 0-619-15997-9

Brief Contents

Table of
Contents

5. Making Decisions   195

6. Repeating Instructions   251

10. Advanced Object-Oriented Programming Features   555

APPENDIX A Compiling and Running an Application from the Command Line

Preface

Microsoft Visual C# .NET Programming: From Problem Analysis to Program Design requires no previous introduction to programming and only a mathematical background of high school algebra. The book uses C# .NET as the programming language for software development; however, the basic programming concepts presented can be applied to a number of other languages. Instead of focusing on the syntax of the C# language, this book uses the C# language to present general programming concepts. It is the belief of the author that once you develop a thorough understanding of one programming language, you can effectively apply those concepts to other programming languages.

Why C#?

C# .NET is a true object-oriented language that includes a rich set of instruction statements. C# was the language used for development of much of .NET, the new Microsoft programming paradigm that includes a collection of more than 2,000 predefined classes that make up the Framework Class Library (FCL). Thus, C# has access to a large collection of predefined classes similar to those available to Java. C# provides tools that make it easy to create graphical user interfaces—similar to the tools Visual Basic programmers have employed for years. C# also provides the pure data crunching horsepower to which C/C++ programmers have become accustomed. But unlike other languages, C# was designed from scratch to accommodate Internet and Windows applications. For these reasons, C# was chosen as the language for this book.

Going Beyond the Traditional CS1 Course

This book was written for the Computer Science 1 (CS1) student and includes all of the basic programming constructs normally covered in the traditional CS1 foundation course for the Computer Science curriculum. But this book goes beyond what is traditionally found in most CS1 textbooks and, because of the inclusion of a number of advanced applications, this textbook could also be used in an intermediate course for students who have already been exposed to some programming concepts.

Advanced Topics

After building a solid programming foundation, this book presents rapid application development techniques that can be used to build a number of advanced types of applications. Illustrating the drag and drop construction approach used with Visual Studio .NET, Windows and Web applications are created. Readers are introduced to the event-driven programming model, which is based on interactively capturing and responding to user input on Windows and Web forms. In the past, CS1 courses and even CS2 courses did not include this model.

As a book for first-time programmers, this book is unusual in introducing applications that retrieve and update data in databases such as those created using Microsoft Access. Other interesting topics include creating and using XML Web Services, programming applications for mobile devices—such as personal digital assistants (PDAs), and developing stand-alone .dll components (class libraries). All of these advanced features are discussed after you have gained a thorough understanding of the basic components found in programming languages.

APPROACH

A problem solving methodology based on object-oriented software development is introduced early and used throughout the book. Programming Examples are presented at the end of each chapter, and each example follows a consistent approach: analyzing the problem specifications, designing a solution, implementing the design, and verifying or validating the solution structures.

The author believes that the best way to learn to program is to experience programming. This assumption drives the material presented in this textbook. As new concepts are introduced, they are described using figures and illustrations. Examples are shown and discussed as they relate to the concept being presented. With a hands-on approach to learning, you practice and solidify the concepts presented by completing the end of the chapter exercises. You are also encouraged throughout the book to explore and make use of the more than 2,000 classes that make up the Framework Class Library (FCL).

Every chapter begins with a list of objectives and a short overview of the previous chapter. Text in each chapter is supplemented with figures and tables to help visual learners grasp the concepts being presented. Each chapter is sprinkled with useful tips and hints on the concepts being presented, and code snippets are embedded as new concepts are introduced in each chapter. In addition, each chapter contains complete working programs illustrating an application using C#. Every chapter ends with a summary of the major points covered in that chapter and review exercises in both objective and subjective formats. Every chapter contains ten programming exercises that give you an opportunity to experience programming.

Using this Book for Two Different Courses

Although this book is primarily intended for a beginning programming course, it will also work well in an intermediate course. For courses introducing students to programming, Chapters 1 through 7 should be covered in detail. Depending on how quickly students are able to grasp the material, the course could end in any of the chapters following Chapter 7. For example, ending with Chapter 8, Introduction to Windows Programming, would give students an opportunity to get excited about continuing their work in programming in upcoming semesters.

For an intermediate course, Chapter 1 could be skipped and students could merely scan Chapters 2, 3, 5 and 6. Scanning these chapters, students could compare and contrast the details of the C# language with programming languages they know. For the intermediate course, Chapters 4 and 7 should be covered, because topics covered in these chapters—Methods and Behaviors, and Arrays and Collections—are often more difficult for the student to grasp. The remainder of the book beginning in Chapter 8 would be included for the intermediate course.

Overview of the Chapters

Chapter 1 briefly reviews the history of computers and programming languages including the evolution of C# and .NET. This chapter introduces data and describes how it is represented. The primary types of hardware components are described and differing types of software are discussed. This chapter explains the difference between structured and object-oriented programming and includes the software development methodology used throughout the remainder of the book.

Chapter 2 describes the different types of applications that can be developed using C#. It discusses the basic elements found in a C# program. It illustrates how to compile, run, and debug an application. After completing Chapter 2, you are ready to write programs. The focus in Chapter 3 is data types and expressions. You gain an understanding of how types, classes, and objects are related. You also learn how to perform arithmetic procedures on the data, how to display formatted data, and how expressions are evaluated using the rules of precedence. Chapter 4 extends the manipulation of the data through introducing methods and behaviors of the data. You learn to write statements that call methods and to write your own instance and class methods. You learn how to pass arguments to methods that return values and to those that do not. Chapters 5 and 6 introduce control structures that alter the sequential flow of execution. Selection control constructs are introduced in Chapter 5. Looping is introduced in Chapter 6. Chapter 7 discusses arrays and collections. Methods of the String and ArrayList class are also included in this chapter. Both single and multi-dimensional arrays are introduced.

Chapters 8 and 9 present a different way of programming, which is based on interactively responding to events. You are introduced to a number of classes in the FCL that are used to create Windows applications. Elements of good design are discussed in Chapter 8. Delegates are explored in Chapter 9. Visual Studio .NET's drag and drop approach to rapid application development is introduced and used in these chapters.

Advanced object-oriented programming features are the focus of Chapter 10. You are introduced to component-based development and learn how to create your own class library files. Inheritance, interfaces, abstract classes, and polymorphic programming are discussed in detail. Advanced features such as overriding, overloading, and the use of virtual methods are also included in Chapter 10.

Exception-handling techniques are introduced in Chapter 11. Chapter 11 also illustrates how data from sources other than the keyboard can be used. Readers learn how to access data stored in files and database tables. The file stream and ActiveX Data Objects (ADO.NET) classes are introduced.

The focus of Chapter 12 is on Web applications. You explore how the design of Web-based applications differs from Windows applications. You discover the differences between static and dynamic Web pages and how HTML and Web server controls differ. In Chapter 12, you learn what a Web service is and how to write one. Also included in Chapter 12 is an introduction to mobile applications that can be viewed with small personal devices such as a personal digital assistant (PDA). Chapter 12 illustrates how validation controls can be used to check users' input values and shows how the ADO.NET classes, introduced in Chapter 11, can also be used with Web applications to access database records.

Appendix A describes how you can compile and execute a C# program from the command line. It includes details on how to download Microsoft's Framework Software Development Kit, a free download that includes everything needed to run C# programs from the command line.

Appendix B assumes development will be done using the Integrated Development Environment (IDE) of Visual Studio .NET. To increase productivity, this appendix presents suggestions for customizing the appearance and behavior of the IDE.

Appendix C lists the Unicode and ASCII (American Standard Code for Information Interchange) character sets. Appendix D shows the precedence of the C# operators and Appendix E lists the C# keywords.

FEATURES

Every chapter in this book includes the following features. These features are both conducive to learning in the classroom and enable you to learn the material at your own pace.

- Four-color interior design shows accurate C# code and related comments.

- Learning objectives offer an outline of the concepts discussed in detail in the chapter.

- Hundreds of visual diagrams throughout the text illustrate difficult concepts.

- Syntax boxes show the general form for different types of statements.

- Numbered examples illustrate the key concepts with their relevant code, and the code is often followed by a sample run. An explanation follows that describes the functions of the most difficult lines of code.

- Notes highlight important facts about the concepts introduced in the chapter.

- Numerous tables are included which describe and summarize information compactly for easy viewing.

- Programming Examples are complete programs featured at the end of the chapter. The examples contain the distinct stages of preparing a problem specification, analyzing the problem, designing the solution, and coding the solution.

- Quick Reviews offer a summary of the concepts covered in the chapter.

- Exercises further reinforce learning and ensure that students have, in fact, absorbed the material.

- Programming Exercises challenge students to write C# programs with a specified outcome.

- Glossary at the end of the book lists all the key terms in alphabetical order along with definitions, for easy reference.

From beginning to end, the concepts are introduced at a pace that is conducive to learning. The writing style of this book is simple and straightforward, and it parallels the teaching style of a classroom. The concepts introduced are described using examples and small programs.

Chapters have two types of programs. The first type includes small programs that are part of the numbered examples and are used to explain key concepts. This book also features numerous case studies called Programming Examples. These Programming Examples are placed at the end of the chapters to pull together many of the concepts presented throughout the chapter. The programs are designed to be methodical and workable. Each Programming Example starts with a Problem Analysis and is then followed by the Algorithm Design. Every step of the algorithm is then coded in C#. In addition to teaching problem-solving techniques, these detailed programs show the user how to implement concepts in an actual C# program. Students are encouraged to study the Programming Examples very carefully in order to learn C# effectively.

All source code and solutions have been written, compiled, and tested by quality assurance with Visual Studio .NET 2003 Professional and Visual C# .NET 2003 Standard Edition, using both Windows 2000 and Windows XP.

Microsoft® Visual C#® .NET 2003 Standard Edition can be packaged with this text. Please contact your Course Technology Sales Representative for more information.

Visual Preview of Key Features

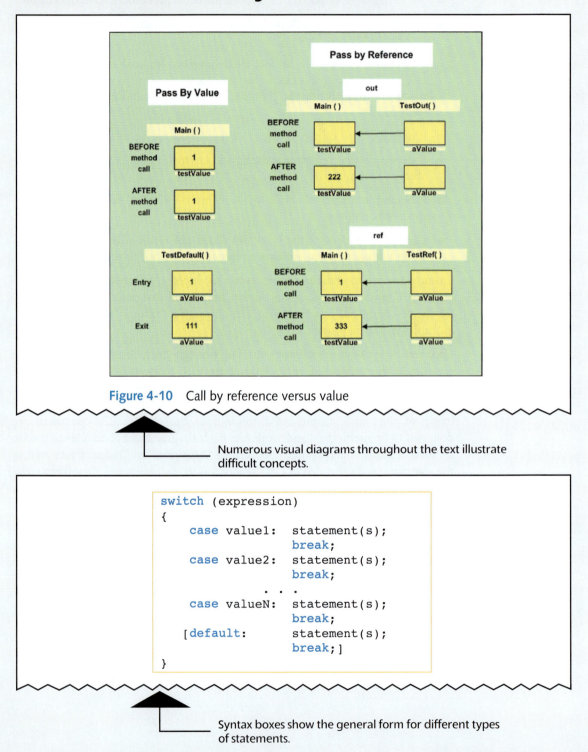

Figure 4-10 Call by reference versus value

Numerous visual diagrams throughout the text illustrate difficult concepts.

```
switch (expression)
{
    case value1:  statement(s);
                  break;
    case value2:  statement(s);
                  break;
               . . .
    case valueN:  statement(s);
                  break;
    [default:     statement(s);
                  break;]

}
```

Syntax boxes show the general form for different types of statements.

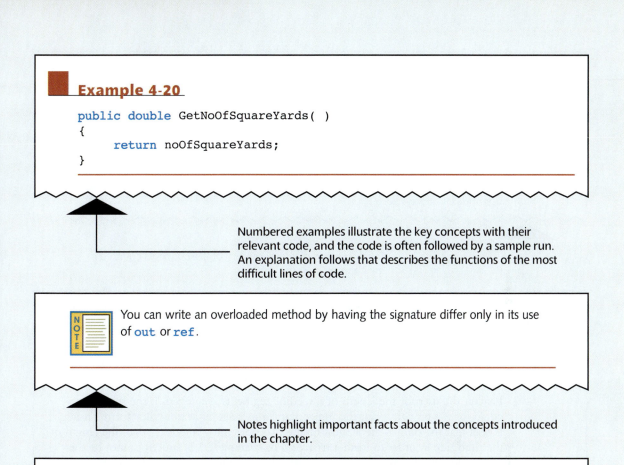

Example 4-20

```
public double GetNoOfSquareYards( )
{
    return noOfSquareYards;
}
```

Numbered examples illustrate the key concepts with their relevant code, and the code is often followed by a sample run. An explanation follows that describes the functions of the most difficult lines of code.

NOTE You can write an overloaded method by having the signature differ only in its use of **out** or **ref**.

Notes highlight important facts about the concepts introduced in the chapter.

PROGRAMMING EXAMPLE: MANATEE APPLICATION

This example demonstrates the use of collections in the analysis, design, and implementation of a program. Array and **string** objects are included. An application is created to monitor manatees, which are still in danger of extinction and are being monitored on a daily basis in some areas. To design this application, a number of **string** methods are used. Parallel arrays are created to store the location, date, and number present at each sighting. The application is designed using two classes, and the problem specification is shown in Figure 7-16.

Programming Examples are complete programs featured at the end of the chapter. The examples contain the distinct stages of preparing a problem specification, analyzing the problem, designing the solution, and coding the solution.

PROGRAMMING EXERCISES

1. Write a program that generates 100 random numbers between 0 and 1000. Display the number of even values generated as well as the smallest, largest, and the range of values. Output should be displayed in a Windows message box.

2. Prompt the user for the length of three line segments as integers. If the three lines could form a triangle, print the integers and a message indicating they form a triangle. Recall that the sum of the lengths of any two sides must be greater than the length of the third side in order to form a triangle. For example, 20, 5, and 10 cannot be the lengths of the sides of a triangle because 5 + 10 is not greater than 20. For line segments that do not form a triangle, print the integers and an appropriate message indicating no triangle can be created. Use a state-controlled loop to allow users to enter as many different combinations as they like.

3. Write a program to calculate the average of all scores entered between 0 and 100. Use a sentinel-controlled loop variable to terminate the loop. After values are entered and the average calculated, test the average to determine whether an A, B, C, D, or F should be recorded. The scoring rubric is as follows:

   A—90-100; B—80-89; C—70-79; D—60-69; F < 60.

1. The value contained within the square brackets that is used to indicate the length of the array must be a(n):

    a. `class`

    b. `double`

    c. `string`

    d. integer

    e. none of the above

2. Which of the following would be the best declaration for an array to store the high temperature for each day of one full week?

    a. `int temp1, temp2, temp3, temp4, temp5, temp6, temp7;`

    b. `int temp [7] = new int [7];`

    c. `temp int [ ] = new temp[7];`

    d. `int [ ] temp = new temp [7];`

    e. `int [ ] temp = new temp [8];`

3. Assume an array called **num** is declared to store four elements. Which of the following statements correctly assigns the value 100 to each of the elements?

    a. `for(x = 0; x < 3; ++x) num [x] = 100`

    b. `for(x = 0; x < 4; ++x) num [x] = 100;`

    c. `for(x = 1; x < 4; ++x) num [x] = 100;`

    d. `for(x = 1; x < 5; ++x) num [x] = 100;`

    e. none of the above

Exercises further reinforce learning and ensure that students have, in fact, absorbed the material.

TEACHING TOOLS

The following supplemental materials are available when this book is used in a classroom setting. All of the teaching tools available with this book are provided to the instructor on a single CD-ROM.

Electronic Instructor's Manual. The Instructor's Manual that accompanies this textbook includes additional instructional material to assist in class preparation, including suggestions for lecture topics.

ExamView®. This textbook is accompanied by ExamView, a powerful testing software package that allows instructors to create and administer printed, computer (LAN-based), and Internet exams. ExamView includes hundreds of questions that correspond to the topics covered in this text, enabling students to generate detailed study guides that include page references for further review. These computer-based and Internet testing components allow students to take exams at their computers, and save the instructor time because each exam is graded automatically.

PowerPoint Presentations. This book comes with Microsoft PowerPoint slides for each chapter. These are included as a teaching aid for classroom presentations, either to make available to students on the network for chapter review, or to be printed for classroom distribution. Instructors can add their own slides for additional topics that they introduce to the class.

Distance Learning. Course Technology is proud to present online courses in WebCT and Blackboard to provide the most complete and dynamic learning experience possible. When you add online content to one of your courses, you're providing a gateway to the 21st century's most important information resource. We hope you will make the most of your course, both online and offline. For more information on how to bring distance learning to your course, contact your local Course Technology sales representative.

Examples Source Code. The complete Visual Studio .NET project files for the examples included within each chapter are available at **www.course.com**, and are also available on the Teaching Tools CD-ROM. The individual source code files are stored with a .cs extension inside the project subdirectory.

Programming Exercises Solution Files. The complete Visual Studio .NET project files for the solutions to all programming exercises included at the end of the chapter are available at **www.course.com**, and are also available on the Teaching Tools CD-ROM. The individual source code files are stored with a .cs extension inside the project subdirectory.

ACKNOWLEDGEMENTS

Special thanks go to a number of people for making this book a reality. The project has been a huge undertaking for me. Without the assistance of a lot of people, it would never have been completed in a timely manner. Betsey Henkels, Developmental Editor, cannot be praised enough for her contribution to the book. Her guidance and hard work kept me grounded. I especially thank Betsey for the early morning and weekend edits that she did to keep the book on schedule. Also, thanks go out to Tricia Boyle, Senior Product Manager, for her positive comments, guidance, and know-how.

I also owe a debt of gratitude to Jennifer Muroff, Managing Editor, who suggested I consider writing the book in the first place. Her faith and confidence in me is greatly appreciated. Thanks to Philippa Lehar, Production Editor, for working with us to help produce a consistently formatted product. Thanks also go out to the Copyeditor, Mark Goodin, and the Quality Assurance Testers, Serge Palladino, Marianne Snow, and Burt LaFontaine for examining the manuscript and source code so methodologically. The book is better because of their careful scrutiny of the manuscript.

Thanks go out to a number of my students for their involvement in the project. Special thanks go to Denise Rutan and Kurt Labarbera for reading the manuscript and solving the programming exercises at the end of chapters. Without their assistance, a number of deadlines would have been missed. Also thanks to another student, Ken Athans, for volunteering to read the chapters and providing suggestions for improvements. His comments were greatly appreciated.

I am very grateful to the following reviewers for their uplifting comments and suggestions for improvements: Randal L. Albert, Oregon Institute of Technology; Corinne Hoisington, Central Virginia Community College; Dennie Van Tassel, Gavilan College; and Matt Weisfeld, Cuyahoga Community College. I hope that the reviewers will see that many of their suggestions were implemented. The textbook is much improved through their contributions.

I would also like to thank my family for their understanding while I was writing. Thanks to my parents, Howard and Alma King, who even though they are hundreds of miles away, have always been sources of encouragement and inspiration to me. And most importantly, a super special thanks goes to David for the pats on the back and the confidence and faith he showed in me that I could complete this project.

1

Introduction to Computing and Programming

Computers have penetrated every aspect of our society and have greatly simplified many tasks. Can you picture yourself typing a paper on an electric typewriter? Would you use an eraser to make your corrections? Would you start from scratch to increase or decrease your margins or line spacing? Can you imagine living in an age without electronic mail? What would you do without an automatic teller machine (ATM) in your neighborhood?

Computers have become such an integral part of our lives that many of their functions are taken for granted. Yet, only a few years ago, word processing, e-mail, and ATMs were unknown. Advances in computing are occurring every day, and the programs that distinguish computers have become very complex. The technology of wireless communication is advancing quickly. Mobile applications for Web-enabled phones, pocket PCs, and personal digital assistants (PDAs) are increasingly in demand. To reach this level of complexity, software development has gone through a number of eras, and today technical advances accumulate faster and faster. What new types of computer services and programs will be integral to our daily lives in the future? This book focuses on creating software programs. Before beginning the journey into software development, a historical perspective on computing is included to help you see the potential for advancements that awaits you.

HISTORY OF COMPUTERS

Computing dates back some 5000 years. Many consider the abacus, which is pictured in Figure 1-1, to be the first computer. Used by merchants of the past and present for trading transactions, the abacus is a calculating device that uses a system of sliding beads on a rack for addition and subtraction.

Figure 1-1   The abacus, the earliest computing device

In 1642, another calculating device, called the Pascaline, was created. The Pascaline had eight movable dials on wheels that could calculate sums up to eight figures long. Both the abacus and Pascaline could perform only addition and subtraction. It was not until the 1830s that the first general-purpose computer, the Analytical Engine, was available.

Charles Babbage and his assistant, Lady Augusta Ada Bryon, Countess of Lovelace, designed the Analytical Engine. Although it was very primitive by today's standards, it was the proto-type for what is known today as a general-purpose computer. The Analytical Engine included input devices, memory storage, a control unit that allowed processing instructions in any sequence, and output devices.

In the 1980s, the U.S. Defense Department named the Ada programming language in honor of Lady Lovelace. Some suggest that she was the world's first programmer. Not so. She was probably the fourth or fifth person to write programs. She did program-ming as a student of Charles Babbage and reworked some of his calculations.

Many computer historians believe the present day to be either the fourth or the fifth gener-ation of modern computing. Each era is characterized by an important advancement. In the mid-1940s, the Second World War, with its need for strategic types of calculations, spurred on the first generation of general-purpose machines. These large, first-generation computers were distinguished by the use of vacuum tubes. They were difficult to program and limited in functionality. The operating instructions were made to order for each specific task.

The invention of the transistor in 1956 led to second-generation computers, which were smaller, faster, more reliable, and more energy efficient than their predecessors. The software industry was born during the second generation of computers with the introduction of FORTRAN and COBOL.

The third generation, 1964–1971, saw computers become smaller, as transistors were squeezed onto small silicon discs (single chips) which were called semiconductors. Operating systems, as they are known today, which allowed machines to run many different programs at once, were also first seen in third-generation systems.

As time passed, chips kept getting smaller and capable of storing more transistors, making computers more powerful and less expensive. The Intel 4004 chip, developed in 1971, placed the most important components of a computer (central processing unit, memory, and input and output controls) on a minuscule chip about half the size of a dime. Many household items such as microwave ovens, television sets, and automobiles benefited from the fourth generation of computing. Figure 1-2 shows an Intel chip.

Figure 1-2   Intel chip

During the fourth generation, computer manufacturers tried to bring computing to general consumers. In 1981, IBM introduced its personal computer (PC). The 1980s saw an expansion in computer use as clones of the IBM PC made the personal computer even more affordable. The number of personal computers in use more than doubled from two million in 1981 to 5.5 million in 1982. Ten years later, 65 million PCs were in use.

> **NOTE** According to the September 2001 *U.S. Census Bureau's Current Population Survey*, 90% of children between the ages of 5 and 17 use computers. In September 2001, 174 million people (or 66% of the population) in the United States used computers. That number continues to grow, up from 51% in August 2000, and 42% in December 1998.

Defining a fifth generation of systems is somewhat difficult because the generation is still young. Computers can now accept spoken word instructions, imitate human reasoning through artificial intelligence, and communicate with devices instantaneously around the globe by transmitting digital media. Mobile applications are growing. By applying problem-solving steps, expert systems assist doctors in making diagnoses. Healthcare professionals are now using handheld devices in patients' rooms to retrieve and update patient records. Using handheld devices, drivers of delivery trucks are accessing global positioning satellites (GPS) to verify locations of customers for pickups and deliveries. Sitting at a traffic light, you can check your e-mail, make airline reservations, remotely monitor and manage household appliances, and access your bank checking and savings accounts. Using wireless local area network (LAN) cards, students can access a professor's notes when they enter the classroom.

Major advances in software are anticipated as Integrated Development Environments (IDEs) such as Visual Studio .NET (pronounced dot net) make it easier to develop applications for the Internet rapidly. Because of the programmability of the computer, the imagination of software developers is set free to conjure the computing functions of the future.

The power of computers rests on the software programs they use. Understanding how a computer processes data is fundamental to your understanding of the software development process. The next section discusses what makes up a computer system.

PHYSICAL COMPONENTS OF A COMPUTER SYSTEM

Looking back historically from the first generation of general-purpose computers through the present, you can see that computer systems share a number of common features. **General-purpose computer** systems are electronic devices that process data and are composed of hardware and software. **Hardware** refers to the physical devices that you can touch. **Software** refers to the programs—the sets of instructions that make the hardware function.

Hardware

Hardware is made up of a system unit, which houses the main circuit board and peripheral devices. The system unit can also contain modems and network and other controller cards. The hardware components facilitate input, processing, storage, and output of data in the form of information. Figure 1-3 shows how these components interact. As shown in the figure, data and programs are input through the keyboard, mouse, or storage devices. Next, processing occurs in the system unit, and the processing results are displayed on the monitor, sent to the printer, or saved to storage devices.

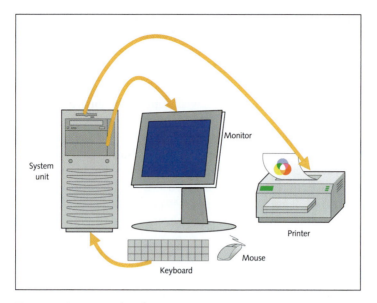

Figure 1-3 Major hardware components

Processor

The **central processing unit (CPU)** is the brain of the computer. Housed inside the system unit on a silicon chip, it is the most important hardware element.

> The CPU is the smallest and most expensive major component inside the system unit.

The CPU has two major roles. It performs the arithmetic and logical comparisons on data and coordinates the operations of the system. Despite its sophistication, it can only carry out very simple instructions such as addition and subtraction or movement of items in memory from one location to another. Much of the power of the system comes from the speed with which the processor is able to carry out its instructions.

Internally, the two major components of the CPU are the control unit (CU) and the arithmetic logic unit (ALU). The **control unit** serves as the traffic cop, directing the flow of information. It is responsible for determining where to get the next instruction. The CU fetches and decodes the instructions and controls the overall operation of the other components of the CPU. The **arithmetic logic unit** performs the actual computations and comparisons on the data. The basic steps of the instruction cycle of the computer are fetch, decode, execute, and store, as is shown in Figure 1-4.

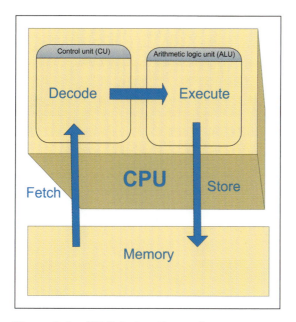

Figure 1-4   CPU's instruction cycle

The **instruction cycle** consists of fetching a program instruction from memory, decoding the instruction, executing it, and then storing the result in memory. One cycle may take one or two clock ticks, with 1 Hz equal to one clock tick per second.

Storage

Computers have two different types of storage: primary and auxiliary. **Primary storage** is the internal or **main memory** of the system. Also commonly called **random-access memory (RAM)**, main memory is simply a device that holds instructions and data. Before data can be used in calculations and before instructions can be executed, they must be inside the computer in main memory. The more RAM a system has, the faster and more efficiently the computer can perform its tasks. Main memory is **volatile**; which means that when the power is turned off, anything placed only in main memory is lost. Main memory is also limited in size; thus, only instructions that are currently being executed or data that is currently being processed is placed in this type of storage.

Memory is divided into sections, or cells, and each cell can hold an equal amount of data. As shown in Figure 1-5, each cell has a unique **address** that can be used to access directly the contents stored inside the cell. You can think of each cell as being made up of eight "switches" set to either on or off. When the switch is in the on position, it is represented by a 1. When the switch is in the off position, it is represented by a 0. The switches are known as bits. The section on data representation describes how data is represented in the cells.

Address	Contents
1000	00100100
1001	00011000
1002	00001100
⋮	⋮
⋮	⋮
2004	00010001
2005	00011100

Figure 1-5   Addressing in memory

Auxiliary storage, also called **secondary storage**, is nonvolatile, permanent memory. It can hold data for long periods of time—even when there is no power to the system. When the system power is interrupted and then turned back on, the data and instructions that were stored on secondary storage media are unharmed. The most common types of secondary storage devices are magnetic disks and optical discs. CDs, DVDs, and flash memory are also forms of secondary storage. The floppy disk, another form of secondary storage device, is being replaced by media such as flash memory keys that plug into your computer. These keys offer much more portable storage capacity, making it easier to transfer data from one computer to another. Hard disk storage media are another type of storage. The more storage capacity the hard disk has, the more functionality the system can offer. This is because most programs are stored (loaded) on the hard disk.

Input and Output Devices

For a computer to produce information, there must be a way to get data inside the machine. The primary input devices are the keyboard, the mouse, and the disk drive. Primary output devices are screens, printers, and disk drives. These devices taken together are sometimes called **peripheral devices**.

You may have noted that magnetic disks and optical discs were categorized as a type of storage. To retrieve and store data and programs on these types of media, the disk drive is used. "Drive" is a common name used by several types of storage media, including magnetic drives such as hard disks, Zip drives, as well as floppy disks and optical drives such CDs and DVDs. Thus, the device drive is used to input data and programs and to output results.

DATA REPRESENTATION

1

You may hear someone say that his computer has a 32-bit processor with 512 megabytes of RAM and 60 gigabytes of hard disk space. Another person tells you her flash memory key holds 128 megabytes. Exactly what does this mean?

Bits

To begin, the word **bit** is a shortening of the words "Binary digIT." Binary means two; thus, a binary digit can hold one of two values, 0 or 1. For data representation, the 1 and 0 correspond to on and off, respectively. When thinking about bits, it may help you to picture a circuit (switch) turned on or turned off. The number 1 represents the circuit as being turned on.

Bytes

A single bit is rarely used alone in computers to represent data. Computer memories are commonly divided into 8-bit groupings. This 8-bit combination is called a **byte**. In the simplest terms, with each of the switches being known as a bit, it takes a combination of eight switches to represent one character, such as the letter A. With eight bits representing one byte and one byte representing one keystroke, it would take 11 bytes to represent the word "programming." You might wonder why it takes eight bits to make a byte. The 8-bit byte is a format that people settled on through trial and error over the past 50 years.

Binary Number System

The computer stores data by setting the switches in a cell of memory to a pattern that represents a character. To represent data, computers use the base-2 number system, also known as the **binary number system**. Our base-10 number system, called the **decimal system**, uses ten symbols ranging from 0 to 9 to represent a value. Base 2 has only two symbols, the values 0 and 1. Therefore, a binary value might look something like 01101001, because it is composed of only 0s and 1s. How do you determine the decimal equivalent value of the binary number 01101001? If you understand the decimal (base-10) positional number system, it is easy to translate those concepts to any other base number system. Figure 1-6 illustrates how 1326 is derived in base 10.

$$10^3 \quad 10^2 \quad 10^1 \quad 10^0$$
$$(1000) \quad (100) \quad (10) \quad (1)$$
$$1 \qquad 3 \qquad 2 \qquad 6$$

	1 times 10^3 (1000)	= 1000
+	3 times 10^2 (100)	= 300
+	2 times 10^1 (10)	= 20
+	6 times 10^0 (1)	= 6
		1326

Figure 1-6   Base–10 positional notation of 1326

Figure 1-7 uses those same concepts with base 2 to illustrate the decimal equivalent of 01101001. In Figure 1-7, you see that the number 01101001 in binary is equivalent to the number 105 in decimal.

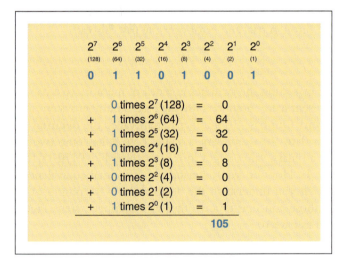

$$2^7 \quad 2^6 \quad 2^5 \quad 2^4 \quad 2^3 \quad 2^2 \quad 2^1 \quad 2^0$$
$$(128) \ (64) \ (32) \ (16) \ (8) \ (4) \ (2) \ (1)$$
$$0 \quad 1 \quad 1 \quad 0 \quad 1 \quad 0 \quad 0 \quad 1$$

	0 times 2^7 (128)	= 0
+	1 times 2^6 (64)	= 64
+	1 times 2^5 (32)	= 32
+	0 times 2^4 (16)	= 0
+	1 times 2^3 (8)	= 8
+	0 times 2^2 (4)	= 0
+	0 times 2^1 (2)	= 0
+	1 times 2^0 (1)	= 1
		105

Figure 1-7   Decimal equivalent of 01101001

You can see from Figure 1-7 that in the binary number system, each bit holds a value of increasing powers of 2. Table 1-1 shows the decimal value when the bits contain various values. As indicated in the table, when all the bits are turned on with a 1 representation, the equivalent decimal value is 255.

Table 1-1 Binary equivalent of selected decimal values

Decimal value	Binary equivalent
0	00000000
1	00000001
2	00000010
3	00000011
4	00000100
5	00000101
6	00000110
7	00000111
8	00001000
...	...
254	11111110
255	11111111

Since it is difficult to read a series of binary numbers, two shorthand versions were developed to make viewing the contents of memory locations easier. Base 16, the **hexadecimal numbering system**, works on powers of sixteen. Base 8, the **octal numbering system**, uses powers of eight. Both are used to express binary numbers more compactly. As with any other positional numbering system, the smallest symbol is 0; the total number of symbols is equal to the base; and our positional notation is used. Hexadecimal has 16 symbols (0-9, A-F). The decimal value 15 is represented by F in hexadecimal. 2C in hex is 44 in our base 10 numbering system, as shown below.

$$2 \quad \rightarrow \quad 2 \text{ times } 16^1 \quad \rightarrow \quad 2 \text{ times } 16 = 32$$

$$+ \quad C \quad \rightarrow \quad 12 \text{ times } 16^0 \quad \rightarrow \quad 12 \text{ times } 1 = 12$$

$$44$$

Using the base-10 positional number system, the value of each digit depends on its position within the number. The octal numbering system uses eight digits.

> **NOTE** Can you determine the octal representation for the decimal value 9? The answer is 11.
> $1 \text{ times } 8^1 + 1 \text{ times } 8^0 = (8 + 1) = 9$

Character Sets

With only eight bits, you can represent 2^8 or 256 different decimal values ranging from 0 to 255. This is 256 different characters or different combinations of 0 and 1. The binary number system is used to represent the language of the computer. The binary number 01000001 is equivalent to the decimal value 65, which represents the uppercase character A. Fortunately, you do not have to retrain yourself to speak that language. The character set used by programmers of C# (pronounced **C sharp**) is called **Unicode**. When the developers created the Unicode character set, instead of using eight bits, they used 16 bits. Now, 2^{16} or 65,536 unique characters can be represented. Unicode includes representation of characters for writing in many different languages in addition to English.

A subset of Unicode, the first 128 characters, corresponds to the **American Standard Code for Information Interchange (ASCII)** character set. ASCII consists of the alphabet for the English language, plus numbers and symbols. For both the ASCII character set and Unicode, the first 32 values (0 through 31) are codes for things such as carriage return and line feed. The space character is the 33rd value, followed by punctuation, digits, uppercase characters, and lowercase characters. Appendix C contains a table showing the decimal representation for the ASCII portion of the Unicode character set. Both the C# and Java languages use the Unicode character set.

Kilobyte, Megabyte, Gigabyte, Terabyte, Petabyte...

Now back to our 32-bit processor with 512 megabytes of RAM and 60 gigabytes of hard disk space. When you start talking about lots of bytes, you get into prefixes such as kilo, mega, and giga, as in kilobyte, megabyte, and gigabyte (also shortened to K, M, and G, as in Kbytes, Mbytes, and Gbytes or KB, MB, and GB). Table 1-2 shows the multipliers.

Table 1-2 Common abbreviations for data representations

Storage capacity	Size in bytes	Abbreviation
Kilobyte	2^{10} (1,024)	KBytes
Megabyte	2^{20} (1,048,576)	MBytes
Gigabyte	2^{30} (1,073,741,824)	GBytes
Terabyte	2^{40} (1,099,511,627,776)	TBytes
Petabyte	2^{50} (1,125,899,906,842,624)	PBytes
Exabyte	2^{60} (1,152,921,504,606,846,976)	EBytes
Zettabyte	2^{70} (1,180,591,620,717,411,303,424)	ZBytes
Yottabyte	2^{80}(1,208,925,819,614,629,174,706,176)	YBytes

Notice that **kilo** is about a thousand, **mega** is about a million, **giga** is about a billion, and so on. So, when you think about a machine that has a 32-bit processor with 512 megabytes of RAM and 60 gigabytes of hard disk space, you know that the machine can process 32 bits at one time, store approximately 512 million characters in memory, and has storage capacity for approximately 60 billion characters on the hard disk.

SYSTEM AND APPLICATION SOFTWARE

1

The real power of the computer does not lie in the hardware, which comprises the physical components that make up the system. The functionality lies in the software available to make use of the hardware. The hardware processes complex patterns of 0s and 1s. The software actually transposes these 0s and 1s into text, images, and documents that people can read.

Software consists of **programs**, which are sets of instructions telling the computer exactly what to do. The instructions might tell the computer to add up a set of numbers, compare two names, or make a decision based on the result of a calculation. Just as a cook follows a set of instructions (a recipe) to prepare a dish, the computer follows instructions—without adding extra salt—to perform a useful task. The next sections describe the two major categories of software, system software and application software.

System Software

System software is loaded when you power on the computer. When thinking of system software, most people think of operating systems. **Operating systems** such as Windows XP, Windows NT, and UNIX are types of programs that oversee and coordinate the resources on the machine. Included are file system utilities, small programs that take care of locating files and keeping up with the details of a file's name, size, and date of creation. System software programs perform a variety of other functions: setting up directories; moving, copying, and deleting files; transferring data from secondary storage to primary memory; formatting media; and displaying data on screens. Operating systems include communication programs for connecting to the Internet or connecting to output devices such as printers. They include user interface subsystems for managing the look and feel of the system.

 Operating systems are one type of system software. They are utility programs that make it easier for you to use the hardware.

Another type of system software includes compilers, interpreters, and assemblers. As you begin learning software development, you will write instructions for the computer using a **programming language**. Modern programming languages are designed to be easy to read and write. They are called **high-level languages** because they are written in English-like statements. The programming language you will be using is **C#**. Other high-level computer programming languages include Visual Basic, FORTRAN, Pascal, C, C++, Java, and J#.

Before the computer can execute the instructions written in a programming language such as C#, the instructions must be translated into machine-readable format. A **compiler** makes this conversion. Figure 1-8 shows what a machine-level instruction looks like.

```
          Machine language instructions

  10110010    10011001
  10001100    11000100    11000110
  10111100    01001100    11011110
  10001100    01000101
  11110100    00101100    11111110
  10101000    11000100    11000001
```

Figure 1-8   A machine language instruction

Just as the English language has rules for sentence construction, programming languages such as C# have a set of rules, called **syntax**, that must be followed. Before translating code into machine-readable form, a compiler checks for rule violations. Compilers do not convert any statements into machine language until all syntax errors are removed. Unlike compilers, which look at entire pieces of code, **interpreters** check for rule violations line by line. If the line does not contain an error, it is converted to machine language. Interpreters are normally slower than compilers. **Assemblers** convert the assembly programming language, which is a low-level programming language, into machine code.

Application Software

Application software consists of programs developed to perform a specific task. Word processors, such as Microsoft Word, are examples of application software. Word was written to help users create professional looking documents by including a number of editing and formatting options. Spreadsheets, such as Excel, are types of application software designed to make numerical calculations and generate charts. Database management systems, such as Oracle or Access, were designed to organize large amounts of data, so that reports could easily be generated. Software that generates payroll checks is considered application software, as is software that helps you register for a class. Games are application software. Application software is used by the banking industry to manage your checking and saving accounts. Programmers use programming languages such as C# to write application software to carry out specific tasks or to solve specific problems. The programs that you write for this book will be application software.

SOFTWARE DEVELOPMENT PROCESS

You will soon be writing programs using C#. How do you start? Many beginning programmers just begin typing without planning or without using any organized sequence of steps. This often leads to increased development time and solutions that may not consistently produce accurate results.

Programming is a process of problem solving. Typing the program statements in a language such as C# is not the hardest part of programming. The most difficult part is coming up with a plan to solve the problem. A number of different approaches, or **methodologies**, are used to solve computer-related problems. Successful problem solvers follow a methodical approach with each programming project. The section that follows describes the organized plan, or methodology, that is used to solve the problems presented in this book.

Steps in the Program Development Process

1. **Analyze the problem.** The first step should be directed toward grasping the problem thoroughly. Analyze precisely what the software is supposed to accomplish. During this phase, you review the problem **specifications**, which describe what the program should accomplish. Specifications often include the desired output of the program in terms of what is to be displayed, saved, or printed. If specifications are ambiguous or need clarification, you may need to ask probing questions. *If you do not know where you are going, how will you know when you have arrived at the correct location?*

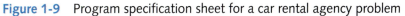 Unless you know what the problem is, there is no way you can solve it. Make sure you understand the problem definition.

A program specification might look like Figure 1-9.

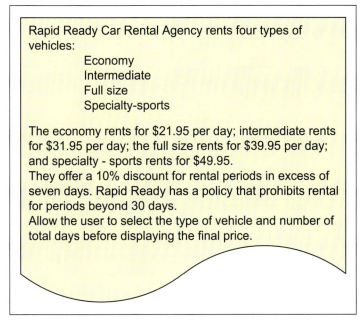

Rapid Ready Car Rental Agency rents four types of vehicles:

        Economy
        Intermediate
        Full size
        Specialty-sports

The economy rents for $21.95 per day; intermediate rents for $31.95 per day; the full size rents for $39.95 per day; and specialty - sports rents for $49.95.
They offer a 10% discount for rental periods in excess of seven days. Rapid Ready has a policy that prohibits rental for periods beyond 30 days.
Allow the user to select the type of vehicle and number of total days before displaying the final price.

Figure 1-9   Program specification sheet for a car rental agency problem

During this first phase, in addition to making sure you understand the problem definition, you must also review the program inputs. You should ask the following types of questions:

- What kind of data will be available for input?
- What types of values (e.g., whole numbers, alphabetic characters, and numbers with a decimal point) will be in each of the identified data items?
- What is the **domain** (range of the values) for each input item?
- Will the user of the program be inputting values?
- If the problem solution is to be used with multiple data sets, are there any data items that stay the same, remain **constant**, with each set?

Before you move to designing a solution, you should have a thorough understanding of the problem. It may be helpful to verbalize the problem definition. It may help to see sample input for each of the data items. Figure 1-10 illustrates how the input data items would be determined during analysis for the car rental agency problem shown in Figure 1-9. Figure 1-10 shows the identifier, or name of the data item, the type, and the domain of values for each item.

Data identifier	Data type	Domain of values
kindOfVehicle	String (characters)	Economy, Intermediate, Full size, Specialty
noOfDays	Integer (whole number)	1...30

Figure 1-10   Data for car rental agency

2. **Design a solution.** Programmers use several approaches, **methods**, during design. Procedural and object-oriented methodologies are the two most commonly used design methods. Some projects are more easily solved using one approach than the other. Both of these approaches will be discussed in the next section. The selection of programming language sometimes weighs in when determining the approach. The language C# was designed to be very object oriented.

1

No matter what size the project is, careful design always leads to better solutions. In addition, careful design normally leads to solutions that can be produced in shorter amounts of time. A **divide and conquer** approach can be used with both methodologies. As the name implies, when you divide and conquer a programming problem, you break the problem into subtasks. Then you conquer each of the subtasks by further decomposing them. This process is also called **top-down design**. Detailed models should be developed as input to subsequent phases.

Using the **object-oriented approach**, the focus is on determining the data characteristics and the methods or behaviors that operate on the data. These logical groupings of members (data and behavior) are referred to as a **class**. These characteristics are placed in a class diagram. Classes and class diagrams will be discussed in the sections that follow. Procedural designs, which are appropriate for simpler problem definitions, use structure charts to show the hierarchy of modules, and flowcharts or pseudocode listings to detail the steps for each of the modules.

Algorithms for the behaviors (object oriented) or processes (procedural) should be developed for both of these methodologies. An **algorithm** is a clear, unambiguous, step-by-step process for solving a problem. These steps must be expressed so completely and so precisely that all details are included. The instructions in the algorithm should be both simple to perform and capable of being carried out in a finite amount of time. Following the steps blindly should result in the same results every time. Figure 1-11 contains a class diagram for the problem specification given in Figure 1-9.

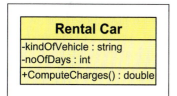

Figure 1-11   Class diagram of car rental agency

You will learn more about class diagrams later in this chapter. Figure 1-11 is divided into three sections with the top portion identifying the name of the class. The middle portion of a class diagram always lists the data characteristics. Data representing the type of vehicle to rent and the number of days for the rental are important to a rental car agency. The bottom portion shows what actions are to be performed with the data items. `ComputeCharges( )` is used to determine the cost of the rental using the type of vehicle and the number of rental days.

An algorithm for `ComputeCharges( )` multiplies the number of rental days by the rate associated with the type of vehicle rented to produce the rental charge. After the algorithm is developed, the design should be checked for correctness. One way to do this is to use sample data and **desk check** your algorithms by mimicking the computer, in other words, walking through the computer's steps. Follow each step precisely, one step at a time. If the problem involves calculations, use a calculator, and follow your design statements exactly. It is important when you desk check not to add any additional steps, unless you go back and revise the algorithm.

During this phase, it may also be helpful to plan and design the look of the desired output by developing a prototype. A **prototype** is a mock-up of screens depicting the look of the final output.

3. **Code the solution.** After you have completed the design and verified that the algorithm is correct, you translate the design into source code. **Source code** consists of program statements written using a programming language, such as C#.

 Source code statements can be typed into the computer using an editor such as Notepad or an **Integrated Development Environment (IDE)**, such as Visual Studio .NET. IDEs include a number of useful development tools: IntelliSense (pop-up windows with completion options); debugging; color coding of different program sections; online help and documentation; and features for running the program.

Whether you speak English, Spanish, or another language, you are accustomed to following language **syntax**, or rules. For example, the syntax of the English language dictates that statements end with periods and include subjects and verbs. When you write in English, you are expected to follow those rules. When you write in the C# programming language, you are expected to follow the rule that every statement should end with a semicolon. It is at this third phase of the program development process (code the solution) that you must concern yourself with language syntax.

Many programmers use an **iterative approach** in the software development process. This means that you may find it necessary to go back to the design stage to make modifications. There even may be times when additional analysis is necessary. If you analyze and design thoroughly before attempting to code the solution, you usually develop a much better program—one that is easier to read and modify.

4. **Implement the code.** During this phase, the typed program statements (source code) are compiled to check for rule violations. Integrated development environments (IDEs) such as Visual Studio .NET supply compilers within the development environment. The output of the compiler is a listing of the errors along with

a brief description of the violation. Before the implementation can go forward, all the syntax errors must be corrected. When rule violations are eliminated, the source code is converted into the Microsoft **Intermediate Language (IL)**. All languages targeting the .NET platform compile into an IL. The language that you will be using in this book, C#, is a new language introduced as part of the .NET platform. Like C#, other languages, such as Java, compile code into an intermediate language. Java's intermediate language is called **bytecode**. Intermediate languages facilitate the use of code that is more platform independent than other languages that compile straight into the machine language of the specific platform.

 If you are using the Visual Studio IDE, you will not be aware of the IL's presence. You simply select options to compile, build, and execute the program to see the output results.

The IL code is between the high-level source code and the **native code**, which is the machine language code of a particular computer. IL code is not directly executable on any computer. It is not in the language of the computer, which means it is not tied to any specific CPU platform. A second step is required before you see the results of the application.

This second step is managed by .NET's **Common Language Runtime (CLR)**. CLR loads predefined .NET classes used by the program into memory and then performs a second compile, called a **just-in-time (JIT) compilation**. This converts the IL code to the platform's native code. The CLR tool used for this is a just-in-time compiler called **JITer**. JITer reads the IL and produces the machine code that runs on the particular platform. Any computer that executes the code must have the CLR installed. The CLR is included with the .NET Framework. Any computer executing .NET code must have the .NET Framework installed. Currently the .NET Framework is available as a free download from the Microsoft Web site. Microsoft is indicating that future releases of its operating systems will come with the .NET Framework, so installing it separately will not be necessary. Figure 1-12 illustrates the steps that must be performed for source code written in C# to be executed.

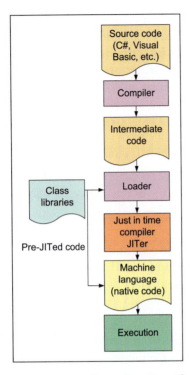

Figure 1-12   Execution steps for .NET

5. **Test and debug**. Even though you have no compiler syntax errors and you receive output, your results might be incorrect. You must test the program to ensure that you get consistent results. The **testing** phases are often shortchanged. Only after thoroughly testing can you be sure that your program is running correctly.

Plan your testing. Good programmers often build **test plans** at the same time they are analyzing and designing their solutions. This test plan should include testing extreme values, identifying possible problem cases, and ensuring that these cases are tested. Once syntax errors are eliminated and results are being produced, you should implement the test plan verifying that the results are accurate. If the application is interacting with a user for input of data, run the program multiple times with the planned test values. For calculations, perform the same operations using a calculator, much as you did during the design phase when you desk checked your algorithm.

During testing, **logic errors** are often uncovered. Logic errors might cause an abnormal termination of the program or just produce incorrect results. These types of errors are often more difficult to locate and correct than syntax errors. A **runtime error** is one form of logic error. Runtime errors normally cause program crashes (stopping execution) and the reporting of error messages. For example, if you attempt to divide by zero, your program will crash. To further complicate matters, a program may sometimes work properly with most test data, but crash when a certain value is entered. This is why it is so important to make sure you thoroughly test all applications. When a logic error is detected, it may be necessary to go back to Step 1, reanalyze the problem specifications, and redesign a solution. As you see in Figure 1-13, the software development process is iterative. As errors are discovered it is often necessary to cycle back to a previous phase or step.

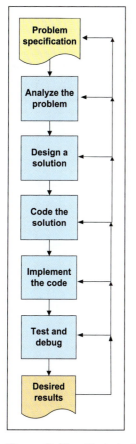

Figure 1-13 Steps in the software development process

PROGRAMMING METHODOLOGIES

How do you do your laundry? How do you prepare for an exam? As you think about those questions, you probably have an answer, and your answer will differ from those of other readers. But, you have some strategy, a set of steps, which you follow to get the job done. You can think of a methodology as a strategy, a set of steps, or a set of directions. Programmers use a numbers of different programming methodologies. The two most popular programming paradigms are structured procedural programming and object-oriented programming. These approaches are discussed in this section.

Structured Procedural Programming

This approach emerged in the 1970s and is still in use today. **Procedural programming** is process oriented—focusing on the processes that data undergoes from input until meaningful output is produced. This approach is very effective for small stand-alone applications. The five steps for software development, which were identified in the preceding section, work well for the structured procedural approach.

During design, processing steps are defined in terms of an algorithm. Any formulas or special processing steps are included in the algorithm. To think algorithmically, programmers use a number of tools. One such tool used is a flowchart. Figure 1-14 shows some of the symbols used in a flowchart for the construction of an algorithm.

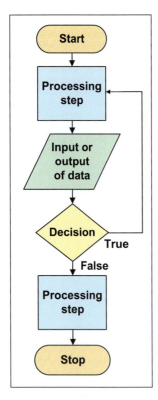

Figure 1-14   Flowchart symbols and their interpretation

Another tool used to develop an algorithm during design is **pseudocode**. As the name implies, with pseudocode, steps are written in "pseudo" or approximate code format, which looks like English statements. The focus is on determining and writing the processes or steps involved to produce the desired output. With pseudocode, the algorithm is written using a combination of English statements and the chosen programming language, such as C#.

Structured programming is associated with a technique called **top–down design** or **stepwise refinement**. The underlying theme or concept is that given a problem definition, you can refine the logic by dividing and conquering. The problem can be divided into subproblems, or procedures. Then each of the subproblems is furthered decomposed. This continues until you reach subproblems that are straightforward enough to be solved easily at the subproblem level. After you arrive at a solution at the lower levels, these solutions are combined to solve the overall problem.

> **NOTE** Consider the analogy of building a house. Using top-down design, this problem might be decomposed into Prepare the Land, Construct the Foundation, Frame the Structure, Install the Roof, Finish the Interior, and Complete the Exterior. Then each of these sub-problems could be further subdivided. An overall contractor could be hired for the project and then subcontractors assigned to each of the subproblem areas. Within each subproblem, additional problems would be defined and separate workers assigned to that area. For example, Finish the Interior might be further divided into Walls, Floors, and so on. Walls would be further decomposed into Hang Sheet Rock, Mud the Walls, Prepare for Paint, Paint the Walls, Paint the Trim, and so on. Again, each of these areas could be subcontracted out.

Programmers using the structured procedural approach normally write each of the subprograms as separate functions or methods that are called by a main controlling function or module. This facilitates the divide-and-conquer approach. With larger problems, the subprograms can be written by different individuals. One of the drawbacks of the procedural approach involves **software maintenance**. When an application is upgraded or changed, programs written using the procedural approach are more difficult to maintain. There is also less opportunity to reuse code than with the object-oriented methodology.

Object-Oriented Programming

Viewed as a newer approach to software development, the concept behind object-oriented programming (OOP) is that applications can be organized around objects rather than processes. This methodology includes a number of powerful design strategies that facilitate construction of more complex systems that model real-world entities. The language C# was designed to take advantage of the benefits of the object-oriented methodology.

With **object-oriented analysis, design, and programming**, the focus is on determining the objects you want to manipulate rather than the processes or logic required to manipulate the data. Remember that the procedural approach focuses on processes. One of the underlying assumptions of the object-oriented methodology is that the world contains a number of entities that can be identified and described. An **entity** is often defined as a person, place, or thing. It is normally a noun. By **abstracting out the attributes** (data) and the **behaviors** (processes on the data), you can divide complex phenomena into understandable entities. An **abstraction** is simply a description of the essential, relevant properties of an entity. For example, you should easily be able to picture in your mind, or conceptualize, the entities of people, school personnel, faculty, student, undergraduate student, graduate student, vehicle, car, book, school, animal, dog, and poodle by describing **characteristics** or attributes, and **behaviors** or actions, about each of these.

Consider the case of a student. A student has these characteristics or attributes: student ID, name, age, GPA, major, and hometown. The characteristics can be further described by identifying what type or kind of data might exist in each of them. For example, alphabetic characters would be found in the name attribute. Whole numbers without a decimal would be found in the age attribute, and numbers with a decimal would be in the GPA attribute.

In addition to abstracting the data properties, you should also be able to think about some of the actions or behaviors of each of the entities identified in the previous paragraph. Behaviors associated with a student include actions such as Apply for Admission, Enroll as Student, Get Final Grade, Change Name, and Determine GPA. Using the object-oriented methodology, these attributes and actions (or characteristics and behaviors) are **encapsulated**, which means that they are combined together to form a class.

A **class diagram** is one of the primary modeling tools used by object-oriented programmers. Figure 1-15 illustrates the Student class diagram using the Unified Modeling Language (UML) notation. The top portion of the diagram identifies the name of the class, which is Student. The section in the center contains the data members and the type of data that would be found in each data member. **Information hiding** is an important component of object-oriented programming. The minus symbol (–) to the left of the data member's name indicates the member is private and accessible to that class only. The bottom portion of the diagram in Figure 1-15 shows actions, or methods, of the Student class. The plus symbol (+) indicates that the behaviors are available outside of the class. This UML notation is used throughout the book for creating class diagrams.

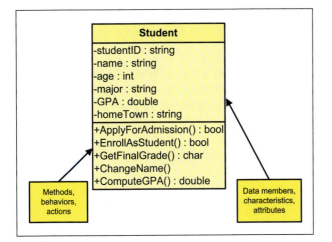

Figure 1-15   Student class diagram

A class is like a template. It is similar to a blueprint for a house. Even though you define all the characteristics of a house in the blueprint, the house does not exist until one is built using that template. Many houses can be created using the same template. In object-oriented terminology, the constructed house is one instance (object) of the blueprint or template. You **instantiate** the blueprint by building a house using that template. Many objects of a particular class can be instantiated. Thus, an **object** is an **instance** of the class.

Examine the expanded example of a student with the following data members:

- Student number: 122223
- Student name: Justin Howard
- Age: 18
- GPA: 3.80
- Major: CS
- Hometown: Winchester, Kentucky

When these data members are associated with the class, an object is created or **constructed**. A second object could be instantiated from that class by giving values to its members (e.g., 228221, Elizabeth Czerwinski, 21, 4.0, ENG, Reno, Nevada).

The object-oriented methodology facilitates designing components, which contain code that can be reused by packaging together the attributes of a data type along with the actions of that type. Through **inheritance**, it is possible to define subclasses of data objects that share some or all of the parent's class characteristics. This is what enables reuse of code. For example, you should be able to visualize that Student is a subset of Person, just as Teacher is a subset of Person. Using object-oriented design, you could abstract out the common characteristics of all people and place them in a superclass. Through inheritance, student and teacher can use the characteristics of person and add their own unique members.

The object-oriented principles are of particular importance when writing software using C#. No program can be written that does not include at least one class. All program statements written using the C# language are placed in a class.

Whether you are using a procedural or object-oriented approach, you should follow the five steps to program development. As with the procedural approach, the object-oriented development process is iterative. During design and subsequent phases, do not hesitate to reconsider analysis and design decisions.

EVOLUTION OF C# AND .NET

Programming Languages

In the 1940s programmers toggled switches on the front of computers to enter programs and data into memory. That is how programming began. Even when they moved to punching 0s and 1s on cards and reading the cards into memory, it could not have been much fun to be a programmer. Coding was very tedious and prone to error. In the 1950s assembly languages replaced the binary notation by using mnemonic symbols to represent the instructions for the computer. Symbols such as MV were used to represent moving the contents of one value in memory to another memory location. Assembly languages were designed to make the programmer's job easier by using these mnemonic symbols instead of binary numbers. However, the instructions depended on the particular CPU architecture. Statements to perform the same task differed from computer to computer. Assembly languages are still considered **low-level programming languages**. As you can see from Figure 1-16, these types of instructions are not easy to read or understand. They are not considered close to the English language, as high-level programming languages such as C# and Java are.

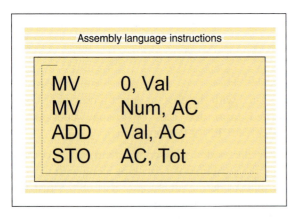

Assembly language instructions

```
MV      0, Val
MV      Num, AC
ADD     Val, AC
STO     AC, Tot
```

Figure 1-16   Assembly language instruction to add two values

High-level languages came into existence in the late 1950s with **FORTRAN** (Formula Translator) and later **COBOL** (Common Business Oriented Language). These languages were considered **high-level languages** because they were designed to be accessible to humans—easy to read and write, and close to the English language. Over the years since then, more than 2,000 high-level languages have come into existence. Some have gone by the wayside, while others have evolved and are still widely used today.

Some of the more noteworthy high-level programming languages are C, C++, Visual Basic, Java, and now C#. **C++** is an extension of C, which actually evolved from BCPL and B in 1973. Dennis Ritchie is credited with developing the C programming language; Bjarne Stroustrup at Bell Labs is considered the father of C++ for his design work in the early 1980s. C++ includes features that enabled programmers to perform object-oriented programming. C++ is used heavily in the computer industry today.

Smalltalk, considered a pure object-oriented language, was developed at the Xerox Palo Alto Research Center (PARC). Visual Basic, introduced in 1991, derived from the BASIC (Beginners All Purpose Symbolic Code) programming language, a language developed in the 1960s. The earlier versions of Visual Basic did not facilitate development using an object-oriented approach. Earlier versions of Visual Basic did, however, facilitate easy creation of Windows-based graphical user interfaces (GUIs). Visual Basic has been used for a great deal of application development because of this.

Java was introduced in 1995 and was originally called Oak. It was originally designed to be a language for intelligent consumer-electronic devices such as appliances and microwave ovens. Instead of being used for that purpose, the business community used Java most heavily for Web applications because of the nature of the bytecode, which enabled machine-independent language compiling. Since the bytecode does not target any particular computer platform and must be converted to the language of the system running the application, this facilitates development of code that runs on many types of computers.

C# is one of the newest programming languages. It conforms closely to C and C++, but many developers consider it akin to Java. There are a number of similarities between the languages. It has the rapid graphical user interface (GUI) features of previous versions of Visual Basic, the added power of C++, and object-oriented class libraries similar to Java. C# was designed from scratch by Microsoft to work with the new programming paradigm, .NET, and was the language used most heavily for the development of the .NET Framework class libraries. C# can be used to develop any type of software component including mobile applications, dynamic Web pages, database access components, Windows desktop applications, Web services, and console-based applications. You will be using C# for the software development in this book; however, the concepts presented can be applied to other languages. The intent of the book is to use the C# language as a tool for learning how to develop software rather than to focus on the syntax of C#.

.NET

When you think about C#, you should also understand its relationship to .NET. **.NET** is an environment in which programs run and was designed to be a new programming paradigm. It is not an operating system, but rather a layer between the operating system and other applications. As such, it provides a platform for developing and running code that is easy to use. Microsoft stated that the vision for .NET was to provide a new programming platform and a set of development tools. The intent was for developers to be able to build distributed component-based applications. By the year 2000, when Microsoft unveiled .NET, many developers had already experienced .NET due to the massive marketing campaign of Microsoft.

Before its official announcement in 2000, .NET was in development for over three years. Microsoft distributed a number of beta versions before the official release. A **beta version** is a working version that has not been fully tested and may still contain **bugs** or errors. It was not until February 2002 that Microsoft finally released the first version of Visual Studio .NET, the Integrated Development Environment (IDE) for developing C# applications. Visual Basic .NET, Visual C++ .NET, Visual J# .NET, and Visual C# .NET all use this same development environment. Figure 1-17 shows Visual Studio with a C# program running. The output of the program "Welcome to Programming!" is shown in the small message box near the bottom of the figure.

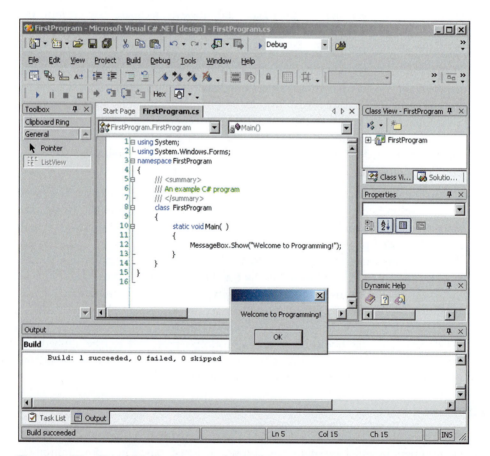

Figure 1-17   Visual Studio Integrated Development Environment

Included in Visual Studio are tools for typing program statements, and compiling, executing, and debugging applications. Appendix B supplies information on some of these Visual Studio tools. The new concepts introduced as part of .NET are outlined in the paragraphs that follow.

Multi-language Independence: .NET supports development using a number of programming languages: Visual Basic, C#, J#, C++, and a number of third-party languages. All the code from each of the languages compiles to the common Microsoft Intermediate Language (IL). Figure 1-18 illustrates the IL created by Visual Studio for the program shown in Figure 1-17. While this may look somewhat unreadable, it provides some useful information. It states that the code size is 12 bytes. The statements beginning with **IL** indicate what is loaded into memory. "Welcome to Programming!" and the System.Windows.Forms class are both loaded.

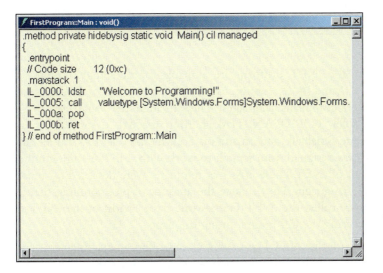

Figure 1-18 Microsoft Intermediate Language (IL)

The Intermediate Language is easily obtained in Visual Studio using a tool called ILDasm, which stands for Intermediate Language Disassembler. This same Intermediate Language would be produced whether the program were written in C#, Visual Basic, or any other .NET-supported languages. This makes newer languages more interoperable than earlier languages, which means that one application can be divided up and written in more than one language. Part of the application might be developed using C++ and another portion developed using C#. When they are compiled, they translate to a common IL. The following list describes some of the common features of the .NET-supported languages:

New Framework Base Classes: The .NET Framework has a class library, which provides a very large collection of over 2,500 reusable types (classes) available to any .NET language.

Dynamic Web Pages and Web Services: .NET was written with the Internet in mind; thus, deploying applications over intranets or the Internet becomes an ordinary, day-to-day operation. Using a new technology, ASP.NET, a set of components called ADO.NET, and having XML support, makes it easier to access relational databases and other data sources as well as to import and export data through the Web.

Scalable Component Development: .NET not only facilitates object-oriented development, but it takes design one step further. With .NET, true component-based development can be performed better and easier than in the past. Segments of code, created as separate entities, can be stored independently, combined, and reused in many applications. That is the beauty behind .NET. .NET provides a relatively seamless way for client programs to use components built using different languages. With .NET, component-based development can become a reality.

WHY C#?

Compilers targeting the .NET platform are available for the programming languages of Visual Basic, C++, C#, and J#. In addition to Microsoft, a number of third-party vendors are also marketing .NET-compliant languages. They include the languages of Alice, APL, COBOL, Pascal, Eiffel, FORTRAN, Haskell, Mercury, ML, Mondrain, Oberon, Perl, Python, RPG, Scheme, Smalltalk, and on and on. So, why use C#? C# was *the* language created for .NET and was designed from scratch to work with .NET. A large number of classes were included as part of .NET. These classes or templates were designed for reuse by any of the .NET-supported languages. They reduce the amount of programming that needs to be done. These classes are called the .NET Framework classes. Most of the .NET Framework classes were written using the C# programming language.

C#, in conjunction with the .NET Framework classes, offers an exciting vehicle to incorporate and use emerging Web standards, such as Hypertext Markup Language (HTML), Extensible Markup Language (XML), and Simple Object Access Protocol (SOAP). As stated earlier, C# was designed with the Internet in mind. Most of the programming tools that were developed before .NET were designed when the Web was in its infancy and thus are not the greatest fit for developing Windows and Web applications.

C# is a simple, object-oriented language. Through using the Visual Studio .NET IDE and the .NET Framework, C# provides an easy way to create graphical user interfaces similar to those Visual Basic programmers have been using for years. C# also provides the pure data crunching horsepower to which C and C++ programmers are accustomed. All of the looping and selection programming constructs are included. C# enables developers to make their packages available over the Internet using many common features previously found only in Java, CGI, or PERL.

 Some characterize C# by saying that Microsoft took the best of Visual Basic and added C++, trimming off some of the more arcane C traditions. The syntax is very close to Java.

Many attribute the success of C++ to its ANSI standardization. C# is following a similar path toward success. On December 13, 2001, the European Computer Manufacturers Association (ECMA) General Assembly ratified C# and its common language infrastructure (CLI) specifications into international standards. This verification proves that C# is not just a fly-by-night language. Originally, development with C# was possible only for the Windows platform; however, a number of projects are in development that port C# to other platforms such as Linux. C# is going to be around for some time. It represents the next generation of languages.

In the next chapters, you will begin developing software using C# as a programming tool. The software development methodology introduced in this chapter will guide the development.

Resources

There are enormous numbers of sites devoted to just C# on the Web. You might start your exploring at one or more of the following sites:

- The Microsoft .NET Web site at *www.microsoft.com/net*
- The MSDN Visual C# home page at *msdn.microsoft.com/vcsharp*
- The .NET Framework Community—GotDotNet at *gotdotnet.com*
- Intel processor information at *www.intel.com*
- Unicode home page at *www.unicode.org*

QUICK REVIEW

1. General-purpose computer systems are electronic devices that process data and are composed of hardware and software.
2. Hardware refers to the physical devices that you can touch. Hardware components facilitate input, processing, storage, and output of data into information that humans can understand.
3. The power of the computer rests with software, which is the set of instructions or programs that give the hardware functionality.
4. The Analytical Engine shaped the model for what is known today as a general-purpose computer because it included input and output devices, memory storage, and a control unit, and it processed instructions.
5. Many consider today's computer technology to be in the fifth generation of modern computing. Each era is characterized by an important advancement.
6. The CPU has two major roles. It performs arithmetic and logical comparisons on data and coordinates the operations of the system.
7. Memory is divided into sections, or cells, which can each hold an equal amount of data. All cells have a unique address. Computer memories are commonly divided into 8-bit groupings. This 8-bit combination is called a byte.

8. Computers use the base-2 number system, also known as the binary number system, to represent data. With only eight bits, you can represent 2^8, or 256, different decimal values ranging from 0 to 255, or 256 different characters.

9. The character set used by C# programmers is called Unicode. 16 bits are used to represent every character uniquely, which means that 2^{16} or 65,536 different characters can be represented.

10. Software can be divided into two categories: system software and application software. Application software is defined as the programs developed to perform a specific task.

11. The type of software most often associated with system software is the operating system. The operating system software is loaded when you turn on the computer. Other types of system software are compilers, interpreters, and assemblers.

12. Programming is a process of problem solving. The hardest part is coming up with a plan to solve the problem.

13. The five problem-solving steps for software development include analyzing, designing, coding, implementing, and testing and debugging the solution.

14. Procedural programming is process oriented and focuses on the processes that data undergoes from input until meaningful output is produced.

15. The underlying theme of top-down design or stepwise refinement is that given any problem definition, the logic can be refined by using the divide-and-conquer approach.

16. Software maintenance refers to upgrading or changing applications.

17. Using an object-oriented analysis approach, the focus is on determining the objects you want to manipulate rather than the logic required to manipulate them.

18. Encapsulation refers to combining attributes and actions or characteristics and behaviors to form a class.

19. An object is an instance of a class.

20. Through inheritance, it is possible to define subclasses of data objects that share some or all of the main class characteristics of their parents or superclasses. Inheritance enables reuse of code.

21. C# was designed from scratch to work with the new programming paradigm, .NET, and was the language used for development of much of .NET.

22. .NET is a software environment in which programs run. It is not the operating system. It is a layer between the operating system and other applications, providing an easier framework for developing and running code.

23. Through using Visual Studio (which is an Integrated Development Environment) and the .NET Framework classes, C# provides an easy way to create graphical user interfaces.

24. Originally, development with C# was possible only for the Windows platform; however, a number of projects are in development that are porting C# to other platforms such as Linux.

EXERCISES

1. Auxiliary storage is _____, which means that when power is turned off, information is _____, whereas RAM is _____.

   a. nonvolatile, not lost, volatile

   b. volatile, not lost, nonvolatile

   c. nonvolatile, lost, volatile

   d. volatile, lost, volatile

   e. volatile, lost, nonvolatile

2. A computer that has a 32-bit processor is able to process how many bytes at one time?

   a. 8

   b. 4

   c. 32

   d. 2

   e. 16

3. The decimal equivalent of 00011010 is:

   a. 32

   b. 36

   c. 26

   d. 3

   e. 256

4. Which of the following is *not* an output device?

   a. hard disk drive

   b. screen

   c. CPU

   d. printer

   e. zip drive

5. The binary equivalent of 11 is:

   a. 00000011

   b. 11000000

   c. 00011011

   d. 00001011

   e. 00011000

6. The character set used by C# programmers is:

   a. Unicode

   b. UML

   c. ASCII

   d. EBCDIC

   e. binary

7. The brain of the computer is the:

   a. program(s)

   b. input device(s)

   c. operating system

   d. CPU

   e. main memory

8. You run a program and it gives you the difference of two values as the output, instead of the sum of the values, as intended. This is what type of error?

   a. syntax

   b. analysis

   c. coding

   d. design

   e. logic

9. The program that translates high-level programming language into machine-readable form is a(n):

   a. application

   b. operating system

   c. C# program

   d. compiler

   e. machine language utility

10. The following strategy reduces the amount of time in development and produces more efficient solutions:

    a. Code the solution as soon as possible.

    b. Design the solution before coding.

    c. Analyze the solution before testing and debugging.

    d. Build a prototype during testing.

    e. Use a simple low-level language for development.

11. In which phase of the software development process would probing questions be used to verify the problem definition?

   a. analysis

   b. design

   c. coding

   d. implementation

   e. testing

12. Cycling back to previous phases as potential problems are uncovered is an example of:

   a. object-oriented programming

   b. stepwise refinement

   c. Intermediate Language

   d. iterative development

   e. structured programming

13. .NET is a(n):

   a. operating system

   b. programming language

   c. compiler

   d. Integrated Development Environment

   e. none of the above

14. The process of changing a working program or upgrading to a new version is referred to as:

   a. maintenance

   b. testing

   c. pseudocode

   d. programming

   e. just-in-time compilation

15. After designing your solution, you should _____ before typing any code.

   a. analyze the problem definition

   b. check for runtime errors

   c. do maintenance on the solution

   d. desk check the solution

   e. determine what .NET class to use

16. With the object-oriented methodology, the data members are referred to as:

   a. attributes or characteristics

   b. characteristics or behaviors

   c. methods or attributes

   d. behaviors or methods

   e. attributes or behaviors

17. Information hiding is possible in object-oriented programming because of:

   a. inheritance

   b. instantiation

   c. objects

   d. classes

   e. encapsulation

18. A megabyte is approximately a _____ bytes. A kilobyte is approximately a _____ bytes, and a gigabyte is approximately a _____ bytes.

   a. million, billion, zillion

   b. thousand, billion, million

   c. billion, thousand, million

   d. zillion, billion, million

   e. million, thousand, billion

19. .NET is considered a powerful development environment because:

   a. It contains over 2000 classes.

   b. Solutions can be developed using different programming languages.

   c. Windows applications can be developed easily.

   d. Component-based development is possible.

   e. All of the above.

20. One feature that differentiates C# from C++ is:

   a. C++ has more brute programming power.

   b. C++ facilitates development of Web applications more quickly.

   c. C# can only be run on Windows platforms.

   d. C# meets ANSI standards.

   e. C# provides an easy way to create graphical user interfaces.

21. How does the analysis phase differ from the design phase during the software development process?

22. Using an ASCII and Unicode table, write down what the decimal equivalent is for the following two characters: C#. Are the decimal values the same for both the ASCII and Unicode character sets?

23. Search the Internet and locate the name of at least one project or software package that has C# available on platforms other than Windows.

24. How is the Java bytecode similar to the Microsoft Intermediate Language?

25. Using abstraction, what attributes would you associate with a vehicle class?

26. Using abstraction, what actions would you associate with a vehicle class?

27. Draw a class diagram of the vehicle class from Exercises #25 and #26.

28. Use the Internet to search for and identify how many different programming languages you find that target the .NET platform. Can you identify three more than those mentioned in this chapter?

29. What is the purpose of the JITer?

30. Describe how procedural programming differs from object-oriented programming.

Your First C# Program

As you learned in Chapter 1, programs are the instructions written to direct a computer to perform a particular task. Each instruction must be written in a specific way. The **syntax**—rules for writing these instructions—is defined by the language in which the program is written. Before results are obtained, these human-readable instructions, called **source code**, must be translated into the machine language, which is the **native code** of the computer. The translation is a two-step process, which begins with the compiler. In this chapter, you write your first C# program, learn how it is compiled, and explore how the final output is produced.

Each instruction statement has a **semantic meaning**—a specific way in which it should be used. This chapter highlights the purpose of the program statements as they appear in an application, because many of these program elements will be used in all applications that you develop using C#. You'll start by investigating the types of applications that can be developed using C# and the .NET platform.

TYPES OF APPLICATIONS DEVELOPED WITH C#

C# can be used to create three different types of software applications:

- Web applications
- Windows graphical user interface (GUI) applications
- Console-based applications

Web Applications

As you remember from Chapter 1, C# was built from the ground up with the Internet in mind. For this reason, programmers can use C# to quickly build applications that run on the Web for end users to view through browser-neutral user interfaces (UIs). As they program in C#, developers can ignore the unique requirements of the platforms—Macintosh, Windows, and Linux—that will be executing these applications and end users will still see consistent results. Using **Web Forms**, which are part of the ASP.NET technology, programmable Web pages can be built that serve as a UI for Web applications. **ASP.NET** is a programming framework that lets you create applications that run on a Web server and delivers functionality through a browser, such as Internet Explorer. Although you can use other languages to create ASP.NET applications, C# takes advantage of the .NET Framework and is generally acknowledged to be the language of choice for ASP.NET development. Much of the .NET Framework Class Library (FCL) is written in the C# programming language. After you learn some problem-solving techniques and the basic features of the C# language, Chapter 12 will introduce you to ASP.NET. Figure 2-1 illustrates an ASP.NET Web page created with C#.

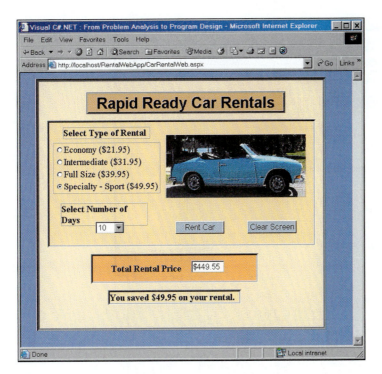

Figure 2-1   Web application written using C#

Windows Applications

Windows applications are designed for desktop use and for a single platform. They run on PC desktops much like your favorite word-processing program. Writing code using C# and classes from the `System.Windows.Forms` namespace, applications can be developed to include menus, pictures, drop-down controls, and other widgets you have come to expect in a modern desktop application. Using the Integrated Development Environment (IDE) of Visual Studio .NET, graphical user interfaces (GUIs) can be developed by dragging and dropping controls such as buttons, text boxes, and labels on the screen. This same drag-and-drop approach is used to create Web applications with Visual Studio .NET. You will begin creating Windows GUI applications in Chapter 8. Figure 2-2 illustrates a windows application written using the C# language.

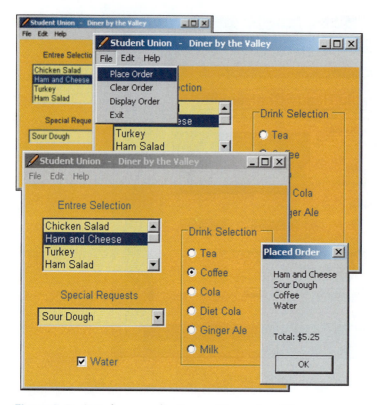

Figure 2-2 Windows application written using C#

Console Applications

Console applications normally send requests to the operating system to display text on the command console display or to retrieve data from the keyboard. From a beginners' standpoint, console applications are the easiest to create and represent the simplest approach to learning software development, because you do not have to be concerned with the side issues associated with building GUIs. Values can be entered as input with minimal overhead, and output is displayed in a console window, as illustrated in Figure 2-3. You will begin by developing console applications, so that you can focus on the details of programming and problem solving in general.

Figure 2-3   Output from Example 2-1 console application

EXPLORING THE FIRST C# PROGRAM

Since the 1970s when the C language was developed, it has been traditional when learning a new language to display "Hello World" on the console screen as the result of your first program. The program in Example 2-1 demonstrates a C# program that does exactly that. The sections that follow explain line by line the elements that make up this first program.

Example 2-1

```
line 1      //  This is traditionally the first program written.
line 2      using System;
line 3      namespace FirstProgram
line 4      {
line 5          class HelloWorld
line 6          {
line 7              static void Main( )
line 8              {
line 9                  Console.WriteLine("Hello World");
line 10             }
line 11         }
line 12     }
```

Readability is important. As far as the compiler is concerned, you could actually type the entire program without touching the Enter key. The entire program could be typed as a single line, but it would be very difficult to read and even more challenging to debug. The style in Example 2-1 is a good one to mimic. Notice that curly braces { } are matched and appear on separate lines, by themselves. Statements are grouped together and indented. Indenting is not required, but is a good practice to follow because it makes the code easier to read. When you type your program, you should follow a consistent, similar style. The output produced from compiling and executing the program appears in Figure 2-3.

ELEMENTS OF A C# PROGRAM

Although the program statements in Example 2-1 make up one of the smallest functional programs that can be developed using C#, they include all the major components found in most programs. An understanding of the features that make up this program will help prepare you to begin developing your own applications. Examine each segment line by line to analyze the program, beginning with line 1.

Comments

The first line of Example 2-1 is a comment:

`line 1    // This is traditionally the first program written.`

 Comments are displayed in **green** throughout the book.

Writing a comment is like making notes for yourself or for readers of your program. Comments are not considered instructions to the computer and therefore have no effect on the running of the program. When the program is compiled, comments are not checked for rule violations; on the contrary, the compiler ignores and bypasses them. Comments do not have to follow any particular rules—with the exception of how they begin and end.

Comments serve two functions: they make the code more readable and they internally document what the program statements are doing. At the beginning of a program, comments are often written to identify who developed the code, when it was developed, and for what purpose the instructions were written. Comments are also used to document the purpose of different sections of code. You can place comments anywhere in the program. Where a portion of the code might be difficult to follow, it is appropriate to place one or more comments explaining the details. In Example 2-1, the only comment is found on line 1.

`line 1    //  This is traditionally the first program written.`

 C# programmers do not normally use line numbers, but they are added here to explain the features.

With C#, three types of commenting syntax can be added to a program: in-line, multi-line, and XML document comments.

In-Line Comments

The comment that appears on line 1 of Example 2-1 is an in-line, or single-line, comment. An **in-line comment** is indicated by two forward slashes **//** and is usually considered a one-line comment. The slashes indicate that everything to the right of the slashes, on the same line, is a comment and should be ignored by the compiler. No special symbols are needed to end the comment. The carriage return (Enter) ends the comment.

Multi-Line Comments

For longer comments, multi-line comments are available. A forward slash followed by an asterisk /* marks the beginning of a **multi-line comment**, and the opposite pattern */ marks the end. Everything that appears between the comment symbols is treated as a comment. Multi-line comments are also called **block comments**. Although they are called multi-line comments, they do not have to span more than one line. Unlike the single-line comment that terminates at the end of the current line when the Enter key is pressed, the multi-line comment requires special characters /* and */ to begin and terminate the comment, even if the comment just appears on a single line. Example 2-2 shows an example of a multi-line comment.

Example 2-2

```
/*  This is the beginning of a multi-line (block) comment. It can
go on for several lines or just be on a single line. No additional
symbols are needed after the beginning two characters. Notice there
is no space placed between the two characters. To end the comment,
use the following symbols. */
```

> **NOTE** C# does not allow you to nest multi-line comments. In other words, you cannot place a block comment inside another block comment. The outermost comment is ended at the same time as the inner comment—as soon as the first */ is typed.

XML Documentation Comments

A third type of comment uses three forward slashes ///. This is an advanced documentation technique used for XML-style comments. **XML (Extensible Markup Language)** is a markup language that provides a format for describing data using tags similar to HTML tags. A C# compiler reads the **XML documentation comments** and generates XML documentation from them.

You will be using the in-line // and multi-line /*   */ comments for the applications you will develop in this book.

Using Directive

The following statement that appears in Example 2-1, line 2 permits the use of classes found in the System `namespace` without having to qualify them with the word System. This reduces the amount of typing that would be necessary without the directive.

```
line 2      using System;
```

Using .NET provides the significant benefit of making available more than 2,000 classes that make up what is called the Framework Class Library (FCL). A `class` contains code that can be reused, which makes programming easier and faster because you don't have to reinvent the wheel for common types of operations. The Framework classes are all available for use by any of the .NET-supported languages, including C#.

> Keywords after they are introduced, such as `class`, are displayed in blue throughout this book. **Keywords** are words reserved by the system and have special predefined meanings. The keyword `class`, for instance, defines or references a C# `class`.

With more than 2,000 classes, it is very unlikely that program developers will memorize the names of all of the classes, let alone the additional names of members of the classes. As you could well imagine, it would be easy for you to use a name in your own application that has already been used in one or more of the Framework classes. Another likely occurrence is that one or more of these 2,000 classes could use the same name. How would you know which `class` was being referenced? .NET eliminates this potential problem by using namespaces.

Example 2-3

Assume you have a `class` called `Captain`. As discussed in Chapter 1, you could abstract out characteristics and behavior attributes of a Captain. If you had an application that was being developed for a football team, the characteristics and behaviors of that kind of Captain would differ greatly from those of the Captain in an application designed for a fire department. Moreover, both sets of characteristics differ from those of a boating Captain. The Captain associated with a military unit, such as the Navy, would also be different. With each possible application, you could use the same name for the Captain `class`. If you gave instructions to a program to display information about a Captain, the program would not know which set of characteristics to display. To clarify whether you are talking about the boat Captain, football team Captain, fire station Captain, or the Navy Captain, you could qualify the keyword by preceding the name with its category. To do so, you could write Boat.Captain, Football.Captain, Fireman.Captain, or Navy.Captain. You would need to precede Captain with its category type every time reference was made to Captain.

By specifying which `namespace` you are building an application around, you can eliminate the requirement of preceding Captain with a dot (.) and the name of the `namespace`. If you simply write "use the boating `namespace`," you do not have to qualify each statement with the prefix name. That is what the `using` directive accomplishes. It keeps you from having to qualify each `class` by identifying within which `namespace` something appears. A `using` directive enables unqualified use of the types that are members of the `namespace`. By typing the using-namespace-directive, all the types contained in the given `namespace` are imported, or available for use within the particular application.

The most important and frequently used `namespace` is `System`. The `System` `namespace` contains classes that define commonly used types or classes. The `Console` `class` is defined within the `System` `namespace`. The `Console` `class` enables programmers to write to and read from the console window or keyboard. The fully qualified name for `Console` is

System.Console. If you remove the using System; directive in line #2, it would be necessary for you to replace

line 9   Console.WriteLine("Hello World");

with

line 9   System.Console.WriteLine("Hello World");

 In addition to including the using directive, the System namespace must be included in the references for a project created using Visual Studio .NET. When a console application is created, Visual Studio .NET automatically references and imports the System namespace.

Namespaces provide scope for the names defined within the group. By including the using directive to indicate the name of the namespace to be used, you can avoid having to precede the class names with the category grouping. Once you add the using System; line, you can use the Console class name without explicitly identifying that it is in the System namespace.

Namespace

Lines 3 through 12 define a namespace called FirstProgram.

```
line 3     namespace FirstProgram
line 4     {
line 12    }
```

The namespace does little more than group semantically related types under a single umbrella. Example 2-1 illustrates how a namespace called FirstProgram is created. FirstProgram is an **identifier**, simply a user-supplied or user-created name. As noted in the previous section, you will create many names (identifiers) when programming in C#. Rules for creating identifiers will be discussed in Chapter 3. You can define your own namespace and indicate that these are names associated with your particular application.

Each namespace must be enclosed in curly braces { }. The open curly brace ({) on line 4 marks the beginning of the FirstProgram namespace. The open curly brace is matched by a closing curly brace (}) at the end of the program on line 12. Within the curly braces, you write the programming constructs.

In the application in Example 2-1, lines 3, 4, and 12 could have been omitted. This program did not define any new programming constructs or names. It is merely using the Console class, which is part of the System namespace. No errors are introduced by adding the additional umbrella, but it was not necessary. Visual Studio .NET automatically adds a namespace umbrella around applications that are created using the IDE.

Class Definition

Lines 5 through 11 make up the **class** definition for this application.

```
line 5          class HelloWorld
line 6          {
line 11         }
```

As C# is an object-oriented language, everything in C# is designed around a **class**, which is the building block of an object-oriented program. C# doesn't allow anything to be defined outside of a **class**. Every program must have at least one **class**. Classes define a category, or type, of object. Many classes are included with the .NET Framework. Programs written using C# can use these predefined .NET classes or create their own classes.

In Example 2-1, the user-defined **class** is titled **HelloWorld**. The example also uses the **Console class**, one of the .NET predefined classes. Every **class** is named. It is tradition to name the file containing the **class** the same name as the **class** name, except the file name will have a .cs extension affixed to the end of the name. C# allows a single file to have more than one **class**; however, it is common practice to place one user-defined **class** per file for object-oriented development.

 Most object-oriented languages, including Java, restrict a file to one **class**. C#, however, allows multiple classes to be stored in a single file.

Classes are used to define controls such as buttons and labels, as well as types of things such as Student, Captain, and Employee. The word **class** is a keyword. Like namespaces, each **class** definition must be enclosed in curly braces { }. The { on line 6 is an open curly brace, which marks the beginning of the **class** definition. The open curly brace is matched by a closing curly brace at the end of the **class** definition on line 11. Within the curly braces, you define the **class** members. A **class** member is generally either a member method, which performs some behavior of the **class**, or a data member, which contains a value associated with the state of the **class**.

Main( ) Method

The definition for the **Main( )** method begins on line 7 and ends with the closing curly brace on line 10.

```
line 7          static void Main( )
line 8          {
line 10         }
```

The **Main( )** method plays a very important role in C#. This is the "entry point" for all applications. This is where the program begins execution. The **Main( )** method can be placed anywhere inside the **class** definition. It begins on line 7 for this example. When a C# program is launched, the execution starts with the first executable statement found in the **Main( )** method and continues to the end of that method. If the application is 2000 lines long with the `Main( )` method beginning on line 1050, the first statement executed for the application is on line 1050.

 All executable applications must contain a `Main( )` method.

The entire contents of line 7 is the heading for the method. A **method** is a collection of one or more statements combined to perform an action. Methods are similar to C++ functions. The heading for the method contains its **signature**, which includes the name of the method and its argument list. Return types and modifiers, such as `public` and `static`, are part of the heading, but not considered part of the signature. The heading line for the `Main( )` method begins with the keyword `static`, which implies that a single copy of the method is created, and that you can access this method without having an object of the `class` available. More details regarding `static` are discussed in subsequent sections. For now, suffice it to say that `Main( )` should include the `static` keyword as part of its heading.

The second keyword in the heading is `void`. Void is the return type. Typically, a method calls another method and can return a value to the calling method. Remember that a method is a small block of code that performs an action. As a result of this action, a value might be returned. If a method does not return a value, the `void` keyword is included to signal that no value is returned. When the method does return a value, the type of value is included as part of the heading. Chapter 3 introduces you to the different data types in C#.

`Main( )` is the name of the method. Methods communicate with each other by sending arguments inside parentheses or as return values. Sometimes no argument is sent, as is the case when nothing appears inside the parentheses.

 Unlike the lowercase main( ) method that appears in the C++ language, in C# `Main( )` must begin with an uppercase 'M'.

In Example 2-1, only one executable statement is included in the body of the method `Main( )`. The body includes all items enclosed inside open and closed curly braces. When a program is executed, the statements that appear in the `Main( )` method are executed in sequential order. Once the end curly brace is encountered, the entire program ends.

Method Body—Statements

The body of this `Main( )` method consists of a single one-line statement found on line 9.

```
line 8          {
line 9                  Console.WriteLine("Hello World");
line 10         }
```

Remember that the purpose of the program in Example 2-1 is to display **"Hello World"** on the output screen. The lines of code in Example 2-1, which have been explained on previous pages of this chapter, are common to most applications you will be developing. Line 9, however, is unique to this application. The body for this method begins on line 8 and ends on line 10.

The statement in the `Main( )` method is a call to another method named "`WriteLine( )`". A method call is the same as a **method invocation**. Like `Main( )`, `WriteLine( )` has a signature. The heading along with the complete body of the method is the **definition of the method**. When called, `WriteLine( )` writes the string argument that appears inside the parentheses to the standard output device, a monitor. After displaying the string, `WriteLine( )` advances to the next line, as if the enter key had been pressed.

 A quick way to identify a method is by looking for parentheses—methods always appear with parentheses ( ). A call to any method, such as `WriteLine( )`, always includes a set of parentheses following the method name identifier, as do signatures for methods.

The string of text, `"Hello World"`, placed inside the parentheses is the method's argument. `WriteLine( )` is defined in the `Console` **class** and can be called with no arguments. To have a blank line displayed on the standard output device, type:

```
Console.WriteLine( );    // No string argument is placed inside ( )
```

The `Console` **class** contains the standard input and output methods for console applications. Methods in this **class** include `Read( )`, `WriteLine( )`, and `Write( )`. The method `Write( )` differs from `WriteLine( )` in that it does not automatically advance the carriage return to the next line when it finishes. The following lines would produce the same result as the single line `Console.WriteLine("Hello World");`

```
Console.Write("Hello");
Console.Write(" ");
Console.WriteLine("World");
```

An invisible pointer moves across the output screen as the characters are displayed. As new characters are displayed, it moves to the next position and is ready to print at that location if another output statement is sent. Notice the second statement in the preceding code, `Console.Write(" ")`. This places a blank character between the two words. After displaying the space, the pointer is positioned and ready to display the *W* in "World." The output for both of the preceding segments of code is:

```
Hello World
```

Usually the characters inside the double quotes are displayed exactly as they appear when used as an argument to `Write( )` or `WriteLine( )`. An exception occurs when an escape character is included. The backslash (`'\'`) is called the **escape character**. The escape character is combined with one or more characters to create a special **escape sequence**, such as `'\n'` to represent advance to next line, and `'\t'` for a tab indention. A number of escape sequences can be used in C#. This is the same set of escape characters found in other languages such as Java and C++. Table 2-1 lists some of the more commonly used escape characters that can be included as part of a string in C#.

Table 2-1 Escape sequences

Escape sequence character	Description
\n	Cursor advances to the next line. Similar to clicking the Enter key.
\t	Cursor advances to the next horizontal tab stop.
\"	Double quote is printed.
\'	Single quote is printed.
\\	Backslash is printed.
\r	Cursor advances to the beginning of the current line.
\a	Alert signal (short beep) is sounded.

When an escape sequence is encountered inside the double quotes, it signals that a special character is to be produced as output. The output of the statement:

```csharp
Console.Write("What goes\nup\nmust come\tdown.");
```

is

```
What goes
up
must come        down.
```

Notice in the `Write( )` method that the argument inside the parentheses has three escape sequences. The backslash is not printed. When the `'\n'` is encountered, the output is advanced to the new line. The space between the words "come" and "down" was placed there as a result of the tab escape sequence (`'\t'`).

Two other methods in the `Console` **class**, `Read( )` and `ReadLine( )`, deserve explanation. Visually they differ from the `WriteLine( )` method in that they have no arguments—nothing is placed inside the parentheses. Both the `Read( )` and `ReadLine( )` methods can return values and are used for accepting input from a standard input device, such as a keyboard.

 Notice in Example 2-1 that the statements in the body of methods end in semicolons. But, no semicolon is placed at the end of method headings, **class** definition headings, or **namespace** definition headings. Note that semicolons appear on lines 2 and 9 in Example 2-1.

Read( ) is often used in a C# program to keep the output screen displayed until the user clicks a key on the keyboard. The **Read( )** method accepts any character from the input device, and as soon as a character is pressed, control passes to the next line in the program. Instead of accepting a single character as the **Read( )** method does, **ReadLine( )** allows multiple characters to be entered. It accepts characters until the Enter key is pressed.

Now that you know what elements make up a C# program, you are almost ready to begin developing your own programs. Figure 2-4 shows how **namespace, class**, method, and statements are related. Notice that the Framework Class Library (FCL) includes a number of different namespaces, such as **System**. Defined within a **namespace** are a number of classes, such as **Console**. Defined within a **class** are a number of methods, such as **WriteLine( )** and **Read( )**. You did not see the statements that made up the **WriteLine( )** method, you saw the **WriteLine( )** method being called. A method can have one or more statements. One of those statement can be a call to another method, such as the case of calling on the **WriteLine( )** method from within the **Main( )** method.

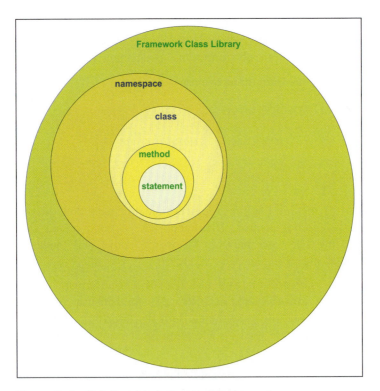

Figure 2-4   Relationship between C# elements

To develop software using C#, the .NET Framework is needed. The Framework includes all the predefined .NET classes. Having so many classes available decreases the amount of new code needed. You can use much of the functionality included in the `class` library. The next section describes how you get the Framework.

INSTALLING THE .NET FRAMEWORK

In the previous sections a working program was examined. To compile, build, and run a C# application, the .NET Framework must be installed. Installation of the Framework places the C# compiler, Common Language Runtime (CLR), and the predefined classes that make up .NET on your computer. Some installation options include:

- You can download the Microsoft .NET Framework Software Development Kit (SDK) from the Microsoft Web site. It is a free download. At the time of writing, the URL for the downloads was *www.microsoft.com/downloads*.

> **NOTE**
> You need to install both the SDK and the Redistributable package in order to write, build, test, and deploy applications. The Redistributable package needs to be installed prior to installing the SDK. The Redistributable package includes everything you need to run applications developed using the .NET Framework. You will find information about how to download and install these packages at the Microsoft Web site.

- Once downloaded, double-click the downloaded file and follow the instructions on the screen to finish installing the .NET Framework SDK on your system. After you complete the installation, be sure to restart your system. The SDK includes the extensive library of .NET classes, C# compiler, Common Language Runtime, and everything you need to build, test, and deploy applications.

- You can use **Visual Studio .NET**. This is a suite of products that includes several programming languages, including C#, along with a large collection of development and debugging tools. All of the .NET languages provide access to the Framework, the common execution engine, and the large `class` library. It is not necessary to download the SDK separately, if you install Visual Studio .NET.

- Several third-party vendors are creating C# compilers. Some of them do not even have to run on a Windows-based platform. On December 13, 2001, the General Assembly of the European Computer Manufacturers Association (ECMA) ratified C# and its Common Language Infrastructure (CLI) specifications into international standards. This opened opportunities for vendors, other than Microsoft, to develop C# compilers. If you want to develop on a Linux platform, you might consider downloading Mono. Another cross-platform implementation of C# is Rotor. In addition to the Windows platform, Rotor has an Apple OSX implementation. At the time of the writing, a large subset of the .NET Framework `class` libraries had been implemented and made available with these options, but not all. A search on the Web using C# and Mono or Rotor takes you to sites where those products can be downloaded.

Of the three listed above, the best option is Visual Studio .NET. It is a complete suite of tools for building applications. After you install the Framework, you need to create a directory to store your applications.

Creating a Place to Store Your Work

This section explains how to create a directory for your C# programs—preferably on the hard disk of your computer or a shared network drive. To create the directory, either open **Windows Explorer** or click the **My Computer** icon on the desktop. To create a storage area, move to the location in which you plan to store your projects. On the **File** menu, click **New>Folder** and type a folder name for your projects. For example, say you plan to store your work at C:\CSharpProjects. Move to the Local Disk (C:\), open the **File** menu, click **New>Folder**, and type **CSharpProjects**. You should perform this step so that you will have an organized pre-determined location to store your work.

 For your own local personal computer, you should follow these instructions for creating a storage area. However, check with your instructor to determine whether different instructions are needed to set up a place to store your work on campus computers. It may be necessary for you to place your work on secondary storage devices such as flash memory keys.

If you do not see the file extension when you browse your files, change the setting to show your file extensions by turning off (deselecting) **Hide Extension for known file types**. One way to do this is to use the **Folder Options** in the **Control Panel**. Using a Windows XP system, click on the **Start** menu in the lower-left corner of the screen, then click **Control Panel>Folder Options>View**. Deselect or uncheck **Hide extensions for known file types**. Select **Apply** to implement the change. Figure 2-5 illustrates making this change in a Windows XP environment.

 Depending on the operating system you are using, the wording may be slightly different. For example, in the Windows 2000 operating system, you deselect **Hide file extensions for known file types**.

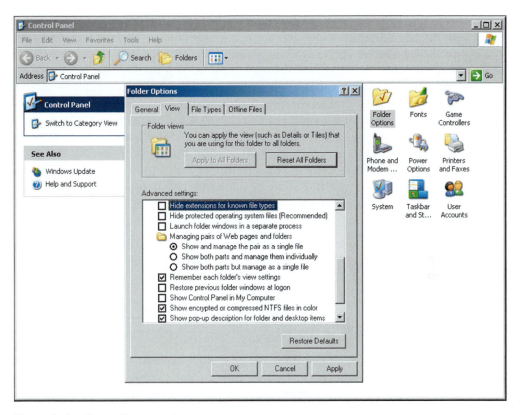

Figure 2-5 Show file extensions

> **NOTE** The file extension includes a dot and two to six characters following the name. Examples are .cs, .csproj, .sys, .doc, .suo, .sln and .exe. The extension identifies the type of information stored in the file. For example, a file ending in .cs is a C# source file. It is helpful to be able to identify files by type.

Typing Your Program Statements

You have a couple of options for writing code using C#. One approach to developing applications is to type the source code statements using a simple text editor (such as Notepad) and follow that up by using the DOS command line to compile and execute the application. This technique offers the advantage of not requiring significant system resources. Appendix A, "Visual Studio Command Line Tools," supplies more detail. All that is needed is the downloaded C# compiler with the .NET Framework, Notepad, and access to the DOS command line. This option also offers the opportunity of using the C# programming language on pre-Windows 2000 operating systems.

A second approach is to use the Visual Studio .NET Integrated Development Environment (IDE), and this chapter introduces you to Visual Studio. The IDE is an interactive environment that enables you to type the source code, compile, and execute without leaving the IDE program. Because of the debugging and editing features that are part of the IDE, you will find it much easier to develop applications if Visual Studio is available. In addition to the rich integrated development environment, Visual Studio includes a number of tools and wizards. To use Visual Studio, you must have at least Windows 2000 or XP Professional operating system loaded on a Pentium II-class 450 or higher MHz computer. The RAM recommendations are 128 MB for Windows 2000 and 256 MB for Windows XP Professional systems. To install Visual Studio, you need approximately 900 MB of available hard disk space. Visual Studio .NET does not run under Windows 98 or earlier operating systems. Appendix B, "Visual Studio IDE," describes many additional features of Visual Studio including suggestions for customizing the IDE.

 You can run Visual Studio on the Windows XP Home edition operating system. However, you will not be able to develop any web applications using this option.

COMPILING, BUILDING, AND RUNNING AN APPLICATION

The preceding sections described the program statements required as a minimum in most console-based applications. To see the results of a program, you must type the statements, or source code, into a file, compile that code, and then execute the application. The next sections examine what happens during the compilation and execution process with and without using the Visual Studio IDE.

Compilation and Execution Process

The **compiler** is used to check the grammar. It makes sure there are no rule violations in the program statements or source code. After the code is successfully compiled, the compiler generates a file that ends with an .exe extension. As noted in Chapter 1, the code in this .exe file has not yet been turned into machine code that is targeted to any specific CPU platform. Instead, the code generated by the compiler is **Microsoft Intermediate Language** (MSIL), often referred to simply as **IL**. In the second required step, the **Just-in-time** compiler **(JITer)** reads the IL code and translates or produces the machine code that runs on the particular platform. After the code is translated in this second step, results can be seen.

Operations going on behind the scene are not readily apparent. For example, after the compiler creates the IL, the code can be executed on any machine that has the .NET Framework installed. Microsoft offers as a free distribution the .NET Framework Redistributable version for deploying applications only. The **Redistributable version** is a smaller download than the SDK and includes the CLR and `class` libraries. Again, this is available at the Microsoft Web site.

The runtime version of the .NET Framework is similar in concept to the Java Virtual Machine (JVM). Like C#, Java's compiler first translates source code into intermediate code called bytecode. The bytecode must be converted to native machine code before results can be seen from an application. With C# the CLR actually translates only the parts of the program that are being used. This saves time. Additionally, after a portion of your IL file has been compiled on a computer, it never needs to be compiled again because the final compiled portion of the program is saved and used the next time that portion of the program is executed.

Compiling the Source Code Using Visual Studio .NET IDE

You can use the built-in editor available with the Visual Studio .NET IDE to type your program statement. You then compile the source code from one of the pull-down menu options in the IDE and execute the application using another menu option in the IDE. Many shortcuts are available. The next section explores how this is done using the Visual Studio .NET IDE.

Begin by opening Visual Studio .NET. Create a new project by either selecting the **New Project** button on the Start page or by using the **File**>**New**>**Project** option.

As shown in Figure 2-6, a list of project types appears in the left window. The right window contains the templates that can be used within the IDE. To develop a C# console application, select **Visual C# Projects** as the Project Type and **Console Application** for the Template. Using the **Browse** button, move to the location where you want to store your projects. The name of the project is HelloWorld.

Whatever name you give the project becomes the namespace's name for this project.

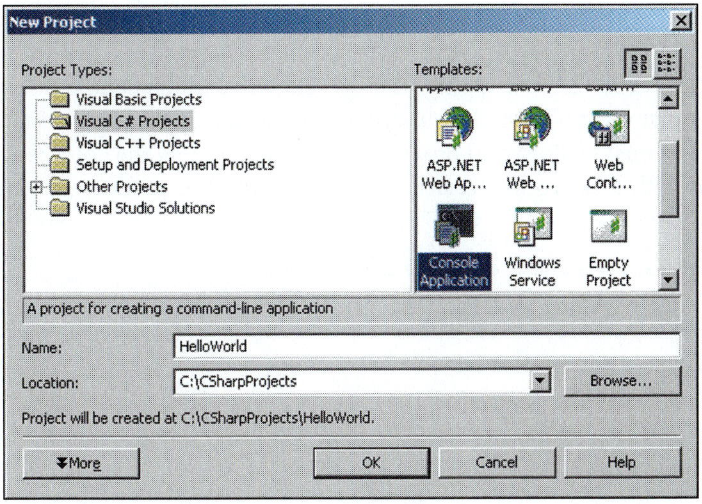

Figure 2-6   Creating a console application

Selecting the template determines what type of code is generated by the IDE. Figure 2-7 shows the code that is created automatically when you create a console application.

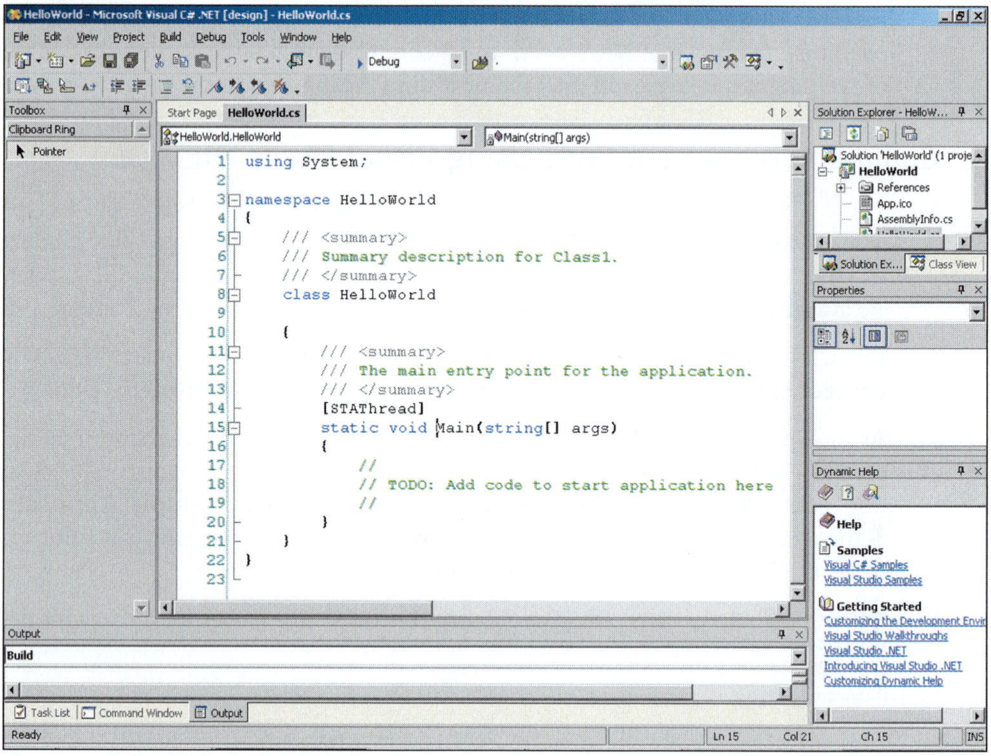

Figure 2-7   Code automatically generated by Visual Studio .NET

As you can see from Figure 2-7, having the IDE generate this much code reduces your typing. The only lines that must be added are those specific to the application being developed. To produce the traditional Hello World program, begin by replacing the comment line in the **Main( )** method with a call to the **WriteLine( )** method to produce the message. The following line

```
// TODO: Add code to start application here
```

is replaced with

```
Console.WriteLine("Hello World");
```

Notice that as soon as you type the period after the `Console` `class`, a smart window listing all of the `Console` methods and properties from which you could choose pops up. This is the **IntelliSense** feature of the IDE. As the name implies, the feature attempts to sense what you are going to type before you type it. When the window pops up, you can quickly select from the pull-down menu without having to complete the typing.

Next, change the name of the **class** and the source code file name. Visual Studio names every **class** Class1 and by default identifies all source code files by that same name. Use the **Solution Explorer** Window to change the source code file name to HelloWorld. Select the **Class1.cs** name. When you right-click on the name in the Solution Explorer Window, you see a rename option as is shown in Figure 2-8. If the Solution Explorer Window is not active on your desktop, select **View>Solution Explorer**. Be sure to include the .cs file extension when you rename the file.

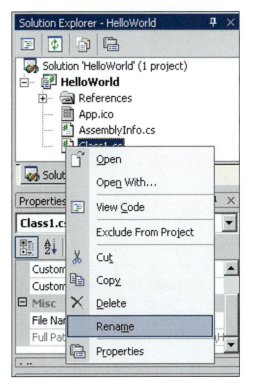

Figure 2-8   Changing the source code name from Class1

Change the name of the **class** by selecting the Class1 **class** name in the source code and replacing it with a new name. For this application, replace Class1 with HelloWorld.

It is not absolutely necessary to change the names of the source code file and `class`. The application can run without making that change; however, to develop good habits you should change the name. It can save you time and grief when applications involve multiple classes.

The statements in Example 2-3 appeared in Example 2-1 and are repeated here without the line numbers so that you can see the final source listing.

Visual Studio generates a couple of other unnecessary lines that can be removed. You will read about them later in this chapter.

Example 2-3

```csharp
// This is traditionally the first program written.

using System;
namespace FirstProgram
{
      class HelloWorld
      {
          static void Main( )
          {
              Console.WriteLine("Hello World");
          }
      }
}
```

Do remember that C# is case sensitive, meaning the name HelloWorld is a totally differ- ent name from helloWorld, even though only one character is different. So be very careful to type the statements exactly as they are shown.

To compile the `HelloWorld` project, select the **Build HelloWorld** option on the **Build** Menu as shown in Figure 2-9. The name `HelloWorld` follows the Build option because `HelloWorld` is the name of the project. Projects that contain more than one `class` are compiled using the Build Solution option.

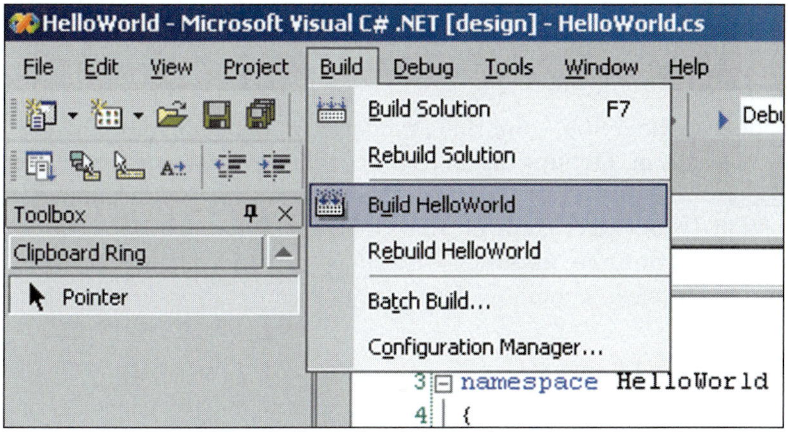

Figure 2-9   Compilation of a project using Visual Studio .NET

To run the application, you can click **Start** or **Start Without Debugging** on the Debug menu bar as illustrated in Figure 2-10. If you attempt to execute code that has not been compiled (using Build), the smart IDE compiles the code first. Therefore, many developers use the shortcut of bypassing the Build step.

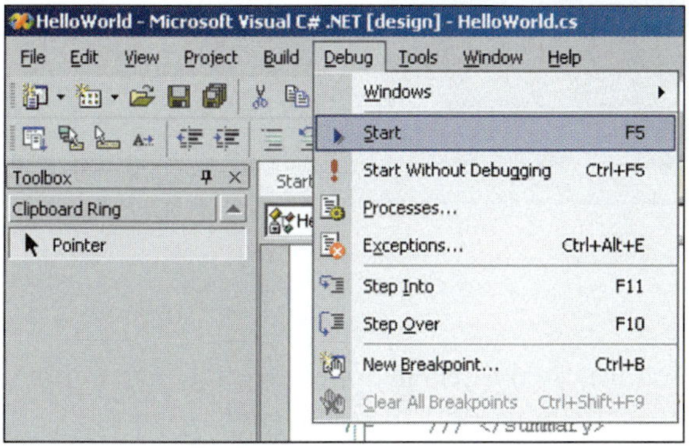

Figure 2-10   Execution of an application using Visual Studio .NET

When you ran the application using the Start option, you probably noticed that the output flashes on the screen and then disappears. You can hold the output screen if you include a call to the `Read( )` method. When this line is executed, the program waits for you to click a key before it terminates. To add this, go back into the source code and place this line as the last statement in the `Main( )` method:

```
Console.Read( );
```

You learned in Chapter 1 that the software development cycle is iterative, and it is sometimes necessary to return to previous phases. After you type the additional statement, recompile, and reexecute when there are no more syntax errors.

Another option to hold the command windows in Visual Studio .NET is to select **Debug>Start Without Debugging** instead of **Debug>Start** to execute your program. Notice in Figure 2-10 that **Start Without Debugging** is the option immediately below the **Start** option. If you select **Debug>Start Without Debugging**, it is not necessary to add the additional `Console.Read( );` statement. When you use the **Start Without Debugging** option for execution, the user is prompted to "Press any key to continue" as illustrated in Figure 2-11.

Several other shortcuts are available to run your program. Notice as you look at the menu option under **Debug** that Ctrl+F5 is listed as a shortcut for **Start Without Debugging**; F5 is the shortcut for **Start**. In addition, if you have the Build Toolbars icons on your screen, a red exclamation point also represents **Start Without Debugging**.

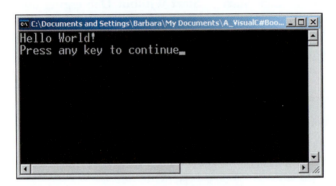

Figure 2-11   Output from Hello World

Visual Studio .NET is a highly sophisticated Integrated Development Environment. Appendix B, "Visual Studio IDE," includes additional information regarding customizing the development environment and using the debugger for development. Reviewing that material now would be wise.

DEBUGGING AN APPLICATION

It is inevitable that your programs will not always work properly immediately. There are several types of errors that can occur and cause you frustration. The major categories of errors—syntax and runtime—are discussed in the next sections.

Syntax Errors

When you type source code statements into the editor, you are apt to make typing errors by misspelling a name or forgetting to end a statement with a semicolon. These types of errors are categorized as **syntax errors** and are caught by the compiler. When you compile, the compiler checks the segment of code to see if you have violated any of the rules of the language. If it cannot recognize a statement, it issues an error message, which is sometimes cryptic, but it should help you fix the problem. Error messages in Visual Studio .NET are more descriptive than those issued at the command line. But, be aware that a single typing error may generate several error messages. Figure 2-12 shows a segment of code, in which a single error causes the compiler to generate three error messages.

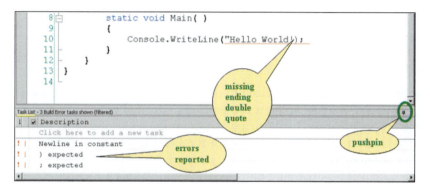

Figure 2-12 Syntax error message listing

The error messages are displayed in the **Task List** window found at the bottom of the IDE. The IDE also underlines the supposed location of the problem. You can also double-click on any of the error messages to go directly to the line flagged by the compiler. If the Task List is not visible on your screen, you can select **Show Tasks>All** or **Show Tasks>Build Errors** on the **View** menu.

A pushpin icon appears in the top-right corner of all tool windows such as that shown in the Task List window. When the pushpin stands up like a thumbtack, the window is docked in place; thus, the Task List window is docked in place in Figure 2-12.

 Tool windows support a feature called Auto Hide. If you click the pushpin so that it appears to be lying on its side, the window minimizes along the edges of the IDE. A small tab with the window name appears along the edge. This frees up space so you can see more of your source code. When you run your application, the Task List window automatically becomes visible again or, if you move your pointer over the named tab, it is redisplayed.

The syntax error shown in Figure 2-12 is a common mistake. The double quote was omitted from the end of the argument to the `WriteLine( )` method at line 17. The error message does not say that, however. When you are reviewing error messages, keep in mind that the message may not be issued until the compiler reaches the next line or next block of code. Look for the problem in the general area that is flagged. Some of the most common errors are failing to end an open curly brace ({) or having an extra end curly brace (}), failing to type a semicolon at the end of a statement (;), and misspelling names. As a good exercise, consider purposefully omitting curly braces, semicolons, and misspelling words. See what kind of error messages each mistake generates. You will then be more equipped to find those errors quickly when you develop more sophisticated applications in the future.

 Since one error may generate several messages, it is probably best to fix the first error and then recompile rather than trying to fix all the errors in one pass.

Runtime Errors

Runtime errors are much more difficult to detect than syntax errors. A program containing runtime errors may compile without any problems, run, and produce results. Many times, logic errors are not identified until you look closely at the results and verify their correctness. If the results are incorrect, the associated error is called a **logic error**. Failing to understand the problem specification fully is the most common culprit in logic errors. It is not enough to produce output; the output must be a correct solution to the problem.

Another potential runtime error type will be introduced when you start working with data in Chapter 3, "Data Types and Expressions." If you are using data for calculations or performing different steps based on the value of data, it is easy to encounter a runtime error. Runtime errors can be minimized during software development by performing a thorough analysis and design before beginning the coding phase. The common strategy of desk checking, introduced in Chapter 1, also leads to more accurate results.

CREATING AN APPLICATION

Now that you understand what is required in most C# programs and how to compile and see your results, work through the following example using the suggested methodology for program development introduced in Chapter 1. In this section, you design a solution for the following problem definition.

Programming Example: ProgrammingMessage

2

The problem specification is shown in Figure 2-13.

Create your first C# Program.

The purpose of this project is to give you practice in following the Steps to Software Development.

The program should output the following phrase:

Programming can be FUN!

Figure 2-13   Problem specification sheet for the ProgrammingMessage example

Analyze the Problem   Do you understand the problem definition? This step is often slighted or glossed over. It is easy to scan the problem definition and think you have a handle on the problem, but miss an important feature. If you do not devote adequate time and energy analyzing the problem definition, much time and expense might be wasted in later steps. This is one, if not the most important, step in the development process. Ask questions to clarify the problem definition if necessary. You want to make sure you fully grasp what is expected.

As you read the problem definition given in Figure 2-13, note that no program inputs are required. The only data needed for this application is a string of characters. This greatly simplifies the analysis phase.

Design a Solution   The desired output, as noted in the problem specification sheet in Figure 2-13, is to display "Programming can be FUN!" on two lines. For this example, as well as any other application you develop, it is helpful to determine what your final output should look like. One way to document your desired output is to construct a **prototype**, or mock-up, of the output. Prototypes range from being elaborate designs created with graphics, word processing, or paint programs, to being quite cryptic sketches created with paper and pencil. It is crucial to realize the importance of constructing a prototype, no matter which method you use. Developing a prototype helps you construct your algorithm. Prototypes also provide additional documentation detailing the purpose of the application. Figure 2-14 shows a prototype of the final output for the ProgrammingMessage example.

Figure 2-14 Prototype for the ProgrammingMessage example

During design it is important to develop an algorithm. The algorithm for this problem could be developed using a flowchart. The algorithm should include a step-by-step solution for solving the problem, which in this case is straightforward and involves merely the output of a string of characters. Figure 2-15 contains a flowchart defining the steps needed for the ProgrammingMessage example.

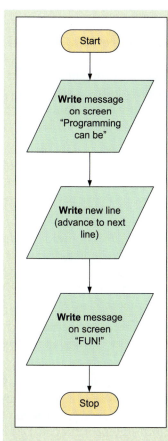

Figure 2-15   Algorithm for ProgrammingMessage example

Another option is to use structured English or pseudocode to define the algorithm. The pseudocode for this problem would be very short. It would include a single line to display the message "Programming can be FUN!" on the output screen.

Using an object–oriented approach to design, the solutions normally entail creating **class** diagrams. No data members would need to be defined for this problem. The **Console class** in the **System namespace** already has methods you can use to display output on a standard output device. Thus, no new methods or behaviors would need to be defined. So, if you were to construct a **class** diagram, it would include only a heading for the **class**. Nothing would appear in the middle or bottom portion of the diagram. Since the diagram does not provide additional documentation or help with the design of this simple problem, it is not drawn.

As noted in Chapter 1, after the algorithm is developed, the design should be checked for correctness. One way to do this is to desk check your algorithms by mimicking the computer and working through the code step by step as if you were the computer. When you step through the flowchart, it should produce the output that appears on the prototype. It is extremely important that you carefully design and check your algorithm for correctness before beginning to write your code. You will spend much less time and experience much less frustration if you do this.

Code the Solution After you have completed the design and verified the algorithm's correctness, it is time to translate the design into source code. You can type source code statements into the computer using a simple editor such as Notepad, or you can create the file using Visual Studio .NET. In this step of the process, you must pay attention to the language syntax rules.

If you create the application using Visual Studio .NET, the IDE automatically generates much of the code for you. Some of that code can be removed or disregarded. For example, do you remember what the three forward slashes signify? These are XML-style comments. You will be using only the in-line comment `//` or multi-line, user-supplied comments `/* */`. You can remove or disregard the XML-style comment lines.

Visual Studio .NET inserts `[STAThread]` on the line preceding the `Main( )` method heading. This indicates that only one thread, or process, is executed at a time from within this application. You can also remove or disregard this line.

Visual Studio .NET also modifies the `Main( )` method's heading from what you saw previously in this chapter. The signature for `Main( )` can have an empty argument list or include "`string[ ] args`" inside the parentheses. For the types of applications you are developing, you do not need to send the additional argument. So, you can also remove or disregard the argument inside the parentheses to `Main( )` at this time.

You may want to change the name of the `class` from `Class1` to a name that better represents what the application is doing. When you typed `ProgrammingMessage` as the project name, the IDE automatically named the `namespace ProgrammingMessage`. The `class` could also be called `ProgrammingMessage`, and this would cause no name clashing problems such as the `namespace` being given the same name as the `class` name. Figure 2-16 illustrates the changes you might want to make to the code generated by Visual Studio .NET.

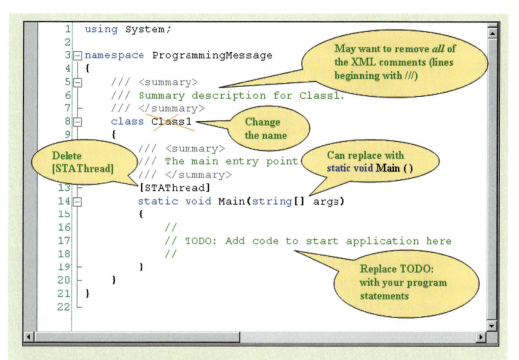

Figure 2-16   Recommended deletions

You would replace the comment lines listed here with the three calls to `Console` methods, which are also listed here:

```
//
// TODO: Add code to start application here
//
```

The only lines that you had to type were found in the `Main( )` body.

```
Console.WriteLine("Programming can be");
Console.WriteLine("FUN!");
Console.Read( );
```

The final program listing looks like this:

```
/*  Programmer:     [supply your name]
    Date:           [supply the current date]
    Purpose:        This class can be used to send messages
                    to the output screen.
*/
using System;
namespace ProgrammingMessage
```

```
{
    class ProgrammingMessage
    {
        static void Main( )
        {
            Console.WriteLine("Programming can be");
            Console.WriteLine("FUN!");
            Console.Read( );
        }
    }
}
```

At the beginning of your program, identify the author of the code, and as a minimum specify the purpose of the project. Note that the statements inside the **Main( )** method are executed in sequential order. The **Read( )** method is executed after the two **WriteLine( )** methods. **Read( )** is used in a program to keep the output screen displayed until the user clicks a key. After a character is clicked on the keyboard, control passes to the next line that marks the end of the application.

Implement the Code During implementation, the source code is compiled to check for rule violations. To compile from within the Visual Studio .NET IDE, use the **Build** menu option. If you have errors, they must be corrected before you can go forward. From within the Visual Studio .NET IDE, select **Start Without Debugging** on the **Debug** menu bar to see the results.

Test and Debug Just because you have no compiler syntax errors and receive output does not mean the results are correct. During this final step, test the program and ensure you have the correct result. The output should match your prototype. Is your spacing correct?

By following the steps outlined in this chapter, you have officially become a C# programmer. The program you created was a simple one. However, the concepts you learned in this chapter are essential to your progress. In Chapter 3 you will begin working with data.

QUICK REVIEW

1. C# can be used to create Web, window, and console applications.
2. Web pages are created using Web Forms, which are part of the ASP.NET technology.
3. Windows applications are considered desktop bound and designed for a single platform.
4. Console applications are the easiest to create. Values can be entered and produced with minimal overhead.
5. C# programs usually begin with a comment or **using** directives, followed by an optional **namespace** grouping and then the required **class** definition.

2

6. All C# programs must define a **class**.

7. Comments are written as notes to yourself or to readers of your program. The compiler ignores comments.

8. It is not necessary to end single in-line comments **//**; they end when the Enter key is pressed. Comments that span more than one line should be enclosed between **/* */**. These are considered block or multiple-line comments.

9. Over 2,000 classes make up the Framework **class** library. A **class** contains data members and methods or behaviors that can be reused.

10. The using-namespace-directive imports all the types contained in the given **namespace**. By specifying the **namespace** around which you are building an application, you can eliminate the need of preceding a **class** with a dot (.) and the name of the **namespace**.

11. Everything in C# is designed around a **class**. Every program must have at least one **class**.

12. A method is a collection of one or more statements taken together that perform an action. In other words, a method is a small block of code that performs an action.

13. The **Main( )** method is the "entry point" for every C# console application. It is the point at which execution begins.

14. The keyword **static** indicates that a single copy of the method is created.

15. The keyword **void** is included to signal that no value is returned. The complete signature of a method starts with the return type, followed by the name of the method, and finally a parenthesized list of arguments. One signature for **Main( )** is **void static Main( )**.

16. **WriteLine( )** writes a string message to the monitor or a standard output device.

17. Methods communicate with each other through arguments placed inside parentheses.

18. Readability is important. Indenting is not required, but it is a good practice because it makes the code easier to read.

19. To see the results of a program, you must type the statements (source code) into a file, compile that code, and then execute the application.

20. Visual Studio .NET Integrated Development Environment (IDE) is an interactive development environment that enables you to type the source code, compile, and execute without leaving the IDE program.

21. One way to document your desired output is to construct a prototype, or mock-up, of your output.

22. The **Read( )** method accepts any character from a standard input device, such as a keyboard. It does nothing with the character.

EXERCISES

1. ASP.NET creates which type of application?

    a. Windows

    b. console

    c. command

    d. Web

    e. services

2. Which beginning symbol(s) identifies the following ten lines as comments?

    a. `/*`

    b. `**`

    c. `//`

    d. `///`

    e. `*/`

3. System is an example of a(n):

    a. object

    b. `class`

    c. method

    d. `namespace`

    e. directive

4. A(n) _____ groups semantically related types under a single name.

    a. object

    b. `class`

    c. method

    d. `namespace`

    e. directive

5. To mark the beginning and end of a block of code, C# programmers use:

    a. [ ]

    b. { }

    c. ( )

    d. begin… end

    e. start… stop

6. Which of the following is a keyword?

    a. `Main( )`

    b. `System`

2

   c. `using`

   d. `WriteLine`

   e. all of the above

7. Which of the following is a signature for a method?

   a. `Main( )`

   b. `Console.WriteLine("Ok");`

   c. `using Programming1`

   d. `static System.Read( )`

   e. none of the above

8. The fully qualified call to the method that allows the user to input a single character is:

   a. `Console.System.Read( )`

   b. `System.Console.Read( )`

   c. `Console.System.Write( )`

   d. `System.Console.Write( )`

   e. `System.Console.ReadLine( )`

9. Source code must be translated into machine code (also called native code). This two-step process begins with a(n):

   a. debugger

   b. editor

   c. interpreter

   d. JITer

   e. compiler

10. A(n) _____ is a mock-up of desired output.

   a. prototype

   b. algorithm

   c. diagram

   d. specification

   e. none of the above

11. What is the name of the feature in Visual Studio .NET that displays in a scrollable list all available methods and properties when the dot is typed after an object name?

   a. Help

   b. Rotor

   c. Mono

   d. IntelliSense

   e. ToolTip

12. To see the results of an application, you _____ the code.

   a. compile

   b. JIT

   c. execute

   d. edit

   e. desk check

13. A console application is characterized by:

   a. containing a `Main( )` `class`

   b. containing a `Main( )` method

   c. featuring a GUI

   d. belonging to the Web Forms `class`

   e. requiring the use of a System.Interface `namespace`

14. A possible signature for `Main( )` is:

   a. `static void Main( )`

   b. `static void Main(string [ ] args )`

   c. `Main( )`

   d. a and b are correct

   e. a, b, and c are correct

15. Which of the following is a call to a method?

   a. `Console.Write;`

   b. `Console.Write["ok"];`

   c. `Write.Console("ok");`

   d. `Console.Write("ok");`

   e. none of the above

16. Identify one syntax error that might occur when you type Example 2-1 into an editor. Identify one logic error that might occur.

17. What is produced when you run the following application?

```
line 1   // Example program - displaying output.
line 2   using System;
line 3   namespace ExerciseI
line 4   {
line 5       class Problem2
line 6       {
line 7             static void Main( )
```

```
line 8               {
line 9                       Console.Write("Go ");
line 10                      Console.Write("Laugh ");
line 11                      Console.WriteLine("Out Loud");
line 12                      Console.Write("Think ");
line 13                      Console.Write("Happy");
line 14              }
line 15      }
line 16  }
```

18. What must be changed in the segment of code in Exercise #17 to cause all of the output to be displayed on one line?

19. Search the Internet and identify the URL of one site, other than Microsoft, that has a C# compiler available for download.

20. Using the program segment in Exercise #17, identify line number(s) in which each of the following can be found:

a. method invocation

b. **namespace**

c. **class** name

d. argument to a method

e. comment

f. identifier

21. Identify the syntax error(s) (if any) in the following:

```
line 1     using System
line 2     namesspace ExerciseI
line 3     {
line 4         Problem2
line 5         {
line 6             static Main( )
line 7             {
line 8                 console.write("ok")
line 9             }
line 10        }
line 11  }
```

22. Explain the relationship between **System**, **Console**, and **Read**.

23. Think algorithmically. Write a set of instructions for each of the activities that follow. Your algorithm should be so complete that you could give it to other people, and they could perform the task specified without asking additional questions.

a. Make a peanut butter and jelly sandwich.

b. Walk to your next class.

c. Purchase a bottle of water from a vending machine.

PROGRAMMING EXERCISES

1. Write a program that produces the following output. Replace the name Tyler Howard with your name.

   Hello, Tyler Howard

2. First develop a prototype, and then write a program that displays the name of the programming language discussed in this text. One possible design is given here.

   ```
   CCCCCCCCCC
   CC                          ##      ##
   CC                      ###############
   CC                          ##      ##
   CC                      ###############
   CC                          ##      ##
   CCCCCCCCCC
   ```

3. Hangman is a favorite childhood game. Design the stick figure for this game and produce a printed listing with your stickman. One possible design follows. You may implement this design or develop an improved version.

   ```
    (^;^)

      |
   ./ | \.

      |
   _/ \_
   ```

4. Every program that you create should begin with internal documentation identifying the assignment. You might want to include some of these items: programming assignment number, your name as developer, program due date, the date the program is turned in, and the purpose of the application. Develop an application that produces a banner containing this information. Your output might look something like the following:

   ```
   **************************************************
   *     Programming Assignment #4                  *
   *     Developer:         Alma King               *
   *     Date Submitted:    September 17             *
   *     Purpose:   Provide internal documentation. *
   **************************************************
   ```

   In addition to printing the output screen banner shown in the preceding code segment, be sure to include appropriate comments as internal documentation to your program.

5. Flags are a symbol of unity and invoke special meaning to their followers. Create a design for a flag, and write a program that displays your design. One possible design follows.

6. Create an application that produces the following output. It should be displayed on three lines, exactly as it appears here.

Today is the FIRST day of the rest of your life.

Live it to the FULLEST!

You may not get a second chance…

7. Exercise 6 presents a popular saying. Produce a listing containing your favorite saying. Double space the output and print the saying one word per line.

8. Print your birth year in one column. For example, if you were born in 1982, your output should look like the following:

1

9

8

2

9. Create an application that displays the following patterns. You may use any character of your choice to construct the pattern.

```
* * * * * * * * *              *                    *
* * * * * * * * *             * * *                 * * *
* * * * * * * * *            * * * * *              * * * * *
* * * * * * * * *           * * * * * * *           * * * * * * *
* * * * * * * * *          * * * * * * * * *        * * * * * * * * *
* * * * * * * * *         * * * * * * * * * * *     * * * * * * *
* * * * * * * * *        * * * * * * * * * * * * *   * * * * *
* * * * * * * * *       * * * * * * * * * * * * * * *  * * *
* * * * * * * * *      * * * * * * * * * * * * * * * * *  *
```

10. Write your initials in block characters to a standard output device. Design your proto-type using the symbol(s) of your choice.

3

Data Types and Expressions

Chapter 2 introduced you to the basic elements of a C# program. You discovered the requirements for developing, compiling, and executing console applications. The applications you created were restricted to displaying text output, and although these are interesting applications, they are quite limited. This chapter focuses on data. **Data** is the raw facts—the basic numbers and characters that are manipulated to produce useful information. In this chapter, you begin to see the power of programming when you write applications to perform calculations. You learn how to declare variables that hold different types of data in memory and see how arithmetic operators react given different kinds of data.

MEMORY LOCATIONS FOR DATA

Programs manipulate data, and data can take the form of a number, single character, or combination of characters. The following are all examples of data:

18, "Brenda", 'A', 3.25, –7, 36724, and 47.23

By themselves, these data items have no value. The number 18 could be an age, temperature, number of students in a class, number of hours you are enrolled in this term, or could represent something totally different. Without identifying and labeling 18, it is a meaningless number. When working with data, the first task is to use an identifier to name the data item.

Identifiers

Identifiers are names of elements that appear in a program, such as data items. Some identifiers are predefined; others are user defined. You have already seen some .NET identifiers when you wrote your first program in Chapter 2. These were not reserved keywords, but simply names selected and used by the developers of the .NET platform and the C# language. The program in Example 2-1 contained the following predefined identifiers: `System`, `Main`, `Console`, and `WriteLine`.

The `namespace` identifier of `ProgrammingI` and the `class` identifier of `HelloWorld` are user-defined identifiers selected by the author of the textbook during the creation of the first project.

Here are the rules for creating an identifier in C#:

1. A combination of alphabetic characters (a–z, and A–Z), numeric digits (0–9), and the underscores (_) can be used. Identifiers can be long; however, many systems consider the first 31 characters unique.

2. The first character in the name may not be a numeric digit.

3. No embedded spaces can be placed between the characters. This means you cannot separate words in a name by a space. Normally you concatenate (append) second and subsequent words onto the identifier by capitalizing the second word.

The underscore character is used between words as a separator by languages such as C++. Even though it is a valid character that can be used in C#, the underscore character is used primarily for defining constant identifiers. You learn about constant literals in this chapter.

4. Table 3-1 shows the **keywords** in C#. Keywords are predefined reserved identifiers that have special meanings to the compiler. They cannot be used as identifiers in your program.

3

Table 3-1 C# keywords

Keywords					
abstract	as	base	bool	break	byte
case	catch	char	checked	class	const
continue	decimal	default	delegate	do	double
else	enum	event	explicit	extern	false
finally	fixed	float	for	foreach	goto
if	implicit	in	int	interface	internal
is	lock	long	namespace	new	null
object	operator	out	override	params	private
protected	public	readonly	ref	return	sbyte
sealed	short	sizeof	stackalloc	static	string
struct	switch	this	throw	true	try
typeof	uint	ulong	unchecked	unsafe	ushort
using	virtual	volatile	void	while	

5. It is permissible to use the "@" symbol as the first character of an identifier, but it has special meaning and should be avoided unless you are writing code that will interface with another programming language. When used, the "@" symbol enables keywords to be used as identifiers.

6. It is smart to use the case of the character to your advantage. C# is case sensitive. The identifier `Rate` is a different from the identifier `rate` and also different from `RATE` or `rATE`.

   With .NET, there are three conventions for capitalizing identifiers, Pascal case, camel case, and uppercase. Using **Pascal case**, the first letter in the identifier and the first letter of each subsequent concatenated word are capitalized. Classes, methods, namespaces, and properties follow the Pascal case naming convention in C#. Variables and objects follow the camel case convention, also referred to as

Hungarian notation. With **camel case**, the first letter of an identifier is lowercase, and the first letter of each subsequent concatenated word is capitalized. The convention in C# is to use camel case for variable and object identifiers. Uppercase is used by constant literals and for identifiers that consist of two or fewer letters.

7. Being descriptive is helpful. Use meaningful names that represent the item being described. If the identifier is used to reference a person's age, call it age, not x. The more descriptive your identifiers, the easier it is for you and others to read your code.

Table 3-2 shows examples of valid identifiers.

Table 3-2 Valid identifiers

Valid identifiers		
studentName	age	numberOfCourses
soc_sec_number	departureTime	course1
AmountOwed	count_of_Values	taxAmount
n	streetAddress	zipCode
roomSize	courseName	x3
moreData	bookTitle	homeRuns
pointsScored	CLUB_NAME	exam4

The compiler will not catch a violation in rule #7 of the previous list. However, this rule is extremely important, and you should follow it. By using meaningful names that describe their contents, programs you develop are more readable and easier to debug and modify. Table 3-3 shows a list of illegal identifiers and a notation indicating why they are invalid.

Table 3-3 Invalid identifiers

Invalid identifiers	Description of violation
soc sec number	Embedded space
int	Reserved keyword
3n	Begins with a digit
room #	Special symbol other than underscore
first-name	Special symbol other than underscore
A number	Embedded space
class	Reserved keyword

The rules for identifiers in C# correspond exactly to those recommended by the Unicode 3.0 standard. The only exception is that Unicode does not recognize that an underscore is allowed as an initial character. This feature was probably included in the C# language because other programming languages such as C++ allow it.

Variables

3

For a computer program to process or manipulate data, the characters and numbers must be stored in random access memory (RAM). Variables are the programming elements that facilitate this storage. A **variable** represents an area in the computer memory where a value of a particular data type can be stored. When you **declare a variable**, you allocate memory for that data item in your program.

Declaring a variable requires that you select an identifier and determine what type of data will appear in the memory cell. The syntax for declaring a variable follows:

```
type identifier;
```

At the same time the variable is declared or created, it may be initialized to a value. This is referred to as a **compile-time initialization**. Notice the word initialization. The variable starts off with the initialized value, but it can be changed. The value being assigned to the variable should be compatible with the data type. The syntax for initializing a variable when it is declared follows:

```
type identifier = expression;
```

 The expression can simply be a value such as 0, or it can include other identifiers in an arithmetic equation. When the variable is going to be used in arithmetic, it is a good idea to initialize it to 0.

With both types of declaration, in addition to naming the data item, you must also determine what type of data will be associated with it. This step notifies the computer of how much storage space to set aside for the data item as well as how to retrieve the data after it is placed in memory.

Literal Values

A variable's value can change. Literals cannot be changed. **Literals** are the numbers, characters, and combinations of characters used in your program. They can be assigned to a variable or used in an expression. Their values stay constant. The number 17 is always 17. The character 'A' is always A. It is possible to copy the value of a literal into a variable and then change the variable; this does not change the value of the original literal. It is also possible to use literals without assigning them to a specific variable.

Every time you declare a variable in the C# language, you are actually **instantiating** a **class** (creating an **object**). If you declare three variables of **int** type, you are instantiating the **class** three times; three **int** objects are created. The following statement creates three **int** objects:

```
int homeWorkScore1;
int examNumber1;
int numberOfPointsScored;
```

 Notice how the camel case naming convention was used to declare the variables of homeWorkScore1, examNumber1, and numberOfPointsScored. The first letter is lowercase. The first character of subsequent words is uppercase. You were instantiating the **int class** when these objects were created.

Literals are often used to give a value to an object's data portion. This can be done when the **object** is created or later in the program statements. A value such as 100 could be assigned to **homeWorkScore1** using the following statement:

```
homeWorkScore1 = 100;
```

Here 100 is a numeric literal. The contents of the memory location where the variable **homeWorkScore1** stored the value 100 can be changed; however, the literal value of 100 cannot be changed. 100 is always 100.

C# differs from languages that include a default value for variables when they are declared. In C#, every variable must be assigned a value before it is used. Otherwise, a syntax error is issued.

The next sections explain how the concept of types, classes, and objects are related to data.

Types, Classes, and Objects

C# is an object-oriented language that makes extensive use of classes and objects. The section that follows explains where types fit into this picture.

Types

C# has a large number of predefined types for use in your programs. When you think about what a type is in the English language, you probably associate type with a label that signifies the sharing of some common characteristics by a group that belongs to that category. Dictionary definitions of the word "type" run something like this: a kind or group that can be differentiated from other kinds or groups by a particular set of characteristics. Example 3-1 should help you build on your understanding of what a type is and the importance of using the correct type.

Example 3-1

You might have or plan to own a certain type of vehicle, such as a Hummer, or a Corvette. Hummer vehicle types have different characteristics from those of the Corvette. A Corvette can travel at a faster pace than a Hummer. But, the Hummer can travel over much rougher terrain. You would not take the Corvette into a mountainous hiking region with the expectation that it could travel over large rocks, whereas a Hummer might do the trick. You would not want to transport four people in a Corvette, but four people could easily fit into a Hummer. Each is considered a vehicle. If you owned both, you could decide which one to use depending on the situation or destination.

For C# there is more than one type of number. One number type is called an **integer**, or `int`. The `int` type is a whole number, between a certain range of values, and contains no decimal point. It can be positive or negative. Another type of number is a **floating-point value**, which can contain a fractional portion. C# supports two types of floating-point types: `float` and `double`. If you wanted to store your grade point average, it would not be appropriate to put that value in an `int`—because an `int` only lets you store the whole number portion. It would be like trying to put more than two people in the Corvette. They just do not fit. If your grade point average is 3.87 and you place the value in an `int` type, it chops off, **truncates**, the .87 and your grade point average becomes 3. You would not be very happy with that, would you?

Classes

Types are actually implemented through classes in C#. The Framework Class Library, which is part of .NET, includes over 2000 classes that you can use in your programs. There is a one-to-one correspondence between a `class` and a type in C#. C# was designed from the ground up to be and is a true object-oriented language. As you learned in Chapter 2, every program must include a `class`. Some programming languages such as C++ and Java support object-oriented development, but are not totally object-oriented languages. These languages may build applications using classes, but separate from classes are their primitive data types, like `double` and `int`, which are not implemented as a `class`.

In C# a simple data type such as a whole number, `int`, is implemented as a `class`. All the basic built-in data types, sometimes referred to as **primitives**, are implemented as classes. In other languages, these primitive data types do not benefit from the inheritance capabilities of being a `class`. As you progress in your software development, you will find this feature of C# of great benefit for object-oriented development.

Objects

As mentioned previously, an `object` is an instance of a `class`. It is an occurrence of the `class`. An instance of the base type `int` would be 21 or 3421. However, a `class` includes more than just the data associated with the type. **Class** is the term used to denote the encapsulation of data and behaviors into a single package or unit. The characteristics of the class's behavior and data can be described. The data portion of the `int`, as indicated previously, is always a whole number value. An `int` can contain values that do not have a decimal portion. The behavior can be described by stating basic arithmetic operations such as addition and subtraction that can be performed on the `int` type. Logical comparisons can determine which is larger than the other, and values can be displayed. Encapsulating (packaging) these data and behavior characteristics into a single unit allows you to describe the built-in `int class`.

Example 3-2

Your current grade point average might be named using an identifier such as GPA. Grade point average normally takes the form of a real number with a fractional component, such as 3.42. In C#, real numbers with decimals are represented using the `double` data type. Your name is another data item composed of a `string` of characters. In C#, the data type `string` is used to represent a grouping of characters. To represent a single character, such as the first initial of your last name, a `char` data type is used. Your age, for example 21, is a whole number without a fractional part. The data type most often used to represent a number without a fractional part is an `int`. Table 3-4 shows the data type, `class`, and `object` (instance) of these data items.

Table 3-4 Relationship between type, class, and object

Description	Identifier	Data type	Class	Object (instance)
grade point average	`gradePointAverage`	`double`	`double`	3.99
current age	`age`	`int`	`int`	19
full name	`studentName`	`string`	`string`	Elizabeth Hill
final grade in a course	`courseGrade`	`char`	`char`	A

You learned in Chapter 2 that every program must define a `class`. There are thousands of classes that make up the .NET Framework Class Library. The next section describes some of the predefined data types that are considered primitive data types in most languages. These value and reference types will be explored: `int`, `double`, `decimal`, `bool`, `char`, and `string`.

PREDEFINED DATA TYPES

The .NET Framework includes a Common Type System (CTS) that is supported by all .NET languages, including C#. This enables cross-language integration of code—meaning a single application can be written using multiple languages, such as C#, J#, and Visual Basic

.NET. The types in the CTS are referred to as common types and are divided into two major categories as seen in Figure 3-1: value types and reference types.

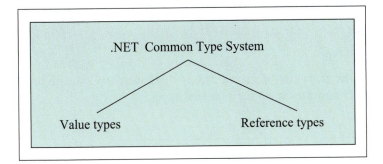

Figure 3-1   .NET common types

When placed in memory, value types contain their own copy of data, in binary notation. The data is stored in the actual memory cell that is addressed by the value type's identifier. In contrast, the contents of reference type memory cells are much different. Reference types contain the address or location in which the sequence of bits is stored. Figure 3-2 shows the difference between how value types are stored and how reference types are stored. An integer value type, such as 2004, representing the year a car was manufactured, is stored directly in the memory cell. To store a string of characters, such as the kind of vehicle, the memory location would contain the address in which "Corvette" is located. The `string` data type is a reference type. The memory location associated with the identifier does not contain the characters "Corvette", but instead the address in which "Corvette" is stored.

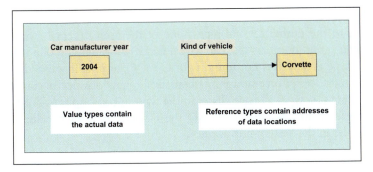

Figure 3-2   Memory representation for value and reference types

Value Types

The **value types** are often called the fundamental data types or primitive data types of the language. They are the common types needed by most applications. In C#, these fundamental types are further subdivided into the following categories:

- Struct types
- Enumerated types

As you look down the hierarchy of Figure 3-3, at the lowest level you find that Integral, Floating-point, and Decimal make up the Numeric types.

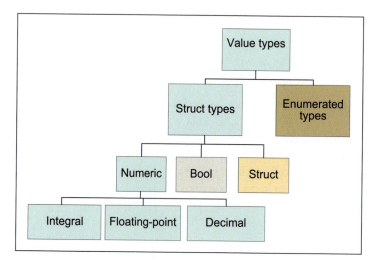

Figure 3-3   Value type hierarchy

Twelve types belong to the numeric value type. Nine of them are Integral (whole number types), two are floating-point (numbers that can have a fractional value), and one is a **decimal** type. The **decimal** type is new; it is not found with C++, C, or Java. It was added to C# to eliminate the problems of loss of precision in mathematical operations that occurred in previous languages. The basic C# types all have aliases in the System **namespace**. Table 3-5 shows the keywords for the built-in C# types, including the numeric type each belongs to in the hierarchy, and the aliases in the System **namespace**.

Table 3-5   C# value data types with .NET alias

C# type	Numeric type	.NET alias type
byte	Integral	System.Byte
sbyte	Integral	System.SByte
char	Integral	System.Char
decimal	Decimal	System.Decimal
double	Floating-point	System.Double
float	Floating-point	System.Single
int	Integral	System.Int32
uint	Integral	System.UInt32
long	Integral	System.Int64
ulong	Integral	System.UInt64
short	Integral	System.Int16
ushort	Integral	System.UInt16

3

INTEGRAL DATA TYPES

All integral values represent whole numbers—values without decimal notation. The value type **int** is used most often to represent a whole number value and will be the primary type used in this textbook. As Table 3-6 illustrates, a value as small as the negative number –2,147,483,648 and as large as 2,147,483,647 can be stored in the **System.int** data type. The primary difference in the integral types is how much storage is needed and whether a negative value can be placed in the data item.

Type names that begin with "u," which stands for unsigned, allow only positive values to be placed in the memory cell.

Table 3-6   Values and sizes for integral types

C# type	Numeric range	Width in bits
byte	0 to 255	8-bit
sbyte	–128 to 127	8-bit
char	U+0000 to U+ffff	16-bit
int	–2,147,483,648 to 2,147,483,647	32-bit
uint	0 to 4,294,967,295	32-bit
long	–9,223,372,036,854,775,808 to 9,223,372,036,854,775,807	64-bit
ulong	0 to 18,446,744,073,709,551,615	64-bit
short	–32,768 to 32,767	16-bit
ushort	0 to 65,535	16-bit

Commas are included in Table 3-6 to add to the readability. However, only the digits 0–9, +, and − are permitted in numeric data types. No formatting symbols, such as commas, are allowed.

Notice in Table 3-6 that the data type **char** is listed as an integral type; however, the range is listed as U+0000 to U+ffff. The **char** keyword is used to declare storage to hold a single Unicode character. A **char** can hold a single value, such as the letter 'A'. If you want to store the three initials representing your first, middle, and last name, you need three **char** variables. You may want to look at Appendix C, "Unicode Character Set (ASCII portion)," which contains a partial listing of the Unicode characters. Most of the known written languages can be represented with the 16-bit Unicode character set.

Example 3-3 shows examples of integral variable declarations.

Example 3-3

```
int studentCount;         // number of students in the class
int ageOfStudent = 20;    // age - originally initialized to 20
int numberOfExams;        // number of exams
int coursesEnrolled;      // number of courses enrolled
```

 Notice that each declaration ends with a semicolon (;). This is because variable declarations are considered statements in the C# language. All statements end in a semicolon.

In Example 3-3, identifiers are chosen that adhere to the rules listed for naming program items. Every line also contains an in-line comment. These comments are unnecessary because the identifiers are self-documenting. If non-descriptive identifiers, such as **x**, **y**, or **s**, are used, comments would be helpful.

 Do not place a comment on every line or with every variable declaration because it creates unreadable code. It is best to include comments when a segment of code needs further explanation.

Each identifier in Example 3-3 consists of two or more words. The second and subsequent words begin with an uppercase character. This naming convention is used throughout the textbook for variable and **object** names. The first character of the identifier begins with a lowercase character.

Class and method names, both user-defined and Framework Class Library (FCL) **class** identifiers, begin with an uppercase character. Constants, which are covered later in this chapter, are named with all uppercase characters, using the underline character to separate words. This is the standard style used by C# programmers.

> **NOTE** Style is composed of a set of personal choices programmers adopt. If you are new to programming, you may want to follow the textbook's style for selecting identifiers; however, your instructors may have different styles that they recommend. Another common naming convention is to separate words with an underscore. The most important thing to remember is that once you select your style, you should use it consistently.

3

FLOATING-POINT TYPES

If you need to keep the decimal portion, the value cannot be stored in an integral data type, such as an `int`. Floating-point values may be specified in scientific notation with an exponent or in standard decimal notation. Very large or small numbers can be specified. The general form of exponential syntax is:

```
n.ne±P
```

With the scientific notation syntax in the preceding example, n is the decimal number; P is the number of decimal positions to move left or right, and the + or − indicate the direction the decimal should be moved. A plus sign indicates that the decimal is moved P positions to the right to form the standard decimal equivalent value. The syntax rules in C# allow the e to be uppercase or lowercase. The ± in the notation indicates that a +, −, or neither can be added. If there is no + or −, + is assumed. Example 3-4 shows examples of converting from scientific to standard decimal notation.

Example 3-4

3.2e+5 is equivalent to 320000

1.76e−3 is equivalent to .00176

6.892e8 is equivalent to 689200000

Because the first value includes an "e+5", the decimal is moved to the right five positions. The second statement in the preceding examples moves the decimal position three positions to the left. The last statement moves the decimal to the right eight positions, which places five significant zeros onto the end of the value.

As Table 3-7 indicates, a value with up to 15 to 16 decimal places can be placed in a **double**. The floating-point types conform to IEEE 754 specifications. For more information, you can read about the IEEE standard at the Web site *www.iee.org*. The following are examples of floating-point variable declarations.

Table 3-7 Values and sizes for floating-point types

Type	Numeric range	Precision	Size
float	$\pm1.5 \times 10^{-45}$ to $\pm3.4 \times 10^{38}$	7 digits	32-bit
double	$\pm5.0 \times 10^{-324}$ to $\pm1.7 \times 10^{308}$	15–16 digits	64-bit

Example 3-5

```
double extraPerson = 3.50;         // extraPerson originally set
                                   // to 3.50
double averageScore = 70.0;        // averageScore originally set
                                   // to 70.0
double priceOfTicket;              // cost of a movie ticket
double gradePointAverage;          // grade point average
float totalAmount = 23.57f;        // note that the f must be placed after
                                   // the value for float types
```

Notice that all but one of the declarations in Example 3-5 uses **double**. In C#, **double** is the default type for floating-point numbers. When a compile-time initialization is included, no suffix is required if you initialize a **double** variable. In the case of the **float**, it is necessary to suffix the number with an 'f' or 'F'. Otherwise the number is assumed to be a **double**. If you fail to suffix the number with an 'f' or 'F' and assign it to a **float** variable, you get a syntax error similar to that shown in Figure 3-4.

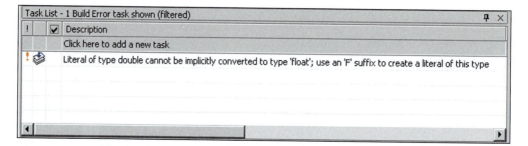

Figure 3-4 Syntax error for failing to use 'F' suffix

The **double** type is used throughout the textbook for all numbers that require a fractional value.

DECIMAL TYPES

The `decimal` value type is new to modern programming languages. It is appropriate for storing monetary data items because it allows both integral (whole) numbers, and a fractional portion. It provides for greater precision than what is found with floating-point types because 128 bits are used to represent the value.

Numbers ranging from positive 79,228,162,514,264,337,593,543,950,335 to negative 79,228,162,514,264,337,593,543,950,335 can be stored in a `decimal` value type. As you can see in Table 3-8, 28 to 29 digits are possible with the `decimal`.

Table 3-8 Value and size for decimal data type

Type	Numeric range	Precision	Size
decimal	1.0×10^{-28} to 7.9×10^{28}	28–29 significant digits	128 bits

As is the case with the `float` type, it is necessary to attach the suffix 'm' or 'M' onto the end of a number to indicate `decimal`. Without the suffix, the number is treated as a `double`. Again, a syntax error message is issued if you try to do compile-time initialization or assign a number to a `decimal` variable without the suffix. No automatic conversion occurs.

Example 3-6

```
decimal endowmentAmount = 33897698.26M;
decimal deficit;
```

Never place commas, dollar signs, or any other special formatting symbols with numbers when they are assigned to value types.

BOOLEAN VARIABLES

Boolean is based on `true/false`, on/off logic. If you look back at the value type hierarchy in Figure 3-3, you see that Boolean inherits from the Value and Struct classes, but not from the Numeric type. The only Boolean type in C# is `bool`. A `bool` variable can have a value of either `true` or `false`. One example of the `bool` type being very useful is in determining when all data has been processed. The variable may be declared as follows.

Example 3-7

```
bool undergraduateStudent;
bool moreData = true;          // used to indicate when all data is
                               // processed. Originally set to true
```

The **bool** type will not accept integer values such as 0, 1, or −1. The keywords **true** and **false** are built into the C# language and are the only allowable values.

 Some languages such as C++ allow Boolean types to hold integers. C# does not.

In addition to numeric and Boolean, there are two other value types: enumeration and structures. These allow you to define your own custom classes. They will be used as you advance in your software development.

DECLARING STRINGS

All the types previously discussed were value types. As shown in Figure 3-1, the .NET common type system also includes reference types. The memory location of value types actually contains the data. With reference types, data is not stored directly in the memory location; instead, the memory location contains a reference to the location in which the data is stored.

C# has two build-in reference types: **string** and **object**. The **string** type represents a string of Unicode characters. Example 3-8 shows how **string** variables are declared. The second and third declarations also include compile-time initializations.

Example 3-8

```
string studentName;
string courseName = "Programming I";
string twoLines = "Line1\nLine2";       // newline escape sequence
                                        // character included
```

The other built-in reference type is **object**. This is probably the most important type of all, because every type inherits characteristics from it. In Chapter 4, you investigate the **object class** when you begin writing your own methods.

 All types inherit the methods ToString( ), Equals( ), Finalize( ), and GetHashCode( ) from the **object class**.

MAKING DATA CONSTANT

When you add the keyword **const** to a declaration, it becomes a constant. Constants are convenient for assigning a value to an identifier; **const** forces the functionality of not allowing the value to be changed. Similar to a variable, the value stored in the memory location can be used throughout the program.. However, the value cannot be altered. The general form of constant syntax is:

```
const type identifier = expression;
```

Some examples of constant declarations are shown in Example 3-9:

Example 3-9

```
const double TAX_RATE = 0.0675;
const int SPEED = 70;
const char HIGHEST_GRADE = 'A';
```

> **NOTE** An advantage of defining a constant is that the value need only be assigned once, during declaration. A constant can be used in many statements. If the value must be changed, only one change is required in the program and that is at the constant declaration location. Once that change is made, the program must be recompiled.

To call attention to the fact that the identifier **TAX_RATE** is a constant instead of a variable, all capital letters are used. To provide a separator between words, the underscore character is used. This is the standard convention used by programmers for naming constants.

ASSIGNMENT STATEMENTS

Variables can be initialized during declaration, or a value can be assigned to them later in the program. However, in C# you must assign a value to a variable before it can be used. No default values are assigned when you declare the variable. To change the value of the variable, an assignment statement is used. An assignment statement takes the form of:

```
variable = expression;
```

The expression can be one of the following:

- Another variable
- Compatible literal value
- Mathematical equation
- Call to a method that returns a compatible value
- Combination of one or more items in this list

The syntax requires that the variable that will hold the result of the expression be placed first—on the left of the equal (=) symbol. The = symbol, when used with an assignment statement or a compile-time initialization, is called an **assignment operator**. The value of the expression on the right side of the assignment operator (=) is determined, and then that value is assigned to the variable on the left side of the = operator.

 Notice that the syntax for an assignment statement requires a variable on the left side of the assignment operator.

If the value on the left side is not compatible with the right side, the C# compiler issues a type mismatch error.

 C# is a strongly typed language. It does a good job of verifying type consistency in an assignment statement. The variable receiving the result of an expression must be either of the same type or a type that can hold the result.

Example 3-10 begins by declaring variables that can be used in assignment statements.

Example 3-10

```csharp
int numberOfMinutes,
    count,
    minIntValue;
```

 If more than one variable is declared of the same type, the identifiers may be separated by commas. The semicolon is placed at the end of the list to indicate the end of the declaration statement.

```csharp
char firstInitial,
     yearInSchool,
     punctuation,
     enterKey,
     lastChar;
double accountBalance,
       weight;
decimal amountOwed,
        deficitValue;
bool isFinished;
string aSaying,
       fileLocation;
```

Once declared, these variables can be assigned literal values as illustrated in the following code segment:

```csharp
numberOfMinutes = 45;
count = 0;
```

```
minIntValue = -2147483648;
firstInitial = 'B';
yearInSchool = '1';
punctuation = ';';
```

Notice that no commas are included with the literal −2147483648. While this seems unreadable, you receive a syntax error message if you add the commas. The variables `firstInitial`, `yearInSchool`, and `punctuation` are of `char` type. Special attention should be paid when using `char` literals. All `char` literals must be enclosed in single quotation marks when used in an assignment statement. Remember, the `char` type can hold any character from the standard keyboard plus many other characters. However, it can only hold one character at a time.

```
enterKey = '\n';            // newline escape character
lastChar = '\u005A';        // Unicode character 'Z'
```

Both of the previous assignments have more than one entry between the single quotes. However, the combination of symbols represents a single character. The `enterKey` variable is assigned the carriage return using the special escape sequence character. The variable `lastChar` is assigned the character 'Z' using its Unicode representation.

Chapter 2 introduced you to some special escape sequences representing characters. You may want to review Table 2-1, which contains many of the valid C# escape sequence characters. The last example in the preceding declarations illustrates how a Unicode character literal can be used to initialize the variable. The numerical value is a hexadecimal number.

```
accountBalance = 4783.68;
weight = 1.7E-3;            //scientific notation may be used
amountOwed = 3000.50m;      //m or M must be suffixed to decimal
deficitValue = -322888672.50M;
```

If you attempt to initialize a `decimal` variable and forget to use the M or m suffix, a compiler error is generated.

```
aSaying = "Today is the first day of the rest of your life!\n ";
fileLocation = @"C:\CSharpProjects\Chapter2";
```

The at symbol (@) can be placed before a `string` literal to signal that the characters inside the double quotation marks should be interpreted verbatim. This eliminates the need to escape the backslash character using the escape character. Without the @ symbol, the `string` literal for the filename would have to be written as "C:\\CSharpProjects\\Chapter2" with two backslashes for what was previously a single backslash.

```
isFinished = false;    // declared previously as a bool
```

The only values that can be placed in a memory location declared as a `bool` are `true` and `false`.

It is also possible to assign one variable's value to another variable. This does not impact the variable on the right side of the assignment operator, as illustrated in Figure 3-5. The `25` from `newValue` replaces the `0` in `count`. A variable can hold only one value at a time.

```
int count = 0,
    newValue = 25;
count = newValue;
```

int count = 0,

   newValue = 25;

count	newValue
0	25

count = newValue;

count	newValue
25	25

Figure 3-5   Impact of assignment statement

Basic Arithmetic Operations

Assignment statements can include mathematical equations. The basic operations of addition, subtraction, multiplication, and division can be performed on real data (floating-point). These operations plus modulation can be performed on integral types. The simplest form of an assignment statement is:

```
resultVariable = operand1 operator operand2;
```

The operands may be variables, constants, or literals. The operators are represented by special symbols shown in Table 3-9.

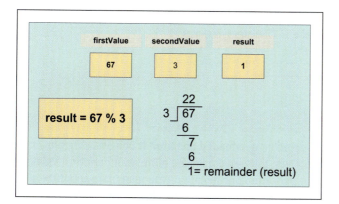

Readability is very important when you write code. Always place a space before and after every arithmetic operator, including the equals symbol (=) . The compiler ignores the white space, but readers of your code appreciate it.

Table 3-9 Basic arithmetic operators

Operator	Operation
+	Addition
–	Subtraction
*	Multiplication
/	Division
%	Modulus

The modulus operator (%) is sometimes referred to as the remainder operator. In most languages, both operands must be of integral type. C# allows you to use floating-point values as operands to the modulus operator. The result produced is the remainder of operand1 divided by operand2. Given the following statements, Figure 3-6 illustrates the results.

```
int firstValue = 67;
int secondValue = 3;
int result;
result = firstValue % secondValue;
```

Figure 3-6 Result of 67 % 3

The modulus operator can be used with negative values; however, you might consider the results strange. For example: –3 % 5 = –3; 5 % –3 = 2; –5 % –3 = –3; The sign of the dividend determines the result.

The results are as you would expect when you use the plus symbol (+) with numeric data. When the + symbol is used with `string` variables, the + symbol concatenates operand2 onto the end of operand1.

```
string result;
string fullName;
string firstName = "Rochelle";
string lastName = "Howard";
fullName = firstName + " " + lastName;
```

As shown in Figure 3-7, the value referenced by `fullName` after the preceding statements are executed is `"Rochelle Howard"`. Notice that a `string` literal containing a single space is placed between the two variables; otherwise, you would have created a full name of `"RochelleHoward"`.

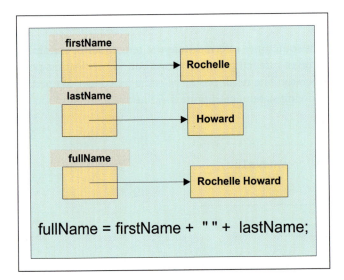

Figure 3-7   String concatenation

> The + symbol is considered an **overloaded operator**. It behaves differently based on the type of operands it receives. If the operands are numeric, it performs addition. If the operands are strings, it performs concatenation. You read more about the `string` data type in Chapter 7, "Arrays and Collections." The plus operator is the only operator from Table 3-9 that can be applied to `string` data types.

Increment and Decrement Operations

A common arithmetic operation is to add or subtract the number one (1) to or from a memory location. **Increment/decrement operators** are used for this. C#, like C++ and Java, has a special unary operator that increments and decrements by one. It is considered a unary operator because it requires a single operand. The basic operators explored in the preceding explanations are all **binary** operators that require two operands.

The symbols used for increment and decrement are **++** and **--**. No space is permitted between the two symbols (**++** or **--**).

```
num++;          // could be written as num = num + 1;
--value1;       // could be written as value = value - 1;
```

The first statement adds **1** to **num**. The second subtracts **1** from **value1**. The increment and decrement operators are often used in situations in which a counter is needed. They are not used to accumulate values, because they always add one or subtract one from the variable.

 In C#, when you use the increment and decrement operators with floating-point types, no syntax error is generated. C# adds or subtracts the number 1 to the variable. You can also use the ++ or -- with a variable of **char** type.

If you use these operators in an arithmetic expression involving additional operands, the placement of the **++** or **--** is important. If they appear as prefixes, or to the left of the variable, the increment or decrement is performed before using them in the expression. When placed before the operand, they are called pre-increment or pre-decrement operators; when placed after the operand, they are called post-increment or post-decrement operators. For example, if the following declaration were made and then each of the **WriteLine( )** methods were called, the output for Example 3-11 would be:

100

101

102

Example 3-11

```
int num = 100;
System.Console.WriteLine(num++);    // Displays 100
System.Console.WriteLine(num);      // Display 101 after the post-
                                    // increment is performed on the
                                    // previous line.
System.Console.WriteLine(++num);    // Displays 102
```

The last value printed is 102. When the next line is executed, **num** has a value of 102. Notice that the incremented value is displayed here because the **++** operator is placed before the identifier. The first call to the **WriteLine( )** method did not display the incremented value. The original value is used as the argument and then the value is incremented.

If **x** is declared to be of type **int** and initialized with a value of **100**, the following statement displays 100 102. The new value stored in **x** is **102** when control goes to the statement following the call to the **WriteLine( )** method.

```
System.Console.WriteLine(x++ + " " +  ++x); // Displays 100 102
```

Look carefully at Example 3-12 to make sure you understand how the placement of the increment and decrement operators impact the result obtained when they are included in an expression involving multiple operations.

Example 3-12

```
int count = 0,
    result = 0,
    firstNum = 10;
count++;
result = count++ * --firstNum + 100;
```

Figure 3-8 shows what is stored in the memory locations after the variables are declared.

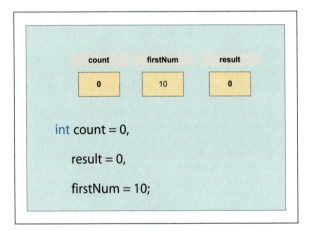

Figure 3-8   Declaration of value type variables

The next statement shown in Example 3-12, **count++;**, is not part of another expression. It really does not matter in this situation whether the **++** is placed before or after **count**. The only memory location affected is count's memory cell. It is incremented by one. Figure 3-9 shows the memory cell after **count++;** is executed.

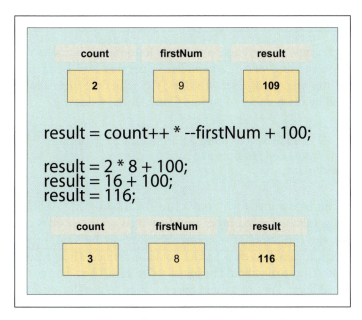

Figure 3-9   Change in memory after count++; statement executed

The last statement in Example 3-12, illustrated in Figure 3-10, is of interest:

```
result = count++ * --firstNum + 100;
```

Notice the ++ is placed after count. The -- comes before firstNum.

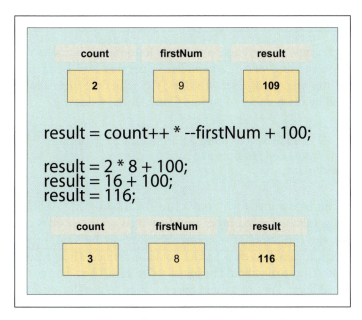

Figure 3-10   Results after statement is executed

The original value of `count`, 2, is used in the multiplication because the `++` comes after the identifier name. After using `count` in the arithmetic, it is incremented by 1, becoming 3. Because the decrement operator comes before the variable `firstNum`, 1 is subtracted from `firstNum` before the multiplication is performed. Thus, 2 is multiplied by 8, and the result is added to 100.

Compound Operations

You commonly write arithmetic operations that modify a variable by using its original value as part of the calculation. Consider the following:

```
answer = 100;
answer = answer + 5;
```

The variable **answer** holds the end result, but it is also used in the computation. **Compound operators** provide a short-cut way to write assignment statements using the result as part of the computation. The last line in the preceding code segment (`answer = answer + 5;`) could be replaced with the following:

```
answer += 5;
```

Both statements take the original value of `answer`, add 5 to it, and store the result back in `answer`.

 In expressions involving multiple operations, the compound operation is always performed last. For example: answer += 45 * 28 + 37 / 16; is equivalent to answer = answer + (45 * 28 + 37 / 16); The original value of answer is not added until the expression on the right of the equal sign is complete.

Accumulation is another type of operation commonly found in applications. You will often find it necessary to keep a running total or accumulate values that a single variable holds. For example, to determine the average of a set of values, the values are normally added to an accumulator and divided by the number of entries. Consider the following:

```
int total = 0;
int newValue;      // statements that enable user to enter
:                  // values for newValue
total = total + newValue;
```

If multiple values are input by the user, each **newValue** could be added to **total**. This is an example of accumulating values. Accumulators are often used with monetary amounts. For example, to accumulate the total amount of money received or the total for an order that includes a number of items, a variable such as **total** could be defined. These types of variables, functioning as accumulators, normally should be initialized to zero. Then they grow, or increase in value with each new addition. The compound operator may be used for these types of situations. Using a compound operator, **newValue** could be added to **total** as shown here:

```
total += newValue;        // same as total = total + (newValue);
```

Table 3-10 shows the compound operators available in C#.

Table 3-10 Compound arithmetic operators

Operator	Operation
+=	Addition
-=	Subtraction
*=	Multiplication
/=	Division
%=	Modulus

Another example of using a compound operator is illustrated with the remainder or modulus operator.

```
answer = 100;
answer %= 3;          // same as answer = answer % 3;
```

The result of the preceding expression would be 1, because that is the remainder of dividing 100 by 3. As stated previously, when a compound operator is used in a statement that contains multiple operations, the variable on the left of the assignment operator is not used until the entire expression on the right side of the assignment symbol is completely evaluated. Consider Example 3-13.

Example 3-13

```
answer = 100;
answer += 50 * 3 / 25 - 4;
```

The value of 100 is not added until the expression is completely evaluated on the right side of the assignment operator. C# then takes the calculated value and adds 100 to it. The result replaces the original 100, storing 102 in **answer**. The order in which the calculations are performed is as follows:

50 * 3 = 150

150 / 25 = 6

6 − 4 = 2

100 + 2 = 102

As with the increment and decrement operators, no space is allowed between the compound operator symbols.

The order in which the calculations are performed is called the **order of operations**. The operations are performed from left to right in Example 3-13. The next section explains why this is not always the case.

ORDER OF OPERATIONS

When multiple arithmetic operators are included in an expression, execution begins with the operator that has the highest level of precedence. The level of precedence is determined by the rules of the language. The C# precedence level for the operators used thus far is shown in Table 3-11.

Table 3-11 Operator precedence

C# category	Operators						Associativity
Unary	+	–	++	--			Right
Multiplicative	*	/	%				Left
Additive	+	–					Left
Assignment	=	*=	/=	%=	+=	-=	Right

As Table 3-11 shows, several operators appear at the same level. For example, *, /, and % are considered equals in terms of order of operations. When an expression contains two or more operators with the same precedence, the associativity of the operators controls the order in which the operations are performed. **Left-associative** means the operations are performed from left to right, so as you move from left to right in an expression, the operation that is encountered first is executed first.

The + and – appear as unary operators in row one and binary operators in row three of Table 3-11.

> **NOTE** As stated previously, unary means one—indicating that only one operand is used with the operator. For example, placing a minus symbol in front of a variable is a unary operation.

As unary operators the – and + operations are executed from right to left negating or indicating that an operand is positive. The binary + and – are left-associative. The assignment category operators, in row four, are **right-associative**.

Parentheses can be used to change the order or operations. If you identify an operation that needs to be processed first, enclose that portion of the expression in a pair of parentheses. Parentheses are also added to increase readability of an expression. Figure 3-11 illustrates the order of operations in which multiple operations of the calculations are performed. Before the arithmetic expression is executed, `answer` is initialized to `10`.

```
int answer = 10;
answer *= 400 + 10  / 2 - (25 + 2 * 4) * 3;
```

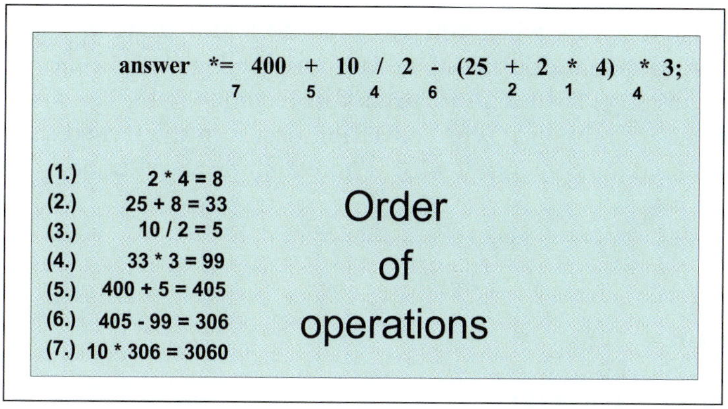

```
          answer  *=  400  +  10  /  2  -  (25  +  2  *  4)  *  3;
                            7      5     4      6       2    1       4

(1.)        2 * 4 = 8
(2.)      25 + 8 = 33           Order
(3.)      10 / 2 = 5
(4.)       33 * 3 = 99            of
(5.)    400 + 5 = 405
(6.)    405 - 99 = 306       operations
(7.) 10 * 306 = 3060
```

Figure 3-11   Order of execution of the operators

Mixed Expressions

C# allows you to mix numeric integral types and floating-point types in an expression. When an expression has operands of different types, the statement is considered a mixed mode expression. Examples include the following:

89 + 76 / 3.25

2 * 7.9 − 5 + 67.99

In the first expression, the division operator has operands of `76`, an integral, and `3.25`, a floating-point type. When the operands are of the same type, the result of the operation will be of that type. However, if the binary operation involves a **double** and an **int**, **implicit type coercion** is performed. Integral types convert to floating-point types. Automatic coercion, by changing the **int** data type into a **double**, occurs for each of the preceding expressions.

It is important to note what is illustrated in Example 3-14—if all the expressions are of integral type on the right side of the equal operator, you cannot just declare the result type to be of floating-point and get the correct floating-point result.

Example 3-14

```
double answer;
answer = 10 / 3;
```

You do not get the results you might expect stored in the answer. The result is 3.0, not 3.333333. Because both of the operands on the right of the assignment operator are integers (whole numbers), integer division is performed. This produces an integer result. After the division is finished, producing 3, it is then assigned to the **double** variable, **answer**, as a Floating-point **double**. Thus, answer becomes 3.0.

Implicit type conversion occurs when you assign an **int** to a **double**. No conversion occurs if you attempt to store a **double** in an **int** variable. Figure 3-12 shows the syntax error for attempting to assign a **double** to an **int** in Example 3-15. The first assignment statement generates an error. Implicit type conversion occurs in the second statement. The variable **value2** can hold the contents of what is stored in **anotherNumber**.

Example 3-15

```
int value1 = 440,
    anotherNumber = 70;
double value2 = 100.60,
    anotherDouble = 100.999;
value1 = value2;              // syntax error as shown in Figure 3-12
value2 = anotherNumber;       // 70.0 stored in value1
```

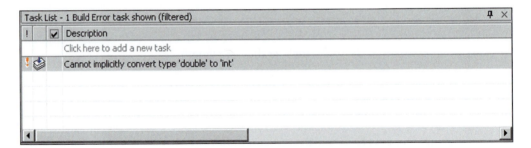

Figure 3-12   Syntax error generated for assigning a double to an int

When one of the operands is a number literal, you can make the literal act like a floating-point type by simply affixing a decimal followed by a zero onto the value as shown in Example 3-16.

Example 3-16

```
int exam1 = 86,
    exam2 = 92,
    exam3 = 91;
double examAverage;
examAverage = (exam1 + exam2 + exam3) / 3.0;
```

The result of the preceding assignment statement is 89.666666. Leave off the .0, so that the assignment statement reads as follows:

```
examAverage = (exam1 + exam2 + exam3) / 3;
```

The result is 89. That could mean the difference between your getting an A in the course versus a B. By simply replacing the 3 with a **3.0**, you get the results you would expect. When the division operator gets an integer representing the sum of the scores and a **double** (3.0), the integer value of 269 is converted to 269.0 for the calculation.

3

This implicit type conversion is made possible by changing the value of the literal. But, this is not always possible. For one reason, you may not have a literal. What if the count of exam scores is stored in a variable? You cannot put a .00 onto the end of an identifier because this generates a syntax error.

If you need to make a mixed-mode assignment with variables, one way to avoid the syntax error produced in Figure 3-12 is to cast the variable in the expression, as explained in the next section.

Casts

C# provides an **explicit type coercion** through type casting or type conversion that can be used with variables. It takes the form of the following:

```
(type) expression
```

Casting makes a variable temporarily behave as if it is a different type. If the value 3 is stored in an **int** memory location, a cast is necessary to produce the correct result for **examAverage**. The type **double** is placed in parentheses before the data item to be cast, as follows:

```
examAverage = (exam1 + exam2 + exam3) / (double) count;
```

By performing a cast on the variables in Example 3-15, the syntax errors would be avoided. Example 3-16 illustrates how this could be done.

Example 3-16

```
int value1 = 0,
    anotherNumber = 0;
double value2 = 100,
    anotherDouble = 100;
value1 = (int) value2;
value2 = (double) anotherNumber;
```

The cast in the last assignment statement in Example 3-16 could have been omitted, because implicit conversion occurs when an **int** is stored in a **double** memory location. Now it is time to put these concepts into an example by developing a sample program.

PROGRAMMING EXAMPLE: CARPETCALCULATOR

This example demonstrates the use of data items in a program. The problem specification is shown in Figure 3-13.

Which carpet fits into your budget? Design an application to determine what it would cost to put new carpeting in a single room. The size of the room is as follows:
Length - 12 feet 2 inches
Width - 14 feet 7 inches

You have narrowed down your choice to two carpet options. They are:
Berber (best) @ $27.95 per square yard
Pile (economy) @ $15.95 per square yard

What will each selection cost you? Display the total cost by type (Berber or Pile).

Figure 3-13 Problem specification sheet for the CarpetCalculator Example

Analyze the Problem

You should review the problem specification in Figure 3–13 and make sure you understand the problem definition. No program inputs are included in this solution. After you learn how data can be entered into your program, you will probably want to revise your solution so that you can run your application any number of times with different types and prices of carpeting. For now, the problem does not require you to input values.

However, data is needed in the program. Begin by determining what kinds of data. What types of values (i.e., whole numbers, numbers with a decimal point, Boolean, alphabetic characters, or strings) will be in each of the identified data items? Are there any constant data items? What would be appropriate identifiers for the variables and constants? What is the range of values or domain of the data item? These are all questions that should be asked. The items listed here describe the data needs for this problem:

- The dimensions of the room are given in feet and inches—whole numbers and integers—representing both values (i.e., 12 feet 2 inches).

3

- The carpet prices are given as a price per square yard. This value is a number with a decimal portion (i.e., 27.95).
- To determine the number of square yards, you must calculate the number of square feet.
- Because the width and length are given in feet and inches, you first convert these measurements (feet and inches) into single units for both the width and length.
- A memory location is needed to store the total square yards. But, to get that value, a memory location is needed to hold total square feet.
- A memory location is needed to hold the total cost of the carpet.

Variables   Table 3-12 lists the data items needed to solve the CarpetCalculator problem.

Table 3-12   Variables

Data item description	Type	Identifier	Domain (range of values)
Length of room in feet	int	roomLengthFeet	positive value < 50
Length of room in inches	int	roomLengthInches	positive value < 12
Width of room in feet	int	roomWidthFeet	positive value < 50
Width of room in inches	int	roomWidthInches	positive value < 12
Length of room	double	roomLength	positive value < 100
Width of room	double	roomWidth	positive value < 100
Number of square feet	double	numOfSquareFeet	positive value < 100
Number of square yards	double	numOfSquareYards	positive value < 100
Carpet price per square yard	double	carpetPrice	positive value < 50.00
Total cost of carpet	double	totalCost	positive value < 1000

Constants   Because this application is not interactive, which means it does not allow the user to input values, decisions have to be made about what data will not change. The number of inches in a foot never changes; the number of square feet in a square yard never changes. Both of these items are defined as constants. The names of the different types of carpet by category are also defined as constants. Notice in Table 3-13 that all uppercase characters are used as identifiers for constants to delineate the constants clearly from the variables. For readability, the underscore character is used as a separator between words.

The actual prices of the different carpets could be defined as constants. Constant definitions are normally placed at the top of the program to make it easy to locate and modify their values when changes are necessary. Instead of declaring the prices as constants, numeric literals are used to initialize the variable's values. After you learn how to enter values interactively as your program is running, you may want to revise your solution so that the price can be inputted by the user. For now, the **27.95** and **15.95** are used as numeric literals for the price.

Table 3-13 Constants

Data item description	Type	Identifier	Value
Number of square feet in one square yard	`int`	`SQ_FT_PER_SQ_YARD`	9
Number of inches in one foot	`int`	`INCHES_PER_FOOT`	12
String of characters representing the best carpet name	`string`	`BEST_CARPET`	`"Berber"`
String of characters representing economy carpet name	`string`	`ECONOMY_CARPET`	`"Pile"`

Design a Solution

The desired output is to display the costs associated with each kind of carpet, given a specific room size. Figure 3-14 shows a prototype for the final output for the **CarpetCalculator** example. The xxx.xx is placed in the prototype to represent the location in which the calculated values should appear.

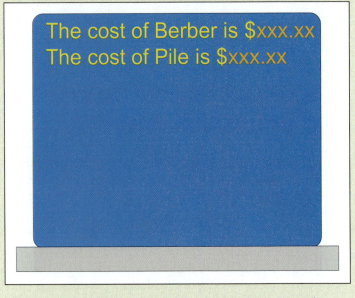
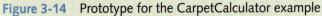

Figure 3-14 Prototype for the CarpetCalculator example

During design, it is important to develop the algorithm showing the step-by-step process to solve the problem. The algorithm for the **CarpetCalculator** example is first developed using a flowchart. Figure 3-15 shows the steps needed to get the desired output. Notice that ovals are used to indicate the start and stop of the application. Rectangles are used to represent processing that will occur, and parallelograms are used for input or output of data. When a flowchart spans multiple pages, a circle connector is used, as is illustrated in Figure 3-15, to connect the diagrams.

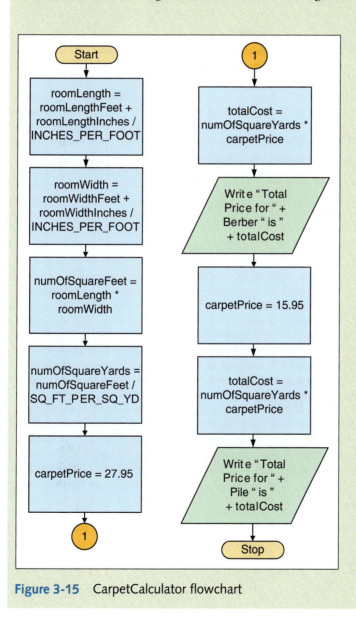

Figure 3-15   CarpetCalculator flowchart

There are a number of techniques and tools used to describe process logic. A flowchart is just one of them. Structured English is another technique. This technique also goes by the name of English Narrative and pseudocode. Flowcharts are primarily used when the solution lends itself to being designed using the traditional, structured approach. Structured English is a tool that is used for that approach, but is also well suited for the object-oriented methodology.

Structured English is an abbreviated, action-oriented version of the English language. There are no syntax rules with Structured English. The emphasis is to write the steps in English as clearly and concisely as possible without consideration for language details. The focus is on writing *what needs to be done*. Figure 3-16 shows the Structured English design for the `CarpetCalculator` example.

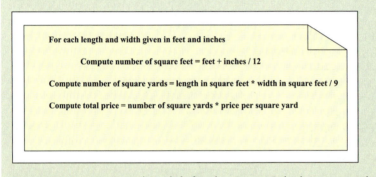

For each length and width given in feet and inches

Compute number of square feet = feet + inches / 12

Compute number of square yards = length in square feet * width in square feet / 9

Compute total price = number of square yards * price per square yard

Figure 3-16   Structured English for the CarpetCalculator example

Structured English is one of the more common tools used with the object-oriented approach to document the process logic. Decision trees and tables are sometimes used in conjunction with Structured English, especially when the solution requires that a number of alternate paths be developed as part of the solution. Chapter 5, "Making Decisions," introduces you to these tools.

The object-oriented approach focuses on the objects (persons, places, and things) that exist in our world. Class diagrams help design and document the data items and behaviors of the objects. Figure 3-17 shows the `class` diagram for the `CarpetCalculator` example. In this chapter, you learned about the data items. The middle section in the `class` diagram includes the identifiers and their data types. Methods are included in the bottom portion of the `class` diagram. **Methods** are procedures for implementing the behaviors in C#. In Chapter 4, "Methods and Behaviors," you learn how to write methods.

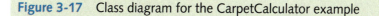

```
                CarpetCalculator
-roomLengthFeet : int
-roomLengthInches : int
-roomWidthFeet : int
-roomWidthInches : int
-roomLength : double
-roomWidth : double
-carpetPrice : double
+DetermineSquareFeet() : double
+DetermineSquareYards() : double
+DeterminePrice() : double
```

Figure 3-17   Class diagram for the CarpetCalculator example

After the algorithm is developed, the design should be checked for correctness. When you desk check your algorithm, use a calculator and write down the results you obtain. Once you implement your design, you can compare the results obtained from the program with the calculator results.

At this point, it may seem that it would be easier simply to perform the calculations using a calculator. Remember that the power of the computer comes into play when you write a set of instructions that can be used with many different data sets. In the next chapter, you learn to call methods that allow you to input data interactively, such as the carpet price and room sizes. This will add much more functionality to your program.

Code the Solution   After you have completed the design and verified the algorithm's correctness, it is time to translate the design into source code. If you are creating your application in Visual Studio .NET, you may want to glance back at Figure 2-19 to review the suggested changes. They included the following:

- After launching Visual Studio .NET, click **File** on the menu bar, click **New**, and then click **Project**. In the Project Type window, select **C#**; and in the Template window, select **Console Application**. Type an appropriate name, such as `CarpetExample`.
- Remove all XML comments (///).
- Remove [STAThread], which appears on the line preceding the `Main( )` method signature.
- Modify the `Main( )` method's signature. You can remove "`string`[ ] args" from within the parentheses.
- Change the name of the `class` from Class1 to a name more representative of the application's operation, such as `CarpetCalculator`.

The final program listing appears as follows:

```csharp
/* CarpetCalculator.cs    Author:        Doyle
 * Calculates the total cost of carpet, given
 * room dimensions in feet and inches and carpet
 * price in price per square yard.
 */
using System;
namespace CarpetExample
{
    class CarpetCalculator
    {
        static void Main( )
        {
            const int SQ_FT_PER_SQ_YARD = 9;
            const int INCHES_PER_FOOT = 12;
            const string BEST_CARPET = "Berber";
            const string ECONOMY_CARPET = "Pile";

            int roomLengthFeet = 12,
                roomLengthInches = 2,
                roomWidthFeet = 14,
                roomWidthInches = 7;

            double roomLength,
                   roomWidth,
                   carpetPrice,
                   numOfSquareFeet,
                   numOfSquareYards,
                   totalCost;

            roomLength = roomLengthFeet +
                roomLengthInches / INCHES_PER_FOOT;
            roomWidth = roomWidthFeet +
                roomWidthInches / INCHES_PER_FOOT;
            numOfSquareFeet = roomLength * roomWidth;
            numOfSquareYards = numOfSquareFeet /
                                SQ_FT_PER_SQ_YARD;
            carpetPrice = 27.95;
            totalCost = numOfSquareYards * carpetPrice;
            Console.Out.WriteLine("The cost of " +
                                BEST_CARPET +
                                " is {0:C}", totalCost);
            Console.Out.WriteLine( );
            carpetPrice = 15.95;
            totalCost = numOfSquareYards * carpetPrice;
```

```
                  Console.Out.WriteLine("The cost of " +
                                         ECONOMY_CARPET +
                                      " is " + "{0:C}",
                                         totalCost);
              Console.Read();
          }
      }
  }
```

3

Readability is important. Notice how the second lines of statements are indented to indicate that the statement has not been completed.

Implement the Code   During implementation, the source code is compiled to check to see if any rule violations have been made. To compile the project, click **Build Solution** from the **Build** Menu if you are using Visual Studio .NET. To run the application, use the **Start Without Debugging** option available under the **Debug** menu.

Test and Debug   During this final step, test the program and ensure you have the correct result. The output should match your prototype. Is your spacing correct? Figure 3-18 shows the output generated from displaying the results of the calculations.

Figure 3-18   Output from the CarpetCalculator program

FORMATTING OUTPUT

The source code listing in the programming example included special formatting with dollar signs. You can format the results through the **Console.Out.Write( )** method, which calls the **String.Format( )** method automatically. You will learn more about calling methods in Chapter 4, "Methods and Behaviors." The **{0:C}** in the following **WriteLine( )** method caused the special formatting.

```
Console.Out.WriteLine("The cost of " + BEST_CARPET
                        + " is {0:C}", totalCost);
```

The currency format is specified using the standard currency format **string** C or c. Place the format **string** inside curly braces – { }. This becomes a part of the **string** literal argument for the **WriteLine( )** method. The first value in the curly brace indicates which argument you want to format. The argument formatted in the programming example was **totalCost**, which is the first argument. You will find that most modern computer programming languages use 0 to reference the first entry. After indicating the argument, you identify the format specification to be used. In this case, it was currency, C.

A **string** is expected for the first argument to the WriteLine( ) method. To increase readability the statement was placed on two lines, with the **string** joined together by the concatenation operator, + sign.

Table 3-14 shows examples using the two most common format strings, c and f.

Table 3-14 Format strings

Character	Description	Examples	Output
C or c	Currency	`Console.Out.Write("{0:c}", 26666.788888);`	$26,666.79
C or c	Currency	`Console.Out.Write("{0:c}", –2);`	($2.00)
C or c	Currency	`Console.Out.Write("{0:c}", 38.8);`	$38.80
F or f	Fixed point	`Console.Out.Write("{0:F4}", 50);`	50.0000
F or f	Fixed point	`Console.Out.Write("{0:F0} {1}", 50, 22);`	50 22

For illustration purposes, literal values were used in the **string** in Table 3-14; however, variables, constants, and expressions can be included in the **Write( )** method as the argument being formatted. The **F**, fixed point, format includes one additional argument. You can indicate how many digits to print to the right of the decimal. The **{0:F4}** indicates that the first argument, argument 0, should be formatted with a fixed point, and that 4 digits should be printed to the right of the decimal. As illustrated in the last row of Table 3-14, when no special formatting is required with an argument, the placeholder is the only entry enclosed inside the curly brace as in **{1}**.

As shown in Table 3-14, negative values are enclosed in parentheses when the currency format **string** is used.

Format strings are positioned in the **string** at the location where the value is to be printed. Consider the following example:

```
Console.Out.WriteLine("Carpet{0:F0} is {1:C}", 9, 14);
```

The result is as follows:

Carpet9 is $14.00

3

No space was printed after the character **t**. The first argument, referenced with a **0** in the format **string** **{0:F0}**, is **9**. That value is printed followed by a space. It was formatted with a fixed point and 0 digits to the right of the decimal. The value **14** is inserted at the location in which the **{1:C}** is inserted. It is formatted with currency.

In conclusion, this chapter concentrated on using data. You will use the concepts you learned in this chapter for the remainder of your software development. In Chapter 4, "Methods and Behaviors," you learn how to write methods that describe the behavior of the data.

QUICK REVIEW

1. Identifiers are names of elements that appear in a program, such as data items. They can include upper and lowercase characters a–z, digits 0–9, underscores, and the at symbol (@). The first character cannot be a digit. No spaces can be included between words. Keywords cannot be used as identifiers.

2. Use meaningful names for identifiers by describing what will appear in memory locations when declaring variables.

3. A variable represents an area in computer memory where the value of a particular data type can be stored. Declaring a variable requires that you select an identifier and determine what type of data will appear in the memory cell.

4. Literals cannot be changed. They are the numbers, characters, and combinations of characters used in your program.

5. Types are actually implemented through classes. This means that classes are used to define types.

6. An **object** is an instance of a **class**. It is an example of the **class**. An instance of the base type **int** would be 21.

7. The value types are often called the fundamental or primitive data types. They are the predefined data types of the language.

8. Value types include nine integral (whole number) types, two floating-point types, and the **decimal** type.

9. All integral values represent whole numbers, which are values without a decimal notation. The value type **int** is used most often.

10. Floating-point values allow you to keep the fractional portion of a data item. They may be specified in scientific notation with an exponent or in standard decimal notation.

11. `decimal` format is suitable for financial and monetary calculations.

12. A `bool` variable can have a value of either **true** or **false**.

13. `string` type represents a combination of Unicode characters.

14. `const` forces the functionality of not allowing the value to be changed.

15. An assignment statement takes the form of variable = expression.

16. Unary operators require a single operand.

17. Pre-increment and post-increment operators of ++ and -- add or subtract the number one (1) to and from a memory location.

18. Compound operators include the assignment operator and are used to modify a variable by using its original value as part of the calculation.

19. The order in which calculations are performed is called the order of operations. Parentheses can be added to an expression to alter the order.

20. Left-associative means the operations are performed from left to right. This means that as you move from left to right in an expression, the operation that is encountered first is executed first.

21. If the binary operation involves both a **double** and an **int**, implicit type coercion is performed.

22. Explicit type coercion through type casting or type conversion takes the form of (type) expression.

EXERCISES

1. Which of the following is a valid identifier?
   a. `namespace`
   b. variable 1
   c. exampleOfAValue
   d. 3value
   e. value#1

2. The number 768 is an example of a _____ type.
   a. `bool`
   b. integral
   c. floating-point
   d. struct
   e. `decimal`

3. Which of the following is a reference type?
   a. `int`
   b. `bool`

   c. **string**

   d. **decimal**

   e. integral

4. The character that *cannot* be used with an identifier is:

   a. −

   b. $

   c. *

   d. #

   e. all of the above

5. Which of the following is a reserved keyword?

   a. Console

   b. Out

   c. int

   d. System

   e. all of the above

6. One of primary differences between **float**, **double**, and **decimal** is:

   a. **float** is used to represent more significant digits.

   b. **double** is normally used with large monetary values.

   c. **decimal** is not used to display negative values.

   d. **double** does not require suffixing a numeric literal with a value such as 'm' or 'f'.

   e. **decimal** is primarily used to represent small monetary values that require a $ for formatting.

7. Which of the following is a valid declaration for a variable to store the name of this textbook?

   a. **string** name of book;

   b. **char** nameOfBook;

   c. boolean nameOfBook;

   d. **string** bookName;

   e. **char** book Name;

8. Types are implemented in C# using:

   a. classes

   b. types

   c. objects

   d. namespaces

   e. programs

3

9. An **object** of the **int class** is:

   a. 47.98

   b. 47

   c. **int class**

   d. type **object**

   e. type integral

10. What would be an appropriate declaration for a memory location to be used as a flag to indicate whether a value has reached its upper limit?

   a. **int** upperLimit;

   b. upperLimit reached;

   c. **bool** upperLimit;

   d. Boolean upperLimit;

   e. **string** upperLimit;

11. Adding the keyword **const** to a declaration:

   a. places a value in memory that cannot be changed.

   b. declares variables of the constant type.

   c. must be done by placing it after the identifier in the declaration.

   d. can only be done with the integral types.

   e. is prohibited in C#.

12. Which statement increases the result by 15?

   a. 15 += result;

   b. 15 =+ result;

   c. result =+ 15;

   d. result += 15;

   e. result = 15 +;

13. What is stored in ans as a result of the arithmetic expression, given the following declarations?

```
int ans = 0, v1 = 10, v2 = 19;
ans = --v2 % v1++;
```

   a. 1.8

   b. 9

   c. 8

   d. 2

   e. none of the above

14. What is stored in ans as a result of the arithmetic expression, given the following declarations?

    int ans = 10, v1 = 5, v2 = 7, v3 = 18;

    ans += v1 + 10 * (v2-- / 5) + v3 / v2;

    a. 18

    b. 32

    c. 28

    d. 30

    e. none of the above

15. Which of the following formats 86 to display with two digits to the right of the decimal?

    a. {0:C}

    b. {0:c}

    c. {0:f2}

    d. all of the above

    e. none of the above

16. Indicate the order of operations for the following assignment statements by placing a number under the assignment operator as illustrated in Figure 3-11.

    a. ans = value1 + value2 * value3 – (value4 + 20 / 5 % 2) * 7;

    b. ans += value1-- * 10;

    c. ans = (((value1 + 7) – 6 * value2) / 2);

    d. ans = value1 + value2 / value3 * value4--;

17. Which of the following are valid identifiers? If they are invalid, indicate why.

    a. intValue

    b. value#1

    c. the first value

    d. _value1

    e. AVALUE

18. For each of the following, declare a variable using the best choice for data type.

    a. a counter for the number of correct responses

    b. the amount of money you owe on a credit card

    c. the name of your hometown

    d. the grade you hope to obtain on the next exam

    e. the grade you hope is recorded at the end of the term for this course

19. For each of the following declarations, write an appropriate compile-time initialization.

a. counter for the number of correct responses begins with zero

b. amount of money you owe on a credit card is zero

c. name of the hometown is the city where your school is located

d. grade on the next exam is 100

e. grade to be recorded at the end of the term for this course is an A

20. Suppose x, y, and z are **int** variables and x = 2, y = 6, and z = 10. What will be in the memory locations of each of the variables after each of the following statements is executed? (For each exercise, use the original declaration.)

	x	y	z
a. z += ++y % 2;	_____	_____	_____
b. x = y + 14 – z / 7;	_____	_____	_____
c. x = y * z / 2 – x * z;	_____	_____	_____
d. x %= --z – y * 2;	_____	_____	_____
e. y = (z – y) * 2 + --y;	_____	_____	_____

21. Suppose x, y, and z are **double** variables and x = 2.5, y = 6.9, and z = 10.0. What will be in the memory locations of each of the variables after each of the following statements is executed? (For each exercise, use the original declaration.)

	x	y	z
a. z *= y++ % 7;	_____	_____	_____
b. x = (**int**) y + (14 – z / 7);	_____	_____	_____
c. x = z / 3 * --y;	_____	_____	_____
d. z /= (int) y / x;	_____	_____	_____
e. z = x + y / 4;	_____	_____	_____

22. What will be the output from each of the following statements?

a. Console.Out.Write("Result is {0:c}", 67);

b. Console.Out.Write("Number {0:f0} is {1:c}", 1, 3);

c. Console.Out.Write("{0:f0}– {1:c}", 1, 3 * 2);

d. Console.Out.Write("{0:f0} result " + "xyz {1:f2}", 1, 25);

e. Console.Out.Write("This is the {0:f0}st example: {1:f2}", 1, 3);

23. Explain how a variable differs from a constant.

24. Explain how type, **class**, and **object** are related to a **string**.

3

25. The following program has several syntax errors as well as style inconsistencies. Correct the syntax errors and identify the style violations.

```
namespace Chapter3
{
  class converter
  {
  static void main(
  {
                CONST int inches = 12;
                int x = 100; y = 10;
                float z = 22.45;
                double ans;
                ans=inches+z*x%y;
                System.out.write("The result is {f2:0} " + "ans");
  }
  }
```

PROGRAMMING EXERCISES

For each of the exercises, be sure to include appropriate comments, choose meaningful identifiers, and use proper indentations in your source code.

1. Design an application that displays the number of square feet in a house. Declare and initialize the length and width of the house to 37 and 22, respectively. Go into your source code and change the initialization values. Rerun the application.

2. Write a program that converts a temperature given in Celsius to Fahrenheit. Test the program by performing a compile-time initialization of 37 for the original Celsius value. Display the original temperature and the formatted converted value. Go into your source code and change the initialization value. Rerun the application.

3. Write a program that converts a temperature given in Fahrenheit to Celsius. Test the program by performing a compile-time initialization of 87 for the Fahrenheit temperature. Display the original temperature and the formatted converted value. Go into your source code and change the initialization value. Rerun the application.

4. Show the output for each of the following data types: `int`, `float`, `double`, and `decimal` with no digits, 2 digits, and 5 digits to the right of the decimal, plus formatted with currency. You will probably want to declare both an integral and floating-point variable to use for your display. Initialize each variable with an appropriate test value. Print one data type per line.

5. Write a program that calculates and prints the take-home pay for a commissioned sales employee. Perform a compile-time initialization and store the name of Jessica Oakley in a variable called employeeName. Jessica received 7% of her total sales. Her federal tax rate is 18%. She contributes 10% to a retirement program and 6% to Social Security. Her sales this week were $28,000. Produce a formatted report showing the amount for each of the computed items. Select appropriate constants. After you finish displaying Jessica Oakley's data, change the values and rerun the application.

6. Write a program that computes the average of 5 exam scores. Declare and perform a compile-time initialization with the 5 values. Use a constant to define the number of scores. Print all scores and the average value formatted with no digits to the right of the decimal. Rerun the application with different values.

7. Write a program that prints the number of quarters, dimes, nickels, and pennies that a customer should get back as change. Run your program once by performing a compile-time initialization using 92 cents for the value to be converted. Go into your source code and change the 92 to 27. Rerun the application.

8. Write a program that declares two integers and initializes them to 199 and 76. Display the sum, difference, product, average, square, and remainder of the values. Rerun the application with different values.

9. Write a program that computes the amount of money the computer club will receive from the proceeds of their candy sales project. They sold 37 cases, which had 12 bars per case. The candy was sold for $0.75 per bar. Each case cost $5.00. They are required to give the student government association 10% of their earnings. Display their proceeds formatted with currency.

10. Write a program that calculates the circumference of a circle. Declare a named constant for PI with a value of 3.14159.

4

Methods and Behaviors

In this chapter, you will:

- O Become familiar with the components of a method
- O Call `class` methods with and without parameters
- O Use predefined methods in the `Console` and `Math` classes
- O Write your own value and non-value returning `class` methods (with and without parameters)
- O Learn about the different methods and properties used for object-oriented development
- O Write your own instance methods to include constructors, mutators, and accessors
- O Call instance methods including constructors, mutators, and accessors
- O Distinguish between value, `ref`, and `out` parameter types
- O Work through a programming example that illustrates the chapter's concepts

In Chapter 3, you learned how to declare variables and data members. You discovered that data is stored in memory in variables. You learned how to perform arithmetic procedures on the data and how expressions are evaluated using the rules of precedence. You also learned how to display formatted data. This chapter focuses on methods. Methods provide the operations, or behavior, for the data members of a **class**. Methods facilitate dividing a problem into manageable units for ease of development and reuse of code. You learn about different types of methods in this chapter, how to call predefined methods, and how to create your own methods and call them. You write methods that perform processing and return the results of their work, you write methods that perform procedures without returning a value, and you write both **class** and instance methods. You learn how to pass arguments to methods and learn about the different types of parameters that can be used with methods. You begin by examining what components make up a method.

ANATOMY OF A METHOD

A method is really nothing more than a group of statements placed together under a single name. Methods are defined inside a **class**. As you learned in Chapter 1, a **class** includes a collection of data and methods. Methods are the members of a **class** that perform an action, and through writing methods you describe the behavior of data. Methods are similar to functions, procedures, and modules found in other programming languages. They allow program statements to be grouped together based on the functionality of the statements and to be called on one or more times when needed.

 Unlike some languages such as C and C++ that allow methods to be defined globally outside a **class**, C# requires all methods to be members of a **class**.

All programs consist of at least one method. For both console and Windows applications, the required method is **Main( )** in C#. **Main( )** is a method you have already written as the entry point into your program. It does not matter where you physically place the **Main( )** method in your program. When your program runs, the first statement in the **Main( )** method is the first statement executed. Control continues in **Main( )** until the end closing curly brace is encountered.

When you wrote programs earlier as part of the body of **Main( )**, you wrote statements that invoked, or called, other methods. Example 4-1 contains calls to two methods: **WriteLine( )** and **Read( )**. **Main( )** is the only user-defined method included in Example 4-1.

Example 4-1

```
/* **********************************************
 * SquareExample.cs        Author:       Doyle
 * Computes the square of a variable initialized
 * at compile time.
 *
 **********************************************/
using System;
namespace Square
{
    public class SquareExample
    {
        public static void Main( )
        {
            int aValue = 768;
            int result;

            result = aValue * aValue;
            Console.WriteLine("{0} squared is {1}",
                                  aValue, result);
            Console.Read( );
        }
    }
}
```

The output of Example 4-1 is:

```
768 squared is 589824
```

> **NOTE** The value in the result variable can be formatted using the number format `string` (n or N). By adding the N format argument to the `string` (`{1:N0}`) a comma is inserted so that the value is more readable.
>
> ```
> Console.WriteLine("{0} squared is {1:N0}", aValue, result);
> ```
>
> produces 768 squared is 589,824
>
> The zero in `{1:N0}` indicates that no digits should be printed to the right of the `decimal` point. The decimal point is not printed either.

The last statement, `Console.Read( )`, in Example 4–1 is added to hold the screen when the program runs. This is necessary if the program is running in Visual Studio .NET using the F5 Start option.

The first line of a method is called the **heading** of the method. Figure 4-1 labels the components that make up the heading.

> **NOTE** You will notice that no semicolon is placed on the end of method headings, such as `Main( )`. Nor do you place semicolons on the end of the `class` headings (e.g., `public class` SquareExample) or `namespace` headings. Semicolons are placed at the end of variable declarations, calls to methods, and assignment statements.

Some programmers refer to the heading for the method as the prototype for the method. The **definition** of the method includes the heading and the body of the method, which is enclosed in curly braces.

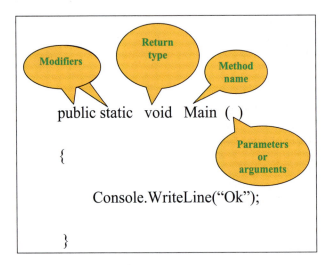

Figure 4-1   Method components

The programs you create include definitions for dozens of methods, calls to those methods, and calls to methods that are part of the .NET FCL (Framework Class Library). The components identified in Figure 4-1 are described in the following section.

Modifiers

Modifiers appear in the headings of methods. They also appear in the declaration heading for classes and `class` members, as shown in Figure 4-1. A modifier is added to a type or a type member's declaration to change or alter it or to indicate how it can be accessed. In Chapter 3, you learned about and used the `const` modifier. `const` is added to a declaration to indicate that a value is constant and cannot be changed. You have previously seen two other types of modifiers: `static` and access.

Static Modifier

You have already encountered **static** used with the `Main( )` method. All `Main( )` method headings must include the **static** modifier. C# issues an error message if you forget to include **static** when you write a `Main( )` method. `Write( )`, `WriteLine( )`, and `ReadLine( )` are all **static** methods of the `Console` **class**. You have to place the **class** name before the method name when it is a static method.

You will soon explore the members of the `Math` **class**. The heading for each of these members includes the **static** keyword. The method in Example 4-2 raises a value to a specified power. Examine its heading.

Example 4-2

```
public static double Pow(double, double)
```

Static is used in this context to indicate that a method belongs to the type itself rather than to a specific **object** of a **class**. This means that it is not necessary to instantiate an **object** of the **class** to use the method member.

> **NOTE**
>
> If a member method is in the same **class** that includes a **static** method, the **static** method can be called by typing its identifier (without an **object** or **class** name). However, if you are calling a **static** method from another **class**, the **class** name must be used with the method name. For example, to call the `Sqrt( )` method of the `Math` **class**, you would write:
>
> ```
> double answer = Math.Sqrt(25);
> ```

Later in this chapter, you create objects of classes. You also learn that methods defined as part of your user-defined **class**, in which objects are instantiated, do not use the **static** keyword.

Methods that use the **static** modifier are called **class** methods. A single copy of the method is made instead of copies for each **object**. Instance methods require that an **object** be instantiated before the method is accessed. When you write your own methods, the **static** modifier can be added; however, for most classes designed for object-oriented applications, the **static** keyword is rarely used. Much of the power of object-oriented development comes from encapsulating (packaging) methods and data members together so that objects can be defined with their own members and be totally independent of each other. By using the **static** modifier, you are violating this important feature. A single copy of a method is created for use with all objects when the method is defined as **static**.

Access Modifiers

Another type of modifier is an access modifier. It specifies the level of accessibility for types and their members. C# includes the following accessibility modifiers:

- `public`
- `protected`
- `internal`
- `protected internal`
- `private`

Public access offers the fewest access limitations; there are basically no restrictions on accessing `public` members or classes. Notice in Example 4-1 that the `class` definition and the `Main( )` method heading include the `public` access modifier. By specifying a `public` access, other classes can reuse your classes in different applications.

Private is the most restrictive access modifier. `Private` members are accessible only within the body of the `class` in which they are declared. Often in object-oriented design, data is defined with a `private` modifier and methods that access the data are declared to have `public` access. By defining the data members as `private`, you restrict access to the data through the members' methods or properties that you learn about in this chapter.

Table 4-1 shows the different accessibility levels of access modifiers.

Table 4-1   C# access modifiers

Modifiers	Explanation of accessibility
`public`	No restrictions
`protected`	Limited to the containing `class` or classes derived from the containing `class`
`internal`	Limited to current project
`protected internal`	Limited to current project or classes derived from `class`
`private`	Limited to containing `class`

When a `class` or a `class` member does not specify a modifier, the default accessibility level of `private` is assumed.

Return Type

The **return** type identifies what type of value is returned when the method is completed. Any of the predefined or valid user-defined types can be returned. Methods can **return** a value when all the statements of the method are complete, or they can simply **return** control to the method that called them, without bringing a value back.

The **return** type is always listed immediately preceding the name of the method, as shown in Figure 4-1. Methods do not have to **return** anything; however, they can **return** at most one data type through the method's name.

 You learn about arrays and collections such as ArrayLists in Chapter 7, "Arrays and Collections." C# allows a method to **return** a collection, however the **return** must be through a single identifier. That identifier can be the name of an array.

If a method does not **return** a value, the **void** keyword is placed at the **return** type location in the method heading as shown in the following line of code:

```
public void DisplayInstructions( )
```

If a **return** type other than **void** is specified in the method heading, there must be a **return** statement included in the body of the method. The value returned must be a compatible value—one that either matches the type in the heading or can be stored in that type.

The **return** statement takes the form:

```
return [value];
```

Note that value is enclosed in square brackets to indicate that it is optional. If the method heading uses **void** as the **return** type, the **return** statement can be omitted or included as follows:

```
return;
```

Whenever the **return** type is not **void**, you must have a **return** value following the **return** keyword. This value can be a literal, arithmetic expression, or variable that holds a value. Example 4-3 illustrates returning a calculated value.

Example 4-3

```
public static double CalculateMilesPerGallon
              (int milesTraveled, double gallonsUsed)
{
    return milesTraveled / gallonsUsed;
}
```

The method heading in Example 4-3 indicates that a **double** value is returned. This is the **double** that follows the **public** keyword. Inside the body of the method, the result of the division produces a compatible **double** value.

The value being returned is sent back to the location in the program that called the method. For example, the value returned from the **CalculateMilesPerGallon( )** method is sent back to the **WriteLine( )** method for display in the call that follows:

```
Console.WriteLine("Miles per gallon = {0:N2}",
                    CalculateMilesPerGallon(289, 12.2));
```

The output produced from the WriteLine( ) method would be:

```
Miles per gallon = 23.69
```

 Your programs are easier to modify and debug if your methods have one entry and one exit. This is a problem-solving technique you should try to include in your design. The implication is that you should try to have only one **return** statement in a method.

Method Name

When naming a method, you follow the rules for creating an identifier, which were described in Chapter 2, "Your First C# Program." Identifiers should be meaningful names that label the overall purpose of the segment of code. Many programmers use the standard convention of naming the method with an action verb phrase. This verb phrase should describe what the method is intending to accomplish. **Pascal case style** is used for **class** and method identifiers. This C# convention specifies that the first character is uppercase when the identifier has at least three characters. Subsequent words that are part of the identifier also begin with an uppercase character. Examples of method identifiers following these style conventions include **CalculateSalesTax( )**, **AssignSectionNumber( )**, **DisplayResults( )**, **InputAge( )**, and **ConvertInputValue( )**.

 C# programs use the **Camel case style** convention for data member identifiers. This style specifies that the first letter of identifiers is lowercase and the first letter of each subsequent concatenated word is capitalized. Examples are **studentName**, **major**, and **yearInSchool**.

Parameters

The items inside the parentheses of the method heading are called the parameters, or arguments. Sometimes a method requires the supply of unique data. For example, if a method is written to calculate the average of three values, the method requires that these three values be sent to it. The **CalculateMilesPerGallon( )** method in Example 4-3 required two arguments: an **int** value for **milesTraveled** and a **double** value for **gallonsUsed**. It is through parameters and arguments that the data can be sent into a method.

When writing a method, you decide what type of unique data is needed for the method. Then place the data type and an identifier for the data type inside the parentheses. You must include matched pairs of types and identifiers inside the parentheses. The two matched pairs of parameters for the `CalculateMilesPerGallon( )` method are as follows:

```
(int milesTraveled, double gallonsUsed)
```

In the body of the method, the identifiers are used to reference where and when the unique data item should be used. For the `CalculateMilesPerGallon( ) method`, `milesTraveled` and `gallonsUsed` were used in an arithmetic expression. The result of the expression is returned to the calling method.

Some programmers make a distinction between parameters and arguments, using the term **parameter** to refer to items appearing in the heading of the method and **argument** for the items appearing in the call to the method. Others make a distinction between arguments and parameters by adding actual and formal onto the terms. **Formal parameters**, or arguments, appear in the heading of a method. **Actual arguments**, or parameters, appear in the call. Think of the actual argument as being the actual data that is sent to the method. The formal parameters are like placeholders; they formally indicate what type of data is expected to be sent for the method to use. This book uses the term "parameters" to refer to the items in the method heading and the term "arguments" for items sent into the method via a method call. For Example 4-3, the arguments for the `CalculateMilesPerGallon( )` method are 289 and 12.2. This is actual data or numbers; however, the actual argument could be an identifier for a variable. It could be an expression involving an arithmetic statement or a call to another method.

Like **return** types, parameters are optional. If no parameters are included, an open and closed parenthesis is used. If more than one parameter is included, they are separated by a comma.

 Some languages place the **void** keyword inside the parentheses in place of the parameter list to indicate that no parameters are needed. C# does not allow this and generates a syntax error.

There are several different types of parameters, which are explored later in this chapter.

Method Body

As you saw in Example 4-1, statements making up the body are enclosed in curly braces. The body for the `DisplayMessage( )` method below consists of two calls to the `Write( )` method in the `Console` class, one call to the `WriteLine( )` method in the `Console` class, and a **return** statement that does not return a value.

```
public void DisplayMessage( )
{
        Console.Write("This is ");
        Console.Write("an example of a method ");
        Console.WriteLine("body. ");
        return;      // no value is returned
}
```

Normally the statements inside the body of a method are executed in sequential order. The body of a method can include statements that declare variables, do arithmetic, and call other methods. These same rules and concepts apply whether you are using your own methods or predefined methods that make up the Framework Class Library (FCL). When the last statement in the method finishes, control is returned to the method that made the call.

 Notice that the `return` type for the `DisplayMessage( )` method is `void`. A `return` statement is included. Return is optional since no value is returned when the method is finished.

Example 4–2 showed you the heading of the `Pow( )` method. It is repeated here:

```
public static double Pow(double, double)
```

This method returns the result of raising a number to a specified power. Two parameters of `double` type are required. These values refer to the base number and an exponent, in that order. These identifiers are inserted in the body of the method at locations where the calculations on the values should occur. When the method is called, the specific values that are sent as arguments replace the placeholders in the body of the method. For example, if you make the following call:

```
double result = Math.Pow(5, 2);
```

the value returned when `Pow( )` is finished is stored in `result`. It would be 25, since $5^2 = 25$.

 You did not see the actual statements that made up its body for the `Pow( )` method. This is one of the beauties of object-oriented development. It is not necessary for you to know how the method produces a result. To use the `Pow( )` method, all you need to know is what type of values to send it and what type of value you can expect to receive back. The black box concept of object-oriented programming hides method implementation details from you.

When an application is run, `Main( )` serves as the controlling method. Execution always starts in the body of the `Main( )` method. Execution begins with the first line in `Main( )` and stops when the closing curly brace in `Main( )` is reached. Lots of other methods can, of course, be executed in your application; however, they must be called from either `Main( )` or from a method that has been called from `Main( )`. In Example 4–1, you saw how control was passed to the `WriteLine( )` and `Read( )` methods by calling, or invoking, these methods.

CALLING CLASS METHODS

Invoking a method means calling the method. When a method call is encountered, the .NET execution engine, the Common Language Runtime (CLR), halts execution in the current method and transfers control to the body of the method called. After completing the called method's body, control is returned back to the location in the calling method that made the call. A call to the method that does not **return** a value uses the following syntax:

```
[qualifier].MethodName(argumentList);
```

 Whenever square brackets are inserted into a syntax reference, the entry is optional. With **static** methods, the qualifier is the **class** name.

4

A qualifier is added to the above syntax notation to indicate that it may be necessary to include a **class** or **object** identifier. Calls to the **WriteLine( )** method have included the **Console class** as the qualifier.

As stated previously, not all methods require an argument list. Both of the following statements are legal calls to the **WriteLine( )** method. The first takes no arguments; the second call sends one data item to the method.

```
Console.WriteLine( );     // No arguments. Writes a blank line
Console.WriteLine("Ok"); // Single argument
```

When the argument list contains more than one data item, the values are separated by commas as follows:

```
Console.WriteLine("Value1({0}) + Value2({1})" +
                  " = Value3({2})", 25, 75, (25 + 75));
```

Output from the last call to the **WriteLine( )** method would be:

```
Value1(25) + Value2(75) = Value3(100)
```

The call included four arguments:

```
1.    "Value1({0}) + Value2({1})" + " = Value3({2})"
2.    25
3.    75
4.    (25 + 75)
```

A call to a method never includes the data type as part of the argument list, but rather the actual data. The actual argument can, of course, take the form of a literal, as shown previously, or it can be a variable or an expression. The expression can be quite sophisticated and even include a call to another method.

If you are developing your applications using Visual Studio .NET, when you call methods you should take advantage of the IntelliSense feature of the IDE. After you enter a **class** or **object** name and then type a dot (.), the list of members is displayed. As you move down the member list, a pop-up window displays information about each member. The **Write( )** method is selected in Figure 4-2. Notice in Figure 4-2 that two icons appear to the left of member names. Methods appear with a three-dimensional fuchsia-colored box. Data members use aqua icons.

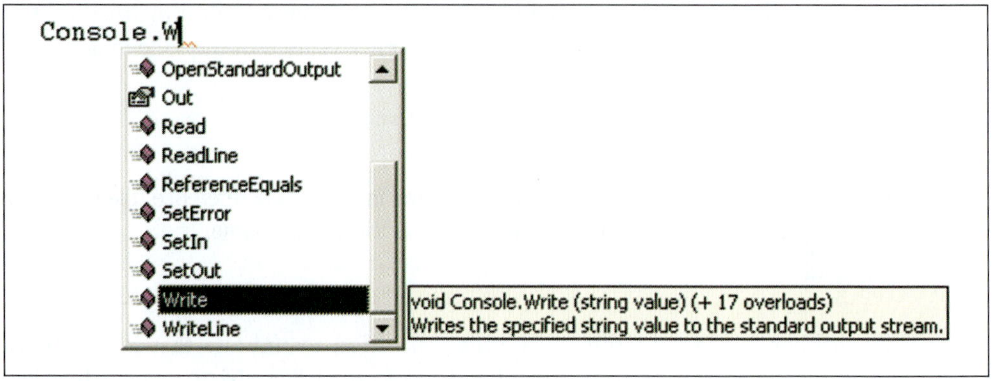

```
Console.W|
     OpenStandardOutput
     Out
     Read
     ReadLine
     ReferenceEquals
     SetError
     SetIn
     SetOut
     Write            │void Console.Write (string value) (+ 17 overloads)
     WriteLine        │Writes the specified string value to the standard output stream.
```

Figure 4-2   Console class members

> **NOTE**   Out is a property of the `Console` **class**. Properties can be distinguished from the other members, such as data and methods, by the icon to the left of their names. You learn more about properties later in this chapter.

In the sections that follow, you explore some of the predefined methods you have already seen and used. This should help you gain a better understanding of how to use those and the other predefined methods that make up the Framework Class Library.

> **NOTE**   To open IntelliSense in Visual Studio .NET quickly, type the first character of any identifier (predefined or user-defined) and then press the Ctrl key and the spacebar. You get a list of members from which to choose. This also works if you type two or three characters before pressing the Ctrl key and spacebar. By typing more characters, you reduce the number listed. To see the names of all the classes in the `System` **namespace**, after you add the **using** directive, press the Ctrl key and the spacebar. By learning to use this feature, you won't mind declaring longer descriptive identifiers and you'll have fewer typing errors.

PREDEFINED METHODS

A key feature of the .NET Framework is the extensive **class** library. Within the library of classes, each **class** has a number of predefined methods. These .NET methods have been thoroughly tested by the .NET developers and provide a great deal of functionality. Avoid making work for yourself by using predefined methods whenever possible.

In the programs you have already seen and developed, the **using** directive made the **System namespace** available. The **Console class** is defined in the **System namespace**. It provides methods for reading characters from, and writing characters to, the console. There are methods for working with individual characters or entire lines of characters. The methods you have used most often are `Write( )` and `WriteLine( )`. They are both **overloaded methods**, which means that there are multiple methods with the same name, but each has a different number or type of parameter.

Write( ) Method

As you saw in Figure 4-2, the IntelliSense feature of Visual Studio .NET shows information about the method in a pop-up window on the right. Use this information to determine how to call the method. The pop-up window includes the signature for the method along with the **return** type and a short description of the member's functionality. The name of the method, modifiers, and the types of its formal parameters make up the **signature**. The `Write( )` method in Figure 4-2 has one formal parameter, a **string** value. Even though the **return** type is displayed first in the pop-up window, the **return** type is not considered part of its signature. Notice that `Write( )` lists **void** as the **return** type.

To add as much functionality as possible to the methods, `Write( )` is overloaded. .NET includes 18 different `Write( )` methods. They all have the same name, but each one has a different signature. Notice how the first line of the pop-up display for Figure 4-2 ends with "(+17 overloads)." This is only one of the 18 `Write( )` method signatures. Example 4-4 lists four of the other `Write( )` signatures. In addition to these four, there are 14 other `Console.Write( )` methods. The implication is that you can send to the method, as an argument, any of the predefined basic types and get the results you would expect displayed on the console.

Example 4-4

```
Console.Write(int)
Console.Write(double)
Console.Write(object)
Console.Write(bool)
```

So how does the CLR know which of these 18 methods to use? The answer is simple, but important for you to understand. When the method is called, the argument used to make the call is matched with the signature to determine which of the methods to execute. Remember, the signature of the method includes the formal parameters, which include the data type that can be used for the method.

In Visual Studio .NET, after you select the `Write( )` member and type the opening parenthesis, IntelliSense displays a drop-down list with a scrollbar that allows the viewing of all 18 signatures. This gives you an opportunity to know what type of argument is needed with a call. Figure 4-3 shows the first of the 18 signatures.

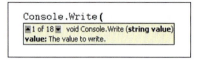

Figure 4-3   IntelliSense display

The `Write( )` method in Figure 4–3 is called by entering the name of the method, an open parenthesis, a **string** value, and a closing parenthesis. In the call, the **string** value can be a **string** literal, **string** variable, or a value of another data type converted to a **string**. From Chapter 2, you learned that a **string** literal is one or more characters enclosed in double quotation marks. A valid call to the `Write( )` method using the displayed over-loaded method from Figure 4–3 would be:

```
Console.Write("Any string value will work!" );
```

The 18 overloaded `Write( )` methods include parameters for common types, such as **int**, **double**, **decimal**, **bool**, and **object**. You should explore the other options.

WriteLine( ) method

As shown previously, the `WriteLine( )` method behaves like the `Write( )` method with the exception that it writes the current end-of-line terminator after it displays the arguments. There are 19 overloaded `WriteLine( )` methods. Example 4-5 includes valid calls to the `WriteLine( )` method.

Example 4-5

```
Console.WriteLine (45);
Console.WriteLine ("An apple a day"
                    + " keeps the doctor away.")
Console.WriteLine (67.28 + 10000);
Console.WriteLine(true);
Console.WriteLine("Score on the next exam: {0}", 100);
```

The output generated from each of the preceding statements is:
```
45
An apple a day keeps the doctor away.
10067.28
True
Score on the next exam: 100
```

> **NOTE** Notice in the output generated for Example 4-5 that True is printed when the `bool` variable is displayed. The first character is capitalized. Yet the valid values for a `bool` variable are `true` and `false`, all lowercase characters. Do not be confused by this inconsistency.

The `Write( )` and `WriteLine( )` methods did not `return` anything when they were called. They performed their tasks and then relinquished control to the next sequential statement in the `Main( )` method. Their task was to write the specified information to the console. No value was returned to the calling method, `Main( )`, when they completed their jobs. Notice that the heading for the `Write( )` method in the pop-up window displayed by IntelliSense shown in Figures 4-1 and 4-2 begins with "`void …`".

4

The `Console class` also includes methods that allow you to enter values from the keyboard. When entered, these values are returned to the program. The two methods used for console input are `Read( )` and `ReadLine( )`. Neither of these methods is overloaded.

Read( )

`Read( )` was used previously to hold the output window open until a character from the keyboard was pressed. This enabled the user of your program to leave the output on the screen as long as necessary.

The pop-up window in Figure 4-4 shows the method heading for `Read( )`.

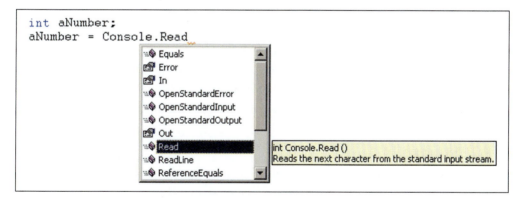

Figure 4-4   Console.Read ( ) signature

As Figure 4-4 shows, the `Read( )` method returns an `int` representing the next character input from the keyboard. The heading for the method in the box on the right displayed using IntelliSense begins with the `int` keyword. The `int` is the Unicode representation of the single `char` value entered. Example 4-6 illustrates what is stored in memory when the `Read( )` method is used.

Example 4-6

```
int aNumber;
Console.Write("Enter a single character: ");
aNumber = Console.Read( );
Console.WriteLine("The value of the character entered: "
                  + aNumber);
```

If the user types the alphabetic character 'a' when prompted, the output is as follows:

```
The value of the character entered: 97
```

This may be a good time for you to review Appendix C, "Unicode Character Set (ASCII portion)." Notice that the Unicode decimal representation for the character 'a' is 97.

To display the actual character entered, you could cast the value as shown in Example 4-7.

Example 4-7

```
Console.WriteLine("The value of the character entered: "
                  + (char) aNumber);
```

If the user types the character 'a' using the cast, the output becomes:

```
The value of the character entered: a
```

Notice that because the **Read( )** method returned a value, provisions had to be made for a location to store the value on **return** from the method. For this, an assignment statement is used. Another option is to include the call to **Read( )** as part of the argument to the **WriteLine( )** method at the location where **aNumber** should be displayed.

The single statement in Example 4-8 could replace all four lines from Example 4-6 and 4-7.

Example 4-8

```
Console.WriteLine("The value of the character entered: "
                  + (char) Console.Read( ));
```

This single line is possible because the **Console.Read( )** method allows the user to enter one character. The **Read( )** method returns an **int**. The **int** value is cast to a **char** for display purposes. This value is then concatenated onto the end of the **string**, with the "+" operator. While the above is syntactically correct and works for entering a single character, it is not as readable. It does not prompt users by telling them to enter a character. Another disadvantage of replacing the four lines with the single line is the fact that the entered value is not stored in a variable; thus, it is only available for use with that specific output statement.

ReadLine( )

The `ReadLine( )` method is much more versatile than the `Read( )` method. Any number of characters can be entered using the `ReadLine( )` method, and it returns all characters up to the current end-of-line terminator, the Enter key.

As Figure 4-5 shows, no arguments are included inside the parentheses to the `ReadLine( )` method. `ReadLine( )` is not an overloaded method. It always returns a **string**. Even if numbers are entered, a **string** representing the concatenation of these numbers is returned. When the user types the number 786 at the keyboard, the result returned is '7' + '8' + '6' or the **string** "786". An extra step is needed before any mathematical operations can be performed on the value. The **string** value must be parsed into an appropriate number type.

 This feature was probably borrowed from Java. All values are entered as strings in Java. This enables values to be entered as strings and checked for typing errors before parsing or translating them into numbers.

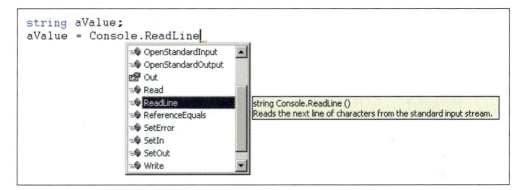

Figure 4-5   Console.ReadLine ( ) signature

Example 4-9 shows calls to the predefined `Write( )`, `ReadLine( )`, `Parse( )`, and `WriteLine( )` methods. An integer is requested. It comes in as a **string** value and must be converted to an **int** using the `Parse( )` method. Parsing must occur before any arithmetic can be performed on the value that was entered.

Example 4-9

```
/* *********************************************
 * AgeIncrementer.cs            Author:     Doyle
 * Displays age one year from now.
 *
 *********************************************/
```

```
using System;
namespace AgeExample
{
    public class AgeIncrementer
    {
        public static void Main( )
        {
            int age;
            string aValue;

            Console.Write("Enter your age: ");
            aValue = Console.ReadLine( );
            age = int.Parse(aValue);
            Console.WriteLine("Your age next year"
                    + " will be {0}", ++age);
            Console.Read( );
        }
    }
}
```

 `int.Parse( )` could be replaced by `Int32.Parse( )`. `Int32` is the `class` name in .NET. The `int` type is an alias for `Int32`. All .NET-supported languages recognize `Int32`.

Parse( )

Another predefined **static** method you will use often is the **Parse( )** method. As stated previously, **Parse( )** returns the number representation of its **string** argument. All numeric types have a **Parse( )** method. In Example 4-9, an **int** value is returned when the **Parse( )** method finishes. **Parse( )** can also be called with a **double object** as illustrated in Example 4-10.

Example 4-10

```
/* *******************************************
 * SquareInputValue.cs          Author:   Doyle
 * Allows an integer value to be input.
 * Computes and displays the square of the
 * value inputted.
 *
 ********************************************/
using System;
namespace Square
{
    class SquareInputValue
    {
```

```
        static void Main( )
        {
            string inputStringValue;
            double aValue;
            double result;

            Console.Write("Enter a value to be "
                            + "squared: ");
            inputStringValue = Console.ReadLine( );
            aValue = double.Parse(inputStringValue);
            result = Math.Pow(aValue, 2);
            Console.WriteLine("{0} squared is {1}",
                                aValue, result);
        }
    }
}
```

4

Calls to methods `char.Parse( )` and `bool.Parse( )` produce similar results, as shown in Example 4-11.

Example 4-11

```
string sValue = "True";
Console.WriteLine(bool.Parse(sValue));      // displays True
string strValue = "q";
Console.WriteLine(char.Parse(strValue));    // displays q
```

If you attempt to parse an incompatible value, a **System.FormatException** error, similar to that shown in Figure 4-6, is generated. The error in Figure 4-6 was generated from `Console.WriteLine(char.Parse(sValue))` when `sValue` referenced `"True"` as in Example 4-11.

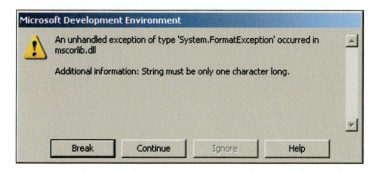

Figure 4-6   System.FormatException runtime error

`sValue` is a **string** variable that contains more than one character. The argument to `char.Parse( )` must be a single-character **string**.

There is more than one way to convert from one base type to another. As part of the .NET Framework Class Library, in the **System namespace**, a number of **static** methods are found in the **Convert class**. These include `Convert.ToDouble( )`, `Convert.ToDecimal( )`, `Convert.ToInt32( )`, `Convert.ToBoolean( )`, and `Convert.ToChar( )`. Used like the `Parse( )` method, they convert data from one base type to another base type. The following converts an entered **string** value to an **int** base type:

```
int newValue = Convert.ToInt32(stringValue);
```

These methods are all overloaded so that the argument to the method can be of varying type. If, for example, you send a **char** argument to the **Convert.ToInt32( )** method, and store the result in an **int** variable, you get the Unicode numeric representation for that character.

Methods in the Math Class

The **Math class** has a number of predefined **static** methods you will find helpful. The **Math class**, like the **Console class**, is located in the **System namespace**. This **class** provides constants and methods for trigonometric, logarithmic, and other common mathematical functions. The **Pow( )** method that you saw previously is a member of the **Math class**. You learned that the first argument to the **Pow( )** method is the base, the number to be raised. The second argument is the exponent, or the specified power value. Table 4-2 identifies, describes, and gives examples of the more commonly used methods from the **Math class**. The signature and the **return** type are included in the third column.

Table 4-2 Math class methods

Method	Description	Method heading
`Abs`	Returns the absolute value of a specified number. Overloaded—can be used with **int**, **double**, **decimal**, **short**, **float**, **sbyte**, and **long**. Example: `Math.Abs(-88.62)` returns the value `88.62`	`public static int Abs(int)`
`Ceiling`	Returns the smallest whole number greater than or equal to the specified number. Example: `Math.Ceiling(88.12)` returns the value 89	`public static double Ceiling (double)`
`Cos`	Returns the cosine of the specified angle measured in radians.	`public static double Cos(double)`

Table 4-2 Math class methods (continued)

Method	Description	Method heading
Exp	Returns e raised to the specified power. e is defined as a constant in the Math class. It has a value of 2.7182818284590452354. Example: `Math.Exp(2)` returns the value `7.38905609893065`	`public static double Exp(double)`
Floor	Returns the largest whole number less than or equal to the specified number. Example: `Math.Floor(88.62)` returns the value 88	`public static double Floor(double)`
Log	Returns the logarithm of a specified number. Two overloaded methods. First one returns the natural (base e) logarithm of a specified number. It takes a single argument of type double. Second (signature to the right) returns the logarithm of a specified number. Example: `Math.Log(4)` returns the value `1.38629436111989`	`public static double Log (double, double)`
Max	Returns the larger of two specified numbers. Overloaded with 11 different methods (byte, decimal, double, short, int, long, sbyte, float, ushort, uint, ulong). All require the same type for both arguments. Example: `Math.Max(87, 13)` returns 87	`public static double Max (double, double)`
Min	Returns the smaller of two numbers. Overloaded—exactly like Max in the previous row. Example: `Math.Min(87, 13)` returns 13	`public static int Min(int, int)`

4

Table 4-2 Math class methods (continued)

Method	Description	Method heading
Pow	Returns a specified number raised to the specified power. Not overloaded. Arguments can be entered as `int`. They are implicitly converted. Return value must be stored in `double`; otherwise, you receive a syntax error. Example: `Math.Pow(5, 3)` returns 125	`public static double Pow` `(double, double)`
Round	Returns the number nearest the specified value. Overloaded. Can return a number with the specified precision indicated by the second argument, as illustrated with the signature to the right. Example: `Math.Round (87.98227657, 4)` returns 87.9823	`public static double Round` `(double, int)`
Sign	Returns a value indicating the sign of a number. -1 for negative values; 1 for positive; 0 for zero values; Overloaded—each returns an `int`. Argument can be used with `double`, `decimal`, `long`, `short`, `sbyte`, `int`, or `float`. Example: `Math.Sign(46.3)` returns 1	`public static int Sign(double)`
Sin	Returns the sine of the specified angle measured in radians.	`public static double Sin(double)`
Sqrt	Returns the square root of a specified number. Return value must be stored in `double`; otherwise, you receive a syntax error. Example: `Math.Sqrt(25)` returns 5	`public static double Sqrt(double)`
Tan	Returns the tangent of the specified angle measured in radians.	`public static double Tan(double)`

Because each of the methods in Table 4-2 is `static`, calls to them must include the `Math class` name as a qualifier.

 You learned about implicit conversion in Chapter 3, "Data Types and Expressions." C# provides for conversion from smaller data types to larger when you send arguments to methods. For example, implicit conversion occurs from `int` to `long`, `float`, `double`, or `decimal` types. Thus, if the formal parameter enclosed inside the parentheses for the method's heading is a `double`, you can usually send an `int` argument when you call the method. The `int` is converted to a `double` by the CLR.

4

The following are examples of valid calls to methods of the `Math class`:

```csharp
double aValue = 78.926;
double result1,
       result2;
result1 = Math.Floor(aValue);// result1 = 78
result2 = Math.Sqrt(aValue); // result2 = 8.88403061678651
Console.Write("aValue rounded to two decimal places"
              + " is {0}", Math.Round(aValue, 2));
```

The output for the last statement is:

```
aValue rounded to two decimal places is 78.93
```

As you look at the examples using the predefined methods from the `Math class`, you can see that they all have something in common. Each of the methods returns a value. Calls to methods returning values usually are placed in an expression or in an output statement. When the value is returned, there has to be a place for the value to be used.

A `class` can define a `static` method, or a `class` can use a `static` method defined in another `class`. If you are calling a method that is a member of the same `class` from where it is being called, the call statement does not have to include the `class` name. If you are calling a `static` method defined in another `class`, the name of the `class` must be included. When you use the methods in the `Math class`, you are using methods that are defined outside the boundaries of your `class`. `Exp( )` is a `static` member of the `Math class`. In the example that follows, it returns `e`, the natural logarithmic base, raised to the 5th power. It is necessary to use the `class` name `Math` as a qualifier.

```csharp
double result;

result = Math.Exp(5);
```

 The `Math class` also has two `static` data field members defined as constants. A call to `static` field members also requires prefixing the member name with the `class` name. Their declarations follow:

```csharp
public const double E  =  2.7182818284590452354;
public const double PI = 3.14159265358979323846;
```

An example of their use is as follows:

```csharp
circumference = 2 * Math.PI * radius;   //use of PI in an
                                        //expression
```

Calls to value returning methods must be placed at a location in your code where the value could be accepted when the method is finished. The call may appear anywhere a compatible value of that type can be placed. The statements in Example 4-12 on lines 4, 6, and 9 illustrate three different places to which the **static** method **Max( )** returns a value.

Example 4-12

```
Line 1     int aValue = 200;
Line 2     int bValue = 896;
Line 3     int result;
Line 4     result = Math.Max(aValue, bValue);
                // result = 896
Line 5     result += bValue *
Line 6             Math.Max(aValue, bValue) -   aValue;
                // result = 896 + (896 * 896  - 200)
                // result = 803512
Line 7     Console.WriteLine("Largest value between {0} "
Line 8           + "and {1} is {2}", aValue, bValue,
Line 9             Math.Max(aValue, bValue));
```

The output generated from lines 7 through 9 is:

```
Largest value between 200 and 896 is 896
```

As shown in Table 4–2, the heading for **Max( )** is

public static int Max(int, int)

As shown with the preceding three statements in lines 4 through 9, values returned from a value returning method can be returned to any location in your program where a variable of that **return** type can be used. The **int** returned in line 4 is assigned to **result**. The **int** returned in line 6 is used as part of an arithmetic expression. The **int** returned in line 9 is an argument to the **WriteLine( )** method.

WRITING YOUR OWN CLASS METHODS

There are many classes containing member methods that make up the .NET FCL. You should explore and make use of them whenever possible. However, for specific tasks relating to building your unique applications, it is often necessary for you to write methods of your own.

The syntax for defining a method follows. The square brackets used with the modifier indicate an optional entry.

```
[modifier(s)] returnType  MethodName(parameterList)
{
    // body of method - consisting of executable statements
}
```

As noted previously, the returnType specifies what kind of information is returned when the body of the method is finished executing. This may be the name of any predefined or user-defined type, such as **int** or **double**. The returnType may also be replaced with the keyword **void**. Void is used to indicate that no value is being returned. Notice that there is only room for one returnType per method. Thus, a method can return at most one value type under its name.

User-defined methods in C# can be classified into two categories:

- Methods that do not return a value, called **void** methods
- Methods that return a value, called value returning methods

You write both types in the sections that follow.

Void Methods

void methods are the simplest to write. No **return** statement is needed in the body of the method.

> **NOTE** It is permissible to use the **return** keyword as the last statement in a non-value return-ing method. Some programmers feel this adds to the readability. If you do include **return**, a semicolon is placed after the keyword. No value is used with non-value returning methods.

The keyword **void** is used for the **return** type in the heading. Example 4-13 illustrates a non-value returning method. This one does not expect any data to be sent into it. No para-meters are included inside the parentheses. The keyword **static** is included so that the methods can be called without instantiating an **object** of the method's **class**. Later in this chapter, you learn how to write nonstatic methods.

Example 4-13

```
public static void DisplayInstructions( )
{
    Console.WriteLine("This program will determine how "
                    + "much carpet to purchase.");
    Console.WriteLine( );
    Console.WriteLine("You will be asked to enter the "
                    + " size of the room and ");
    Console.WriteLine("the price of the carpet, "
                    + "in price per square yards.");
    Console.WriteLine( );
}
```

Non-value returning methods may include parameters. Example 4-14 illustrates a **void** method that requires that data be sent to it when it is called.

4

Example 4-14

```
public static void DisplayResults(double squareYards,
                                  double pricePerSquareYard)
{
    Console.Write("Total Square Yards needed: ");
    Console.WriteLine("{0:N2}", squareYards);
    Console.Write("Total Cost at {0:C} ",
                    pricePerSquareYard);
    Console.WriteLine(" per Square Yard: {0:C}",
                        (squareYards *
                         pricePerSquareYard));
}
```

To call these non-value returning methods, simply enter the method's identifier followed by a set of parentheses. If the method has parameters, the call will include actual arguments inside the parentheses. These methods are **class** methods; they include the **static** keyword in the heading. Calls to methods in Examples 4-13 and 4-14 follow:

```
DisplayInstructions( );
DisplayResults(16.5, 18.95);
```

NOTE The 16.5 and 18.95 could be replaced by **double** variables containing values.

Notice how each of these methods is called without qualifying it with a **class** or **object** name. This is possible when a **static** method is called from within the **class** where it resides as a member. This is different from the calls to methods in the **Console** and **Math** classes.

Value Returning Method

Every method that has a **return** type other than **void** must have a **return** statement in the body. A compatible value of the type found in the heading follows the **return** keyword. As stated previously, this **return** does not actually have to appear as the last statement; however, it is good practice to design your methods so they have one entry and one exit. Placing the **return** as the last statement helps you follow this guideline. Example 4-15 illustrates a value returning method that does not require any arguments. To call this method, no data need be passed to it.

Example 4-15

```
public static double GetLength( )
{
    string inputValue;
    int feet,
        inches;
    Console.Write("Enter the Length in feet: ");
    inputValue = Console.ReadLine( );
    feet = int.Parse(inputValue);
    Console.Write("Enter the Length in inches: ");
    inputValue = Console.ReadLine( );
    inches = int.Parse(inputValue);
    return (feet + (double) inches / 12);
}
```

4

Three variables are declared in the **GetLength( )** method in Example 4-15. They are considered local variables. A local variable exists only inside the method where it is declared. The scope of the variable covers the location where it is declared to the ending curly brace of the method. The **scope** of an identifier is simply the region of the program in which that identifier is usable. Scope applies to methods as well as variables. An attempt to use any of the local variables declared in the **GetLength( )** method in another method results in a syntax error stating that the identifier is unknown.

It is possible to use exactly the same name as an identifier for a local variable that has already been used for an instance variable or a parameter identifier. When this happens, the innermost declaration takes scope when you are inside that method. Thus the local variable would be visible and the other(s) hidden. If, for example, the identifier **feet** is used as a variable in the **Main( )** method and that same identifier, **feet**, is declared as a variable inside the **GetLength( )** method, no syntax error is generated. Instead, the **feet** variable declared in the **GetLength( )** method is visible as long as execution is inside that method. When the method is completed, the **GetLength( )** **feet** identifier becomes out of scope. You can think of it as "dying" or no longer existing as soon as the ending curly brace is encountered. As soon as that happens, if control returns back to **Main( )** where the other **feet** is declared, the **Main( )** method's **feet** goes back into scope and becomes visible again.

Like non-value returning methods, one or more data items may be passed as arguments to these types of method as illustrated in Example 4-16.

Example 4-16

```
public static double DeterminePrice(double squareYards,
                        double pricePerSquareYard )
{
    return (pricePerSquareYard * squareYards);
}
```

Calls to value returning methods require a location for the value to be returned. As you saw previously, calls can be placed in assignment statements, output statements, or anywhere a value can be used. If the method has parameters, the call includes the actual data inside the parentheses. Since the **static** keyword appears in the heading, these are still considered **class** methods. Calls to methods in Examples 4-15 and 4-16 follow:

```
double roomLength;
roomLength = GetLength( );
Console.WriteLine(" Total cost of the carpet: {0:C}",
                  DeterminePrice(squareYards, pricePerSquareYard));
```

Signatures of methods that appeared in Examples 4-13 through 4-16 follow. The signature consists of the name of the method, modifiers, and the formal parameter types.

```
public static DisplayInstructions( );
public static DisplayResults(double, double);
public static GetLength( );
public static DeterminePrice(double, double);
```

The complete program listing using the **class** methods introduced as part of the **CarpetExampleWithClassMethods** class is shown in Example 4-17. Notice that there is no **GetLength(   )** method in the program listing. Instead a method named **GetDimension( )** is used to get both the length and width. The heading for the method includes a **string** parameter representing which side, length, or width is being entered. This method is called twice. It is called first with the **string** argument of "Length" and second with "Width" as the argument. The value that is returned from the **GetDimension(   )** method each time is stored in different variables.

Example 4-17

```
/* CarpetExampleWithClassMethods.cs
 * Author:   Doyle
 * Calculates the total cost of carpet. User
 * inputs room dimensions and carpet price.
 */
using System;
namespace CarpetExampleWithClassMethods
{
    public class CarpetWithClassMethods
    {
        public static void Main( )
        {
            double roomWidth;
            double roomLength;
            double pricePerSqYard;
            double noOfSquareYards;
```

```
        DisplayInstructions( );

        // Call getDimension( ) to get the length
        roomLength = GetDimension("Length");

        // Call getDimension( ) again to get the
        // width
        roomWidth = GetDimension("Width");
        pricePerSqYard = GetPrice( );
        noOfSquareYards =
         DetermineSquareYards(roomWidth, roomLength);
        DisplayResults(noOfSquareYards,
                          pricePerSqYard);
    }

    public static void DisplayInstructions( )
    {
        Console.WriteLine("This program will "
                          + "determine how much "
                          + "carpet to purchase.");
        Console.WriteLine( );
        Console.WriteLine("You will be asked to "
                          + "enter the size of "
                          + "the room ");
        Console.WriteLine("and the price of the "
                          + "carpet, in price per"
                          + " square yds.");
        Console.WriteLine( );
    }

    public static double GetDimension(string side )
    {
        string inputValue;      // local variables
        int feet,               // needed only by this
            inches;             // method

        Console.Write("Enter the {0} in feet: ",
                        side);
        inputValue = Console.ReadLine( );
        feet = int.Parse(inputValue);
        Console.Write("Enter the {0} in inches: ",
                        side);
        inputValue = Console.ReadLine( );
        inches = int.Parse(inputValue);

        // Note: cast required to avoid int division
        return (feet + (double) inches / 12);
    }
```

4

```
public static double GetPrice( )
{
    string inputValue;          // local variables
    double price;

    Console.Write("Enter the price per Square"
                    + "Yard: ");
    inputValue = Console.ReadLine( );
    price = double.Parse(inputValue);
    return price;
}

public static double DetermineSquareYards
                        (double width, double length)
{
    const int SQ_FT_PER_SQ_YARD = 9;

    double noOfSquareYards;
    noOfSquareYards = length * width
                            / SQ_FT_PER_SQ_YARD;
    return noOfSquareYards;
}

public static double DeterminePrice
                (double squareYards,
                 double pricePerSquareYard)
{
    return (pricePerSquareYard * squareYards);
}

public static void DisplayResults
                (double squareYards,
                 double pricePerSquareYard)
{
    Console.WriteLine( );
    Console.Write("Square Yards needed: ");
    Console.WriteLine("{0:N2}", squareYards);
    Console.Write("Total Cost at {0:C} ",
                pricePerSquareYard);
    Console.WriteLine(" per Square Yard: "
                    + "{0:C}",
                    DeterminePrice(squareYards,
                        pricePerSquareYard));
}
    }
}
```

Figure 4-7 shows the output produced when the user types 16 feet, 3 inches for length; 14 feet, 7 inches for width; and 14.95 for `price`.

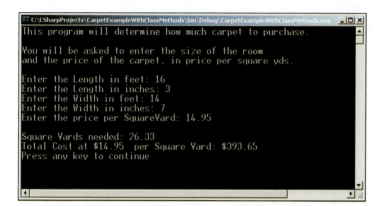

Figure 4-7   Output from CarpetExampleWithClassMethods

 Notice that Figure 4-7 includes as the last line "Press any key to continue." This is placed there because the program was run in Visual Studio .NET using the Debug - >Start feature without the Debugging option (Ctrl+F5) in contrast to the Start (F5) option. This was done to hold the output screen without adding the extra call to the `Read( )` method as the last statement in the `Main( )` method.

THE OBJECT CONCEPT

C# is an object-oriented language. All the code that you wrote for your applications has been placed in a `class`. Thus far you have not really taken advantage of the object-oriented approach to systems development. Remember that one of the underlying assumptions of the object-oriented methodology is that a number of entities exist that can be identified and described. An **entity**, usually associated with a person, place, or thing, is normally a noun. The entity can be defined in terms of its current state and behaviors. By abstracting out the attributes (data) and the behaviors (processes on the data), you can create a `class` to serve as a template from which many objects of that type can be instantiated. Then, just as you declare objects of the `int` type and use all its predefined methods, after you define your own classes, you can declare objects of your user-defined types and use the methods that you define.

To program an object-oriented solution, a few new concepts are needed. First, instead of thinking about what processes need to be programmed, begin by determining what objects are needed in the solution. From that, determine what data characteristics will belong to the objects and what kind of behaviors the data will need to perform. When you are defining a `class`, you find that there are common features that are included with your object-oriented solutions, as described in the following sections.

Private Member Data

You learned in Chapter 3, "Data Types and Expressions," to declare variables. Those variables were defined inside the `Main( )` method. In this chapter you saw how methods other than `Main( )` could define local variables. The variables declared in these methods and in `Main( )` were only visible inside the body of the method in which they were declared. When you define a `class` and determine what data members it should have, you declare instance variables or fields that represent the state of an `object`. These fields are declared inside the `class`, but not inside any specific method. They become visible to all members of the `class`, including all of the method members.

Normally the data, instance variables, are defined to have a **`private`** access. This enables the `class` to protect the data and allow access to the data only through the `class` member methods. Example 4-18 shows where the instance variables are declared. As illustrated in Example 4-18, data fields are normally declared first inside the body of the `class` definition. In the examples that follow, the `CarpetCalculator` is revisited using an object-oriented approach.

Example 4-18

```
public class CarpetCalculator
{
    private double pricePerSqYard;
    private double noOfSquareYards;
    :
```

WRITING YOUR OWN INSTANCE METHODS

When you write an instance method, you do not use the **`static`** keyword in the heading. To call an instance method, however, an **`object`** must be instantiated and associated with the method. In addition to the kinds of methods previously introduced that were categorized as value or non-value returning methods and methods with or without arguments, there are several special types of methods that are only affiliated with instance methods. They are described in the sections that follow.

Constructor

Object-oriented design of applications facilitates reuse of code. Once the `class` is defined, you create instances, examples, of the `class`. This is called **instantiating the `class`**. An instance of a `class` is called an **`object`**. When you instantiate the `class`, you actually create an instance of the `class`, an **`object`** that takes up space and exists. It is through a special method, called a **constructor**, that you use to create instances of a `class`. Constructors differ from other methods in two ways:

- Constructors do not `return` a value, but the keyword `void` is not included. You receive an error message if you type `void`.

- Constructors use the same identifier as the `class` name.

A `public` access modifier is always associated with constructors so that other classes can instantiate objects of their type. Constructors are often overloaded. When you write a `class`, you do not have to write a constructor; one is automatically created for you that is called the default constructor. It has no functionality, other than the fact that it can be used to create an instance of the `class`. Default values are assigned to each member data field if the default constructor is used to create an `object` of the `class` type. No parameters are included with this one. It has no body, simply open and closed curly braces.

To add full functionality to your classes, you normally write one or more constructors for all classes in which objects will be instantiated. If you write even one constructor, you lose the default that is created automatically. When you write your constructors, think about how objects will be created of that `class` type. If you had a `Student class`, you may want a constructor that lets you create a `Student object` that is given an `ID`. You may want another constructor that lets you create a `Student object` that is given a `name`. Another constructor might be useful given `name` and `ID`. Thus, for a `Student class`, at least four constructors might be designed as shown here:

```
Student (string name)          // Constructor- one string parameter
Student (int ID)               // Constructor- one int parameter
Student (string name, int ID)  // Constructor- two
                               // parameters
Student ( )                    // default constructor
```

 You should design your classes to be as flexible and full-featured as possible. One way to do this is to include multiple constructors.

A fifth constructor could be designed with the first argument being `ID` followed by the `string` for the `name`. Its signature would be different from the constructor that has the `string` parameter listed first. As with overloaded methods, signatures must differ for constructors. You could not have one constructor that has the two `string` parameters of `firstName` and `lastName` and then define another constructor that took `string` parameters of `lastName` and `firstName`. Their signatures would be the same. Both would have two strings for their parameter list.

 The default constructor does not have to have an empty body. You often place one or more statements in this method to initialize the `private` member data.

Example 4-19 shows three constructors for the `CarpetCalculator` `class`.

Example 4-19

```
// Constructor with no parameters—Default constructor
public CarpetCalculator( )
{
    //empty body
}
// Constructor with two parameters
public CarpetCalculator(double amountNeeded, double price)
{
    noOfSquareYards = amountNeeded;
    pricePerSqYard = price;

}
// Constructor with one parameter
public CarpetCalculator(double price)
{
  pricePerSqYard = price;
}
```

All three constructors used the same identifier, that is, the name of the `class`. They each have different signatures. One requires no arguments, one requires one argument, and the third requires two arguments. By writing three separate constructors, more flexibility is offered an application that chooses to use this `class`. An `object` of the `class` can be created by giving a price and the number of square yards needed; an `object` can be created sending it just the price; or, an `object` can be created without any arguments.

It might seem like overkill to write a method that does not have a body, but this is a common practice. If you define at least one constructor, you should write another constructor that takes no arguments, the default constructor. Otherwise, you are limiting the functionality of your `class`. By having a constructor with no arguments, you can create instances of the `class` without setting the current state of its data members. When this happens, the default values for the specific types are used.

 A default constructor can have a body; it normally does not have parameters. Parameterless constructors are useful for assigning default values to data members.

Accessor

To access the current state or value of an `object` member's data, special methods called accessors can be used. Accessors are also referred to as **getters**. They access the value of a data member, without changing it. **Accessors** are used because instance variables, data members of a `class`, are normally defined using a `private` modifier. As you saw in Table 4-1, `private` limits access to members of the `class`. However, the idea behind object-oriented development is that objects communicate with each by exchanging information. Objects that are instances of one **class** may need to access members in another **class**. They do this through calling methods. Because methods are usually defined as **public**, this communication is possible.

An accessor normally returns just the current value of a data member so that the current value can be used by other classes. Many bodies of accessor methods consist of a single **return** statement, as illustrated in Example 4-20.

Example 4-20

```
public double GetNoOfSquareYards( )
{
     return noOfSquareYards;
}
```

 Java programmers often include an accessor method for each **private** data member that is to be accessible from outside the **class**. This is unnecessary in C#. A new property member is included. This reduces the number of accessors needed. You learn about properties later in this chapter.

A standard naming convention is to add "Get" onto the front of the instance variable identifier and use that name for the accessor method name that retrieves the data item. Example 4-20 shows an accessor method for `noOfSquareYards`. The identifier for the accessor is `GetNoOfSquareYards( )`.

Mutators

To change the current state or value of an **object** member's data, special methods called mutators can be used. **Mutators** are sometimes called **setters**. A mutator normally is written to include one parameter that represents the new value a data member should have. Like accessors, mutators are needed because of the **private** accessibility of instance variables. Example 4-21 shows two overloaded mutators. The first example is the more common way to write a mutator. The body of the method consists of a single assignment statement.

Example 4-21

```
public void SetNoOfSquareYards(double squareYards)
{
     noOfSquareYards = squareYards;
}
public void SetNoOfSquareYards(double length,
                                  double width)
{
     const int SQ_FT_PER_SQ_YARD = 9;
     noOfSquareYards = length * width / SQ_FT_PER_SQ_YARD;
}
```

> C#'s new property members also reduce the number of mutators needed.

A standard naming convention is to add "Set" to the front of the instance variable identifier; that name becomes the mutator method name. In Example 4-21 the instance variable being changed is `noOfSquareYards`; the identifier for the mutator is `SetNoOfSquareYards( )`.

Property

One of the new features included in C# is a property. A property looks like a data field, but it does not directly represent a storage location. Properties are more closely aligned to methods. They provide a way to set or get **private** member data. Example 4-22 includes the property for `pricePerSqYard`.

Example 4-22

```
public double Price
{
    get
    {
        return pricePerSqYard;
    }
    set
    {
        pricePerSqYard = value;
    }
}
```

A standard naming convention in C# for properties is to use the same name as the instance variable or field. The exception is that the property identifier starts with an uppercase character. To call attention to the fact that the names do not have to match, Example 4-22 did not follow that convention. Following the naming convention, the property would be named `PricePerSqYard`.

When you define a property, you can define the **set** without the **get** or the **get** without the **set**. It is not necessary to include both. The body of the **get** must return a value of the property type. If you include only the **get**, the property is considered a read-only property because the value of the instance variable cannot be changed through the property. The execution of the **get** is equivalent to reading the value of the field. Once the set property for a variable is defined, you can change the **private** instance variable's data using that property in any **class** that instantiates an **object**. For example, if an instantiated **object** is named `Berber`, to change the `pricePerSqYard` you could write:

```
Berber.Price = 25.99;
```

The body of the **set** portion in the property is similar to a mutator. Remember that the mutator method's **return** type is **void**. Mutators normally have one argument representing the value to be assigned to the instance variable. The **set** portion of the property uses an implicit parameter, called **value**. The type of **value** is always the same as the **private** member that is being associated with the property. **get**, **set**, and **value** are not keywords. However, it is not necessary to declare **value**, **get**, or **set**. They have special meaning when used with properties. No parentheses or parameter is placed after the property identifier.

 Once the properties are declared, they can be used as if they were fields of the **class**. You see more examples of their use in the next section.

4

As previously noted, by including properties for logical member data, the number of mutator and accessor methods needed is reduced.

CALLING INSTANCE METHODS

Once a **class** template has been defined to include **private** member data, **public** methods, and **public** properties, many different applications can use the **class**. To do so, objects of the **class** are instantiated using the **class** constructor.

Calling the Constructor

Normally, the first method called is the constructor. This is the method that actually creates an **object** instance of the **class**. The syntax for this is:

```
ClassName objectName = new ClassName(argumentList);
```

or

```
ClassName objectName;
objectName = new ClassName(argumentList);
```

It is more usual to call the constructor in a single statement as shown first.

Example 4-23 creates three objects and calls the three different constructor methods defined in Example 4-19.

Example 4-23

```
CarpetCalculator plush = new CarpetCalculator( );
CarpetCalculator pile =
            new CarpetCalculator(37.90, 17.95);
CarpetCalculator Berber = new CarpetCalculator(17.95);
```

Each of the preceding statements does two things:

- Declares an **object** of a specific **class**

- Calls the constructor to create an instance of the **class**

The keyword **new** is used as an operator to call constructor methods. The first line in Example 4-23 is a call to the default constructor for the `CarpetCalculator` **class**. An **object** named **plush** is created. Only the system default values for **double** are used to initialize the instance variables. Table 4-3 shows the default values of the value types assigned to variables when no arguments are sent to member data.

Table 4-3   Value type defaults

Value type	Default value
bool	false
byte	0
char	'\0' (null)
decimal	0.0M
double	0.0D
float	0.0F
int	0
long	0L
short	0
uint	0
ulong	0
ushort	0

 Using uninitialized variables in C# is not allowed.

The second call to the constructor sends two arguments. An **object** named **pile** is created, and an **object** named **Berber** is created with the third constructor. The actual argument of 17.95 is used to initialize the **private** member `pricePerSquareYard`.

Calling Accessor and Mutator Methods

All instance methods are called in exactly the same manner as **class** methods, with one exception. If the method is being called from another **class** that has instantiated an **object** of the **class**, the method name is preceded by the **object** name. If another member of the same **class** is using the method, all that is needed is the name of the method.

One of the methods of the **CarpetCalculator class** is **SetNoOfSquareYards( )**. Another **class**, called **CarpetCalculatorApp**, has instantiated an **object** of the **CarpetCalculator class** by using the last constructor from Figure 4-19, shown again as follows:

```
CarpetCalculator Berber = new CarpetCalculator(17.95);
```

A call to the **SetNoOfSquareYards( )** method requires the name of the **object**, a dot, and the name of the **method** as shown in the code that follows. This is a non–value returning method. You should note it is a mutator method.

```
Berber.SetNoOfSquareYards(27.83);
```

If the method is returning a value, as accessors do, there must be a place for the value to be returned. Again the method is called by typing the objectName, a dot, and the methodName. Example 4-24 shows a call to an accessor method, which has a **return** value.

Example 4-24

```
Console.WriteLine("{0:N2}",
        Berber.GetNoOfSquareYards( ));
```

The value representing the number of square yards is printed on **return** from the accessor method.

Member properties are normally defined with a **public** access. To reference a **set** member property, you can use the name of the property field in an assignment statement as in

```
PropertyName = value;
```

You can reference the **get** portion of the property as if it were an instance variable. Line 2 in Example 4-25 shows how the property **Price**, which was declared in Example 4-22, is used.

Example 4-25

```
Line 1    Console.Write("Total Cost at {0:C} ",
Line 2                    Berber.Price);
Line 3    Console.WriteLine(" per Square Yard: {0:C}",
Line 4            Berber.DetermineTotalCost( ));
```

Notice that the use of the property in line 2 differs from a method call. No parentheses are used with the property.

In the last nine examples you saw instance methods, instance data fields, and properties defined and called. Most of the examples were code snippets for an object-oriented solution to the `CarpetCalculator` problem. The complete listing for the object-oriented solution for the application follows. The solution consists of two files.

When you create an application that has two files, be sure to include only one **Main( )** method. Only one of the files is used as the startup control file. The first file in this solution is the `CarpetCalculator` **class**, which defines the **class** template for a carpet **object**. It includes **private** data, **public** methods, and **public** property definitions. The second file is an example application, which instantiates an **object** of the `CarpetCalculator` **class**.

 In Visual Studio, add a second file to your application by clicking Project >Add Class. Only one file in your application can have a **Main( )** method.

The complete program listing follows in Example 4-26.

Example 4-26

```
/* CarpetCalculator.cs
 * Author:  Doyle
 * Defines the template for the
 * CarpetCalculator class to include constructors,
 * accessors, mutators, and properties
 */

using System;
namespace Carpet
{
    public class CarpetCalculator
    {
        private double pricePerSqYard;
        private double noOfSquareYards;

        // Property of the pricePerSqYard data field
        public  double Price
        {
            get
            {
                return pricePerSqYard;
            }
            set
            {
                pricePerSqYard = value;
            }
        }
```

```
// Default Constructor
public CarpetCalculator( )
{
    //empty body
}

// Constructor
public CarpetCalculator(double amountNeeded,
                        double price)
{
    noOfSquareYards = amountNeeded;
    pricePerSqYard = price;
}

// Constructor
public CarpetCalculator(double price)
{
    pricePerSqYard = price;
}

public double DetermineTotalCost( )
{
    return (pricePerSqYard * noOfSquareYards);
}

// One of the overloaded Mutator methods
public void SetNoOfSquareYards(double length,
                               double width)
{
    const int SQ_FT_PER_SQ_YARD = 9;

    noOfSquareYards = length * width
                      / SQ_FT_PER_SQ_YARD;
}

// One of the overloaded Mutator methods
public void SetNoOfSquareYards
                        (double squareYards)
{
    noOfSquareYards = squareYards;
}

// Accessor method
public double GetNoOfSquareYards( )
{
    return noOfSquareYards;
}
    }
}
```

4

The following file uses the `CarpetCalculator class`:

```csharp
/* CarpetCalculatorApp.cs
 * Author:  Doyle
 * This class instantiates an object
 * of the CarpetCalculator class. It
 * demonstrates how to access and use
 * the members of the class.
 */
using System;
namespace Carpet
{
    public class CarpetCalculatorApp
    {
        public static void Main( )
        {
            CarpetCalculator Berber =
                        new CarpetCalculator(17.95);

            double roomWidth;
            double roomLength;

            DisplayInstructions( );

            // Call GetDimension( ) to get the length
            roomLength = GetDimension("Length");

            // Call GetDimension( ) again to get the width
            roomWidth = GetDimension("Width");
            Berber.SetNoOfSquareYards
                        (roomLength, roomWidth);
            DisplayResults(Berber);
        }
        static void DisplayInstructions( )
        {
            Console.WriteLine("This program will"
                        + " determine how much "
                        + "carpet to purchase.");
            Console.WriteLine( );
            Console.WriteLine("You will be asked to "
                        + "enter the size of the "
                        + "room and the price of the");
            Console.WriteLine("carpet, in price per "
                        + "square yds.");
            Console.WriteLine( );
        }
```

```
static double GetDimension(string side)
{
    string inputValue;      // local variables
    int feet,               // needed only by this
        inches;             // method

    Console.Write("Enter the {0} in feet: ",
                        side);
    inputValue = Console.ReadLine( );
    feet = int.Parse(inputValue);
    Console.Write("Enter the {0} in inches: ",
                        side);
    inputValue = Console.ReadLine( );
    inches = int.Parse(inputValue);

    // Note: cast required to avoid int division
    return (feet + (double) inches / 12);
}

static void DisplayResults
                    (CarpetCalculator carpet )
{
    Console.WriteLine( );
    Console.Write("Square Yards needed: ");
    Console.WriteLine("{0:N2}",
                    carpet.GetNoOfSquareYards( ));
    Console.Write("Total Cost at {0:C} ",
                    carpet.Price);
    Console.WriteLine(" per Square Yard: "
                    + "{0:C}",
                    carpet.DetermineTotalCost( ));
}
}
}
```

Figure 4-8 shows the output for the preceding application when the user enters a room measurement of 12 feet, 2 inches for length, and 14 feet, 3 inches for the width.

Figure 4-8   Output from Carpet example using instance methods

TYPES OF PARAMETERS

The examples using parameters presented thus far used value parameters. C# offers both call by value and call by reference parameters. Call by value is the default type. With **call by value**, a copy of the original value is made and stored in a separate, different memory location. If the method changes the contents of the variable sent to it, this does not affect the original value stored in the variable from the calling method. The original value is retained when control passes back to the calling method. There are three other types of parameters available in C#:

- **ref**

- **out**

- **params**

The **params** parameter is discussed when arrays are presented in Chapter 7, "Arrays and Collections." The **params** type facilitates sending a varying number of arguments into a method. The other two, **ref** and **out**, are useful now. Earlier you learned that when a method was called, you could receive only one data type back as a **return** type. This holds true for receiving the value back through the name of the method. Only one **return** type can be specified. However, think about a situation in which you might write a method that allows the user to enter several values. If only one of those values could be returned to the calling segment, how would you decide which one to **return**? What happens to the other values? If you need a method to **return** more than one value, the values can be returned through parameters, in particular call by reference parameters. The **ref** and **out** keywords facilitate this process.

Both **ref** and **out** cause a method to refer to the same variable that was passed into the method. Instead of making a copy of the original value and storing the copied value in a different memory location, as happens when you send in a value parameter, when you use ref or out the method gains access to the original memory location. Any changes made to the data in the method are reflected in that variable when control passes back to the calling method.

The keywords differ in that the ref keyword cannot be used unless the original argument is initialized. This restriction does not exist for out. The out is useful for methods that allow users to enter new values in a method, when those values are needed by the calling method.

When you use the keywords ref and out, call by reference is assumed. With call by reference, you send the address of the argument to the method. You must include either ref or out in both the call and in the method's heading parameter list. They must match. In other words, you may not use ref in the heading and out in the call. This is different from languages like C++, in which you just indicate a reference parameter in the method heading. The actual call in C# must also include the keyword.

 Java does not have reference parameters. Java's objects simulate call by reference, but the language does not offer call by reference for its primitive types.

All three types, value, ref and out are demonstrated in Example 4-27 that follows.

Example 4-27

```csharp
/* Parameters.cs
 * Author    Doyle
 * This class demonstrates the
 * differences between the
 * default, ref, and out
 * parameter types */
using System;
namespace Parameters
{
    public class ParameterClass
    {
        public static void TestDefault(int aValue)
        {
            aValue = 111;
            Console.WriteLine("In TestDefault -"
                            + "Value: "
                            + "{0}", aValue);
        }
        public static void TestOut(out int aValue)
        {
            aValue = 222;
            Console.WriteLine("In TestOut - "
                            + "Value: "
                            + " {0} ", aValue);
        }
```

```
public static void TestRef(ref int aValue)
{
   aValue = 333;
   Console.WriteLine("Inside TestRef -"
                        + "Value: "
                        + "{0} ", aValue);
}
public static void Main( )
{
   int testValue = 1;
   Console.WriteLine("Original "
                        + "Value: {0} ",
                        testValue);
   TestDefault(testValue);
   Console.WriteLine("Upon return from "
                  + "TestDefault Value: {0}",
                     testValue);
   Console.WriteLine( );
   Console.WriteLine("Original Value: {0}",
                           testValue);
   TestRef(ref testValue);
   Console.WriteLine("Upon return from "
                        + "TestRef Value: {0}",
                        testValue);
   Console.WriteLine( );

   // variable does not have to be initialized
   // for out parameter type
   int testValue2;
   // however, you cannot display its value yet!
   //   Console.WriteLine("Original "
   //                     + "Value: {0}", testValue2);
   TestOut(out testValue2);
   Console.WriteLine("Upon return from "
                        + "TestOut Value: {0}",
                        testValue2);
   Console.Read( );
}
   }
}
```

The output shown in Figure 4-9 illustrates how value parameters remain unchanged. They retain their original value in the calling method. This is because a copy is actually made of the original value. On **return** to the calling method, the original retained values are visible.

Arguments sent using **ref** and **out** are changed when control is returned to the calling method. The **out** parameter does not have to be initialized before the call; however, the **out** parameter must be assigned a value before the method returns. C# does not allow the use of uninitialized variables.

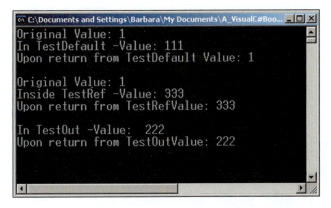

Figure 4-9   Output from ParameterClass example

Figure 4-10 illustrates graphically the difference between call by value and call by reference. It also calls attention to the fact that the **out** parameter type does not have to be initialized before the call. Please notice that the program statements from Example 4-27 are used for this figure.

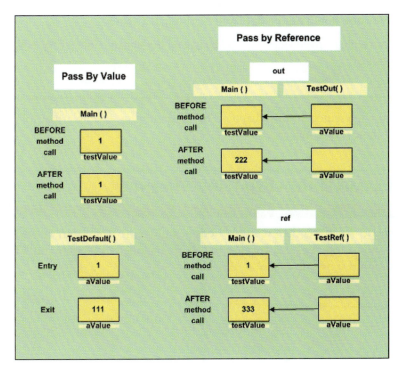

Figure 4-10   Call by reference versus value

In the preceding program example, Example 4-27, notice how one of the calls to the `Console.WriteLine( )` method appears as a comment. In Visual Studio .NET, two tools are available that allow you to select a segment of code with only one click, commenting or uncommenting the section. This can be useful during debugging. The icon circled in Figure 4-11 is used for commenting as the ToolTip shows. Uncomment appears to the right.

Figure 4-11 Visual Studio .Net comment out icon

The lines in the preceding code were commented out to eliminate a syntax error. The contents of `testValue2` could not be displayed until it had a value.

> **NOTE** You can write an overloaded method by having the signature differ only in its use of `out` or `ref`.

Much material is presented in this chapter. The programming example that follows makes use of most of these new concepts.

PROGRAMMING EXAMPLE: REALESTATEINVESTMENT

This example demonstrates the use of methods in a program. Both **static** and instance methods are used. Properties that are new to C# are included in the solution. The problem specification is shown in Figure 4-12.

How much cash flow profit is a rental investment generating? Create an application to determine what the cash flow is for a real estate investment used as a rental.

Design an object-oriented solution. Use two classes.

For the real estate property class, characteristics such as the year the home was built, purchase price, and street address will help identify the current state of an object. The real estate object also has a monthly income amount from rent and a monthly expense characteristic. Include a method to determine what the monthly earnings, or cash flow, is based on deducting the total monthly expenses from the monthly rental income.

In the second class, instantiate an object of the real estate property class. Call the constructor that creates an object using year built, purchase price, and street address. Allow the user to input the yearly taxes and insurance expenses. The monthly utilities costs should also be considered. In this application class, calculate a monthly expense based on the inputted values. Set the appropriate data field in the real estate property object.

Write code in the application class to display the property address and the expected cash flow for a given month.

Figure 4-12   Problem specification for RealEstateInvestment example

Analyze the Problem

You should review the problem specification in Figure 4-12 and make sure you understand the problem definition. Several values must be entered into the program. These values must be entered as **string** variables and then parsed into numeric fields, so that arithmetic can be performed.

Two separate classes are to be developed. Creating a separate **class** for the real estate **object** enables this **class** to be used by many different applications. One application is to produce a listing showing the cash flow from the investment. Other applications might include determining total investment dollar amounts or locations of investments. If the characteristics of real estate objects are abstracted out, many applications can reuse the **class**.

Variables   Tables 4-4 and 4-5 list the data items needed for the RealEstateInvestment problem.

Table 4-4   Instance variables for the RealEstateInvestment class

Data item description	Type	Identifier
Year the home was built	`int`	yearBuilt
Location of the home	`string`	streetAddress
Original purchase price	`double`	purchasePrice
Total expenses for average month	`double`	monthlyExpense
Rental premium per month	`double`	incomeFromRent

The `class` that is using the RealEstateInvestment `class` also needs data. As noted in the problem specification, the application `class` allows the user to enter values for expenses. Table 4-5 identifies some of the local variables needed by the application `class`.

Table 4-5   Local variables for the property application class

Data item description	Type	Identifier
Cost of insurance per year	`double`	insurance
Amount of taxes per year	`double`	taxes
Estimated monthly utility costs	`double`	utilities
String value for inputting values	`string`	inValue

Constants   The rental rate is set as a constant value. The identifier and preset constant value will be

RENTAL_AMOUNT = 1000.00.

Design a Solution

The desired output is to display the address of a property and the expected cash flow for a given month. Figure 4-13 shows a prototype of the desired final output. The xxx.xx is placed in the prototype to represent the location in which the calculated values should appear.

Figure 4-13   Prototype

The object–oriented approach focuses more on the **object**. The real estate property has both data and behavior characteristics that can be identified. Class diagrams are used to help design and document these characteristics. Figure 4-14 shows the **class** diagrams for the RealEstateInvestment example.

Figure 4-14   Class diagrams

The **class** diagrams show neither the properties needed nor the local variables that might be needed by specific **class** methods. As you learned earlier, properties are new to C# and reduce the need to write mutators and accessors for the **private** instance variables. Table 4-6 lists the data members that will have properties defined and indicates whether both **get** and **set** are needed. The name of the property is also shown.

Table 4-6 Properties for the RealEstateInvestment class

Data member identifier	Property identifier	Set	Get
yearBuilt	YearBuilt		
streetAddress	StreetAddress		
purchasePrice	PurchasePrice		
monthlyExpense	MonthlyExpense		
incomeFromRent	IncomeFromRent		

The data members of **yearBuilt**, **streetAddress**, and **purchasePrice** are read-only instance variables. After an **object** of the **class** is instantiated with these values, they cannot be changed. Notice that the identifiers for the properties match the data member with the exception that the first character in the property name is capitalized.

During design it is important to develop the algorithm showing the step-by-step process to solve the problem. Structured English, also called pseudocode, is suited for the object-oriented methodology. In addition to the **Main( )** method, two additional methods— **DetermineMonthlyEarnings( )** and **GetExpenses( )**—need to be designed. Figure 4-15 shows the Structured English design for the RealEstateInvestment example.

```
                 Main( )
Construct RealEstateInvestment object invest1
         yearBuilt = 1998
         purchasePrice = 150000
         streetAddress = "65th Street"

set invest1.MonthlyExpense = GetExpenses( );
set invest1.IncomeFromRent = RENTAL_AMOUNT;

Write "Property Location: "+
         invest1.StreetAddress
Write "Earnings For Month:
invest1.DetermineMonthlyEarnings( )
```

A. PropertyApp Class

```
                GetExpenses( )

Write message to enter insurance rate
Read insurance rate into string inValue
insurance = parse(inValue)

Write prompt to enter taxes
Read tax amount into string inValue
taxes = parse(inValue)

Write prompt to enter utilities charges
Read utilities charges into string inValue
utilities = parse(inValue)

return (insurance / 12 + taxes  / 12 +
         utilities)
```

B. PropertyApp Class

```
DetermineMonthlyEarnings( )

return (incomeFromRent - monthlyExpense)
```

C. RealEstateInvestment Class

Figure 4-15   Structured English for the RealEstateInvestment example

After the algorithm is developed, the design should be checked for correctness. When you desk check your algorithm, begin in `Main( )`. When you encounter method calls, keep your location in that method, go to the called method, and perform the statements. When you finish with the called method, return back to your saved location.

Test your algorithm with the following data:

Insurance: 650.00

Taxes: 1286.92

Utilities: 250.00

Use a calculator and write down the results you obtain. Once you implement your design, you can compare these results with those obtained from your program output.

Code the Solution

After you complete the design and verify the algorithm's correctness, it is time to translate the design into source code. For this application, you are creating two separate files—one for each **class**. Only one of the classes will have a **Main( )** method. If you create the **RealEstateInvestment class** first, delete the **Main( )** method from that file. To add a second **class**, click Project>Add Class.

The final application listing for both files appears here:

```csharp
/* RealEstateApp.cs          Author:      Doyle
 * This class constructs an
 * object of the RealEstateInvestment
 * class. It tests several properties and
 * methods of the class.
 * A static method is used in
 * the application class to
 * input expenses.
 *  */
using System;
namespace PropertyApplication
{
    public class RealEstateApp
    {
      public static void Main( )
      {
        const double RENTAL_AMOUNT = 1000.00;

        RealEstateInvestment invest1 = new
            RealEstateInvestment (2004,  150000, "65th Street");

        invest1.MonthlyExpense = GetExpenses( );
        invest1.IncomeFromRent = RENTAL_AMOUNT;
        Console.WriteLine( );
        Console.WriteLine("Property Location: {0}",
                        invest1.StreetAddress);
```

```csharp
                    Console.WriteLine("Earnings For Month: {0:C}",
                                invest1.DetermineMonthlyEarnings( ));
                Console.Read( );
            }

            public static double GetExpenses( )
            {
                double insurance;
                double taxes;
                double utilities;
                string inValue;
                Console.Write("Yearly Insurance: ");
                inValue = Console.ReadLine( );
                insurance = double.Parse(inValue);
                Console.Write("Yearly Tax: ");
                inValue = Console.ReadLine( );
                taxes = double.Parse(inValue);
                Console.Write("Monthly Utilities: ");
                inValue = Console.ReadLine( );
                utilities = double.Parse(inValue);
                return (insurance / 12 + taxes / 12  + utilities);
            }
        }
}

/* RealEstateInvestment.cs
 * Author:        Doyle
 * This class defines a template
 * for a real estate object to
 * include instance data members,
 * public properties,
 * constructors, and a method to
 * determine the monthly earnings.
 */
using System;
namespace PropertyApplication
{
    class RealEstateInvestment
    {
        private string streetAddress;
        private int yearBuilt;
        private double purchasePrice;
        private double monthlyExpense;
        private double incomeFromRent;
```

4

```csharp
// Read-only property
public double YearBuilt
{
    get
    {
        return yearBuilt;
    }
}

// Read-only property
public string StreetAddress
{
    get
    {
        return streetAddress;
    }
}

// Read-only property
public double PurchasePrice
{
    get
    {
        return purchasePrice;
    }
}

// Property acting as mutator and accessor
public double MonthlyExpense
{
    set
    {
        monthlyExpense = value;
    }
    get
    {
        return monthlyExpense;
    }
}

// Property acting as mutator and accessor
public double IncomeFromRent
{
    set
    {
        incomeFromRent = value;
    }
}
```

```
        get
        {
            return incomeFromRent;
        }
    }

    // default constructor
    public RealEstateInvestment ( )
    {
    }

    // constructor used to create property object
    public RealEstateInvestment (int year, double price,
                                        string address)
    {
        yearBuilt = year;
        purchasePrice = price;
        streetAddress = address;
    }

    // returns the earnings for a given month
    public double DetermineMonthlyEarnings( )
    {
        return incomeFromRent - monthlyExpense;
    }
    }
}
```

Implement the Code   Compile the source code. If you have any rule violations, make corrections until no errors are present. Run the application entering the values indicated previously (650.00, 1286.92, 250.00).

Test and Debug

During this final step, test the program and ensure you have the correct result. The output for the test values should match your prototype. Is your spacing correct? Figure 4-16 shows the output generated from the preceding source code.

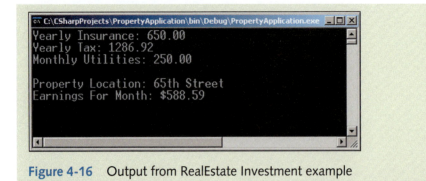

Figure 4-16 Output from RealEstate Investment example

QUICK REVIEW

1. Methods are the members of a **class** that describe the behavior of the data.

2. The method **Main( )** is required for both console and Windows applications.

3. **Main( )** should include the **static** keyword.

4. The heading to a method may consist of modifiers, a **return** type, method identifier, and parameters. The body of the method is enclosed in curly braces.

5. When the **static** modifier is included with a method, it becomes a **class** method.

6. Instance methods require that an **object** be instantiated before they access the method.

7. Private members are accessible only within the body of the **class** in which they are declared.

8. Often in object-oriented development, data is defined with a **private** modifier, and methods that access the data are declared to have **public** access.

9. The **return** type identifies what type of value is returned when the method is completed. Any of the predefined or valid user-defined types can be returned.

10. The **void** keyword specifies that the method does not **return** a value.

11. Many programmers employ the standard convention of using an action verb phrase to name methods.

12. Formal parameters appear in the heading of a method. Actual arguments appear in the call. The actual arguments are the actual data that is sent to the method.

13. The signature of a method consists of the name of the method, modifiers, and the types of its formal parameters. It does not include the **return** type.

14. Overloaded methods are methods with the same name but a different number or type of parameters.

15. The `ReadLine( )` method returns all characters up to the current end-of-line terminator, the Enter key. It returns a `string` that must be parsed into a number before the value can be used in arithmetic.

16. Variables declared in the `Main( )` method and other methods are considered local variables and are visible only inside the body of the method in which they are declared.

17. Constructors are special methods that create instances of a `class`. Constructors do not return a value, but you should not include the keyword `void`.

18. Constructors use the same identifier as the `class` name. The keyword `new` is an operator that calls constructor methods.

4

19. Use `public` access with constructors and most other methods. Use the `private` access modifier with data members.

20. The default constructor has no body and is automatically created if you do not write one. If you write even one constructor, you lose the default and have to write it.

21. Accessors are methods that access the value of a `private` data member without changing it. Accessors are also referred to as getter methods.

22. Mutators are used to change the current state of `object` members' data. Mutator methods are also referred to as setters.

23. A property looks like a data field and provides a way to set or get `private` member data. You can define the `set` without the `get` or visa versa. It is not necessary to include both.

24. If a value is being returned from a method, such as with an expression or output statement, there must be a location in which the value can be accepted when the method is finished. The call actually may appear anywhere a compatible value of that type can be placed.

25. To call non-value returning methods, simply type the method's name. If it is a `static` method, qualify it with the `class` name. If it is an instance method, qualify the identifier with an `object`. If the method has parameters, the call includes actual arguments inside the parentheses, without the types.

26. C# offers both call by value and call by reference. Call by value is the default if no keyword is added in the heading. Call by reference is possible through using the `ref` and `out` keywords. They must appear both in the heading and in the call. `ref` requires that the argument be initialized before it is sent.

EXERCISES

1. Functions or modules found in other languages are similar to _____ in C#.

   a. modifiers

   b. parameters

   c. arguments

   d. methods

   e. classes

2. Which of the following is a required component of the method heading?

   a. modifiers

   b. parameters

   c. arguments

   d. void

   e. identifier

3. Which of the following modifiers is the most restrictive?

   a. private

   b. static

   c. public

   d. internal

   e. protected

4. Which of the following would be the most appropriate method identifier?

   a. Calculate Final Grade

   b. MilesPerGallon

   c. InValueMethod

   d. PrintReport

   e. Method1

5. Which of the following calls the predefined Floor( ) method found in the Math class?

   public static double Floor(double)

   a. answer = Floor(87.2);

   b. answer = Math.Floor(87.2);

   c. Floor(87.2);

   d. Math.Floor(double);

   e. Math.Floor(87.2);

6. Given the following statement, what would be the best heading for the `DetermineAnswer( )` method?

```
int aValue,
    result;
result = DetermineAnswer(27.83, aValue);
```

a. `public void DetermineAnswer(27.83, aValue)`

b. `public int DetermineAnswer( )`

c. `public int DetermineAnswer(double, int )`

d. `public double int DetermineAnswer( )`

e. `public void DetermineAnswer(double, int)`

7. After completing the called method's body, control is returned:

a. back to the location in the calling method that made the call

b. to the last statement in the method that made the call

c. to the first statement in the method that made the call

d. to the `Main( )` method

e. to the method that is listed next in the printed source code

8. Which of the following is a valid overloaded method for `determineHighestScore`?

```
int DetermineHighestScore(int val1, int val2)
```

a. `void DetermineHighestScore(int val1, int val2)`

b. `int DetermineScore(int val1, int val2)`

c. `void DetermineHighestScore(double val1, double val2)`

d. `double DetermineHighestScore(int val1, int val2)`

e. `int GetHighestScore(int val1, int val2)`

9. What is the signature of the following method?

```
public void SetNoOfSquareYards(double squareYards)
{
        noOfSquareYards = squareYards;
}
```

a. `public void SetNoOfSquareYards(double squareYards)`

b. `public SetNoOfSquareYards(double squareYards)`

c. `SetNoOfSquareYards`

d. `public SetNoOfSquareYards(double)`

e. `SetNoOfSquareYards(double)`

10. Instance variables are the same as:

a. `private` member data

b. local variables

c. properties

d. arguments

e. parameters

11. What would the heading for a constructor for the following `class` look like?

`public class Employee {`

a. `public void Employee( )`

b. `public Employee( )`

c. `public static Employee( )`

d. `private void Employee( )`

e. `private Employee( )`

12. The following is probably an example of a _____.

`public double GetYards( )`

a. constructor

b. mutator

c. property

d. accessor

e. `class` definition

13. If you follow the standard C# naming conventions, the property name for the following instance variable would be:

`private string name;`

a. `propertyName`

b. `nameProperty`

c. `getName`

d. `name`

e. `Name`

14. Which of the following would be a valid call to the default constructor for the following `class`?

`public class Employee {`

a. `Employee employee1 = new Employee( );`

b. `Employee employee1= new undergrad( );`

c. `Employee employee1;`

d. `Employee employee1= new Employee(default);`

e. Not enough information is given to be able to answer.

15. Given the following `class` definition, what would be a valid heading for a mutator?

`public class Student {`
`private string name;`
`private double gpa; }`

a. `public double SetGpa(double gpaValue)`

b. `public void SetGpa(double gpaValue)`

c. `public double SetGpa( )`

d. `public void GetGpa(double gpaValue)`

e. `public double SetGpa( )`

16. If a method is to be used to enter two values, which of the following would be the most appropriate heading and call?

a. heading: `public void InputValues(out int val1, out int val2)`

   call: `InputValues(out val1, out val2);`

b. heading: `public void InputValues(int val1, int val2)`

   call: `InputValues(val1, val2);`

c. heading: `public void InputValues(ref int val1, ref int val2)`

   call: `InputValues(ref val1, ref val2);`

d. heading: `public int int InputValues( )`

   call: `val1 = InputValues( );`
   `val2 = InputValues( );`

e. none of the above

17. Which of the following is *not* a modifier in C#?

a. `const`

b. `Private`

c. `public`

d. `static`

e. `protected`

18. Normally member data use a _____ access modifier, and methods use a _____ access modifier for object-oriented solutions.

    a. protected   public

    b. private   protected

    c. public   protected

    d. public   private

    e. private   public

19. Given the following task, which of the following would be the most appropriate class method?

    A method receives three whole numbers as input. The values represent grades. They should be unchangeable in the method. The method should return the average with a fractional component.

    a. static double determineGrade(int grade1, int grade2, int grade3)

    b. double determineGrade(int grade1, int grade2, int grade3)

    c. static int int int determineGrade(double finalAverage)

    d. static double determineGrade(ref int grade1, ref int grade2, ref int grade3)

    e. static void determineGrade( )

20. Given the following task, which of the following would be the most appropriate class method?

    Results have been calculated for **taxAmount** and **totalSales**. Write a **class** method heading that accepts these values as input for display purposes.

    a. public static displayResults( )

    b. public displayResults( )

    c. public static void displayResults( )

    d. public static void displayResults(double taxAmount, double totalSales)

    e. public static void displayResults(taxAmount, totalSales)

21. Use the following method headings to answer the questions below:

```
public static int determineResult(int value1, ref double value2)
public static void displayResult(int value1, double value2)
public static int getValue( )
```

a. How many parameters does each method have?

b. What is the **return** type for each of the methods?

c. If the methods belong to a **class** identified as GardenTool, write valid calls to each of the preceding methods.

d. Can objects use any of the preceding methods? If so, which one(s) and how?

e. Which of the preceding methods will have a **return** statement as part of its body?

22. Given the following code snippet:

```
public class Camera                          Line 1
{                                            Line 2
    private double zoom;                      Line 3
    private double lensSpeed;                 Line 4
    public   double Zoom                      Line 5
    {                                        Line 6
        get                                   Line 7
      {                                      Line 8
        return zoom;                          Line 9
      }                                      Line 10
    }                                        Line 11
    public Camera ( )                         Line 12
    {                                        Line 13
    }                                        Line 14
    public Camera (double zCapacity,          Line 15
                    double ls)                Line 16
    {                                        Line 17
        int xValue = 2;                       Line 18
        zoom = zCapacity * xValue;            Line 19
        lensSpeed = ls;                       Line 20
    }                                        Line 21
    public double getLensSpeed( )             Line 22
    {                                        Line 23
        return lensSpeed;                     Line 24
    }                                        Line 25
```

Identify the following items by line number:

a. method headings

b. property identifier

c. default constructors

d. formal parameters

e. local variables

23. Write **class** methods to do the following:

   a. Display three full lines of asterisks on the screen.

   b. Accept as an argument your age, and display that value along with an appropriate label.

   c. Accept two floating-point values as arguments. Display the values formatted with three digits to the right of the decimal.

   d. Accept three **int** arguments and return their sum.

   e. Accept no arguments and return no values. Initialize a local Boolean variable to **true**. Have the method print the Boolean's value.

24. What will be produced from the following predefined **Math class** method calls?

   a. `Console.WriteLine(Math.Abs(-98887.234));`

   b. `Console.WriteLine(Math.Pow(4,3));`

   c. `Console.WriteLine(Math.Sign(-56));`

   d. `Console.WriteLine(Math.Sqrt(81));`

   e. `Console.WriteLine(Math.Min(-56, 56));`

25. The following program has several syntax errors as well as style inconsistencies. Correct the syntax errors and identify the style violations.

```
/* ******************************************
 * AgeIncrementer.cs                Author: Doyle
 * Prompts the users for their ages in
 * a class method. Prints the value
   entered back in the Main( ) method.

using System;
namespace AgeExample
{
public class AgeIncrementer
{
public static void Main( )
    {

    int AGE;
    string aValue;

    age = GETAge(aValue);
    Console.WriteLine("Your age next year will be {0}",
                ++age);
    Console.Read( );
    }
```

```
public static GETAge( )
{
        Console.Write("Enter your age: ");
        aValue = Console.ReadLine( );
        age = int.Parse(aValue);

        return int AGE;
}
}
}
```

4

PROGRAMMING EXERCISES

1. Write an application that calls a **class** method to display information about your school. Items you might include are the name of your school, number of students enrolled, and school colors. The display should be aesthetically pleasing.

2. Design a message display application. Allow users to enter their favorite sayings in **class** method. Return the saying back to the **Main( )** method. Call another method, sending the saying. From that method, display the message surrounded by two lines of asterisks.

3. Create a **class** representing a student. Include characteristics such as first and last name, overall GPA, classification, and major. Write at least two constructors. Include properties for each of the data items. Create a second **class** that instantiates the first **class** with information about yourself. In the second **class**, create a **class** method that displays your name and GPA.

4. Design an application using methods that display the number of square feet in a house. Allow the user to enter values for the length and width of the house. Use **class** methods for entering values, performing the computation, and displaying the results. The results should include the original measurements entered by the user.

5. Write a program that converts a temperature given in Celsius to Fahrenheit. Allow the user to enter values for the original Celsius value. Display the original temperature and the formatted converted value. Use appropriate methods for entering, calculating, and outputting results.

6. Write a program that prints the number of quarters, dimes, nickels, and pennies that a customer should get back as change. Allow the user to enter any value less than $1.00 in a method. Call on separate methods for each of the calculations.

7. Write a program that allows the user to enter two integers. Write separate methods that produce the sum, product, average, and squared result of the values. Call the squared result with both values that were entered.

8. Write a program that computes the amount of money the computer club will receive from proceeds of their granola bar sales project. Allow the user to enter the number of cases sold and the sale price per bar. Each case contains 12 bars; each case costs $5.00. The club is required to give the student government association 10% of their earnings. Display their proceeds formatted with currency. Write appropriate methods for your solution.

9. Write a program that calculates and prints the take-home pay for a commissioned sales employee. Allow the user to enter values for the name of employee and the sales amount for the week. Employees receive 7% of the total sales. Federal tax rate is 18%. Retirement contribution is 10%. Social Security tax rate is 6%. Use appropriate constants, design an object-oriented solution, and write constructors. Include at least one mutator and one accessor method; provide properties for the other instance variables. Create a second **class** to test your design.

10. Write a program that creates a student **class** consisting of student ID and three exam scores. In a separate implementation **class**, allow the user to enter the values. Call the constructor to create an instance of the student **class**. Include appropriate properties. Do not allow the ID to be changed after an **object** has been constructed. Provide a method in the student **class** to compute and **return** the overall exam average. Print all scores and the average value formatted with no digits to the right of the decimal from the implementation **class**. Use a single **class** method to enter all data.

5 Making Decisions

General-purpose programming languages provide three categories of programming statements. These categories are referred to as the **basic programming constructs**. Simple sequence, which you have already used, is one of them. Most language statements are designed with this construct. In a method, execution begins with the first statement and continues sequentially one statement after the next until the end of the method is encountered. The **simple sequence** construct follows this sequence. This chapter introduces you to a second construct, which is the selection statement. The **selection statement** is used for decision making and allows you to deviate from the sequential path laid out with simple sequence and perform different statements based on the value of an expression. The third basic construct, iteration, is introduced in Chapter 6. **Iteration** or looping enables you to write instructions that can be repeated.

Methods were introduced to you in Chapter 4. In this chapter, you write methods that use two kinds of selection statements: **if...else** and **switch**. You examine one-way, two-way, nested, multi-way, and compound forms of **if** statements. You explore situations where **switch** statements should be used instead of **if...else** statements. You learn about the ternary conditional operator that can be used in your methods to write selection statements. By the time you finish this chapter, your methods will include statements that perform simple and complex decisions.

BOOLEAN RESULTS AND BOOL DATA TYPES

Chapter 3 introduced you to Boolean variables, represented in C# using the **bool** data type. You learned that the **bool** type holds values of either **true** or **false**. Boolean variables are central to both selection and iteration control constructs. Their values can be tested and used to determine alternate paths. However, many times selection statements are written that do not actually use a Boolean variable, but instead produce a Boolean result.

Boolean Results

Consider the following statements in Example 5-1. They are written in pseudocode.

You will remember that pseudocode is "near code," but does not satisfy the syntax requirements of any programming language.

Example 5-1

1. if (gradePointAverage is greater than 3.80)

   awardType is assigned deansList

2. if (letterGrade is equal to 'F')

   display message "You must repeat course"

3. if (examScore is less than 50)

   display message "Do better on next exam"

The three statements in Example 5-1 have common features. First, they each include a conditional expression, enclosed inside parentheses. **Conditional expressions** produce a Boolean result. The result is either **true** or **false**. The first conditional expression is (**gradePointAverage** is greater than 3.80). Either **gradePointAverage** is greater than 3.8 (**true**) or it is not (**false**); similarly, **letterGrade** is equal to F (**true**) or it is not (**false**). The same holds for **examScore**. It does not matter how close the score is to 50. The result is **true** when **examScore** is less than 50. At other times it is **false**. That is a requirement of a conditional expression. It must evaluate to **true** or **false**.

The second common feature of the three statements in Example 5-1 is that they each include an additional statement following the condition expression. This second line is executed when the conditional expression evaluates to **true**. No statement is included for any of the statements in Example 5-1 for the situation when the expression evaluates to **false**. The conditional expression, sometimes called "**the test**," uses English-equivalent words to represent the comparisons to be made. This is because the statements in Example 5-1 are written using pseudocode or Structured English. You learn how to transpose these words into C# relational and equality operators later in this chapter.

Boolean Data Type

A variable declared to be of **bool** type holds the value of **true** or **false**. When a **bool** variable is used in a conditional expression, you do not have to add symbols to compare the variable against a value. You simply write the **bool** variable name as the expression. Take, for example, the Boolean variable declared as shown in the following code snippet:

```
bool salariedEmployee;
```

Once declared, a conditional expression could be used to determine whether **salariedEmployee** held the values **true** or **false**. The conditional expression would read:

```
if (salariedEmployee)
```

It is not necessary to write **if** (**salariedEmployee** is equal to **true**) because **salariedEmployee** is defined as a **bool** type.

Boolean Flags

Boolean data types are often used as flags to signal when a condition exists or when a condition changes. To create a flag situation, declare a **bool** data type variable and initialize it to either **true** or **false**. Then use this variable to control processing. As long as the value of the Boolean variable remains the same, processing continues. When some planned condition changes, the Boolean data type is changed and processing stops. For example, `moreData` declared as a Boolean, initialized to **true**, can be changed to **false** when all of the data has been processed.

```
bool moreData = true;
:                       // Other statement(s) that might change the
:                       // value of moreData to false.
if (moreData)           // Execute statement(s) following the if
                        // when moreData is true.
```

The expressions you have seen thus far used English-equivalent words for the conditional expression. In sections that follow, you examine operators used for conditional expressions and learn how to implement selection statements in C#.

CONDITIONAL EXPRESSIONS

A conditional expression is also referred to as a **test condition**. To determine, for example, who receives an **A** on an exam, a relational test is made between two operands. The first operand is an exam score, and the second is a value like 90, or some predetermined cutoff value for an **A**. After this conditional expression is written, it can be used with hundreds of different exam scores to determine who gets the **A**.

When you write an expression to be tested, you must first determine the operands. Unless a **bool** data type is used, two operands are required for equality and relational tests. You saw this same requirement of two operands when you used binary arithmetic operators such as multiply * and divide / to perform multiplication and division.

```
answer = x * y;                 // Here x and y are both operands

examScore greater than 89       // examScore and 89 are operands
finalGrade is equal to 'A'      // finalGrade and 'A' are operands
```

To construct a conditional expression, after you identify the operands, determine what type of comparison to make. In Example 5-1, pseudocode demonstrated how to compare a variable against a value. However, to write those statements in C#, you use special symbols to represent the operations. The next section describes the types of operators that can be used.

Equality, Relational, and Logical Tests

You can use equality, relational, and logical operators in conditional expressions. To determine whether two values are the same, use the equality operator.

Equality Operators

Two equal symbol characters == are used as the **equality operator** in C# for comparing operands. No space is inserted between the symbols. Recall that the single equal symbol (=), called the **assignment operator**, is used to assign the result of an expression to a variable. You cannot use the assignment operator in a selection statement in C#.

> **NOTE** Languages such as Java and C++ allow you to use a single equal symbol inside a conditional expression. This often creates an error that takes time to find. Failing to put two equal symbols in a conditional expression leads to an assignment being made. The side effect of this is that the expression always evaluates to `true`, unless the assignment statement assigns zero to a variable. You never have this problem in C#, because C# issues a syntax error if you use the assignment operator in a location where the equality operator is expected.

An exclamation point followed by a single equal symbol (!=) represents **NOT equal**. As with the equality operator, no space is embedded between the exclamation point and equal symbol. Table 5-1 shows examples of the use of equality operators.

Table 5-1 Equality operators

Symbol	Meaning	Example	Result
==	equal	(1 == 2)	false
!=	NOT equal	(4 != (19 % 5))	false

Notice how an arithmetic operator is part of one of the operands in the last row of Table 5-1. The expression 19 % 5 produces 4 as a remainder; thus 4 != (19 % 5) returns `false`. The operand may also include a call to a value returning method. You can use any valid executable statement that produces or returns a value as an operand. Consider the next conditional expression. When `operand1` has a value of 25, the expression returns `true` (5^2 is equal to 25). When `operand1` is not 25, the expression returns `false`.

```
(operand1 == Math.Pow(5,2))
```

> **NOTE** While not a requirement when comparing a variable to a literal value, it is conventional to place the variable in the first operand location with a value in the second location.

When you use the equality operator with integral values, such as variables of type `int`, the results produced are what you would expect; however, you need to be cautious of making equality comparisons with floating-point (`float` and `double`) and `decimal` types. In the following code segment, consider the compile-time initialization of `aValue` followed by the conditional expression:

```
double aValue = 10.0  / 3.0;
(aValue == 3.33333333333333)
```

The expression returns `false`. Floating-point division does not produce a finite value. Due to rounding, you often get unpredictable results when comparing floating-point variables for equality.

The `==` and `!=` are **overloaded operators**. You learned about overloaded methods in Chapter 4. Overloaded operators are defined to perform differently based on their operands. In addition to being defined for numeric data types, `==` and `!=` are defined for strings in C#. The operators perform a completely different function when the operands are of `string` data type in contrast to numeric type. When strings are compared, the first character in the first operand is compared against the first character in the second operand. If they are the same, the comparison moves to the second characters. The characters are compared lexicographically using the Unicode character set.

 Words are placed in a dictionary in lexicographical order. The word "Able" comes before "Ada" in the dictionary. The Unicode uppercase character A comes before the lowercase character a.

Example 5-2

```
           ↓                                    ↓
("The class name is CS158" == "The class name is cs158")
```

Example 5-2 returns `false` because the uppercase character `C` at position 19 has a Unicode value of 67, while the lowercase `c` at that same position on the right side of the comparison operator has a value of 99.

 You may want to review Appendix C, "Unicode Character Set," which contains the `decimal` equivalent for many of the Unicode characters.

In Example 5-2, up to position 19, the strings are considered equal. When the characters at position 19 are compared, the result of the expression (`false`) is determined, and no additional comparison beyond position 19 is needed.

 Many languages require you to use special `string` methods, such as `strcmp( )`, to make equality comparisons on `string` variables. C# makes it much easier for you to write instructions comparing the contents of `string` variables for equality.

Relational Operators

Relational operators allow you to test variables to see if one is greater or less than another variable or value. Table 5-2 lists the relational symbols used in C#. The symbol's meaning and an example expression using each operator is included.

Table 5-2 Relational symbols

Symbol	Meaning	Example	Result
>	greater than	(8 > 5) (1 > 2)	true false
<	less than	(1 < 2) ('z' < 'a')	true false
>=	greater than or equal	(100 >= 100) (14 >= 7)	true true
<=	less than or equal	(100 <= 100) (27 <= 7)	true false

For comparing numbers, the relational operators <, >, <=, and >= produce a straightforward result as shown in Table 5-2. When you compare characters declared using **char**, they are compared lexicographically using the Unicode character set. A comparison to determine whether the lowercase character **z** is less than **a** produces **false**, because **z** has a Unicode **decimal** equivalent of 122 and **a** has a value of 97. You cannot compare **string** operands using the relational symbols <, >, >=, or <= in C#.

Remember from Chapter 3, "Data Types and Expressions," that strings in C# are reference types. Instead of the **string** character values being stored in binary form at the memory location of the variable's identifier, the memory location of a **string** identifier contains the address in which the string of characters is stored. Normally when you compare reference type variables, you get a comparison of the addresses.

 The **string class** in C# has a number of useful methods for dealing with strings. You learn about these methods in Chapter 7. The **Compare( )** method is used for relational comparisons of strings. If you want to look ahead, many methods of the **string class** are listed in Table 7-3.

For debugging, it is often easier to follow and read simple relational comparisons than compound comparisons. You study this in more detail in a later section in this chapter. With additional thought, most numeric comparisons involving the compound relational operators of <= and >= can be revised. By simply adding or subtracting from the endpoint, the comparison can be written in a simpler form. Consider the following two statements, which yield exactly the same comparison.

Example 5-3

```
(examScore >= 90)      // Avoid compounds if you can
(examScore > 89)       // Better test—does the same as above
```

Both of the expressions in Example 5-3 return **true** for values larger than 89. The first line contains a compound expression (`examScore greater than 90 or examScore equal to 90`). By simply subtracting 1 from 90, you can write a simpler conditional expression as shown in line 2 of Example 5-3.

 Develop good style by surrounding operators with a space. This includes arithmetic, logical, and relational symbols. Readability is enhanced if you type a space before and after every operator, e.g., `x > 5; y == z; aValue = bValue + 3`.

Table 5-3 in Example 5-4 presents several conditional expressions. Both relational and equality operators are used. A result of the expression with an explanation is included.

Example 5-4

For each expression example, use the following declaration of variables:

```
int aValue = 100,
    bValue = 1000;
char cValue = 'A';
string sValue = "CS158";
decimal money = 50.22m;
double dValue = 50.22;
```

Table 5-3 Results of example conditional expressions

Expression	Result	Explanation
`(money == 100.00)`	syntax error	Type mismatch. Money is `decimal`, 100.00 is `double`. Receive an error message that says "== cannot be applied to `double` and `decimal`"
`(money == 50.22m)`	true	Must suffix the `decimal` number with M or m
`(money != dValue)`	syntax error	Type mismatch. Money is `decimal`, dValue is `double`. Receive an error message that says "== cannot be applied to `double` and `decimal`"
`(aValue > bValue)`	false	100 is not greater than 1000
`(sValue < "CS")`	syntax error	< cannot be used with `string` operand
`(aValue > (bValue - 999))`	true	100 is greater than 1

Table 5-3 Results of example conditional expressions (continued)

Expression	Result	Explanation
(aValue > dValue)	true	Integer aValue is converted to double and compared correctly
(aValue < money)	false	Integer aValue is converted to decimal and compared correctly
(cValue = 'F')	syntax error	Cannot use single equal symbol (=) for condition comparison. Single equal symbol (=) is used for assignment.
(cValue < 'f')	true	Unicode A has a value of 65; Unicode f has a value of 102

5

In C#, the == and != are defined to work with strings to compare the characters lexicographically. This is not the case for other reference variables. In addition, the relational operators such as <, >, <=, and >= are not defined to work with strings.

Logical Operators

Conditional expressions may be combined with logical conditional operators to form complex expressions. The **logical operators** in C# are &, &&, |, ||, and !. Just as you communicate a compound expression in English, you can combine expressions with AND or OR in C#. To add two points to **examScore** that range between 70 and 90, you might write the following pseudocode:

```
if (examScore > 69 AND examScore < 91)
    examScore = examScore + 2
```

When expressions are combined with AND, both expressions must evaluate to `true` in order for the entire compound expression to return `true`. C# uses two ampersands && and two pipes || to represent AND and OR, respectively. These two operators are called the **conditional logical operators**. As shown in Table 5-4, unless both expression operands are `true`, the compound expression created using the && evaluates to `false`.

Table 5-4 Conditional logical AND &&

Expression1	Expression2	operand1 && operand2
true	true	true
true	false	false
false	true	false
false	false	false

> Table 5-4 is sometimes referred to as a truth table.

When combining logical operators with relational tests, developers often make the mistake of omitting the variable for the second and subsequent conditions being tested. In English, you would probably say, "if examScore is greater than 69 and less than 91." You normally do not repeat the variable being tested. In C#, you must repeat the variable. It is incorrect to write:

```
(examScore > 69 < 91)                              //Invalid
```

It is also incorrect to write:

```
(69 < examScore < 91)                              //Invalid
```

The correct way to write the expression is:

```
((examScore > 69) && (examScore < 91))             //Correct way
```

> It is not necessary to use the two innermost parentheses. Later in this chapter, in Table 5-7, you explore the order of operations. The relational operators (< and >) have a higher precedence than the logical && and || operators, meaning the comparisons would be performed prior to the &&. Including the parentheses adds to the readability.

As illustrated in Table 5-5, || only returns a **false** result when both of the operands are **false**. At all other times, when either one of the operands evaluates to **true**, the entire compound expression evaluates to **true**.

Table 5-5 Conditional logical OR ||

Expression1	Expression2	operand1 || operand2
true	true	true
true	false	true
false	true	true
false	false	false

Compound expressions using the || must also have a complete expression on both sides of the logical symbol. The following is invalid:

```
(letterGrade == 'A' || 'B')                        //Invalid
```

The correct way to write the conditional expression is:

```
((letterGrade == 'A') || (letterGrade == 'B'))     //Correct way
```

Parentheses can be added to conditional expressions to improve readability.

The ! symbol is the **logical negation operator**. It is a unary operator that negates its operand and is called the **NOT operator**. It returns `true` when `operand1` is `false`. It returns `false` when `operand1` is `true`.

Given the following declaration:

```
char letterGrade = 'A';
```

5

When the NOT operator (!) is placed in front of the conditional expression, the statement returns `false` as shown in the line that follows:

```
( ! (letterGrade == 'A'))
```

The conditional expression first yields a `true` result (`letterGrade is equal to 'A'`). Adding the NOT operator ! negates that result. Thus, the expression evaluates to `false`.

As illustrated in Table 5-6, the NOT operator ! returns the logical complement, or negation, of its operand.

Table 5-6 Logical NOT !

Expression1	! operand1
true	false
false	true

As with the logical `&&` and `||`, the ! operator can also be difficult to follow. It is easier to debug a program that includes only positive expressions. An extra step is required in problem solving if you have to analyze a negated result.

This section on compound conditions is included to give you an understanding of reading complex expressions. As you learn in the sections that follow, you can often avoid writing complex expressions that use logical operators with the use of a multi-way or nested selection statement. This may take more thought than just combining a number of conditional expressions with a logical operator. However, because compound conditions can be difficult to debug, you should explore other options whenever possible.

Short-Circuit Evaluation

In C# the `&&` and `||` operators are also called the **short-circuiting logical operators**. These operators enable doing as little as is needed to produce the final result through short-circuit evaluation. With **short-circuit evaluation**, as soon as the value of the entire expression is known, evaluation stops. A conditional expression is evaluated from left to right. With expressions involving **&&**, if the first evaluates as **false**, there is no need to evaluate the second. The result will be **false**. With expressions involving **||**, if the first evaluates as **true**, there is no need to evaluate the second. The result will be **true**. Using the initialized variables, consider the expressions that follow in Example 5-5.

Example 5-5

```
int examScore = 75;
int homeWkGrade = 100;
double amountOwed = 0;
char status = 'I';
:
((examScore > 90) && (homeWkGrade > 80))          // Line 1 - false
((amountOwed == 0) || (status == 'A'))            // Line 2 - true
```

When the first part of the expression (**examScore > 90**) in line 1 evaluates to **false**, there is no need to evaluate the second. The result of the entire expression is **false**. If the first part of the expression in line 1 evaluates to **true**, the second expression has to be evaluated. Both must be **true** in order for the entire expression to evaluate to **true**.

Line 2 is a logical OR; thus, if the first part of the expression evaluates to **true**, there is no need to evaluate the second. The result of the entire expression is **true** as soon as one of them evaluates to **true**. With short-circuit evaluation, the computer is able to stop evaluating as soon as the value of the expression is known.

C# also includes the **&** and **|** operators. They both compute the logical AND or OR of their operands, just as the **&&** and **||** do. The difference between them is that **&&** and **||** do short-circuit evaluation, while **&** and **|** do not. They are useful for situations that involve compound or complex expressions in which you want the entire expression to be performed, whether the result of the conditional expression returns **true** or not. Consider the following:

```
((aValue > bValue) & (count++ < 100))
```

Using the logical AND (**&**) always results in 1 being added to **count**, whether **aValue** is greater than **bValue** or not. Replacing the **&** with **&&** produces the same result for the entire expression, however, the side effect of incrementing **count** may not happen. Using the **&&** and doing short-circuit evaluation would only enable 1 to be added to **count** when the first part of the expression (**aValue > bValue**) evaluates to **true**. With **&&**, if (**aValue > bValue**) evaluates to **false**, the second expression is not executed.

IF...ELSE SELECTION STATEMENTS

The **if selection statement**, classified as one-way, two-way, or nested, is used in combination with a conditional expression. The `if` statement facilitates specifying alternate paths based on the result of the conditional expression. The expressions might involve values entered at run time or calculations made using data. The sections that follow illustrate how you can include these types of selection statements in your programs.

One-Way If Statement

A **one-way selection statement** is used when an expression needs to be tested. When the result of the expression is `true`, additional processing is performed. The general format for a one-way `if` statement is:

5

```
if (expression)
    statement;   // actions to be performed when the expression
                 // evaluates to true.
```

In C# the expression must be enclosed in parentheses. Notice that no semicolon is placed at the end of the line containing the expression. The expression must produce a Boolean result when evaluated—a result that can be evaluated as `true` or `false`. Thus, the expression can be a Boolean variable or a conditional expression involving two or more operands. With a one-way `if` statement, when the expression evaluates to `false`, the statement immediately following the conditional expression is skipped or bypassed. No special statement(s) is included for the `false` result. Execution continues with the segment of code following the `if` statement.

If the expression evaluates to `true`, the statement is performed and then execution continues with the same segment of code following the `if` statement as when the expression evaluates to `false`.

With the preceding syntax illustration, `statement` represents the action(s) that takes place when the expression evaluates as `true`. To associate more than one statement with the `true` result, enclose the statements inside curly braces. These statements are referred to as the `true` statements. By enclosing the `true` statements inside curly braces, you are marking the beginning and ending of the statements to be executed when the expression evaluates to `true`.

Consider the following example.

Example 5-6

```
if (examScore > 89)
{
    grade = 'A';
    Console.WriteLine("Congratulations - Great job!");
}
Console.WriteLine("I am displayed, whether the expression "
                    + "evaluates true or false");
```

When **examScore** is equal to 89 or any smaller value, the expression evaluates to **false**, and the **true** statements inside the curly braces are skipped. The **WriteLine( )** method following the closing curly brace is executed. When **examScore** is equal to 95, the **true** statements are executed and then the **WriteLine( )** following the closing curly brace is executed.

Consider the following revision to Example 5-6:

```
if (examScore > 89)
                        // missing opening curly brace '{'
    grade = 'A';
    Console.WriteLine("Congratulations - Great job!");
                        // missing closing curly brace '}'
Console.WriteLine("I am displayed, whether the expression "
                    + "evaluates true or false");
```

Here, the **Console.WriteLine("Congratulations - Great job!");** is always executed. Indentation is for readability only. If the curly braces are omitted, no syntax error or warning is issued. The congratulations message would be displayed for *all* values of **examScore** (even **examScore** of zero).

 Some programmers enclose all statements associated with **if** statements in curly braces. This includes the single line **true** statements. This way they do not forget to surround the body with { }.

The flow of execution in a one-way **if** statement is illustrated in Figure 5-1. When the expression evaluates to **true**, the **true** statement(s) is (are) executed. As the figure shows, execution continues at the same location whether the expression evaluates to **true** or **false**.

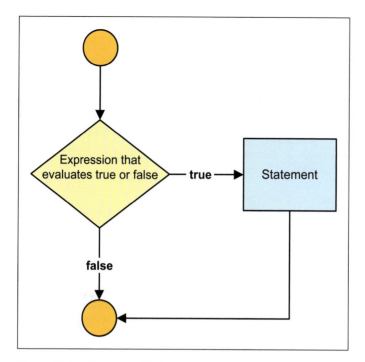

Figure 5-1   One-way if statement

Example 5-7

A company issues $1000.00 bonuses at the end of the year to all employees who have sold over $500,000.00 in products. The following code segment is a program that allows users to enter their sales figure. It determines whether a bonus is due and displays a message indicating whether a bonus is awarded or not.

```
/* BonusCalculator.cs        Author:      Doyle
 * Allows the user to input their
 * gross sales for the year. This value
 * is checked to determine whether
 * a bonus is in order.
 **********************************/
using System;
namespace BonusApp
{
    class BonusCalculator
    {
      static void Main( )
      {
          string inValue;
```

```
decimal salesForYear;
decimal bonusAmount = 0M;

Console.WriteLine("Do you get a bonus this year?");
Console.WriteLine( );
Console.WriteLine("To determine if you are due "
                      + "one,");
Console.Write("enter your gross sales figure: ");
inValue = Console.ReadLine();
salesForYear = Convert.ToDecimal(inValue);
if(salesForYear > 500000.00M)
{
   Console.WriteLine( );
   Console.WriteLine("YES...you get a bonus!");
   bonusAmount = 1000.00M;
}
Console.WriteLine("Bonus for the year: {0:C}",
                      bonusAmount);
Console.ReadLine( );
      }
   }
}
```

Because this application involves money, the new data type, **decimal**, is used to hold the value entered and the bonus amount. Notice how the special suffix of **M** is placed on the end of the initialization when the variable is declared. The declaration is repeated here:

decimal bonusAmount = 0M;

It is also necessary to place **M** on the end of the **decimal** numeric literal used as part of the expression being evaluated:

if (salesForYear > 500000.00M)

It is again necessary to include the **M** when an assignment statement stores the **decimal** 1000.00M in the bonusAmount memory location:

bonusAmount = 1000.00M;

 The special symbols m and M stand for money. Numeric literals used with **decimal** variables require the M; otherwise, a syntax error message is issued.

As you examine Example 5-7, note a call to a method in the **Convert class**. In Chapter 4 you were introduced to the **Parse( )** method to convert values stored in **string** variables into numeric types. You can also use the **Convert class** for this conversion. **Convert** is in the **System namespace** and has methods for converting one **base** type into another **base** type. The **Convert.ToDecimal( )** method was used in Example 5-7 to change the inputted **string** value into a **decimal** value. To convert to an integer, use `Convert.ToInt32( )`, and to convert to a **double**, use `Convert.ToDouble( )`. As discussed in Chapter 4, if you are using Visual Studio .NET, make sure to use the IntelliSense feature. You can explore the many methods and their overloads available in the `Convert` **class**.

For Example 5-7, the output produced when the user enters 600000 is shown in Figure 5-2.

Figure 5-2   BonusApp with salesForYear equal to 600000.00

The problem definition indicates that sales must be over $500,000.00 before a bonus is awarded. The output produced when 500000.00 is entered is shown in Figure 5-3.

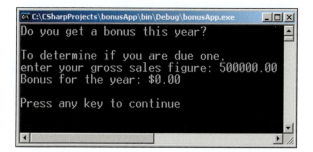

Figure 5-3   BonusApp with salesForYear equal to 500000.00

Beginning programmers often mistakenly place a semicolon at the end of the parenthesized expression being evaluated. If you do this, your program runs, and no syntax error message is issued. However, you are creating a **null (empty) statement body** in place of the **true** statement. The logic is basically indicating, "Do nothing when the expression evaluates to **true**." If you are using Visual Studio .NET and place a semicolon in the wrong place, as shown in Figure 5-4, you get a red indicator, alerting you to the potential problem. Most other language IDEs do not warn you that this problem may exist.

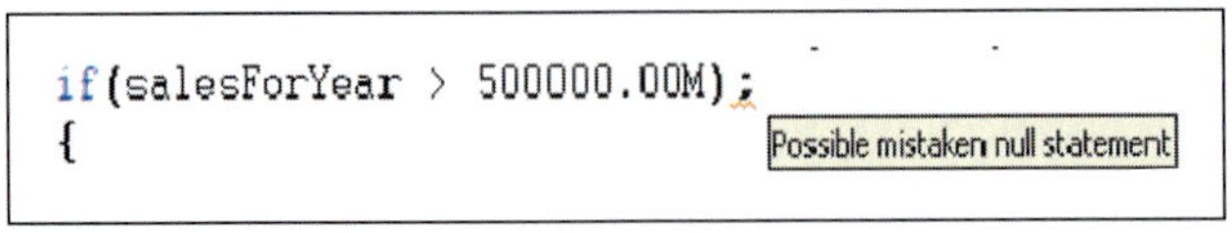

```
if(salesForYear > 500000.00M);
{                              Possible mistaken null statement
```

Figure 5-4 IntelliSense pop-up message

In Visual Studio .NET, when you move your pointer over the red warning, IntelliSense pops up the message, "Possible mistaken null statement."

The one-way **if** statement does not provide an alternate set of steps for a situation in which the expression evaluates to **false**. That option is available with the **two-way if statement**.

Two-Way if Statement

An optional **else** clause can be added to an **if** statement to provide statements to be executed when the expression evaluates to **false**. With a **two-way if statement**, either the **true** statement(s) is (are) executed or the **false** statement(s), but not both. After completing the execution of one of these statements, control always transfers to the statement following the **if** block. The general format for a two-way **if** statement is:

```
if (expression)        //NOTE: no semicolon is placed on this line
    statement;         //executed when expression is true
else
    statement;         //executed when expression is false
```

Notice there is no need to repeat the expression with the **else**. Many beginning programmers write the following:

```
if (aValue == 100)
    Console.WriteLine("The value is 100");
else (aValue != 100)   // INCORRECT! Do not repeat the expression
    Console.WriteLine("The value is not 100");
```

The correct way to include the **else** is to place it on a line by itself without any expression. On the lines that follow the **else**, include the statements that are to be performed when the expression evaluates to **false**. Here is the correct way to write the selection statement:.

```
if (aValue == 100)
    Console.WriteLine("The value is 100");
else
    Console.WriteLine("The value is not 100");
```

As with the one-way **if** statement, you may include more than one statement by enclosing statements in curly braces.

 Readability is important. Notice the indentation used with one- and two-way **if** statements. The statements are aligned with the conditional expression. Smart indenting can be set in Visual Studio, so that the alignment is automatic.

Figure 5-5 illustrates the flow of execution in a two-way **if** statement.

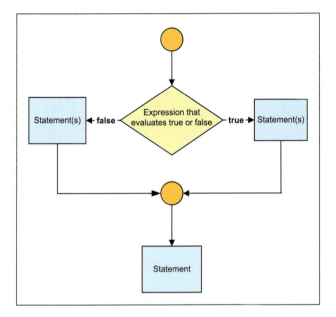

Figure 5-5   Two-way if statement

When the expression evaluates to **true**, the **true** statements are executed. As the figure shows, execution continues at the same location for both, whether the **true** statements are executed or the **false** statements. Consider the following example.

Example 5-8

```
if (hoursWorked > 40)
{
    payAmount = (hoursWorked - 40) * payRate * 1.5 + payRate * 40;
    Console.WriteLine("You worked {0} hours overtime.",
                        hoursWorked - 40);
}
```

```
else
    payAmount = hoursWorked * payRate;
Console.WriteLine("I am displayed, whether the expression "
                  + "evaluates true or false");
```

As shown in Example 5-8, it is permissible to have a block of statements with the **true** portion and a single statement for the **false** portion. No curly braces are required for the **false** statement in this example; however, adding the curly braces may improve readability.

Consider the following example that uses a two-way **if** statement in a **class** method. The user is prompted to enter two values. A two-way **if** statement is used to determine which is the largest. That value and its square root are displayed.

Example 5-9

```
/* LargestValue.cs            Author:        Doyle
 * Allows the user to input two values.
 * Determine the largest of the two values.
 * Prints the largest and its square root.
 * *********************************** */
using System;
namespace LargestValue
{
    class LargestValue
    {
        static void Main( )
        {
            int value1,
                value2,
                largestOne;

            InputValues(out value1, out value2);
            largestOne = DetermineLargest(value1, value2);
            PrintResults(largestOne);
        }

        public static void InputValues(out int v1, out int v2)
        {
            string inValue;

            Console.Write("Enter the first value: ");
            inValue = Console.ReadLine();
            v1 = Convert.ToInt32(inValue);
            Console.Write("Enter the second value: ");
            inValue = Console.ReadLine();
            v2 = Convert.ToInt32(inValue);
        }
```

```
public static int DetermineLargest(int value1, int value2)
{
    int largestOne;     //local variable declared to
                        //facilitate single exit from method
    if (value1 > value2)
    {
        largestOne = value1;
    }
    else
    {
        largestOne = value2;
    }
    return largestOne;
}
public static void PrintResults(int largestOne)
{
    Console.WriteLine( );
    Console.WriteLine("The largest value entered was "
                        + largestOne);
    Console.WriteLine("Its square root is {0:f2}",
    Math.Sqrt(largestOne));
    Console.ReadLine( );
}
}
}
```

When you are writing selection statements, try to avoid repeating code. Instead of duplicating statements for both the **true** and **false** statements, pull out common statements and place them before or after the selection statement. You might have been tempted to solve the problem presented for Example 5-9 with the following two-way **if** statement:

```
if (value1 > value2)
{
    Console.WriteLine("The largest value entered was "
                        + value1);
    Console.WriteLine("Its square root is {0:f2}",
                        Math.Sqrt(value1));
}
else
{
    Console.WriteLine("The largest value entered was "
                        + value2);
    Console.WriteLine("Its square root is {0:f2}",
                        Math.Sqrt(value2));
}
```

The calls to the `Console.WriteLine( )` method for displaying the largest value and its square root are included only once in Example 5-9. They appear twice in the last segment.

Another solution that is not modularized, but eliminates the repeating code, is as follows:

```
int largest;
if (value1 > value2)
{
    largest = value1;
}
else
{
    largest = value2;
}
Console.WriteLine("The largest value entered was "
                    + largest);
Console.WriteLine("Its square root is {0:f2}",
                            Math.Sqrt(largest));
```

All three ways of writing the selection statement produce the same output. The modularized version in Example 5-9 is the preferred approach of the three. Figure 5-6 shows the output produced when the program is run with **25** entered for the first value and **16** entered for the second value.

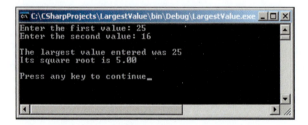

Figure 5-6   Output from LargestValue problem

What does the program in Example 5-9 print when the values entered are the same?

Because **value1** is not greater than **value2**, the **else** statement is executed and **value2** is stored in **largestOne**. If you want to display a message indicating their values are the same, you need to add one more conditional expression as part of the **if** statement. This additional test would be to determine whether **value2** is greater than **value1**. The expression would be added as the **else** statement. Adding this second test would enable you to include a second **else** statement. The last **else** would not be entered unless both of the conditional expressions evaluated to **false**—and in this case, the values are the same. If you make this revision, the logic would need to be revised for displaying the largest value. One approach would be to return the negative value of **value1** or **value2**, when they have the same values. It does not matter which one gets returned since their values are the same. The `PrintResults( )` method could test the `largestOne` variable. When it is negative, a message could be printed indicating the values are the same. The additional test is as follows:

```
if (value1 > value2)
{
    largestOne = value1;
}
else
    if (value1 < value2)
    {
        largestOne = value2;
    }
    else
        largestOne = -(value1);
```

Sometimes a single variable may need to be tested for multiple values. A nested `if...else` statement, like that described previously, can be used for this. You may also want to test a different variable inside the `true` (or `false`) statements. A nested `if...else` statement is also used for this. You learn more about nested `if...else` statements in the section that follows:

Nested If...else Statement

Any statement can be included with the statements to be executed when the expression evaluates to `true`. The same holds for the `false` statements. Therefore, it is acceptable to write an `if` within an `if`. Many different expressions can be evaluated in a single `if` statement. When you place an `if` within an `if`, you create a **nested `if...else` statement**, also referred to as a **nested `if` statement**.

With a nested `if` statement, multiple expressions can be tested. As long as the expressions evaluate to `true`, the `true` statements continue to be evaluated. When another `if` statement is one of the statements in the block being executed, another evaluation is performed. This continues as long as additional `if` statements are part of the `true` statements.

As with the two-way, only one segment of code is executed. You never execute the `true` and its associated `false` statements. When the block is completed, all remaining conditional expressions and their statements are skipped or bypassed. After completing the execution of that block, control always transfers to the statement immediately following the `if` block. The syntax for a nested `if...else` statement follows that of the two-way. The difference is that with a nested `if...else`, the statement may be another `if` statement:

```
if (expression)        //NOTE: no semicolon is placed on this line
    statement;         // could be another if statement
else
    statement;         // could be another if statement
```

In a nested **if...else**, the inner **if** statement is said to be nested inside the outer **if**. However, the inner **if** may also contain another **if** statement. There are no restrictions on the depth of nesting. The limitation comes in the form of whether you and others can read and follow your code. The mark of a good program is that it is readable.

Example 5-10 shows how a nested **if...else** is used to determine the bonus amount to be issued to employees.

Example 5-10

```
// For hourlyEmployees working more than 40 hours, a bonus of $500
// is issued. If hourlyEmployee has not worked more than 40 hours,
// issue a bonus of $100. For those non-hourlyEmployees, issue a
// $300 bonus if they have been employed longer than 10 years;
// otherwise issue a $200 bonus.
bool hourlyEmployee;
double hours,
       bonus;
int yearsEmployed;

if (hourlyEmployee)
    if (hours > 40)
        bonus = 500;
    else
        bonus = 100;
else
    if (yearsEmployed > 10)
        bonus = 300;
     else
        bonus = 200;
```

No equality operator is needed in the first conditional expression. That is because a Boolean variable, **hourlyEmployee**, is used.

The logic for Example 5-10 could be written using four one-way **if** statements as shown in Example 5-11. Here each statement uses the **&&** operator.

Example 5-11

```
if (hourlyEmployee && hours > 40)
    bonus = 500;
if (hourlyEmployee && hours <= 40)
    bonus = 100;
if ((!hourlyEmployee) && yearsEmployed > 10)
    bonus = 300;
if ((!hourlyEmployee) && yearsEmployed <= 10)
    bonus = 200;
```

The single nested **if...else** solution in Example 5-10 is much more efficient than the four statements in Example 5-11. In Example 5-11, every one of the statements is evaluated, even if the first one evaluates to **true**. In Example 5-10, when the first two lines evaluate to **true**, 500 is assigned to **bonus** and no additional evaluations are performed.

> Notice how a statement written using a logical **&&** can be rewritten as a nested **if...else**.
>
> ```
> if (hourlyEmployee && hours > 40)
> ```
>
> produces the same result as
>
> ```
> if (hourlyEmployee)
>       if (hours > 40)
> ```

5

When programming a nested **if...else** statement, it is important to know which **else** matches which **if** statement. The rule for **lining up**, or matching, elses is that an **else** goes with the closest previous **if** that does not have its own **else**. By properly lining up the **else** clauses with their corresponding **if** clauses, you encounter fewer logic errors that necessitate debugging. Example 5-12 illustrates the importance of properly lining up **if** and **else** clauses. Can you match each **else** with the correct **if**?

Example 5-12

```
if (aValue > 10)                          Line 1
if (bValue == 0)                          Line 2
amount = 5;                               Line 3
else                                      Line 4
if (cValue > 100)                         Line 5
if (dValue > 100)                         Line 6
amount = 10;                              Line 7
else                                      Line 8
amount = 15;                              Line 9
else                                      Line 10
amount = 20;                              Line 11
else                                      Line 12
if (eValue == 0)                          Line 13
amount = 25;                              Line 14
```

As shown in Example 5-13 the **else** in line 12 matches the **if** in Line 1; Line 10 matches line 5. What value would be stored in **amount** if **aValue**, **bValue**, **cValue**, **dValue**, and **eValue** were all equal to **0**? Did you get 25 when you traced the logic? Look at Example 5-13. By properly lining up the **else** clauses with their corresponding **if** clauses, the answer can be determined much more quickly.

Example 5-13

```
if (aValue > 10)                        Line 1
    if (bValue == 0)                    Line 2
        amount = 5;                     Line 3
    else                                Line 4
        if (cValue > 100)               Line 5
            if (dValue > 100)           Line 6
                amount = 10;            Line 7
            else                        Line 8
                amount = 15;            Line 9
        else                            Line 10
            amount = 20;                Line 11
else                                    Line 12
    if (eValue == 0)                    Line 13
        amount = 25;                    Line 14
```

The rule indicates that an **else** matches up with the closest previous **if** that does not already have an **else** attached to it. However, you can use braces to attach an **else** to an outer **if** as shown in Example 5-14.

Example 5-14

```
if (average > 59)
{
    if (average < 71)
        grade = 'D';
}
else
    grade = 'F';
```

The braces enclose the **true** statement associated with the expression of (**average > 59**). The inner **if** statement is ended as a statement when the closing curly brace is encountered.

Consider the statements in Example 5-15 that determine a grade based on testing the value in **average**.

Example 5-15

```
if (average > 89)
    grade = 'A';
else
    if (average > 79)
        grade = 'B';
    else
        if (average > 69)
            grade = 'C';
```

```
else
    if (average > 59)
        grade = 'D';
    else
        grade = 'F';
```

Pay particular attention to the conditional expressions in Example 5-15. It is not necessary for the second expression to be a compound expression using `&&`. You do not have to write `if (average > 79 && average <= 89)`. Make sure you understand that execution would never have reached the expression of `(average > 79)` unless the first expression was `false`. If the `average` is not greater than 89, it must be either equal to 89 or less than 89.

As you reviewed Example 5-13 and 5-15, you probably wondered what happens when you keep indenting. Your statements soon start to go off to the right, out of sight. A solution to this problem used by many programmers is to write a series of `else...if` statements when they have a long nested multi-way statement.

The lines in Example 5-15 could be written with a series of `else...if` statements as shown in Example 5-16. This prevents the indentation problem.

Example 5-16

```
if (average > 89)
    grade = 'A';
else if (average > 79)
    grade = 'B';
else if (average > 69)
    grade = 'C';
else if (average > 59)
    grade = 'D';
else
    grade = 'F';
```

Examples 5-15 and 5-16 are multi-way `if` statements. A single variable is tested using a relational operator.

A nested `if...else` statement could also be written using the equality operator in the conditional expression. Consider the following example that displays the `weekDay` name based on testing an integer variable holding a number representing the day.

Example 5-17

```
if (weekDay == 1)
    Console.WriteLine("Monday");
else if (weekDay == 2)
    Console.WriteLine("Tuesday");
else if (weekDay == 3)
    Console.WriteLine("Wednesday");
```

```
else if (weekDay == 4)
    Console.WriteLine("Thursday");
else if (weekDay == 5)
    Console.WriteLine("Friday");
```

When you have a single variable, such as **weekDay**, being tested for equality against four or more values, a **switch** statement can be used. A **switch** statement is not an option for the nested **if...else** solution presented in Example 5-16. A **switch** statement only works for tests of equality.

SWITCH SELECTION STATEMENTS

The **switch statement** is considered a multiple selection structure. It also goes by the name **case statement**. The **switch** or **case** statement allows you to perform a large number of alternatives based on the value of a single variable. This variable or expression must evaluate to an integral or **string** value. It cannot be used with a **double, decimal**, or **float**. But is appropriate for **short, int, long, char**, and **string** data types. The general format of the **switch** statement follows:

```
switch (expression)
{
    case value1:   statement(s);
                   break;
    case value2:   statement(s);
                   break;
              . . .
    case valueN:   statement(s);
                   break;
    [default:      statement(s);
                   break;]
}
```

With the **switch** statement, the expression is sometimes called the **selector**. Its value determines, or selects, which of the cases will be executed. When a **switch** statement is executed, the expression is evaluated and its result compared to each case's value.

The **case** value must be a constant literal of the same type as the expression. You cannot use a variable in the value spot for the **case**. Nor can you use an expression, such as **x < 22**, in the value spot for the **case**. If the expression is a **string** variable, the value is enclosed in double quotes. If the expression is a **char** variable, the value is enclosed in single quotes. For integers, the number is typed without any special surrounding symbols.

The comparison to the **case** values is from top to bottom. The first **case** value that matches the expression results in that case's statements being executed. If no match is made, the statements associated with **default** are executed. Default is optional, but usually it is a good idea to include one. The **default** statements are only executed when there is no match of any of the **case** values.

The curly braces are required with a `switch` statement. That is different from an `if` statement in which they are only required when more than one statement makes up the `true` statement or the `false` statement body. A syntax error is generated if you fail to use curly braces to surround the cases with the `switch` statement.

The last statement for each `case` and the `default` is a **jump statement**. The `break` keyword is used for this jump. There are other types of jump statements covered in the next chapter. When `break` is encountered, control transfers outside of the `switch` statement.

Unlike other languages that allow you to leave off a `break` and **fall through** executing code from more than one `case`, C# requires the `break` for any `case` that has an executable statement(s). You cannot program a `switch` statement in C# to fall through and execute the code for multiple cases.

C# also differs from some other languages in that it requires that a `break` be included with the `default` statement. If you do not have a `break` with a `default` statement, a syntax error is issued. Many languages do not require the `break` on the last `case` because the `default` is the last statement. A natural fallout occurs.

Example 5-18

```
switch(weekDay)
{
    case 1:     Console.WriteLine("Monday");
                break;
    case 2:     Console.WriteLine("Tuesday");
                break;
    case 3:     Console.WriteLine("Wednesday");
                break;
    case 4:     Console.WriteLine("Thursday");
                break;
    case 5:     Console.WriteLine("Friday");
                break;
    default:    Console.WriteLine("Not Monday through Friday");
                break;
}
```

C# allows strings to be used in expressions for `switch` statements. Consider the following program example that displays the full name of a state based on comparing its 2-character abbreviation to a series of `string` literals.

Example 5-19

```
/* StatePicker.cs       Author:       Doyle
 * Allows the user to enter a state
 * abbreviation. A switch statement
 * is used to display the full name
 * of the state.
 * ******************************/
```

5

```
using System;
namespace StatePicker
{
    class StatePicker
    {
        static void Main( )
        {
            string stateAbbrev;

            Console.WriteLine("Enter the state abbreviation. ");
            Console.WriteLine("Its full name will"
                              + " be displayed");
            Console.WriteLine( );
            stateAbbrev = Console.ReadLine();

            switch(stateAbbrev)
            {
              case "AL":  Console.WriteLine("Alabama");
                          break;
              case "FL":  Console.WriteLine("Florida");
                          break;
              case "GA":  Console.WriteLine("Georgia");
                          break;
              case "IL":  Console.WriteLine("Illinois");
                          break;
              case "KY":  Console.WriteLine("Kentucky");
                          break;
              case "MI":  Console.WriteLine("Michigan");
                          break;
              case "OK":  Console.WriteLine("Oklahoma");
                          break;
              case "TX":  Console.WriteLine("Texas");
                          break;
              default:    Console.WriteLine("No match");
                          break;
            }
        }
    }
}
```

When **stateAbbrev** has a value of NV, no error message is issued; **Nevada** is not printed either. Instead, **No match** is displayed on the console screen. Also, notice that **Alabama** is not displayed when **stateAbbrev** has a value of **al**. The **case** value must match the characters exactly; otherwise, the **default** option executes.

Multiple **case** values can be associated with the same statement(s), and it is not necessary to repeat the statement(s) for each value. When more than one **case** is associated with the same statement(s), you group common cases together and follow the last **case** value with the executable statement(s) to be performed when any of the previous cases match. In Example 5-19, it would be useful to display **Alabama** for **AL**, **al**, **Al**, and maybe **aL**. All four of the cases could be associated with the same executable statement that displays **Alabama**, as shown here:

```
case "AL":
case "aL":
case "Al":
case "al": Console.WriteLine("Alabama");
                break;
```

You can place the executable statements for that group with the last **case** value. When you do this, you have effectively created a logical OR situation. In Example 5-20 the result of the expression is compared against 1, 2, 3, 4, and 5. If it matches any of those values, **Failing Grade** is written. Notice that the **break** statement is required as soon as a **case** includes an executable statement. No fall through is permitted if the previous **case** label has code.

5

Example 5-20

```
switch(examScore / 10)
{
    case 1:
    case 2:
    case 3:
    case 4:
    case 5:   Console.WriteLine("Failing Grade");
              break;
    case 6:
    case 7:
    case 8:   Console.WriteLine("Passing Grade");
              break;
    case 9:
    case 10:  Console.WriteLine("Superior Grade");
              break;
    default:  Console.WriteLine("Problem Grade");
              break;
}
```

The preceding **case** statement could be replaced with the following compound multi-way **if** statement:

```
if (((examScore / 10) == 1) || ((examScore / 10) == 2) ||
    ((examScore / 10) == 3) || ((examScore / 10) == 4) ||
    ((examScore / 10) == 5))
      Console.WriteLine("Failing Grade");
```

```
else if (((examScore / 10) == 6) || ((examScore / 10) == 7)
            || ((examScore / 10) == 8))
            Console.WriteLine("Passing Grade");
else if (((examScore / 10) == 9) || ((examScore / 10) == 10))
            Console.WriteLine("Superior Grade");
else Console.WriteLine("Problem Grade");
```

Which do you find the most readable? A solution for this problem could also be written using ten separate one-way **if** statements. When an expression can be designed using the equality operator and involves more than three comparisons, the **switch** statement is almost always the best choice.

You cannot use the **switch** statement to test for a range of values. The only way to do this would be to list every value using the **case** keyword. Also, the **case** value must be a constant literal; it cannot be a variable. The following code segment creates a syntax error:

```
int score,

        high = 90;
switch (score)
{
        case high:      // Syntax error. Case value must be a constant
```

You could write **case** 90:, but not **case** high:

 You must ensure that the expression type is the same as the **case** value type. For example, you can use a **char** variable as the selector. Each character literal value used as the **case** value must be enclosed in single quotation marks.

TERNARY OPERATOR ? :

Also called the **conditional operator**, the **ternary operator** **?** **:** provides another way to express a simple **if...else** selection statement. The operator consists of a question mark **?** and a colon **:**. The general format for this conditional expression is:

```
expression1  ?  expression2  :  expression3;
```

The expression that comes before the question mark, **expression1**, is evaluated first. When **expression1** evaluates to **true**, **expression2**, following the question mark, is executed; otherwise **expression3**, following the colon, is executed.

An example of a statement using the conditional operator is as follows:

```
grade = examScore > 89 ? 'A' : 'C';
```

This reads **if examScore** is greater than **89**, assign **A** to **grade** ; otherwise, assign **C** to **grade**. When **examScore** has a value of 75, the first expression, **examScore > 89**, evaluates to **false**; thus, expression3, **C**, following the colon is executed, and **C** is assigned to the grade memory location.

It performs the same operation as:

```
if (examScore > 89)
    grade = 'A';
else
    grade = 'C';
```

 The conditional operator is often used in an assignment statement.

Consider the following example.

Example 5-21

Most service companies have a minimum charge they use for making house calls. Take, for example, a washing machine repairperson. He may charge $50.00 per hour; however, his minimum charge for traveling to your home is $100.00. Thus, when it takes him less than two hours, the charge is $100. A conditional expression to calculate the charges follows:

```
double charges,
       timeAtSite = 3.5;
charges = timeAtSite < 2.0 ? 100.00 : timeAtSite * 50.00;
```

The value stored in **charges** would be 175. The first expression (**timeAtSite < 2.0**) evaluates to **false**; thus the last expression (**timeAtSite * 50.00**) is evaluated and 175 is stored in **charges**.

 The conditional operator is not as readable as the **if** statement. It is used more often than other forms of the selection statement.

ORDER OF OPERATIONS

When an expression contains multiple operators, the **precedence of the operators** controls the order in which the individual operators are evaluated. For example, you saw in Chapter 3 that an expression such as **value1 + value2 * value3** is evaluated as **value1 + (value2 * value3)** because the * operator has higher precedence than the + operator. In Table 3-1, the operators used primarily for arithmetic were presented. Table 5-7 adds the operators presented in this chapter.

Table 5-7 Operator precedence

Category	Operator	Precedence
Unary	+ - ! ~ ++x --x	Highest
Multiplicative	* / %	
Additive	+ -	
Relational	< > <= >=	
Equality	== !=	
Logical AND	&	
Logical OR	|	
Conditional AND	&&	
Conditional OR	||	
Conditional	? :	
Assignment	= *= /= %= += -=	Lowest

The operators listed in Table 5-7 appear from highest to lowest precedence. Except for the assignment operators, all binary operators are **left-associative**, meaning that operations are performed from left to right. For example, `aValue + bValue - cValue` is evaluated as `(aValue + bValue) - cValue` .

The assignment operators and the conditional operator `? :` are **right-associative**, meaning that operations are performed from right to left. For example, `firstValue = secondValue = thirdValue` is evaluated as `firstValue = (secondValue = (thirdValue))`. Precedence and associativity can be controlled using parentheses. It was not necessary to include the parentheses in the previous example because the order of operations of the language determined the order. Parentheses could have certainly been added to increase readability, but they were not necessary.

Example 5-22 includes an example of a selection statement using many of the operators presented in this chapter. The actual order in which the operations are performed is given following the declaration and conditional expression.

Example 5-22

```
int value1 = 10, value2 = 20, value3 = 30, value4 = 40, value5 = 50;
if (value1 > value2 || value3 == 10 && value4 + 5 < value5)
    Console.WriteLine("The expression evaluates to true");
```

The above expression is evaluated in the following order:

1. (value4 + 5) → (40 + 5) → 45

2. (value1 > value2) → (10 > 20) → false

3. ((value4 + 5) < value5) → (45 < 50) → true

4. (value3 == 10) → (30 == 10) → **false**

5. ((value3 == 10) && ((value4 + 5) < value5)) → **false** && **true** → **false**

6. ((value1 > value2) || ((value3 == 10) && ((value4 + 5) < value5)))
   → **false** || **false** → **false**

Because the expression evaluates to **false**, the line following the **if** statement is skipped or bypassed. The executable statement after the **Console.WriteLine( )** would be the next one performed after the expression is evaluated.

PROGRAMMING EXAMPLE: SPEEDINGTICKET APPLICATION

This programming example demonstrates an application that calculates fines for traffic tickets issued on campus. A nested **if...else** selection statement is used in the design. Figure 5-7 shows the problem definition.

Consider the situation of issuing parking tickets on campus and determining the fines associated with the ticket.

All students are charged an initial $75.00 when ticketed. Additional charges are based on how much over the speed limit the ticket reads. On campus there is a 35 miles per hour (MPH) speed limit on most streets. Two roads are posted with a speed limit at 15 MPH. Fines are expensive on campus. After the initial $75 fee, an extra $87.50 is charged for every 5 MPH students are clocked over the speed limit.

The traffic office feels seniors have been around for a while and should know better than to speed on campus. They add even more fees to their fine. At the same time, they try to cut freshmen a little slack. Seniors are charged an extra $50 when they get caught speeding, unless they are traveling more than 20 MPH over the speed limit. Then it is an additional $200 added to their fine.

If freshmen are exceeding the speed limit but not by 20 MPH or more, they get a $50 deduction off their fines. But, freshmen, sophomores, and juniors traveling over 20 MPH over the speed limit are fined an additional $100.

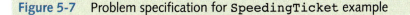

Figure 5-7   Problem specification for **SpeedingTicket** example

Analyze the Problem

You should review the problem specification in Figure 5-7 and make sure you understand the problem definition. The purpose of the application is to calculate a fine based on the reported speed, speed limit, and classification of a student.

Two separate classes are developed. One **class** is designed to include characteristics of the ticket. The other **class** instantiates objects of the **Ticket class** and is used to test the **Ticket class** to ensure that all possible situations have been taken into consideration. Several different conditional expressions must be constructed to determine the fine.

The application or client **class** should test for each classification type and for speeds over and under 20 miles over the speed limit. This **class** produces an output listing showing the ticket cost given a number of test cases.

Variables Tables 5-8 and 5-9 list the data items needed for the **SpeedingTicket** example.

Table 5-8 Instance variables for the Ticket class

Data item description	Data type	Identifier
Street speed limit	int	speedLimit
Speed traveling when ticketed	int	speed
Fine associated with ticket	decimal	fine

The application **class** that is using the **Ticket class** also needs data. The application **class** allows the user to enter values for the speed limit, the speed at which the speeder was traveling, and the speeder's classification. Table 5-9 identifies some of the local variables needed by the application **class**.

Table 5-9 Local variables for the SpeedingTicket application class

Data item description	Data type	Identifier
Year in school—classification	char	classif
Street speed limit	int	speedLimit
Speed traveling when ticketed	int	speed
string input value	string	inValue

Constants The cost of each five miles over the speed limit is a set amount that everyone pays. It is defined as a constant value in the `Ticket` `class`. Setting it as a constant allows quick modification to the memory location when the minimum charges change. The identifier and preset constant value are

```
COST_PER_5_OVER = 87.50
```

Design a Solution

The desired output is to display the fine amount. Figure 5-8 shows a prototype for what the final output should be. The xxx.xx is placed in the prototype to represent the location in which the calculated value should appear. For many applications, it is also useful to display the values used in calculations.

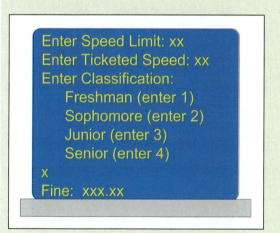
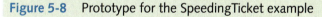

Figure 5-8   Prototype for the SpeedingTicket example

As you read in earlier chapters, the object-oriented approach focuses attention on the design of the **object**. A **Ticket object** has both data and behavior characteristics that can be identified. Given the characteristics of student classification, speed limit, and ticketed speed, the **Ticket** object's major action or behavior is to set the fine amount. Class diagrams are used to help design and document these characteristics. Figure 5-9 shows the **class** diagrams for the **SpeedingTicket** example.

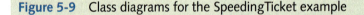

Ticket

-speed : int
-speedLimit : int
-fine : decimal

+SetFine() : void

TicketApp

-classif : char
-speed : int
-speedLimit : int

+GetInputValues()

Figure 5-9 Class diagrams for the SpeedingTicket example

The **class** diagrams show neither the properties needed nor the local variables that might be needed by specific **class** methods. For example, a **string** value is needed for inputting data in the **TicketApp class**. It is not included on the **class** diagram.

During design it is important to develop an algorithm showing the systematic process to solve the problem. This can be done using any of the design tools presented in previous chapters. Pseudocode for the **SetFine( )** method, which contains a nested **if**, is shown in Figure 5-10.

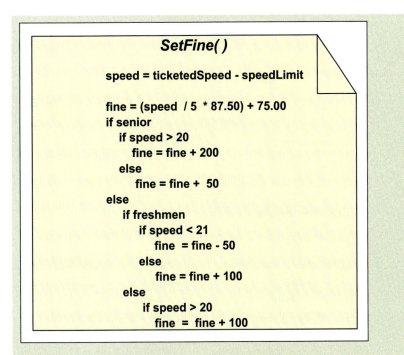

Figure 5-10   Pseudocode for the SetFine() method

The problem definition indicates that for every 5 miles over the speed limit the additional fine is \$87.50. A whole number value representing the overage is needed. For example, if the `speedLimit` is 35 and the `ticketedSpeed` is 42, only one additional fee of \$87.50 is added to the fine. If the `ticketedSpeed` is 45, two additional \$87.50 fees are added. This value is determined by doing integer division. An assumption for the pseudocode is that all variables, except `fine`, are of type `int`. This forces the division to be integer division.

$42 - 35 = 7$ miles over the limit

$7 / 5 = 1$

Notice that the result is not 1.40, because integer division produces an integer result.

When you are designing a solution that requires a nested `if...else`, sometimes it is easier to develop your algorithm if you graphically map out the different options. A flowchart could be used. Another option is a **decision tree**, which is a design tool that allows you to represent complex procedures visually. Nodes are used to represent decision points, and lines branch out from the nodes to represent either further conditions or, eventually, the action to be taken based on the conditions expressed to the left. Figure 5-11 shows a decision tree for part of this application. It pictures the logic involved to determine the additional fee based on classification of student and the number of miles traveling over the speed limit.

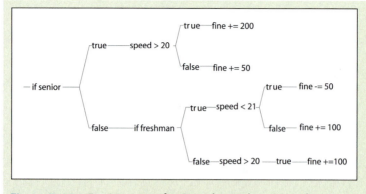

Figure 5-11   Decision tree for SpeedingTicket example

You should always desk check your design. It is especially important when selection statements are included as part of your solution. With the `SpeedingTicket` example, a large number of expressions are combined; thus, it is imperative that you walk through the logic and make sure the calculations are being performed properly. One way to do this is to develop a table with columns for all inputted and calculated values. Include a row for all possible combinations of unique paths through the nested `if`. If you have developed a decision tree, it is easier to determine which cases need to be tested. End points, such as for speeds over 20 miles per hour above the speed limit, can be especially troublesome. Make sure you include rows testing those values. After you identify values to be tested, use a calculator to fill in the calculated values. Then, go back and reread the problem definition. Are those the correct calculated values? Table 5-10 includes the values selected to test the `SpeedingTicket` algorithm. This can be considered a test plan. Not only do you want to see how your algorithm handles these specific values, but once you implement your design, be sure to run and test your application using the identified values for speed limit, ticketed speed, and classification. Compare the results with those obtained from your program output.

Table 5-10   Desk check of SpeedingTicket algorithm

Speed limit	Ticketed speed	Classification (1=Freshman 2=Sophomore 3=Junior 4=Senior)	Fine
35	42	1	112.50
35	55	2	475.00
35	57	1	525.00

Table 5-10 Desk check of SpeedingTicket algorithm (continued)

Speed limit	Ticketed speed	Classification (1=Freshman 2=Sophomore 3=Junior 4=Senior)	Fine
35	47	2	250.00
35	55	1	425.00
35	57	2	525.00
35	44	4	212.50
35	39	4	125.00
35	58	4	625.00
35	55	4	475.00
35	38	1	25.00

Code the Solution   After you complete the design and verify the algorithm's correctness, it is time to translate the design into source code. For this application you are creating two separate files—one for each **class**. As you learned in Chapter 4, only one of the classes has a **Main( )** method.

The final application listing for both files is as follows:

```
/* Ticket.cs        Author:        Doyle
 * Describes the characteristics of a
 * speeding ticket to include the speed
 * limit, ticketed speed, and fine amount.
 * The Ticket class is used to set the
 * amount for the fine.
 * **********************************/
using System;
namespace TicketSpace
{
    public class Ticket
    {
        private const decimal COST_PER_5_OVER = 87.50M;
        private int speedLimit;
        private int speed;
        private decimal fine;
        public Ticket()
        {
        }
```

```
public Ticket(int speedLmt, int reportedSpeed)
    {
        speedLimit = speedLmt;
        speed = reportedSpeed - speedLimit;
    }
    public decimal Fine
    {
        get
        {
            return fine;
        }
    }

    public void SetFine(char classif)
    {
        fine = (speed / 5  * COST_PER_5_OVER) + 75.00M;
        if (classif == '4')
            if (speed > 20)
                fine += 200;
            else
                fine += 50;
        else
            if (classif == '1')
                if (speed < 21)
                    fine  -= 50;
                else
                    fine += 100;
            else
                if (speed > 20)
                    fine += 100;
    }
  }
}

/* TicketApp.cs          Author:      Doyle
 * Instantiates a Ticket object
 * from the inputted values of
 * speed and speed limit. Uses
 * the year in school classification
 * to set the fine amount.
 * * *******************************/
using System;
namespace TicketSpace
{
   public class TicketApp
   {
```

```csharp
static void Main( )
{
    int speedLimit,
        speed;
    char classif;

    speedLimit = InputSpeed("Speed Limit", out speedLimit);
    speed = InputSpeed("Ticketed Speed", out speed);
    classif = InputYearInSchool( );

    Ticket myTicket = new Ticket(speedLimit, speed);

    myTicket.SetFine(classif);
    Console.WriteLine("Fine: {0:C}", myTicket.Fine);
}


public static int InputSpeed(string whichSpeed, out int s)
{
    string inValue;
    Console.Write("Enter the {0}: ", whichSpeed);
    inValue = Console.ReadLine();
    s = Convert.ToInt32(inValue);
    return s;
}
public static char InputYearInSchool ( )
{
    string inValue;
    char yrInSchool;

    Console.WriteLine("Enter your classification:" );
    Console.WriteLine("\tFreshmen (enter 1)");
    Console.WriteLine("\tSophomore (enter 2)");
    Console.WriteLine("\tJunior (enter 3)");
    Console.Write("\tSenior (enter 4)");
    Console.WriteLine();
    inValue = Console.ReadLine();
    yrInSchool = Convert.ToChar(inValue);
    return yrInSchool;
}
}
}
```

5

Figure 5-12 shows the output produced for a ticket issued to a junior traveling at a speed of 45 MPH in a 35 MPH zone.

Figure 5-12   Output from the SpeedingTicket example

As indicated in Table 5-10, a number of different test cases should be run to verify the correctness of your solution. Just because you are getting output, does not mean your solution is correct. Compare your results with the desk checked calculated results. Are they the same? Have you considered all possible combinations?

QUICK REVIEW

1. The three basic programming constructs include simple sequence, selection, and iteration.

2. The selection statement allows you to deviate from the sequential path and perform different statements based on the value of one or more variables.

3. The two types of selection statements are the **if...else** and **switch** statements. C# also provides the ternary operator **? :** for conditional expressions.

4. With selection statements, indentation is for readability only. Curly braces are used when you have more than one expression to be evaluated.

5. The result of expressions used with selection statements is either **true** or **false**.

6. Testing a Boolean variable does not require the use of an equality operator. If **salariedEmployee** is of type **bool**, you can write **if (salariedEmployee)**. It is not necessary to include the **==** operator.

7. When you compare characters or strings, the Unicode character set is used.

8. You can compare **string** operands using the equality operators **==** and **!=**. The relational symbols **>, <, >=,** or **<=** are not defined for strings.

9. Conditional expressions may be combined with logical conditional operators, `&&` or `||`, to form more complex expressions.

10. C# uses the `&&` and `||` operators to represent AND and OR, respectively.

11. With short-circuit evaluation, as soon as the value of the entire expression is known, the common language runtime (CLR) stops evaluating the expression. For complex expressions using `&&`, when the first part of the expression evaluates to `false`, there is no need to evaluate the second.

12. In C#, there is no conversion between the `bool` type and other types; thus, when `x` is defined as `int`, you cannot type `if (x)`.

13. New programmers often mistakenly place a semicolon at the end of the parenthesized expression being evaluated. This makes a null (empty) statement, but does not create a syntax error.

14. With a two-way `if` statement, either the `true` statement(s) is executed or the `false` statement(s), but not both. After the execution of the statement(s) is (are) finished, control always transfers to the statements following the `if` block.

15. Any statement, including another `if` statement, can be included within the statements to be executed when the expression evaluates to `true`. The same holds for the `false` statements.

16. When determining which `else` matches which `if`, follow this rule: the `else` matches up with the closest `if` that does not already have an attached `else`.

17. Use a series of `else...if` for a long nested, multi-way statement.

18. The `switch` statement is considered a multiple selection structure that allows a large number of alternatives to be executed. The `switch` can be used for equality comparisons only.

19. The `case` value with a `switch` statement must be a constant literal of the same type as the expression. It cannot be a variable.

20. With a `switch` statement, the occurrence of the first `case` value that matches the expression causes that case's statement(s) to be executed. If no match is made with any of the `case` values, the statements associated with `default` are executed.

21. Having a `default` is not required, but it is a good idea always to include one.

22. There is no way to program a `switch` statement in C# to fall through to the code for the next `case`. After code is associated with a `case`, there must be a `break`. If used, the `default` statements must also end with a `break`.

23. Multiple cases in a `switch` statement can be associated with the same statements. This works like having a logical OR operator between each of the cases.

24. The `switch` statement only works for equality testing. You cannot use it to test for a range of values, or to perform a relational test.

25. Also called the conditional operator, the ternary operator ? : provides a shorthand way to express a simple if...else selection statement.

26. When an expression contains multiple operators, the precedence of the operators controls the order in which the individual operators are evaluated.

27. Equality operators have a lower precedence than relational operators. Therefore, && has a higher precedence than ||, but both && and || have lower precedence than the relational or equality operators. The very lowest precedence is the assignment operators.

EXERCISES

1. The result of the expression if (aValue == 10) is:

   a. true or false

   b. 10

   c. an integer value

   d. aValue

   e. determined by an input statement

2. Which expression is evaluated first in the following statement?

   ```
   if( a > b && c == d || a == 10 && b > a + 7)?
   ```

   a. a > b

   b. b && c

   c. d || a

   d. a + 7

   e. none of the above

3. What is the output for **total** after the following segment of code executes?

   ```
   int num = 4,
       total = 0;
   switch (num)
   {
       case 1:
       case 2:        total = 5;
                      break;
       case 3:        total = 10;
                      break;
       case 4:        total = total + 3;
                      break;
       case 8:        total = total + 6;
                      break;
   ```

```
    default:      total = total + 4;
                  break;
    }
Console.WriteLine("The value of total is " + total);
```

a. 0

b. 3

c. 13

d. 28

e. none of the above

4. What is the displayed when the following code executes?

```
score = 40;
if (score > 95)
    Console.WriteLine("Congratulations!");
    Console.WriteLine("That's a high score!");
    Console.WriteLine("This is a test question!");
```

a. This is a test question!

b. Congratulations!

   That's a high score!

   This is a test question!

c. That's a high score!

   This is a test question!

d. Congratulations!

   That's a high score!

e. none of the above

5. Which statement in C# allows you to do the following: properly check the variable code to determine whether it contains the character C, and if it does, display "This is a check" and then advance to a new line?

a. `if code is equal to C`

   `Console.WriteLine("This is a check");`

b. `if (code = "C")`

   `Console.WriteLine("This is a check");`

c. `if (code == 'C')`

   `Console.WriteLine("This is a check");`

d. `if (code == C)`

   `Console.WriteLine("This is a check");`

e. none of the above

6. What will be displayed from executing the following segment of code? You may assume the user enters a grade of 90 from the keyboard.

```
int testScore;
if (testScore < 60);
    Console.WriteLine("You failed the test!");
if (testScore > 60)
    Console.WriteLine("You passed the test!");
else
    Console.WriteLine("You need to study for "
                        + "the next test!");
```

a. You failed the test!

b. You passed the test!

c. You failed the test!

   You passed the test!

d. You failed the test!

   You need to study for the next test!

e. none of the above

7. The _____ operator represents the logical AND.

a. ++

b. ||

c. &&

d. @

e. none of the above

8. What does the following program segment display?

```
int f = 7, s = 15;
f = s % 2;
if (f != 1)
{
   f = 0;
   s = 0;
}
else if (f == 2)
{
   f = 10;
   s = 10;
}
```

```
else
{
  f = 1;
  s = 1;
}
Console.WriteLine(" " + f + " " + s);
```

a. 7 15

b. 0 0

c. 10 10

d. 1 1

e. none of the above

9. The symbol (=) is:

a. the operator used to test for equality

b. used for comparing two items

c. used as part of an assignment statement

d. considered a logical compound operator

e. all of the above

10. Incorrect use of spacing with an **if** statement:

a. detracts from its readability

b. causes a syntax error message

c. can change the program logic

d. causes a logic error message

e. all of the above

11. Which logical operator (op) is defined by the following table? (T and F denote **true** and **false**.)

P	Q	P op Q
T	T	T
T	F	F
F	T	F
F	F	F

a. NOT

b. AND

c. OR

d. not enough information is given

e. none of the above

12. Examine the code to complete the following question. (Be careful.)

```
if (A == B);
    C = 3;
```

When will C get the value of 3?

a. when A is equal to B

b. when A is not equal to B

c. never

d. every time the program is executed

e. not enough information is given

13. Consider the following **if** statement, which is syntactically correct, but uses poor style and indentation:

```
if (x >= y) if (y > 0) x = x * y; else if (y < 4) x = x - y;
```

Assume that **x** and **y** are **int** variables containing the values 9 and 3, respectively, before execution of the preceding statement. After execution of the statement, what value does **x** contain?

a. 9

b. 1

c. 6

d. 27

e. none of the above

14. After execution of the following code, what will be the value of **inputValue**?

```
int inputValue = 0;
if (inputValue > 5)
    inputValue += 5;
else if (inputValue > 2)
        inputValue += 10;
else inputValue += 15;
```

a. 15

b. 10

c. 25

d. 0

e. 5

15. If you intend to place a block of statements within an **if** statement, you must use _____ around the block.

a. parentheses

b. square brackets

c. quotation marks

d. curly braces

e. none of the above

16. Given the following segment of code, what will be the output?

```
int x = 5;
if (x == 2)
    Console.WriteLine("Brown, brown, run aground.");
else
    Console.WriteLine("Blue, blue, sail on through.");
Console.WriteLine("Green, green, nice and clean.");
```

a. Brown, brown, run aground.

b. Blue, blue, sail on through.

c. Brown, brown, run aground.

Blue, blue, sail on through.

d. Blue, blue, sail on through.

Green, green, nice and clean.

e. none of the above

17. What is the result of the following conditional expression when aValue = 100 and bValue = 7?

```
result = aValue > bvalue + 100 ? 1000 : 2000;
```

a. 0

b. 1000

c. 2000

d. 7

e. none of the above

18. Given the switch statement, which of the following would be the first if statement to replace the first test in the switch?

```
switch (control)
{
  case 11 :   Console.WriteLine("eleven");
              break;
  case 12 :   Console.WriteLine("twelve");
              break;
  case 16 :   Console.WriteLine("sixteen");
              break;
}
```

a. if (case = 11)

b. if (case == 11)

c. if (control == 11)

d. if (switch == 11)

e. none of the above

19. Which of the following statements about logical operators is correct?

a. Logical AND yields **true** if and only if both of its operands are either **true** or **false**.

b. Logical OR yields **true** if either or both of its operands are **true**.

c. Logical OR is represented in C# by **&&** .

d. Logical NOT is represented in C# by **|** .

e. none of the above

20. The **string** data type can be used:

a. as an operand for the **==** or **!=**

b. as an expression in the **switch** statement to be evaluated

c. as an operand for the **>** or **<** operator

d. a and b are correct

e. all of the above

21. Assuming a is 5, b is 6, and c is 8, which of the following is **false**?

a. `a == 5;`

b. `7 <= (a + 2);`

c. `c <= 4;`

d. `(1 + a) != b;`

e. `c >= 8;`

f. `a >= 0;`

g. `a <= (b * 2);`

22. Could a **switch** statement be designed logically to perform the same tests as the following nested **if**? If so, explain how it could be done.

```
if (aValue == 100)
    Console.WriteLine("Value is 100");
else
    if (aValue < 100)
        Console.WriteLine("Value is less than 100");
```

23. Rewrite the following **switch** statement as a nested **if** statement using a series of **else…if** statements.

```
string birdName;
switch (birdName)
{
    case "Pelican":
            Console.WriteLine("Lives near water.");
            break;
    case "Cardinal":
            Console.WriteLine("Beautiful in the snow.");
            break;
```

```
        case "Owl":
                Console.WriteLine("Night creature.");
                break;
        case "Eagle":
                Console.WriteLine("Keen vision");
                break;
        case "Flamingo":
                Console.WriteLine("Pretty and pink.");
                break;
        default:
                Console.WriteLine("Can fly.");
                break;
    }
```

5

24. Rewrite the following compound expression as nested **if** statements.

```
if ((aValue > bValue) && (bValue == 10))
    Console.WriteLine("Test complete");
```

25. Write conditional expressions to perform the following tests.

    a. When **amountOwed** is greater than 1000.00 display an overdue message.

    b. When **amountOfRain** is greater than 5 inches, add 5 to **totalCount**. When it is between 3 and 5 inches, add 3 to **totalCount**. When it is less than 3 inches add 1 to **totalCount**.

    c. When **middleInitial** is equal to the character **z**, display message "You're one in a thousand"; otherwise check to see if it is equal to the character 'a'. When it is equal to the character **a**, display the message "A common initial".

    d. When **balance** > 100 and **transaction** < 50, subtract **transaction** from **balance**. When **balance** is not greater than 100, add **transaction** to **balance**.

PROGRAMMING EXERCISES

1. Write a program that allows the user to input two values. Perform a conditional test to find the smallest value. Be sure to check whether the values entered are the same. If they are the same, display a message that indicates this; otherwise, display the smallest value.

2. Write a program that allows the user to input a month number. Display the name of the month associated with the number entered and the number of days of that month. For this exercise, use 28 for February. If the user inputs an invalid entry, display an appropriate message.

3. Write a program to calculate and display your average and grade. Allow the user to enter five scores. After values are entered, and the average calculated, test the result to determine whether an A, B, C, D, or F should be recorded. The scoring rubric is as follows: A—90–100; B—80–89; C—70–79; D—60–69; F < 60.

4. Write a program that calculates the take-home pay for an employee. The two types of employees are salaried and hourly. Allow the user to input the employee type. If an employee is salaried, allow the user to input the salary amount. If an employee is hourly, allow the user to input the hourly rate and the number of hours clocked for the week. For hourly employees, overtime is paid for hours over 40 at a rate of 1.5 of the base rate. For all employees' take-home pay, federal tax of 18% is deducted. A retirement contribution of 10% and a social security tax rate of 6% should also be deducted. Use appropriate constants. Design an object-oriented solution. Create a second **class** to test your design.

5. A large Internet merchandise provider determines its shipping charges based on the total purchases. As the total increases, the shipping charges proportionally decrease. This is done to encourage more purchases. The following chart is used to determine the charge for shipping.

   $0–$250.00: $5.00

   $250.01–$500.00: $8.00

   $500.01–$1000.00: $10.00

   $1000.01–$5000.00: $15.00

   over $5000.00: $20.00

   Write a program that allows users to enter their total purchases and to determine their shipping charges. Your program should calculate and display their shipping charges.

6. Write an application that computes the area of a circle, rectangle, and cylinder. Display a menu showing the three options. Allow users to input which figure they want to see calculated. Based on the value inputted, prompt for appropriate dimensions and perform the calculations using the following formulas:

   Area of a circle = PI * radius ^{2}

   Area of a rectangle = length * width

   Area of a cylinder = PI * radius ^{2} * height

   Write a modularized solution, which includes **class** methods for inputting data and performing calculations.

7. Create an application with four classes. Three of the classes should contain data and behavior characteristics for circle, rectangle, and cylinder. The fourth **class** should allow the user to input a figure type from a menu of options. Prompt for appropriate values based on the inputted figure type, instantiate an **object** of the type entered, and display characteristics about the **object**.

8. Design a solution that prints the amount of pay a commissioned salesperson takes home. The more sales documented, the larger the commission rate. Allow the user to input a total sales amount for the week. Compute the commission based on the following table. Display the pay amount formatted with commas, decimals, and a dollar symbol.

   $0–$1000: 3%

   $1001–$5000: 5%

   $5001–$10000: 6%

   over $10000: 7%

   Be sure to design your solution so that all possible situations are accounted for and tested. What values did you enter and test to verify your program's correctness?

9. Write a program that allows the user to input three-digit hexadecimal values. Convert the value inputted to its **decimal** equivalent. Your program should display the original hex value and the corresponding **decimal** value.

10. People sometimes give their telephone number using one or more alphabetic characters. Write a program that takes a single letter and displays the corresponding number. Look at your telephone to determine which numbers correspond to which characters. Notice that the letters 'q' and 'z' are not used. If the user enters one of those letters, display a message indicating that the value does not match a number. Allow both uppercase and lowercase characters to be entered. Test your program using your own phone number.

6

Repeating Instructions

In this chapter, you will:

Chapter 5 introduced you to the second type of programming construct, the selection statement. You learned that the two common forms of selection statements, `if...else` and `switch`, can change the sequential order in which statements are performed. You learned that a conditional expression with a selection statement produces a Boolean result that can be tested and used to determine alternate paths in your program.

Recall that the first programming construct is the simple sequence and that the second construct is the selection statement. The third construct is called repetition, iteration, or looping. In this chapter, you discover why loops are so valuable and how to write loop control structures. You learn about different kinds of loops and determine when one type is more appropriate than another.

WHY USE A LOOP?

One of the major strengths of programming languages can be attributed to loops. The programming examples you have seen thus far could have been solved more quickly through manual calculations. Take, for example, calculating your course grade average. With a calculator in hand, you could certainly add together your scores and divide by the number of entries. However, if you were assigned this task for everyone in your class or everyone at your school, you could see the value of being able to write one set of instructions that can be repeated with many different sets of data.

C# has a rich set of looping structures. These constructs, sometimes called **repetition** or **iteration structures**, enable you to identify and block together one or more statements to be repeated based on a predetermined condition. For looping, C# includes the C-style traditional `while`, `do...while`, and `for` statements that are found in many other programming languages. New to C-style languages is the `foreach` loop construct used to process collections of data stored under a common name in structures such as arrays, which you will learn about in Chapter 7. The sections that follow introduce you to the different types of loops and show you how they can be used in your programs.

USING THE WHILE STATEMENT

Probably the simplest and most frequently used loop structure to write is the `while` statement. The general form of the `while` statement is:

```
while (conditional expression)
    statement(s);
```

The conditional expression, sometimes called the **loop condition**, is a logical condition to be tested. It is enclosed in parentheses and is similar to the expressions you use for selection statements. The conditional expression must return a Boolean result of `true` or `false`. An interpretation of the `while` statement is "`while` condition is `true`, perform statement(s)."

The statement following the conditional expression makes up the body of the loop. The body of the loop is performed as long as the conditional expression evaluates to `true`. Like the selection construct, the statement following the conditional expression can be a single statement or a series of statements surrounded by curly braces { }.

> **NOTE** Some programmers use curly braces to surround all loop bodies, even loop bodies consisting of a single statement. Consistently using curly braces increases readability. It also reduces the chance of forgetting to include the curly braces when the body contains multiple statements.

Notice that there is no semicolon after the conditional expression. If you place a semicolon there, you do not get a syntax error, but your program will run. If you are using Visual Studio .NET and place a semicolon on the line containing the conditional expression, a red mark is placed under the semicolon. This should alert you that there might be a problem. When you move your mouse pointer over the red mark, IntelliSense displays this message: "Possible mistaken `null` statement." You saw this same warning when a semicolon was placed at the end of the selection statement expression.

Placing the semicolon at the end of the conditional expression produces a loop that has no body, or an **empty bodied loop**. Placing a semicolon at the end of the conditional expression can create an infinite loop situation. Your program will run and run and run, accomplishing nothing. An **infinite loop** is a loop that has no provisions for termination.

> **NOTE** You can usually kill an infinite loop by closing the window or pressing the Esc key. If that does not work, try the key combinations Ctrl+C or Ctrl+Break. You may have to press the two keys simultaneously. The easiest way to do this is to hold down the Ctrl key and then press the second key. If that does not work, open the Windows Task Manager by pressing Ctrl+Alt+Del and press the End Task button in the Close Program dialog box. Sometimes this causes you to lose unsaved work. Thus, it is a good idea to save your work before running applications that contain loops.

The `while` statement is a **pretest** loop, which means that the conditional expression is tested before any of the statements in the body of the loop are performed. If the conditional expression evaluates to `false`, the statement(s) in the body of the loop is (are) never performed. If the conditional expression evaluates to `true`, the statements are performed, and then control transfers back to the conditional expression. It is reevaluated and the cycle continues. Figure 6-1 illustrates the flow of execution in a pretest loop.

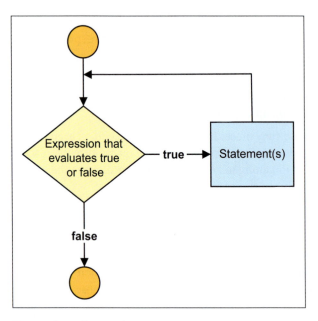

Figure 6-1 Pretest loop

Counter-Controlled Loop

Many programs you develop require that you write one or more statements that must be performed more than once. When you know the number of times the statements must be executed, you can create a **counter-controlled loop**. With a counter-controlled loop, a variable simulating a counter is used as the **loop control variable** to keep track of the number of iterations. Example 6-1 adds values to an accumulator. The variable, **sum**, is initialized to zero and the positive integers 1 through 10 are added to the **sum** memory location, one value at a time.

Example 6-1

```
/* SummedValues.cs        Author: Doyle
 * Demonstrates use of a loop to add 10
 * integers. Displays the total after
 * the loop body is completed.
 */
using System;
namespace SummedValues
{
    class SummedValues
    {
        static void Main( )
```

```
{
    int sum = 0;                              //Line 1
    int number = 1;                           //Line 2
    while (number < 11)                       //Line 3
    {                                         //Line 4
        sum = sum + number;                   //Line 5
        number++;                             //Line 6
    }                                         //Line 7
    Console.WriteLine("Sum of values "        //Line 8
                        + "1 through 10"       //Line 9
                        + " is " + sum);       //Line 10
}
}
}
```

The output of this code is:

Sum of values 1 through 10 is 55

To include a counter-controlled loop in your program, you must design the conditional expression so that you can exit the loop after a certain number of iterations. Normally on the outside of the loop, before the conditional expression, the loop control variable is initialized. On line 2 in Example 6-1, number is initialized to 1. The variable number is the loop control variable. On line 3, its value is evaluated and used to determine whether the loop should be executed.

When the while statement on line 3 is reached, the conditional expression of (number < 11) produces a true result, so the statements in the body of the loop are performed. Notice that the last line in the loop, line 6, increments the loop control variable, number, by one. When the closing curly brace is encountered on line 7, control transfers back to the conditional expression on line 3. The conditional expression is reevaluated and again produces a true result. This cycle—test, perform body of loop, test—is continued as long as the conditional expression evaluates to true. When the loop control variable, number, becomes 11, the conditional expression evaluates to false (11 is not less than 11). At this point, control transfers to line 8, the statement following the loop. Here, beginning on line 8, the WriteLine( ) method displays the sum of the values.

What would happen if line 6, the following line, is omitted?

number++;

If you answered "an infinite loop," you are correct. Without changing the loop control variable used in the conditional expression by increasing its value, the expression would never evaluate to false. Careful thought must focus on how the loop will end with a normal termination. Without incrementing the counter used in the conditional expression, the loop would go on indefinitely.

Why not put the following statement, which began on line 8, inside the loop body?

```
Console.WriteLine("Sum of values 1 through 10 is " + sum);
```

The final value of **sum** would be printed if the **WriteLine( )** method is placed in the body of the loop. However, you would also have nine additional printed lines. Every time **sum** changes, a line would be printed showing its new value. Thus, it is better to print the result after all the calculations have been performed.

You could modify Example 6-1 to allow the user to input the first and last values to be summed. Both operands in the conditional expression could be variables. Example 6-2 prompts the user for the boundaries.

Example 6-2

```csharp
/* InputEndPointsWithWhile.cs        Author: Doyle
 * Demonstrates use of a loop to add any range
 * of values. User inputs start and stop values.
 * Displays the result after the loop is
 * completed.
 */
using System;
namespace InputEndPointsWithWhile
{
    class InputEndPointsWithWhile
    {
        static void Main( )
        {
            int sum = 0;
            int startValue,
                endValue;
            string inValue;
            Console.Write("Enter the beginning value. ");
            inValue = Console.ReadLine();
            startValue = Convert.ToInt32(inValue);
            Console.Write("Enter the last value. ");
            inValue = Console.ReadLine();
            endValue = Convert.ToInt32(inValue);
            Console.Write("Sum of values {0} through {1} ",
                            startValue, endValue);
            while (startValue < endValue + 1)
            {
                sum = sum + startValue;
                startValue++;
            }
            Console.WriteLine("is {0}", sum);
        }
    }
}
```

There are a couple of interesting issues to consider with Example 6-2. The conditional expression now reads:

```
while (startValue < endValue + 1)
```

The same result could have been achieved using

```
while (startValue <= endValue)
```

Both cases call attention to the fact that the value entered by the user as the last number should be added to the total. If the conditional expression read `while(startValue < endValue)`, the loop would not be executed for the last value. An **off-by-one error** would have occurred. This is a common problem associated with counter-controlled loops. It is important to think through test cases and check endpoints to ensure they have been taken into consideration. You should always check the initial and final values of the loop control variable and verify that you get the expected results at the boundaries. Without adding one onto the endpoint or using the compound relational operator, the result would be incorrect.

Why did the solution print the range of values (`startValue` and `endValue`) before the loop executed? The following statement appeared before the loop:

```
Console.Write("Sum of values {0} through {1} ",
              startValue, endValue);
```

The loop control variable, `startValue`, is changed inside the loop. Its original value is lost and no longer available when the loop is finished. Thus, to display the beginning value, you would need either to store it in a different memory location (that does not change) or to print it before the loop body.

If you are going to print the boundaries before the loop, why not go ahead and place the following statement before the loop in Example 6-2?

```
Console.WriteLine("is {0}", sum);
```

Zero would be printed for `sum` if you print it before the loop. The variable `sum` gets the accumulated value from the loop body; thus, it does not make sense to print the value until after the calculations are performed and the loop is completed.

Figure 6-2 shows the results of an execution of Example 6-2 when 14 and 33 are entered as the range of values.

6

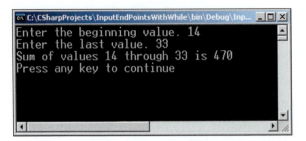

Figure 6-2   Example of output from user-entered loop boundaries

Sentinel-Controlled Loop

Although you do not always know ahead of time how many times the loop should be performed, this is a requirement for a counter-controlled loop. Another option is a **sentinel-controlled loop**. Sentinel-controlled loops are often used for inputting data when you do not know the exact number of values to be entered. If your program inputs multiple homework scores, for example, you might display a message telling the users to enter a negative value to indicate they are finished entering scores. You would never have a negative score; thus, this would be an appropriate sentinel value.

Sentinel-controlled loops are also referred to as **indefinite loops**, because the number of repetitions is not known before the loop's execution. To design an indefinite loop, select a sentinel value to use in the expression. A **sentinel value** is an extreme value, a dummy value. It is a value that should not be processed—like a negative value when only positive scores are to be processed.

The sentinel value is used as the operand in the conditional expression for an indefinite loop. A sentinel-controlled loop gives you the advantage of not needing to know how many times the loop will be performed. When all the data has been processed, the sentinel value can be entered indicating the loop should terminate normally. Example 6-3 demonstrates how a sentinel-controlled loop can be used to input any number of data values.

Example 6-3

```
/* InputValuesLoop.cs        Author: Doyle
 * Demonstrates loop for inputting values
 */
using System;
namespace InputValuesLoop
{
    class InputValuesLoop
```

```
{
    static void Main( )
    {
        string inValue = "";   //Initialized to null

        Console.Write("This program will let you enter");
        Console.Write(" value after value. To Stop, enter");
        Console.WriteLine(" -99");
        while (inValue!= "-99")
        {
            Console.WriteLine("Enter value (-99 to exit)");
            inValue = Console.ReadLine();
        }
    }
}
}
```

6

As with the counter-controlled loop, it is necessary to set up the conditional expression in Example 6-3. This must be done before the loop executes. This time the variable used to hold the inputted values, inValue, is initialized to null (""); no value is placed between the double quotes. The variable inValue could have been initialized to any value, other than -99. However, it had to be initialized.

 C# does not allow you to use unassigned values. If you failed to initialize inValue, you would have received the error message, "Use of unassigned local variable inValue," when you attempted to use inValue in the conditional expression.

In Example 6-3, the conditional expression continues to evaluate as true as long as the user does not enter -99. Notice how the input statement is placed as the last statement in the loop body. The placement is important. If calculations were part of the loop body, it would have been necessary to **prime the read** on the outside of the loop. This means that you would input a value before going into the body of the loop. Doing this allows the first statements in the loop to be the statements processing that entered value. Then, as the last statement in the body of the loop, another ReadLine( ) method is included. If you do not place the ReadLine( ) at the end as the last statement, you end up processing the sentinel value. As soon as the user enters the -99, or the sentinel value, you want to stop processing data. Placing the ReadLine( ) as the last line in the body enables the conditional expression to evaluate to false as soon as the -99 is entered. Example 6-4 illustrates this important point by summing the values entered.

Example 6-4

```
/* PrimeRead.cs                          Author: Doyle
 * Sentinel loop to sum values
 */
namespace PrimeRead
{
   class PrimeRead
   {
       static void Main( )
       {
           string inValue = "";          //Initialized to null
           int sum = 0,
               intValue;
           Console.Write("This program will let you enter");
           Console.Write(" value after value. To Stop, enter");
           Console.WriteLine(" -99");
           Console.WriteLine("Enter value (-99 to exit)");
           inValue = Console.ReadLine();    // Priming read
           while (inValue!= "-99")
           {
               intValue = Convert.ToInt32(inValue);
               sum += intValue;
               Console.WriteLine("Enter value(-99 to exit)");
               inValue = Console.ReadLine( );
           }
           Console.WriteLine("Total values entered {0}", sum);
       }
   }
}
```

Suppose the input is:

10

12

40

5

1

-99

The output for this code with the above input is:

Total values entered 68

When you implement a sentinel-controlled loop, it is imperative that you tell the user what value to type to end the loop. You should include this information inside the loop body. This is especially true if a large number of values are being entered. You do not want the user to have to guess or try to remember how to terminate the program.

> **NOTE** To tell users what value to enter to terminate, you display a message using a `Write( )` or `WriteLine( )` method before the `ReadLine( )`. Otherwise, how will they know what value to enter to stop?

In Chapter 11, you learn how to process data batched together and stored on a storage medium, such as your hard drive. Sentinel-controlled loops are useful for loops that process data stored in a file. The sentinel value is placed as the last entry in the file. Here it is unnecessary to display a message indicating how to stop. The loop conditional expression looks exactly like that used for interactive input of data. The conditional expression matches the selected sentinel value.

6

Windows Applications Using Loops

Many C# applications developed in industry today create a Windows application designed with a graphical user interface (GUI). So far, the output you have displayed has been in the form of a console window instead of a Windows form or Web page. Take note that all of the programming concepts you are learning are useful for any type of application; however, as you will learn in later chapters, an event-driven model is used with Windows applications. An **event-driven model** manages the interaction between the user and the GUI by handling the repetition for you. Sending your output to the console made it possible for you to learn the basics of programming before focusing on the interface design.

C# has a predefined **class** called **MessageBox** that can be used to display information to users through its **Show( )** method member. The output generated by the **MessageBox.Show( )** method more closely resembles the windows you are accustomed to seeing and using. In later chapters of this book, all applications are built around windows. The example that follows produces a table showing values one through ten and their squares. The results are displayed in a dialog box window instead of the console to give you the flavor of displaying output to a Windows dialog box.

Example 6-5

```
/* SquaredValues.cs    Author: Doyle
 * Displays values 1 through 10
 * along with their squares.
 */
using System;
using System.Windows.Forms; //Namespace for Windows Forms class
namespace SquaredValues
{
    class SquaredValues
    {
```

```
static void Main( )
{
    int counter = 0;
    string result ="";
    while (counter < 10)
    {
        counter++;
        result += " \t"        // Notice the use of += to build
                + counter      // the string for the MessageBox
                + " \t"
                + Math.Pow(counter, 2)
                + "\n";
    }
    MessageBox.Show(result, "1 through 10 and their "
                            + "squares");
    }
  }
}
```

Figure 6-3 shows the output of this program. The figure contains text representing the program's looped output and a title bar. The two buttons, an "X" indicating "close" and an OK button, are added automatically by the predefined **MessageBox.Show( )** method.

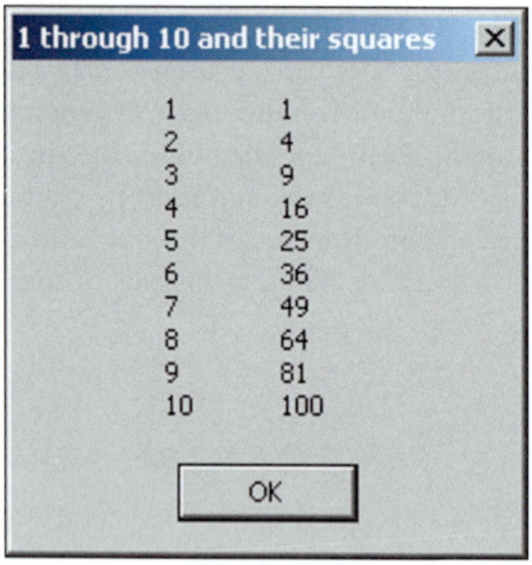

Figure 6-3   MessageBox dialog output

To use the **MessageBox class** in your console application, you must do two things:

1. Add a reference to the System.Windows.Forms.dll assembly in your project. This can be done by opening the Solution Explorer tab in Visual Studio .NET and right-clicking on the References folder as shown in Figure 6-4.

> **NOTE** Adding a reference to the System.Windows.Forms.dll will be done automatically for you later in this chapter when you create Windows applications. This is accomplished by selecting a Windows Application Project type template instead of the Console Applications type template. Adding the reference is required now because you are adding this `class` to your console application.

If the Solution Explorer is not present on your screen, you can open it from the View menu bar.

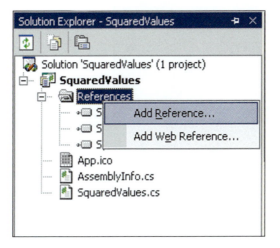

Figure 6-4   Add a reference to a project

As shown in Figure 6-5, a list of .NET assemblies appears after you double-click Add Reference. Scroll down the list and select System.Windows.Forms.dll. The `MessageBox` `class` is located in this assembly. Click OK to close the Add Reference dialog box.

Figure 6-5   Class libraries of .NET

After you select the System.Windows.Forms.dll component, you can use the **MessageBox class**, but you need to specify the full name of the **namespace** in which the **class** is located, starting at the system level. If you do not perform Step 2 that follows, any reference to the **Show( )** message of the **MessageBox** would require the fully qualified name of:

```
System.Windows.Forms.MessageBox.Show( )
```

2. By adding a **using** directive, you can use types defined in the **System.Windows.Forms namespace** without qualifying the name. The following **using** directive is added to the Example 6-5 program:

```
using System.Windows.Forms;
```

> Notice that it is not enough just to include the **using** directive; you must also add the reference to the assembly.

The **Show( )** method of the **MessageBox class** displays a predefined dialog box that can contain text, captions for the title bar, special buttons, and icons. Message boxes are normally used to display small messages, but can also be used to accept input in the form of allowing users to make selections from buttons. Message boxes are considered dialog boxes and can display and accept simple clicks on Yes, No, Cancel, Abort, and OK buttons. Using your selection statement, you can write an expression to determine which button is clicked. In later chapters, you learn to create forms for larger quantities of input. Your forms will contain text boxes, labels, list boxes, combo boxes, menus, radio buttons, and many other types of controls. For now, the `MessageBox` limits input to dialog types of controls.

The `Show( )` method of the `MessageBox` `class` is overloaded. In its simplest form, a `string` of text is displayed on the dialog box window. The call to the `MessageBox.Show( )` method in Example 6-5 includes two arguments as follows:

```
MessageBox.Show(result, "1 through 10 and their squares");
```

The first argument, `result`, is the `string` that is displayed in the window. The variable `result` gets its value from inside the loop body. Text is concatenated onto the end of the result with each pass through the loop body. Tabs and newline characters (`'\t'` and `'\n'`) are added for spacing. A tab is concatenated as the first character for each pass through the loop. A newline character (Enter key) is concatenated as the last character for each pass through the loop. After all values are placed in the result, its contents are displayed in the window when the `Show( )` method is called. The contents appear in tabular form because of the tabs and newline characters.

The second argument, `"1 through 10 and their squares"`, is placed as a caption in the title bar of the window as illustrated in Figure 6-3. As noted previously, `Show( )` is overloaded; you can include a button as a third argument. Table 6-1 lists valid options for the buttons that can appear as arguments to the `Show( )` method.

Table 6-1   Dialog button arguments

MessageBox buttons	Description of contents
`MessageBoxButtons.AbortRetryIgnore`	Abort, Retry, and Ignore buttons
`MessageBoxButtons.OK`	OK button [default]
`MessageBoxButtons.OKCancel`	OK and Cancel buttons
`MessageBoxButtons.RetryCancel`	Retry and Cancel buttons
`MessageBoxButtons.YesNo`	Yes and No buttons
`MessageBoxButtons.YesNoCancel`	Yes, No, and Cancel buttons

 Using IntelliSense in Visual Studio .NET, you can see the button property values shown in Table 6-1, as well as the options for different icons that can be included in the `MessageBox`.

You can add a button as the third argument as follows:

```
MessageBox.Show(result, "1 through 10 and their "
                    + "squares",
                MessageBoxButtons.YesNoCancel);
```

Buttons for Yes, No, and Cancel are included on the `MessageBox` dialog box.

As you examine Figure 6-3, notice the last line of output is the value 10. However, the conditional expression indicated that the loop is executed as long as the counter is less than 10. The loop terminates when the counter became 10. So why did 10 and its square print? Also, note that the variable `counter` is initialized to 0, but the first line displayed in Figure 6-3 is for a value of 1. The loop has been included again below so that you can examine it closely.

Example 6-6

```
while (counter < 10)
{
    counter++;
    result += " \t"
            + counter
            + " \t"
            + Math.Pow(counter, 2)
            + "\n";
}
```

Notice where the counter is incremented and where the concatenation occurs. Because the counter is incremented to one as the first statement, the zero is never concatenated. The last time the conditional expression evaluates to **true** is when counter is equal to 9, since (9 < 10) is **true**. Because the counter is incremented to 10 inside the loop, before concatenation, the value for 10 is printed. You should pay careful attention to the placement of the update for your loop control variable as well as the conditional expression you write to allow for normal termination.

The `MessageBox` is a dialog box. As you know, dialogue implies conversation between two or more individuals, so a dialog box is designed for user intervention. When the line of code containing the `MessageBox.Show( )` method is executed, processing stops until the user responds by clicking the OK button on the `MessageBox`. This method call is placed on the outside of the loop in Example 6-5. Placement inside the loop would have necessitated a click from the user every time the `MessageBox.Show( )` call was executed. The user would have had to click OK ten times if the method call had been included inside the loop body. That is why the values produced inside the loop body were concatenated onto the end of a string variable. Only one call to the `MessageBox.Show( )` method is included, and that is on the outside of the loop body.

The overloaded method of `MessageBox.Show( )` can be sent one of the button types from Table 6-1 and a fourth argument of an icon as shown in Example 6-7.

Example 6-7

```
MessageBox.Show(result, "1 through 10 and their "
                + "squares",
            MessageBoxButtons.YesNoCancel,
            MessageBoxIcon.Information);
```

Figure 6-6 shows the output produced when the `Show( )` method of Example 6-7 replaces that which appears in the full program from Example 6-5.

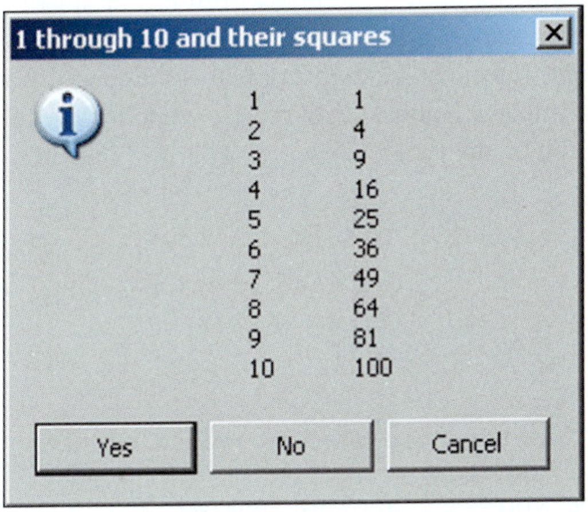

Figure 6-6   Button and icon arguments to MessageBox.Show( )

The .NET framework **class** library includes several predefined icons that can be included as the fourth argument to the `MessageBox.Show( )` method. Table 6-2 lists those you need to know.

Table 6-2   Dialog icon arguments

MessageBoxIcons	Description of symbol contents
MessageBoxIcon.Asterisk	Lowercase letter *i* in a circle
MessageBoxIcon.Error	White *X* in a circle with a red background
MessageBoxIcon.Exclamation	Exclamation point in a triangle with a yellow background
rMessageBoxIcon.Hand	White *X* in a circle with a red background
MessageBoxIcon.Information	Lowercase letter *i* in a circle
MessageBoxIcon.Question	Question mark in a circle
MessageBoxIcon.Stop	White *X* in a circle with red background
MessageBoxIcon.Warning	Exclamation point in a circle with yellow background

State-Controlled Loops

Similar to sentinel-controlled loops, **state-controlled loops** stop when a certain state is reached. Instead of requiring that a dummy value be entered after all values are processed, as is often a requirement for a sentinel-controlled loop, another type of special variable is used with a state-controlled loop. This special variable is used in the conditional expression for the loop. It is evaluated to determine when its state changes.

The variable used with a state-controlled loop usually differs from the variable used to store the data that is being processed. It must be initialized and then evaluated to see when it changes state. When it does, the loop is terminated. In Example 6-8 the special Boolean variable `moreData` is used. For this example, a Boolean data type is used; however, that is not a requirement for the variable. It can be of any type.

Example 6-8

```
bool moreData = true;
while (moreData)
{
    . . .
// moreData is updated inside the loop when a condition changes that
// indicates the loop should stop.
    if (MessageBox.Show("Do you want another number ?",
                        "State Controlled Loop",
                        MessageBoxButtons.YesNo,
                        MessageBoxIcon.Question)
            == DialogResult.No) // Test to see if No clicked
        {
            moreData = false;
        }
}
```

Sometimes state-controlled loops are referred to as **flag-controlled loops**. After initializing a variable to a value, flag-controlled loops remain unchanged until it is time for the loops to stop running. In Example 6-8, `moreData` is initialized to `true` when it is declared. Inside the loop, an `if` statement is used to test for a `DialogResult.No` value. The statement `moreData = false;` is executed when the user clicks No on the `MessageBox` dialog box. The next time the conditional expression `while(moreData)` is evaluated, the variable has changed state, so the loop terminates normally.

Example 6-9 illustrates the use of a state-controlled loop to print any number of random positive integers less than 100.

Example 6-9

```
/* StateControlled.cs     Author: Doyle
 * One or more random integers are
 * printed. User is prompted to
 * determine when to stop printing
 * random values.
 */
```

```csharp
using System;
using System.Windows.Forms;
namespace StateControlled
{
    class StateControlled
    {
        static void Main( )
        {
            bool moreData = true;
            Random numb = new Random( );
            int s = numb.Next(100); // Returns positive number < 100

            while(moreData)
            {
                Console.Write("{0}   ", s);
                if (MessageBox.Show("Do you want another number?",
                                    "State Controlled Loop",
                                    MessageBoxButtons.YesNo,
                                    MessageBoxIcon.Question)
                        == DialogResult.No)
                {
                    moreData = false;
                }
                else
                {
                    s = numb.Next(100);
                }
            }
        }
    }
}
```

One of the overloaded methods of the Random class is Next( ). Used with an int argument, it returns a nonnegative random number between zero and the argument included in the call. In Example 6-9, the random number returned is a value less than 100.

Another one of the overloaded Next( ) methods in the Random class allows you to send two arguments. These values specify the range of values for the random number.

```csharp
s = numb.Next(300, 1000);       // Returns random number
                                // between 300 and 1000.
```

The random numbers generated during one sample run of the application presented in Example 6-9 are shown in Figure 6-7.

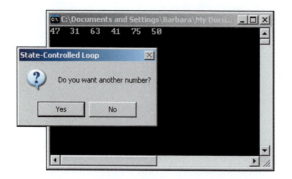

Figure 6-7   State-controlled loop of random numbers

USING THE FOR STATEMENT LOOP

Another pretest looping structure is the **for** statement. It is considered a specialized form of the **while** statement and is usually associated with counter-controlled types of loops; however, it can be used to create other types of loop structures. The general form of the **for** statement is:

```
for (statement; conditional expression; statement)
     statement;
```

The statements and expressions with the **for** loop are interpreted as follows:

```
for (initialize; test; update)
     statement;
```

Figure 6-8 illustrates the flow of execution in a **for** statement.

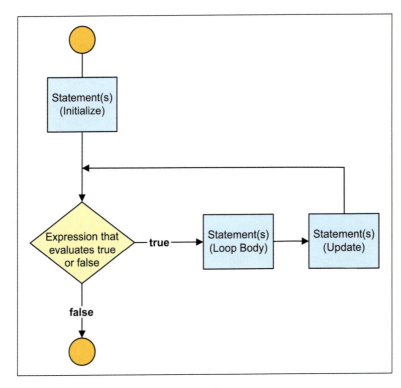

Figure 6-8 Flow of control with a for statement

6

When a variable must be incremented or updated with each pass through the loop, the **for** statement is the preferred loop structure. When a **for** statement is reached in your program, the loop is executed as shown in Figure 6-9.

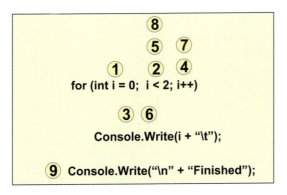

Figure 6-9 Step of the for statement

1. The initialize statement is executed first and only once.

> **NOTE**
> By separating the statements with commas, you can include more than one executable statement in the initialize location. The semicolon ends the initialization portion. Usually, however, the only variable initialized here is the loop control variable.

2. The test is performed. Because the **for** statement is a pretest loop, the test is performed before the loop body is executed. When the conditional expression evaluates to **false**, the rest of the **for** statement (the update and body of the loop) is bypassed and control transfers to the statement following the **for** statement.

3. When the conditional expression evaluates to **true**, the body of the loop is performed.

4. The update statement is executed. Often this involves incrementing a variable.

5. Steps 2, 3, and 4 are repeated until the conditional expression evaluates to **false**.

As stated, Figure 6-9 numbers the steps that a **for** statement goes through when it executes. The conditional expression is (i < 2). The body of the loop is executed twice for values of i = 0 and i = 1. When i is updated to 2, the conditional expression no longer evaluates to **true**. The body is bypassed and control transfers to the statement following the **for** loop.

The for statement is a compact method of writing the same kind of loop that can be written using while; it packages together the initialization, test, and update all on one line. Take for example the while statement in Example 6-10 that displays three columns of text for all values between 0 and 10. It displays the counter value, counter's square, and counter's cubed value.

Example 6-10

```
int counter = 0;

while (counter < 11)
{
    Console.WriteLine("{0}\t{1}\t{2}",
                      counter,
                      Math.Pow(counter,2),
                      Math.Pow(counter,3));

    counter++;
}
```

The output of this code is:

0	0	0
1	1	1
2	4	8
3	9	27
4	16	64
5	25	125
6	36	216
7	49	343
8	64	512
9	81	729
10	100	1000

This is a very common type of application. It could be rewritten using a **for** statement as shown in Example 6-11.

Example 6-11

```
for (int counter = 0; counter < 11; counter++)      //Line 1
{
      Console.WriteLine("{0}\t{1}\t{2}",              //loop body
                        counter,
                        Math.Pow(counter,2),
                        Math.Pow(counter,3));
}
```

The output of this code that uses the **for** statement is exactly the same as that shown from the **while** loop in Example 6-10.

In Example 6-11, everything is included on line 1 except the statements to be looped or the body of the loop. The loop body contains one statement; thus, the curly braces could have been omitted without any change in the output.

In Example 6-11, the loop control variable is declared and initialized at the same time. This is often done with **for** loops when the variable is used only as a loop control variable. Be aware that if you do this, you cannot use the variable that is declared in the **for** statement outside of the **for** statement. The variable **counter** only exists in the **for** block. The scope of the variable declared in the **for** initializer is the initializer, test expression, increment/update portion, and is inside the loop body. **Scope** refers to the region in the program in which you can use the variable. Trying to use it beyond the ending curly brace of the **for** body produces the syntax error shown in Figure 6-10.

6

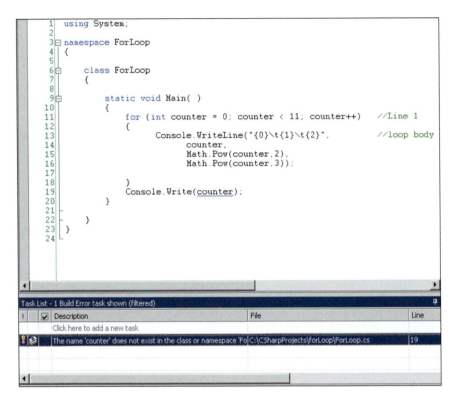

```
 1   using System;
 2
 3   namespace ForLoop
 4   {
 5
 6       class ForLoop
 7       {
 8
 9           static void Main( )
10           {
11               for (int counter = 0; counter < 11; counter++)    //Line 1
12               {
13                   Console.WriteLine("{0}\t{1}\t{2}",             //loop body
14                       counter,
15                       Math.Pow(counter,2),
16                       Math.Pow(counter,3));
17
18               }
19               Console.Write(counter);
20           }
21
22       }
23   }
24
```

Task List - 1 Build Error task shown (filtered)

!	☑	Description	File	Line
		Click here to add a new task		
❗	◈	The name 'counter' does not exist in the class or namespace 'Fo	C:\CSharpProjects\forLoop\ForLoop.cs	19

Figure 6-10 Syntax error

In addition to declaring variables as part of the initialization of the **for** statement, some pro-grammers declare variables inside the curly braces. You should avoid doing this for two rea-sons. First, with every iteration through the loop, a new memory location must be set aside for that identifier. Imagine having a loop executed 1000 times. One thousand different memory cells would be declared, but they all hold the same kind of information as that pre-viously declared. It would be best to declare variables on the outside of the loop body.

The second problem involves the visibility of the variable. If it is declared inside a block, it dies or becomes no longer available on the outside the block. C# performs **automatic garbage collection**. Once the loop is finished, the variable is no longer available. Its space is released back to the operating system for reuse. The variable is visible and usable inside the block in which it is defined. If it is needed outside the loop body, it is best to declare the variable outside the loop body.

The conditional expression is located in the center of the **for** statement after the first semi-colon. The increment or update of the control variable is placed as the last entry, after the sec-ond semicolon. This compact arrangement makes it easier to read and modify, because you do not have to go searching through your code to find the lines associated with the loop control variable.

The update does not have to be a simple increment by one. It does not even have to be a single statement. It can be any valid executable statement. This is also true for the initialize statement. You can put multiple entries in the initialize and update portion or you can omit one or both of them. The following five statements illustrate valid ways the initialize, test, and update portions can be written.

```
1. for (int counter = 0, val1 = 10;  counter < val1; counter++)
```

Here both `counter` and `val1` are declared and initialized as part of the `for` statement. Notice their declaration is separated by a comma and that `int` is not repeated with `val1`. If these identifiers are used in another declaration outside the `for` statement, a syntax error message is issued, such as the one shown in Figure 6-11.

6

A local variable named 'counter' cannot be declared in this
scope because it would give a different meaning to 'counter',
which is already used in a 'parent or current' scope to denote
something else

Figure 6-11   Redeclaration error message

The second statement shows that you do not have to include an expression for the initialize portion. The semicolon is required. When you place a semicolon without anything to the left of it as shown below, it indicates that no statement or a `null` statement is associated with the initialize portion.

```
2. for ( ; counter < 100; counter+=10)   // No initialization
```

The other parts of the `for` statement may also have more than one or no statements for expressions included, as shown with statement 3.

```
3. for (int j = 0;  ; j++)              // No conditional
                                        // expression
```

The infinite loop created in statement 3 requires an abnormal termination. As you learn in the sections that follow, either a **break** or **continue** is needed in the body or the user must terminate this running loop; thus, you should rarely omit the conditional expression.

```
4. for ( ; j < 10; counter++, j += 3)   // No initialization and
                                        // compound update
```

The last statement indicates that more than one update can be included by separating the statements with commas. Notice that no semicolon is included after the update. No semicolon is placed after the parentheses ending the initialize, test, and update expressions unless you have a `null` body loop or no statements to loop.

Syntactically you are permitted to have a null-bodied loop. If you choose to have this, do not hide the semicolon. It is best to place the semicolon on a line by itself (not at the end of the line containing the conditional expression) with a comment indicating that the body is `null`. For example, the following loop adds values 0 through 100. If the result, sum, is to be displayed outside the loop, it must also be declared outside the loop. It cannot be declared in the initializer portion.

```
for (int aNum = 0; aNum < 101;   sum += aNum, aNum++)
        ;                           // No statements in the loop body
```

5. `for (int j = 0, k = 10; j < 10 && k > 0;   counter++, j += 3)`

To include more than one test as part of the conditional expression, you must use the `&&` operator as a separator between the expressions. It is not enough to just separate the conditional expressions by a comma. Of course, the logical OR operator could also be used. However, you should be cautious. With the `||` operator, only one of the expressions must evaluate to `true` for the loop body to be executed. It is easy to create an infinite loop.

Floating-point variables can be used for the initialization, conditional expressions, and increments of loops. It is syntactically correct to write:

```
for (double d = 15.0; d < 20.0; d += 0.5)
{
    Console.Write(d + "\t");
}
```

The output produced using the floating-point values is as follows:

15   15.5   16   16.5   17   17.5   18   18.5   19   19.5

You can also change the loop control variable inside the loop and alter the execution. If you add 2.0 to the loop control variable, you change the result produced by the loop as follows:

```
for (double d = 15.0; d < 20.0; d += 0.5)

{
    Console.Write(d + "\t");
    d += 2.0;

}
```

The output produced is:

15   17.5

You can also change the value of the variables used in the conditional expression inside the loop body. Each iteration through the loop is an independent activity. If, for example, you modify the variables d and endValue, which are used as the test to terminate the loop, the loop is altered by the new values, as shown in the following code segment:

```
double endValue = 20.0;

for (double d = 15.0; d < endValue; d += 0.5)
{
    Console.Write(d + "\t");
    d += 2;
    endValue = 30;
}
```

The output produced is:

15   17.5   20   22.5   25   27.5

6

 While it is legal to change endValue, be careful, because it is easy to create an infinite loop. Also notice in the previous example that each iteration through the loop made the same assignment of endValue = 30. This was inefficient.

The **for** loop is the preferred structure used with arrays. Arrays are the topic of the next chapter.

USING THE FOREACH STATEMENT

The **foreach** statement is new to the C++/Java line of programming languages. It is used to iterate or move through a collection, such as an array. An **array** is a data structure that allows multiple values to be stored under a single identifier. Values are usually accessed in the array using the identifier and an index representing the location of the element relative to the beginning of the first element. The **foreach** loop offers another option for traversing through the array. This chapter introduces the **foreach** loop because it is a looping structure available in C#; however, the next chapter explores the concept in greater detail.

To use the **foreach** statement, a collection must be available. You have not used or seen any collections yet; thus, the discussion that follows will be brief, but continued in the next chapter. The general form of the **foreach** statement is:

```
foreach (type identifier in expression)
        statement;
```

The expression in the preceding syntax box is the collection, such as the array. The type is the kind of values found in the array. The identifier is a user-supplied name used as an iteration control variable to reference the individual entries in the collection. The **foreach** statement offers a shortcut to moving through a group of data items. With the **for** statement, you understood that it was necessary to increment a loop control variable and test an expression to determine when all data had been processed. Neither of those statements is required with the `foreach` loop. In Example 6-12 an array called **number** contains five different values. Using the `foreach` statement all five values are printed.

Example 6-12

```
int [ ] number = {2, 4, 6, 8, 10};

foreach(int val in number)
{
        Console.WriteLine(val);
}
```

The output of this code is:

2

4

6

8

10

 Note the following restriction on the `foreach` statement: You cannot change values in the collection. The access to the elements is read-only.

Do not be alarmed if you don't totally understand Example 6-12. As mentioned previously, the `foreach` statement will be revisited when you learn about arrays in the next chapter. For now, recognize that the loop body is executed for every element in the array or collection. Like the other forms of looping structures, after the iteration has been completed for all the elements in the collection, control is transferred to the next statement following the `foreach` block.

USING THE DO...WHILE STRUCTURE

All of the loop structures you have learned up to this point are considered pretests. The `do...while` is the only posttest loop structure available in C#. The general form of the `do...while` statement is:

```
do
{
    statement;
}
while(conditional expression);
```

With a posttest, the statements are executed once before the conditional expression is tested. When the conditional expression evaluates to **true**, the statement(s) are repeated. When the expression evaluates to **false**, control is transferred to the statement following the **do...while** loop expression. Notice that the loop body is always executed at least once regardless of the value of the conditional expression.

Figure 6-12 illustrates the flow of execution in a posttest loop.

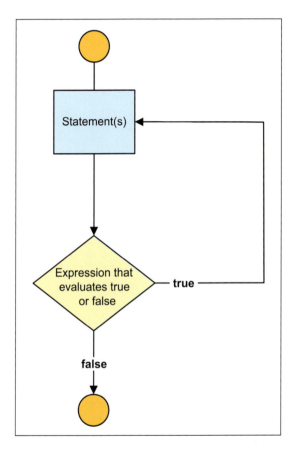

Figure 6-12   Do...while loop

A **do...while** loop is used in Example 6-13 to display numbers and their squares. The first value printed is 10. Each iteration through the loop decreases the counter by one until the counter reaches zero.

Example 6-13

```csharp
int counter = 10;
do                          // No semicolon on this line
{
    Console.WriteLine(counter + "\t" + Math.Pow(counter, 2));
    counter--;
}
while (counter > 0);
```

The output of this code is:

10	100
9	81
8	64
7	49
6	36
5	25
4	16
3	9
2	4
1	1

No semicolon is placed on the line containing the **do** keyword. A semicolon is placed on the last line. It appears on the same line as the **while** keyword. As with the other looping structures, the curly braces are optional; however, with the **do...while** loop you will not forget to block the loop body when you have more than one statement as you might with the other formats. As shown in Figure 6-13, C# issues a syntax error if you have more than one statement between the **do** and **while** without including the curly braces.

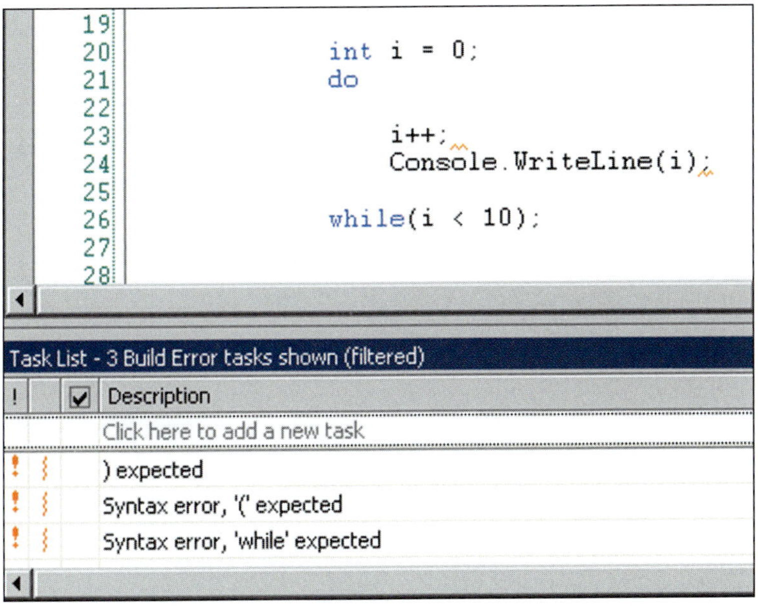

```
19
20              int i = 0;
21              do
22
23                  i++;
24                  Console.WriteLine(i);
25
26              while(i < 10);
27
28
```

Task List - 3 Build Error tasks shown (filtered)

!	✔	Description
		Click here to add a new task
!	§	) expected
!	§	Syntax error, '(' expected
!	§	Syntax error, 'while' expected

Figure 6-13   Curly brace required

The `do...while` loop can be used to implement a counter-controlled loop as shown in Example 6-13. It can also be used to implement a sentinel- or flag-controlled loop. You will see an example of this in the nested loop section. The only difference between this structure and the `while` structure is in the placement of the conditional expression. For posttest loops, the conditional expression is placed at the end of the loop body.

NESTED LOOPS

Any statement can be included within the body of a loop, which means another loop can be nested inside an outer loop. When this occurs, the inner nested loop is totally completed before the outside loop is tested a second time. You often need nested loops when working with arrays, especially multidimensional arrays, which are covered in Chapter 7. Example 6-14 illustrates a nested loop using two `for` statements.

Example 6-14

```
int inner;
for (int outer = 0; outer < 3; outer++)
{
    for(inner = 10; inner > 5; inner --)
    {
```

```
            Console.WriteLine("Outer: {0}\tInner: {1}", outer, inner);
        }
    }
```

The output of this code is:

Outer: 0   Inner: 10

Outer: 0   Inner: 9

Outer: 0   Inner: 8

Outer: 0   Inner: 7

Outer: 0   Inner: 6

Outer: 1   Inner: 10

Outer: 1   Inner: 9

Outer: 1   Inner: 8

Outer: 1   Inner: 7

Outer: 1   Inner: 6

Outer: 2   Inner: 10

Outer: 2   Inner: 9

Outer: 2   Inner: 8

Outer: 2   Inner: 7

Outer: 2   Inner: 6

In Example 6-14 the `Console.WriteLine( )` method is executed 15 times. As shown from the output, after the variable `outer` is initialized to zero and evaluated to determine whether `outer` is less than 3, the innermost loop is executed five times. The variable `inner` takes on the values of 10, 9, 8, 7, and 6. When `inner` is updated to 5, the second `for` statement, in the innermost loop, evaluates to `false` (`inner > 5`). That loop is now completed.

The `for` statement using the variable `inner` is the executable statement for the outermost `for` loop. After the innermost `for` statement is completed, control transfers back to the update portion of the outside `for` loop. Here the variable `outer` is updated. Another evaluation of `outer` occurs to determine whether `outer` is less than 3. Because it is less, control transfers back into the nested innermost `for` loop. Here the entire `for` statement is executed again. Notice the identifier `inner` is redeclared and reinitialized to 10. The sequence of evaluating the conditional expression using the variable `inner`, executing the body of the loop and updating `inner`, which is the control variable, continues until the innermost conditional expression again evaluates to `false`. At that point `outer`, the loop control variable in the outermost loop, is updated and the outermost conditional expression is evaluated again. This cycle continues until the outermost **for** loop expression evaluates to **false**.

Example 6-15 shows another nested loop. This program allows any number of n factorial (n!) calculations. First, a loop is used to calculate n!, which represents the product of the first n positive integers. If n, for example, has a value of 3, 3! is 3 * 2 * 1, or 6. When n is 6, n! is 6 * 5 * 4 * 3 * 2 * 1 or 720. One approach to determine the product is to use a loop and multiply n * n- 1 * n- 2 * ...* 1. Because this is a loop that requires that a variable be updated by decrementing a loop control variable with each pass through the loop, a **for** loop is used.

A nested loop allows the user to calculate more than one n!. The design choice for Example 6-15 is "at least one calculation should be run." A posttest loop structure is used for the outermost nested loop. At the end of the first pass, the user is asked whether another value is to be calculated. The do...while loop is used as the outer loop control. A for statement is used for the inner loop. The for loop, doing the individual calculations, is placed in a class method. This method is called with each new value entered by the user. Example 6-15 follows.

6

Example 6-15

```
/* NFactorial.cs       Author: Doyle
 * Computes n factorial -
 * the product of the first n
 * positive integers.
 */
using System;
namespace NFactorial
{
    class NFactorial
    {
        static void Main( )
        {
            int result;                                      //Line 1
            string moreData;                                 //Line 2
            int n;                                           //Line 3

            DisplayInformation( );                           //Line 4

            do                                               //Line 5
            {                                                //Line 6
                n = InputN( );                               //Line 7
                CalculateNFactorial(n, out result);          //Line 8
                DisplayNFactorial(n, result);                //Line 9
                moreData = PromptForMoreCalculations( );     //Line 10
            }                                                //Line 11
            while(moreData == "y");                          //Line 12
        }                                                    //Line 13
        public static void DisplayInformation( )             //Line 14
```

```
    {                                                  //Line 15
        Console.WriteLine("n! represents the "         //Line 16
                          + "product of the "          //Line 17
                          + "first n integers");       //Line 18
     }

    public static void CalculateNFactorial(int n,      //Line 19
                                    out int result)    //Line 20
    {                                                  //Line 20
        result = 1;                                    //Line 21
        for(int i = n; i > 0; i--)                     //Line 22
        {                                              //Line 23
            result *= i;                               //Line 24
        }                                              //Line 25
    }                                                  //Line 26

    public static int InputN( )                        //Line 27
    {                                                  //Line 28
        string inValue;                                //Line 29
        int n;                                         //Line 30

        Console.Write("\nEnter the number to "         //Line 31
                      + "use to compute n! ");         //Line 32
        inValue = Console.ReadLine();                  //Line 33
        n = Convert.ToInt32(inValue);                  //Line 34
        return n;                                      //Line 35
    }
    public static void DisplayNFactorial(int n,        //Line 36
                                    int result)        //Line 37
    {                                                  //Line 37
        Console.WriteLine("{0}! is {1}.", n,result);   //Line 38
    }                                                  //Line 39

    public static string PromptForMoreCalculations( )  //Line 40
    {                                                  //Line 41
        string moreData;                               //Line 42
        Console.WriteLine("\nDo you want to calculate" //Line 43
                          + " another factorial?");    //Line 44
        Console.WriteLine("Enter y for another "       //Line 45
                          + "calculation. "            //Line 46
                          + "\nAny other"              //Line 47
                          + " character to stop.");    //Line 48
        moreData = Console.ReadLine();                 //Line 49
        return moreData;                               //Line 50
    }                                                  //Line 51
   }                                                   //Line 52
}                                                      //Line 53
```

Figure 6-14 shows the output of running the program for Example 6-15 with 9, 5, and 3. To exit the outer loop, the character **N** was entered when the user was prompted to "Enter y for another calculation..." beginning on line 45. Any character value, other than the character y, is entered to exit the loop.

```
C:\CSharpProjects\NFactorial\bin\Debug\NFactorial.exe                 _ □ ×
n! represents the product of the first n integers

Enter the number to use to compute n! 9
9! is 362880.

Do you want to calculate another factorial?
Enter y for another calculation.
Any other character to stop.
y

Enter the number to use to compute n! 5
5! is 120.

Do you want to calculate another factorial?
Enter y for another calculation.
Any other character to stop.
y

Enter the number to use to compute n! 3
3! is 6.

Do you want to calculate another factorial?
Enter y for another calculation.
Any other character to stop.
n
Press any key to continue
```

Figure 6-14   Nested loop output

Notice that the **CalculateNFactorial(int n, out int result)** method shown on lines 19-26 contains the **for** statement used as the inner nested loop. This is where **n!** is calculated. It produces **result** by initializing the loop control variable, **i**, to n on line 22. The variable n stores the user-inputted entry that represents the factorial to be calculated. With each iteration of the loop, the loop control variable is multiplied by **result**. The out keyword is included in the method call and method heading for the variable **result**, indicating **result** does not contain a value on entry into the method.

The first statement in the **CalculateNFactorial( )** method initializes **result** to 1. During each iteration through the loop, the update portion of the **for** statement decrements the loop counter. The conditional expression is reevaluated to determine whether the calculations are finished. This cycle of execute body, update loop control variable, and evaluate expression continues until the loop control variable reaches 0. When this occurs, the innermost **for** statement is completed. This also completes the **CalculateNFactorial( )** method. Control transfers back to the outer loop at line 9, which calls another method `DisplayNFactorial( )`, to display the original value of n and `result`, the product of the calculations. After control returns to the `Main( )` method, the `PromptForMoreCalculations( )` method found on lines 40–51 is called next. It returns a value indicating whether the loop body should be executed again or not.

UNCONDITIONAL TRANSFER OF CONTROL

C# provides a couple of options to alter the flow of control in a program. You have been introduced to the **break** statement. It is used with the **switch** selection statement to provide an immediate exit from the **switch** structure. You can also place a **break** statement in the body of a loop to provide an immediate exit. If you do, when the **break** statement is reached, control immediately transfers to the statement on the outside of the loop body. The conditional expression is never evaluated again. Example 6-16 illustrates what happens when a **break** statement is placed inside a loop.

 When you use a **break** statement with a nested loop, the **break** takes you out of the innermost loop in which the **break** is placed.

Example 6-16

```csharp
int total = 0;
for (int nValue = 0; nValue < 10; nValue++)
{
    if (nValue == 5)
    {
        break;
    }
    total += nValue;
    Console.Write(nValue + "\t");
}
Console.WriteLine("\nTotal is equal to {0}.", total);
```

The output for this code is:

0   1   2   3   4

Total is equal to 10.

When the conditional expression (`nValue == 5`) evaluates to **true**, the break statement is executed, which stops the loop body. The loop conditional expression (`nValue < 10`) is never evaluated again. The statement (`Console.WriteLine("\nTotal is equal to {0}.", total);`) is executed.

For the preceding example, you would get the same result if you modified the conditional expression to (`nValue < 5`).

Another unconditional transfer of control option used with loops is the **continue** statement, discussed in the next section.

Continue Statement

The **continue** statement, like the **break**, is a form of jump statement. When a **continue** is reached, a new iteration of the nearest enclosing **while**, **do…while**, **for**, or **foreach** statement is started. Physically, it does not matter where the execution is. It could be at the top or bottom of the loop body. When **continue** is reached and executed, the rest of that iteration of the loop body is not performed. Continue immediately transfers control straight to the conditional expression for an evaluation.

 With the **for** statement, transfer is back to the top of the next iteration, which actually causes the update portion to be performed before the reevaluation of the conditional expression.

The general form of the statement is:

```
continue;
```

Example 6-17 adds and prints only odd values. When the conditional expression (`nValue % 2 == 0`) evaluates to **true**, the **continue** statement is executed which causes the loop body to halt at that location. The remaining statements in the loop are skipped and control transfers back to update `nValue`. The variable `total` is not incremented and the `Console.WriteLine(nValue)` is not executed for that iteration through the loop.

Example 6-17

```csharp
int total = 0;
for (int nValue = 0; nValue < 10; nValue++)
{
    if (nValue % 2 == 0)
    {
        continue;
    }
    total += nValue;
    Console.Write(nValue + "\t");
}
Console.WriteLine("\nTotal is equal to {0}.", total);
```

The output for this code is:

```
1       3       5       7       9
Total is equal to 25.
```

Notice that the difference between the **break** and **continue** statements is that the **continue** statement does not stop the execution of the loop body, but rather, halts that iteration and transfers control to the next iteration of the loop.

The other jump statements in C# are **goto**, **throw**, and **return**. You learn about the **throw** statement with exception handling in Chapter 11. You have used the **return** statement in your value returning methods. The **goto** statement transfers control to a statement that is marked by a label. The **goto** statement has a bad reputation. It is associated with poorly designed spaghetti code that is difficult to debug and maintain. You should not use a **goto** jump statement in your programs.

The **break** and **continue** statements should also be used sparingly. It is appropriate and a requirement that you use a **break** statement with a **switch** statement. However, when you use **break** and **continue** statements with a loop, you are violating the **single entry and single exit** guideline for developing a loop. What this means is that there should be only one way to enter a loop and one way to exit. When you exit a loop from multiple locations, it becomes more difficult to debug. The loop might end because the condition evaluates to **false** or it might end prematurely because of the **break**. This adds complications when you are trying to walk through the logic.

DECIDING WHICH LOOP TO USE

The decision regarding which type of loop to use is sometimes a personal choice; however, there are some considerations you might want to acknowledge and allow to overrule your personal biases. Remember that the body of the **do...while** is always executed at least once. Thus, you should avoid using this form if there is the possibility that the loop body should not be executed when certain types of data are input into your program. Conversely, if you know your loop will always be executed at least once, the **do...while** is a good option.

If a numeric variable is being changed by a consistent amount with each iteration through the loop, the compactness of the **for** statement may work best. The initialization, conditional expression, and update can all be located on the same line. While theformat allows for multiple entries for all three of these entries, a good rule of thumb is that the **for** statement initialization, condition, and update should be able to be placed on one line. Remember, readability is always an important consideration.

The **while** statement can be used to write any type of loop. It can implement counter-controlled loops just as the **for** statement can. The **while** statement is also useful for applications requiring state- and sentinel-controlled loops. So it is always a good option. It offers the advantage of being a pretest type. With all of the loops, you want to ensure that you understand and design the condition that is used to end the loop as well as how the condition is updated or changed.

PROGRAMMING EXAMPLE: LOANAPPLICATION

This example demonstrates the use of loops in the analysis, design, and implementation of a program. Both pretest and posttest forms of loops are included in the example. The pretest form is used to calculate individual loan details. It is nested inside the posttest through method calls. Static and instance methods, properties, and selection statements are included. Figure 6-15 outlines the problem specification.

6

Create an application that will allows a loan amount, interest rate, and number of finance years to be entered for a given loan. Determine the monthly payment amount. Calculate how much interest will be paid over the life of the loan. Display an amortization schedule showing the new balance after each payment is made.

Design an object-oriented solution. Use two classes. For the Loan class, characteristics such as the amount to be financed, rate of interest, period of time for the loan, and total interest paid will identify the current state of a loan object. Include methods to determine the monthly payment amount, return the total interest paid over the life of the loan, and return an amortization schedule.

In the second class, instantiate an object of the loan class. Allow the user to input data about more than one loan. Display in the LoanApp class the payment amount, amortization schedule, and the total amount of interest to be paid.

Figure 6-15   Problem specification for the LoanApplication example

Analyze the Problem

You should review the problem specification in Figure 6-15, and make sure you understand the problem definition. Several values are put into the program to represent the loan amount, rate, and the time period of the loan. These values are entered as `string` variables and then parsed or converted into numeric fields so the calculations can be performed.

Two separate classes are to be developed. Creating a separate `class` for the `Loan` `object` enables the `class` to be used by other applications. The `class` includes an algorithm for producing an amortization schedule. It also includes a stand-alone method to determine the total interest paid over the life of the loan.

Data

Tables 6-3 and 6-4 list the data field members needed for the LoanApplication problem.

Table 6-3 Instance field members for the Loan class

Data item description	Type	Identifier
Amount of loan	double	loanAmount
Interest rate	double	rate
Total interest paid	double	totalInterestPaid
Monthly payment amount	double	paymentAmount
Current balance of the loan	double	balance
Current amount paid toward principal	double	principal
Number of payments	int	numPayments
Interest for the current month	double	monthInterest

The client **class** that is using the **Loan class** will need additional data. As noted in the problem specification, the client or application **class** allows the user to enter values for the loan. Table 6-4 identifies some of the local variables needed by the application **class**.

Table 6-4 Local variables for the LoanApp class

Data item description	Type	Identifier
Amount of loan	double	loanAmount
Interest rate	double	interestRate
Number of years to finance loan	int	years
More calculations loop state-controlled variable	char	anotherLoan

The top three entries in Table 6-4 will be used to instantiate an **object** of the **Loan class**. After the values are entered and converted to numeric values, the loan constructor will be called to create a **Loan object**.

Constants

No constants are used for this application.

Formulas

Formulas are needed to calculate the following:

1. numPayments = years * 12
2. term = $(1 + rate / 12.0)^{numberOfPayments}$
3. paymentAmount = loanAmount * rate / 12 * term / (term − 1.0)
4. monthInterest = rate / 12 * balance
5. principal = payment − interestPerMonth
6. balance = balance − amountAppliedToPrincipal
7. totalInterestPaid = totalInterestPaid + monthInterest

Design a Solution

6

The desired output is to display the monthly payment amount, an amortization schedule, and the total interest paid over the life of the loan. Figure 6-16 shows a prototype for the final output. The xxx's are placed in the prototype to represent the location in which the calculated values should appear.

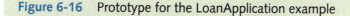

Figure 6-16   Prototype for the LoanApplication example

The object-oriented approach focuses on the **object**. The loan application has both data and behavior characteristics that can be identified. Class diagrams are used to help design and document these characteristics. Figure 6-17 shows the **class** diagrams for the loan application example.

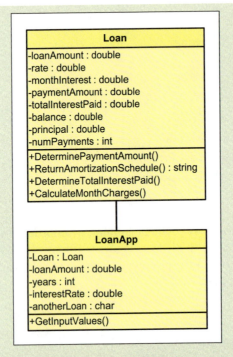

Figure 6-17   Class diagrams

The **class** diagrams do not show the properties or the local variables that might be needed by specific methods. Table 6-5 lists the data members that will have properties defined, and indicates whether both **get** and/or **set** will be needed. The name of the property is also shown.

Table 6-5 Properties for the Loan class

Data member identifier	Property identifier	Set	Get
paymentAmount	PaymentAmount		
loanAmount	LoanAmount		
rate	Rate		
numPayments (in months)	Years		
totalInterestPaid	TotalInterestPaid		

The property members `PaymentAmount` and `TotalInterestPaid` are set as read-only properties, because they are calculated values involving more than just the individual data member.

Figures 6-18 and 6-19 show the Structured English, or pseudocode, used to design the step-by-step processes for the behaviors of the methods for the LoanApplication example.

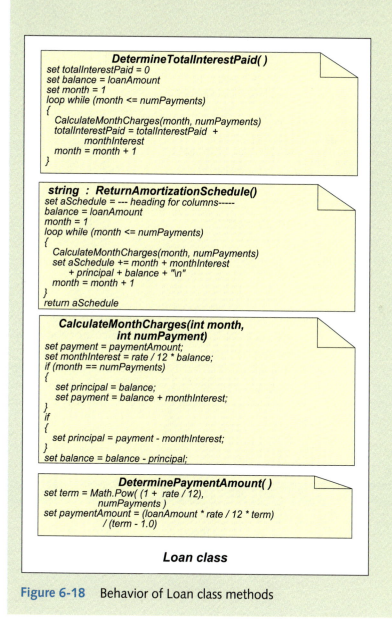

Figure 6-18   Behavior of Loan class methods

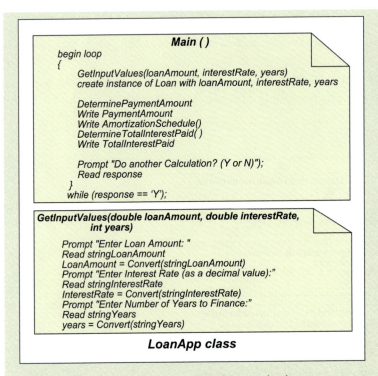

Figure 6-19 Behavior of LoanApp class methods

After the algorithm is developed, the design should be checked for correctness. With previous applications, you have been able to use a standard calculator and compare results you produce with your program against values you produce with a calculator. Sometimes you need additional resources to verify the correctness of your output. On the Internet, you can find amortization tables, and you can also use financial calculators to test your results. Table 6-6 contains values that can be used to verify the correctness of the programming example.

Table 6-6 LoanApp test values

Loan amount	Interest rate	Years	Payment amount	Total interest
50000	.08	10	606.64	22,796.56
22000	.05	5	415.17	2,910.03
150000	.055	30	851.68	156,606.06
12000	.06	3	365.06	1,142.28
10000	.05	2	438.71	529.13

Once you implement your design, you can compare these results with those obtained from your program output. This is sometimes called a desk run.

Code the Solution

After you complete the design and verify the algorithm's correctness, it is time to translate the design into source code. For this application you are creating two separate files—one for each class. The final application listing for both files is as follows:

```
/* Loan.cs
 * Creates fields for the amount of loan, interest
 * rate, and number of years. Calculates amount of payment
 * and produces an amortization schedule.
 */
using System;
using System.Windows.Forms;
namespace Loan
{
    public class Loan
    {
        private double loanAmount;
        private double rate;
        private int numPayments;
        private double balance;
        private double totalInterestPaid;
        private double paymentAmount;
        private double principal;
        private double monthInterest;

        // Default constructor
        public Loan()
        {
        }

        // Constructor
        public Loan(double loan, double interestRate, int years)
        {
            loanAmount = loan;
            if(interestRate < 1)
                rate = interestRate;
            else                    //In case directions aren't followed
                rate = interestRate / 100;   // convert to decimal
            numPayments = 12 * years;
            totalInterestPaid = 0;
        }
```

6

```csharp
// Property accessing payment amount
public double PaymentAmount
{
    get
    {
        return paymentAmount;
    }
}

// Property setting and returning loan amount
public double LoanAmount
{
    set
    {
        loanAmount = value;
    }
    get
    {
        return loanAmount;
    }
}

// Property setting and returning rate
public double Rate
{
    set
    {
        rate = value;
    }
    get
    {
        return rate;
    }
}

// Property to set the numPayments, given years to finance.
// Returns the number of years using number of payments
public int Years
{
    set
    {
        numPayments = value * 12;
    }
    get
    {
        return numPayments / 12;
    }
}
```

```csharp
// Property for accessing total interest to be paid
public double TotalInterestPaid
{
    get
    {
        return totalInterestPaid;
    }
}

// Determine payment amount based on number of years,
// loan amount, and rate
public void DeterminePaymentAmount( )
{
    double term;

    term = Math.Pow((1 +  rate / 12.0), numPayments);
    paymentAmount = (loanAmount *  rate / 12.0 * term)
                        / (term - 1.0);
}

// Returns a string containing an amortization table
public string ReturnAmortizationSchedule()
{
    string aSchedule = "Month\tInt.\tPrin.\tNew";
            aSchedule += "\nNo.\tPd.\tPd.\tBalance\n";

    balance = loanAmount;


    for (int month = 1; month <= numPayments; month++)
    {
        CalculateMonthCharges(month, numPayments);
        aSchedule += month
                    + "\t"
// "F" and "f" are the format strings for fixed point
                    + monthInterest.ToString("F")
                    + "\t"
                    + principal.ToString("F")
                    + "\t"
                    + balance.ToString("C")
// "C" and "c" are the currency format strings
                    +"\n";
    }
    return aSchedule;
}
```

6

```csharp
        // Calculates monthly interest and new balance
        public void CalculateMonthCharges(int month,
                                                int numPayments)

        {
            double payment = paymentAmount;

            monthInterest = rate / 12 * balance;
            if (month == numPayments)
            {
                principal = balance;
                payment = balance + monthInterest;
            }
            else
            {
                principal = payment - monthInterest;
            }
            balance -= principal;
        }


        // Calculates interest paid over the life of the loan
        public void DetermineTotalInterestPaid( )
        {
            totalInterestPaid = 0;
            balance = loanAmount;

            for (int month = 1; month <= numPayments; month++)
            {
                CalculateMonthCharges(month, numPayments);
                totalInterestPaid += monthInterest;
            }
        }
    }
}


/* LoanApp.cs
 * Used for testing Loan class.
 * Prompts user for loan amount,
 * interest rate, and time period
 * for loan. Calls method to display
 * payment amount and amortization
 * schedule. Allows more than
 * one loan calculation.
 * */
using System;
using System.Windows.Forms;
namespace Loan
{
```

```csharp
class LoanApp
{
    static void Main( )
    {
        int years;
        double loanAmount;
        double interestRate;
        string inValue;
        char anotherLoan = 'N';

        do
        {
            GetInputValues(out loanAmount,
                              out interestRate, out years);

            Loan ln = new
                Loan(loanAmount, interestRate, years);
            ln.DeterminePaymentAmount( );
            Console.WriteLine( );
            Console.WriteLine(ln.ReturnAmortizationSchedule());
            ln.DetermineTotalInterestPaid( );
            Console.WriteLine("Payment Amount: {0:C}",
                                    ln.PaymentAmount);
            Console.WriteLine("InterestPaid over Life"
                            "of Loan: {0:C}",
                            ln. TotalInterestPaid);
            Console.Write("Do another Calculation? (Y or N)");
            inValue = Console.ReadLine( );
            anotherLoan = Convert.ToChar(inValue);
        }
        while ((anotherLoan == 'Y')|| (anotherLoan == 'y'));
    }

    // Prompts user for loan data
    static void GetInputValues(out double loanAmount,
                                    out double interestRate,
                                    out int years)
    {
        string sValue;

        Console.Write("Loan Amount: ");
        sValue = Console.ReadLine( );
        loanAmount = Convert.ToDouble(sValue);
        Console.Write("Interest Rate (as a decimal value): ");
        sValue = Console.ReadLine( );
        interestRate = Convert.ToDouble(sValue);
        Console.Write("Number of Years to Finance: ");
```

6

```
                    sValue = Console.ReadLine( );
                    years = Convert.ToInt32(sValue);
            }
        }
}
```

Using the input values from the last row of Table 6-6, the output is shown in Figure 6-20.

```
C:\CSharpProjects\Loan\bin\Debug\Loan.exe                    _ □ ×
Loan Amount: 10000
Interest Rate (as a decimal value): .05
Number of Years to Finance: 2

Month   Int.    Prin.   New
No.     Pd.     Pd.     Balance
1       41.67   397.05  $9,602.95
2       40.01   398.70  $9,204.25
3       38.35   400.36  $8,803.89
4       36.68   402.03  $8,401.86
5       35.01   403.71  $7,998.15
6       33.33   405.39  $7,592.76
7       31.64   407.08  $7,185.69
8       29.94   408.77  $6,776.91
9       28.24   410.48  $6,366.44
10      26.53   412.19  $5,954.25
11      24.81   413.90  $5,540.34
12      23.08   415.63  $5,124.71
13      21.35   417.36  $4,707.35
14      19.61   419.10  $4,288.25
15      17.87   420.85  $3,867.41
16      16.11   422.60  $3,444.81
17      14.35   424.36  $3,020.45
18      12.59   426.13  $2,594.32
19      10.81   427.90  $2,166.41
20      9.03    429.69  $1,736.73
21      7.24    431.48  $1,305.25
22      5.44    433.28  $871.97
23      3.63    435.08  $436.89
24      1.82    436.89  $0.00

Payment Amount: $438.71
Interest Paid over Life of Loan: $529.13
Do another Calculation? (Y or N)
```

Figure 6-20   LoanApplication output

 The output is formatted using the fixed point F and currency C format strings. They are the arguments to the ToString( ) method.

QUICK REVIEW

1. The three programming constructs found in most programming languages are simple sequence, selection, and iteration.

2. Based on a predetermined condition, iteration enables you to identify and block together one or more statements to be repeated.

3. The looping structures available in C# include `while`, `do...while`, `for`, and `foreach` statements. The `do...while` loop is a posttest. The others are pretest loop structures. With pretest, the conditional expression is tested before any of the statements in the body of the loop are performed.

4. When you know the number of times the statements must be executed, you can use a counter-controlled loop.

5. An infinite loop does not have provisions for normal termination.

6. With counter-controlled loops, it is important to think through test cases and check endpoints to ensure they have been used to avoid off-by-one errors.

7. Sentinel-controlled loops are also referred to as indefinite loops. They are useful when the number of repetitions is not known before the loop's execution. For interactive input, a sentinel value is selected and the user is told to input that value to stop. The sentinel value should not be processed.

8. The `MessageBox.Show( )` method is used to display information to users in a format that resembles Windows applications.

9. A state-controlled loop, also referred to as flag-controlled loop, uses a special variable—not the variable used to store the data that is being processed. With a state-controlled loop, the body of the loop is stopped when the special variable's value is changed.

10. The `for` statement is considered a specialized form of the `while` statement. It packages together the initialization, test, and update—all on one line.

11. The `foreach` statement is new and is used to iterate or move through a collection, such as an array. It does not require a loop control variable to be incremented and tested to determine when all data has been processed.

12. With the `do...while` posttest loop structure, the statements are executed once before the conditional expression is tested.

13. A loop can be included within the body of another loop. When this occurs, the innermost nested loop is completed totally before the outside loop is tested a second time.

14. C# offers a number of jump statements that can alter the flow of control in a program. They include `break`, `continue`, `goto`, `throw`, and `return` statements.

15. When a `continue` statement is reached, it starts a new iteration of the nearest enclosing `while`, `do...while`, `for`, or `foreach` loop statement.

16. The `break` and `continue` statements should be used sparingly with loops.

6

17. Regarding decisions about which type of loop to use—if you know your loop will always be executed at least once, then do...while is good option. When a numeric variable is being changed by a consistent amount with each iteration through the loop, the for statement may be the best option. The while statement can be used to write any type of loop.

EXERCISES

1. Loops are needed in programming languages:

   a. to facilitate sequential processing of data

   b. to enable a variable to be analyzed for additional processing

   c. to process files stored on hard drives

   d. to allow statements to be repeated

   e. all of the above

2. To write a sentinel-controlled loop to compute the average temperature during the month of July in Florida, the best option for a sentinel value would be:

   a. 67

   b. 0

   c. 100

   d. "high temperature"

   e. none of the above

3. Which loop structure must be used with a collection or array?

   a. foreach

   b. for

   c. while

   d. do...while

   e. none of the above

4. If a loop body must be executed at least once, which loop structure would be the best option?

   a. foreach

   b. for

   c. while

   d. do...while

   e. none of the above

5. If a loop body uses a numeric value that is incremented by three with each iteration through the loop until it reaches 1000, which loop structure would probably be the best option?

   a. `foreach`

   b. `for`

   c. `while`

   d. `do...while`

   e. none of the above

6. When used with a `while` statement, which jump statement causes execution to halt inside a loop body and immediately transfers control to the conditional expression?

   a. `break`

   b. `goto`

   c. `return`

   d. `continue`

   e. none of the above

7. Which of the following is a valid C# pretest conditional expression that enables a loop to be executed as long as the `counter` variable is less than `10`?

   a. `do while (counter < 10)`

   b. `while (counter < 10)`

   c. `foreach (counter in 10)`

   d. `for (counter < 10)`

   e. all of the above

8. Which of the following `for` statements would be executed the same number of times as the following `while` statement?

```
int num = 10;
while(num > 0)
{
      Console.WriteLine(num);
      num--;
}
```

   a. `for (num = 0; num < 10; num++)`

   b. `for (num = 1; num < 10; num++)`

   c. `for (num = 100; num == 10; num+=10)`

   d. `for (num = 10; num < 0; num--);`

   e. none of the above

9. What would be the output produced from the following statements?

```
int aValue = 1;
do
{
        aValue++;
        Console.Write(aValue++);
}    while (aValue < 3);
```

a. 123

b. 234

c. 1234

d. 23

e. none of the above

10. If aValue, i, and n are type `int` variables, what does the following program fragment do?

```
aValue = 0; n = 10;
for  (i = n;  i > 0;  i --)
     if (i % 2 == 0)
           aValue = aValue + i;
```

a. Computes the sum of the integers from 1 through n

b. Computes the sum of the integers from 1 through n – 1

c. Computes the sum of the even integers from 1 through n

d. Computes the sum of the odd integers from 1 through n

e. none of the above

11. To produce the output

2 4 6 8 10

which should be the loop conditional expression to replace the question marks?

```
int n = 0;
do
{
        n = n + 2;
        Console.Write("{0}\t", n);
}    while (????);
```

a. n < 11

b. n < 10

c. n < 8

d. n > = 2

e. n > 8

12. What would be the output produced from the following statements?

```
int i = 0;
while (i < 0)
{
    Console.Write("{0}\t", i);
    i++;
}
Console.Write("{0}\t", i);
```

 a. 0

 b. an infinite loop

 c. an error

 d. 0 0

 e. none of the above

13. Which of the following represents a pretest loop?

 a. while

 b. do...while

 c. for

 d. a and b above

 e. a and c above

14. If you intend to place a block of statements within a loop body, you must use
 _____ around the block.

 a. parentheses

 b. square brackets

 c. quotation marks

 d. curly braces

 e. none of the above

Questions 15-17 refer to the following program segment.

```
int z = 0,    g = 0,    s = 0,       t= 0,    i = 0;
string sValue;
while (i < 5)
{
    inValue = Console.ReadLine( );
    t = Convert.ToInt32(inValue);
    s = s + t;
    if (t  > -1)
        g = g + 1;
    else
        z = z + 1;
    i = i + 1;
}
}
```

6

15. How many times is the loop body of the **while** statement executed?

    a. once

    b. never

    c. four times

    d. five times

    e. until a number 5 or larger is entered

16. The value stored in variable **z** at the end of the execution of the loop could best be described as:

    a. the number of positive items entered

    b. the sum of all positive items entered

    c. the number of negative items entered

    d. the sum of all negative items entered

    e. the sentinel value

17. The loop can best be categorized as a:

    a. counter-controlled loop

    b. sentinel-controlled loop

    c. state-controlled loop

    d. flag-controlled loop

    e. none of the above

18. How many lines of output will be printed by the following program fragment?

```
for (i = 0; i < 5; i ++)
    for (j = 0;  j < 4;  j++)
            Console.WriteLine("{0}\n{1}", i, j);
```

    a. 20

    b. 40

    c. 9

    d. 12

    e. none of the above

19. How many lines of output will be printed by the following program fragment?

```
for (i = 0; i < 5; i += 2)
    for (j = 0;  j < 4;  j = j + 2)
            Console.WriteLine("{0}\n{1}", i, j);
```

    a. 20

    b. 40

    c. 9

    d. 12

    e. none of the above

20. What would be the result of the following conditional expression?

```
int i = 0;

while (i < 10) ;

i++;
Console.Write(i);
```

    a. 123456789

    b. 012345678910

    c. 0123456789

    d. an infinite loop

    e. none of the above

21. Convert the following do...while loop into a for loop and a while loop. Did the logic change? If so, explain.

```
int counter = 100;
do
{
        Console.WriteLine(counter);
        counter--;
}
while (counter > 0);
```

22. Write a for loop to display every third number beginning with 10 and continuing through 100.

23. Write a sentinel-controlled while loop that allows any number of temperatures to be entered. The average temperature should be calculated and displayed.

24. Create a loop body that generates random numbers between 25 and 75. Write a state-controlled loop that adds all these randomly generated numbers until a value larger than 60 is generated. When the loop stops, display the number of acceptable generated values and the sum of those values.

25. Desk run or trace the following code segment, showing every value that goes into each variable.

```
for (i = 0; i < 3; i ++)
        for (j = 4;  j > 0;  j-)
                Console.WriteLine ("{0}\t{1}", i, j);
```

PROGRAMMING EXERCISES

1. Write a program that generates 100 random numbers between 0 and 1000. Display the number of even values generated as well as the smallest, largest, and the range of values. Output should be displayed in a Windows message box.

2. Prompt the user for the length of three line segments as integers. If the three lines could form a triangle, print the integers and a message indicating they form a triangle. Recall that the sum of the lengths of any two sides must be greater than the length of the third side in order to form a triangle. For example, 20, 5, and 10 cannot be the lengths of the sides of a triangle because 5 + 10 is not greater than 20. For line segments that do not form a triangle, print the integers and an appropriate message indicating no triangle can be created. Use a state-controlled loop to allow users to enter as many different combinations as they like.

3. Write a program to calculate the average of all scores entered between 0 and 100. Use a sentinel-controlled loop variable to terminate the loop. After values are entered and the average calculated, test the average to determine whether an A, B, C, D, or F should be recorded. The scoring rubric is as follows:

   A—90-100; B—80-89; C—70-79; D—60-69; F < 60.

4. Create an application that determines the total due including sales tax and shipping. Allow the user to input any number of item prices. Sales tax of 7% is charged against the total purchases. Shipping charges can be determined from the following chart. Display an itemized summary containing the total purchase charge, sales tax amount, shipping charge, and grand total.

$0–$250.00	$5.00
$250.01–$500.00	$8.00
$500.01–$1000.00	$10.00
$1000.01–$5000.00	$15.00
over $5000.00	$20.00

5. Write a program that allows the user to input any number of hexadecimal characters. Within the loop, convert each character entered to its decimal equivalent. Treat each inputted character as a separate value. Display the original hex value and the corresponding decimal value. Use a sentinel value to control the loop.

6. People sometimes give their telephone numbers using one or more alphabetic characters. Write a program that accepts a 10-digit telephone number that may contain one or more alphabetic characters. Display the corresponding number using numerals. The numbers and letters are associated as follows on your telephone:

   ABC: 2

   DEF: 3

   GHI: 4

   JKL: 5

   MNO: 6

   PRS: 7

   TUV: 8

   WXY: 9

If the user enters a letter that is not on the telephone (q or z) as part of the number, display a message indicating that the value does not match a number. Allow both upper- and lowercase characters to be entered.

7. Write a program that produces a multiplication table. Allow the user to input the first and last base values for the multiplication table. Display a column in the table beginning with the first base inputted value. The last column should be the ending base value entered. Produce 15 rows of computations. The first row should be for 1 times the beginning base, 1 times the (beginning base value + 1), through 1 times the ending base value. The last row should be for 15 times the beginning base, 15 times the (beginning base value + 1), through 15 times the ending base value. Base values can range from 2 through 8. Display an aesthetically formatted multiplication table.

8. Create an application that contains a loop to be used for input validation. Valid entries are between 10 and 50. Test your program with values both less than and greater than the acceptable range.

9. Determine what the population will be in Davidville in five years. Projections for the city's growth indicate that for the next five years, there will be a constant increase of 4%. This year the population in Davidville is 23,962. Display a table with the growth expectations for the next five years.

10. Allow the user to input two values: a character to be used for printing an isosceles triangle and the size of the peak for the triangle. For example, if the user inputs # for the character and 6 for the peak, you should produce the following display:

```
#
##
###
####
#####
######
#####
####
###
##
#
```

7

Arrays and Collections

In previous chapters you were introduced to the basics of programming. You learned about the three programming constructs of simple sequence, selection, and iteration. You learned to handle data and declare memory locations to store and access values using an identifier. In this chapter you discover how to work with collections of data that are referenced by a single identifier name. You learn about one type of collection, called an array, which is similar to a vector in mathematics or cells in a spreadsheet in that each entry can be referenced by the location of the item in the collection. You create single, multidimensional, and parallel arrays that can hold multiple data values. Using an index to reference the location of the item, you learn how to access single values and iterate through collections to process all the values. You are introduced to members of the **ArrayList class** for creating collections that can grow and shrink. You learn about special properties and methods of this **class** and the .NET **Array class**.

In this chapter, you also do additional programming using strings and learn about some of the predefined **string** methods available with the .NET Framework Class Library for accessing and modifying collections of character data items.

Array Basics

It is not always efficient to have unique names for every memory location. Suppose, for example, you have 14 homework scores. A unique identifier could be associated with each one. The declaration would look something like the following:

```
int score1,
    score2,
         . . .
    score14;
```

If you want to allow the user to input the values and compute the average, 14 separate prompts to input a score, 14 calls to the **ReadLine( )** method, and 14 parse or convert method calls would need to be written. Another option you are probably considering would be to use a loop. You could write a loop body to input a value into a memory location and add that value to an accumulator. The loop body could read all 14 values. If you use the same memory location to store the second value, the second value replaces the first value. The third value replaces the second, and so on. This seems to be the most reasonable approach. Instead of having 14 distinct **ReadLine( )** statements, you could place one method call inside a counter-controlled loop and have it execute 14 times.

If the only output needed is the average, a loop with a single variable is the most efficient way to write your algorithm. However, what if you want to determine and display how far each score is from the average of all scores? Or, what if you want to drop the lowest score? Or, what if you need all the values for additional processing later in the program? For these situations, using a single value presents a problem. The average cannot be calculated until you accumulate all the values. If all values are read into a single memory location, the first score is no longer available as soon as the second score is read. There is no way to determine how far the first value is from the average, until you calculate the average. For this type of problem, it would be best to retain the values in memory in addition to accumulating them. This brings you back to the need for the 14 different memory locations. What if there were 50 scores, or 1000 scores? You certainly would not want to write declaration statements for `score1`, `score2`, `score3`, `score4`, through `score1000`.

This is where an array is useful. An **array** is a data structure that may contain any number of variables. In the C# language, the variables must be of the same type. A single identifier, or name, is given to the entire structure. The individual variables in the array are called the **elements** of the array and are accessed through an index. The **index**, also called the **subscript** of the array, references the location of the variable relative to the first element in the array. Elements in an array are sometimes referred to as **indexed** or **subscripted variables**.

In C#, all arrays are objects of the base type, `Array class` (`System.Array`). The `Array class` includes a number of built-in methods and properties that add functionality for creating, manipulating, searching, and sorting arrays. You learn about these members in the sections that follow.

7

ARRAY DECLARATION

You create an array in much the same way you instantiate an `object` of a user-defined `class`—by using the `new` keyword at the time of declaration. You can also specify during declaration the number of individual elements for the array. The format for creating an array is as follows:

```
type [ ] identifier = new type [integral value];
```

All data values placed in an array must be of the same **base type**. The type can be one of the predefined types like `int` or `string`, or some other .NET `class`. The type can also be a `class` that you create in C#. The integral value is used to specify the number of elements. This is called the **length** or **size of the array**. This integral value can be a constant literal, a variable, or an expression that produces an integral value. Because the integral value is indicating the actual number of elements for which space will be allocated, the value must be positive. It must represent an integer, a whole number, or an expression that maps to a whole number. To create an array to hold the 14 homework scores discussed previously, you could write:

```
int [ ] score = new int[14];
```

Figure 7-1 shows what happens when you create an array to hold 14 elements of `int` type using `score` as an identifier. When you create the array, you declare the identifier type and also allocate space for a specific number of elements.

```
int [ ] score = int [14];
```

score

score[0] score[1] score[2] score[3]   score[12] score[13]

Figure 7-1   Creation of an array

The arrow in the Figure 7-1 is used to indicate that the identifier, `score`, actually references the first element in the array, `score[0]`, by containing the address in which `score[0]` is located. Array elements are normally stored in contiguous, side-by-side, memory locations. The first index in all arrays is 0.

 Java and all C-style languages use zero-based arrays—meaning the first element is indexed by 0.

Notice that the last element of all arrays is always referenced by an index with a value of the length of the array minus one. `Length` of `score` is 14; first element is `score[0]`; last element is `score[13]`.

 In C#, when creating an array, the location of the square bracket is different from C++, which includes the square brackets after the identifier. Java allows you to place the square bracket before or after the identifier when you declare an array.

C# allows you to declare an array without instantiating it. The general form of the declaration is:

```
type [ ] identifier;
```

No value is placed inside the square bracket [ ]. This does not create the array as shown in Figure 7-2. It simply defines the base type for the array and associates an identifier with it. No values are referenced. When you look at Figure 7-2, remember that arrays are reference types. Score declares an array that has no values to reference.

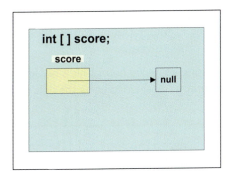

Figure 7-2   Declaration of an array

A separate step is required before you can access the array. This step is to instantiate the array by indicating how many elements to allocate. This is sometimes referred to as **dimensioning the array**. The general form of the second step is:

```
identifier = new type [integral value];
```

Adding the additional statement of `score = new int [14];` to the preceding declaration produces the same result you saw in Figure 7-1. The keyword `new` allocated 14 memory locations for `score` to reference.

 You can declare and allocate space for an array in two steps or combine the steps into one statement. When you are declaring an array that will be a field member of a `class`, it is normally declared with the `class`, but instantiated when an `object` of the `class` is created at runtime.

With the exception of the first line, which declares an integer used for the length of two of the arrays, the remaining statements in Example 7-1 create different array references.

Example 7-1

```
const int SIZE = 15;
string [ ] lastName = new string [25];
double [ ] cost = new double [1000];
double [ ] temperature = new double [SIZE];
int [ ] hmWkScore;
hmWkScore = new int [SIZE + 15];
```

Twenty-five different last names could be stored under the single identifier `lastName`. One thousand different prices of type **double** could be stored using `cost`. Because `SIZE` is declared to be a constant with a value of 15, 15 temperatures could be stored. As shown with the last declaration, any expression that produces an integral value can be used to create an array. Thirty different locations are allocated for hmWkScore.

 Array identifiers are normally defined using a singular noun. This is because you normally access individual elements in the array as opposed to using the data structure as a grouped collection.

Some languages, such as C++, do not allow the length of an array to be determined at runtime. It is legal in C# to use a variable, such as arraySize, as the length indicator. You could prompt the user for the number of values that will be entered and use that entry for the declaration, as shown in Example 7-2.

Example 7-2

```
Console.Write("How many scores will you enter? ");
string sSize = Console.ReadLine( );
int arraySize = Convert.ToInt32(sSize);
int [ ] score = new int[arraySize];
```

 In C# the length of an array cannot be changed. After it is instantiated with a length, dynamic resizing is not an option.

Array Initializers

Just as you use **compile-time initialization** with variables, you can initialize the elements of an array during declaration. The general form of the initialization follows:

```
type[ ] identifier = new type[ ] {value1, value2, ...valueN};
```

Values are separated by commas and must be assignment compatible to the element type. Thus, if the type is specified as an int and you include values with a decimal point as part of the initialization, you receive an error indicating, "cannot implicitly convert type double to int." It is legal to have an array defined as a type double and include values without decimals. This does not violate the assignment compatibility rule. You get implicit conversion from int to double.

A more standard way to declare and initialize the elements of an array follows. It is considered a shortcut to specifying the size and at the same time placing values in the array. This option is especially useful when the data will not change.

```
type [ ] identifier = {value1, value2, ...valueN};
```

The length of the array is determined by the number of values placed inside the curly braces. Example 7-3 creates and initializes three arrays of different types. Each statement illustrates a different way to perform the initialization.

Example 7-3

```
int [ ] anArray = {100, 200, 400, 600};
char [ ] grade = new char[ ] {'A', 'B', 'C', 'D', 'F'};
double [ ] depth = new double [2] {2.5, 3};
```

The first statement creates an array of four elements. The initial values are 100, 200, 400, and 600. Notice that the keyword new is not included here, and the type is not repeated. The second statement shows that the type of the value used for initialization must be compatible with the declaration type. Because char is the specified declaration type, all initialization values are enclosed in single quotes. Five elements are created using the grade identifier. No length specifier is required. But notice that this differs from the declaration of anArray in that the new keyword is used and the type is specified with open and closed square brackets. The last statement creates an array with a length of two. The value 3 is assignment compatible with the double type. Figure 7-3 shows the memory contents after the initialization.

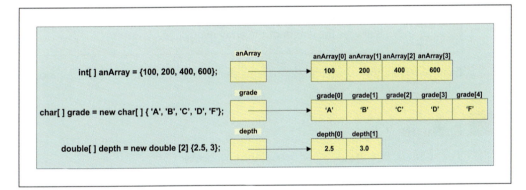

Figure 7-3   Methods of creating and initializing arrays at compile time

In Figure 7-3 the depth array is shown with a length indicator of 2, and two initial values are included in the declaration. Remember, the length indicator is not required when you do a compile-time initialization. However, if you include the length indicator, it must match the number of values included. Otherwise a syntax error is issued. The following example does not compile and generates an error:

```
double[ ] waterDepth = new double [200] {0, 3};   //invalid
```

Two values were used for initialization; however, the declaration indicated **200** elements were to be allocated.

ARRAY ACCESS

To access an array element, you must specify which element is to be accessed by suffixing the identifier with an index enclosed in square brackets. With C# the index of the first element is always 0. The index references the physical location of the element relative to the beginning element. To place a value in the first element of **score**, the following assignment statement could be made:

```
score[0] = 100;
```

Figure 7-1 shows the index values. The **score** array can hold 14 elements.

Example 7-4

```
total = score[0] + score[1] + score[2] + score[3] + score[4] +
        score[5] + score[6] + score[7] + score[8] + score[9] +
        score[10] + score[11] + score[12] + score[13];
```

> Notice that the last element was referenced by score[13]. There is no score[14]. Fourteen elements are referenced by score. The first one is score[0]. The last valid index is always the length of the array minus one.

Example 7-5 shows a better way to sum the values. A counter-controlled loop with a variable for the index is used.

Example 7-5

```
for (int  i = 0; i < score.Length; i++)
{
        total += score[i];
}
```

This produces exactly the same result as Example 7-4.

> C# always performs bounds checking on array indexes. Some languages let you store or access values outside the originally declared legal bounds of the array. This is not possible in C#.

One of the special properties in the **Array class** is Length. It returns an **int** representing the total number of elements in an array. For Example 7-5, Length returned 14. The loop control variable, i, is evaluated before each iteration through the loop to determine whether it is less than 14 (**score.Length**).

 Notice that the conditional expression that was used with the **for** statement used less than (<) instead of less than or equal to (<=). Since Length returns a number representing the size of the array, the last valid index should always be one less than Length. Thus as soon as the index is equal to Length, the loop should terminate.

If you create an array to hold 14 elements and include the following assignment statement:

```
score [14] = 100;    //runtime error, no location 14
```

a message similar to that shown in Figure 7-4 is generated, which indicates that the index was outside the boundaries of the array.

7

Just-In-Time Debugging   ☒

An exception 'System.IndexOutOfRangeException' has occurred in
DisplayArrayContents.exe.

Possible Debuggers:

DisplayArrayContents - Microsoft Visual C# .NET [design] - DisplayArray
New instance of Microsoft CLR Debugger
New instance of Microsoft Development Environment

☑ Set the currently selected debugger as the default.

Do you want to debug using the selected debugger?

    Yes   No

Figure 7-4   Index out of range exception

You receive this "Unhandled Exception" error message if you try to access the array using an index value larger than the array length minus one, a nonintegral index value, or a negative index value. This is a runtime error, not caught during compilation.

Example 7-6 creates an array to hold ten elements. Values are input, average is calculated, and then a table is produced showing the original value entered and how far that value is from the overall average.

Example 7-6

```csharp
/* AverageDiff.cs        Author: Doyle
 * Ten scores are entered. Average is calculated.
 * A table is printed showing how far each
 * value is from the average.
 */
using System;
using System.Windows.Forms;
namespace AverageDiff
{
    class AverageDiff
    {
        static void Main( )
        {
            int total = 0;
            double avg;
            double distance;
            string inValue;
            int [ ] score = new int[10];              //Line 1

            // Values are entered
            for (int i = 0; i < score.Length; i++)    //Line 2
            {
                Console.Write("Enter Score{0}: ",
                              i + 1);                 //Line 3
                inValue = Console.ReadLine( );
                score[i] = Convert.ToInt32(inValue);  //Line 4
            }

            // Values are summed
            for (int i = 0; i < score.Length; i++)
            {
                total += score[i];                    //Line 5
            }
```

```
        avg = total / score.Length;                    //Line 6
        Console.WriteLine( );
        Console.WriteLine("Average: {0}",
                            avg);

        // Output is the array
        // element and how far the value is
        // from the mean (absolute value).
        Console.WriteLine( );
        Console.WriteLine("Score\tDist. from Avg.");
        for (int i = 0; i < score.Length; i++)
        {
            distance = Math.Abs((avg - score[i]));      //Line 7
            Console.WriteLine("{0}\t\t{1}",
                                score[i], distance);     //Line 8
        }
    }
  }
}
```

7

In Example 7-6 on line 1, the array is declared and space is allocated for 10 scores. Line 2 uses the `Length` property of the `System.Array` class as the expression for the loop control variable (`i < score.Length`). This loop is used to accumulate scores. `score.Length` returns 10; thus, ten iterations of the loop are performed. The property `score.Length` is also used as the divisor representing the number of scores in the calculation of `avg` on line 6.

The loop control variable, `i`, is displayed with 1 added to its value on line 3. Here it is used as part of the prompt to the user concerning which score to enter. Instead of first displaying "`Enter Score0`", the display reads "`Enter Score1`". The last prompt displays "`Enter Score10`". Adding 1 to the index produces less confusing output for the user who does not realize that the first score is associated with location zero.

The statement labeled line 4, also part of the loop body, assigns the converted integer to the array. Line 5 does another assignment statement when the array value is added to `total`. In the loop body a single array element is sent as an argument to the `Math.Abs( )` method on line 7.

Line 8, inside another loop, displays the contents of each element. The loop control variable serves as the index to the array indicating which element to access. Figure 7-5 shows the output produced from one test run of Example 7-6.

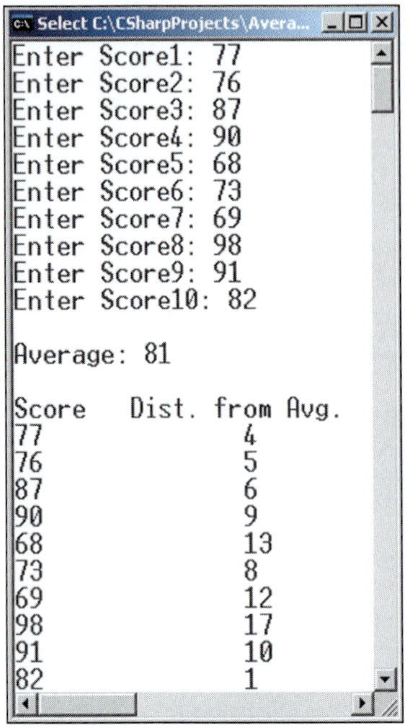

Figure 7-5 Output from AverageDiff example

Sentinel-Controlled Access

What if you do not know how many scores will be entered? What size array do you create? The size or length of the array cannot change after it is allocated. If you do not know how many values will be entered, you could ask the user to count the number of entries and use that value for the size when you allocate the array. Another approach is to create the array large enough to hold any number of entries. Then tell users to enter a predetermined sentinel value after they enter the last value. If you use this approach, you need to increment a counter as values are entered so that you know how many elements are stored in your array. The **Length** property would not be helpful for this type of application. It could not be used as a loop control value because **Length** returns whatever the array is dimensioned to hold. Example 7-7 illustrates filling an array when you do not know how many values will be entered. A sentinel value of **-99** is used to terminate the loop.

Example 7-7

```
/* UnknownSize.cs    Author: Doyle
 * Any number of scores, up to 100,
 * can be entered.
 */
```

```csharp
using System;
namespace UnknownSize
{
    class UnknownSize
    {
      static void Main( )
      {
            int [ ] score = new int[100];
            string inValue;
            int scoreCnt = 0;
            Console.Write("Enter Score{0}: "
                        + "((-99 to exit)) ",
                        scoreCnt + 1);
            inValue = Console.ReadLine( );

            while(inValue != "-99")
            {
                score[scoreCnt] = Convert.ToInt32(inValue);
                ++scoreCnt;
                Console.Write("Enter Score{0}: "
                            + "((-99 to exit)) ",
                            scoreCnt + 1);
                inValue = Console.ReadLine( );
            }
            Console.WriteLine("The number of scores: "
                            + scoreCnt);
      }
    }
}
```

7

> NOTE
>
> In Chapter 6, you learned about the importance of priming the read (placing a call to the ReadLine( ) method on the outside of the loop body) and then placing a second ReadLine( ) method call as the last statement in the loop body. This keeps you from processing the sentinel value.

Using Foreach with Arrays

The **foreach** loop can be used to iterate through an array. However, it can be used for read-only access to the elements. You were briefly introduced to the **foreach** loop structure in Chapter 6. Remember that the general format is as follows:

```csharp
foreach (type identifier in expression)
        statement;
```

The **foreach** loop cannot be used to change the contents of any of the elements in an array. You can use it to add the values of the elements as illustrated in Example 7-8.

Example 7-8

```
int total = 0;
double avg;
foreach(int val in score)
{
        total += val;
}
Console.WriteLine("Total: " + total);
avg = (double)total / scoreCnt;
Console.WriteLine("Average: " + avg);
```

The identifier, **val**, is the iteration variable. It represents a different array element with each loop iteration. Remember that the type used in the **foreach** expression should match the array type. Because the **score** array contains **int** elements, **val** is declared of that type. During the first iteration through the loop, **val** references **score[0]**. A compile-time error occurs if one of the statements in the **foreach** loop body attempts to change the iteration variable or pass the iteration variable as a **ref** or **out** parameter. Example 7-9 displays **red**, **blue**, and **green** on separate lines.

Example 7-9

```
string [ ] color = {"red", "green", "blue"};
foreach(string val in color)
        Console.WriteLine(val);
```

ARRAY CLASS

Through access to the elements using indexed values, C# supports the easy handling of arrays that other languages provide. But you get more than just indexed access. All arrays, of any type, inherit characteristics from the **Array class**, which includes a number of predefined methods and properties. Table 7-1 lists some of these predefined methods from the **System.Array class**. The third column gives examples of the use of each method. You will want to explore methods, especially those that are overloaded, using the online Help features in Visual Studio .NET. Much of the information in Table 7-1 came from that documentation. As you explore the **Array class** methods, you will find a number of other members not listed in Table 7-1. The **Array class** serves as the base array **class** for all languages that target the Common Language Runtime. Having its properties and methods available across languages provides power to each of the .NET languages, and this power is available with minimal programming. For example, an entire collection of data can be sorted with a call to one of the **Array class** member methods.

Table 7-1   System.Array class methods

Method	Description	Examples

BinarySearch
 (System.Array array,
    object value)
	Class method. Overloaded. Searches a one-dimensional sorted array for a value, using a binary search algorithm. Returns index location or negative value if not found.	```double [ ] waterDepth = {2.4, 3.5, 6.8};```
		 ```double x = 6.8;```
		 ```int i = Array.BinarySearch```
		 ``` (waterDepth, x);```
		 ```Console.WriteLine (myIndex);```
		 ```//Displays 2 (This is the index of```
		 ```//6.8.)```

Clear
 (System.Array array,
    int firstIndex,
    int length)
	Class method. Sets elements in the array to zero, to false, or to a null reference depending on the element type. Start at firstIndex, go length positions.	```Double [ ] waterDepth = {2.4, 3.5, 6.8};```
		 ```Array.Clear (waterDepth, 1, 1);```
		 ```//Sets a range of array elements```
		 ```//beginning at index 1, for a```
		 ```//length of 1, to Zero```
		 ```Console.WriteLine (waterDepth[1]);```
		 ```//Displays 0```

Clone( )	Creates a copy of the array. Returns an object.	```double [ ] waterDepth = {2.4, 3.5, 6.8};```
		 ```double [ ] w = new Double [3];```
		 ```object o = waterDepth.Clone( );```
		 ```w = (double[ ]) o;```
		 ```//Object cast to an array```

Copy (System.Array
    sourceArray,
    int firstIndexSource,
    System.Array
    targetArray,
    int firstIndexTarget,
    int lengthToCopy)
	Class method. Overloaded. Copies a section of one array to another array.	```double [ ] waterDepth = {2.4, 3.5, 6.8};```
		 ```double [ ] w = new Double [3];```
		 ```Array.Copy (waterDepth, 0, w, 0, 3);```
		 ```//Copies three elements from waterDepth```
		 ```//to w. Begins```
		 ```//copy at index 0 in waterDepth;```
		 ```//begins placement at```
		 ```//index 0 in w array.```

CopyTo (System.Array
    targetArray, int
    targetArrayStartLocation)
	Copies elements of a one-dimensional array to another one-dimensional array starting at the specified destination array index. (Destination must be large enough to hold elements.)	```double [ ] waterDepth = {2.4, 3.5, 6.8};```
		 ```double [ ] w = new Double [5];```
		 ```waterDepth.CopyTo (w, 2);```
		 ```Console.WriteLine (w[3]);```
		 ```//Displays 3.5 (copy started at w[2])```

GetValue(int index)	Overloaded. Gets the value of the specified element in the current array.	```double [ ] waterDepth = {2.4, 3.5, 6.8};```
		 ```Console.WriteLine```
		 ``` (waterDepth.GetValue(1));```
		 ```//Displays 3.5```

7

Table 7-1 System.Array class methods (continued)

Method	Description	Examples
IndexOf(System.Array array, object value)	Class method. Overloaded. Returns the index of the first occurrence of a value in a one-dimensional array or in a portion of the array.	```double [ ] waterDepth = {2.4, 3.5, 6.8};``` ```int i = Array.IndexOf (waterDepth, 3.5);``` ```Console.WriteLine (i);``` ```//Displays1``` ```//Returns -1 when the value is not``` ```//found in the array```
LastIndexOf(System.Array array, object value)	Class method. Overloaded. Returns the index of the last occurrence of a value in a one-dimensional array or in a portion of the array.	```double [ ] waterDepth = {2.4, 3.5, 6.8,``` ``` 2.4};``` ```int i = Array.LastIndexOf``` ``` (waterDepth, 2.4);``` ```Console.WriteLine (i);``` ```//Displays 3```
Reverse(System.Array array)	Class method. Overloaded. Reverses the order of the elements in a one-dimensional array or in a portion of the array.	```double [ ] waterDepth = {2.4, 3.5, 6.8};``` ```Array.Reverse (waterDepth);``` ```foreach (double wVal in waterDepth)``` ``` Console.Write (wVal + "\t");``` ```//Displays 6.8 3.5 2.4```
SetValue(object value, int indexLocation)	Overloaded. Sets the specified element in the current array to the specified value.	```double [ ] waterDepth = {2.4, 3.5, 6.8};``` ```waterDepth.SetValue (55, 0);``` ```foreach (double wVal in waterDepth)``` ``` Console.Write (wVal + "\t");``` ```//Displays 55 3.5 6.8```
Sort(System.Array array)	Class method. Overloaded. Sorts the elements in one-dimensional array objects.	```double [ ] waterDepth = {12.4, 3.5, 6.8};``` ```Array.Sort (waterDepth);``` ```foreach (double wVal in waterDepth)``` ``` Console.Write (wVal + "\t");``` ```//Displays 3.5 6.8 12.4```

Some of the descriptions listed in column 2 of Table 7-1 indicate "Class method." You have used **class** methods from the **Math class**. To call a **class** method, you prefix the method name with the **class** name. As you review the examples in column 3, notice that these **class** method calls require **Array** to be listed before the method name.

Example 7-10 demonstrates the use of **Sort( )**, **Reverse( )**, and **Copy( )** methods. Values are concatenated onto a **string** inside a **foreach** loop structure. On the outside of the loop, the **string** is displayed with one call to the **MessageBox.Show( )** method.

Example 7-10

```
/* UsePredefinedMethods.cs    Author: Doyle
 * Demonstrates use of methods from the
 * System.Array class.
 */
using System;
using System.Windows.Forms;
namespace UsePredefinedMethods
{
    class UsePredefinedMethods
    {
        static void Main( )
        {
            double [ ] waterDepth = {45, 19, 2, 16.8,
                                     190, 0.8, 510, 6, 18 };
            string outputMsg = "";
            string caption = "System.Array Methods Illustrated";
            double [ ] w = new double [20];

            // Displays contents of Array waterDepth
            outputMsg += "waterDepth Array\n\n";
            foreach(double wVal in waterDepth)
                    outputMsg += wVal
                                + "\n";
            MessageBox.Show(outputMsg, caption);

            // Copies 5 values from waterDepth,
            // beginning at indexed location 2.
            // Place values in Array w, starting
            // at index location 0.
            Array.Copy(waterDepth, 2, w, 0, 5);

            // Sorts Array w in ascending order
            Array.Sort (w);

            // Displays Array w sorted
            outputMsg = "Array w Sorted\n\n";
            foreach(double wVal in w)
            {
                if (wVal > 0)
                    outputMsg += wVal
                                + "\n";
            }
            MessageBox.Show(outputMsg, caption);

            // Reverses the elements in Array w
            Array.Reverse(w);
```

7

```
            // Displays Array w in descending order
            outputMsg = "Array w Reversed\n\n";
            foreach(double wVal in w)
            {
                if (wVal > 0)
                    outputMsg += wVal
                               + "\n";
            }
            MessageBox.Show(outputMsg, caption);
        }
    }
}
```

As documented in Example 7–10, five values from `waterDepth`, beginning at indexed location 2, are placed in array w, starting at index location 0.

The output produced from Example 7–10 is shown in Figure 7–6.

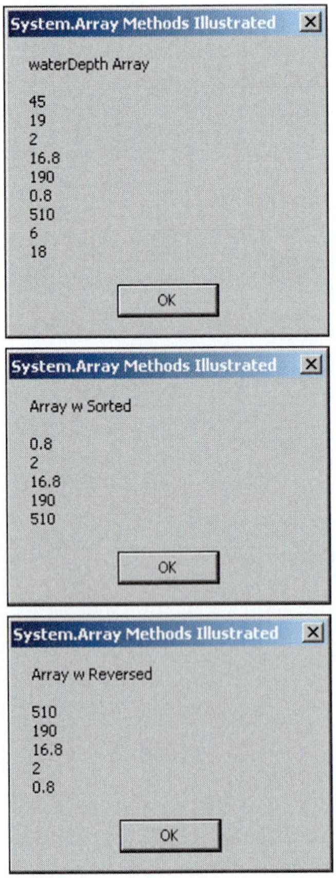

Figure 7-6   Output from Examples 7-10 and 7-12

To use the MessageBox class, you need to Add a Reference to the System.Windows.Forms class using the Solution Explorer window.

ARRAYS AS METHOD PARAMETERS

You can write your own methods and send arrays as arguments much as you did with the calls to the predefined methods of the **Array class**. As you review the code in Example 7-10, notice that three separate segments of code are used for displaying output, and they all look similar. Except for the different headings above the array, the only difference is that the **waterDepth** array is displayed once. Two other times, the array **w** is displayed. Why not write one method and call it three times? The general format used for the heading of a method that includes an array as a parameter is:

```
modifiers returnType identifier (type [ ] arrayIdentifier...)
```

An illustration of a method heading is shown in Example 7-11.

Example 7-11

```
void DisplayArrayContents (double [ ] anArray)
```

The array identifier and type are included in the parameter heading. The length or size of the array is not included. Open and closed square brackets are required to indicate that the parameter is an array.

 When you work with Visual Studio .NET, the code generator adds an array parameter to the Main( ) method heading (Main(string[] args)). This enables arguments to be sent into the program when it is first opened. When this occurs, the array identifier args can be used in the program like any other array.

Pass by Reference

Recall that arrays are reference variables. The array identifier memory location does not actually contain the values, but rather an address indicating the location of the elements in the array. When you pass an array to a method, by default, you pass a reference to the address of the array elements. The importance of this feature is the fact that if the method changes one or more of the elements, the changes are made to the actual data. Thus, any changes made to array elements in a called method change the same array elements created in the calling method.

The actual call to the method expecting an array as an argument simply includes the identifier. It does not include the size or the square brackets. A call to the `DisplayArrayContents( )` method shown in Example 7-11 would be as follows:

```
DisplayArrayContents (waterDepth);
```

Recall that `waterDepth` is a `double` [ ] array.

Example 7-12 illustrates how the output statements can be placed in a method and called three times with different arguments each time. The first call sends the `waterDepth` array. The last two calls send the `w` array.

Example 7-12

```
/* StaticMethods.cs    Author: Doyle
 * Demonstrates use of methods from the
 * System.Array class.
 */
using System;
using System.Windows.Forms;
namespace StaticMethods
{
    class StaticMethods
    {
        public const string CAPTION = "System.Array Methods
                                   Illustrated";
        static void Main( )
        {
            double [ ] waterDepth = {45, 19, 2, 16.8,
                                 190, 0.8, 510, 6, 18 };
            double [ ] w = new Double [20];

            DisplayOutput(waterDepth, "waterDepth Array\n\n" );

            // Copies values from waterDepth to w
            Array.Copy(waterDepth, 2, w, 0, 5);

            // Sorts Array w in ascending order
            Array.Sort (w);
            DisplayOutput(w, "Array w Sorted\n\n" );

            // Reverses the elements in Array w
            Array.Reverse(w);
            DisplayOutput(w, "Array w Reversed\n\n");
        }
```

```
// Displays an array in a MessageBox
public static void DisplayOutput(double [ ] anArray,
                                 string msg)
{
    foreach(double wVal in anArray)
        if (wVal > 0)
            msg += wVal
                + "\n";
    MessageBox.Show(msg, CAPTION);
}
}
}
```

Notice how **CAPTION** is defined as a **public** constant data member in the **StaticMethods class**. The declaration appears above the **Main( )** method in Example 7-12. Doing this enabled each of the method members to have access to the **string** of characters without having to pass a value for the **CAPTION** to each method.

The parameter identifier **anArray** in the **DisplayOutput( )** method is used as a placeholder for an array argument. The arrays are of different lengths, but this does not create a problem. Every element in the array is being processed using the **foreach** statement in the method. When array **w** is sent into the method, it is necessary to use the selection statement (**if (wVal > 0)**); otherwise, twenty lines are displayed. The **foreach** loop traverses through every element in the array. **Array w** is dimensioned to have a length of **20**. Without the **if** statement, a number of **0** values are displayed when no other initialization values are given.

 Zero is used as the default value by the constructor for integer arrays. That includes **sbyte**, **byte**, **short**, **ushort**, **int**, **uint**, **long**, and **ulong**; their default value is **0**. The default constructor values for **decimal**, **float**, and **double** are **0.0M**, **0.0F**, and **0.0D**, respectively. False is the default for **bool**.

Figure 7-6 shows output from Example 7-12. It is exactly the same as the output produced from Example 7-10. The last example, Example 7-12, is more streamlined. Because array parameters are automatically treated as pass by reference, no additional keywords such as **ref** or **out** are required with the argument or parameter list.

Remember, when you pass by reference, or call by reference, you pass the address of the identifier. A call or pass by value sends the actual data.

Consider the following that allocates memory for five elements:

```
int [ ] temperature = new int[5];
```

The following method could be used to input values into the **temperature** array:

```
public static void InputValues(int [ ] temp)
{
      string inValue;

      for(int i = 0; i < temp.Length; i++)
      {
            Console.Write("Enter Temperature {0}: ", i + 1);
            inValue = Console.ReadLine( );
            temp[i] = int.Parse(inValue);
      }
}
```

A call to the method to input values follows:

```
InputValues(temperature);
```

Figure 7-7 shows the result of inputting 78, 82, 90, 87, and 85.

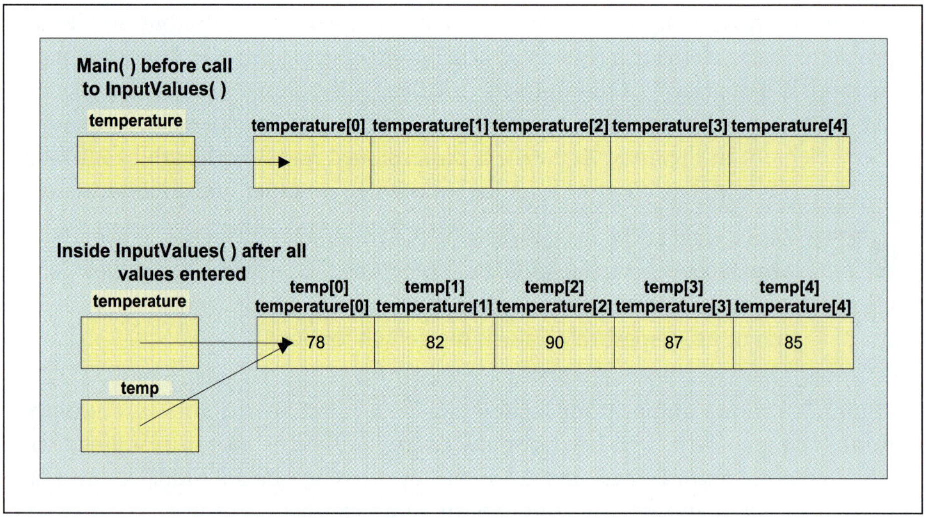

Figure 7-7   Array contents after the InputValues( ) method is called

When the **InputValues( )** method is called, a reference to **temperature** is sent.

In Chapter 4, you learned that when an argument is sent using call by value, a copy of the argument's contents is made. The copy of the values is stored in new memory locations accessible only within that method. Changes made to the values do not impact the variables in the calling module. On return from the called method, the original value of the argument is unchanged. It contains the same value it had before the execution of the method.

With call by reference, no copy is made of the contents. A copy is made of the reference (address) to the location in which the array is stored, and the copy stored in a variable. As shown in Figure 7-7, the formal parameter, `temp`, references the same location in memory as `temperature` does. The values entered into the `temp` array in the `InputValues( )` method are stored in the memory cells referenced by `temperature`.

Array Assignment

The assignment operator = may not work as you would think it should when used with reference types such as arrays. If an additional array is defined and an assignment is made, the assignment operator and the array reference the same elements. Individual elements are not copied to another memory location. Consider the following statements that could be written after the `temperature` array is filled with values:

```
int [ ] t = new int[5];
t = temperature;
t[1] = 44;
```

Figure 7-8 illustrates the result of the assignment statements. Any reference to `temperature[1]` accesses `44`.

7

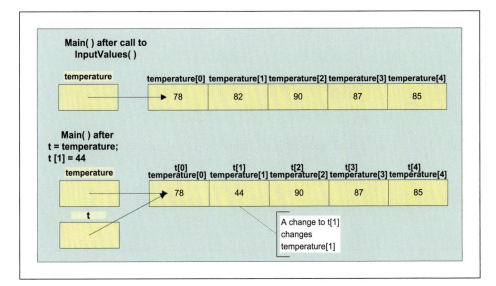

Figure 7-8   Assignment of an array to reference another array

Example 7-13 includes the complete code listing from the program statements used in Figures 7-7 and 7-8, which illustrate the assignment and use of arrays as method parameters.

Example 7-13

```
/* PassingArray.cs        Author:   Doyle
 * Demonstrates passing
 * arrays to methods - references
 */
using System;
namespace PassingArray
{
    class PassingArray
    {
        static void Main( )
        {
            int [ ] temperature = new int[5];
            int [ ] t = new int[5];

            InputValues(temperature);

            //Array t will reference the same array
            //as the temperature array
            t = temperature;
            t[1] = 44;
            Console.WriteLine(temperature[1]);
        }

        public static void InputValues(int [ ] temp)
        {
            string inValue;

            for(int i = 0; i < temp.Length; i++)
            {
                Console.Write("Enter Temperature {0}: ", i + 1);
                inValue = Console.ReadLine( );
                temp[i] = int.Parse(inValue);
            }
        }
    }
}
```

Params Parameters

In Chapter 4 you were briefly introduced to the **params** parameter type. When a method uses the **params** modifier, the parameter is considered a **parameter array**. It is used to indicate that the number of arguments to the method may vary.

If you include the **params** argument in the method heading, the array identifier it is used with must be the last parameter listed in the method heading. The identifier cannot be defined as a **ref** or **out** parameter.

The keyword **params** appears only in the formal parameter list of the method heading. By including it, the method may be called one time with a single value. Another call to the same method could send 10 or 100 values or an array of values. A variable number of arguments are accepted when **params** is included. It makes the method very flexible. Example 7-14 shows how a method defined with a parameter array can be called with both simple value arguments and with an array.

Example 7-14

```
/* VaryingArguments.cs        Author:   Doyle
 * This example demonstrates the use
 * of the params keyword. A varying
 * number of arguments can be sent
 * to a method.
 */
using System;
namespace VaryingArguments
{
    class VaryingArguments
    {
        public static void Main( )
        {
            DisplayItems(1, 2, 3, 5);
            int[] anArray = new int[5] {100, 200,
                                        300, 400, 500};
            DisplayItems(anArray);
            DisplayItems(1500, anArray[1] * anArray[2]);
        }
        public static void DisplayItems(params int[] item)
        {
            for ( int i = 0 ; i < item.Length ; i++ )
            {
                Console.Write(item[i] + "\t");
            }
            Console.WriteLine( );
        }
    }
}
```

7

The first call to the `DisplayItems( )` method includes four arguments (`1, 2, 3, 5`). They match the `DisplayItems( )` heading of (`params int[] item`). The second call sends an array as an argument during the method call. The last call sends two arguments; the first is `1500`, a constant literal. The second argument for the last call is an expression that involves multiplying 200 times 300 (`anArray[1] * anArray[2]`). This result is an integer; thus, all are acceptable arguments when the `params` keyword is included in the parameter list. The output produced is as follows:

```
1       2      3      5

100     200    300    400    500

1500    60000
```

ARRAYS IN CLASSES

Arrays can be used as fields or instance variables in classes. Normally, the base type is declared with the other instance variable. But, space is allocated when an **object** of that **class** is instantiated. Consider the following list of data members of the **Player class**. In addition to the descriptive characteristics about a player, an array for **pointsScored** is defined.

```
public class Player
{
        private string lname;
        private string fname;
        private string id;
        private int[ ] pointsScored;
        private int numberOfGames;
        private double avg;
```

After the **Player class** is defined, any number of games and associated points scored per game could be used to instantiate an **object** of the **class**. As you think about the characteristics of a player, you realize that you cannot say that all team players play 50 games or 5 games; thus, no space is allocated in the **pointsScored** array for a certain number of games. Because this is an instance member, allocate space when you construct an **object** of the **class**. This enables the **class** to be more flexible and usable by a larger number of applications.

Because one player might have played in 50 games and another player only 37, you need to know how many different **pointsScored** elements to instantiate or allocate. In addition to the default constructor, a constructor is defined that receives the number of games a player played. This is sent in as an argument from the application through **numGames**. Thus if **numGames** has a value of 10, a 10-element array for **pointsScored** should be allocated (one per game). The constructor contains parameters for all instance variables, except the average. This is a calculated value.

The heading for the constructor follows:

```
public Player (string ln, string fn, string iden,
                int [ ] s, int numGames)
```

You might think you could just use the value of s.Length to determine the number of games instead of sending in the number of games argument. Remember that Length returns the total number of dimensioned elements, even those that are unused. The Length value does not represent how many elements are nonzero.

Space is allocated for the pointsScored array using the numGames argument. The following Player member method is used:

```
public void FillPointsScoredArray(int [ ] s)
{
        pointsScored = new int [numberOfGames];
        for (int i = 0; i < pointsScored.Length; i++)
            pointsScored[i] = s[i];
}
```

Before the preceding method can be called, an **object** of the **Player class** has to be constructed. A value would already be associated with the field member **numberOfGames**. The first statement in the body of the **FillPointsScoredArray( )** method instantiates the array **object** by allocating space for the number of elements using that instance field member. The last statement then copies the elements from the array **s**, which was sent into the method, to the instance array member, **pointsScored**.

The length of **s** could not be used as a loop control variable because it does not accurately indicate how many actual values are sent into the method. **Length** is the number of dimensioned elements, which was **1000** in the application using the **Player class**. Remember, one of the goals of creating classes is to be able to reuse the **class** with different applications. The current **Player class** determines the average points scored by a player. Additional methods could be written to return the number of games played, the high and low scores, the number of games in which the player scored at least 10 points, and so on. A parallel array could be created to associate **pointsScored** with the opponent name.

Parallel arrays are two or more arrays that have a relationship. The relationship is established using the same subscript or index to refer to the elements. For example, opponent X's name might be stored in a **string** array at index location C. Then the number of points the player made against opponent X would be stored at that same indexed location C in another array. Parallel arrays are especially useful for storing related data when the related data is of different types.

With parallel arrays anArrayOne[0] is related to anArrayTwo[0], anArrayOne[1] is related to anArrayTwo[1], anArrayOne[2] is related to anArrayTwo[2], etc.

Consider the following declarations:

```
string [] firstName = new string [3]
                {"George", "Hillary", "David"};
string [] lastName = new string [3]
                {"Bush", "Clinton", "Letterman"};
```

The two arrays are parallel arrays. `firstName[0]` goes with `lastName[0]`. These two memory locations could be concatenated with a separating space to form "George Bush". `firstName[1]` goes with `lastName[1]`, and `firstName[2]` goes with `lastName[2]`.

Array of User-Defined Objects

Just as you can create arrays of predefined types, such as `int`, you can create arrays of user-defined classes. What if you had data on twelve different players? Using the `Player class`, an array of `Player` objects could be created as follows:

```
Console.Write("How many players? ");
inValue = Console.ReadLine( );
playerCnt = Convert.ToInt32(inValue);
Player[ ] teamMember = new Player[playerCnt];
```

First, values are made available for an individual player for the following: last name (`ln`), first name (`fn`), identification number (`iden`), points scored (`points`), and the number of games played (`gameCnt`). Then the constructor for the `Player class` can be called using the following statement:

```
playerNumber = 1;
teamMember [playerNumber] = new Player(ln, fn, iden,
                                    points, gameCnt);
```

Of course a loop could be designed to instantiate multiple `Player` objects. The variable `playerCnt` could be used as the loop control terminating variable.

Arrays as Return Types

Arrays can be sent to methods as arguments, and methods can have arrays as their return types as well. The following heading to the `GetScores( )` method returns an array containing the points scored list for one `Player object`. Notice the square bracket in the heading preceding the identifier for the method.

```
public static int [ ] GetScores(ref int gameCnt)
```

A call to this method would be as follows:

```
int [ ] points = new int [1000];
points = GetScores(ref gameCnt);
```

GetScores( ) is used by an application that instantiates an object of the Player type. The full code listing appears in Example 7-15. GetScores( ) is defined as a static method (class method) that returns a filled array. An assumption that no player would play more than 1000 games is made. A reference variable, scoreCnt, is included as an argument so that the actual number of games is available when an **object** of the Player **class** is constructed.

You will remember that a method can return a single type. A decision had to be made whether to return the array or to return the variable storing gameCnt. The choice was made to use the array as a return type to demonstrate how an array type can be returned. However, a more efficient solution is to send the array into the method as an argument and return gameCnt through the method name. The reason the last option is a better choice is based on the following. To return an array through the return type of the method, another array must be declared and space allocated locally for it in the method. This additional space for the size of the array is unnecessary if the array is sent as an argument because arrays are always passed by reference. Sending the array as an argument passes the address of the one declared in the calling method and eliminates the need to declare a local array.

Example 7-15 contains a listing of the Player application. It consists of two files. The first file describes characteristics of a Player. The second file is an application instantiating an array of Player objects. In addition to storing information about multiple Player objects, this file contains code to access the Player members. Player **class** is listed first.

Example 7-15

```
/* Player.cs      Author:  Doyle
 * Creates class with characteristics
 * about one player. Includes name
 * and ID fields, plus points scored.
 * Any number of games can be used
 * to instantiate an object of this class.
 * Average calculated based on the
 * number of points associated with
 * one player.
 */
using System;
namespace PlayerApp
{
    public class Player
    {
        private string lname;
        private string fname;
        private string id;
        private int[ ] pointsScored;
        private int numberOfGames;
        private double avg;
```

```csharp
// Default constructor
public Player( )
{
}

// Constructor accepts any size
// pointsScored array.
public Player (string ln, string fn,
          string iden,  int [ ] s, int numGames)
{
    numberOfGames = numGames;
    FillPointsScoredArray(s);
    ComputeAverage( );
    lname = ln;
    fname = fn;
    id = iden;
}

// Property returning calculated average
public double Average
{
    get
    {
        return avg;
    }
}

public string FName
{
    get
    {
        return fname;
    }
    set
    {
        fname = value;
    }
}

public string LName
{
    get
    {
        return lname;
    }
```

```
            set
            {
                lname = value;
            }
        }

        public string ID
        {
            get
            {
                return id;
            }
            set
            {
                id = value;
            }
        }

        public void FillPointsScoredArray(int [ ] s)
        {
            pointsScored = new int [numberOfGames];
            for (int i = 0; i < pointsScored.Length; i++)
                pointsScored[i] = s[i];
        }

        public void ComputeAverage( )
        {
            int total = 0;

            foreach(int s in pointsScored)
                total += s;
            if(pointsScored.Length > 0)
                avg = total / pointsScored.Length;
        }
    }
}
/*PlayerApp.cs      Author: Doyle
 * Application that instantiates
 * Player class. Creates an array
 * of player objects that can be
 * used to display individual
 * records or do stats
 * on the entire team.
 */
```

7

```csharp
using System;
namespace PlayerApp
{
    class PlayerApp
    {
        static void Main()
        {
            string ln,
                   fn,
                   iden;
            string inValue;

            int playerCnt,
                loopCnt = 0,
                gameCnt;
            int [ ] points = new int [1000];

            Console.Write("How many players? ");
            inValue = Console.ReadLine( );
            playerCnt = Convert.ToInt32(inValue);

            Player[ ] teamMember = new Player[playerCnt];
            while(loopCnt < playerCnt)
            {
                GetIdInfo(out ln, out fn, out iden);
                gameCnt = 0;
                points = GetScores(ref gameCnt);
                teamMember [loopCnt] = new Player(ln, fn, iden,
                                                 points, gameCnt);

                loopCnt++;
            }
            DisplayStats(teamMember);
        }

        public static int [ ] GetScores(ref int gameCnt)
        {
            int [ ] points = new int [1000];
            string inValue;

            Console.Write("Game {0}: "
                        + "((-99 to exit)) ",
                          gameCnt + 1);
            inValue = Console.ReadLine( );
```

```
            while(inValue != "-99")
            {
                points[gameCnt] = Convert.ToInt32(inValue);
                ++gameCnt;
                Console.Write("Game {0}: "
                                + "((-99 to exit)) ",
                                gameCnt + 1);
                inValue = Console.ReadLine( );
            }
        return points;
        }

        public static void GetIdInfo(out string ln,
                            out string fn, out string iden)
        {
            Console.WriteLine( );
            Console.Write("Player First Name: ");
            fn = Console.ReadLine( );
            Console.Write("Player Last Name: ");
            ln = Console.ReadLine( );
            Console.Write("Player ID Number: ");
            iden = Console.ReadLine( );
        }

        public static void DisplayStats(Player[ ]teamMember)
        {
            Console.WriteLine();
            Console.WriteLine("Player\t\tAvg Points ");
            Console.WriteLine("----------------------------");
            foreach(Player pl in teamMember)
            {
                Console.Write("{0} {1}\t", pl.FName, pl.LName);
                Console.WriteLine("{0}", pl.Average);
            }
        }
    }
}
```

7

Remember that the properties with the sets and gets are added to enable client applications to access the **private** data members. By including them in your programs, you make your classes more usable.

The output from one test run of **PlayerApp** is shown in Figure 7-9.

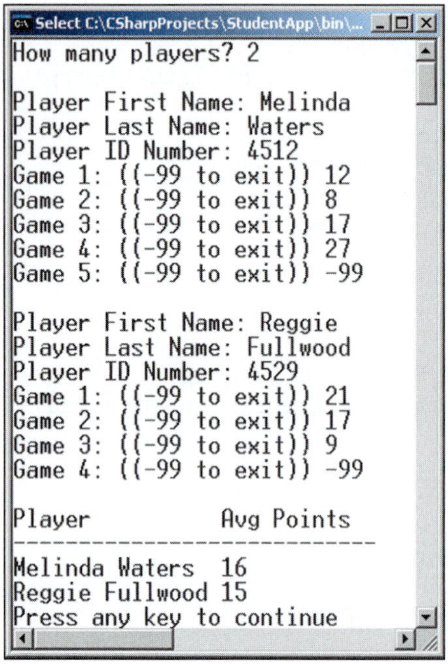

Figure 7-9 PlayerApp output

Notice how Reggie Fullwood ended up with whole numbers (integers) representing his average points. If you do the arithmetic ((21 + 17 + 9) / 3 = 15.666666667), you would think that a different result would be produced. As you examine Example 7-15, you should observe that the result is stored in a `double`, but integer division was performed in the `ComputeAverage( )` method when an `int` (`total`) was divided by an `int` (`pointsScored.Length`). The result is an `int`. It is then assigned to a `double`. In order to produce a floating-point result, one of those variables should have been cast to a `double`, that is ((`double`) `total` / `pointsScored.Length`).

Figure 7-10 shows how the data from **PlayerApp** is represented in memory.

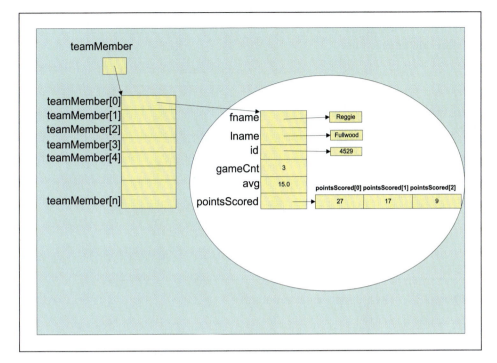

Figure 7-10   PlayerApp memory representation

As you review the figure, note the difference between value types such as `avg` and `gameCnt`. Array **objects** and **string** types contain a reference to the location of the stored values.

TWO-DIMENSIONAL ARRAYS

One-dimensional arrays are useful for storing lists of data. Because the data is stored in contiguous memory locations, elements are referenced by an index representing the location relative to the beginning element of the array. Two-dimensional and other multidimensional arrays follow the same guidelines you learned with one-dimensional arrays. Two kinds of two-dimensional arrays can be created using C#. Rectangular is the first type, and this type is supported by most languages. The second type is called a jagged or ragged array. Two-dimensional arrays are referenced much like you reference a matrix.

Rectangular Array

A **rectangular two-dimensional array** is usually visualized as a table divided into rows and columns. Much like a spreadsheet in which the rows and columns intersect, data is stored in individual cells. Figure 7-11 shows a table you might create to store calories consumed for a seven-day period. The table contains three columns and seven rows. Each cell holds one integer value.

Calories consumed	Breakfast	Lunch	Dinner
Sunday	900	750	1020
Monday	300	1000	2700
Tuesday	500	700	2100
Wednesday	400	900	1780
Thursday	600	1200	1100
Friday	575	1150	1900
Saturday	600	1020	1700

Figure 7-11   Two-dimensional structure

A structure can be created in memory to hold these values using a two-dimensional array. The format for creating such a data structure is:

```
type [ , ] identifier = new type [integral value, integral value];
```

As was a requirement for a one-dimensional array, all data values placed in a two-dimensional array must be of the same base type. Two integral values are required for a two-dimensional array. These values specify the number of rows and columns for allocating storage to be referenced by the identifier name. To create an array in C# to hold the data from Figure 7-11 you write:

```
int [ , ] calories = new int[7, 3];
```

This allocates storage for 21 elements. The first index represents the number of rows; the second represents the number of columns. Notice how a comma is used as a separator between the row and column for both the declaration base type and again to separate the number of rows and columns.

 You will receive a syntax error if you try to use the C-style method for two-dimensional array declaration. The following is not permitted in C#: `int anArray[ ] [ ].`

Just as with one-dimensional arrays, you can perform compile-time initialization of the elements. C# is a **row major language**, meaning data is stored in contiguous memory locations by row. All elements from row 0 are placed in memory first followed by all elements from row 1, and so on. To initialize the calories array with the values shown in Figure 7-11 you write:

```
int [,] calories = {{900, 750, 1020}, {300, 1000, 2700},
                    {500, 700, 2100}, {400, 900, 1780},
                    {600, 1200, 1100}, {575, 1150, 1900},
                    {600, 1020, 1700}};
```

Notice how each row is grouped using curly braces. A comma is used to separate rows. You receive a syntax error if you use curly braces indicating you have an "incorrectly structured array initializer". Figure 7-12 further illustrates the result of the preceding statement.

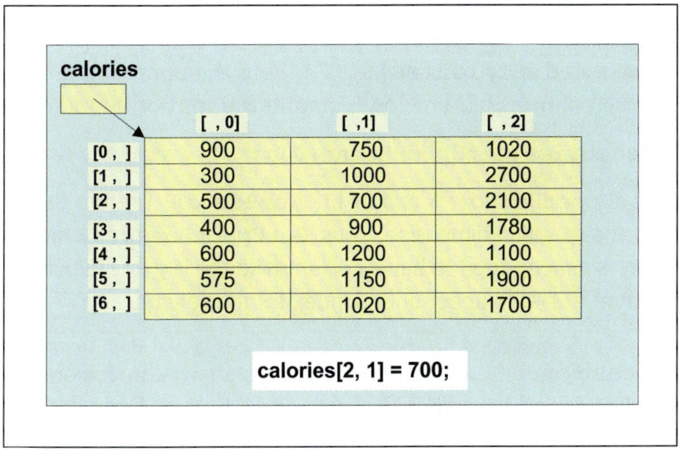

calories

	[,0]	[,1]	[,2]
[0 ,]	900	750	1020
[1 ,]	300	1000	2700
[2 ,]	500	700	2100
[3 ,]	400	900	1780
[4 ,]	600	1200	1100
[5 ,]	575	1150	1900
[6 ,]	600	1020	1700

calories[2, 1] = 700;

Figure 7-12   Two-dimensional calories array

> Data is not really stored in memory in a table such as this. Values are stored side by side in contiguous memory locations using a row major format.

The identifier `calories` contains a reference to `calories[0, 0]`. The `Length` property can be used with multidimensional arrays to get the total number of elements in all dimensions. The following statement displays 21:

```
Console.WriteLine(calories.Length);   // Length used here returns 21
```

Another useful member of the **Array class** is the `GetLength()` method. It can be called to return the number of rows or columns. Arrays are also zero based for specifying their dimensions. With a two-dimensional array, the first dimension (indexed by 0) represents the number of rows and the second dimension (indexed by 1) represents the number of columns. `GetLength(0)` returns the number of rows and `GetLength(1)` returns the number of columns, as shown in the following code segment:

```
Console.WriteLine(calories.GetLength(1)); // displays 3 (columns)
Console.WriteLine(calories.GetLength(0)); // displays 7 (rows)
Console.WriteLine(calories.Rank);         // returns 2 (dimensions)
```

 The property `Rank` returns the number of dimensions of the array.

You can also get the upper bounds index using another **Array class** member. With the array dimensioned as

```
int [ , ] calories = new int [7, 3];
```

the last element (1700) is located at `calories[6, 2]`. Thus the upper bound for the row is 6. The upper bound for the column is 2. The lower bound is 0 for both dimensions.

```
Console.WriteLine(calories.GetUpperBound(0)); // returns 6  (row)
```

 The methods `GetUpperBound( )` and `GetLowerBound( )` return the upper or lower bounds of the specified dimension. Thus, `GetUpperBound(1)` returns 2 because the array is dimensioned to have 3 columns so the largest index that could be used for the column is 2—the upper bound index for the column.

The **foreach** loop structure can be used to iterate through a two-dimensional array. Using the same format as noted previously, an identifier of the base type is defined. To display each of the values from the two-dimensional array, a **foreach** loop could be used as follows:

```
foreach (int cal in calories)
       Console.Write(cal + " ");
```

The output produced is in row major format—meaning every element in row 0 is printed before any element from row 1, as follows:

900 750 1020 300 1000 2700 500 700 2100 400 900 1780 600 1200 1100 575 1150 1900 600 1020 1700

 You do not get the whole collection printed if you type `Console.Write(calories);` instead the `ToString( )` method of the **object class** is called. `ToString( )` is defined in the **object class** to return an object's type. Thus, you would get `System.Int32[ ]` printed if you typed `Console.Write(calories)`.

The `foreach` loop is used for read-only access. To change values you need a different loop with two indexes. To clear each cell, you could write:

```
for (int r = 0; r < calories.GetLength(0); r++)
    for (int c = 0; c < calories.GetLength(1); c++)
        calories[r, c] = 0;
```

The nested loop body is executed 21 times. During the last iteration through the loop body, r has a value of six, and c has a value of two.

Jagged Array

When the number of columns in the rows must differ, a jagged, or **ragged array** can be created. **Jagged arrays** differ from rectangular arrays in that rectangular arrays always have a rectangular shape, like a table. Jagged arrays are called "**arrays of arrays.**" One row might have five columns; another row 50 columns. To create a jagged array, you can create a one-dimensional array of type **Array**, and initialize each of the one-dimensional arrays separately. Example 7-16 illustrates the creation of a jagged array.

7

Example 7-16

```
int[ ] [ ] anArray = new int[4] [ ];
anArray [0] = new int[] {100, 200};
anArray [1] = new int[] {11, 22, 37};
anArray [2] = new int[] {16, 72, 83, 99, 106};
anArray [3] = new int[] {1, 2, 3, 4};
```

The `GetLength( )`, `GetUpperBound( )`, and `GetLowerBound( )` methods can be used with jagged arrays. Jagged arrays are used exactly like rectangular arrays, except that rows may have a different number of elements.

MULTIDIMENSIONAL ARRAYS

You are really only limited by your imagination as far as the number of dimensions for which you can allocate arrays in C#. The major requirement is the fact that all data values placed in an array must be of the same base type. A two-dimensional array is actually a multidimensional array; however, it is such a common type of structure that it often is put in its own category.

To declare a three-dimensional array, three integral values are used. They specify the number of planes, rows, and columns to set aside for the array. As with single-dimensional arrays, three-dimensional arrays are referenced by the identifier name.

The format for creating a three-dimensional array is:

```
type [ , , ] identifier =
          new type [integral value, integral value, integral value];
```

What if you wanted to create the **calories** table to hold four weeks of statistics? A three-dimensional array could be defined to hold the data. The first dimension could represent the number of weeks, the second the number of days, and the third the number of meals. To create the array in C# to hold that extra data, you write:

```
int [ , , ] calories = new int [4, 7, 3];
```

Figure 7-13 shows what the array would look like.

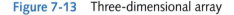

	calories			
		[,,0]	[,,1]	[,,2]
	[,0,]	900	750	1020
	[,1,]	300	1000	2700
	[,2,]	500	700	2100
[0, ,]	[,3,]	400	900	1780
	[,4,]	600	1200	1100
	[,5,]	575	1150	1900
	[,6,]	600	1020	1700
		[,,0]	[,,1]	[,,2]
	[,0,]	890	1900	785
	[,1,]	450	1000	2005
	[,2,]	400	1200	2100
[1, ,]	[,3,]	400	900	1780
	[,4,]	600	1200	1500
	[,5,]	500	750	1900
	[,6,]	600	890	1200
		[,,0]	[,,1]	[,,2]
	[,0,]	850	750	1350
	[,1,]	300	1000	2330
	[,2,]	350	800	2100
[2, ,]	[,3,]	400	900	1080
	[,4,]	600	1250	1100
	[,5,]	575	1000	2140
	[,6,]	500	870	1600
		[,,0]	[,,1]	[,,2]
	[,0,]	500	1500	1020
	[,1,]	400	1100	2700
	[,2,]	170	700	2100
[3, ,]	[,3,]	400	1240	1780
	[,4,]	600	1100	1100
	[,5,]	575	1150	1750
	[,6,]	575	1500	2100

calories[1,1,2] = 2005;

Figure 7-13   Three-dimensional array

This allocates storage for 84 elements (4 * 7 * 3). You will notice that the upper bounds on the indexes are 3, 6, and 2; the lower bound is 0 for all three.

An additional column could be added to the array to hold the total calories for each day by dimensioning the array as follows:

```
int [ , , ] calories = new int [4, 7, 4];
// Loop to place the row total in the last column, indexed by 3
for (int wk = 0; wk < calories.GetLength(0); wk++)
{
    for (int da = 0; da < calories.GetLength(1); da++)
    {
        for (int ml = 0; ml < calories.GetLength(2) - 1; ml++)
        {
            calories [wk, da, 3] += calories [wk, da, ml];
        }
    }
}
```

7

 Reexamine the first line in the preceding code segment, and note that the dimension representing the number of columns was changed from 3 to 4. This enables the total calories for each row to be stored in this column.

The length integral value of the last dimension was changed from 3 to 4 to hold the total per day. Now each row has the meal count for breakfast, lunch, and dinner, and the total count.

The nested loop adds columns indexed with 0 through 2 of each row and stores the result in the column indexed by 3. The conditional expression of the innermost loop uses (`calories.GetLength(2)` - 1) for the evaluation. `GetLength(2)` returns the length of the third dimension, or rank. This returns 4 because there are now 4 columns in the row. But notice that 1 is subtracted from that value, because the last column should not be added. It is holding the total. Thus the loop is executed for `ml` = 0, `ml` = 1, and `ml` = 2. When `ml` is equal to 3, `ml` is no longer less than 3 (`ml` < `calories.GetLength(2)` - 1), and the inner loop is complete for that iteration.

`calories.GetLength(0)` returns the dimension for the number of planes or weeks. It returns 4. `GetLength(1)` returns the dimension for the number of rows per plane or days per week. It returns 7. As was noted, `GetLength(2)` returns the dimension for the number of columns per row or meals per day. It returns 4. The program listing for the calorie counter application is included as Example 7-17.

Example 7-17

```
/* CalorieCounter.cs     Author:  Doyle
 * Demonstrates multidimensional array
 * through a calorie counter program.
 * Initializes array with values.
 * Accumulates calories per day and
 * displays report by day.
 */
using System;
namespace CalorieCounter
{
    class CalorieCounter
    {
        static void Main( )
        {
            int [, ,] calories = { { {900, 750, 1020, 0},
                                     {300, 1000, 2700, 0},
                                     {500, 700, 2100, 0},
                                     {400, 900, 1780, 0},
                                     {600, 1200, 1100, 0},
                                     {575, 1150, 1900, 0},
                                     {600, 1020, 1700, 0}  },

                                   { {890, 1900, 785, 0},
                                     {450, 1000, 2005, 0},
                                     {400, 1200, 2100, 0},
                                     {400, 900, 1780, 0},
                                     {600, 1200, 1500, 0},
                                     {500, 750, 1900, 0},
                                     {600, 890, 1200, 0}   },

                                   { {850, 750, 1350, 0},
                                     {300, 1000, 2330, 0},
                                     {350, 800, 2100, 0},
                                     {400, 900, 1080, 0},
                                     {600, 1250, 1100, 0},
                                     {575, 1000, 2140, 0},
                                     {600, 870, 1600, 0}   },

                                   { {500, 1500, 1020, 0},
                                     {400, 1100, 2700, 0},
                                     {170, 700, 2100, 0},
                                     {400, 1240, 1780, 0},
```

```
                                    {600, 1100, 1100, 0},
                                    {575, 1150, 1750, 0},
                                    {575, 1500, 2100, 0}  }  };
        AccumulateCalories(calories);
        DisplayTotals(calories);
    }

    public static void AccumulateCalories(int [, ,] calories)
    {

        for (int wk = 0; wk < calories.GetLength(0); wk++)
            for (int da = 0; da < calories.GetLength(1); da++)
                for (int ml = 0;
                        ml < calories.GetLength(2) - 1; ml++)
                    calories [wk, da, 3] +=
                                calories [wk, da, ml];
    }

    public static void DisplayTotals(int [, ,] calories)
    {
        string [ ] dayName = {"Sun", "Mon", "Tue",
                              "Wed", "Thr", "Fri",
                              "Sat"};

        Console.WriteLine("Week#\tDay#\tTotalCalories");
        for (int wk = 0; wk < calories.GetLength(0); wk++)
            for (int da = 0; da < calories.GetLength(1); da++)
                Console.WriteLine("{0}\t{1}\t{2}",
                                    wk + 1,
                                    dayName[da],
                                    calories [wk,  da, 3]);

    }
  }
}
```

7

The display from this listing includes the name of the day instead of the day number. A selection statement could have been used to test the day number and print the value. A much more efficient solution is to use the index from the calories array for the day number as the index to another one-dimensional **string** array holding the day names. This is illustrated in Example 7-17. Figure 7-14 shows the output.

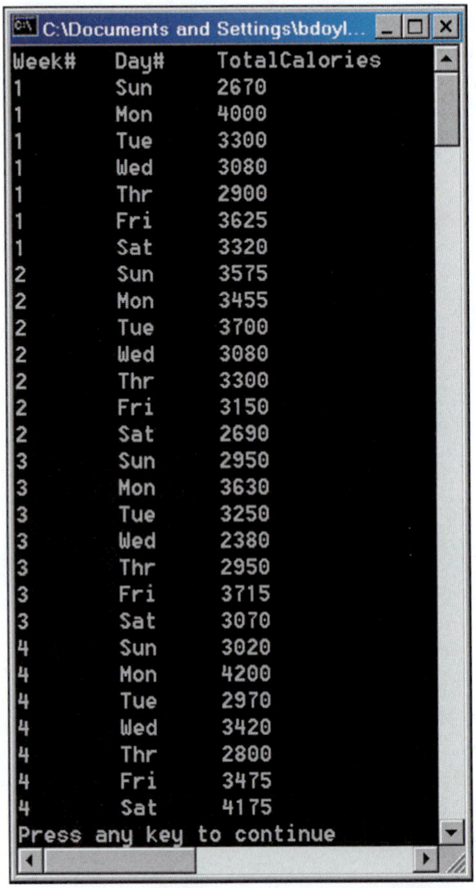

Figure 7-14   Sample run from the CalorieCounter application

This section began by stating that you are only limited by your imagination in terms of the number of dimensions you can include in a C# application. Of course, at some point space becomes an issue. You can now envision creating a **calories** structure for each month, and you might be interested in comparing calorie intake by month. This could be a fourth dimension in your array. The same rules of creation, access, and use with methods that apply to a two-dimensional array apply to fourth- and fifth-dimensional arrays.

ARRAYLIST CLASS

One of the limitations of the traditional array is the fact that you cannot change the size or length of an array after it is created. To give you more flexibility .NET includes another **class**, the **ArrayList class**, which facilitates creating a listlike structure that can dynamically increase or decrease in length. Like traditional arrays, indexes of **ArrayList** objects are zero based. The **class** includes a large number of predefined methods; Table 7-2 lists some of them. Explore the C# documentation to learn about the parameters of these methods and about the other methods and properties of the **ArrayList class**.

Table 7-2 ArrayList members

Methods or properties	Description
Add( )	Adds a value onto the end
BinarySearch( )	Overloaded. Uses a binary search algorithm to locate a value
Capacity	Property. Gets or sets the number of elements that the **ArrayList** can contain
Clear( )	Removes all elements
Clone( )	Creates a copy
Contains( )	Determines whether an element is in the **ArrayList**
Count	Property. Gets or sets the number of elements that the **ArrayList** actually contains
GetRange( )	Returns an **ArrayList** that is a subset of another **ArrayList**
IndexOf( )	Overloaded. Returns the index of the first occurrence of a value
Insert( )	Inserts an element at a specified index
InsertRange( )	Inserts the elements of an **ArrayList** into another **ArrayList** at the specified index
Item	Property. Gets or sets the element at the specified index
LastIndexOf( )	Overloaded. Returns the index of the last occurrence of a value
Remove( )	Removes the first occurrence of a specified object
RemoveAt( )	Removes the element at the specified index
RemoveRange( )	Removes a range of elements
Repeat( )	Returns an **ArrayList** whose elements are copies of the specified value
Reverse( )	Overloaded. Reverses the order of the elements
Sort( )	Overloaded. Sorts the elements or a portion of them
ToArray( )	Overloaded. Copies the elements to a new array
TrimToSize( )	Sets the capacity to the actual number of elements

7

The **ArrayList class** is similar to the vector **class** found in other languages in that you push and pop elements on and off using the Add( ) and Remove( ) methods.

Example 7-18 includes a program that creates an object of the **ArrayList class**. String values were added as elements. Any predefined or user-defined type can be used as an **ArrayList object**.

Example 7-18

```
/* ArrayListExample.cs    Author:  Doyle
 * Instantiates the ArrayList class.
 * Adds and removes values. Demonstrates
 * displaying items using an index.
 */
using System;
using System.Collections;
public class ArrayListExample
{
    public static void Main( )
    {
        ArrayList anArray = new ArrayList();

        anArray.Add("Today is the first day of the rest "
                    + "of your life!");
        anArray.Add("Live it to the fullest!");
        anArray.Add("ok");
        anArray.Add("You may not get a second chance.");

        Console.WriteLine("Count of elements in array:    {0}",
                          anArray.Count);
        anArray.RemoveAt(2);
        Console.WriteLine("New Count (after removing ok): {0}",
                          anArray.Count);
        Console.WriteLine( );
        DisplayContents(anArray);
    }

    public static void DisplayContents(ArrayList ar)
    {
        for(int i = 0; i < ar.Count; i++)
            Console.WriteLine(ar[i] );
        Console.WriteLine();
    }
}
```

The example demonstrates how items are added and removed from the structure. The output from one sample run is shown in Figure 7-15.

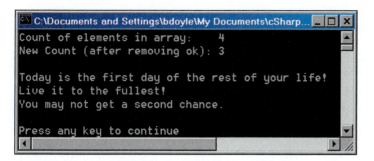

Figure 7-15   Sample run from the ArrayList example

> **NOTE**
> By now you should know and be fully aware that you must include parentheses ( ) with methods. No parentheses are used with property members in C#.

STRING CLASS

You have been using the **string** data type since the beginning of this book. The **string** data type is included in this chapter because strings are used to store a collection of Unicode characters.

> **NOTE**
> Unicode assigns a unique numeric value for characters. It is the universal character encoding scheme used by the .NET languages. Unicode makes it easier to develop applications that can be used across the world because it includes most international characters.

You can instantiate an **object** using **string** or **String**. This works because **string** is an alias for the **System.String class** in the .NET Framework. The keyword in C#, which turns blue in Visual Studio, is **string**. It is used throughout the book to represent the type.

You have already learned that the **string** is a reference type. Normally with reference types, equality operators, **==** and **!=**, compare the object's references, instead of their values. However, the equality operators function differently with **string** than with other reference objects. The equality operators are defined to compare the contents or values referenced by the **string** type instead of comparing their addresses.

Unlike some languages that require you to store collections of characters as **char** arrays, the C# **string** type allows individual characters to be accessed using an index with [ ], but you can also process variables of **string** type as a group of characters. As with array objects, when you access an individual element in a **string**, the first character is indexed by zero. However, you have the best of both worlds with strings in C#. You can access the individual characters using an index, but **string** variables are objects of the **string class**. Thus, in addition to [ ] and the + used for concatenation, you have many predefined methods and properties that make **string** objects functional and flexible.

Objects of the **string class** store an immutable series of characters. They are considered **immutable** because once you give a **string** a value; it cannot be modified. Methods that seem to be modifying a **string** are actually returning a **new string** containing the modification. Table 7–3 shows some of the members of the **string class**, using the following declarations:

```
string sValue = "C# Programming";
object sObj;
string s = "C#";
```

Column three in Table 7–3 illustrates the result produced by an example of the methods and properties.

Table 7-3 Members of the string class

Methods and properties	Description	Example

Clone( )	Returns a reference to this instance of string.	sObj = sValue.Clone( );
		Console.WriteLine(sObj);
		//Displays C# Programming

Compare( )	Overloaded. Class method. Compares two strings.	if (string.Compare(sValue, s) > 0)
		    Console.WriteLine("sValue has
		higher Unicode chars.");
		//Displays sValue has higher Unicode
		//chars.

Concat( )	Overloaded. Class method. Concatenates one or more string(s).	string ns = string.Concat(sValue, s);
		Console.WriteLine(ns);
		//Displays C# ProgrammingC#

Copy( )	Class method. Creates a new copy of a string with the same values as the source string.	s = string.Copy(sValue);
		Console.WriteLine(s);
		//Displays C# Programming

EndsWith( )	Determines whether the end of this instance matches the specified string.	bool result = sValue.EndsWith("#");
		Console.WriteLine(result);
		//Displays False

Equals( )	Overloaded. Determines whether two strings have the same value.	bool result = sValue.Equals(s);
		Console.WriteLine(result);
		//Displays False

Table 7-3   Members of the string class (continued)

Methods and properties	Description	Example
Format( )	Overloaded. Class method. Replaces each format specification in a string with the textual equivalent of the corresponding object's value.	```double nu = 123.45678;``` ```string nn = string.Format("{0:F2}", nu);``` ```//Displays 123.45```
IndexOf( )	Overloaded. Returns the index of the first occurrence of a string, or one or more characters, within this instance.	```Console.WriteLine (sValue.IndexOf("#"));``` ```//Displays 1```
Insert( )	Inserts a specified instance of a string at a specified index position.	```s = sValue.Insert(3,".NET ");``` ```Console.WriteLine(s);``` ```//Displays C# .NET Programming```
LastIndexOf( )	Overloaded. Returns the index of the last occurrence of a specified character or string.	```Console.WriteLine``` ```(sValue.LastIndexOf("P"));``` ```//Displays 3```
Length(property)	Gets the number of characters.	```Console.WriteLine(sValue.Length);``` ```//Displays 14```
PadLeft( )	Overloaded. Right-aligns the characters in the string, padding on the left with spaces or a specified character.	```s = sValue.PadLeft(20, '#');``` ```Console.WriteLine(s);``` ```//Displays ######C# Programming```
PadRight( )	Overloaded. Left-aligns the characters in the string, padding on the right with spaces or a specified character.	```s = sValue.PadRight(20, '#');``` ```Console.WriteLine(s);``` ```//Displays C# Programming######```
Remove( )	Deletes a specified number of characters beginning at a specified position.	```s = sValue.Remove(3, 8);``` ```Console.WriteLine(s);``` ```//Displays C# ing```

7

Table 7-3 Members of the string class (continued)

Methods and properties	Description	Example

Replace( )	Overloaded. Replaces all occurrences of a character or string with another character or string.	`s = sValue.Replace("gram", "GRAM");`
		`Console.WriteLine(s);`
		`//Displays   C# ProGRAMming`

Split( )	Overloaded. Identifies the substrings in the string that are delimited by one or more characters specified in an array, then places the substrings into a string array.	`string [ ] sn = sValue.Split(' ');`
		`foreach (string i in sn)`
		`    Console.WriteLine(i);`
		`//Displays        C#`
		`//               Programming`

StartsWith( )	Determines whether the beginning of the string matches the specified string.	`Console.WriteLine`
		`(sValue.StartsWith("C#"));`
		`//Displays   True`

Substring( )	Overloaded. Retrieves a substring from the string.	`Console.WriteLine`
		`(sValue.Substring(3, 7));`
		`//Displays   Program`

ToCharArray( )	Copies the characters in the string to a character array.	`char[ ] cArray =`
		`sValue.ToCharArray(0, 2);`
		`Console.WriteLine(cArray);`
		`//Displays   C#`

ToLower( )	Overloaded. Returns a copy of the string in lowercase.	`Console.WriteLine(sValue.ToLower( ));` `//Displays     C# programming`

ToString( )	Overloaded. Converts the value of the instance to a string.	`int x = 234;`
		`s = x.ToString( );`
		`Console.WriteLine(s);`
		`//Displays   234`

ToUpper( )	Overloaded. Returns a copy of the string in uppercase.	`Console.WriteLine(sValue.ToUpper( ));` `//Displays     C# PROGRAMMING`

Trim( )
TrimEnd( )
TrimStart( )
	Overloaded. Removes all occurrences of a set of specified characters from the beginning and end.	`s = sValue.Trim('g', 'i', 'n', 'm', 'C');`
		`Console.WriteLine(s);`
		`//Displays   # Progra`

> Notice that the methods identified as `class` methods in column two prefix the name of the method with the `string` data type.

Most `string` member arguments that take a `string object` accept a `string` literal. C# has two types of `string` literals. You have used one of them, the quoted literal. Quoted `string` literals appear between double quotation marks (" ") and are the most common type found in languages. The other type, @-quoted `string` literals, start with the at symbol (@) and are also enclosed in double quotation marks. The @-quoted `string` literals are referred to as the **verbatim** `string` **literal** because the characters between the double quotes are interpreted verbatim. There are two differences between the quoted and @-quoted string literal. With the @-quoted literal, escape sequence characters, such as `'\t'` and `'\n'`, are not recognized as special characters. The second difference is that @-quoted enables you to use a keyword for an identifier.

Using the @-quoted literal with the statement here:

```
Console.WriteLine( @"hello \t world");
//Displays     hello \t world
```

Without the @-quoted literal:

```
(Console.WriteLine("hello \t world");
//Displays     hello     world
```

Tables 7-2 and 7-3 included a number of the extremely useful methods and properties of the `ArrayList` and `String` classes. Others members exist. Do not reinvent the wheel and write code for functions that already exist. These members have been tried and tested. The key to using the members is to experiment and play with them. The C# online documentation with Visual Studio includes many examples that you will want to explore.

PROGRAMMING EXAMPLE: MANATEE APPLICATION

This example demonstrates the use of collections in the analysis, design, and implementation of a program. Array and `string` objects are included. An application is created to monitor manatees, which are still in danger of extinction and are being monitored on a daily basis in some areas. To design this application, a number of `string` methods are used. Parallel arrays are created to store the location, date, and number present at each sighting. The application is designed using two classes, and the problem specification is shown in Figure 7-16.

Create an application that will be used to monitor the number of manatees in a given waterway. A team of researchers flies from four to six times per month over a regional waterway and logs sightings of manatees. The waterway is mapped into different viewing locations. The researchers record the date, location, and count of the number of manatees present at that location.

Determine which day had the highest sightings at a given location. Print that date with the actual name of the month. Also include the count associated with the highest sighting. Plan your application so that the average number of sightings for a given location can be determined.

Design an object-oriented solution. Use two classes. For the manatee sighting class, characteristics such as the location, date of viewing, count of manatees, average number of sightings, and date of maximum sighting should be included. Methods to determine the average, month with the highest number of sightings, and associated month name should be part of the application.

In the second class, instantiate an object of the manatee sighting class. Allow the user to input data about a given location. Test the member of the manatee sighting class.

Figure 7-16 Problem specification for Manatee example

Analyze the Problem

You should review the problem specification in Figure 7-16 and make sure you understand the problem definition. Several values will be entered into the program to represent location, date, and counts of sighted manatees. These dates and counts will be entered into arrays and used to instantiate an object of the **ManateeSighting class**.

Data Table 7-4 lists the data field members needed for the manatee sighting problem.

Table 7-4 Instance field members for the **ManateeSighting** class

Data item description	Type	Identifier
Sighting location	string	location
Date of flight	string []	sightDate
Number of manatees sighted	int []	manateeCount
Average count per location	double	avg
Maximum seen at one location	int	maxCnt
Date maximum seen at one location	string	maxDate
Month where most seen at one location	string	monthWithMostSightings

A second **class** will be created to test the **ManateeSighting class**. To do this, additional data is needed by the **class** using the **ManateeSighting class**. As noted in the problem specification, the application **class** allows the user to enter values so that the **ManateeSighting class** can be instantiated. Local variables for location and arrays for date and count are declared in the application **class**. The two arrays will be dimensioned to a maximum number of 20 entries. The number of actual records will be used to construct the **ManateeSighting** object. For testing purposes, a single location will be entered. The application could be modified to create arrays of data about multiple locations.

Design a Solution

The desired output is to display the location, number of sightings during the most active month, and date (including the month name) in which the most manatees were sighted. Figure 7-17 shows a prototype of what the final output might look like.

7

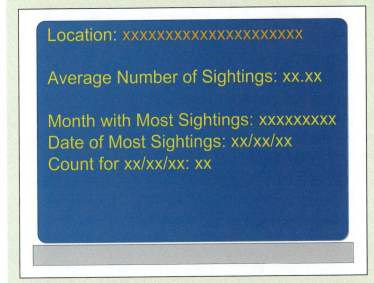

Location: xxxxxxxxxxxxxxxxxxxxxx

Average Number of Sightings: xx.xx

Month with Most Sightings: xxxxxxxxx
Date of Most Sightings: xx/xx/xx
Count for xx/xx/xx: xx

Figure 7-17   Prototype

Class diagrams are used to help design and document both data and behavior characteristics. Figure 7-18 shows the **class** diagrams for the manatee application example.

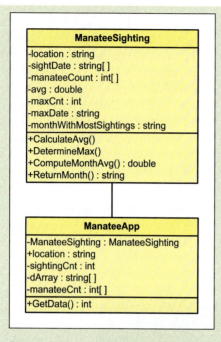

Figure 7-18 Class diagrams

The **class** diagrams do not show the properties or the local variables that might be needed by specific methods. Table 7-5 lists the data members that have properties defined indicating whether get and/or set will be needed. The name of the property is also shown in the table.

Table 7-5 Properties for the `ManateeSighting` class

Data member identifier	Property identifier	Set	Get
`location`	`Location`		
`monthWithMostSightings`	`MonthWithMostSightings`		
`avg`	`Avg`		
`maxCnt`	`MaxCnt`		
`maxDate`	`MaxDate`		

The property members `MonthWithMostSightings`, `MaxCnt`, `MaxDate`, and `Avg` are set as read-only properties. This is because they are calculated values involving more than just the individual data member.

Figure 7-19 shows the Structured English, or pseudocode, used to design the step-by-step processes for the behaviors of the methods of the `ManateeApp` example.

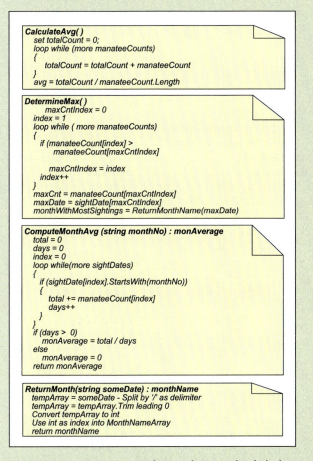

```
CalculateAvg( )
    set totalCount = 0;
    loop while (more manateeCounts)
    {
        totalCount = totalCount + manateeCount
    }
    avg = totalCount / manateeCount.Length
```

```
DetermineMax( )
        maxCntIndex = 0
    index = 1
    loop while ( more manateeCounts)
    {
        if (manateeCount[index] >
            manateeCount[maxCntIndex]

            maxCntIndex = index
        index++
    }
    maxCnt = manateeCount[maxCntIndex]
    maxDate = sightDate[maxCntIndex]
    monthWithMostSightings = ReturnMonthName(maxDate)
```

```
ComputeMonthAvg (string monthNo) : monAverage
    total = 0
    days = 0
    index = 0
    loop while(more sightDates)
    {
        if (sightDate[index].StartsWith(monthNo))
        {
            total += manateeCount[index]
            days++
        }
    }
    if (days > 0)
        monAverage = total / days
    else
        monAverage = 0
    return monAverage
```

```
ReturnMonth(string someDate) : monthName
    tempArray = someDate - Split by '/' as delimiter
    tempArray = tempArray.Trim leading 0
    Convert tempArray to int
    Use int as index into MonthNameArray
    return monthName
```

Figure 7-19   ManateeSighting class methods behavior

After the algorithm is developed, the design should be checked for correctness. You might develop a table now with test values using a standard calculator. Desk check the pseudocode to ensure you are getting the results expected. After your program is running, you can validate the correctness by comparing results you produce with your program against values you produced with the calculator during your design walkthrough.

Code the Solution After you complete the design and verify the algorithm's correctness, translate the design into source code. For this application you are creating two separate files—one for each class. The final application listing for both files is as follows:

```csharp
/* ManateeSighting.cs          Author: Doyle
 * This class defines manatee characteristics to include
 * location, count, and date of sightings. Methods to
 * determine the month with most sightings and
 * average number of sightings per location included.
 */
using System;
namespace ManateeApp
{
    public class ManateeSighting
    {
        private string location;
        private string [ ] sightDate;
        private int [ ] manateeCount;
        private double avg;            // average count for location
        private int maxCnt;            // maximum count for location
        private string maxDate;        // date maximum recorded
        private string monthWithMostSightings;

        // Default constructor
        public ManateeSighting( )
        {

        }
        // Constructor
        public ManateeSighting(string loc, string[ ] date,
                               int [ ] cnt, int numOfFlights)
        {

            sightDate = new string[numOfFlights];
            manateeCount = new int[numOfFlights];

            Array.Copy(date,0,sightDate,0,numOfFlights);
            Array.Copy(cnt,0,manateeCount,0,numOfFlights);
            location = loc;
        }

        // Properties
        public string Location
        {
            get
            {
                return location;
            }
        }
```

```csharp
        set
        {
            location = value;
        }
    }
    public string MonthWithMostSightings
    {
        get
        {
            DetermineMax( );
            return monthWithMostSightings;
        }
    }
    public double Avg
    {
        get
        {
            CalculateAvg( );
            return avg;
        }
    }
    public int MaxCnt
    {
        get
        {
            DetermineMax( );
            return maxCnt;
        }
    }
    public string MaxDate
    {
        get
        {
            DetermineMax( );
            return maxDate;
        }
    }

    // Determines the average number of sightings per location
    public void CalculateAvg( )
    {
        int total = 0;
        foreach (int c in manateeCount)
                    total += c;
        avg = total / manateeCount.Length;
    }
    // Determines the maximum number of manatees
    // sighted on any one given date. Uses a parallel
```

7

```csharp
// array to determine the actual date.
// Calls method to set the month name.
public void DetermineMax( )
{
    int maxCntIndex = 0;
    for(int i = 1; i < manateeCount.Length; i++)
        if(manateeCount[i] > manateeCount[maxCntIndex])
            maxCntIndex = i;
    maxCnt = manateeCount[maxCntIndex];
    maxDate = sightDate[maxCntIndex];
    monthWithMostSightings = ReturnMonth(maxDate);
}


// Given a month number the average is computed
// for a given location.
public double ComputeMonthAvg(string mon)
{
    int total = 0;
    int days = 0;
    double monAverage;
    for(int i = 0; i < sightDate.Length; i++)
    {
        if(sightDate[i].StartsWith(mon))
        {
            total += manateeCount[i];
            days++;
        }
    }
    if (days > 0)
        monAverage = total / days;
    else
        monAverage = 0;
    return monAverage;
}


// Given a date in the format of mm/dd/yyyy
// the name of the month is returned.
public string ReturnMonth(string someDate)
{
    string [ ] monthName = {"January", "February", "March",
                            "April", "May", "June", "July",
                            "August", "September",
                            "October",
                            "November", "December"};

    string[ ] dateParts = someDate.Split('/');
    dateParts[0] = dateParts[0].TrimStart('0');
```

```
                    return monthName[Convert.ToInt32(dateParts[0]) - 1];
            }
        }
}


/* ManateeApp.cs        Author: Doyle
 * This is the client program that uses the
 * ManateeSighting class. Users are prompted
 * for location, date, and sightings. The
 * ManateeSighting class is tested using
 * this class by calling many of the methods
 * and properties.
 */
using System;
namespace ManateeApp
{
    public class ManateeApp
    {
        static void Main(string[] args)
        {
            string location;
            int sightingCnt;
            string [ ] dArray = new String[ 20];
            int [ ] manateeCnt = new int[20];
            sightingCnt = GetData(out location, dArray,
                            manateeCnt);

            ManateeSighting m = new ManateeSighting(location,
                        dArray, manateeCnt, sightingCnt);

            Console.WriteLine( );
            Console.WriteLine( );
            Console.WriteLine("Location:  {0}", m.Location);
            Console.WriteLine("Average number of Sightings: {0}",
                        m.Avg);
            Console.WriteLine( );
            Console.WriteLine("Month with Most Sightings : {0}",
                        m.MonthWithMostSightings);
            Console.WriteLine("Date of the Most Sightings : {0}",
                        m.MaxDate);
            Console.WriteLine("Count for {0}: {1}", m.MaxDate,
                        m.MaxCnt);


        }
```

```csharp
        public static int GetData(out string location,
                string [ ] dArray, int [ ] manateeCnt)
    {
        int i;
        Console.Write("Location: ");
        location = Console.ReadLine( );
        Console.Write("How many records for {0}? ", location);
        string inValue = Console.ReadLine( );
        int loopCnt = Convert.ToInt32(inValue);
        for (i = 0; i < loopCnt; i++)
        {
            Console.Write("Date (mm/dd/yyyy): ");
            dArray[i] = Console.ReadLine( );
            Console.Write("Number of Sightings: ");
            inValue = Console.ReadLine();
            manateeCnt[i] = Convert.ToInt32(inValue);
        }
        return i;
    }
}
}
```

The output from one test run is shown in Figure 7–20.

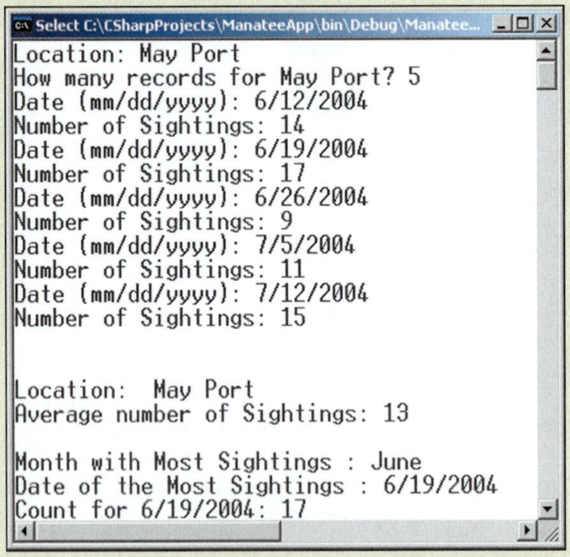

Figure 7-20   ManateeApp application output

QUICK REVIEW

1. An array may contain any number of variables of the same type. One common identifier names the entire structure.

2. The individual variables in the array are called the elements of the array.

3. To access an array element, use an index enclosed in square brackets. The index (or subscript) references the location of the variable relative to the beginning location. The first index is always zero.

4. With C# the size or length of the array cannot change after it is allocated, but you can use a variable to declare the size of an array.

5. During the declaration, specify the number of individual elements for which space must be allocated and use an identifier representative of the contents (normally a singular name).

6. When you use an array as a method parameter, the array identifier and type are specified; however, the length or size of the array is not included. Open and closed square brackets are required. The call to that method includes the name of the array only.

7. `Array class` has a number of predefined methods that perform sort, binary search, copy, and reverse. All arrays, of any type, inherit them.

8. Include `params` with a parameter to indicate that the number of arguments may vary.

9. With the `foreach` statement, the identifier represents the array element for which iteration is currently being performed. The type used in the `foreach` expression must match the array type.

10. Arrays can be sent as arguments to methods, and in addition, a method can have an array as its return type.

11. Array `objects` and `string` types are reference instead of value types.

12. Two-dimensional and other multidimensional arrays follow the same guidelines as one-dimensional arrays.

13. A two-dimensional array is usually visualized as a table divided into rows and columns. The first index represents the number of rows.

14. When the number of columns in rows may need to differ, a jagged, or ragged array can be used. It is called an "array of arrays."

15. `ArrayList class` creates a listlike structure that can dynamically increase or decrease in length. Like traditional arrays, indexes of `ArrayList` objects are zero based. A number of predefined methods are included.

16. To create a multidimensional array, specify the type and the number of dimensions per rank. These values are separated by commas. A three-dimensional array would be defined with `type [ , , ] identifier = new type [length_of_planes, length_of_rows, length_of_columns]`.

7

17. The **string class** stores an immutable series of characters. After you give a **string** a value, it cannot be modified.

18. The **string** type is an alias for the **System.String class** in the .NET Framework. You can access the individual characters using an index, with the first index being zero.

19. String variables are objects of the **string class**; thus, a number of predefined methods including the following can be used: **Trim( ), ToUpper( ), ToLower( ), Substring( ), Split( ), Replace( ), Insert( ),** and **Copy( ).**

EXERCISES

1. The value contained within the square brackets that is used to indicate the length of the array must be a(n):

   a. **class**

   b. **double**

   c. **string**

   d. integer

   e. none of the above

2. Which of the following would be the best declaration for an array to store the high temperature for each day of one full week?

   a. **int temp1, temp2, temp3, temp4, temp5, temp6, temp7;**

   b. **int temp [7] = new int [7];**

   c. **temp int [ ] = new temp[7];**

   d. **int [ ] temp = new temp [7];**

   e. **int [ ] temp = new temp [8];**

3. Assume an array called **num** is declared to store four elements. Which of the following statements correctly assigns the value **100** to each of the elements?

   a. **for(x = 0; x < 3; ++x) num [x] = 100**

   b. **for(x = 0; x < 4; ++x) num [x] = 100;**

   c. **for(x = 1; x < 4; ++x) num [x] = 100;**

   d. **for(x = 1; x < 5; ++x) num [x] = 100;**

   e. none of the above

4. Choose the statement that does *not* apply to the following declaration:

```
double [ ] totalCostOfItems =
    {109.95, 169.95, 1.50, 89.95};
```

a. declares a one-dimensional array of floating-point values

b. specifies the size of the array as five

c. sets the array element `totalCostOfItems [1]` to `169.95`

d. declares an area in memory where data of **double** type can be stored

e. all are correct

5. What value is returned by function `result`?

```
int result(int[ ] anArray, int num)
{
    int i,
        r;
    for (r = 0, i = 1;  i < num;  ++i)
        if (anArray[i]  >  anArray [r] )
            r = i;
    return (r);
}
```

a. the index of the largest of the first **num** elements of array **anArray**

b. the value of the largest of the first **num** elements of array **anArray**

c. the index of the smallest of the first **num** elements of array **anArray**

d. the value of the smallest of the first **num** elements of array **anArray**

e. the index of the last element greater than its predecessor within the first **num** elements of array **anArray**

6. Which is the effect of the following program segment?

```
int[ ] anArray = new int[50];
int i, j, temp;
string inValue;
for (i = 0;  i < 50;  ++i)
{
    Console.Write("Enter Value");
    inValue = Console.ReadLine( );
    anArray[i] = int.Parse(inValue);
}
temp = 0;
for (i = 1;  i < 50;  ++i)
        if (anArray[i] < anArray[0])
            ++temp;
```

a. arranges the elements of array **anArray** in ascending order

b. counts the number of elements of array **anArray** greater than its initial element

c. reverses the numbers stored in the array

d. puts the largest value in the last array position

e. none of the above

7. Using the following declaration:

```
char [ , ] n = {{'a', 'b', 'c', 'd', 'e'},
                {'f', 'g', 'h', 'i', 'j'}};
```

What does n[1, 1] refer to?

a. a

b. f

c. b

d. g

e. none of the above

8. An array is a list of data items that _____.

a. all have the same type

b. all have different names

c. all are integers

d. all are originally set to null ('\0')

e. none of the above

9. Using the following declaration:

```
int [ ] x = {12, 13, 14, 15, 16, 17, 18, 19};
```

What does x[8] refer to?

a. 19

b. 18

c. '\0'

d. 0

e. none of the above

10. Which of the following adds 42 to the element at the fifth physical spot?

```
int [ ] x = {12, 13, 14, 15, 16, 17, 18, 19};
```

a. x[5] += 42;

b. x[4] += 42;

c. x[5 + 42];

d. x = 42 + 5;

e. none of the above

11. How many components are allocated by the following statement?

```
double [ , ] values = new double [3, 2];
```

a. 32

b. 3

c. 5

d. 6

e. none of the above

12. What output is produced by the following code?

```
int i;
int [ ] anArray = new int [5];
for (i = 0; i < anArray.Length; i++)
    a[i] = 2 * i;
for (i = 0; i < anArray.Length; i++)
    Console.Write(a[i] + "  ");
```

a. 2 2 2 2 2

b. 2 4 6 8 10

c. 0 2 4 6 8 10

d. 0 2 4 6 8

e. none of the above

13. If you declare an array as `int [ ] anArray = new int[5];`

you can double the value stored in `anArray [2]` with the statement:

a. `anArray [2] = anArray [5] * 2;`

b. `anArray = anArray * 2;`

c. `anArray [2] *= anArray [2];`

d. `anArray [2] *= 2;`

e. none of the above

14. With the following declaration:

```
int [ , ] points =
    {{300, 100, 200, 400, 600},
     {550, 700, 900, 800, 100}};
```

The statement `points [1, 3] = points [1, 3] + 10;` will

a. replace the 300 amount with 310 and 900 with 910

b. replace the 500 amount with 510

c. replace the 900 amount with 910

d. replace the 800 amount with 810

e. none of the above

7

15. With the following declaration:

    ```
    int [ , ] points =
            {{300, 100, 200, 400, 600},
             {550, 700, 900, 200, 100}};
    ```

    The statement `points [0, 4] = points [0, 4-2];` will

    a. replace the 400 amount with 2

    b. replace the 300 and 600 with 2

    c. replace the 600 with 200

    d. result in an error

    e. none of the above

16. With the following declaration:

    ```
    int [ , ] points =
            {{300, 100, 200, 400, 600},
             {550, 700, 900, 200, 100}};
    ```

    The statement `Console.Write(points [1, 2] + points [0, 3]);` will

    a. display 900400

    b. display 1300

    c. display `"points[1, 2] + points[0, 3]"`

    d. result in an error

    e. none of the above

17. When you pass a single integer array element to a method, the method receives:

    a. a copy of the array

    b. the address of the array

    c. a copy of the value in the element

    d. the address of the element

    e. none of the above

18. When you pass the entire array to a method, the method receives:

    a. a copy of the array

    b. the address of the array

    c. a copy of the first value in the array

    d. the address of each of the elements in the array

    e. none of the above

19. To convert all the uppercase letters in a **string** to their lowercase counterpart, you can use the _____ method of the **string class**.

a. **IsLower( )**

b. **ConvertLower( )**

c. **Lower( )**

d. **ToLower( )**

e. none of the above

20. Which method in the **Array class** can be used to return the index of the first occurrence of a value in a one-dimensional array?

a. **IndexOf( )**

b. **LastIndex( )**

c. **FirstIndex( )**

d. **Search( )**

e. none of the above

21. Which method in the **Array class** can be used to get or set the number of elements that an **ArrayList** can contain?

a. **Length( )**

b. **Size( )**

c. **Dimension( )**

d. **Rank( )**

e. **Capacity( )**

22. Which class includes methods to create a dynamic one-dimensional structure?

a. **Array**

b. **string**

c. **array**

d. **ArrayList**

e. all of the above

23. A correct method call to a method that has the following heading would be:

int result(int[ ] anArray, int num)

a. **Console.Write(result(anArray, 3));**

b. **result(anArray, 30);**

c. **Console.Write(result(anArray[ ], 3));**

d. **result(anArray[ ], 30);**

e. none of the above

24. With arrays a limitation on the **foreach** statement is that it can:

    a. only be used for read-only access

    b. only be used with integral type arrays

    c. not be nested

    d. only be used with arrays smaller than 1000 elements

    e. not be used with dynamic arrays

25. A valid call to the following method using a **params** parameter is:

    ```
    public static void DoSomething(params int[] item)
    ```

    a. `DoSomething(4);`

    b. `DoSomething(anArray);`

    c. `DoSomething(4, 5, 6);`

    d. a and c are correct

    e. all are correct

26. Use the following **string** to answer questions a through e.

    ```
    string sValue = "Today is the first Day of "
                    + "your life."
    ```

    a. Create a new **string** that has all lowercase characters except the word Day. Day should be all uppercase.

    b. Create a new **string** array that contains the eight elements. Each word from the sValue **string** should be in a separate array cell.

    c. Remove the period from the last array element created in Step b. Display the contents of the new array verifying its removal.

    d. Surround the sValue **string** with three asterisks on each end.

    e. Replace the word **first** with the word **best** in the sValue **string**.

27. Using the following declaration:

    ```
    int [ ] anArray = {34, 55, 67, 89, 99};
    ```

    What would be the result of each of the following output statements?

    a. `Console.WriteLine(anArray.Length);`

    b. `Console.WriteLine(anArray[2]);`

    c. `Console.WriteLine(anArray[anArray.Length -2]);`

    d. `Console.WriteLine(anArray[2 +1] * anArray[0]);`

    e. `Console.WriteLine(anArray.Rank);`

28. Using the following declarations, write solutions for Steps a through e.

```
int [ ] bArray = new int [10];
int [ , ] cArray = new int [ 2, 3];
string [ , , ] dArray = new string [ 5, 2, 6];
```

   a. Write a **foreach** loop to display the contents of **bArray**.

   b. Write a **for** loop to increment each element in **bArray** by 5.

   c. Write a **foreach** loop to display the contents of **cArray**.

   d. Can you use a **foreach** loop to initialize all elements of **cArray** with zero? If so, show your code. If not, explain why.

   e. Write a **foreach** loop to display the contents of **dArray**.

29. Create array declarations for the following problem specifications.

   a. An array to hold the names of five font strings. Initialize the array with your favorites.

   b. An array to hold 12 state names. Initialize with the 12 states closest to your campus.

   c. An array to hold the 10 most common single character middle initials.

   d. An array to store a key for an exam consisting of 15 true/false questions.

   e. Parallel arrays to hold up to 100 checking account check numbers, dates, and check amounts.

30. Explain the difference between the .NET **Array class** and the **ArrayList class**.

PROGRAMMING EXERCISES

1. Write a program that reads data into an array of type **int**. Valid values are from 0 through 10. Your program should determine how many values were inputted. Output a list of distinct entries and a count of how many times that entry occurred.

Use the following test data:

1 7 2 4 2 3 8 4 6 4 4 7

2. Write a program that accepts any number of integer input values. Total the values. Display a report showing the original value input and the percentage it contributes to the total. You may prompt the user for the number of values to be inputted.

3. Write a program that allows users to enter their first and last names separated by a space. Display the names they input in uppercase characters with the last name first, followed by a comma, and then the first name. For a little more challenge, design your solution to accommodate the fact that sometimes users enter a middle name or initial.

4. Create three arrays of type **double**. Do a compile-time initialization and place ten different values in two of the arrays. Write a program to store the product of the two arrays in the third array. Produce a display using the **MessageBox class** that shows the contents of all three arrays using a single line for an element from all three arrays.

5. Write a program that allows the user to enter any number of names, last name first. Using one of the predefined methods of the **Array class**, order the names in ascending order. Display the results.

6. Areway ouyay away izwhay ithway Igpay Atinlay? (Translated: "Are you a whiz with Pig Latin?") Write a program that converts an English phrase into a pseudo–Pig Latin phrase (that is Pig Latin that doesn't follow all the Pig Latin syntax rules). Use predefined methods of the **Array** and **string** classes to do the work. For simplicity in your conversion place the first letter as the last character in the word and prefix the characters "ay" onto the end. For example, the word "example" would become "xampleeay", and "method" would become "ethodmay." Allow the user to input the English phrase. After converting it, display the new Pig Latin phrase.

7. Create an application that sorts a collection of integers and performs a binary search for one of the elements. Perform a compile-time initialization of your array with 15 unsorted values. Test your application by searching for values that do not exist in the array as well as values that are present.

8. Write a program that accepts ten homework scores with a value of 0 through 10. Store the values in an array. Create a second array representing what percentage of 100 these scores represent. Calculate and display the average based on the 100 percent array excluding the lowest and highest scores.

9. Write a program that creates a two-dimensional array with ten rows and two columns. The first column should be filled with ten random numbers between 0 and 100. The second column should contain the squared value of the element found in column 1. Using the **Show( )** method of the **MessageBox class**, display a table.

10. Write a program that displays the number of students that can still enroll in a given class. Design your solution using parallel arrays. Test your application with the following data:

Class name	Current enrollment	Maximum enrollment
CS150	18	20
CS250	11	20
CS270	09	25
CS300	04	20
CS350	20	20

8

Introduction to Windows Programming

In this chapter, you will:

- O Differentiate between the functions of Windows applications and console applications
- O Learn about graphical user interfaces
- O Become aware of some elements of good design
- O Use C# and Visual Studio .NET to create Windows-based applications
- O Create Windows forms and be able to change form properties
- O Add control objects such as buttons, labels, and text boxes to a form
- O Work through a programming example that illustrates the chapter's concepts

If you have read and completed the exercises in the previous chapters, you now have a solid programming foundation and can build fairly sophisticated console-based applications. These types of applications are excellent for learning the basic elements of programming and are appropriate for many types of small, utility applications today. However, you probably consider them boring. In your daily life, you have become accustomed to using modern programs that look and act like Windows applications. In this chapter, you learn to create those types of applications.

Building Windows-based applications was a complicated endeavor in the past; this is no longer the case. Included in the .NET Framework Class Library is an entire subsystem of classes that enables you to create highly interactive, attractive, graphical user interface (GUI) applications. Using Visual Studio .NET, it is easy to perform drag-and-drop constructions. In the next two chapters, you are introduced to many classes in the **System.Windows.Forms namespace** including control classes such as **Label**, **Button**, and **TextBox** that can be placed on a Windows **Form** container **class**. A different way of programming based on interactively responding to events such as mouse clicks will be introduced. In Chapter 9, you extend this knowledge by creating applications that are more event-driven and are used for capturing and responding to user input. By the time you complete Chapter 9, you will be building fun, interactive Windows-based applications.

CONTRASTING WINDOWS AND CONSOLE APPLICATIONS

When a Windows application executes, it functions differently from the console-based applications you have been writing. With a console-based application, each line in the **Main( )** method is executed sequentially. Then the program halts. Method calls might branch to different locations in your program; however, control always returns back to the **Main( )** method. When the closing curly brace is encountered in **Main( )**, execution halts with console-based applications. With your console applications, the program initiates interaction with the operating system by calling the operating system to get data using the **ReadLine( )** method. It calls on the operating system to output data through method calls such as **WriteLine( )** or **Write( )**.

For both Windows and console applications, execution begins with the first statement in the **Main( )** method. However, with a Windows application, instead of the program executing sequential statements from top to bottom, the application, once launched, sits in what is called a process loop waiting for an event to execute. An **event** is a notification from the operating system that an action, such as the user clicking the mouse or pressing a key, has occurred. Instead of calling on the operating system with a request, as console applications do, **Windows applications** receive messages from the operating system that an event has occurred. With Windows applications, you write methods called **event handlers** to indicate what should be done when an event such as a mouse click on a button or the press of a key occurs.

You might design a window that includes several locations on your screen where a user could input different values. You might have many different buttons on that same screen, with one labeled Compute. With Windows applications, you register events about which you want your program to receive notification. For example, you might want your program to be notified when the user clicks the Compute button. For this situation, you would write in your program a method called an event handler, indicating what should be done when that Compute button is clicked. If this is the only event-handler method you include, your program, once launched, would be in a process loop—or wait state—until that Compute button was clicked.

The body of the event-handler method for the Compute button might include statements to perform a calculation and then display the formatted results on the Windows form. When the user clicks the Compute button, an event is fired. The operating system sends a message to your program indicating that the event you registered has occurred. The associated method to handle the event is then executed automatically.

Think about your own experience using any Windows-based program. Take for example your word-processing program. Once launched, the program appears to be sitting idle allowing you to type forever. It is in a process loop once it is launched. When you select an option from one of the menus, an event is fired. Select an option such as Find or Search and a dialog box prompts you to enter the word for the search. Another event is fired when you press the Enter key indicating you have finished typing the search word. This event-handler method performs the search in your document. Until you clicked on the menu bar, the program was just waiting for a notification from the operating system that an event of interest had occurred.

Unlike console-based applications that exit after all statements have been sequentially executed, Windows-based applications, once they are launched, sit idly waiting for notification of a registered event. The program remains in the operating system environment in a process loop. This means your program could be minimized, resized, or closed like other Windows applications. Someone could surf the Web for hours while your program was still running, or write an English paper using another application. Your program's code would be ready and still waiting for an event to be fired when the user made the program's window active again.

Another important difference is sequential order. Unlike the sequential nature you expect with console-based applications, in which one statement executes followed by the next, no sequential order exists with methods that handle events for Windows applications. If you have many options on your screen, or many buttons, you do not know which one the user will click first or whether any of them will be clicked. Again, think about your experiences using a Windows-based word processor. Each time you use the program, you select different options or use different menu selections.

With Windows applications, many different types of events may be fired. As a developer, you select actions your program should respond to and write event handlers for those events. If

8

you have five buttons on the screen, button1 may not be the one clicked first every time. These event-handler methods may be executed in a different order every time your application runs.

Windows applications not only function differently, they also look different. Windows applications tend to have a consistent user interface—one that is considered more user-friendly than what you find with console-based applications. In many cases, the user interface of a Windows application is considered as important as the application's power behind the scenes.

GRAPHICAL USER INTERFACES

Have you ever tried to use a computer program and said to yourself "Okay, what do I do next?" or been unable to exit a program or perform some function that you knew the program was supposed to be able to do? The culprit was probably the interface. The **interface** is the front end of a program. It is the visual image you see when you run a program. The interface is what allows users to interact with your program. Although a program may be powerful and offer rich functionality, those functions may remain unused unless they present the user with easy methods of interaction. Often users of programs actually identify the interface as the program itself, when in reality, the interface is just one facet of the program.

The interfaces you designed thus far have not been graphical. Your program interaction was primarily limited to accepting input through the `ReadLine( )` method and displaying output in the form of a single font at the DOS console window. In this chapter, the interface changes. Instead of interacting with the black console screen, you design Windows-based, graphical user interface (GUI) applications. These types of applications are displayed on a Windows form as shown in Figure 8-1.

Figure 8-1   Windows-based form

A **graphical user interface (GUI)** can include menus, buttons, pictures, and text in many different colors and sizes. Think of the form in Figure 8-1 as a container waiting to hold additional controls, such as buttons or labels. **Controls** are objects that can display and respond to user interaction. In Figure 8-1, the form has a title bar, complete with an icon on the left, a textual caption in the title bar, and the typical Windows minimize, maximize, and close buttons. The C# code used to create this blank form is shown in Example 8-1.

Example 8-1

```csharp
// Windows0.cs          Author: Doyle
// Demonstrates creating blank container form
using System.Windows.Forms;                        // Line 1

namespace Windows0
{
        public class Form1 : Form                  // Line 2

        {
                public Form1( )                    // Line 3

                {
                        Text = "Simple Windows Application";// Line 4

                }
                static void Main( )
                {
                        Form1 winForm = new Form1( );      // Line 5

                        Application.Run(winForm);          // Line 6

                }
        }
}
```

The code in Example 8-1 could be written using an editor such as Notepad and executed from the command line. This is not recommended for developing Windows-based applications. The Visual Studio .NET Integrated Development Environment (IDE) automatically generates all the code needed for a blank Windows form for you. If you do not use the IDE, you lose out on the built-in, drag-and-drop construction capabilities and the ease of modifying controls during design. The program listing in Example 8-1 is much smaller than what is generated from Visual Studio. Later in the chapter you will have a chance to compare Example 8-1 with the code Visual Studio actually generates. Before doing that and before exploring the rich Visual Studio .NET environment, it is useful to evaluate what is actually required to create a Windows application in C#.

Examine the statements in Example 8-1. Notice that the `using` directive labeled line 1 imports types or classes from the `System.Windows.Forms namespace`. This is where most of the classes for developing Windows-based application are organized. By including this directive, you avoid having to fully qualify references to classes organized under the `System.Windows.Forms namespace`.

> The Windows applications you will be creating will always refer to the `System.Windows.Forms namespace`. Visual Studio .NET automatically adds this reference, and it imports the `namespace` for you when you create a Windows Application Project using the IDE.

The `class` heading definition labeled line 2 looks a little different from what you have seen previously. It includes not only the `class` name, but a colon followed by another `class` name. The second `class` is called the `base class`; the first is called the **derived class**. Look closely at this statement again.

```
public class Form1 : Form                              // Line 2
```

The colon is used in the definition to indicate that the new `class` being defined, `Form1`, is derived from a `base class` named `System.Windows.Forms.Form`. The default name given for a Windows application `class` in Visual Studio is `Form1`. You do not have to change the `class` name, but you may want to so that the name better represents the application.

> Because the `namespace` `System.Windows.Forms` was included in the `using` directive, the fully qualified name of `System.Windows.Forms.Form` can be written as `Form`. You will find, however, that Visual Studio inserts the fully qualified name when you look at the code generated by the IDE.

When a `class` is **derived** from another `class`, the new `class` inherits all the functionality of the `base class`. `Form` is a predefined .NET `class` that includes a number of methods and properties used to create a basic Windows screen. `Form1` inherits the characteristics of the `Form class`. You learn more about inheritance in Chapter 10 when you study advanced object-oriented concepts. For now, think about inheritance as it relates to your family tree. Just as you can inherit traits from your father, such as hair color or height, `Form1` inherits methods and properties from the predefined `System.Windows.Forms.Form class`. As you reexamine the form created for Figure 8-1 using Example 8-1, notice that it includes fully functional close, minimize, and maximize boxes in the upper-right corner of the form. No new code had to be written to add these features. `Form1` inherited this functionality from the `Form class`. Remember that one of the beauties of object-oriented programming is not having to reinvent the wheel. Inheriting characteristics from `base` classes adds functionality to your program without the burden of your having to do additional coding.

Unlike your family tree, in which you inherit traits from two distinctively different individuals, your mother and your father, in C# and all .NET languages you are limited to single inheritance. Thus, you cannot just add a second or third colon (on line 2 for Example 8-1) and follow that with additional `class` names. You are limited to deriving from one `base class`. You learn more about this in Chapter 10.

Looking again at Example 8-1, line 3 begins the section of code defining the constructor for the `Form1 class`. Remember that a constructor has the same name as the `class` name—`Form1`. Constructors are called automatically when an `object` of the `class` is created. This constructor has one statement in its body, which is:

```
Text = "Simple Windows Application";                    // Line 4
```

`Text` is a property that can be used to set or get the caption of the title bar for the window. Observe that the string

```
"Simple Windows Application"
```

appears on the title bar in Figure 8-1.

8

You created your own property attributes using set and get when you defined your own classes. Windows forms and controls offer a wide variety of changeable properties including `Text`, `Color`, `Font`, `Size`, and `Location`. Much of the power of Visual Studio .NET lies in having these properties readily available and easy to change or add through IntelliSense.

As with console-based applications, execution for Windows-based programs begins in the `Main( )` method. In Example 8-1, line 5, the first statement in the `Main( )` method body instantiates or creates an `object` of the `Form1 class`. The object's identifier is `winForm`. That statement is listed again as follows:

```
Form1 winForm = new Form1( );                           // Line 5
```

The last statement in the body of `Main( )`, on line 6, calls the `Run( )` method. `Run( )` is a `class` method of the `Application class`. The call is as follows:

```
Application.Run(winForm);                               // Line 6
```

The `Application class` is also defined as part of the `System.Windows.Forms namespace`. The `object` that is instantiated from the `Form1 class` is sent as the argument to its `Run( )` method. It is this method call that causes the `object`, `winForm`, to be displayed as a window on your screen. This statement displays the form and places the application in a process loop so that it receives messages from the operating system when events of interest to the application are fired.

Unlike instance methods, `class` methods, or `static` methods, are not called with an `object`. Class methods are not owned by any specific `object`. To call `static` methods, the method name is suffixed by the `class` name. `Application` is a `class` that has `static` methods (`class` methods) to start and stop applications. The `Run( )` method starts an application; the `Exit( )` method stops an application and closes all of its windows.

The amount of development time for Windows applications is greatly reduced when you use Visual Studio .NET and C#. Because it is easy to add controls, sometimes beginning programmers get bogged down or carried away designing GUIs. Thus, before jumping into examining the different controls that can be added to the form, the next section presents some design issues that you should think about before dropping any control onto a form using Visual Studio .NET.

ELEMENTS OF GOOD DESIGN

As you start developing Windows applications, your goal should be to develop applications that are usable, that permit users to spot items in the windows quickly, and that enable users to interact with your program. Appearance matters! An attractively laid out screen with good visual organization gives users control. This is of utmost importance.

A large field of research in the field of computing is focused on **human–computer interaction (HCI)**. HCI concentrates on the design and implementation of interactive computing systems for human use. Explaining HCI fully is beyond the scope of this book, but it is a good topic for you to explore further, because it involves issues that you should consider and incorporate into your interfaces from the beginning. A few of the more important HCI considerations are presented in the following sections.

Consistency

This is listed first because it is extremely important. Do you know how to close a Windows-based program? Sure you do. One way is to click the box labelled "X" in the top-right corner of an active Windows application. The "X" performs the same functionality for all applications and is consistently located in that same place. Do you know which menu option to use to save your work? Again, you probably answered "Yes." Save is almost always located under the File menu option for all Windows-based applications. Consistent placement of items is important. Consistent sizing of items is important. Consistent appearance of items that are performing the same functionality is also important. These are good design features to mimic. Buttons that are providing the same functionality should be consistently located in the same general area, be sized consistently, and be designed to look consistent.

Unless you are trying to call attention to an item, keep the item the same as other items. To bring attention to an item, use contrast, make it look different, or place it in a different location; otherwise you should be consistent with your design of graphical user interfaces.

Alignment

Use alignment for grouping items. When you place controls on a form, place similar items together. They can be lined up to call attention to the fact that they belong together. Place similar items together and align them in the same column or same row. Use indentation to show subordination of items.

Use blank spaces to aid in grouping. Adding blank space between controls can make the difference between an attractively laid out GUI and one that is cluttered and difficult to use. Align controls with their identifying labels.

Avoid Clutter

The Windows `Form` `class` is considered a container on which controls such as buttons, text, labels, text boxes, and pictures can be placed. As you are about to learn, it is easy to fill the window with controls. Pay attention to the amount of information being placed on the form. Do not crowd a form with too many controls. Buttons to be clicked should be large enough for easy use. Make sure text is legible. Use intuitive labels that are descriptive of the control they are identifying. Fonts should be large enough to be legible.

8

Color

Think about your color combinations. Background colors and foreground text colors should contrast with each other. Avoid using bright colors (such as reds), especially for backgrounds; this can result in user eye fatigue. You can use color as an attention getter, but do not abuse it. Color can play a significant role in your design. A great deal of research has focused on how colors impact the GUI, and you will probably want to explore this topic further.

Target Audience

You should begin thinking about the design of an interface in terms of who will be using it. Your target audience should be taken into consideration. Another consideration for the design of an application is where it will be displayed. C# is being used to design mobile applications for handheld devices. A GUI should be different if it is going to be displayed on a WAP (Wireless Access Protocol)-enabled device such as a personal digital assistant (PDA) or a cell phone. You would want to place fewer controls and minimal graphics on such an application. The design of your interface for rich Windows applications that can be run on workstations equipped with large hard drives that hold graphical images should also differ from the design for Web applications that run on thin client systems over a browser. (A thin client is designed to be small because it works with a server designed to perform most of the data processing.) For one thing, the amount of download overhead should be taken into consideration for a Web application. Thin client systems often do not have much computing power and can be limited in their storage capacity. You will explore Web applications in Chapter 12.

New to Visual Studio .NET 2003 are built-in design templates for creating small device and mobile Web applications. These two new templates are added to the original console, Windows, and Web applications templates.

With every application that you design, you should always think about the design considerations discussed in this section. There are a number of useful Web sites focused on human-computer interaction. At the time of writing this text, *www.hcibib.org* was one of the more exhaustive sites. It includes a number of software developer resources such as an online bibliography, published HCI guidelines, plus links to a number of professional affiliations focusing on HCI and personal pages of designers sharing their design suggestions.

USE C# AND VISUAL STUDIO .NET TO CREATE WINDOWS-BASED APPLICATIONS

Although you could certainly manually create very sophisticated Windows applications in C# using an editor such as Notepad, this is not recommended. Visual Studio automatically generates much of the general service plumbing code that you would have to add to locate your controls on the screen. This makes writing Windows applications using Visual Studio much simpler. To create a Windows application in Visual Studio .NET, after clicking **New Project** on the File menu, select Visual C# Projects as the project type and Windows Application from the Templates Window as shown in Figure 8-2.

Figure 8-2   Visual Studio New Windows application

> **NOTE** The illustration shown in Figure 8-2 shows the project types available in Visual Studio .NET 2003. You see fewer project templates listed if you are using Version 1.1.

You can browse to the location where you want to store your work and type a name for the project.

> **NOTE** If you have not done so already, you may want to consider creating a working directory on your hard drive at the root level for your projects. Visual Studio and some operating systems can be a little finicky when you use spaces and special symbols such as the pound character (#) in your file or directory names, so you should probably avoid doing that. Notice that the location of all projects created for this book is C:\CSharpProjects.

After you click the OK button, Visual Studio automatically generates the code to create a blank Windows `Form` `object`. The IDE opens the Form Designer showing the form as illustrated in Figure 8-3, which is ready to receive control objects.

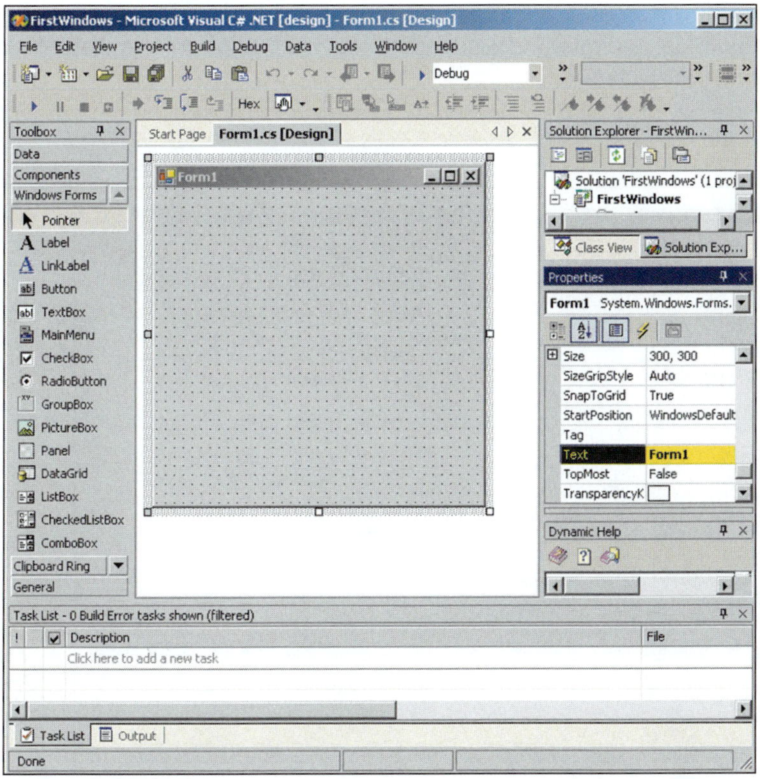

8

Figure 8-3   Initial design screen

If you do not see the constructed form, but instead see the program statements, your system may be set to show the Code Editor first. To see the graphical user interface form, select the Designer option from the View menu (or press Shift+F7).

Based on how you have Visual Studio configured, your screen may not look exactly like Figure 8-3. As a minimum, you will probably want to have the Toolbox and Properties windows accessible when you design your applications. Some developers prefer a larger screen to see their source code or find it distracting to have such a full screen of windows visible. You have many options for docking and hiding the windows shown in Figure 8-3. This figure has the Toolbox, Solution Explorer, Class View, Properties, Dynamic Help, Form Designer, and Task List windows visible. If you click the pushpin icon on the title bar of a specific window, the Auto Hide feature minimizes that window, but leaves a tab for it along the end of the IDE. In Auto Hide mode, when you hover the mouse pointer over the tab, the window is displayed. Figure 8-4 calls attention to the pushpin icon. The Toolbox and Task List windows are displayed in a dockable state snapped in place. Solution Explorer, Properties, and Dynamic Help windows are tab-docked in Auto Hide state. To put the window in Auto Hide state, click on its pushpin icon, and the pushpin is shown laying on its side.

  When a window is in Auto Hide state, if you move your mouse pointer over the tab, the window is re-displayed. At other times only the tab is visible. To take a window out of Auto Hide, re-display the window and click the pushpin icon so that it is standing up as shown in Figure 8-4.

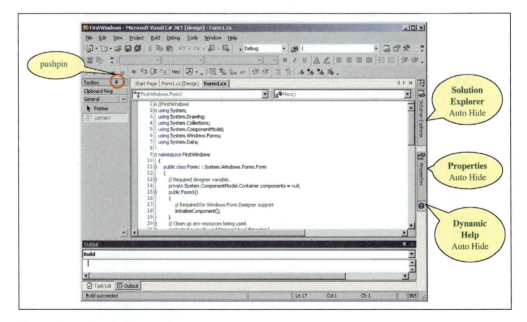

Figure 8-4   Dockable windows

Remember that to display the program statements, you can select Code from the View menu or press F7.

WINDOWS FORMS

Windows Forms enable you to use a more modern object–oriented approach to developing Windows applications. The .NET model is based on an extensive collection of `Control` classes available, including a `Form` `class` which is used as a container to hold other controls. The top-level window for an application is called a "form" in C#. If that top-level window opens another window, it is also considered a "form." The large collection of properties and methods that make up a rich programmable interface to forms is available to classes inheriting from `Form`. The code written for Example 8-1 to change the title bar caption is

```
Text = "Simple Windows Application";                    // Line 4
```

Using Visual Studio, all you have to do is find the appropriate property (`Text`) in the Properties window and type the value for the caption. You do not have to worry about whether the property's name begins with an uppercase character or is spelled correctly. You can select it from an alphabetized list. In Figure 8-3, notice the bright yellow box highlighting the `Text` property. Changing that property is as easy as clicking in the box and typing the new title bar caption. As soon as you finish typing and click outside of the box, the Form Designer form is updated with this new caption. The section that follows explores some of the other properties you can change for the `Form` container `class`.

 If the Designer window is not visible, select Designer from the View menu or press Shift+F7.

Windows Form Properties

Figure 8-5 displays a list of some of the properties that can be set for the `Form1` `object`. The Properties window is used to view and change the design time properties and events of an `object`.

> **NOTE** If your Properties window is not visible, select Properties Window from the View menu or press F4.

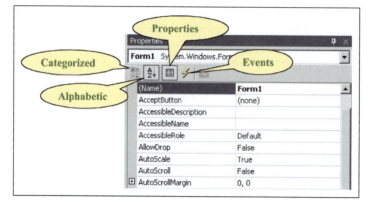

Figure 8-5 Properties

In Figure 8-5, many of the properties have a plus symbol (+) to the left of the property name indicating that the property can be expanded (only one is currently visible in the cropped image). Groups of properties are collapsed together for easier navigation through the property list. If you click the plus symbol, the group expands. For example, clicking the plus symbol to the left of the **Location** property reveals space where values can be typed for **x** and **y**. These values represent the **x** coordinate and **y** coordinate respectively for the location of the top-left corner of the form.

In Figure 8-5, there are five buttons or icons immediately above the list of properties. The second button, the Alphabetic button, is selected. Properties appear listed in alphabetic order for this illustration. Many developers prefer to see the properties listed by category. As Figure 8-5 illustrates, the button to the left of the Alphabetic button rearranges the Properties window by category. The lightning bolt, labeled Events, is used to display the list of events that can be programmed for a selected **object**. The third button from the left in Figure 8-5 is the Property button. This is selected, instead of the Events button, indicating that the list of properties are being displayed. Take a look at Figure 8-6, which contains a partial list of events that can be associated with a **Form1 object**.

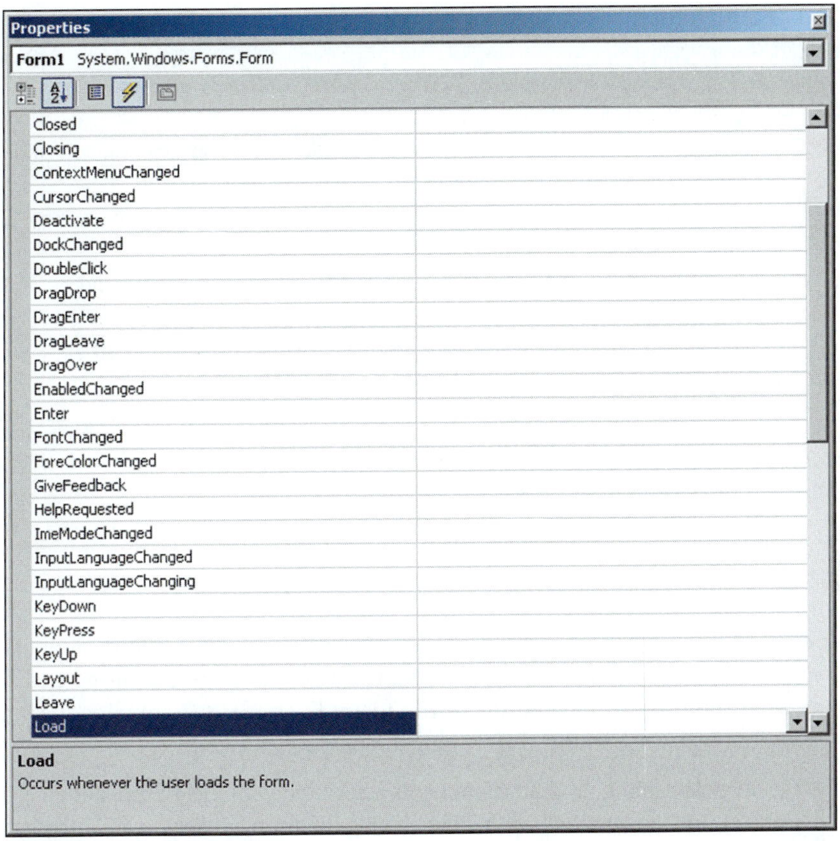

Figure 8-6 Form1 events

To illustrate how Visual Studio automatically generates code when property values are changed, Table 8-1 lists changes made to the respective properties of **Form1**. These changes are applied to the project that was started in Figure 8-2. Changing the property is as simple as moving the cursor to the edit box to the right of the property identifier and typing or selecting a value. Many properties have a drop–down list of values available for selection. All changes to the property values can be made in the Properties window at design time. You do not have to enter any source code statements.

 You can, however, set the properties using program statements. As you review the code generated by Visual Studio .NET, note how each property that you set by selecting or typing a value in the Properties window generates one or more lines of code.

Table 8-1 Form1 property changes

Property name	Actions performed on the FirstWindows properties
AutoScroll	Selected true
BackColor	Selected a peach color from a drop-down color picker window under the custom tab
Font	Selected Arial from a drop-down list of fonts; changed the size to 12 point; selected bold style
ForeColor	Selected a blue color from a drop-down color selection window under the custom tab
Location	Changed the x coordinate and y coordinate from 0,0 to 30,30
MaximizeBox	Selected false
Size	Changed the x coordinate and y coordinate from 300,300 to 400,400
StartPosition	Using a drop-down menu option, changed the value from WindowsDefault to CenterScreen
Text	Typed "First Windows Application"

As you can see from examining the property names in Table 8-1, the developers of Visual Studio .NET did a good job selecting intuitive names for most of the properties. The names represent what the property would do to the form. Example 8-2 contains the source code listing generated by Visual Studio .NET after the properties are set.

 One way to see the program statements associated with the Form1 design is to select Code on the View menu bar. Double-clicking the form, while you are in design mode, takes you to the Code Editor, but with the undesired side effect that a Form1_load( ) event-handler method heading and an empty body are added to your code.

The code shown in Example 8-2 is completely generated by Visual Studio .NET. Changes were made to the comments. The XML comments inserted by Visual Studio were deleted and new in-line comments added.

Example 8-2

```
//FirstWindows
using System;
using System.Drawing;
using System.Collections;
using System.ComponentModel;
using System.Windows.Forms;
using System.Data;
```

```csharp
namespace FirstWindows
{
    public class Form1 : System.Windows.Forms.Form
    {
        // Required designer variable.
        private System.ComponentModel.Container components = null;
        public Form1( )
        {
            // Required for Windows Form Designer support.
            InitializeComponent( );
        }
        // Clean up any resources being used.
        protected override void Dispose(bool disposing)
        {
            if(disposing)
            {
                if (components != null)
                {
                    components.Dispose( );
                }
            }

            base.Dispose(disposing);
        }

#region Windows Form Designer generated code
        // Required method for Designer support-do not modify
        // the contents of this method with the Code Editor.
        private void InitializeComponent( )
        {
            // Form1
            this.AutoScaleBaseSize = new System.Drawing.Size(8, 19);
            this.AutoScroll = true;
            this.BackColor =
                System.Drawing.Color.FromArgb(((System.Byte)(255)),
                ((System.Byte)(224)), ((System.Byte)(192)));
            this.ClientSize = new System.Drawing.Size(392, 373);
            this.Font = new System.Drawing.Font("Arial", 12F,
                System.Drawing.FontStyle.Bold,
                System.Drawing.GraphicsUnit.Point,
                ((System.Byte)(0)));
            this.ForeColor = System.Drawing.Color.Blue;
            this.Location = new System.Drawing.Point(30, 30);
            this.MaximizeBox = false;
            this.Name = "Form1";
            this.StartPosition =
                System.Windows.Forms.FormStartPosition.CenterScreen;
            this.Text = "First Windows Application";
        }
#endregion
```

```
    // The main entry point for the application.
    [STAThread]
    static void Main( )
    {
        Application.Run(new Form1( ));
    }
  }
}
```

 Right-clicking on the form, when you are using the Form Designer, also displays a menu that allows you to switch to the Code Editor where you can access the source code.

You run Windows applications like console applications by selecting Start or Start without Debugging from the Debug menu in Visual Studio .NET. You can also use the shortcuts, F5 and Ctrl+F5, to run your applications. When you run the program in Example 8-2, a peach-colored window titled **"First Windows Application"** is displayed in the center of your screen. The maximize button on the title bar is grayed out. The `StartPosition` property overrode the `Location` property values set. As you examine the drop-down menu options for `StartPosition`, notice that `Manual` is one of the values that can be selected. Selecting `Manual` enables the `Location` property to change where the form is displayed.

 You can look ahead at Figure 8-7 to see what the form looks like with its title caption added, the Windows maximize button grayed out, and the color set to peach. Figure 8-7 includes just one additional MessageBox dialog box layered on top of the form. It is added in the examples that follow.

Inspecting the Code Generated by Visual Studio .NET

Notice the two lines in Example 8-2 that begin with the pound (#) symbol. The first one says `#region Windows Form Designer generated code`. About twenty lines below that line, you find `#endregion`. This term, `#region`, is one of the preprocessor directives that can be included in C#. A **preprocessor directive** indicates something that should be done before processing. Preprocessor directives are often associated with conditionally skipping sections of source files or reporting certain types of errors.

According to the C# language reference specifications, the term "preprocessor" is used just for consistency. C# does not have the separate preprocessing step you find with C++ and other languages that identify statements that begin with # as preprocessor directives.

The `#region` preprocessor directive in C# is used to explicitly mark sections of source code that you can expand or collapse. If you were viewing the code in the Visual Studio

.NET Code Editor, observe that to the left of the directive a minus (-) or plus (+) symbol appears. Clicking the (-) symbol causes the entire block of code between the # symbols to be collapsed and be replaced by a comment labeled **"Windows Form Designer generated code"**. Clicking (+) expands the listing.

 You can create your own regions using the #region preprocessor directive. All you have to do is add a label naming your region following #region. To end the block, use #endregion, as is done with the #region Windows Form Designer generated code . . . #endregion. This can aid the readability and maintainability of the code.

Comparing the Code of Example 8-1 to Example 8-2

Comparing the source code statements generated from Visual Studio .NET for Example 8-2 against the program created manually for Example 8-1 reveals a couple of differences. Visual Studio .NET uses a method named **InitializeComponent( )** to build the form at runtime. All the properties that are set during design are placed in this method. Notice that the only statement in the constructor for Example 8-2 is a call to the **InitializeComponent( )** method.

```
// Constructor from Example 8-2
public Form1( )
{
    // Required for Windows Form Designer support.
    InitializeComponent( );
}
```

In Example 8-1, you will remember that the Text property was actually set in the constructor method. No **InitializeComponent( )** method was created.

```
// Constructor from Example 8-1
public Form1( )
{
    Text = "Simple Windows Application";
}
```

In the **InitializeComponent( )** method of Example 8-2, each of the properties was suffixed with the keyword **this**, which refers to the current instance of a **class**. In Example 8-2, **this** referred to the current instance of **Form1**. In Example 8-2, the **this** keyword could have been completely eliminated from the program listing without changing anything.

 When you are writing code using Visual Studio IDE, typing the keyword **this** followed by a period brings up IntelliSense. A listing of the members of the **class** is displayed for selection. You will find this extremely useful. It keeps you from having to remember the correct spelling of identifiers associated with your **class** members.

Notice that Visual Studio also imported several other namespaces:

```
using System;
using System.Drawing;
using System.Collections;
using System.ComponentModel;
using System.Windows.Forms;
using System.Data;
```

Because these namespaces were included, it is really not necessary to qualify each **class** name fully. Removing the **this** keyword and removing the fully qualified **namespace** names enables the `InitializeComponent( )` method to read as shown in Example 8-3.

Example 8-3

```csharp
private void InitializeComponent( )
{
    AutoScaleBaseSize = new Size(8, 19);
    AutoScroll = true;
    BackColor = Color.FromArgb(((Byte)(255)),
        ((Byte)(224)), ((Byte)(192)));
    ClientSize = new Size(392, 373);
    Font = new Font("Arial", 12F, FontStyle.Bold,
        GraphicsUnit.Point, ((Byte)(0)));
    ForeColor = Color.Blue;
    Location = new Point(30, 30);
    MaximizeBox = false;
    Name = "Form1";
    StartPosition = FormStartPosition.CenterScreen;
    Text = "First Windows Application";
    // Additional statements
}
```

This code is much more readable than the code generated from Visual Studio. However, it is not worth your effort to take time to remove the verbage. Do not lose sight of the fact that all of the code was automatically generated from the Visual Studio .NET Form Designer after properties were set from the Properties window. This certainly cuts down on the development time. Nevertheless, it is important that you are able to read the code and make modifications as necessary.

Take a look at the calls to the `Run( )` method included in the program listing generated by Visual Studio .NET. This is the only statement in the `Main( )` method. In Example 8-2, no actual identifier was associated with an **object** of the `Form1` type.

```csharp
//From Example 8-2
Application.Run(new Form1( ) );
```

The **new** keyword creates an anonymous (unnamed) instance of **Form1**, but notice where this occurs—as an argument to the **Run( )** method. There is really no need to identify an **object** of the **Form1** type by name, and this **Form1 object** identifer is not used anywhere else. Thus, the approach taken in the **Main( )** method in Example 8-2 is more streamlined than in Example 8-1. The two statements that made up the **Main( )** method body from Example 8-1 are displayed again in the following code segment for comparison purposes.

```
// From Example 8-1
Form1 winForm = new Form1( );                              // Line 5
Application.Run(winForm);                                  // Line 6
```

One additional method, **Dispose( )**, is added by the Form Designer as is shown in Example 8-2. The .NET Common Language Runtime (CLR) performs memory management. The CLR's automatic garbage collector releases memory from the application after the program is halted. The purpose of this **Dispose( )** method is to clean up or release unused resources back to the operating system.

Windows Form Events

The topic of Chapter 9 is handling events. However, it is useful to have a brief introduction to them here so that you can add some functionality to your Windows form. Figure 8-6 showed a partial list of events to which objects of the **Form1 class** could respond. Visual Studio makes it very simple to add code to respond to events. One way to add a method is to find the event in the list of events (from the Properties window with the lightning bolt (Events) selected) and double-click on the event name. When you do this, code is automatically added to your program by the Visual Studio .NET Form Designer.

Notice in Figure 8-6 that one of the events listed is **Closing**. Double-clicking on the **Closing** event adds the following code as the last line to the **InitializeComponent( )** method:

```
this.Closing +=
     new System.ComponentModel.CancelEventHandler(this.Form1_Closing);
```

The preceding statement is registering the **Closing** event so that your program is notified when a user is closing the application. You will learn more details about events in Chapter 9. For now, just realize that this line is necessary if you want to have your program receive a message from the operating system when a user clicks the "X" to close your application. Visual Studio adds the statement automatically for you when you double-click **Closing**, while you are using the Form Designer and have the form selected.

The other code automatically generated by the Form Designer and added to the program listing when you double-click the **Closing** event is the actual event-handler method heading and an empty body, as shown in the following code segment:

```
private void Form1_Closing(object sender,
                    System.ComponentModel.CancelEventArgs e)
{

}
```

8

Also notice that when you double–click on an event name such as **Closing**, the Code Editor window becomes the active window.

> **NOTE** A tab is placed behind the Code Editor window for Form Designer. Clicking the tab allows you to move between the Code Editor and the Form Designer. Figure 8-4 shows the tabs; they appear to the right of the labeled pushpin.

The cursor is placed inside the empty body of the **Form1_Closing** method. The IDE is waiting for you to program what is to occur when the user is closing your application. Take note! This is the first time you have needed to type any code since you started developing the FirstWindows application. The following line is typed as the body for the **Form1_Closing( )** method:

```
MessageBox.Show("Hope you are having fun!");
```

Figure 8-7 shows the output produced when the user clicks the close button.

Figure 8-7   Output produced when the Close button causes the event-handler method to fire

At this point, the form is still blank. The next section introduces you to controls such as buttons and labels that can be placed on the form to add functionality to your Windows application.

CONTROLS

The real strength of using C# for Windows applications lies in the number of controls that you can add to your applications. The `System.Windows.Forms namespace` includes many classes that you can add to your form representing controls with names such as `Button`, `Label`, `TextBox`, `ComboBox`, `MainMenu`, `ListBox`, `CheckBox`, `RadioButton`, and `MonthCalendar`. It is important to understand the concept that these controls are all classes. Each comes with its own bundle of predefined properties and methods. Each fires events—some of which you should write methods for—indicating what to do when its event is fired. An example is the `Button class`, which fires click events when an `object` of the `class` is clicked. As stated previously, if you use Visual Studio .NET, most of the standard service plumbing code is added automatically for you. All you add is code for the special processing that should occur when a particular `Button object` is clicked.

 You are going to find it very easy to work with Visual Studio and Windows applications using an object-oriented approach.

8

All of the control classes that can be added to a form are derived from the `System.Windows.Forms.Control class`. Figure 8-8 shows the `class` hierarchy of namespaces for the `Control` classes. With `Object` being the `base class` from which all classes ultimately are derived, Figure 8-8 illustrates that all the Windows control classes derive from a `class` named `Control`.

 In C#, `object` is an alias for `System.Object` in the .NET framework. Thus, instead of using `Object` to refer to this top-level `base class`, you use `object` with a lowercase 'o'.

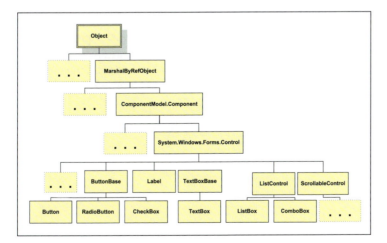

Figure 8-8   Control class hierarchy

Remember, when a **class** is derived from another **class**, it inherits the characteristics of all of its ancestor classes—meaning its parent **class**, the parent of the parent, and so on.

The dots on the classes in Figure 8-8 indicate that other classes are derived from the **class**. For example, a number of other classes are derived from the **class** **Object**; other classes are derived from the **MarshalByRefObject** and **ComponentModel.Component** classes. If you examine the .NET documentation, you find a total of 22 classes that are derived from **System.Windows.Form.Control**. The classes shown in Figure 8-8 are those that represent some of the more basic GUI controls. They are discussed in the sections that follow and in Chapter 9.

Another important concept to recognize is that the **Form** **class** is actually a derived **class** of the **ContainerControl class**. The **ContainerControl class** is a derived **class** of the **ScrollableControl class**, which is a derived **class** of **Control**. Figure 8-8 showed the **ScrollableControl class** with dots to indicate that other classes are derived from it. The reason this is important to you will be revealed when you learn about all the properties, methods, and event members that the **Control class** has predefined. Thus, not only **Button**, **Label**, and **TextBox** objects have access to these members, but also, **Form** objects inherit members of the **Control class**.

The Form Designer helps you organize the layout of the form window. While in Design view, you can select controls from the Toolbox window and drag and drop them onto your form container. You can actually write your own control classes and have them included on the Toolbox window. And a number of third-party vendors also sell controls that can be added to your Toolbox window to increase functionality. Figures 8-9 and 8-10 show the standard controls included when you install Visual Studio .NET.

A large number of additional controls are available, beyond those included when you install Visual Studio. To customize a specific Toolbox, select that Toolbox tab, such as Windows Forms, and right-click on any of its controls. A menu option displays that includes a Customize Toolbox option. You can select new .NET predefined controls or deselect those that you do not need access to on your desktop. You can even write your own controls (or buy controls from other vendors) and add them to the Toolbox.

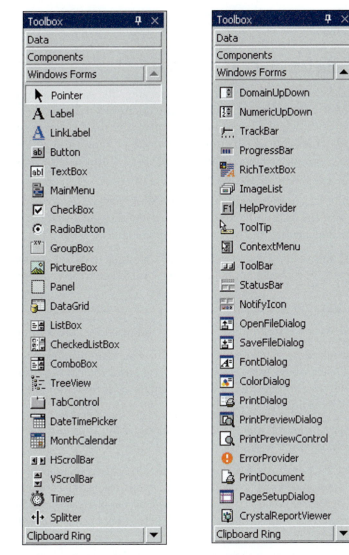

Figure 8-9   Controls—part I   **Figure 8-10**   Controls—part II

The illustration shown in Figure 8-10 shows the controls available in Visual Studio .NET 2003. You may see a slightly different listing if you are using Version 1.1 or if the Toolbox has been previously customized by another user.

If your Toolbox window is not visible, one way to activate it is to select **Toolbox** from the View menu. The Windows form controls in the Toolbox are only visible when you are using

8

the Designer. If the Code Editor is active, you must select the Designer tab to gain access to the Windows form controls.

Place, Move, Resize, and Delete Control Objects

Two procedures are used to place a control on your form. After the control is selected, you can either double-click the control or drag and drop the control to the correct location. If you use the double-click approach, the control is always placed in the top-left corner of the form—even if it overlaps other controls. To move the control, position the mouse pointer over the control until you see the standard Windows crossbars. With the left mouse button pressed, you can drag the control to its new location.

In Design view, you can resize controls using the standard Windows conventions of positioning the mouse pointer over the resizing handles. When you get the double-sided arrow, hold down the left mouse button and drag the border to the desired size.

 Select multiple controls using your mouse by either drawing an outline around the controls that are to be formatted or holding down the ctrl key while you click on the controls.

Another option available to you is to use the Properties window and set the `Size` property.

To delete a control, first select the control by clicking on it. The sizing handles become visible. Now clicking the Delete or Backspace key not only removes the control visually from the Form Designer view, but also removes all the constructor code and associated property changes relating to the selected `object`.

When you copy and paste controls on the form, you normally must always move the `object` to the new position after it is pasted.

 Just as you spent time designing a prototype for a console-based application, you should design a prototype for your Windows form. Randomly placing controls on your form leads to unorganized source code. It is probably best to place all labels, then all buttons, and so on. That way, like items are grouped together in your program listing.

Several menu options under the Format menu are extremely helpful during design, including Align, Make Same Size, Horizontal Spacing, and Vertical Spacing. After the control(s) is (are) selected, the Align selections include options such as Align Lefts, Align Rights, and Centers. The Make Same Size selection is especially useful for sizing buttons for consistency.

 Note that when you select more than one control to format, the *last* control selected is the one used as the template for the action. For example if `label1`, `label2`, and `label3` are all large, but `label4` is small, and you click on `label4` last when you are identifying controls to resize, clicking Make Same Size changes `label1`, `label2`, and `label3` to the size of `label4`. This also holds true for the Align options.

The Horizontal and Vertical Spacing options enable you to increase or decrease the amount of blank space displayed between objects. If multiple objects are selected, using these tools helps you have an equal amount of space between your controls.

> **NOTE** Be sure to practice using the tools available under the Format menu. Using the Align, Make Same Size, and Horizontal and Vertical Spacing options can greatly reduce your development time for the GUI and lead to more professional looking designs.

Methods and Properties of the Control Class

You recall that object-instantiated `Form` classes that derive from the `System.Windows.Form.Control class` inherit a number of predefined methods and properties from the `Control class`. This includes `Form` objects as well as `Button`, `Label`, `TextBox`, and the other objects from classes shown in Figure 8-8. Table 8-2 describes some of the more interesting properties that the control objects have available to them through inheritance from the actual `Control class`.

> **NOTE** Using the Form Designer you are able to configure the properties for the form and the controls that are on the form.

8

Table 8-2 System.Windows.Form.Control class properties

Property	Description
Anchor	Gets or sets which edges of the control are anchored to the edges of its container
BackColor	Gets or sets the background color for the control
BackgroundImage	Gets or sets the background image displayed in the control
CanFocus	Gets a value indicating whether the control can receive focus—read-only
Enabled	Gets or sets a value indicating whether the control can respond to user interaction
Font	Gets or sets the font of the text displayed by the control
ForeColor	Gets or sets the foreground color of the control
Location	Gets or sets the coordinates of the upper-left corner of the control relative to the upper-left corner of its container
Name	Gets or sets the name of the control
Size	Gets or sets the height and width of the control
TabIndex	Gets or sets the tab order of the control within its container
Text	Gets or sets the text associated with the control
Visible	Gets or sets a value indicating whether the control is displayed

The Control `class` has over 75 properties and over 100 methods. Not all are useful for every `class` that derives from it. Thus, you will not see all of the `Control` members listed in the Properties window for classes that derive from it. For example, the `Label` `object` has its own `Image`, `ImageIndex`, and `ImageList` properties. It does not use Control's `BackgroundImage` method to get or set its background image.

Table 8-3 includes a short list of methods in the `System.Windows.Form.Control` `class` that derived classes inherit. You should explore the online documentation available in Visual Studio .NET to learn about other members. All of the information from Tables 8-2 and 8-3 is developed from the Visual Studio MSDN documentation.

Table 8-3 System.Windows.Form.Control methods

Method	Description
Focus( )	Sets the input focus to the control
Hide( )	Conceals the control from the user
Select( )	Activates a control
Show( )	Displays the control to the user

 One of the most powerful features of Visual Studio .NET IDE is the extensive help available. Activate Dynamic Help from the Help menu bar. Once it is active, watch the Help Window. In Design view, every movement of the cursor displays a new topic. You can also position your cursor over controls or properties and press F1 to cause the online documentation to pop up.

The `Show( )` method functions the same way as setting the `Visible` property to `true`; `Hide( )` does the same thing as setting the `Visible` property to `false`.

The `System.Windows.Form.Control` `class` also has a number of predefined events, many of which you will examine in Chapter 9. The `System.Windows.Form.Control` click events will be used in this chapter with `Button` objects.

Derived Classes of the System.Windows.Form.Control Class

All the controls that you add to a form are objects or instances of one of the .NET predefined classes. Figure 8-11 identifies some of the basic user interface controls that can be added to a form. Look at each of the controls. They are named and briefly described.

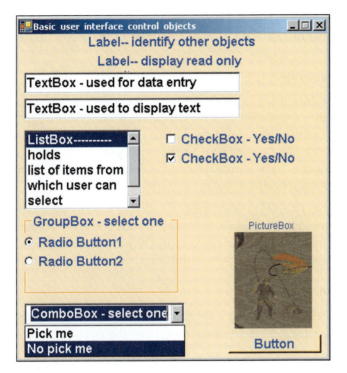

Figure 8-11   GUI controls

In the sections that follow, these GUI components are discussed in detail, and you create a small GUI application that can be used to compute the tax due on a purchase.

Label

As the name implies, `Label` objects are normally used to provide descriptive text or labels for another control. They can also be used to display information at runtime. Using Visual Studio, you can drag and drop the `Label` object onto your form. After it is added, you can set its properties to customize it for your application. The actual text caption that appears on the `Label` control object is placed there using the `Text` property. The `TextAlign` property enables you to position the caption within the label control area. The `Label` object can be programmed to be visible based on runtime dynamics using the `Visible` property. By default the `Visible` property is set to `true`. `Font`, `Location`, and any of the other `Control` properties shown in Table 8-2 can be modified using the Form Designer in Visual Studio.

If you prefer, you can manually add statements to instantiate and place control objects on your Windows forms, instead of using the Form Designer in Visual Studio .NET. As long as the `System.Windows.Forms` `namespace` is imported and referenced, you can create a `Label` object manually (without having to qualify the name fully) by calling the default constructor and instantiating an `object` as follows:

```
Label labelName = new Label( );
```

If you add a control such as a **Label** or **Button object** manually, a second step is required. To make the label viewable on the form, it must be added to the **Form object**. This is accomplished as follows:

```
this.Controls.Add(labelName);
```

When a form is created, it includes an instance of the **ControlCollection class**. This **class** is used to manage the controls that are added to the form. The **ControlCollection class** has a special inherited property named **Controls** that can be used to get the collection of controls on the form. The **ControlCollection class** also has methods such as **Add( )**, which adds controls to a form; **Clear( )**, which removes all controls; and **Remove( )**, which removes a specific control from a form.

If you use Visual Studio .NET to add your controls, you do not have to worry about all the details of getting the control registered with the **ControlCollection object**, because that code is added automatically for you. This is certainly the easiest, most efficient approach, and will be the method used for the remainder of the chapter.

Creating a TaxApp Form

To experience adding labels and changing their properties, a Visual Studio project named **TaxApp** has been created. Table 8-4 lists the properties set for the **Form object**.

Table 8-4 TaxApp Form1 properties

Property	Changes with explanation
BackColor	Selected blue from the Custom tab; could have typed 192, 192, 255 (RGB code for that selection)
Font	Selected Bookman Old Style, regular, 12 point; changed the font on the form, so that all controls added to this container would have this value set
GridSize	Replaced 8, 8 with 5, 5 for finer granularity
Size	Changed the size of the window from 300, 300 to 300, 280
Text	Typed "Windows Tax App" for the title bar caption

Adding Label Objects to Your TaxApp Form

Four **Label** objects are dragged to the form using the **Label** icon in the Toolbox.

The **Text** property for each is selected and values typed. Each of the individual objects needs to be resized so that the text can be displayed. The **label1 object** Font property is set to a size of 14 points with a bold style. This is done by clicking on the **Font** property and selecting these values from a drop-down list. The **TextAlign** property for **label1** is set to **TopCenter**.

After `label2`, `label3`, and `label4` objects' `Text` properties are changed and they are sized properly, the Align option from the Format menu is used to line them up in the same general area. One of the properties set was `GridSize`. By typing a small number (5, 5), a finer grain or more dots are displayed; thus, alignment is more precise. Using the Align option, you must line up objects after identifying those that should be aligned with each other. This can be accomplished by holding the Ctrl key and clicking on each of the objects you want to format. An alternate approach is to hold down the left mouse button and use the mouse to draw a box around the objects to be impacted. When you release the mouse button, you should ensure that the correct objects are selected.

 If you select too many objects, deselect one or more by pressing the Ctrl key and clicking on the objects to be deselected. You also have an Undo option under the Edit menu, which enables you to back out of a step.

While `label2`, `label3`, and `label4` are still selected, the vertical spacing between the labels is formatted using Format, Vertical Spacing, Make Equal. This is much simpler than trying to align your objects visually and drag them to new locations. Figure 8-12 shows the `Label` objects that are added and formatted.

8

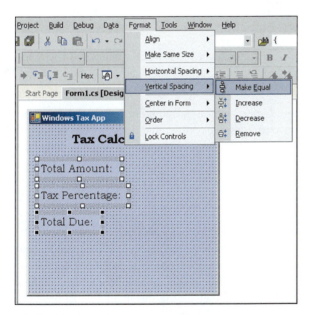

Figure 8-12   Formatting Label objects

One additional `Label` `object`, `label5`, is added to the `TaxApp` form container for the actual tax percentage amount. Because the tax rate is a constant value, the number can be placed on the form at design time. The number can also be used in calculations. This way users are not required to enter the value.

A good design principle to follow is to keep data entry to a minimum. Limit the amount of typing required by users, and do not have them enter values that can be calculated or obtained from other sources. This reduces the chances that typing errors will corrupt your solutions. It also reduces the amount of coding that might have to be done to deal with data entered in inconsistent formats. If you were to ask users to enter the tax rate for seven and one half percent, one user might enter 0.075; others might enter 7.5%, 7.50%, 7.5 %, 7.5, or 07.50. Entries stored as constants eliminate the need to program for these potential formatting inconsistencies.

After `label5` is added to the form, its properties are changed as shown in Table 8-5.

Table 8-5 TaxApp label5 object properties

Property	Changes with explanation
`BackColor`	Selected medium blue from Custom tab; changed the value to 50, 50, 192
`Font`	Selected style of bold italic
`ForeColor`	Selected light blue from Custom tab; could have typed 128, 128, 255 (RGB code for that selection)
`Text`	Typed "7.5%"

Since labels are not programmed for functionality with this application, the **Name** property of the **Label** objects is not changed. The default identifer names (`label1`, `label2`, ...) are left as is.

> **NOTE** Labels are sometimes used to display messages to users during runtime. They are especially useful for displaying error messages or text that does not appear with each run of an application. But, labels are most often used primarily to describe other controls on the form.

TextBox

The `TextBox` control **object**, shown in Figure 8-11, can be used to enter data or display text during runtime. This is the probably the most commonly used control because it can be used for both input and output. Like most other objects of the `Control` **class**, the `Text` property is used to get or set the **string** value in the control. Normally a single line of text is shown in a `TextBox` **object**; however, by changing the `MultiLine` property to **true**, the `TextBox` **object** can show several lines. There is also a `ScrollBars` property. When this property is used in combination with setting the `MultiLine` property to **true**, you can designate whether vertical or horizontal scrollbars are added. You can also restrict the number of characters the `TextBox` **object** can display by typing a value for the `MaxLength` property.

The **PasswordChar** property is used with **TextBox** objects and is fun to work with. By typing a single character such as an asterisk (*), you can mask the characters entered by the user. This is perfect for creating or entering data such as passwords. The **PasswordChar** property only works when the **MultiLine** property is set to **false**.

 Set the value of the **PasswordChar** property to **'0'** if you do not want the control to mask characters as they are typed.

Another property, **CharacterCasing**, can be set so that all characters retrieved by the **TextBox.Text** property are converted to uppercase or lowercase. This is useful when you are comparing the results entered from a user against a specific value. By using the **CharacterCasing** property you eliminate many of the extra comparisons that might be necessary.

There are many interesting properties that can be used with a **TextBox object**. Table 8-6 includes some of them. They were adapted from the Visual Studio MSDN documentation.

8

Table 8-6 TextBox properties

Property	Description
AcceptsReturn	Gets or sets a value indicating whether the Enter key creates a new line of text in a multiline **TextBox** control
AcceptsTab	Gets or sets a value indicating whether the Tab key inserts a tab into text of a multiline **TextBox** control
CharacterCasing	Gets or sets whether the **TextBox** control modifies the case of the characters as they are typed
Lines	Gets or sets the lines of text in a **TextBox** control
MaxLength	Gets or sets the maximum number of characters the user can type or paste into the **TextBox** control
Modified	Gets or sets a value indicating that the **TextBox** control has been modified since creation or when its contents were last set
MultiLine	Gets or sets a value indicating whether this is a multiline **TextBox** control
PasswordChar	Gets or sets the character used to mask characters in a single line **TextBox** control
ReadOnly	Gets or sets a value indicating whether text in the **TextBox** is read-only
ScrollBars	Gets or sets which scroll bars should appear in a multiline **TextBox** control
TextAlign	Gets or sets how text is aligned in a **TextBox** control
WordWrap	Indicates whether a multiline **TextBox** control automatically wraps words to the beginning of the next line

The `Modified` property is not listed in the Properties window because it is used to get or set the value indicating whether the contents of the text box control have been modified by the user since the control was created or its contents were last set.

Remember that in addition to the **TextBox** properties listed in Table 8-6, all the **Control** properties and methods shown in Tables 8-2 and 8-3 are available for use with **TextBox** objects. Several other methods including **AppendText( )**, which adds text to the end of the current text of the **TextBox**, and **Clear( )** can be used with **TextBox** objects. There are many interesting events that can be responded to with **TextBox** objects, and you will read about many of them in Chapter 9.

Add TextBox Objects to Your TaxApp Form

Two **TextBox** objects are added to the **TaxApp** form. The first is used as an input control allowing the user to enter the total purchase amount. The second is used to display the results of the calculation. Because the values entered or displayed in the **TextBox** objects must be referenced programmatically, one of the first properties to set is the **Name** property. **TextBox textBox1** is renamed **txtPurchase**, and **textBox2** is renamed **txtTotalDue**.

 Remember that to set properties, the Properties window must be active. If you do not see it on your screen, it can be displayed from the View menu. Then click on the control that you want to change and move down the list of properties in the Properties window until you locate the property. Type or select the new setting.

Table 8-7 lists the other properties set for the two **TextBox** objects.

Table 8-7 TaxApp TextBox objects property changes

Object	Property	Changes with explanation
textBox1	Name	Typed txtPurchase
textBox2	Name	Typed txtTotalDue
txtPurchase	Text	All spaces; deleted the characters so no value is displayed
txtPurchase	TextAlign	Selected right
txtTotalDue	Enabled	Selected false
txtTotalDue	Text	All spaces; deleted the characters so no value is displayed
txtTotalDue	TextAlign	Selected right

> **NOTE** As controls, such as text boxes and labels, are placed on the form, they are aligned and sized using **Format>Align**, **Format>Make Same Size**, **Format>Center in Form**, and the other options available under the Format menu. You are encouraged to experiment and learn to use these options.

As you build your Windows applications, in addition to seeing what the output looks like in the Form Designer, you can run the application at any stage as soon as you start the project by selecting the Windows application template.

The output produced from **TaxApp** (after adding the **Label** and **TextBox** objects and setting their properties) is shown in Figure 8-13. Notice that the gridlines do not appear when the program is run.

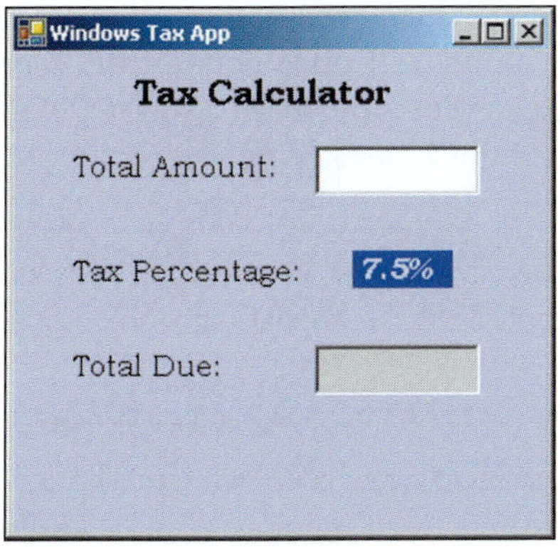

Figure 8-13   TaxApp with Label and Button objects

> **NOTE** If you accidentally double-click on the form when you are using the Form Designer, it brings up the Code Editor. Entering the Code Editor this way has the undesirable side effect of creating a `Form1_Load( )` method heading for you. The creation of the event does not create an error when you run your application, but it clutters your program listing with an empty method and a statement that registers the event. If you remove the method heading, you should also remove the statement that registered the form load event (`this.Load += new System.EventHandler(this.Form1_Load);`). This same side effect occurs if you double-click other controls such as labels or text boxes. The `label_click( )` or `textbox_textChanged( )` methods are added.

At design time you change the **Text** property by pointing and clicking in the **Text** property box. But, how do you use the Total Amount value entered by the user? How do you place text in the **TextBox** object beside the Total Due **Label** object? This cannot be done at design time. It needs to change based on the value the user enters for Total Amount. You are about to experience the programming power of using C# and Visual Studio. Any and all of the properties you changed during design can be accessed as part of a program statement and changed dynamically when your program runs. To experience this powerful characteristic of C#, you will now add a button that performs some calculations and displays the result in the Total Due **TextBox** object.

Button

Button objects are added to your form to increase functionality. They enable a user to click a button to perform a specific task. When it is clicked by a user, the event-handler method is automatically called up—if the button has an event-handler method—and is registered as an event to which your program is planning to respond. You place code in the event-handler method to perform any action you choose. A click event is normally associated with a mouse click; however, the click event can be fired when the Enter key or spacebar is pressed if the button has the focus.

 Having focus means being selected for the next activity. When an object has focus, it often appears different from the other controls. It can appear highlighted or selected with a box surrounding it.

Like other control objects, **Button** objects have a number of properties, methods, and events. They also inherit the properties, methods, and events listed previously in Tables 8-2 and 8-3 from the **Control class**. The **Enabled** property, inherited from the **Control class**, can be used to get or set a value indicating whether the control can respond to user interaction. The **Focused** property is used to determine whether the control has focus or is the one currently selected. The **Focus( )** method from the **Control class** is useful with **Button** objects to set the input focus to that control. **TabIndex**, also inherited from **Control**, is useful for setting or getting the tab order of the controls on a form container. Selecting View Tab Order from the View menu shows the sequential order of how the user moves through the application if the Tab key is used. By default the tab order is the same order as the order of how the controls are added to the form. You can change this order when you are in View Tab Order by clicking the controls sequentially to establish the new order. As you do this, a number representing the **TabIndex** property is displayed beside the control.

 You can also set the tab order from the Properties window or by writing program statements. A Label object participates in the tab order in that you can set its **TabIndex**. However, labels never receive focus—meaning the control is not stopped at when you press the Tab key. Instead, it is skipped and the next control, that can take focus, is selected.

For a complete list and description of the `Button` members, you should explore the C# documentation provided with Visual Studio .NET.

Add Button Objects to Your TaxApp Form

A `Button object` is dragged to the bottom of the form and its center is aligned with the center of label1, the heading for the form. The `Button` object's `Name` property is set to `btnCompute`. As noted previously, when you plan to name a control `object`, this should be one of the first things that is done after it is placed on the form container. Under most circumstances, it will not create problems for you if the `Name` is not set first. However, with buttons, if you add a click event before naming the control, you may have to go into the code generated by Form Designer and manually modify the name of the event-handler methods and registrations to have them match the new button name. Table 8-8 lists the properties that are set at design time for the `button1 object`.

Table 8-8 TaxApp button1 properties

Property	Changes with explanation
Name	Typed btnCompute
BackColor	Selected Navy
Font	Selected style of bold, point size of 14
ForeColor	Selected yellow from Custom tab; could have typed 255, 255, 128 (RGB code for that selection)
TabIndex	3
Text	Typed "Compute"

After setting the properties, you probably need to resize the `Button object` so that the text is displayed properly. The `txtPurchase TextBox` object's `TabIndex` property is also set to 1. You may need to realign it with the `label1` text heading. You can do this by selecting both control objects and clicking **Format>Align>Centers**. Remember that it *does* matter what the GUI looks like.

Add a `Click` event for the `btnCompute object`. This can be done by double-clicking on the actual `Button object` in the Form Designer. Another option is to display all the events using the lightning bolt on the Properties window and then double-click on the `Click` event as illustrated in Figure 8-14.

Figure 8-14   Events

> **NOTE**
> If you add the button click event using the list of available events as shown in Figure 8-14, you need to select the Properties icon in that window to reshow the list of properties. The Properties icon appears to the left of the lightning bolt.

When you double-click on the **Click** event you are taken to the **btnCompute_Click( )** method in the Code Editor. This is where you write your program statements describing the actions to be taken when the user clicks the Compute button.

As you think about what program statements need to be written and in what order, you should understand that the first action should be retrieval of the values that are entered into the **txtPurchase TextBox object**. The **Text** property can be used to accomplish this. Values retrieved with the **Text** property are of **string** type and require conversion before arithmetic is performed. The statements that appear in Example 8-4 can be added to the **btnCompute_Click( )** method to retrieve the purchase price and store it in a **double** variable for processing.

Example 8-4

```
private void btnCompute_Click(object sender, System.EventArgs e)
{
      string inValue;
      double purchaseAmt;
      inValue = txtPurchase.Text;
      purchaseAmt = double.Parse(inValue);
      // More program statements
```

You will recall that the actual percentage value associated with the tax rate is displayed in a **Label object**. The **Text** property for this **object** was used to set the value. The **Text** property can also be used to get the **string** value. However, in addition to the numeric amount representing the tax rate percentage, a special character, the percent symbol (%), was used to set the value. It is displayed and is retrieved with the **Text** property.

You learned about many **string** processing methods in Chapter 7. One of them listed in Table 7-3 is the **Remove( )** method. It can be used to remove characters from a **string** beginning at a specific location. You also learned in Chapter 7 about the **Length** property. **Length** is used to return the number of characters in the **string**. The percent symbol (%) is the last character in the string. Remember that the first character for a **string** is indexed by zero. Thus, the last character of the **string**, where the '**%**' character is located, is indexed by **Length-1**.

Two arguments are included with the **Remove( )** method. The first argument is the index of where character removal should begin. For this example, removal should start at **Length-1**. The second argument, 1, specifies how many characters to remove. Only one character, the '**%**', needs to be removed before converting the **string** into a **double** type for calculations. The statements in Example 8-5 are added to the **btnCompute_Click( )** method to retrieve and place the numeric value representing the tax percentage rate into the variable identified by **percent**.

Example 8-5

```
double percent;
inValue = label5.Text;    // inValue previously declared as string
inValue = inValue.Remove(inValue.Length-1, 1);
percent = double.Parse(inValue) / 100;
```

The last three lines in Example 8-5 could be written in one statement as shown in Example 8-6. Both produce the same results.

Example 8-6

```
percent = (double.Parse(label5.Text.Remove
         (label5.Text.Length-1, 1))) / 100;
```

Now that you have both values stored in the **double** variable, simple arithmetic can be performed and the result displayed in the **txtTotalDue TextBox object**. Example 8-7 includes those statements.

Example 8-7

```
double ans;
ans = (purchaseAmt *  percent) + purchaseAmt;
txtTotalDue.Text = String.Format("{0:C}",ans).ToString();
```

Figure 8-15 shows the output produced after the user enters a value and clicks the **Compute** button.

Figure 8-15   Tax calculator output

One additional property was set for the form to allow the Enter key to be associated with the **Compute** button. **AcceptButton** was set to **btnCompute**. Now pressing the Enter key is the same as clicking the **Compute Button object**. The complete program listing for **TaxApp** is shown in Example 8-8. Remember that the Form Designer automatically generated the code for the program based on dropping and dragging controls from the Toolbox window and setting properties using the Properties window during design. The body of the **btnCompute_Click( )** is the only code written manually.

Example 8-8

```csharp
// TaxApp              Author: Doyle
// A tax calculator is produced. Labels are used
// to display descriptive captions. A text box object
// is used for input and displaying results. One
// button click event method is programmed.
using System;
using System.Drawing;
using System.Collections;
using System.ComponentModel;
using System.Windows.Forms;
using System.Data;
namespace TaxApp
{
    public class Form1 : System.Windows.Forms.Form
    {
      private System.Windows.Forms.Label label1;
      private System.Windows.Forms.Label label2;
      private System.Windows.Forms.Label label3;
      private System.Windows.Forms.Label label4;
      private System.Windows.Forms.Label label5;
      private System.Windows.Forms.TextBox txtPurchase;
      private System.Windows.Forms.TextBox txtTotalDue;
      private System.Windows.Forms.Button btnCompute;
      private System.ComponentModel.Container
              components = null;
      public Form1( )
      {
        InitializeComponent( );
      }

      // Clean up any resources being used.
      protected override void Dispose(bool disposing)
      {
        if(disposing)
        {
            if (components != null)
            {
                components.Dispose( );
            }
        }
        base.Dispose(disposing);
      }
```

8

```csharp
#region Windows Form Designer generated code
private void InitializeComponent( )
{
    this.label1 = new System.Windows.Forms.Label( );
    this.label2 = new System.Windows.Forms.Label( );
    this.label3 = new System.Windows.Forms.Label( );
    this.label4 = new System.Windows.Forms.Label( );
    this.label5 = new System.Windows.Forms.Label( );
    this.txtPurchase = new
        System.Windows.Forms.TextBox( );
    this.txtTotalDue = new
        System.Windows.Forms.TextBox( );
    this.btnCompute = new System.Windows.Forms.Button( );
    this.SuspendLayout( );

    // label1
    this.label1.Name = "label1";
    this.label1.Font = new System.Drawing.Font
        ("Bookman Old Style",
        14.25F, System.Drawing.FontStyle.Bold,
        System.Drawing.GraphicsUnit.Point,
        ((System.Byte)(0)));
    this.label1.Location = new
        System.Drawing.Point(60, 10);
    this.label1.Size = new System.Drawing.Size(160, 23);
    this.label1.TabIndex = 0;
    this.label1.Text = "Tax Calculator";
    this.label1.TextAlign =
        System.Drawing.ContentAlignment.TopCenter;

    // label2
    this.label2.Location = new System.Drawing.Point(30, 50);
    this.label2.Name = "label2";
    this.label2.Size = new System.Drawing.Size(125, 26);
    this.label2.TabIndex = 0;
    this.label2.Text = "Total Amount:";

    // label3
    this.label3.Location = new System.Drawing.Point(30, 105);
    this.label3.Name = "label3";
    this.label3.Size = new System.Drawing.Size(135, 23);
    this.label3.TabIndex = 0;
    this.label3.Text = "Tax Percentage:";
```

```
// label4
this.label4.Location = new System.Drawing.Point(30, 155);
this.label4.Name = "label4";
this.label4.Size = new System.Drawing.Size(95, 26);
this.label4.TabIndex = 0;
this.label4.Text = "Total Due:";

// label5
this.label5.BackColor =
    System.Drawing.Color.FromArgb(((System.Byte)(50)),
    ((System.Byte)(50)), ((System.Byte)(192)));
this.label5.Font = new System.Drawing.Font
    ("Bookman Old Style", 12F,
    (System.Drawing.FontStyle.Bold |
    System.Drawing.FontStyle.Italic),
    System.Drawing.GraphicsUnit.Point,
    ((System.Byte)(0)));
this.label5.ForeColor =
    System.Drawing.Color.FromArgb(((System.Byte)(128)),
    ((System.Byte)(128)), ((System.Byte)(255)));
this.label5.Location = new
    System.Drawing.Point(185, 105);
this.label5.Name = "label5";
this.label5.Size = new System.Drawing.Size(55, 20);
this.label5.TabIndex = 0;
this.label5.Text = "7.5%";

// txtPurchase
this.txtPurchase.Location =
    new System.Drawing.Point(165, 50);
this.txtPurchase.Name = "txtPurchase";
this.txtPurchase.Size = new System.Drawing.Size(90, 26);
this.txtPurchase.TabIndex = 1;
this.txtPurchase.Text = "";
this.txtPurchase.TextAlign =
    System.Windows.Forms.HorizontalAlignment.Right;

// txtTotalDue
this.txtTotalDue.Enabled = false;
this.txtTotalDue.Location = new
    System.Drawing.Point(140, 155);
this.txtTotalDue.Name = "txtTotalDue";
this.txtTotalDue.Size = new
    System.Drawing.Size(115, 26);
this.txtTotalDue.TabIndex = 0;
this.txtTotalDue.Text = "";
this.txtTotalDue.TextAlign =
    System.Windows.Forms.HorizontalAlignment.Right;
```

8

```csharp
// btnCompute
this.btnCompute.BackColor = System.Drawing.Color.Navy;
this.btnCompute.Font = new System.Drawing.Font
    ("Bookman Old Style", 14.25F,
    System.Drawing.FontStyle.Bold,
    System.Drawing.GraphicsUnit.Point,
    ((System.Byte)(0)));
this.btnCompute.ForeColor =
    System.Drawing.Color.FromArgb(((System.Byte)(255)),
    ((System.Byte)(255)), ((System.Byte)(128)));
this.btnCompute.Location = new
    System.Drawing.Point(87, 205);
this.btnCompute.Name = "btnCompute";
this.btnCompute.Size = new
    System.Drawing.Size(107, 23);
this.btnCompute.TabIndex = 2;
this.btnCompute.Text = "Compute";
this.btnCompute.Click += new
    System.EventHandler(this.btnCompute_Click);

// Form1
this.AcceptButton = this.btnCompute;
this.AutoScaleBaseSize = new
    System.Drawing.Size(9, 19);
this.BackColor =
    System.Drawing.Color.FromArgb(((System.Byte)(192)),
    ((System.Byte)(192)), ((System.Byte)(255)));
this.ClientSize = new System.Drawing.Size(292, 253);
this.Controls.AddRange
    (new System.Windows.Forms.Control[]
                {this.btnCompute,
                 this.txtTotalDue,
                 this.txtPurchase,
                 this.label5,
                 this.label4,
                 this.label3,
                 this.label2,
                 this.label1});
this.Font = new System.Drawing.Font
    ("Bookman Old Style", 12F,
    System.Drawing.FontStyle.Regular,
    System.Drawing.GraphicsUnit.Point,
    ((System.Byte)(0)));
this.Name = "Form1";
this.Text = "Windows Tax App";
this.ResumeLayout(false);
}
#endregion
```

```csharp
// The main entry point for the application.
[STAThread]
static void Main()
{
    Application.Run(new Form1());
}

private void btnCompute_Click(object sender,
                                System.EventArgs e)
{
    string inValue;
    double purchaseAmt,
           percent,
           ans;

    inValue = txtPurchase.Text;
    purchaseAmt = double.Parse(inValue);

    inValue =  label5.Text;
    inValue = inValue.Remove(inValue.Length-1, 1);
    percent = double.Parse(inValue) / 100;

    ans = (purchaseAmt * percent) + purchaseAmt;
    txtTotalDue.Text =
            String.Format("{0:C}",ans).ToString();
}
}
}
```

8

PROGRAMMING EXAMPLE: TEMPAGENCY APPLICATION

This example demonstrates the design and implementation of a graphical user interface for a Windows application. Two classes are constructed to separate the business logic from the presentation details. The first class defines a template for a typical payroll employee object. It includes the behaviors for determining withholding deductions and calculating the net take-home pay; thus, the business logic is described in this Employee class. The other class instantiates an object of the Employee class and instantiates a Windows Form object to represent the graphical user interface. Using the .NET predefined Control classes, labels, text boxes, and button objects are added to the Form object. The problem specification for the TempAgency application is shown in Figure 8-16.

> XYZ JobSource is in the business of matching computer systems analysts and programmers with employers needing temporary help. They pay a flat rate of $150.00 per hour to their contract analysts and programmers. Contractors are paid on a weekly basis or at the completion of a project, whichever comes first. Each contractor logs his or her own hours. They have asked you to develop a Windows application to be used by the contractors to determine how much money they will take home for a given period in time.
>
> XYZ JobSource is located in a city that does not pay local sales tax. The company pays no benefits in terms of insurance or retirement. They are required by law to deduct Social Security taxes and federal income taxes from each check. The amount of Social Security deductions is calculated at 7.85% of the gross pay. The amount of federal withholding is based on the number of dependent allowances. The following formula is used: fed deduction = (grossPay - (grossPay * 5.75% * number of dependents)) * 25%. They also charge a membership fee to each contractor of 13% of their gross pay.
>
> Design a GUI that will accept as input the contractor's name, number of dependents, and the number of hours worked. Display the gross pay, deductions, and net pay.

Figure 8-16   Problem specification for TempAgency

Analyze the Problem

You should review the problem specification in Figure 8-16 and make sure you understand the problem definition. Several values will be entered into the program to represent the name, number of hours worked, and number of dependents for an employee. The business logic is separated from the user interface by using two separate classes. This enables other applications to use the **Employee class**. Actual checks for the XYZ JobSource temp agency may need to be printed, payroll records saved, and other reports generated. By separating the logic from the design of the GUI presentation, the **Employee class** can be reused for many other applications.

Data   Table 8-9 lists the data field members needed for the **Employee class**. In addition to these entered values, instance variables to store deductions and pay amounts are needed.

Table 8-9 Instance field members for the Employee class

Data description	Type	Identifier
Employee name	string	employeeName
Number of hours worked	double	noOfHours
Number of dependents	int	noOfDependents
Social Security deduction	double	socialSecurity
Federal income tax deduction	double	federalTax
Agency fee for contract	double	agencyFee
Gross amount before deductions	double	gross
Net take home after deductions	double	net

Constants   Several values such as hourly rate, Social Security, and federal withholding tax rates are the same for all employees. The user does not have to enter these values at runtime; instead, constants can be defined for the values in the **Employee class**. Any objects instantiated of that **class** can then have access to the amounts, as shown in Table 8-10.

8

Table 8-10 Constant field members for the Employee class

Data description	Type	Identifier	Value
Hourly rate	double	RATE	150.00
Federal tax deduction percentage	double	FEDERAL_TAX	0.25
Social Security deduction percentage	double	SOCIAL_SECURITY_RATE	0.0785
Dependent allowance percentage	double	DEPENDENT_ALLOWANCE	0.0575
Agency fee for the contract	double	AGENCY_CHARGE	0.13

A second **class** is created for the user interface. This **class** allows the user to enter their name, number of dependents, and number of hours worked. Local variables must be declared to hold these values. After values are entered and calculations performed, an area on the form displays the results. Thus, objects that can be used to display gross and net pay along with calculated deductions are needed. During design, a prototype is developed to determine the location of the objects on the form.

Design a Solution

The desired output is to display the gross and net pay along with deductions. Figure 8-17 shows a prototype for the form. It illustrates what types of objects are needed and gives an approximation of where they should be placed.

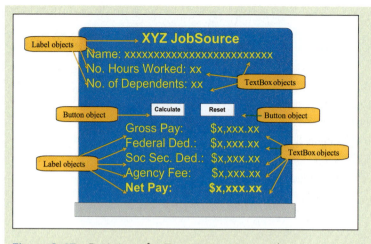

Figure 8-17 Prototype for TempAgency example

During design, it is also useful to determine which **object** types are used to create the interface. The GUI is used for both input and output of data. Not all objects show on the screen at the same time. The labels and text boxes below the buttons are initially set to be invisible to the user. Only after the Calculate button is clicked do those objects show on the monitor. When they show, the labels and text boxes associated with the number of hours worked and the number of dependents are hidden.

When the Reset button is pressed, the text box for the name is cleared and the labels and text boxes above the buttons show. All objects below the buttons are hidden.

An abstraction for a typical employee has both data and behavior characteristics that can be identified. For this application, one of the major actions or behaviors of an **object** of the **Employee class** is to calculate the gross pay using the number of hours and the number of dependents. These values can be retrieved from the **TextBox** objects. Methods to determine the deductions for the agency, Social Security, and federal tax contributions are needed, as well as a method to calculate the net take-home pay. Class diagrams are used to help design and document these characteristics. Figure 8-18 shows the **class** diagrams for the **TempAgency** example.

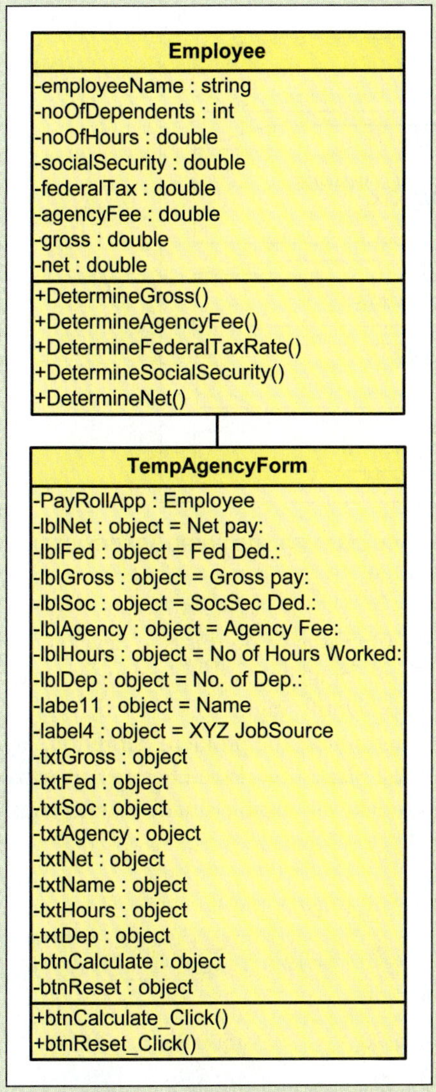

Employee

-employeeName : string
-noOfDependents : int
-noOfHours : double
-socialSecurity : double
-federalTax : double
-agencyFee : double
-gross : double
-net : double

+DetermineGross()
+DetermineAgencyFee()
+DetermineFederalTaxRate()
+DetermineSocialSecurity()
+DetermineNet()

TempAgencyForm

-PayRollApp : Employee
-lblNet : object = Net pay:
-lblFed : object = Fed Ded.:
-lblGross : object = Gross pay:
-lblSoc : object = SocSec Ded.:
-lblAgency : object = Agency Fee:
-lblHours : object = No of Hours Worked:
-lblDep : object = No. of Dep.:
-labe11 : object = Name
-label4 : object = XYZ JobSource
-txtGross : object
-txtFed : object
-txtSoc : object
-txtAgency : object
-txtNet : object
-txtName : object
-txtHours : object
-txtDep : object
-btnCalculate : object
-btnReset : object

+btnCalculate_Click()
+btnReset_Click()

Figure 8-18 Class diagrams for TempAgency example

The **class** diagrams do not show the properties needed or the local variables that might be needed by specific **class** methods.

During design, it is important to develop an algorithm showing the systematic process for the business logic of the application. Pseudocode for the **Employee** methods is shown in Figure 8–19.

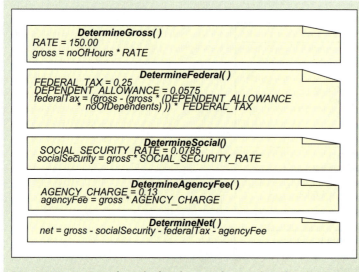

Figure 8-19 Pseudocode for the Employee class for the TempAgency example

You should always desk check your design. One way to do this is to develop a test plan of values to use for testing. A table with columns for all entered and calculated values can be developed as shown in Table 8–11. After you identify values to be tested, use a calculator to fill in the calculated values. Then, go back and reread the problem definition. Are those the correct calculated values? Notice that the test plan is developed before any actual coding. This ensures that you design the solution to take all possible situations into consideration.

Table 8-11 Desk check test plan of TempAgency example

noOFDependents	noOfHours	gross	socialSecurity	federalTax	agencyFee	net
1	10	1500.00	117.75	353.44	195.00	833.81
0	40	6000.00	471.00	1500.00	780.00	3249.00
1	40	6000.00	471.00	1413.75	780.00	3335.25
2	40	6000.00	471.00	1327.50	780.00	3421.50
3	40	6000.00	471.00	1241.25	780.00	3507.75
6	20	3000.00	235.50	491.25	390.00	1883.25
4	40	6000.00	471.00	1155.00	780.00	3594.00
2	30	4500.00	353.25	995.63	585.00	2566.13
0	50	7500.00	588.75	1875.00	975.00	4061.25
2	50	7500.00	588.75	1659.38	975.00	4276.88

Table 8-11 Desk check test plan of TempAgency example (continued)

noOFDependents	noOfHours	gross	socialSecurity	federalTax	agencyFee	net
9	25	3750.00	294.38	452.34	487.50	2515.78
3	2	300.00	23.55	62.06	39.00	175.39

Once you implement your design, be sure to run and test your application using the values you identified when you developed the test plan. Compare the results you obtain during your desk check using a calculator with the output produced from your program.

Code the Solution   After you complete the design and verify the algorithm's correctness, it is time to translate the design into source code. For this application, you are creating two separate files—one for each **class**.

If you are using Visual Studio .NET, much of the code for the user interface **class** can be generated for you by the Form Designer. If you do not have Visual Studio, you can type assignment statements for the property values. For example, the first statement in Table 8-12 could be typed as:

```
AcceptButton = btnCalculate;
```

The statement that the Visual Studio Form Designer generates when you use the Properties window to set the **AcceptButton** is:

```
this.AcceptButton = this.btnCalculate;
```

Both produce the same result when the application is run. Thus, even though Visual Studio was used to produce the code listing that follows, the program statements could all be written using an editor such as Notepad and executed from the DOS command line. Appendix A includes details for compiling and executing from the command line. Table 8-12 shows the different **Control** objects' properties and values that are set at design time.

8

Table 8-12 Properties set for TempAgency example

Type of object	Identifier	Property	Value
Form	TempAgencyForm	AcceptButton	btnCalculate
Form	TempAgencyForm	BackColor	blue(0,0,192)
Form	TempAgencyForm	CancelButton	btnReset
Form	TempAgencyForm	Font	ComicSansMS, size 12, style regular
Form	TempAgencyForm	ForeColor	light yellow(255,255,192)

Table 8-12 Properties set for TempAgency example (continued)

Type of object	Identifier	Property	Value
Form	TempAgencyForm	Text	Typed "PayRoll Application"
Label	label1	Text	Typed "Name: "
Label	lblHours	Text	Typed "No. of Hours Worked: "
Label	lblDep	Text	Typed "No. Of Dependents: "
Label	label4	Font	Comic Sans MS, size 14, style bold
Label	label4	Text	Typed "XYZ JobSource"
Label	lblNet	Text	Typed "Net Pay: "
Label	lblNet	Visible	false
Label	lblFed	Text	Typed "Federal Ded: "
Label	lblFed	Visible	false
Label	lblGross	Text	Typed "Gross Pay: "
Label	lblGross	Visible	false
Label	lblAgency	Text	Typed "Agency Fee: "
Label	lblAgency	Visible	false
Label	lblSoc	Text	Typed "Soc Sec. Ded: "
Label	lblSoc	Visible	false
TextBox	txtHours	AcceptsReturn	true
TextBox	txtNet	FontStyle	Bold
TextBox	txtName	AcceptsReturn	true
TextBox	txtName	Text	true
TextBox	txtHours	Text	All spaces; deleted the characters so no value is displayed
TextBox	txtHours	TextAlign	Right
TextBox	txtDep	Text	All spaces; deleted the characters so no value is displayed
TextBox	txtDep	TextAlign	Right
TextBox	txtGross	Text	All spaces; deleted the characters so no value is displayed
TextBox	txtGross	TextAlign	Right
TextBox	txtGross	Visible	False
TextBox	txtGross	BackColor	blue (192,192,255)

Table 8-12 Properties set for TempAgency example (continued)

Type of object	Identifier	Property	Value
TextBox	txtFed	Text	All spaces; deleted the characters so no value is displayed
TextBox	txtFed	TextAlign	Right
TextBox	txtFed	Visible	False
TextBox	txtFed	BackColor	blue (192,192,255)
TextBox	txtSoc	Text	All spaces; deleted the characters so no value is displayed
TextBox	txtSoc	TextAlign	Right
TextBox	txtSoc	Visible	False
TextBox	txtSoc	ForeColor	blue (192,192,255)
TextBox	txtAgency	Text	All spaces; deleted the characters so no value is displayed
TextBox	txtAgency	TextAlign	Right
TextBox	txtAgency	Visible	False
TextBox	txtAgency	BackColor	blue (192,192,255)
TextBox	txtNet	Text	All spaces deleted the characters so no value is displayed
TextBox	txtNet	TextAlign	Right
TextBox	txtNet	BackColor	blue (192,192,255)
Textbox	txtNet	Visible	False
Button	btnCalculate	Text	Typed "Calculate Take-Home Pay"
Button	btnCalculate	ForeColor	Yellow
Button	btnReset	Text	Typed "Reset Display"
Button	btnReset	ForeColor	Yellow

8

The final application listing for both files appears in the following code segment. The first **class**, **Employee**, was written without the aid of the Form Designer. Most of the code for the second **class**, **TempAgencyForm**, was generated by the Form Designer in Visual Studio .NET as properties were set. The bodies for the last three methods, **btnCalculate_Click( )**, **btnReset_Click( )**, and **setVisibility( )**, were added to the generated code.

> **NOTE**
>
> When you create your application using Visual Studio, your solution may vary from what is shown in the example code. For example, some of your property value settings may differ due to the fact that you may drag and drop your controls to different locations, or you may select the controls in a different order. You may see more or different comments than what appears in the code listing. Also, due to space constraints some lines of code must be formatted to appear on two or more lines.

```csharp
// Employee.cs            Author: Doyle
// Employee class includes data characteristics of
// name, number of dependents, number of hours worked,
// deductions for Social Security, federal tax, and agency fee
// Methods to calculate gross, net, and deductions
using System;
namespace PayRollApp
{
    public class Employee
    {
        private const double RATE = 150.00d;
        private const double FEDERAL_TAX = 0.25d;
        private const double SOCIAL_SECURITY_RATE = 0.0785d;
        private const double DEPENDENT_ALLOWANCE = 0.0575d;
        private const double AGENCY_CHARGE = 0.13d;

        private string employeeName;
        private int noOfDependents;
        private double noOfHours;
        private double socialSecurity;
        private double federalTax;
        private double agencyFee;
        private double gross;
        private double net;

        // Default constructor
        public  Employee( )
        {

        }

        // Constructor - when the object is created, calculate
        // values for private member data items.
        public Employee(string name, double hours, int dep)
        {
            employeeName = name;
            noOfHours = hours;
            noOfDependents = dep;
```

```csharp
        DetermineGross( );
        DetermineAgencyFee( );
        DetermineFederalTaxRate( );
        DetermineSocialSecurity(   );
        DetermineNet( );
    }

    // Property used to access or change EmployeeName
    public string EmployeeName
    {
        set
        {
            employeeName = value;
        }
        get
        {
            return employeeName;
        }
    }

    // Property used to access number of dependents
    public int NoOfDependents
    {
        set
        {
            noOfDependents = value;
        }
        get
        {
            return noOfDependents;
        }
    }

    // Property used to access or change hours worked
    public double NoOfHours
    {
        set
        {
            noOfHours = value;
        }
        get
        {
            return noOfHours;
        }
    }
```

8

```csharp
        // Property used to access Social Security tax amount
        public double SocialSecurity
        {
            get
            {
                return socialSecurity;
            }

        }
        // Property used to access gross pay
        public double Gross
        {
            get
            {
                return gross;
            }
        }

        // Property used to access federal income tax amount
        public double FederalTax
        {
            get
            {
                return federalTax;
            }
        }

        // Property used to access agency fee
        public double AgencyFee
        {
            get
            {
                return agencyFee;
            }
        }

        // Property used to access net pay
        public double Net
        {
            get
            {
                return net;
            }
        }
```

```csharp
// Using the same constant value for a flat hourly rate,
// calculate gross pay prior to any deductions.
public void DetermineGross( )
{
    gross = noOfHours * RATE;
}

// Calculate agency fee based on gross pay
public void DetermineAgencyFee( )
{
    agencyFee = gross * AGENCY_CHARGE;
}

// Calculate federal tax due
public void DetermineFederalTaxRate( )
{
    federalTax = (gross - (gross * (DEPENDENT_ALLOWANCE
                        * noOfDependents) )) *
                    FEDERAL_TAX;
}

// Calculate Social Security taxes
public void  DetermineSocialSecurity( )
{
    socialSecurity = gross * SOCIAL_SECURITY_RATE;
}
// Calculate take home pay after deductions
public void DetermineNet( )
{
    net =  gross - socialSecurity - federalTax - agencyFee;
}
```

8

> **NOTE** The program listing for the file containing the source code for the `class` that creates the graphical user interface appears next.

```csharp
// TempAgencyForm.cs          Author: Doyle
// Builds the Graphical User Interface
// Includes button, label, text box, and form objects
using System;
using System.Drawing;
using System.Collections;
using System.ComponentModel;
using System.Windows.Forms;
using System.Data;
```

```csharp
namespace PayRollApp
{
    public class TempAgencyForm : System.Windows.Forms.Form
    {
        private System.Windows.Forms.Label label1;
        private System.Windows.Forms.Label label4;
        private System.Windows.Forms.Label lblNet;
        private System.Windows.Forms.Label lblFed;
        private System.Windows.Forms.Label lblGross;
        private System.Windows.Forms.Label lblSoc;
        private System.Windows.Forms.Label lblAgency;
        private System.Windows.Forms.TextBox txtGross;
        private System.Windows.Forms.TextBox txtFed;
        private System.Windows.Forms.TextBox txtSoc;
        private System.Windows.Forms.TextBox txtAgency;
        private System.Windows.Forms.TextBox txtNet;
        private System.Windows.Forms.Button btnCalculate;
        private System.Windows.Forms.TextBox txtName;
        private System.Windows.Forms.TextBox txtHours;
        private System.Windows.Forms.TextBox txtDep;
        private System.Windows.Forms.Label lblHours;
        private System.Windows.Forms.Label lblDep;
        private System.Windows.Forms.Button btnReset;

        // Required designer variable
        private System.ComponentModel.Container components = null;

        public TempAgencyForm( )
        {
            InitializeComponent( );
        }

        // Clean up any resources being used
        protected override void Dispose(bool disposing)
        {
            if(disposing)
            {
                if (components != null)
                {
                    components.Dispose( );
                }
            }
            base.Dispose(disposing);
        }
        #region Windows Form Designer generated code
```

```csharp
// Required method for Designer support - do not modify
private void InitializeComponent( )
{
    this.label1 = new System.Windows.Forms.Label( );
    this.lblHours = new System.Windows.Forms.Label( );
    this.lblDep = new System.Windows.Forms.Label( );
    this.label4 = new System.Windows.Forms.Label( );
    this.lblNet = new System.Windows.Forms.Label( );
    this.lblFed = new System.Windows.Forms.Label( );
    this.lblGross = new System.Windows.Forms.Label( );
    this.lblSoc = new System.Windows.Forms.Label( );
    this.lblAgency = new System.Windows.Forms.Label( );
    this.txtName = new System.Windows.Forms.TextBox( );
    this.txtHours = new System.Windows.Forms.TextBox( );
    this.txtDep = new System.Windows.Forms.TextBox( );
    this.txtGross = new System.Windows.Forms.TextBox( );
    this.txtFed = new System.Windows.Forms.TextBox( );
    this.txtSoc = new System.Windows.Forms.TextBox( );
    this.txtAgency = new System.Windows.Forms.TextBox( );
    this.txtNet = new System.Windows.Forms.TextBox( );
    this.btnCalculate = new System.Windows.Forms.Button( );
    this.btnReset = new System.Windows.Forms.Button( );
    this.SuspendLayout( );

    // label1
    this.label1.Location = new System.Drawing.Point(8, 48);
    this.label1.Name = "label1";
    this.label1.TabIndex = 0;
    this.label1.Text = "Name:";

    // lblHours
    this.lblHours.Location = new
            System.Drawing.Point(8, 80);
    this.lblHours.Name = "lblHours";
    this.lblHours.Size = new System.Drawing.Size(176, 23);
    this.lblHours.TabIndex = 1;
    this.lblHours.Text = "No. of Hours Worked:";

    // lblDep
    this.lblDep.Location = new
            System.Drawing.Point(8, 120);
    this.lblDep.Name = "lblDep";
    this.lblDep.Size = new System.Drawing.Size(160, 23);
    this.lblDep.TabIndex = 2;
    this.lblDep.Text = "No. of Dependents:";
```

8

```
// label4
this.label4.Font = new
        System.Drawing.Font("Comic Sans MS",
        14.25F, System.Drawing.FontStyle.Bold,
        System.Drawing.GraphicsUnit.Point,
        ((System.Byte)(0)));
this.label4.ForeColor = System.Drawing.Color.Yellow;
this.label4.Location = new
        System.Drawing.Point(144, 0);
this.label4.Name = "label4";
this.label4.Size = new System.Drawing.Size(160, 23);
this.label4.TabIndex = 3;
this.label4.Text = "XYZ JobSource";

// lblNet
this.lblNet.Location = new
        System.Drawing.Point(136, 392);
this.lblNet.Name = "lblNet";
this.lblNet.TabIndex = 4;
this.lblNet.Text = "Net Pay:";
this.lblNet.Visible = false;

// lblFed
this.lblFed.Location = new
        System.Drawing.Point(144, 288);
this.lblFed.Name = "lblFed";
this.lblFed.Size = new System.Drawing.Size(112, 23);
this.lblFed.TabIndex = 5;
this.lblFed.Text = "Federal Ded:";
this.lblFed.Visible = false;

// lblGross
this.lblGross.Location = new
        System.Drawing.Point(136, 256);
this.lblGross.Name = "lblGross";
this.lblGross.TabIndex = 6;
this.lblGross.Text = "Gross Pay:";
this.lblGross.Visible = false;

// lblSoc
this.lblSoc.Location = new
        System.Drawing.Point(144, 320);
this.lblSoc.Name = "lblSoc";
this.lblSoc.Size = new System.Drawing.Size(120, 23);
this.lblSoc.TabIndex = 7;
this.lblSoc.Text = "Soc Sec. Ded:";
this.lblSoc.Visible = false;
```

```
// lblAgency
this.lblAgency.Location = new
            System.Drawing.Point(144, 352);
this.lblAgency.Name = "lblAgency";
this.lblAgency.TabIndex = 8;
this.lblAgency.Text = "Agency Fee:";
this.lblAgency.Visible = false;

// txtName
this.txtName.AcceptsReturn = true;
this.txtName.Location = new
            System.Drawing.Point(64, 40);
this.txtName.Name = "txtName";
this.txtName.Size = new System.Drawing.Size(280, 30);
this.txtName.TabIndex = 9;
this.txtName.Text = "";

// txtHours
this.txtHours.AcceptsReturn = true;
this.txtHours.ForeColor =
            System.Drawing.SystemColors.WindowText;
this.txtHours.Location = new
            System.Drawing.Point(184, 80);
this.txtHours.Name = "txtHours";
this.txtHours.Size = new System.Drawing.Size(32, 30);
this.txtHours.TabIndex = 10;
this.txtHours.Text = "";
this.txtHours.TextAlign =
        System.Windows.Forms.HorizontalAlignment.Right;

// txtDep
this.txtDep.Location = new
            System.Drawing.Point(184, 120);
this.txtDep.Name = "txtDep";
this.txtDep.Size = new System.Drawing.Size(32, 30);
this.txtDep.TabIndex = 11;
this.txtDep.Text = "";
this.txtDep.TextAlign =
        System.Windows.Forms.HorizontalAlignment.Right;

// txtGross
this.txtGross.BackColor =
        System.Drawing.Color.FromArgb
        (((System.Byte)(192)), ((System.Byte)(192)),
        ((System.Byte)(255)));
this.txtGross.Location = new
            System.Drawing.Point(224, 248);
this.txtGross.Name = "txtGross";
```

8

```csharp
this.txtGross.Size = new System.Drawing.Size(120, 30);
this.txtGross.TabIndex = 12;
this.txtGross.Text = "";
this.txtGross.TextAlign =
    System.Windows.Forms.HorizontalAlignment.Right;
this.txtGross.Visible = false;

// txtFed
this.txtFed.BackColor =
    System.Drawing.Color.FromArgb
    (((System.Byte)(192)), ((System.Byte)(192)),
    ((System.Byte)(255)));
this.txtFed.Location = new
    System.Drawing.Point(264, 288);
this.txtFed.Name = "txtFed";
this.txtFed.Size = new System.Drawing.Size(80, 30);
this.txtFed.TabIndex = 13;
this.txtFed.Text = "";
this.txtFed.TextAlign =
    System.Windows.Forms.HorizontalAlignment.Right;
this.txtFed.Visible = false;

// txtSoc
this.txtSoc.BackColor =
    System.Drawing.Color.FromArgb
    (((System.Byte)(192)), ((System.Byte)(192)),
    ((System.Byte)(255)));
this.txtSoc.Location = new
        System.Drawing.Point(264, 320);
this.txtSoc.Name = "txtSoc";
this.txtSoc.Size = new System.Drawing.Size(80, 30);
this.txtSoc.TabIndex = 14;
this.txtSoc.Text = "";
this.txtSoc.TextAlign =
    System.Windows.Forms.HorizontalAlignment.Right;
this.txtSoc.Visible = false;

// txtAgency
this.txtAgency.BackColor =
    System.Drawing.Color.FromArgb
    (((System.Byte)(192)), ((System.Byte)(192)),
    ((System.Byte)(255)));
this.txtAgency.Location = new
    System.Drawing.Point(264, 352);
this.txtAgency.Name = "txtAgency";
this.txtAgency.Size = new System.Drawing.Size(80, 30);
this.txtAgency.TabIndex = 15;
this.txtAgency.Text = "";
```

```csharp
this.txtAgency.TextAlign =
      System.Windows.Forms.HorizontalAlignment.Right;
this.txtAgency.Visible = false;

// txtNet
this.txtNet.BackColor =
      System.Drawing.Color.FromArgb
      (((System.Byte)(192)), ((System.Byte)(192)),
      ((System.Byte)(255)));
this.txtNet.Font = new
            System.Drawing.Font("Comic Sans MS",
            12F, System.Drawing.FontStyle.Bold,
            System.Drawing.GraphicsUnit.Point,
            ((System.Byte)(0)));
this.txtNet.Location = new
            System.Drawing.Point(224, 392);
this.txtNet.Name = "txtNet";
this.txtNet.Size = new System.Drawing.Size(120, 30);
this.txtNet.TabIndex = 16;
this.txtNet.Text = "";
this.txtNet.TextAlign =
      System.Windows.Forms.HorizontalAlignment.Right;
this.txtNet.Visible = false;

// btnCalculate
this.btnCalculate.ForeColor =
      System.Drawing.Color.Yellow;
this.btnCalculate.Location = new
            System.Drawing.Point(48, 184);
this.btnCalculate.Name = "btnCalculate";
this.btnCalculate.Size = new
            System.Drawing.Size(128, 56);
this.btnCalculate.TabIndex = 17;
this.btnCalculate.Text = "Calculate Take-Home Pay";
this.btnCalculate.Click += new
      System.EventHandler(this.btnCalculate_Click);

// btnReset
this.btnReset.DialogResult =
      System.Windows.Forms.DialogResult.Cancel;
this.btnReset.ForeColor = System.Drawing.Color.Yellow;
this.btnReset.Location = new
            System.Drawing.Point(264, 184);
this.btnReset.Name = "btnReset";
this.btnReset.Size = new System.Drawing.Size(128, 56);
this.btnReset.TabIndex = 18;
this.btnReset.Text = "Reset Display";
```

8

```
        this.btnReset.Click += new
            System.EventHandler(this.btnReset_Click);

        // TempAgencyForm
        this.AcceptButton = this.btnCalculate;
        this.AutoScaleBaseSize = new
            System.Drawing.Size(8, 23);
        this.BackColor =
            System.Drawing.Color.FromArgb
            (((System.Byte)(0)), ((System.Byte)(0)),
            ((System.Byte)(192)));
        this.CancelButton = this.btnReset;
        this.ClientSize = new System.Drawing.Size(492, 473);
        this.Controls.AddRange(new
            System.Windows.Forms.Control[] {
            this.btnReset, this.btnCalculate, this.txtNet,
            this.txtAgency, this.txtSoc, this.txtFed,
            this.txtGross, this.txtDep, this.txtHours,
            this.txtName, this.lblAgency, this.lblSoc,
            this.lblGross, this.lblFed, this.lblNet,
            this.label4, this.lblDep, this.lblHours,
            this.label1});
        this.Font = new System.Drawing.Font
            ("Comic Sans MS", 12F,
              System.Drawing.FontStyle.Regular,
              System.Drawing.GraphicsUnit.Point,
              ((System.Byte)(0)));
        this.ForeColor =
            System.Drawing.Color.FromArgb
            (((System.Byte)(255)), ((System.Byte)(255)),
            ((System.Byte)(192)));
        this.Name = "Form1";
        this.Text = "PayRoll Application";
        this.ResumeLayout(false);
    }
#endregion

    // The main entry point for the application.
    [STAThread]
    static void Main( )
    {
        Application.Run(new TempAgencyForm( ));
    }
}
```

```csharp
// Button click event handler for the Calculate button
private void btnCalculate_Click
                (object sender, System.EventArgs e)
{
    int dep;
    double hours;
    hours = double.Parse((txtHours.Text));
    dep = int.Parse((txtDep.Text));
    Employee anEmployee =
        new Employee(txtName.Text, hours, dep );
    txtGross.Text = anEmployee.Gross.ToString("C");
    txtSoc.Text = anEmployee.SocialSecurity.ToString("C");
    txtFed.Text = anEmployee.FederalTax.ToString("C");
    txtAgency.Text = anEmployee.AgencyFee.ToString("C");

    txtNet.Text = anEmployee.Net.ToString("C");
    txtName.Enabled = false;
    txtHours.Visible = false;
    txtDep.Visible = false;
    lblHours.Visible = false;
    lblDep.Visible = false;
    setVisibility(true);
}

// Button click event handler for the Reset button
private void btnReset_Click
                (object sender, System.EventArgs e)
{
    txtName.Clear( );
    txtHours.Clear( );
    txtDep.Clear( );
    txtName.Enabled = true;
    txtHours.Visible =true;
    txtDep.Visible =true;
    lblHours.Visible = true;
    lblDep.Visible =true;
    setVisibility(false);
}

// Used by both the btnCalculate and btnReset to
// change the visibility on the objects below the buttons
private  void setVisibility(bool visibilityValue)
{
    lblGross.Visible = visibilityValue;
    lblSoc.Visible = visibilityValue;
    lblFed.Visible = visibilityValue;
    lblAgency.Visible = visibilityValue;
    lblNet.Visible = visibilityValue;
```

8

```
            txtGross.Visible = visibilityValue;
            txtSoc.Visible = visibilityValue;
            txtFed.Visible = visibilityValue;
            txtAgency.Visible = visibilityValue;
            txtNet.Visible = visibilityValue;
        }
    }
}
```

Figure 8-20 shows the original user interface as values are entered. Notice the focus is on the Calculate button. The Enter or Tab keys can be used to move down the form. Also, the Enter key or a mouse click can be used to fire the `btnCalculate_Click( )` event as long as the button has the focus.

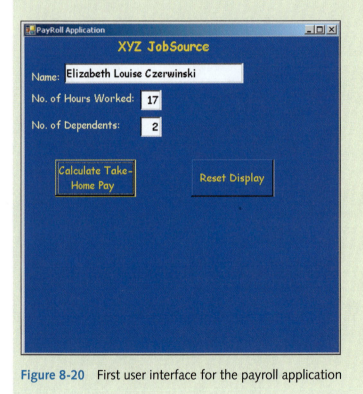

Figure 8-20   First user interface for the payroll application

Figure 8-21 shows the result of clicking the Calculate button. Comparing Figure 8-20 with Figure 8-21, notice that the number of hours and the number of dependents are hidden, so they are not visible in Figure 8-21. The text box containing the name is also disabled (grayed out) so that no new values can be typed. Values representing the results of the calculations are now displayed in Figure 8-21.

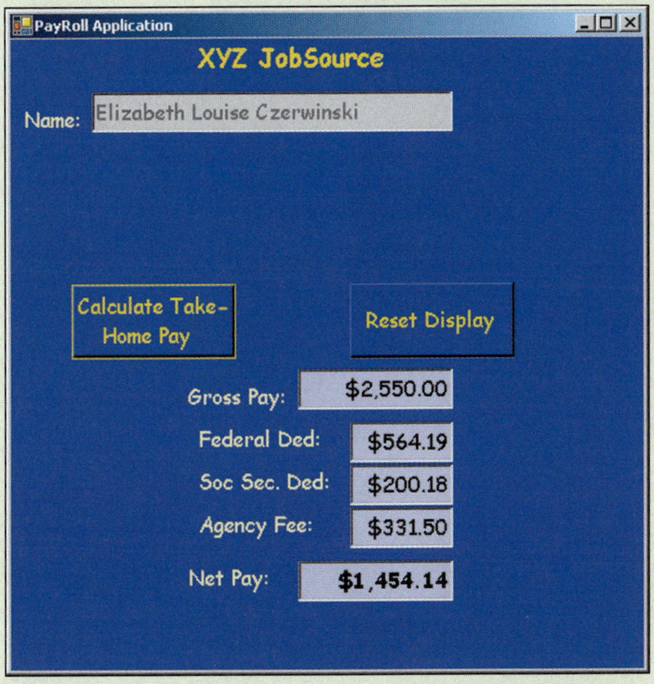

Figure 8-21   Output produced when the Calculate button is clicked

Figure 8-22 shows the result of clicking the Reset button.

8

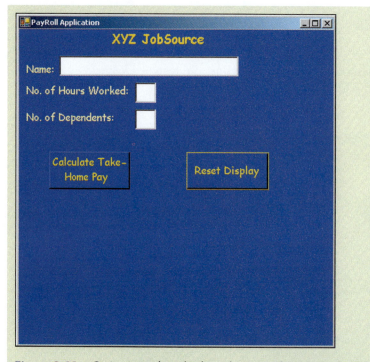

Figure 8-22 Output produced when the Reset button is clicked

The Reset button clears the text boxes and readies the form for new input. Once the values are erased, you will notice that the primary difference between Figure 8-20 (prior to entering the data) and 8-22 is that in Figure 8-22, the focus is on the Reset button. As you study the solution, what changes might you make to build the graphical user interface to be more user-friendly? One potential change would be to set the focus to the Name text box (where the name is entered) when the Reset button is clicked. Another change would be to the size of the form. It could be initially set to be smaller for data entry and then larger for the display of results. A number of other properties could be set to enhance the program. You are encouraged to play, experiment, and experience the effect of modifying properties for the application.

Quick Review

1. Console applications and Windows applications interact differently with the operating system. With console applications, the program calls on the operating system to perform certain functions such as inputting or outputting of data. In contrast, Windows applications are event driven. They register events with the operating system. When the event occurs, they receive notification from the operating system.

2. An event is a notification from the operating system that an action has occurred, such as the user clicking the mouse or pressing a key on the keyboard.

3. With Windows applications, you write methods called event handlers to indicate what should be done when an event such as a click on a button occurs.

4. Another important difference in a Windows application is that unlike the sequential nature you can plan on with console-based applications, in which one statement executes and is followed by the next, no sequential order exists with event-handling methods for Windows applications.

5. As the front end of a program, the interface is the visual image you see when you run a program. Windows applications not only function differently from console applications, they look different, and can therefore be used to create a friendlier user interface.

6. Windows-based GUI applications are displayed on a Windows form. `Form` is a container waiting to hold additional controls, such as a buttons or labels. Controls are objects that can display and respond to user actions.

7. The Visual Studio .NET Integrated Development Environment (IDE) automatically generates for you all the code needed for a blank Windows form. The amount of development time for Windows applications is greatly reduced when you use Visual Studio .NET and C#, because it is easy to add controls by dropping and dragging them onto the form container.

8. When you have a `class` defined that has the `class` name, followed by a colon and then another `class` name, you have inheritance. The second `class` is called the `base` `class`; the first is called the derived `class`. The second `class` listed inherits the characteristics of the first `class`. In C# and all .NET languages, you are limited to single inheritance.

9. Your design should take into consideration the target audience. Use consistency in the design unless there is a reason to call attention to something. Alignment should be used to group items. Avoid clutter and pay attention to color.

10. Properties of the Form `class` include `AutoScroll`, `BackColor`, `Font`, `ForeColor`, `Location`, `MaximizeBox`, Size, `StartPosition`, and `Text`. `Text` is used to set the caption for the title bar of the form.

11. A preprocessor directive indicates that something should be done before processing. C# does not have a separate preprocessing step. The `#region` preprocessor directive in C# is used to explicitly mark sections of source code that you can expand or collapse.

8

12. The `System.Windows.Forms` namespace includes many classes representing controls with names such as `Button`, `Label`, `TextBox`, `ComboBox`, `MainMenu`, `ListBox`, `CheckBox`, `RadioButton`, and `MonthCalendar` that you can add to your form. Each comes with its own bundle of predefined properties and methods, and each fires events.

13. The `Control` class has a number of properties including `Anchor`, `BackColor`, `Enabled`, `Font`, `ForeColor`, `Location`, `Name`, `Size`, `TabIndex`, `Text`, and `Visible`. Names of properties are quite intuitive.

14. The `Control` class has a number of methods, including `Focus( )`, `Hide( )`, `Select( )`, and `Show( )`.

15. Controls that you add to a form are objects or instances of one of the predefined classes such as `Label`, `TextBox`, and `Button`. They inherit the properties, methods, and events from the `Control` class.

16. `Label` objects are normally used to provide descriptive text for another control. In addition to the inherited members, they have their own unique properties, methods, and events.

17. `TextBox` objects are probably the most commonly used controls, because they can be used for both input and output. In addition to the inherited members, they have their own unique properties, methods, and events.

18. `Button` objects are added to your form to add functionality. Users can click `Button` objects to perform a specific task. In addition to the inherited members, they have their own unique properties, methods, and events.

EXERCISES

1. One of the differences between a console application and a Windows application is:
   a. Arrays can only be used with console applications.
   b. One font size is used with console applications.
   c. Variables must be declared with console applications.
   d. Windows applications require that program statements be placed in a `class`.
   e. Execution always begins in the `Main( )` method for console applications.

2. Which namespace includes most of the `Control` classes for developing Windows applications?
   a. `System;`
   b. `System.Windows.Controls`
   c. `System.Windows.Components.Forms`
   d. `System.Windows.Forms`
   e. `System.Windows.Drawing;`

3. Which of the following inherits members from the `Control class`?

    a. `Label`

    b. `Form`

    c. `Textbox`

    d. a and c

    e. all of the above

4. The _____ is the front end of a program that represents the presentation layer or the visual image of the program.

    a. interface

    b. control

    c. Visual Studio

    d. IDE

    e. framework

5. A(n) _____ is a notification from the operating system that an action has occurred, such as the user clicking the mouse or pressing a key.

    a. method call

    b. message

    c. event

    d. GUI

    e. handler

6. Which of the `Control` objects is viewed as a container that can hold other objects when you design a Windows application?

    a. `Control`

    b. `Button`

    c. `Window`

    d. `Frame`

    e. `Form`

7. Which property is used to set the caption for the Windows title bar?

    a. `Caption`

    b. `Text`

    c. `Title`

    d. `TitleBar`

    e. `WindowTitle`

8

8. The **class** heading **public class** AForm : Form indicates that:

   a. **Form** is a derived **class** of the **AForm class**.

   b. **AForm** is the **base class** for the **Form class**.

   c. The **class** being defined is identified as **Form**.

   d. **AForm** inherits the members of the **Form class**.

   e. none of the above

9. If the name of the **class** is **graphicalForm**, the following:

   public graphicalForm( )

   is an example of a(n):

   a. accessor method

   b. property

   c. constructor

   d. mutator method

   e. data member

10. You would use an IDE such as Visual Studio to construct Windows applications because it has the following capability:

    a. drag-and-drop construction

    b. IntelliSense features

    c. access to Properties window listing properties and events

    d. access to Toolbox for dropping controls

    e. all of the above

11. **Click** is an example of a(n):

    a. event

    b. property

    c. method

    d. control

    e. handler

12. Visual Studio has a number of windows that can be viewed during design. The window used to hold controls that are dragged and dropped during construction is called the:

    a. Property

    b. Code Editor

    c. Form Designer

    d. Solution Explorer

    e. Class View

13. If the `System.Windows.Forms` namespace is imported, the following statement:

    `this.textbox1 = new System.Windows.Forms.TextBox ( );`

    can be written as:

    a. `this.textbox1 = new TextBox ( );`

    b. `textbox1 = new TextBox ( );`

    c. `textbox1 = new System.Windows.Forms.TextBox ( );`

    d. all of the above

    e. none of the above

14. The statement that actually constructs or instantiates a `Button` object is:

    a. `this.button1 = new System.Windows.Forms.Button( );`

    b. `private System.Windows.Forms.Button button1;`

    c. `this.Controls.AddRange(this.button1);`

    d. `button1.Name = "A button";`

    e. `button1.Click += new System.EventHandler`
       `(this.button1_Click);`

15. The statement that registers a `Button` object click event with the operating system is:

    a. `this.button1ClickEvent = new System.Windows.Forms.Button( );`

    b. `private System.Windows.Forms.Button button1ClickEvent;`

    c. `this.Controls.AddRange(this.button1ClickEvent);`

    d. `button1.Click = "Register Me";`

    e. `button1.Click += new System.EventHandler`
       `(this.button1_Click);`

16. The property of the `TextBox` control that is used to set all characters to uppercase is:

    a. `CharacterCasing`

    b. `Text`

    c. `ToUpper`

    d. `UpperCase`

    e. `ConvertToUpper`

17. Which of the following might be the heading for an event-handler method?

    a. `private void btn1_Click(object sender, System.EventArgs e)`

    b. `Application.Run(new TempAgencyForm());`

    c. `btnCalculate.Click += new`
       `System.EventHandler(this.btnCalculate_Click);`

    d. `this.btnCalculate = new System.Windows.Forms.Button();`

    e. none of the above

8

18. Which of the following design considerations leads to more user-friendly presentation layers for GUIs?

    a. Avoid clutter.

    b. Be consistent with font, color, and placement.

    c. Design for the target audience.

    d. Use contrast to call attention to something.

    e. all of the above

19. The `#region...` `#endregion` is an example of a C#_____.

    a. Windows `class` declaration statement

    b. required statement for creating Windows applications

    c. reference to a `namespace` called `region`

    d. preprocessor directive

    e. collapsible segment of code that must be used for Windows applications

20. During design, how can you separate the business logic from the presentation layer?

    a. Create two forms, one for input, and the other for output.

    b. Create two objects using an object-oriented approach.

    c. Create at least two methods.

    d. Create separate classes for each.

    e. all of the above

21. Describe at least three ways Windows applications differ from console applications.

22. Identify which property could be set so that a `Form object` would perform the following function:

    a. Change the background color for the form.

    b. Set the default font to Courier for all controls that are added.

    c. Change the size of the window to 400 by 400.

    d. Associate a name of `designForm` with the `Form object`.

    e. Position the window near the center of the screen.

23. Describe what might be done to respond to a button click event?

24. List at least five issues to consider when you plan the design of graphical user interfaces.

25. Describe the process that must occur to get a `TextBox object` added to a `Form object`. In your description, consider not only how the process is performed with Visual Studio, but also what steps would be necessary to do it manually.

PROGRAMMING EXERCISES

1. Create a Windows application that contains a **Button object** labeled OK and a **TextBox object** labeled Name. Change the properties of the **Form object** to have a different background color of your choosing. Change the **Font** property to a font of your choice. Initially clear the text from the text box. Align the controls so they are aesthetically pleasing.

2. To the project developed in the preceding exercise, add an event handler for the **Button object** so that when the user clicks the OK button, the value entered is cleared, the **Form object** changes color, and a message is displayed on a **Label object** prompting the user to input a value for their name.

3. Create a Windows application that sets the **Form object** properties of **ForeColor**, **BackColor**, **Size**, **Location**, **Text**, and **AcceptButton**. The form should contain one button labeled Click Me. When the user clicks the **Button object**, a **MessageBox** should be displayed indicating the button has been clicked.

4. Create a Windows application that contains two **TextBox** objects and two **Button** objects. The text boxes should be used to allow the user to input two numeric values. The buttons should be labeled Add and Multiply. Create event-handler methods that retrieve the values, perform the calculations, and display the result of the calculations on a **Label object**. The **Label object** should initially be set to be invisible. Additional **Label** objects will be needed for the **TextBox object** captions.

5. Create a Windows application that contains two **TextBox** objects and one **Button object**. The text boxes should be used to allow the user to input the x, y coordinates to indicate where the form should be positioned. When the user clicks the button, the window should be moved to that new point.

   Hint: One easy way to do this is to set the location using an instance of the **Point class** when the user clicks the button. To do this you could allow the user to input values for both x and y into two separate text box objects. Once retrieved, they would need to be parsed or converted to their integer equivalent. Then use the numeric values for x and y to set the location by typing **this.Location = new Point(x,y);**

6. Create a Windows application that contains **TextBox** objects for first name, last name, and title, plus one **Button object**. The text boxes should be used to allow the users to input their names. When the **Button object** is clicked, the user names should be displayed in a **Label object** formatted with one space between the title, first, and last names.

8

7. Create a Windows application that contains two **TextBox** objects and two **Button** objects. One of the **TextBox** objects and one of the buttons are initially invisible. The first text box should be used to input a password. The text box should be masked to some character of your choosing so that the characters entered by the user are not seen on the screen. When the user clicks the first button, the second **TextBox object** and **Button object** should be displayed with a prompt asking the user to reenter his or her password. Now, when the user clicks the second button, have the application compare the values entered to make sure they are the same. Display an appropriate message indicating whether they are the same or not.

8. Create a Windows application with one **TextBox object** and one **Button object**. The **TextBox object** should allow you to enter your favorite saying. When the button is clicked, the saying should be displayed in a **Label object** in all uppercase characters.

9. Create a Windows application that functions like a banking account register. Separate the business logic from the presentation layer. The graphical user interface should allow the user to input the account name, number, and balance. Provide **TextBox** objects for withdrawals and deposits. A **Button object** should be available for clicking to process withdrawal and deposit transactions showing the new balance.

10. Create the higher/lower guessing game using a graphical user interface. Allow users to keep guessing until they guess the number. Choose two colors for your game: one should be used to indicate that the value the users guessed is higher than the target; the other is used to indicate that the value the users guessed is lower than the target. With each new guess, change the form color based on whether the guess is higher than the target or lower. Keep a count of the number of guesses. When they hit the target, display a **MessageBox** indicating the number of guesses it took. Several approaches can be used to seed the target: one is to generate a random number by constructing an **object** of the **Random class**. For example, the following stores a random whole number between 0 and 100 in **target**:

```
Random r = new Random();
int target = r.Next(0,100);
```

9

Programming Based on Events

In Chapter 8, you wrote your first real Windows-based application and learned how easy it is to develop graphical user interfaces using C# and Visual Studio .NET's drag-and-drop construction approach. In addition, you learned that included as part of the .NET Framework `class` library are a number of predefined classes located in the `System.Windows.Forms` `namespace` that enable you to add controls such as `Label`, `Button`, and `TextBox` objects to an `object` of the Windows `Form` container `class`. And finally, you learned a new way of programming based on interactively responding to events such as button clicks.

In this chapter, you extend this knowledge by writing additional event-handling methods for capturing and responding to user input. You create applications that have menus and other widgets such as list boxes, radio buttons, combo boxes, and check boxes that can be displayed and responded to. You explore other types of events that are triggered or raised for Windows applications.

This chapter begins by introducing you to delegates. An understanding of their use makes you more aware of what goes on behind the scenes with events. The remainder of the chapter focuses on adding controls to Windows applications and programming their events. By the time you complete Chapter 9, you are creating very sophisticated, highly interactive, Windows-based applications.

DELEGATES

Delegates form the foundation for events in C#. **Delegates** are special types of .NET classes whose instances store references (addresses) to methods as opposed to storing actual data. Delegates are used in applications other than Windows applications that respond to GUI events; however, it is their relationship to events that makes them interesting and worth presenting in this section.

Defining Delegates

The `delegate base class` type is defined in the `System namespace`. A couple of syntactical differences exist between delegates and the other predefined and user-defined classes that you have already used. First, the declaration for a `delegate` looks more like a method declaration than a `class` definition; however, it has no body. It begins with the keyword `delegate`. It ends with a parenthesized list of parameters followed by a semicolon. Every `delegate` type has a signature, which may include zero or more parameters. Remember that a **signature** for a method includes its name, number of parameters, and parameter types. The signature of a method does not include the `return` type. Like methods, a `delegate` may include a `return` type or the keyword `void` as part of its heading. However, unlike a method, the `return` type of a delegate becomes part of its identifying signature. Example 9-1 defines a `delegate` type that takes no arguments and returns a `string`.

Example 9-1

```
delegate string ReturnsSimpleString( );
```

When you define a `delegate` type, you identify what types of methods the `delegate` represents. This identification is accomplished through the `delegate` signature, which is very important. It indicates what the method signatures must look like if they are to be referenced by the `delegate`.

 In C#, you can think of the `delegate` as a way of defining or naming a method signature.

Given the signature for the `delegate` defined in Example 9-1, any method that has zero parameters and returns a `string` could be referenced by the `ReturnsSimpleString` `delegate`. Example 9-2 shows the heading and body for a prospective method.

Example 9-2

```
// Method that returns a string.
static string EndStatement( )
{
    return " in 10 years.";
}
```

Compare the heading for the `EndStatement( )` method shown in Example 9-2 with the `delegate` in Example 9-1. Both return strings. Both have zero parameters. The `delegate` does not specify what the statements must be in the body of the method, and it does not specify what the name of the method must be, just what the signature must look like.

 A `delegate` is implemented in C# as a `class`; however, an instance of the `delegate` `class` is also referred to as a `delegate`, rather than as an `object`. The fact that both the `class` type and the instance type go by the same name can be confusing.

Creating Delegate Instances

To associate the `delegate` with the method, a `delegate` instance is defined using the method name as the argument inside the parentheses. One way you have previously identified methods from field and property instances is by recognizing that the method name identifier is followed by a set of parentheses. When you write a method name without parentheses, you are referencing the address of the method. Example 9-3 instantiates the `ReturnsSimpleString` `delegate` with the `EndStatement( )` method as the argument.

9

Example 9-3

```
ReturnsSimpleString  saying3 = new ReturnsSimpleString(EndStatement);
```

> **NOTE** The constructor for a delegate of the delegate class always takes just one parameter. This is because you are sending the name of a method for the constructor to reference.

Notice that the `EndStatement` argument does not include the parentheses, even though `EndStatement` is a method. A reference to the address of the method is sent as an argument. The address stored is the entry point in memory where the method begins when it is called.

Using Delegates

After completing the instantiation in Example 9-3, the delegate identifier `saying3` references the `EndStatement( )` method. Any use of `saying3( )` calls the `EndStatement( )` method. Example 9-4 illustrates this.

Example 9-4

```
MessageBox.Show(saying3( ));
```

A call to the `Show( )` method of the `MessageBox` class calls the delegate instance, `saying3( )`, which calls the `EndStatement( )` method to display "in 10 years." Calling the `EndStatement( )` method in the `Show( )` method produces the same output. This is a simple example, but illustrates how a delegate is used to call a method. Example 9-4 did not directly call the `EndStatement( )` method; however, the statements from its body were those executed.

The program in Example 9-5 illustrates defining a single delegate type, instantiating three delegate instances, and calling up the three delegates. Without looking closely, the arguments to the `Show( )` method appear to be normal method calls. In reality, the methods are called through the delegates. Notice that the delegate instance name and a set of parentheses form the argument to the `Show( )` method.

Example 9-5

```
// DelegateExample.cs         Author: Doyle
// After defining a delegate class, 3 delegate
// instances are instantiated. Delegates are
// used as arguments for the Show( ) method.
using System;
using System.Windows.Forms;
```

```
namespace DelegateExample
{
    delegate string ReturnsSimpleString( );
    class DelegateExample
    {
        static void Main ( )
        {
            int age = 18;
            ReturnsSimpleString saying1 =
                new ReturnsSimpleString(AHeading);
            ReturnsSimpleString saying2 =
                new ReturnsSimpleString(
                (age + 10).ToString);
            ReturnsSimpleString saying3=
                new ReturnsSimpleString(EndStatement);
            MessageBox.Show(saying1( ) +
                saying2( ) + saying3( ));
        }
        // Method that returns a string.
        static string AHeading( )
        {
            return "Your age will be ";
        }

        // Method that returns a string.
        static string EndStatement( )
        {
            return " in 10 years.";
        }
    }
}
```

9

The signatures for the methods and the **delegate class** match.

> **NOTE** Notice that the second instance of the **delegate**, saying2, is associated with a
> .NET predefined method of the **object class**. Remember that the ToString( )
> method takes no arguments and returns a **string**. Its signature matches the
> ReturnsSimpleString( ) **delegate**.

The methods are said to be wrapped by the **delegate**. When the **delegate** is used, it passes a method, instead of data, as an argument to the **Show( )** method. Figure 9–1 shows the output produced when you execute the program from Example 9-5.

Figure 9-1   Output from delegate example

It is possible to have the **delegate** **wrap** more than one method, so that when a **delegate** is used, multiple methods are called, one after the other. This type of **delegate** is called a **multicast delegate**. The **+=** and **-=** operators are used to add or remove methods to and from the **delegate** chain or invocation list. One requirement for multicast delegates is that the **return** type be **void**.

The real advantage or power of the **delegate**, however, is that the same **delegate** can call different methods during runtime. When the program is compiled, the method or methods that will be called are not determined. This is why delegates work so well in an event-driven arena, where you do not know, for example, which event occurs first or which control gets attention first.

> Delegates were introduced with Microsoft Visual J++. Their closest counterparts in another language are the function pointers in C++.

Relationship of Delegates to Events

Think about what the word "delegate" means in the English language; you associate it with something or someone who acts as a bridge between two things. A **delegate** serves as a bridge with event-driven applications. It acts as an intermediary between objects that are raising or triggering an event, and the **object** that captures the event and responds to it. You can think of events as special forms of delegates in C#, because they enable you to place a reference to event-handler methods inside a **delegate**. Once this reference is made, or the event is registered, the **delegate** is used to call the event-handler method when an event, such as a button click, is fired.

This behind the scenes plumbing is dealt with in C# without much programmer intervention. In fact, if you are using Visual Studio .NET, all of the code, with the exception of the statements that appear in the event-handler methods, is automatically generated for you when you identify the events about which your program must receive notification.

EVENT HANDLING IN C#

In Chapter 8, you wrote program statements for methods that were executed when a button was clicked. The Form Designer in Visual Studio did much of the work for you. Two things were added to your program when you double-clicked on a **Button** control **object** during design (or selected its click event from the Event list in the Properties window). First, the button click event was registered as being of interest, and second, an event-handler method heading was generated. This process is called **event wiring**. You associate a method in your program to an event, such as the user clicking the button. Then, this method is automatically called when the event occurs.

Now that you know about delegates, if you examine the code generated by Visual Studio .NET, you understand how the **delegate** is used to register the event. The code that appears in Example 9-6 is generated when you double-click a button in the Form Designer. **System.EventHandler** is a **delegate** type. This code associates the two methods, **button1_Click( )**, and **button2_Click( )**, with that **delegate**.

Example 9-6

```
this.button1.Click += new
    System.EventHandler(this.button1_Click);
this.button2.Click += new
    System.EventHandler(this.button2_Click);
```

 The keyword **this** is added to all code generated by Visual Studio .NET. This keyword is used to indicate the current instance of a **class**. For the Windows applications you are developing in this chapter, think of **this** as the current instance of the form. So, for Example 9-6, when you notice **this.button1.Click**, you should mentally associate that with "the current form's" **button1.Click**.

When Visual Studio adds the event-handler method heading, the body of the method is empty. You add the program statements to the body of the method indicating what actions to perform when the button is clicked. Example 9-7 shows the event-handler method for **button1_Click**.

Example 9-7

```
private void button1_Click(object sender, System.EventArgs e)
{
}
```

9

These methods have a **return** type of **void** with two parameters; the **delegate** System.EventHandler( ) has a **return** type of **void** and two parameters. Their signatures match.

Event-Handler Methods

Example 9-7 includes the heading for the event-handler method. All event-handler methods normally have the same signature. They do not return anything; they have a **return** type of **void**. They take two parameters. The first parameter, **object sender**, represents the source that raises the event, and the second parameter is the data for the event. Accessible data, for example, for a **MouseEventArg** event includes which mouse button (left, right, or both) was clicked, how many clicks, and the x-coordinates and y-coordinates for where the mouse pointer was positioned on the screen when the mouse button was clicked. This data can be obtained from the second argument.

The **delegate** maintains a list of the registered event handlers for an event. To identify the events about which you are interested in receiving notification, register the event and specify what actions to perform when the event occurs by typing the body of the event-handler method. The event handlers are called using delegates.

The sections that follow highlight the most interesting of the many events (other than button click events) that you can include in your application to add functionality. An application will be created using Visual Studio .NET; controls will be added, their properties set, and their events programmed.

LISTBOX CONTROL OBJECTS

The **ListBox** control is a very powerful widget that can be added to Windows applications. **ListBox** controls can be used to display a list of items from which the user can make single or multiple selections. A scroll bar is automatically added to the control if the total number of items exceeds the number that can be displayed. You can add or remove items to and from the **ListBox** control at design time or dynamically at runtime.

Create a Form to Hold ListBox Controls

So that you can experience working with a **ListBox object**, a new project is created in Visual Studio .NET using the Windows application template. A blank form is automatically generated. The **Name** property for the form is set to **ClubForm**. The **Font** property for **ClubForm** is set to 12 points. This property is set on the **Form1 object** so that other objects that are added to **ClubForm** will already be set; this becomes the default font for the application. This procedure ensures consistency in **Font** selection across controls. Of course, the **Font** can be set for individual controls if there is a need for one or more to be different. The **BackColor** blue (**128, 128, 255**) is set for **ClubForm**. The **Text** property is set to **Computer Club Outing Sign Up**.

Remember, you need to use the Form Designer window to set the properties at design time. If you are in the Code Editor instead of the Form Designer, select Designer from the View menu or press Shift+F7.

A `TextBox object` is dragged onto the `ClubForm object` and placed at the bottom of the form. The `Name` property is set to `txtBoxResult`. This text box stores the result of the list box selection. The `Text` property is set to all blanks (`""`). A `Label object` is added to `ClubForm` to the left of the `TextBox object` with its `Text` property set to `"Result"`.

Adding a ListBox Control Object

A `ListBox object` is dragged onto the `ClubForm object`. Its `Name` property is set to `lstBoxEvents`. The background color for the control is set using the `BackColor` property. It is set to yellow (`255,255,192`). The `ForeColor` property is set to blue (`0,0,192`) so that the font for characters displays in blue. The `Items` property is used to set the initial values for the list box. Clicking on the button with the ellipsis to the right of the word `Collection` in the `Items` property displays the String Collection Editor window. Values for the list box are typed on separate lines using this editor. Figure 9-2 shows the window after values were typed for the list box collection. The following `string` values are typed, each on separate lines; "Movie", "Dance", "Boat Tour", "Dinner", "Hike", "Amusement Park", and "Sporting Event".

9

String Collection Editor		
Enter the strings in the collection (one per line):		
Amusement Park		
Boat Tour		
Dance		
Dinner		
Hike		
Movie		
Sporting Event		

Properties	
lstBoxEvents	System.Windows.Form
AccessibleRole	Default
AllowDrop	False
Anchor	Top, Left
BackColor	255, 255, 19
BorderStyle	Fixed3D
CausesValidation	True
ColumnWidth	0
ContextMenu	(none)
Cursor	Default
DataSource	(none)
DisplayMember	(None)
Dock	None
DrawMode	Normal
Enabled	True
Font	Microsoft Sans Serif
ForeColor	0, 0, 192
HorizontalExtent	0
HorizontalScrollba	False
ImeMode	NoControl
IntegralHeight	True
ItemHeight	20
Items	**(Collection)**

OK   Cancel   Help

Figure 9-2   String Collection Editor

The **Sorted** property is set to **true** for the **ListBox** **object**. This keeps you from having to type values into the collection as sorted items. By setting the **Sorted** property to **true**, they are displayed sorted—as if you had typed them in that order. The control **object** is sized by clicking on the **object** and using the standard Windows sizing handles to drag the **object** so that four of the strings are shown. If the window is too small to show all choices, a scroll bar is automatically added to **ListBox** objects when the application is run.

 After the controls are placed in their general location, use the **Format>Align** menu options to line up associated controls so they are consistently placed on the same row or column. Select multiple controls by drawing a box around the controls using your mouse as the selection tool, or hold the Ctrl key as you select multiple controls.

Register a ListBox Event

To add functionality, you need to register an event for the **ListBox** control **object**. To give you an example, you might want to know when the item selection changes. When it does, you might want to display or use the selection. In the Form Designer, when you double-click on a control, you register the default event for that specific control. An event-handler method for that registered event is added to your source code.

 You may not want to program a method for the default event for a control. It may be a different event that is of interest. The default event for a **Button** **object** is the Button Click event. Thus, when you double-click on a button in the Form Designer, the buttonName_Click event is registered. This is usually the event of interest for Button objects. Clicking on the Event icon (lightning bolt) in the Properties window shows you a selection of events that can be registered for the **object** selected.

Double-clicking on the **ListBox** control adds the line shown in Example 9-8, which registers the **SelectedIndexChanged** event as being of interest.

Example 9-8

```
this.lstBoxEvents.SelectedIndexChanged += new
        System.EventHandler (this.lstBoxEvents_SelectedIndexChanged);
```

The Form Designer also adds the empty-bodied method shown in Example 9-9 to your program.

Example 9-9

```
private void lstBoxEvents_SelectedIndexChanged(object sender,
                                        System.EventArgs e)
{
}
```

ListBox Event Handlers

One of the properties of the `ListBox` `class` is `SelectedItem`. It returns an `object` representing the selected `string` item. If you retrieve the selection using this property, the `object` must be converted to a `string object` to display it in the Result `TextBox`. The `Text` property of the `txtBoxResult` `object` is used to display the selection. The statement in Example 9-10 is added to the body of the `listBox1_SelectedIndexChanged( )` method so that when the event is fired, the selection is displayed.

Example 9-10

```
private void lstBoxEvents_SelectedIndexChanged(object sender,
                                               System.EventArgs e)
{
    this.txtBoxResult.Text =
        this.lstBoxEvents.SelectedItem.ToString( );
}
```

The `ToString( )` method was used to convert the item `object` to a `string` for displaying; the `Text` property can also be used to retrieve the data from a `ListBox` control `object`. If you use the `Text` property as opposed to the `SelectedItem` property, there is no requirement of adding the `ToString( )` method. Thus, the body of the `listBox1_SelectedIndexChanged` method could read as shown in Example 9-11.

9

Example 9-11

```
private void lstBoxEvents_SelectedIndexChanged(object sender,
                                               System.EventArgs e)
{
    this.txtBoxResult.Text = this.lstBoxEvents.Text;
}
```

Figure 9-3 shows the output generated from Example 9-11 after the `SelectedIndexChanged` event is fired. Notice that the items appear in alphabetical order. The `Sorted` property rearranged the items.

Figure 9-3   SelectedIndexChanged event fired

Multiple Selections with a ListBox Object

The `ListBox` control **object** offers the advantage of allowing users to make multiple selections. The `SelectionMode` property has selection values of `MultiSimple` and `MultiExtended`, in addition to `None` and `One`. By default, the property is set to `One`. With a `MultiSimple` selection, the only way to make a selection is by using the spacebar and clicking the mouse. `MultiExtended` allows users to make selections using the Ctrl key, Shift key, and arrow keys in addition to using the spacebar and clicking the mouse. Multiple selections are allowed in Figure 9-4. The text box shows that Boat Tour, Dinner, and Hike selections were all highlighted.

Figure 9-4   Multiple selections within a ListBox object

After the `SelectionMode` property is set to `MultiExtended`, the event-handler method must be changed to display each of the items selected. Example 9-12 shows the revision to the method.

Example 9-12

```csharp
private void lstBoxEvents_SelectedIndexChanged(object sender,
                                    System.EventArgs e)
{
    string result  = " ";
    foreach(string activity in lstBoxEvents.SelectedItems)
    {
        result  += activity + "   ";
    }
    this.txtBoxResult.Text = result;
}
```

Using the **foreach** loop construct, the selected items are concatenated one item at a time onto a **string** instance named **result**.

 Remember that when you use + (the plus symbol) with data stored in a **string** type, the characters are appended onto the end of the result **string** instead of being used in calculations.

Notice that the characters were not appended straight to the **Text** property of the **TextBox** **object** in Example 9-12. Instead, they were placed in an intermediate memory location (**result**) to enable multiple selections. Each time the event is fired (the selection is changed), the result **string** is reinitialized (**result = " "**). On the outside of the loop, after values have been concatenated, the **Text** property of the **TextBox** **object** was assigned the **string** value.

Adding Items to a ListBox at Runtime

The **ListBox** control **object** is a fairly sophisticated control. It can hold data of any type. Values returned using the **SelectedItem** and **SelectedItems** properties are returned as objects; thus, you can easily store numbers in the **ListBox**. Once they are retrieved as objects, they can be cast into an **int** or **double** for processing.

The **ListBox** control can have values added or removed at runtime. To add a value when the program is running, you use the **Add( )** method with the **Items** property as shown in Example 9-13.

9

Example 9-13

```
lstBoxEvents.Items.Add("string value to add");
```

Figure 9-5 shows the form allowing the user to enter another activity. The text from the **TextBox object** is added as a selection to the **ListBox**. Two events were fired before the output being displayed in Figure 9-5 was produced. The first event that was fired was the button click. This event-handler method added the user-entered **string** to the **ListBox**. The second event that was fired when the user clicked a selection from the list box displays the selections in the Result text box. Notice the new selection that was typed. "Picnic" now appears as an option. It was also selected from the list box.

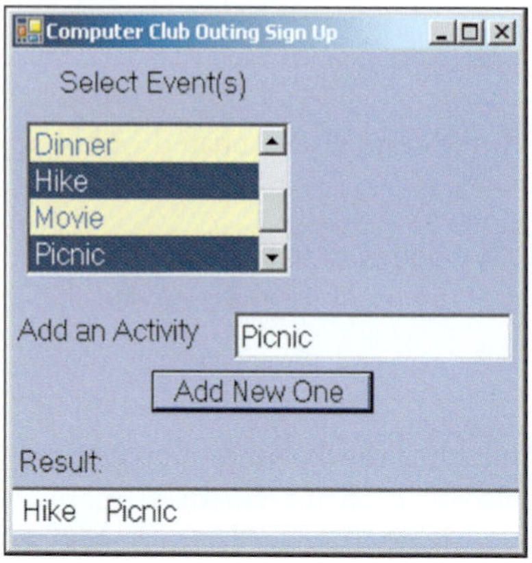

Figure 9-5 Add( ) method executed inside the buttonClick event

The new **btnNew_Click( )** event-handler body retrieves the text that is typed by the user from **txtBoxNewAct** and adds it to the **ListBox object**. The method is shown in Example 9-14.

Example 9-14

```
private void btnNew_Click(object sender, System.EventArgs e)
{
    lstBoxEvents.Items.Add(txtBoxNewAct.Text);
}
```

Example 9-15 shows the complete program listing for the application with a couple of minor modifications included. The modifications are discussed following the source listing.

Example 9-15

```csharp
// ListBoxExample.cs     Author: Doyle
// This application includes Button, Label,
// TextBox, and ListBox objects.
// SelectedIndexChanged and Click events fired.
using System;
using System.Drawing;
using System.Collections;
using System.ComponentModel;
using System.Windows.Forms;
using System.Data;
namespace ListBoxExample
{
    public class ClubForm : System.Windows.Forms.Form
    {
        private System.Windows.Forms.Label label2;
        private System.Windows.Forms.ListBox lstBoxEvents;
        private System.Windows.Forms.TextBox txtBoxResult;
        private System.Windows.Forms.Label label1;
        private System.Windows.Forms.Label label3;
        private System.Windows.Forms.TextBox txtBoxNewAct;
        private System.Windows.Forms.Button btnNew;
        private System.ComponentModel.Container
            components = null;
        public ClubForm( )
        {
            InitializeComponent( );
        }
        protected override void Dispose(bool disposing)
        {
            if(disposing)
            {
                if (components != null)
                {
                    components.Dispose( );
                }
            }
            base.Dispose(disposing);
        }
#region Windows Form Designer generated code
        private void InitializeComponent( )
        {
            this.lstBoxEvents = new
                System.Windows.Forms.ListBox( );
            this.label1 = new System.Windows.Forms.Label( );
            this.label2 = new System.Windows.Forms.Label( );
            this.label3 = new System.Windows.Forms.Label( );
```

9

```
this.txtBoxResult = new
    System.Windows.Forms.TextBox( );
this.txtBoxNewAct = new
    System.Windows.Forms.TextBox( );
this.btnNew = new System.Windows.Forms.Button( );
this.SuspendLayout( );

// lstBoxEvents
this.lstBoxEvents.BackColor =
    System.Drawing.Color.FromArgb
    (((System.Byte)(255)), ((System.Byte)(255)),
    ((System.Byte)(192)));
this.lstBoxEvents.ForeColor =
    System.Drawing.Color.FromArgb
    (((System.Byte)(0)), ((System.Byte)(0)),
    ((System.Byte)(192)));
this.lstBoxEvents.ItemHeight = 20;
this.lstBoxEvents.Items.AddRange(new object[]
    { "Amusement Park",
      "Boat Tour",
      "Dance",
      "Dinner",
      "Hike",
      "Movie",
      "Sporting Event" } );
this.lstBoxEvents.Location =
    new System.Drawing.Point(8, 40);
this.lstBoxEvents.Name = "lstBoxEvents";
this.lstBoxEvents.SelectionMode =
    System.Windows.Forms.SelectionMode.MultiExtended;
this.lstBoxEvents.Size =
    new System.Drawing.Size(152, 84);
this.lstBoxEvents.Sorted = true;
this.lstBoxEvents.TabIndex = 1;
this.lstBoxEvents.SelectedIndexChanged +=
    new System.EventHandler
    (this.lstBoxEvents_SelectedIndexChanged);

// label1
this.label1.Location = new
    System.Drawing.Point(0, 216);
this.label1.Name = "label1";
this.label1.Size = new
    System.Drawing.Size(72, 23);
this.label1.TabIndex = 4;
this.label1.Text = "Result:";
```

```
// label2
this.label2.Location = new
    System.Drawing.Point(24, 8);
this.label2.Name = "label2";
this.label2.Size = new
    System.Drawing.Size(120, 24);
this.label2.TabIndex = 2;
this.label2.Text = "Select Event(s)";

// label3
this.label3.Location = new
    System.Drawing.Point(0, 144);
this.label3.Name = "label3";
this.label3.Size = new
    System.Drawing.Size(120, 23);
this.label3.TabIndex = 5;
this.label3.Text = "Add an Activity";

// txtBoxResult
this.txtBoxResult.Location =
    new System.Drawing.Point(-2, 240);
this.txtBoxResult.Name = "txtBoxResult";
this.txtBoxResult.Size =
    new System.Drawing.Size(296, 26);
this.txtBoxResult.TabIndex = 3;
this.txtBoxResult.Text = "";

// txtBoxNewAct
this.txtBoxNewAct.Location =
    new System.Drawing.Point(128, 144);
this.txtBoxNewAct.Name = "txtBoxNewAct";
this.txtBoxNewAct.Size =
    new System.Drawing.Size(160, 26);
this.txtBoxNewAct.TabIndex = 6;
this.txtBoxNewAct.Text = "";

// btnNew
this.btnNew.Location =
    new System.Drawing.Point(80, 176);
this.btnNew.Name = "btnNew";
this.btnNew.Size = new
    System.Drawing.Size(128, 23);
this.btnNew.TabIndex = 7;
this.btnNew.Text = "Add New One";
this.btnNew.Click +=
    new System.EventHandler(this.btnNew_Click);

// ClubForm
this.AcceptButton = this.btnNew;
```

9

```csharp
                this.AutoScaleBaseSize =
                    new System.Drawing.Size(8, 19);
                this.BackColor = System.Drawing.Color.FromArgb
                    (((System.Byte)(128)), ((System.Byte)(128)),
                    ((System.Byte)(255)));
                this.ClientSize = new
                    System.Drawing.Size(292, 273);
                this.Controls.AddRange
                    (new System.Windows.Forms.Control[]
                                    { this.btnNew,
                                      this.txtBoxNewAct,
                                      this.label3,
                                      this.label1,
                                      this.txtBoxResult,
                                      this.label2,
                                      this.lstBoxEvents } );
                this.Font =
                    new System.Drawing.Font
                    ("Microsoft Sans Serif",
                    12F, System.Drawing.FontStyle.Regular,
                    System.Drawing.GraphicsUnit.Point,
                    ((System.Byte)(0)));
                this.Name = "ClubForm";
                this.Text = "Computer Club Outing Sign Up";
                this.ResumeLayout(false);

        }
#endregion

        static void Main( )
        {
            Application.Run(new ClubForm( ));
        }

        private void lstBoxEvents_SelectedIndexChanged
                    (object sender, System.EventArgs e)
        {

          // Single selection option
          // this.txtBoxResult.Text =
          //      this.lstBoxEvent.Text;
            string result  = " ";
            foreach (string activity  in
                lstBoxEvents.SelectedItems)
            {
                result  += activity + "     ";
            }
            this.txtBoxResult.Text = result;
        }
```

```
    private void btnNew_Click(object sender,
                              System.EventArgs e)
    {
        lstBoxEvents.Items.Add(txtBoxNewAct.Text);
        txtBoxNewAct.Clear( );
    }
  }
}
```

To add functionality, the **btnNew Button object** was set as the value for the **AcceptButton** property of the **Form object**. This enables the user to press the Enter key after typing in new entries. Now the Enter key functions in the same way as clicking the left mouse button on the **btnNew Button object**. The **btnNew_Click()** event is fired when the user clicks the mouse or presses the Enter key. In the **btnNew_Click()** event-handler method, the **TextBox object** was also cleared using the **Clear()** method. This was done after the value was typed into the **TextBox object**, retrieved, and added to the **ListBox object**. Table 9-1 includes a list of properties set for the **ListBoxExample** application.

Table 9-1 ListBoxExample property values

Name	Object type	Property	Value
ClubForm	Form	AcceptButton	btnNew
ClubForm	Form	BackColor	Blue (128,128,255)
ClubForm	Form	Font	SansSerif, 12
ClubForm	Form	Text	Typed "Computer Club Outing Sign Up"
lstBoxEvents	ListBox	BackColor	Yellow (255,255,192)
lstBoxEvents	ListBox	ForeColor	Blue (0,0,192)
lstBoxEvents	ListBox	SelectionMode	MultiExtended
lstBoxEvents	ListBox	Sorted	true
lstBoxEvents	ListBox	TabIndex	1
lstBoxEvents	ListBox	Items (Collection)	Typed "Amusement Park", "Boat Tour", "Dance", "Dinner", "Hike", "Movie", "Sporting Event"
label1	Label	Text	Typed "Result"
label2	Label	Text	Typed "Select Event(s)"
label3	Label	Text	Typed "Add an Activity"
txtBoxResult	TextBox	Text	All spaces. Deleted the characters, so no value is displayed

Table 9-1 ListBoxExample property values (continued)

Name	Object type	Property	Value
txtBoxNewAct	TextBox	Text	All spaces. Deleted the characters, so no value is displayed
btnNew	TextBox	Text	Typed "Add New One"

Example 9-15 just touched the surface for what you can do with **ListBox** objects. You will want to explore this **class** further. The **Items**, **SelectedItems**, and **SelectedIndices** properties are useful for getting a collection of selected items from the **ListBox** object. In addition to being useful for entering values at design time, the **ListBox** object is a control that can be populated with new values at runtime. By including the **Add( )** method inside a loop, values entered by the user or read from a file can be added to the control while the application is running. Table 9-2 describes some of the more interesting properties of the **ListBox** class.

 The information included in Tables 9-2 and 9-3 was adapted from the MSDN documentation.

Table 9-2 ListBox properties

Property	Description
Items	Gets the values (items) in the list box
MultiColumn	Gets or sets a value indicating whether the list box supports multiple columns
SelectedIndex	Gets or sets the zero-based index of the currently selected item
SelectedIndices	Gets a collection that contains the zero-based indexes of all currently selected items
SelectedItem	Gets or sets the selected item
SelectedItems	Gets a collection containing the currently selected items
SelectionMode	Gets or sets the method in which items are selected (MultiExtended, MultiSimple, One, None)
Sorted	Gets or sets a value indicating whether the items are sorted alphabetically
Text	Gets or searches for the text of the currently selected item

Table 9-3 gives a partial list of methods and events of the **ListBox** object. Remember that the **ListBox** object also inherits members from the **Control** class. Tables 8-2 and 8-3, in Chapter 8, listed many of the **Control** class members. You should review those tables.

Table 9-3   ListBox methods

Method (and event)	Description
ClearSelected( )	Unselects all items
Enter (Event)	Occurs when the control is entered
FindString( )	Finds the first item that starts with the specified string
FindStringExact( )	Finds the first item that exactly matches the specified string
GotFocus (Event) [inherited from Control]	Occurs when the control receives focus
KeyPress (Event) [inherited from Control]	Occurs when a key is pressed while the control has focus
Leave (Event) [inherited from Control]	Occurs when the input focus leaves the control
MouseEnter (Event) [inherited from Control]	Occurs when the mouse pointer enters the control
MouseHover (Event) [inherited from Control]	Occurs when the mouse pointer hovers over the control
MouseLeave (Event) [inherited from Control]	Occurs when the mouse pointer leaves the control
SelectedIndexChanged (Event) [default event]	Occurs when the SelectedIndex property has changed
SetSelected( )	Selects or clears the selection for the specified item

A similar control, but one with additional functionality, is the **ComboBox**. The **ComboBox** class is discussed in the next section; the differences between the **ComboBox** class and **ListBox** controls are highlighted.

COMBOBOX CONTROL OBJECTS

In many cases, the **ListBox** controls and **ComboBox** controls can be used interchangeably. They share many of the same properties and methods because they both are derived from the **System.Windows.Forms.ListControl** class. The **ListBox** control is usually used when you have all the choices available at design time. You saw in previous code segments that values can be added to the **ListBox** using the **Add( )** method. For the example illustrated in Figure 9-5, an additional control **object** was required. The **TextBox** provided a place on the form for the user to enter a new value. Once retrieved, it was then added to the **ListBox**.

A **ComboBox** facilitates displaying a list of suggested choices; however, it has an added feature. **ComboBox** objects contain their own text box field as part of the **object**. This makes it easy to add a new value at runtime. In addition, **ComboBox** objects save space on a form. Figure 9-6 shows the difference in appearance between the two controls.

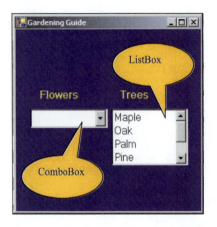

Figure 9-6   ComboBox and ListBox objects

 A new Windows application is created to illustrate features of the **ComboBox** and **ListBox**. The **Text**, **Name**, **Font**, **BackColor**, **ForeColor**, and **Size** properties were all set for the new **Form** **object**.

Add ComboBox Objects

When you place the **ComboBox** **object** on the form, it looks like a **TextBox** **object** because the top line is left blank for the entry of typed text. The default setting for the property that determines its appearance (the **DropDownStyle** property) is **DropDown**. If you accept the default setting, the user can either type a new entry into the **object** or select from the list of items that you assign to the control during design. Another **DropDownStyle** option, **DropDownList**, disables new text from being entered into the **ComboBox** **object** and offers additional navigational options for viewing the list.

DropDown is set as the `DropDownStyle` for Figure 9-7. A new option can be typed. The full list of choices is not displayed until the user clicks the down arrow button.

Figure 9-7   ComboBox list of choices

Handling ComboBox Events

Another difference between the `ComboBox` and `ListBox` is the `ComboBox` allows a single selection to be made. This can be either the new typed value or one of the choices displayed from the drop-down selection. As with the `ListBox` control **object**, `SelectedIndexChanged( )` is the default event-handler method. When a value such as `"Sunflower"` is typed into the `ComboBox`, the `SelectedIndexChanged( )` event-handler method is not triggered or raised. A new event must be registered to respond to values being typed into the text portion. One way to deal with this is to have a `KeyPress( )` event-handler method executed when new values are entered.

Registering a KeyPress Event

A `KeyPress( )` event occurs when the user presses a key. Actually, the event is fired with each and every keystroke. This event is registered for the `ComboBox` **object** so that if values are typed into the text area, they can be retrieved and processed. Example 9-16 shows the two events being registered for the `ComboBox` control. Notice that the `Name` property for the `ComboBox` **object** was set to `cmboFlowers`.

Example 9-16

```
this.cmboFlowers.SelectedIndexChanged += new System.EventHandler
            (this.cmboFlowers_SelectedIndexChanged);
this.cmboFlowers.KeyPress += new
            System.Windows.Forms.KeyPressEventHandler
            (this.cmboFlowers_KeyPress);
```

 If you are using Visual Studio .NET, the code in Example 9-16 is generated for you. The complete program listings are included in this chapter and in Chapter 8 for all Windows application programs. This is done so that programs can be recreated without Visual Studio. Some of the example code listings appear very long—however, if you are using Visual Studio, most of the code is automatically added for you. This generated code gives all Windows applications a consistent look and feel.

Programming Event Handlers

To access text from the **ComboBox** and the **ListBox** objects shown in Figure 9-7, three event-handler methods are programmed. New **TextBox** objects are added to store the values retrieved from these controls. Both the **cmboFlowers_SelectedIndexChanged()** method and the **cmboFlowers_KeyPress( )** method use the **Text** property to get the value from the **ComboBox** object. After retrieving the value, both methods set the text for the associated **TextBox** object. The body for both of those event handlers contains the following statement:

```
this.txtBoxResultFlowers.Text = cmboFlowers.Text;
```

Using Collection Indexes

Because the **ListBox** object allows multiple selections, the **Text** property cannot be used. It retrieves a single selection. **Text** gets the first one selected. To retrieve all of the choices you have a couple options. You can use the **SelectedItems**, **SelectedIndices**, or **Items** methods to retrieve a collection of items selected. These collections are zero-based structures such as an array. You can access them as you would access an element from an array by taking advantage of their array-like nature.

 SelectedIndices is a collection of indexes. Thus, if the first, third, and seventh items were selected, the **SelectedIndices** collection would contain 1, 3, 7.

It is possible to use an **int** to traverse through the collection of **SelectedIndices** as shown in Example 9-17.

```csharp
private void lstBoxTrees_SelectedIndexChanged(object sender,
                                        System.EventArgs e)
{
    this.txtBoxResultTrees.Text = " ";
    foreach(int i in lstBoxTrees.SelectedIndices)
    {
            this.txtBoxResultTrees.Text +=
                this.lstBoxTrees.Items[i] + " ";
}
```

Compare the event-handler method shown in Example 9-17 to the **ListBox SelectedIndexChanged( )** event-handler method shown in Example 9-12. Example 9-12 accessed the items using the **SelectedItems** property as opposed to the **SelectedIndices** property. Instead of accessing the selection by retrieving the items, the statements in Example 9-17 retrieved the indexes. The output produced from the application after adding these event-handler methods is shown in Figure 9-8.

9

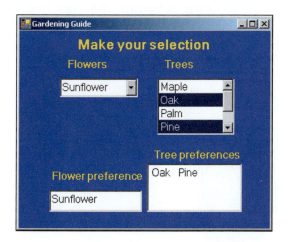

Figure 9-8 KeyPress and SelectedIndexChanged events fired

Sunflower was not placed in the collection list at design time; it is typed when the program is launched. The **KeyPress( )** event-handler method fired (multiple times). Remember **KeyPress( )** is fired for each and every character pressed. Thus, it is fired when the character *S* is typed; it is fired again when the character *u* is typed, and so on. So the **KeyPress( )** method is executed multiple times to get the characters from the combo box and display them in the text box. This **KeyPress( )** method uses the **Text** property of the **ComboBox** to get the selection and the **Text** property of the **TextBox object** to set the value for display purposes.

Two selections were made from the **ListBox object**. The **SelectedIndexChanged( )** method set the text of the **TextBox object** by concatenating (+=) the selections into the **Text** property.

Most Windows applications include a number of menu options. In the next section, you add menus to this application and learn how easy it is to add traditional menus found on most Windows applications.

MENU CONTROL OBJECTS

Menus offer the advantage of taking up minimal space on your window. They enable you to add more functionality to your application through offering additional options to the user. In the **System.Windows.Forms namespace**, a number of classes are available that inherit from the **Menu class**. These classes are used to add layers of menus to your applications.

Adding Main Menus

One of the classes is the **MainMenu class**. Using the Visual Studio .NET Toolbox window, it is easy to drag and drop a **MainMenu** control **object** to your form. When you do this, an icon representing the **MainMenu object** is placed below the design window. To add the text for the menu option, select this **mainMenu** icon and then click on the form in the top left corner—where the menu should display as illustrated in Figure 9-9. A menu structure is displayed so that you can type the text for the options.

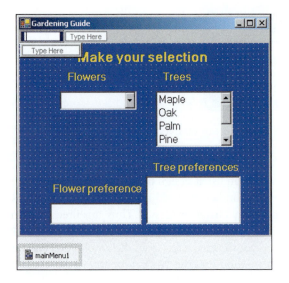

Figure 9-9   First step to creating a MainMenu

The menu structure is created by typing the text for the menu option in the prompted text box. This is the blank text box in the upper-left corner immediately below the icon that appears on the title bar as shown in Figure 9-9. This **class** enables you not only to create the top-level structure, but also to type options for drop-down subordinate menus. Notice the phrase "Type Here" in Figure 9-9. Moving to the right or below the current text box selection enables you to type either a subordinate menu option (below it) or another top-level menu option to the right. Additional drop-down options can be typed from the lower layers so that you can create a menu structure exactly like you see in applications such as your word-processing program.

With most Windows application menus, shortcuts are available for selections. When you type the text that is to appear in the menu, preceding a character with an ampersand (&) places an underline under the next character typed. As shown in Figure 9-10, the ampersand is typed between the *F* and *o* for the Format option. This makes Alt+o the shortcut for Format. This enables the option to be selected by pressing the Alt key plus the key that you type following the ampersand. For example, instead of typing **File**, type **&File**. This creates a shortcut of Alt+F for the File menu. You will see <u>F</u>ile displayed when you press the Alt key. To the right of File, **F&ormat** is typed followed by **&Help**. Under File, **Exit** was typed. As an option under the Format menu, **Font** was typed, followed by **Color**. Under Help, **About** was typed.

9

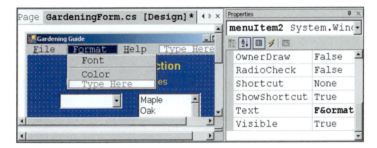

Figure 9-10 Creating a shortcut for a menu item

> **NOTE** A special **Shortcut** property for menu items exists. You can set other shortcuts using the Properties window. Selecting the box to the right of **Shortcut** in the Properties window reveals a drop-down list of characters. You can associate one of the function keys, or combinations of the Alt, Shift, Ctrl+Shift, or Ctrl keys, with any of the keys on the keyboard to any menu option.

> **NOTE** If you add shortcuts, you would want to include them as part of the text for the menu option. For example, if you associate Ctrl+S with save, the text for the menu for save should not just read "Save", but read "Save Ctrl+S"; otherwise, how will users know what shortcuts you have programmed for them?

You are accustomed to seeing separators between menu options. These are easily created in Visual Studio .NET by right-clicking on the text label below the needed separator as illustrated in Figure 9-11. When launched, a separator appears between the Font and Color options.

Figure 9-11   Adding a separator

After you type the text that will appear on the menu, you must set the **Menu** property on the form to the name of the **MainMenu object**. Otherwise, the menu does not display when you launch the application. The default, **mainMenu1**, is selected from the Properties window (using the **Menu** property for the form) as shown in Figure 9-12.

Properties		🔲 ×
GardeningForm System.Windows.Forms.Form		
AcceptButton	(none)	
CancelButton	(none)	
KeyPreview	False	
Language	(Default)	
Localizable	False	
⊟ Window Style		
ControlBox	True	
HelpButton	False	
⊞ Icon	(Icon)	
IsMdiContainer	False	
MaximizeBox	True	
⊞ Menu	mainMenu1	

Menu
The main menu of the form. This should be set to a component of type 'MainMenu'.

Figure 9-12   Setting the Menu property for the form

Once you finish laying out the structure, the **Name** property can be set for each menu. This is especially important if the menu item will be wired to an event, because the name of the control becomes part of the name of the event-handler method.

 To wire a method to an event such as a menu option means you are associating the event to a specific method. Once the method is wired to the menu option, the method is executed automatically when the menu option is clicked. When the menu option is clicked, it can be said that the event triggers, happens, or is fired. This is one of the underlying concepts behind event-driven applications.

Properties names such as **menuExit, menuFont, menuColor,** and **menuHelp** were set in the Properties window after selecting each individual option in the Form Designer. **Click** events are registered by double-clicking on the option. Form Designer generates individual click event-handler methods. The click event method name for the **menuExit** option is **menuExit_Click( )**; the event handler for the **menuFont** option is **menuFont_Click( )**.

 If you name a menu option *after* wiring its event handler to the menu option, the event-handler method name does not carry the name of the control. This does not impact the results—just leads to less readable code. You can actually change the method name to match the new name for the control; however, if you do this, you must also change the method name in the statement that wires the event handler to the **object**.

9

The click event-handler methods for the **Exit** and **About** menu options are shown in Example 9-18.

Example 9-18

```
private void menuExit_Click(object sender, System.EventArgs e)
{
        Application.Exit( );
}

private void menuAbout_Click(object sender, System.EventArgs e)
{
        MessageBox.Show("Gardening Guide Application\n\n\nVersion"
                        +" 1.0",
                         "About Gardening");
}
```

A message dialog box is displayed when the user clicks the **About** option. All windows are closed and the program terminated when the user clicks the Exit option.

Adding Predefined Standard Windows Dialog Boxes

Included as part of .NET are a number of preconfigured dialog boxes. They include boxes that look like the standard Windows File Open, File Save, File Print, File Print Preview, Format Font, and Format Color dialog boxes. They are added to your application by dragging and dropping the control **object** on your form. Figure 9-13 shows a partial list of controls highlighting the **FontDialog** and **ColorDialog** controls.

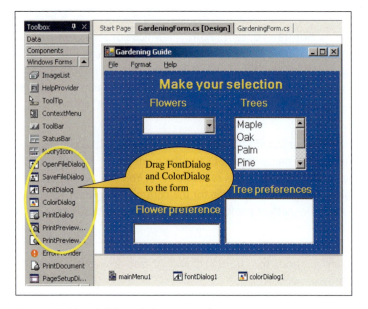

Figure 9-13   Adding dialog controls to menu options

To see the effect of the **Font** and **Color** menu options, a new **Label object** is placed on the **Form**. Its **Name** property is set to **lblOutput**. The **Text** property for **lblOutput** is set to **"Add Water!"**.

Double-clicking on the **Font** and **Color** menu options registers click events and generates event-handler methods. Example 9-19 shows the body of these methods.

Example 9-19

```csharp
private void menuFont_Click(object sender, System.EventArgs e)
{
    fontDialog1.Font = lblOutput.Font;
    if(fontDialog1.ShowDialog( ) != DialogResult.Cancel)
    {
        lblOutput.Font = fontDialog1.Font ;
    }
}
```

```
private void menuColor_Click(object sender, System.EventArgs e)
{
    colorDialog1.Color = lblOutput.ForeColor;
    if(colorDialog1.ShowDialog( ) != DialogResult.Cancel)
    {
        lblOutput.ForeColor = colorDialog1.Color;
    }
}
```

The first statement in the **menuFont_Click( )** method retrieves the current **Font** setting from the **Label** object's **Font** property. This value is shown as the selected option when the dialog box is displayed. The first statement in the **menuColor_Click( )** method retrieves the current **ForeColor** property setting for the **Label object**. Again, this value is used when the Color dialog box is displayed. For this example, the Color dialog box originally has a box around the yellow color, which is the value set as the **ForeColor** on the **Form** property. The **if** statement in Example 9-19 is checking to make sure the Cancel button has not been clicked. If it has been clicked, no change is made; otherwise, the **Font** and **ForeColor** are set to the selections made by the user.

Launching the program and selecting the **Color** menu option, after changing the **Font**, displays a window as shown in Figure 9-14. Clicking on the pink color changes the **ForeColor** for the **Label** to that selection.

9

Figure 9-14   Color dialog menu option

The Font dialog box displayed from the Format menu in the Gardening Guide is shown in Figure 9-15. It contains the styles, sizes, effects, and a sample output window for viewing. Notice that Informal Roman, Bold Italic, 28 point, and underline effects were all chosen. The `Label object` containing the text "Add water!" is changed to reflect these selections.

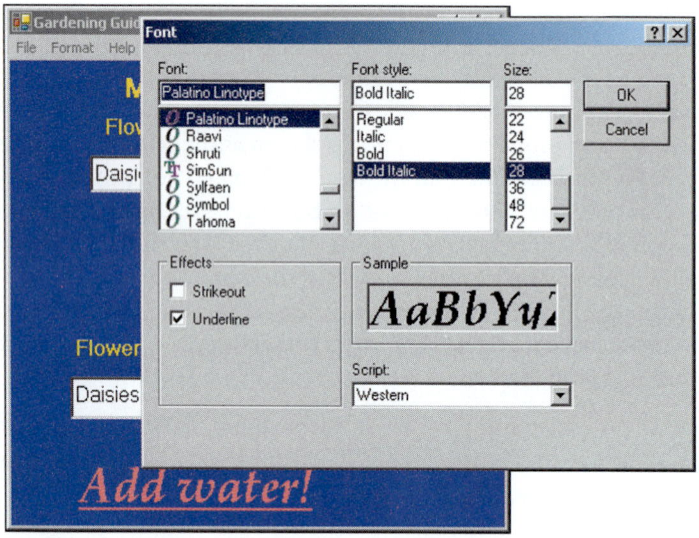

Figure 9-15 Font dialog box menu option

> **NOTE**
> You can add color selections to the `Font` dialog box by setting the `ShowColor` property of the FontDialog `object` to `true`. Your program statement would read: `fontDialog1.ShowColor = true;` By that same token, you could remove the `Effects` selections by setting the `ShowEffects` property to `false`. Doing this removes the check boxes for Strikeout and Underline.

You could certainly change any or all of the fonts and colors on the form using the name of the control `object` in your program statements. The `lblOutput Label object` is the only one modified by the font and color selections at runtime. The complete source code listing for this application is given in Example 9-20.

Example 9-20

```
// GardeningForm.cs          Author: Doyle
// Menu, ListBox, ComboBox, Label, and TextBox
// objects are included in the design. KeyPress( ),
// Click( ), and SelectedIndexChanged( ) events
```

```csharp
// are programmed. Font and Color dialog boxes
// are added.
using System;
using System.Drawing;
using System.Collections;
using System.ComponentModel;
using System.Windows.Forms;
using System.Data;
namespace GardeningForm
{
    public class GardeningForm : System.Windows.Forms.Form
    {
        private System.Windows.Forms.Label label1;
        private System.Windows.Forms.Label label2;
        private System.Windows.Forms.ListBox lstBoxTrees;
        private System.Windows.Forms.ComboBox cmboFlowers;
        private System.Windows.Forms.Label label3;
        private System.Windows.Forms.TextBox
            txtBoxResultTrees;
        private System.Windows.Forms.TextBox
            txtBoxResultFlowers;
        private System.Windows.Forms.Label label4;
        private System.Windows.Forms.Label label5;
        private System.Windows.Forms.MainMenu mainMenu1;
        private System.Windows.Forms.MenuItem menuItem1;
        private System.Windows.Forms.MenuItem menuItem2;
        private System.Windows.Forms.MenuItem menuItem3;
        private System.Windows.Forms.MenuItem menuAbout;
        private System.Windows.Forms.MenuItem menuFont;
        private System.Windows.Forms.MenuItem menuColor;
        private System.Windows.Forms.MenuItem menuExit;
        private System.Windows.Forms.FontDialog fontDialog1;
        private System.Windows.Forms.Label lblOutput;
        private System.Windows.Forms.ColorDialog
            colorDialog1;
        private System.Windows.Forms.MenuItem menuItem4;
        private System.ComponentModel.Container components =
            null;
        public GardeningForm( )
        {
            InitializeComponent( );
        }
        protected override void Dispose(bool disposing)
        {
            if(disposing)
            {
```

9

```csharp
                if (components != null)
                {
                    components.Dispose( );
                }
            }
            base.Dispose(disposing);
        }
        #region Windows Form Designer generated code
        private void InitializeComponent( )
        {
            this.lstBoxTrees = new
                System.Windows.Forms.ListBox( );
            this.cmboFlowers =
                new System.Windows.Forms.ComboBox( );
            this.label1 = new System.Windows.Forms.Label( );
            this.label2 = new System.Windows.Forms.Label( );
            this.label3 = new System.Windows.Forms.Label( );
            this.txtBoxResultTrees =
                new System.Windows.Forms.TextBox( );
            this.txtBoxResultFlowers =
                new System.Windows.Forms.TextBox( );
            this.label4 = new System.Windows.Forms.Label( );
            this.label5 = new System.Windows.Forms.Label( );
            this.mainMenu1 = new
                System.Windows.Forms.MainMenu( );
            this.menuItem1 = new
                System.Windows.Forms.MenuItem( );
            this.menuExit = new
                System.Windows.Forms.MenuItem( );
            this.menuItem2 = new
                System.Windows.Forms.MenuItem( );
            this.menuFont = new
                System.Windows.Forms.MenuItem( );
            this.menuColor = new
                System.Windows.Forms.MenuItem( );
            this.menuItem3 = new
                System.Windows.Forms.MenuItem( );
            this.menuAbout = new
                System.Windows.Forms.MenuItem( );
            this.fontDialog1 = new
                System.Windows.Forms.FontDialog( );
            this.lblOutput = new
                System.Windows.Forms.Label( );
            this.colorDialog1 = new
                System.Windows.Forms.ColorDialog( );
            this.menuItem4 = new
                System.Windows.Forms.MenuItem( );
            this.SuspendLayout( );
```

```csharp
// lstBoxTrees
this.lstBoxTrees.ItemHeight = 20;
this.lstBoxTrees.Items.AddRange(new object[]
                        {   "Maple",
                            "Oak",
                            "Palm",
                            "Pine",
                            "Spruce",
                            "Walnut"});
this.lstBoxTrees.Location =
    new System.Drawing.Point(216, 72);
this.lstBoxTrees.Name = "lstBoxTrees";
this.lstBoxTrees.SelectionMode =
System.Windows.Forms.SelectionMode.MultiExtended;
this.lstBoxTrees.Size = new
    System.Drawing.Size(120, 84);
this.lstBoxTrees.TabIndex = 1;
this.lstBoxTrees.SelectedIndexChanged +=
    new System.EventHandler
    (this.lstBoxTrees_SelectedIndexChanged);

// cmboFlowers
this.cmboFlowers.Items.AddRange(new object[]
                        {   "Roses",
                            "Orchids",
                            "Tulips",
                            "Daisies ",
                            "Asters",
                            "Mums"});
this.cmboFlowers.Location =
    new System.Drawing.Point(64, 72);
this.cmboFlowers.Name = "cmboFlowers";
this.cmboFlowers.Size = new
    System.Drawing.Size(121, 28);
this.cmboFlowers.KeyPress += new
    System.Windows.Forms.KeyPressEventHandler
    (this.cmboFlowers_KeyPress);
this.cmboFlowers.SelectedIndexChanged +=
    new System.EventHandler
    (this.cmboFlowers_SelectedIndexChanged);

// label1
this.label1.Font = new System.Drawing.Font
    ("Microsoft Sans Serif",
    12F, System.Drawing.FontStyle.Bold,
    System.Drawing.GraphicsUnit.Point,
    ((System.Byte)(0)));
```

9

```
this.label1.Location = new
    System.Drawing.Point(72, 40);
this.label1.Name = "label1";
this.label1.TabIndex = 3;
this.label1.Text = "Flowers";

// label2
this.label2.Font = new System.Drawing.Font
    ("Microsoft Sans Serif",
    12F, System.Drawing.FontStyle.Bold,
    System.Drawing.GraphicsUnit.Point,
    ((System.Byte)(0)));
this.label2.Location = new
    System.Drawing.Point(224, 40);
this.label2.Name = "label2";
this.label2.TabIndex = 4;
this.label2.Text = "Trees";

// label3
this.label3.Font = new System.Drawing.Font
    ("Microsoft Sans Serif",
    15.75F, System.Drawing.FontStyle.Bold,
    System.Drawing.GraphicsUnit.Point,
    ((System.Byte)(0)));
this.label3.Location = new
    System.Drawing.Point(88, 8);
this.label3.Name = "label3";
this.label3.Size = new
    System.Drawing.Size(224, 23);
this.label3.TabIndex = 5;
this.label3.Text = "Make your selection";

// txtBoxResultTrees
this.txtBoxResultTrees.Location =
    new System.Drawing.Point(200, 200);
this.txtBoxResultTrees.Multiline = true;
this.txtBoxResultTrees.Name =
    "txtBoxResultTrees";
this.txtBoxResultTrees.ScrollBars =
    System.Windows.Forms.ScrollBars.Horizontal;
this.txtBoxResultTrees.Size =
    new System.Drawing.Size(148, 72);
this.txtBoxResultTrees.TabIndex = 6;
this.txtBoxResultTrees.Text = "";

// txtBoxResultFlowers
this.txtBoxResultFlowers.Location =
    new System.Drawing.Point(48, 240);
this.txtBoxResultFlowers.Multiline = true;
```

```csharp
this.txtBoxResultFlowers.Name =
    "txtBoxResultFlowers";
this.txtBoxResultFlowers.Size =
    new System.Drawing.Size(144, 32);
this.txtBoxResultFlowers.TabIndex = 7;
this.txtBoxResultFlowers.Text = "";

// label4
this.label4.Font =
    new System.Drawing.Font
    ("Microsoft Sans Serif",
    12F, System.Drawing.FontStyle.Bold,
    System.Drawing.GraphicsUnit.Point,
    ((System.Byte)(0)));
this.label4.Location = new
    System.Drawing.Point(48, 208);
this.label4.Name = "label4";
this.label4.Size =
    new System.Drawing.Size(144, 23);
this.label4.TabIndex = 8;
this.label4.Text = "Flower preference";

// label5
this.label5.Font = new System.Drawing.Font
    ("Microsoft Sans Serif",
    12F, System.Drawing.FontStyle.Bold,
    System.Drawing.GraphicsUnit.Point,
    ((System.Byte)(0)));
this.label5.Location = new
    System.Drawing.Point(208, 176);
this.label5.Name = "label5";
this.label5.Size = new
    System.Drawing.Size(136, 23);
this.label5.TabIndex = 9;
this.label5.Text = "Tree preferences";

// mainMenu1
this.mainMenu1.MenuItems.AddRange
    (new System.Windows.Forms.MenuItem[]
                        { this.menuItem1,
                            this.menuItem2,
                            this.menuItem3 } );

// menuItem1
this.menuItem1.Index = 0;
this.menuItem1.MenuItems.AddRange
    (new System.Windows.Forms.MenuItem[]
    { this.menuExit });
this.menuItem1.Text = "&File";
```

9

```
// menuExit
this.menuExit.Index = 0;
this.menuExit.Text = "Exit";
this.menuExit.Click += new
    System.EventHandler(this.menuExit_Click);

// menuItem2
this.menuItem2.Index = 1;
this.menuItem2.MenuItems.AddRange
    (new System.Windows.Forms.MenuItem[]
                        {   this.menuFont,
                            this.menuItem4,
                            this.menuColor } );
this.menuItem2.Text = "F&ormat";

// menuFont
this.menuFont.Index = 0;
this.menuFont.Text = "Font";
this.menuFont.Click += new System.EventHandler
    (this.menuFont_Click);

// menuColor
this.menuColor.Index = 2;
this.menuColor.Text = "Color";
this.menuColor.Click += new System.EventHandler
    (this.menuColor_Click);

// menuItem3
this.menuItem3.Index = 2;
this.menuItem3.MenuItems.AddRange
    (new System.Windows.Forms.MenuItem[]
                        {this.menuAbout});
this.menuItem3.Text = "&Help";

// menuAbout
this.menuAbout.Index = 0;
this.menuAbout.Text = "About";
this.menuAbout.Click += new System.EventHandler
    (this.menuAbout_Click);

// lblOutput
this.lblOutput.Location = new
    System.Drawing.Point(48, 296);
this.lblOutput.Name = "lblOutput";
this.lblOutput.Size = new
    System.Drawing.Size(304, 48);
this.lblOutput.TabIndex = 10;
this.lblOutput.Text = "Add water!";
```

```csharp
// menuItem4
this.menuItem4.Index = 1;
this.menuItem4.Text = "-";

// GardeningForm
this.AutoScaleBaseSize = new
    System.Drawing.Size(8, 19);
this.BackColor =
    System.Drawing.Color.MediumBlue;
this.ClientSize = new
    System.Drawing.Size(392, 353);
this.Controls.AddRange
    (new System.Windows.Forms.Control[]
    { this.lblOutput,
      this.label5,
      this.label4,
      this.txtBoxResultFlowers,
      this.txtBoxResultTrees,
      this.label3,
      this.label2,
      this.label1,
      this.cmboFlowers,
      this.lstBoxTrees } );
this.Font = new System.Drawing.Font
    ("Microsoft Sans Serif",
    12F, System.Drawing.FontStyle.Regular,
    System.Drawing.GraphicsUnit.Point,
    ((System.Byte)(0)));
this.ForeColor = System.Drawing.Color.Yellow;
this.Menu = this.mainMenu1;
this.Name = "GardeningForm";
this.Text = "Gardening Guide";
this.ResumeLayout(false);
}
#endregion

static void Main( )
{
    Application.Run(new GardeningForm( ));
}

private void cmboFlowers_SelectedIndexChanged
    (object sender, System.EventArgs e)
{
    this.txtBoxResultFlowers.Text =
        this.cmboFlowers.Text;
}
```

9

```csharp
private void cmboFlowers_KeyPress
    (object sender,
     System.Windows.Forms.KeyPressEventArgs e)
{
        this.txtBoxResultFlowers.Text =
            cmboFlowers.Text;
}

private void lstBoxTrees_SelectedIndexChanged
    (object sender, System.EventArgs e)
{
    this.txtBoxResultTrees.Text = " ";
    foreach(int i in lstBoxTrees.SelectedIndices)
    {
        this.txtBoxResultTrees.Text +=
                this.lstBoxTrees.Items[i] + "    ";
    }
}

private void menuExit_Click(object sender,
                                System.EventArgs e)
{
    Application.Exit( );
}

private void menuAbout_Click(object sender,
                                System.EventArgs e)
{
    MessageBox.Show
        ("Gardening Guide Application\n\n\nVersion"
        " 1.0", "About Gardening");
}

private void menuFont_Click(object sender,
                                System.EventArgs e)
{
    fontDialog1.Font = lblOutput.Font;
    if(fontDialog1.ShowDialog( ) !=
       DialogResult.Cancel)
    {
        lblOutput.Font = fontDialog1.Font ;
    }
}

private void menuColor_Click(object sender,
                                System.EventArgs e)
{
    colorDialog1.Color = lblOutput.ForeColor;
    if(colorDialog1.ShowDialog( ) !=
       DialogResult.Cancel)
```

```
            {
                lblOutput.ForeColor = colorDialog1.Color;
            }
        }
    }
}
```

 As you review the source code for Example 9-20, keep in mind that the Visual Studio Form Designer automatically generated most statements. The only statements that you as a developer need to add are explained in the previous sections.

As you review the code, you will find that a number of properties were set for the different objects of the **GardeningForm** application. To aid you in reviewing these settings, Table 9-4 includes a list of properties and the values used to set them. You should match the entries in the table with the program statements in Example 9-20. Doing so will help you better read and understand the program statements.

Table 9-4 GardeningForm property values

Name	Object type	Property	Value
GardeningForm	Form	BackColor	Medium Blue
GardeningForm	Form	Font	Microsoft Sans Serif, 12
GardeningForm	Form	Menu	mainMenu1
GardeningForm	Form	Text	Typed "Gardening Guide"
lstBoxTrees	ListBox	Items (Collection)	Typed "Maple", "Oak","Palm", "Pine","Spruce", "Walnut"
lstBoxTrees	ListBox	SelectionMode	MultiExtended
cmboFlowers	ComboBox	Items (Collection)	Typed "Roses", "Orchids", "Tulips", "Daisies", "Asters", "Mums"
label1	Label	Text	Typed "Flowers"
label2	Label	Text	Typed "Trees"
label3	Label	Text	Typed "Make your Selection"
txtBoxResultTrees	TextBox	Multiline	true
txtBoxResultTrees	TextBox	ScrollBars	Horizontal

9

Table 9-4 GardeningForm property values (continued)

Name	Object type	Property	Value
txtBoxResultTrees	TextBox	Text	(left blank)
txtBoxResultFlowers	TextBox	Multiline	true
txtBoxResultFlowers	TextBox	Text	(left blank)
label4	Label	Text	Typed "Flower preference"
label5	Label	Text	Typed "Tree preferences"
mainMenu1	mainMenu	MenuItems	menuItem1, menuItem2, menuItem3
menuItem1	menuItem	Text	Typed "&File"
menuExit	menuItem	Text	Typed "Exit"
menuItem2	menuItem	Text	Typed "F&ormat"
menuItem2	menuItem	MenuItems	menuFont, menuItem4, menuColor
menuFont	menuItem	Text	Typed "Font"
menuColor	menuItem	Text	Typed "Color"
menuItem3	menuItem	Text	Typed "&Help"
menuAbout	menuItem	Text	Typed "About"
lblOutput	Label	Text	Typed "Add water!"

The Program in Example 9-20 wired a number of objects to event-handler methods. Table 9-5 shows the event handlers that are registered for specific objects. Two events are registered for the ComboBox object.

Table 9-5 GardeningForm events

Object	Event-handler method
lstBoxTrees	SelectedIndexChanged( )
comboFlowers	SelectedIndexChanged( )
comboFlowers	KeyPress( )
menuExit	Click( )
menuFont	menuFont_Click( )
menuColor	menuColor_Click( )
menuAbout	menuAbout_Click( )

Again, for each entry in the table, you should first locate the statement in the Example 9-20 that registers the method as being the event handler for the particular `object`. Secondly, locate the actual method that is raised when the event is fired.

You have now wired and programmed `Click( )`, `KeyPress( )`, and `SelectedIndexChanged( )` events. `RadioButton` and `CheckBox` objects fire a different type of event. When their values are changed, they raise `CheckedChanged( )` events. These types of events are discussed in the next section.

CHECKBOX AND RADIOBUTTON OBJECTS

Radio buttons and check boxes are two types of objects commonly used in Windows applications. They are often grouped together for discussion; however, they differ in appearance and functionality. You first explore `CheckBox` objects.

CheckBox Objects

`CheckBox` objects can be added to a Windows form application in the same manner as other objects. If you are using Visual Studio .NET, you drag and drop the control. If you are developing in a simple text editor, such as Notepad, instantiate an `object` of the `CheckBox` `class` using the `new` operator. Check boxes usually appear as small boxes that allow users to make a yes/no or `true`/`false` selection. After the objects are placed on the form, `Name` and `Text` properties are normally set for each of the `CheckBox` objects.

Previous applications used a separate event-handler method for every `object` added to the form. You can, however, write an event-handler method and wire it to more than one control. This is illustrated in the next example. You might want to look ahead to Figure 9-19 to see what the final solution looks like.

 A new project is started. It is also a Windows application. This one allows users to register for swim, snorkel, or dive lessons. The form enables the user to select his or her skill level. The Text property for the Form `object` is set to "Registration Form". The Name property is set to RegForm and the BackColor property is set to DarkBlue.

Adding CheckBox Objects

A `TextBox` `object` is added near the bottom of the form to display the final charge for the lessons. Swim lessons cost $50; snorkel lessons cost $25; scuba diving lessons cost $100. A user can select more than one lesson. Three `CheckBox` objects are added to the form. Their `Name` properties are set to `ckBoxSwim`, `ckBoxSnorkel`, and `ckBoxDive`. The `Text` property on each is set to represent the type of lessons along with a cost (that is, Swim—$50, Snorkel—$25, and Dive—$100). A `Label` `object` is used to describe the `TextBox` where the total charges will be displayed. Another `Label` `object` is added near the top of the form describing the `TextBox` `object` to its right, which will accept as input the user's name. Additional

Label objects are added above and below the check boxes with text of "Select lesson" and "Check all that apply".

After the Text properties are set for the controls, the Checked property of the CheckBox objects is reviewed. The Checked property is set to either **true** or **false** depending on whether a check mark appears or not. This property can be set at design time. At runtime the Checked property can be set or inspected using an **if** statement to determine which selections are checked by users. All CheckBox objects remain set at their default **false** value.

Registering CheckBox Object Events

The default event-handler method for CheckBox objects is CheckChanged( ). Double-clicking on one of the CheckBox objects registers a CheckChanged( ) event for that one CheckBox object. The method that is fired checks all the check boxes to see which are checked. This code could be copied and pasted to different methods or the one method could be wired to all three objects. The last option is a better approach. If you copy and paste the code to three methods, any minor modifications that you make require you to make those changes to all three different methods. A runtime or logic error is easily created by this scenario. It is easy to forget to make those slight changes to all three methods. A better approach is to wire a single method to multiple objects.

In Visual Studio .NET, the Form Designer prefixes the name of the event-handler method with the name of the object to which the method is wired. You can change the name of the method so that the method appears to be used by all three objects and not just associated with one object. If you do this, a second step is required. You cannot just change the name of the method in the method heading. You must also change the name of the method in the statement that registered the method to handle the event.

For this example, the original heading for the event-handler method for the Swim CheckBox object was:

```
private void ckBoxSwim_CheckedChanged
                (object sender, System.EventArgs e)    {    }
```

The heading of the ckBoxSwim_CheckedChanged( ) method was changed to:

```
private void ComputeCost_CheckedChanged
        (object sender, System.EventArgs e)    {    }
```

 The characters ckBoxSwim were replaced by ComputeCost so that the new method name is ComputeCost_CheckedChanged( ). This makes the code more readable. You could have actually wired the other two events to the method without changing any names; however, it would be more difficult to read and modify later, because it would appear that the method was associated with the Swim CheckBox object only.

If you change the name of the method, the second step you must take uses the new name to register the event for the Swim **CheckBox object**. Originally the statement read:

```
this.ckBoxSwim.CheckedChanged +=
     new System.EventHandler(this.ckBoxSwim_CheckedChanged);
```

It was changed to:

```
this.ckBoxSwim.CheckedChanged +=
     new System.EventHandler(this.ComputeCost_CheckedChanged);
```

 Notice that you are only changing the method name inside the parentheses. You do not change the name of the **object** on the left side of the += symbols.

Once those changes are made, you can write the body for the method that will be fired when any of the **CheckBox object** states change. Example 9-21 shows this method.

Example 9-21

```
// Event handler to be used by all three CheckBoxes
private void ComputeCost_CheckedChanged
                         (object sender, System.EventArgs e)
{
    decimal cost = 0;
    if (this.ckBoxSwim.Checked)
    {
        cost += 50;
    }
    if (this.ckBoxSnorkel.Checked)
    {
        cost += 25;
    }
    if (this.ckBoxDive.Checked)
    {
        cost += 100;
    }
    this.txtResult.Text = cost.ToString("C");
}
```

 Notice that a nested **if** statement is not used here because the user might click one, two, or all three. A nested **if** would exit the selection statement as soon as one condition evaluated to **true**.

Wiring One Event Handler to Multiple Objects

The Swim `CheckBox` `object` is wired to the `ComputeCost_CheckedChanged( )` method. You changed the name associated with the event-handler method. Now with two clicks you can wire the other events. First select the Snorkel `CheckBox` `object` as shown in Figure 9-16. Using the Visual Studio Properties window, click on the Events Icon (lightning bolt). Move down to the `CheckedChanged` event. Click the down arrow associated with that event and select `ComputeCost_CheckedChanged`. Follow the same steps for the Dive `CheckBox` `object`.

> **NOTE** Actually, this is the only event-handler method written so far; thus, it is the only one available to choose.

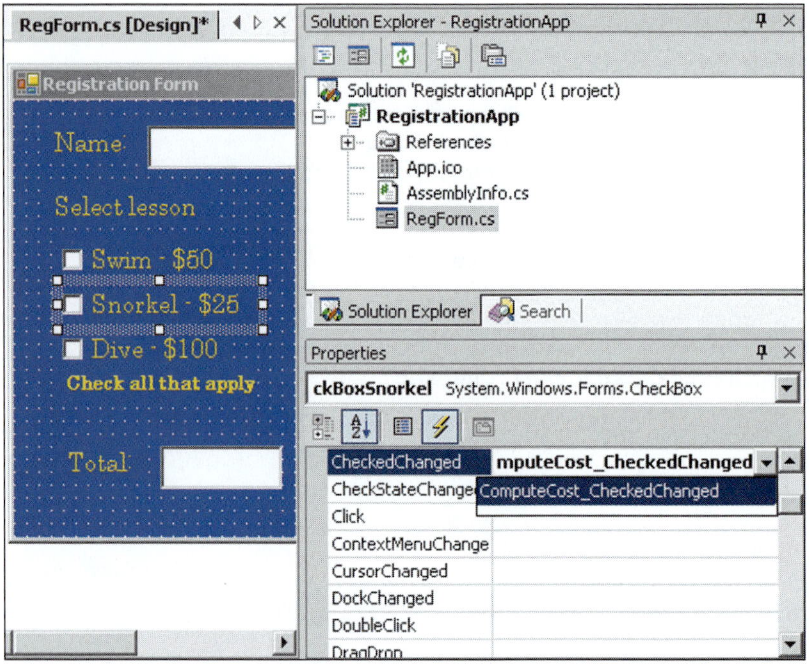

Figure 9-16   Wiring the event-handler method

When you launch the application, changes to any of the `CheckBox` objects fire the `ComputeCost_CheckedChanged( )` method. Figure 9-17 shows the output from the application.

Figure 9-17   ComputeCost_CheckedChanged( ) method raised

> Notice in Figure 9-17 that a number of `Form` properties were set. These properties were set when the `Form` object was initially created. The `Name`, `BackColor`, `ForeColor`, `Text`, `Font`, and `Size` properties should almost always be set.

GroupBox Objects

`CheckBox` objects may be grouped together using the `GroupBox` control. This is beneficial for visual appearance. It also helps during design because you can move or set properties that impact the entire group. However, it does not provide any additional functionality for `CheckBox` objects.

A `GroupBox` control should be placed on the form before you add the `RadioButton` objects to it. If you add the `RadioButton` objects first and then try to add the `GroupBox` control object on top of the `RadioButton` objects, it does not work as smoothly. If you add the `GroupBox` control object last, you need physically to drag the `RadioButton` objects onto the top of the `GroupBox` control object.

> Do not forget about the useful tools under the Format Menu. The Align, Make Same Size, Horizontal Spacing, Vertical Spacing, and Center in Form tools save you hours of time. Remember, it does matter what your interface looks like!

RadioButton Objects

There are differences between the `RadioButton` and `CheckBox` objects, other than their visual representation. `RadioButton` controls appear as small circles on the `Form` object. They are used to give users a choice between two or more options. Remember that it is appropriate to select more than one `CheckBox` object. Not so, with `RadioButton` objects. Normally you group `RadioButton` objects by placing them on a `Panel` or `GroupBox` control.

Adding RadioButton Objects

To build on the application developed in the previous section containing the `CheckBox` objects, a `GroupBox` control is placed on the form. It should be placed there before adding objects to the group. `GroupBox` control objects provide an identifiable grouping for other controls. After it is dragged onto the form, a `GroupBox` control `object` must usually be resized. Using Visual Studio you can drag three `RadioButton` objects on top of the `GroupBox`.

 Once the `RadioButton` objects are placed on the `GroupBox`, you can set properties of the `GroupBox` and impact all members of the group. Want to make them invisible? Set the `Visible` property of the `GroupBox`. It is not necessary to set all of the members. Want to change the font color of all radio buttons—just change the `GroupBox` `Font` property.

Setting the `Text` property for the `GroupBox` adds a labeled heading over the group of radio buttons without your having to add an additional `Label` `object`. Whatever value you type for the `Text` property for `RadioButton` objects is used to label the control. By default the text appears to the right of the small circle as shown in Figure 9-18. If you want the text in the label to display to the left of the small circle, set the `RightToLeft` property to Yes for the `RadioButton` control. For this example, the `GroupBox` `Text` property was set to `"Skill level"`; `RadioButton` `Text` properties are set to `"Beginner"`, `"Interme-diate"`, and `"Advanced"`. An extra `Label` `object` is added to the bottom right to display messages regarding special discounts or extra charges associated with different skill levels. The new `Label` object's `Text` property is set to `""`. Figure 9-18 shows the form in Design view after the `Text` properties are set for the newly added `GroupBox` and `RadioButton` objects.

Figure 9-18　GroupBox and RadioButton objects added

Notice the box drawn around the `RadioButton` objects. This is added by the `GroupBox` control object. The heading that appears over the radio buttons is the `Text` property for the `GroupBox`.

The middle `RadioButton` object is set as the default by selecting **true** for its `Checked` property. This is done during design using the **Checked** property, located in the Properties window list of properties. You change the value by selecting **true** from the drop-down list. Double-clicking on the property name also toggles the setting between **false** (default) and **true**. The Visual Studio Form Designer inserts the following line of code in your program:

`this.radInterm.Checked = true;`

 If you plan to have more than one set of `RadioButton` objects on your form, each set must be associated with a different `Panel` or `GroupBox` control object. This is necessary to allow mutually exclusive selections from different categories. For example, if you had one set of buttons for skill level and another set for age group (1 year to 5 years; 6 years to 10 years; over 10 years), to allow selection from both categories, the two categories of radio buttons must be connected to two different group boxes or panels.

Registering RadioButton Object Events

Like `CheckBox` objects, `RadioButton` objects raise a number of events, including `Click( )` and `CheckedChanged( )` events. For this application, the skill level helps determine the cost of the lessons. The prices shown on the form are actually for registrants of intermediate skill level. Those with an advanced skill level are discounted $15; beginners are charged an extra $10. Because the skill level is used to determine the cost of lessons, the `RadioButton Click` event is wired to the same event-handler method that was written for the `CheckBox` objects. Modifications are made to the method to reflect the additional problem specification.

Wire the `Click` event for each of the `RadioButton` objects—just as you wired the Scuba and Dive `CheckBox` objects. This can be done in Visual Studio .NET by displaying the list of events (click on the **Event** lightning bolt icon) in the Properties window. Select the `Click( )` event and then use the down arrow to select the event-handler method `ComputeCost_CheckedChanged( )`. This is still the only event-handler method available to be displayed as shown in Figure 9-19. No other event-handler methods have been written for this application. The `Click` event for the `RadioButton` objects is wired to the `ComputeCost_CheckedChanged( )` method in Figure 9-19.

9

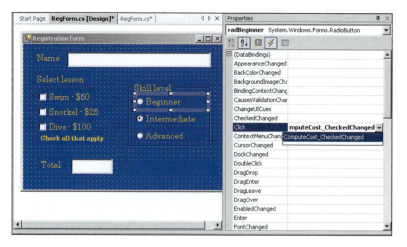

Figure 9-19 Wired Click event

Example 9-22 shows the additional statements added to the end of the `ComputeCost_CheckedChanged( )` method to take the skill level into consideration. The `Checked` property is used again. This time it is inspected to determine which `RadioButton` object is selected.

Example 9-22

```
if (this.radBeginner.Checked)
{
    cost +=10;
    this.lblMsg.Text = "Beginner — Extra $10" +
                        " charge";
}
else
    if (this.radAdvanc.Checked)
{
    cost -=15;
    this.lblMsg.Text = "Advanced - Discount" +
                        " $15";
}
else
{
    this.lblMsg.Text = "   ";
}
```

 Notice that a nested `if` statement is used here with the `RadioButton` objects. Unlike the `CheckBox` objects, only one selection is possible. Thus, as soon as an expression evaluates to `true`, there is no need to test the other expressions.

Example 9-23 includes the complete program listing. Although it seems long, the Form Designer in Visual Studio generates much of the code.

Example 9-23

```csharp
// RegForm.cs          Author: Doyle
// CheckBox and RadioButton objects
// added to Windows Form.
// Illustrates wiring several methods to
// the same event handler.
using System;
using System.Drawing;
using System.Collections;
using System.ComponentModel;
using System.Windows.Forms;
using System.Data;
namespace RegistrationApp
{
    public class RegForm : System.Windows.Forms.Form
    {
        private System.Windows.Forms.Label label1;
        private System.Windows.Forms.Label label2;
        private System.Windows.Forms.Label label3;
        private System.Windows.Forms.TextBox textBox1;
        private System.Windows.Forms.CheckBox ckBoxSwim;
        private System.Windows.Forms.CheckBox ckBoxSnorkel;
        private System.Windows.Forms.CheckBox ckBoxDive;
        private System.Windows.Forms.Label lblResult;
        private System.Windows.Forms.TextBox txtResult;
        private System.Windows.Forms.GroupBox groupBox1;
        private System.Windows.Forms.Label lblMsg;
        private System.Windows.Forms.RadioButton radAdvanc;
        private System.Windows.Forms.RadioButton radInterm;
        private System.Windows.Forms.RadioButton
            radBeginner;
        private System.ComponentModel.Container components =
            null;

        public RegForm( )
        {
            InitializeComponent( );
        }
        protected override void Dispose(bool disposing)
        {
            if(disposing)
            {
```

9

```csharp
            if (components != null)
            {
                components.Dispose( );
            }
        }
        base.Dispose(disposing);
    }
    #region Windows Form Designer generated code

    private void InitializeComponent( )
    {
        this.label1 = new System.Windows.Forms.Label( );
        this.ckBoxSwim = new
            System.Windows.Forms.CheckBox( );
        this.ckBoxSnorkel = new
            System.Windows.Forms.CheckBox( );
        this.label2 = new System.Windows.Forms.Label( );
        this.ckBoxDive = new
            System.Windows.Forms.CheckBox( );
        this.label3 = new System.Windows.Forms.Label( );
        this.textBox1 = new
            System.Windows.Forms.TextBox( );
        this.lblResult = new
            System.Windows.Forms.Label( );
        this.txtResult = new
            System.Windows.Forms.TextBox( );
        this.groupBox1 = new
            System.Windows.Forms.GroupBox( );
        this.radAdvanc = new
            System.Windows.Forms.RadioButton( );
        this.radInterm = new
            System.Windows.Forms.RadioButton( );
        this.radBeginner = new
            System.Windows.Forms.RadioButton( );
        this.lblMsg = new System.Windows.Forms.Label( );
        this.groupBox1.SuspendLayout( );
        this.SuspendLayout( );

        // label1
        this.label1.Font = new System.Drawing.Font
            ("Century", 9F,
            System.Drawing.FontStyle.Bold,
            System.Drawing.GraphicsUnit.Point,
            ((System.Byte)(0)));
        this.label1.Location = new
            System.Drawing.Point(32, 168);
        this.label1.Name = "label1";
        this.label1.Size = new
            System.Drawing.Size(128, 23);
```

```
this.label1.TabIndex = 0;
this.label1.Text = "Check all that Apply";

// ckBoxSwim
this.ckBoxSwim.Location = new
    System.Drawing.Point(32, 88);
this.ckBoxSwim.Name = "ckBoxSwim";
this.ckBoxSwim.Size = new
    System.Drawing.Size(112, 24);
this.ckBoxSwim.TabIndex = 1;
this.ckBoxSwim.Text = "Swim - $50";
this.ckBoxSwim.CheckedChanged += new
    System.EventHandler
    (this.ComputeCost_CheckedChanged);

// ckBoxSnorkel
this.ckBoxSnorkel.Location =
    new System.Drawing.Point(32, 116);
this.ckBoxSnorkel.Name = "ckBoxSnorkel";
this.ckBoxSnorkel.Size = new
    System.Drawing.Size(128, 24);
this.ckBoxSnorkel.TabIndex = 2;
this.ckBoxSnorkel.Text = "Snorkel - $25";
this.ckBoxSnorkel.CheckedChanged += new
    System.EventHandler
    (this.ComputeCost_CheckedChanged);

// label2
this.label2.Location = new
    System.Drawing.Point(24, 56);
this.label2.Name = "label2";
this.label2.Size = new
    System.Drawing.Size(112, 23);
this.label2.TabIndex = 3;
this.label2.Text = "Select Lesson ";

// ckBoxDive
this.ckBoxDive.Location = new
    System.Drawing.Point(32, 144);
this.ckBoxDive.Name = "ckBoxDive";
this.ckBoxDive.Size = new
    System.Drawing.Size(112, 24);
this.ckBoxDive.TabIndex = 4;
this.ckBoxDive.Text = "Dive - $100";
this.ckBoxDive.CheckedChanged += new
    System.EventHandler
    (this.ComputeCost_CheckedChanged);
```

9

```
// label3
this.label3.Location = new
    System.Drawing.Point(24, 16);
this.label3.Name = "label3";
this.label3.Size = new
    System.Drawing.Size(64, 23);
this.label3.TabIndex = 5;
this.label3.Text = "Name:";

// textBox1
this.textBox1.Location = new
    System.Drawing.Point(88, 16);
this.textBox1.Name = "textBox1";
this.textBox1.Size = new
    System.Drawing.Size(280, 27);
this.textBox1.TabIndex = 6;
this.textBox1.Text = "";

// lblResult
this.lblResult.Location = new
    System.Drawing.Point(32, 216);
this.lblResult.Name = "lblResult";
this.lblResult.Size = new
    System.Drawing.Size(56, 23);
this.lblResult.TabIndex = 7;
this.lblResult.Text = "Total:";

// txtResult
this.txtResult.Location =
    new System.Drawing.Point(96, 216);
this.txtResult.Name = "txtResult";
this.txtResult.Size = new
    System.Drawing.Size(80, 27);
this.txtResult.TabIndex = 8;
this.txtResult.Text = "";
this.txtResult.TextAlign =
 System.Windows.Forms.HorizontalAlignment.Right;

// groupBox1
this.groupBox1.Controls.AddRange
    (new System.Windows.Forms.Control[]
    {  this.radAdvanc,
       this.radInterm,
       this.radBeginner});
this.groupBox1.ForeColor =
    System.Drawing.Color.Yellow;
this.groupBox1.Location =
    new System.Drawing.Point(208, 72);
```

```
this.groupBox1.Name = "groupBox1";
this.groupBox1.Size = new
    System.Drawing.Size(160, 120);
this.groupBox1.TabIndex = 9;
this.groupBox1.TabStop = false;
this.groupBox1.Text = "Skill Level";

// radAdvanc
this.radAdvanc.Location = new
    System.Drawing.Point(16, 88);
this.radAdvanc.Name = "radAdvanc";
this.radAdvanc.Size = new
    System.Drawing.Size(136, 24);
this.radAdvanc.TabIndex = 2;
this.radAdvanc.Text = "Advanced";
this.radAdvanc.Click += new System.EventHandler
    (this.ComputeCost_CheckedChanged);

// radInterm
this.radInterm.Checked = true;
this.radInterm.Location = new
    System.Drawing.Point(16, 56);
this.radInterm.Name = "radInterm";
this.radInterm.Size = new
    System.Drawing.Size(136, 24);
this.radInterm.TabIndex = 1;
this.radInterm.TabStop = true;
this.radInterm.Text = "Intermediate";
this.radInterm.Click += new System.EventHandler
    (this.ComputeCost_CheckedChanged);

// radBeginner
this.radBeginner.Location =
    new System.Drawing.Point(16, 24);
this.radBeginner.Name = "radBeginner";
this.radBeginner.Size = new
    System.Drawing.Size(136, 24);
this.radBeginner.TabIndex = 0;
this.radBeginner.Text = "Beginner";
this.radBeginner.Click += new
    System.EventHandler
    (this.ComputeCost_CheckedChanged);

// lblMsg
this.lblMsg.Font = new
    System.Drawing.Font("Century",
    9.75F, System.Drawing.FontStyle.Italic,
    System.Drawing.GraphicsUnit.Point,
    ((System.Byte)(0)));
```

9

```csharp
            this.lblMsg.ForeColor =
                System.Drawing.Color.GreenYellow;
            this.lblMsg.Location = new
                System.Drawing.Point(192, 224);
            this.lblMsg.Name = "lblMsg";
            this.lblMsg.Size = new
                System.Drawing.Size(192, 24);
            this.lblMsg.TabIndex = 10;

            // RegForm
            this.AutoScaleBaseSize = new
                System.Drawing.Size(8, 20);
            this.BackColor = System.Drawing.Color.DarkBlue;
            this.ClientSize = new
                System.Drawing.Size(392, 273);
            this.Controls.AddRange(
                new System.Windows.Forms.Control[]
                {   this.lblMsg,
                    this.groupBox1,
                    this.txtResult,
                    this.lblResult,
                    this.textBox1,
                    this.label3,
                    this.ckBoxDive,
                    this.label2,
                    this.ckBoxSnorkel,
                    this.ckBoxSwim,
                    this.label1});
            this.Font = new
                System.Drawing.Font("Century", 12F,
                System.Drawing.FontStyle.Regular,
                System.Drawing.GraphicsUnit.Point,
                ((System.Byte)(0)));
            this.ForeColor = System.Drawing.Color.Yellow;
            this.Name = "RegForm";
            this.Text = "Registration Form";
            this.groupBox1.ResumeLayout(false);
            this.ResumeLayout(false);
        }
        #endregion

        static void Main( )
        {
            Application.Run(new RegForm( ));
        }
```

```csharp
// Handles events for RadioButton and
// CheckBox objects
private void ComputeCost_CheckedChanged
    (object sender, System.EventArgs e)
{
    decimal cost = 0;
    this.lblMsg.Text = "   ";
    if (this.ckBoxSwim.Checked)
    {
        cost += 50;
    }
        if (this.ckBoxSnorkel.Checked)
    {
        cost += 25;
    }
    if (this.ckBoxDive.Checked)
    {
        cost += 100;
    }
    if(this.radBeginner.Checked)
    {
        cost += 10;
        this.lblMsg.Text = "Beginner — Extra $10" +
                            " charge";
    }
    else
        if(this.radAdvanc.Checked)
    {
        cost -= 15;
        this.lblMsg.Text = "Advanced - Discount" +
                            " $15";
    }
    else
    {
        this.lblMsg.Text = "   ";
    }
    this.txtResult.Text = cost.ToString("C");
}
    }
}
```

A sample run of the application appears in Figure 9-20.

9

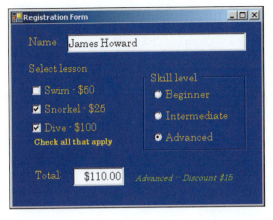

Figure 9-20   ComputeCost_CheckedChanged( ) and Click( ) events raised

Users may select one or more lessons; however, only one skill level is permissible.

PROGRAMMING EXAMPLE: DINERGUI APPLICATION

This example demonstrates event-driven applications that include the design and implementation of a graphical user interface. Two classes are constructed to separate the business logic from the presentation details. The first **class** defines a template for a food order **object**. It includes behaviors for processing an order that includes selections for entrée, drink, and special requests. The **class** assigns prices to each item selected and determines the overall price of the order. The other **class** instantiates an **object** of the Order **class** and instantiates a Windows **Form object** to represent the graphical user interface. Using the .NET predefined **Control** classes, **Label**, **ComboBox**, **ListBox**, **RadioButton**, **CheckBox**, and **Menu** objects are added to the **Form object**. The problem specification for the DinerGUI application is shown in Figure 9-21.

The manager of the Diner by the Valley campus deli plans to have a computer available for students to place their orders when they enter the campus center. They have a limited menu selection available that includes sandwiches and drinks. The manager wants the computer screen to allow the students to select from a list of available sandwich and drink options. A large board is located on the wall at the location where the computer will reside. It shows the menu of items available and lists the price of each item.

A user-friendly interface is needed. Water is available for each order at no charge, but it must be ordered. In addition to white bread, they have whole wheat and rye bread. No charge is included for different bread types; however, they do consider that selection a special request. The interface should enable special requests such as bread types to be selected. Students should be able to enter other special requests such as "Hold the onion" or "Hold the mayo."

Design a GUI that accepts as input food and drink selections. The manager would like to have options for showing the total cost of the order, displaying the current order selections, or allowing students to change their minds about each of the selections.

Figure 9-21   Problem specification for DinerGUI example

Analyze the Problem

You should review the problem specification in Figure 9-21 and make sure you understand the problem definition. Several values will be selected from GUI controls to represent the entrée and drink selections, as well as preferences for water and special requests. The business logic is separated from the user interface using two classes. The data members for the **Order class** are shown in Table 9-6.

Data

Table 9-6 lists the data field members needed for the **Order class**.

Table 9-6 Order class data fields

Data description	Type	Identifier
Entrée selection	string	entree
Water preference	bool	waterSelection
Drink preference	string	drinkSelection
Special requests	string	specialRequest
Entrée price	decimal	entreePrice
Drink price	decimal	drinkPrice
Total cost of the order	decimal	totalCharge

A second **class**, OrderGUI, is created for the user interface. This **class** allows the user to select an entrée and a drink, enter special requests, and request water. During design, a prototype is developed to determine which controls would be most appropriate for each selection.

Drink selections are constant and include "Milk", "Juice", "Soda", "Lemonade", "Tea", and "Coffee". Menu options may change occasionally and should not be statically placed on the graphical user interface. Current options are: "Chicken Salad", "Ham and Cheese", "Turkey", "Vegetable Wrap", "Tuna Salad", "Avocado and Cheese", "Club", "Peanut Butter & Jelly", "Grilled Cheese", and "Reuben".

Design a Solution

The desired output is to produce a graphical user interface that allows a user to pick from a number of selections while placing an order. According to the problem definition, menu options should be available to clear the entire order or just part of it. After the items are selected, the total price and items selected should be displayed. These options can also appear as selections from the menu bar. Figure 9-22 shows a prototype of the form that illustrates the types of objects to be used and approximates their placement.

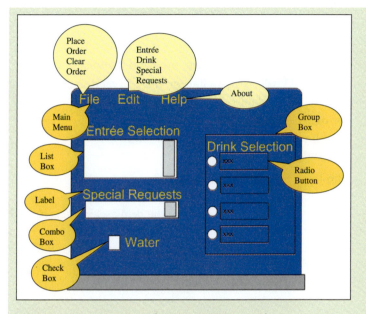

Figure 9-22 Prototype for DinerGUI example

During design, determine which **object** types will be used to create the interface. The **MainMenu object** was selected rather than a number of buttons so that the screen does not become cluttered. Menus offer the advantage of requiring less real estate on your screen. The entrées are displayed in a **ListBox object**. A scroll bar is automatically added when the number of entries exceeds the available space. The text selections for the **ListBox object** are loaded at runtime to enable the diner manager to change the menu options in the **class** that deals with the business logic and keep that separate from the actual display.

Special requests are stored in a **ComboBox object**, because it enables users either to choose from a list of options or to type a new entry. The water selection is a yes/no format; thus, a **CheckBox object** is used. **RadioButton** objects are used for drink selection. The buttons are placed in a **GroupBox** so that only one drink is selected.

9

Menu options include the following features:

File

- **Place the order**—Displays the current order and the total price of the order
- **Clear the order**—Deselects all options on the GUI and sets all of the individual selections back to their defaults
- **Display the order**—Displays the current order
- **Exit**—Closes all windows and exits the application

Edit

- **Entrée**—Displays a message indicating that the entrée selection is cleared, clears the entrée selection, and deselects the selected entrée
- **Drink**—Displays a message indicating that the drink selection is cleared, clears the drink selection, and deselects the selected drink
- **Special Request**—Displays a message indicating that the special request selection is cleared, clears the special request selection, and deselects the selected special request, or clears the text area if a value is typed

Help

- **About**—Displays the name of the application along with the version number

The `Order` `class` has both data and behavior characteristics that can be identified. The major actions or behaviors of an `Order` `object` are to set instance variables using the selection from the GUI objects, determine the individual prices, and determine the overall charge for the order. Class diagrams are used to help design and document these characteristics. Figure 9-23 shows the `class` diagrams for the `DinerGUI` example.

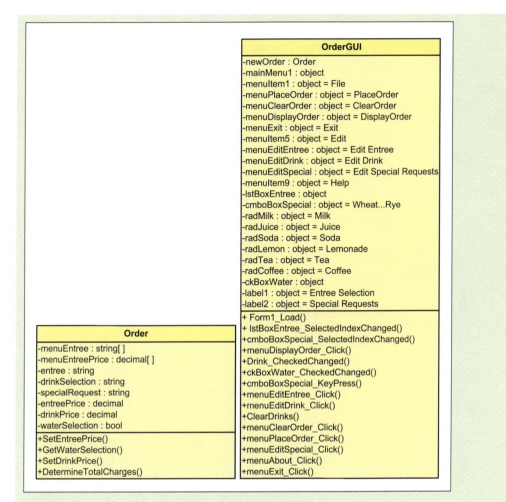

OrderGUI
-newOrder : Order
-mainMenu1 : object
-menuItem1 : object = File
-menuPlaceOrder : object = PlaceOrder
-menuClearOrder : object = ClearOrder
-menuDisplayOrder : object = DisplayOrder
-menuExit : object = Exit
-menuItem5 : object = Edit
-menuEditEntree : object = Edit Entree
-menuEditDrink : object = Edit Drink
-menuEditSpecial : object = Edit Special Requests
-menuItem9 : object = Help
-lstBoxEntree : object
-cmboBoxSpecial : object = Wheat...Rye
-radMilk : object = Milk
-radJuice : object = Juice
-radSoda : object = Soda
-radLemon : object = Lemonade
-radTea : object = Tea
-radCoffee : object = Coffee
-ckBoxWater : object
-label1 : object = Entree Selection
-label2 : object = Special Requests
+ Form1_Load()
+ lstBoxEntree_SelectedIndexChanged()
+cmboBoxSpecial_SelectedIndexChanged()
+menuDisplayOrder_Click()
+Drink_CheckedChanged()
+ckBoxWater_CheckedChanged()
+cmboBoxSpecial_KeyPress()
+menuEditEntree_Click()
+menuEditDrink_Click()
+ClearDrinks()
+menuClearOrder_Click()
+menuPlaceOrder_Click()
+menuEditSpecial_Click()
+menuAbout_Click()
+menuExit_Click()

Order
-menuEntree : string[ ]
-menuEntreePrice : decimal[ ]
-entree : string
-drinkSelection : string
-specialRequest : string
-entreePrice : decimal
-drinkPrice : decimal
-waterSelection : bool
+SetEntreePrice()
+GetWaterSelection()
+SetDrinkPrice()
+DetermineTotalCharges()

Figure 9-23   Class diagrams for DinerGUI example

The **class** diagrams do not show the properties or the local variables that may be required for specific **class** methods. They do not show which event–handler methods are associated with particular objects.

> There are a number of ways to document collaboration between objects using an object-oriented approach. They include sequence, collaboration, state transition, and activity diagrams. Systems analysts often use these diagrams to design an application. Development of these types of models is beyond the scope of this book; however, you are encouraged to research and learn about them.

During design, it is important to develop algorithms showing the step-by-step process for the business logic of the application. Pseudocode for the **Order class** methods is shown in Figure 9-24.

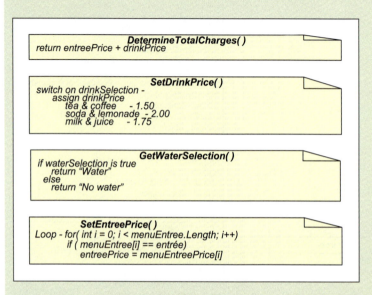

Figure 9-24   Pseudocode for the Order class for the DinerGUI example

Many of the objects on the interface must be registered with event-handler methods. It is important that you spend time thinking about what should happen when each event is fired. Figures 9-25, 9-26, and 9-27 show pseudocode for the event handlers of the GUI **class**.

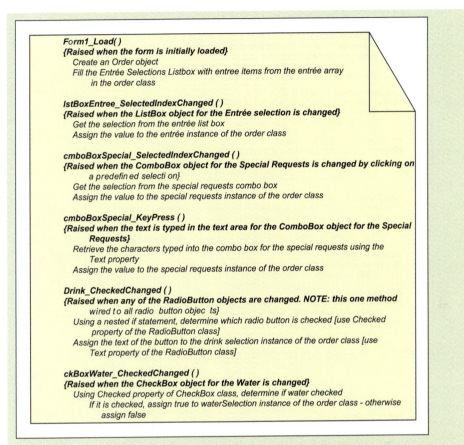

Figure 9-25 Pseudocode for RadioButton, CheckBox, ListBox, and ComboBox object event handlers

9

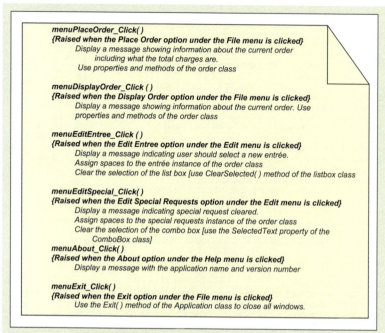

Figure 9-26   Pseudocode for menu object event handlers

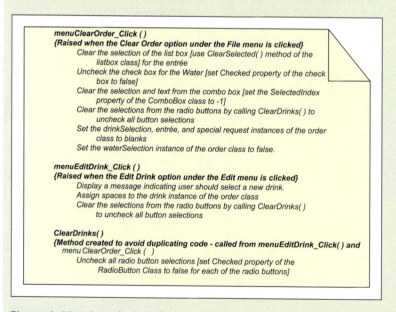

Figure 9-27   Pseudocode for menu object event handlers and the Clear( ) method

You should always desk check your design. Develop your test plan for testing the application. Walk through your logic, and ensure you have accounted for each of the events that need to be programmed. Reread the problem specification and ensure you have taken all issues into consideration.

Once you implement your design, be sure to run and test your application using your test plan.

Code the Solution After completing the design and verifying the algorithm's correctness, you translate the design into source code. For this application, two separate files, one for each **class**, are created. Form Designer can generate much of the code for the user interface **class**. Control objects' property values are as shown in Table 9-7.

Table 9-7 DinerGUI property values

Name	Object type	Property	Value
OrderGUI	Form	Text	Typed "Student Union - Diner by the Valley"
OrderGUI	Form	BackColor	Goldenrod
OrderGUI	Form	Menu	mainMenu1
OrderGUI	Form	Font	Arial, 9.75
OrderGUI	Form	Icon	PEN04.ICO
mainMenu1	mainMenu	MenuItems	menuItem1, menuItem5, menuItem9
menuItem1	menuItem	Text	Typed "File"
menuItem1	menuItem	MenuItems	menuPlaceOrder, menuClearOrder, menuDisplayOrder, menuExit
menuPlaceOrder	menuItem	Text	Typed "Place Order"
menuClearOrder	menuItem	Text	Typed "Clear Order"
menuDisplayOrder	menuItem	Text	Typed "Display Order"
menuExit	menuItem	Text	Typed "Exit"
menuItem5	menuItem	MenuItems	menuEditEntree, menuEditDrink, menuEditSpecial
menuItem5	menuItem	Text	Typed "Edit"
menuEditEntree	menuItem	Text	Typed "Entree"

9

Table 9-7 DinerGUI property values (continued)

Name	Object type	Property	Value
menuEditDrink	menuItem	Text	Typed "Drink"
menuEditSpecial	menuItem	Text	Typed "Special Requests"
menuItem9	menuItem	Text	Typed "Help"
menuAbout	menuItem	Text	Typed "About"
lstBoxEntree	ListBox	BackColor	Khaki
label1	Label	Text	Typed "Entrée Selection"
groupBox2	GroupBox	Controls	radMilk, radJuice, radSoda, radLemon, radTea, radCoffee
radMilk	RadioButton	Text	Typed "Milk"
radJuice	RadioButton	Text	Typed "Juice"
radSoda	RadioButton	Text	Typed "Soda"
radLemon	RadioButton	Text	Typed "Lemonade"
radTea	RadioButton	Text	Typed "Tea"
radCoffee	RadioButton	Text	Typed "Coffee"
cmboBoxSpecial	ComboBox	Items (Collection)	Typed "Whole Wheat", "Pumpernickel", "Seedless Rye", "Pita","Sour Dough"
cmboBoxSpecial	ComboBox	BackColor	Khaki
label2	Label	Text	Typed "Special Requests"
ckBoxWater	CheckBox	Text	Typed "Water"

If you do not have Visual Studio, you can type assignment statements for the properties, making the assignments indicated in Table 9-7. For example, the first two properties could be set by typing:

```
Text = "Student Union   -   Diner by the Valley";
BackColor = Color.Goldenrod;
```

If the System.Drawing namespace is imported and referenced, it is not necessary to fully qualify the name. When the Form Designer generates the code to set these two properties, the statements read:

```
this.Text = "Student Union   -   Diner by the Valley";
this.BackColor = System.Drawing.Color.Goldenrod;
```

Both produce the same result with this application.

The complete source listing for both files is given next. The first **class**, `Order`, was written manually. Much of the code for the second **class**, `OrderGUI`, was created by Visual Studio Form Designer. After the event-handler methods were registered by Visual Studio .NET Form Designer, code was written for each of the methods following the pseudocode developed during the design of the application.

```csharp
// Order.cs      Author: Doyle
// Creates an order class with
// entree, drink, and special request
// data members. Methods to calculate
// total cost of order and set each
// data member included.

using System;
using System.Windows.Forms;
namespace Diner
{
    public class Order
    {
        public string [ ] menuEntree  = new
            string [ ] {"Chicken Salad",
                        "Ham and Cheese",
                        "Turkey", "Vegetable Wrap",
                        "Tuna Salad",
                        "Avocado and Cheese",
                        "Club", "Peanut Butter & Jelly",
                        "Grilled Cheese", "Reuben"};

        public decimal [ ]  menuEntreePrice = new
            decimal [ ] {4.50m, 5.00m, 4.75m,
                         4.00m, 4.50m, 4.00m, 5.50m,
                         3.75m, 3.50m, 5.00m };

        private string entree;
        private bool waterSelection;
        private string drinkSelection;
        private string specialRequest;
        private decimal entreePrice;
        private decimal drinkPrice;

        // Default constructor
        public Order( )
        {
            entree = "";
            waterSelection = false;
```

9

```csharp
            specialRequest = "";
            drinkPrice = 0;
            entreePrice = 0;
    }

    // Property for entree
    public string Entree
    {
        get
        {
            return entree;
        }
        set
        {
            entree = value;
            SetEntreePrice( );
        }
    }

    // Property for special requests
    public string SpecialRequest
    {
        get
        {
            return specialRequest;
        }
        set
        {
            specialRequest = value;
        }
    }

    // Property for Water selection
    public bool WaterSelection
    {
        set
        {
            waterSelection = value;
        }
    }

    // Property for Drink selection
    public string DrinkSelection
    {
        get
        {
            return drinkSelection;
        }
```

```csharp
        set
        {
            drinkSelection = value;
            SetDrinkPrice( );
        }
    }

    // Read-only property for entree price
    public decimal EntreePrice
    {
        get
        {
            return entreePrice;
        }
    }

    // Read-only property for drink price
    public decimal DrinkPrice
    {
        get
        {
            return drinkPrice;
        }
    }

    // Once the entree is set, store the entree price
    public void SetEntreePrice( )
    {
        for (int i = 0; i < menuEntree. Length;  i++)
        {
            if (menuEntree[i] ==  entree)
            {
                entreePrice = menuEntreePrice[i];

            }
        }
    }

    // Return the water selection
    public string GetWaterSelection( )
    {
        string waterOrNot;
        if (waterSelection)
        {
            waterOrNot = "Water";
        }
```

```csharp
        else
        {
            waterOrNot = "No Water";
        }
        return waterOrNot;
    }

    // Once the drink is set, store the drink price
    public void SetDrinkPrice( )
    {
        switch(drinkSelection)
        {
            case "Tea" :
            case "Coffee" :
                drinkPrice = 1.50m;
                break;
            case "Soda" :
            case "Lemonade" :
                drinkPrice = 2.00m;
                break;
            case "Milk" :
            case "Juice" :
                drinkPrice = 1.75m;
                break;
        }
    }

    // Return the total cost of the order
    public decimal DetermineTotalCharges( )
    {
        return entreePrice + drinkPrice;
    }
  }
}
```

The source listing for the **OrderGUI class** is shown next.

> **NOTE** Remember that much of the code in the following listing was generated by the Form Designer in Visual Studio .NET. The complete listing is shown so that you can see the program statements added for the set properties. It is also included for those readers developing applications using a simple editor such as Notepad.

```csharp
// OrderGUI.cs    Author: Doyle
// Create the graphical user interface
// to take an order and display the
// total cost.
using System;
using System.Drawing;
```

```csharp
using System.Collections;
using System.ComponentModel;
using System.Windows.Forms;
using System.Data;
namespace Diner
{
    public class OrderGUI : System.Windows.Forms.Form
    {
        private Order newOrder;
        private System.Windows.Forms.MainMenu mainMenu1;
        private System.Windows.Forms.MenuItem menuItem1;
        private System.Windows.Forms.MenuItem menuItem5;
        private System.Windows.Forms.MenuItem menuItem9;
        private System.Windows.Forms.Label label1;
        private System.Windows.Forms.GroupBox groupBox2;
        private System.Windows.Forms.Label label2;
        private System.Windows.Forms.MenuItem
            menuPlaceOrder;
        private System.Windows.Forms.MenuItem
            menuClearOrder;
        private System.Windows.Forms.MenuItem
            menuDisplayOrder;
        private System.Windows.Forms.MenuItem menuExit;
        private System.Windows.Forms.MenuItem
            menuEditEntree;
        private System.Windows.Forms.MenuItem menuEditDrink;
        private System.Windows.Forms.MenuItem
            menuEditSpecial;
        private System.Windows.Forms.MenuItem menuAbout;
        private System.Windows.Forms.ListBox lstBoxEntree;
        private System.Windows.Forms.ComboBox
            cmboBoxSpecial;
        private System.Windows.Forms.CheckBox ckBoxWater;
        private System.Windows.Forms.RadioButton radCoffee;
        private System.Windows.Forms.RadioButton radTea;
        private System.Windows.Forms.RadioButton radLemon;
        private System.Windows.Forms.RadioButton radSoda;
        private System.Windows.Forms.RadioButton radJuice;
        private System.Windows.Forms.RadioButton radMilk;
        private System.ComponentModel.Container components =
            null;

        public OrderGUI( )
        {
            InitializeComponent( );
        }
```

9

```csharp
protected override void Dispose(bool disposing)
{
    if(disposing)
    {
        if (components != null)
        {
            components.Dispose( );
        }
    }
    base.Dispose(disposing);
}

#region Windows Form Designer generated code
private void InitializeComponent( )
{
    System.Resources.ResourceManager resources = new
        System.Resources.ResourceManager
        (typeof(OrderGUI));
    this.mainMenu1 = new
        System.Windows.Forms.MainMenu( );
    this.menuItem1 = new
        System.Windows.Forms.MenuItem( );
    this.menuPlaceOrder = new
        System.Windows.Forms.MenuItem( );
    this.menuClearOrder = new
        System.Windows.Forms.MenuItem( );
    this.menuDisplayOrder = new
        System.Windows.Forms.MenuItem( );
    this.menuExit = new
        System.Windows.Forms.MenuItem( );
    this.menuItem5 = new
        System.Windows.Forms.MenuItem( );
    this.menuEditEntree = new
        System.Windows.Forms.MenuItem( );
    this.menuEditDrink = new
        System.Windows.Forms.MenuItem( );
    this.menuEditSpecial = new
        System.Windows.Forms.MenuItem( );
    this.menuItem9 = new
        System.Windows.Forms.MenuItem( );
    this.menuAbout = new
        System.Windows.Forms.MenuItem( );
    this.lstBoxEntree = new
        System.Windows.Forms.ListBox( );
    this.label1 = new System.Windows.Forms.Label( );
    this.groupBox2 = new
        System.Windows.Forms.GroupBox( );
```

```csharp
this.radCoffee = new
    System.Windows.Forms.RadioButton( );
this.radTea = new
    System.Windows.Forms.RadioButton( );
this.radLemon = new
    System.Windows.Forms.RadioButton( );
this.radSoda = new
    System.Windows.Forms.RadioButton( );
this.radJuice = new
    System.Windows.Forms.RadioButton( );
this.radMilk = new
    System.Windows.Forms.RadioButton( );
this.cmboBoxSpecial = new
    System.Windows.Forms.ComboBox( );
this.label2 = new System.Windows.Forms.Label( );
this.ckBoxWater = new
    System.Windows.Forms.CheckBox( );
this.groupBox2.SuspendLayout( );
this.SuspendLayout( );

// mainMenu1
this.mainMenu1.MenuItems.AddRange
    (new System.Windows.Forms.MenuItem[]
    {this.menuItem1,
     this.menuItem5,this.menuItem9});

// menuItem1
this.menuItem1.Index = 0;
this.menuItem1.MenuItems.AddRange
    (new System.Windows.Forms.MenuItem[]
    {this.menuPlaceOrder,
     this.menuClearOrder,
     this.menuDisplayOrder, this.menuExit});
this.menuItem1.Text = "File";

// menuPlaceOrder
this.menuPlaceOrder.Index = 0;
this.menuPlaceOrder.Text = "Place Order";
this.menuPlaceOrder.Click += new
    System.EventHandler
    (this.menuPlaceOrder_Click);

// menuClearOrder
this.menuClearOrder.Index = 1;
this.menuClearOrder.Text = "Clear Order";
this.menuClearOrder.Click += new
    System.EventHandler
    (this.menuClearOrder_Click);
```

9

```
// menuDisplayOrder
this.menuDisplayOrder.Index = 2;
this.menuDisplayOrder.Text = "Display Order";
this.menuDisplayOrder.Click += new
    System.EventHandler
    (this.menuDisplayOrder_Click);

// menuExit
this.menuExit.Index = 3;
this.menuExit.Text = "Exit";
this.menuExit.Click += new
    System.EventHandler(this.menuExit_Click);

// menuItem5
this.menuItem5.Index = 1;
this.menuItem5.MenuItems.AddRange
    (new System.Windows.Forms.MenuItem[]
    {this.menuEditEntree, this.menuEditDrink,
     this.menuEditSpecial});
this.menuItem5.Text = "Edit";

// menuEditEntree
this.menuEditEntree.Index = 0;
this.menuEditEntree.Text = "Entree";
this.menuEditEntree.Click += new
    System.EventHandler
    (this.menuEditEntree_Click);

// menuEditDrink
this.menuEditDrink.Index = 1;
this.menuEditDrink.Text = "Drink";
this.menuEditDrink.Click += new
    System.EventHandler
    (this.menuEditDrink_Click);

// menuEditSpecial
this.menuEditSpecial.Index = 2;
this.menuEditSpecial.Text = "Special Requests";
this.menuEditSpecial.Click += new
    System.EventHandler
    (this.menuEditSpecial_Click);

// menuItem9
this.menuItem9.Index = 2;
this.menuItem9.MenuItems.AddRange
    (new System.Windows.Forms.MenuItem[]
    {this.menuAbout});
this.menuItem9.Text = "Help";
```

```
// menuAbout
this.menuAbout.Index = 0;
this.menuAbout.Text = "About";
this.menuAbout.Click += new
    System.EventHandler(this.menuAbout_Click);

// lstBoxEntree
this.lstBoxEntree.BackColor =
    System.Drawing.Color.Khaki;
this.lstBoxEntree.ItemHeight = 16;
this.lstBoxEntree.Location = new
    System.Drawing.Point(23, 42);
this.lstBoxEntree.Name = "lstBoxEntree";
this.lstBoxEntree.Size = new
    System.Drawing.Size(156, 68);
this.lstBoxEntree.TabIndex = 0;
this.lstBoxEntree.SelectedIndexChanged += new
    System.EventHandler
    (this.lstBoxEntree_SelectedIndexChanged);

// label1
this.label1.Location = new
    System.Drawing.Point(41, 18);
this.label1.Name = "label1";
this.label1.Size = new
    System.Drawing.Size(120, 23);
this.label1.TabIndex = 1;
this.label1.Text = "Entree Selection";

// groupBox2
this.groupBox2.Controls.AddRange
    (new System.Windows.Forms.Control[]
    {this.radCoffee, this.radTea, this.radLemon,
     this.radSoda, this.radJuice,
     this.radMilk});
this.groupBox2.Location = new
    System.Drawing.Point(205, 50);
this.groupBox2.Name = "groupBox2";
this.groupBox2.Size = new
    System.Drawing.Size(120, 176);
this.groupBox2.TabIndex = 3;
this.groupBox2.TabStop = false;
this.groupBox2.Text = "Drink Selection";

// radCoffee
this.radCoffee.Location = new
    System.Drawing.Point(8, 144);
this.radCoffee.Name = "radCoffee";
```

9

```
this.radCoffee.TabIndex = 5;
this.radCoffee.Text = "Coffee";
this.radCoffee.CheckedChanged += new
    System.EventHandler
    (this.Drink_CheckedChanged);

// radTea
this.radTea.Location = new
    System.Drawing.Point(8, 120);
this.radTea.Name = "radTea";
this.radTea.TabIndex = 4;
this.radTea.Text = "Tea";
this.radTea.CheckedChanged += new
    System.EventHandler
    (this.Drink_CheckedChanged);

// radLemon
this.radLemon.Location = new
    System.Drawing.Point(8, 96);
this.radLemon.Name = "radLemon";
this.radLemon.TabIndex = 3;
this.radLemon.Text = "Lemonade";
this.radLemon.CheckedChanged += new
    System.EventHandler
    (this.Drink_CheckedChanged);

// radSoda
this.radSoda.Location = new
    System.Drawing.Point(8, 72);
this.radSoda.Name = "radSoda";
this.radSoda.TabIndex = 2;
this.radSoda.Text = "Soda";
this.radSoda.CheckedChanged += new
    System.EventHandler
    (this.Drink_CheckedChanged);

// radJuice
this.radJuice.Location = new
    System.Drawing.Point(8, 48);
this.radJuice.Name = "radJuice";
this.radJuice.TabIndex = 1;
this.radJuice.Text = "Juice";
this.radJuice.CheckedChanged += new
    System.EventHandler
    (this.Drink_CheckedChanged);
```

```csharp
// radMilk
this.radMilk.Location = new
    System.Drawing.Point(8, 24);
this.radMilk.Name = "radMilk";
this.radMilk.TabIndex = 0;
this.radMilk.Text = "Milk";
this.radMilk.CheckedChanged += new
    System.EventHandler
  (this.Drink_CheckedChanged);

// cmboBoxSpecial
this.cmboBoxSpecial.BackColor =
    System.Drawing.Color.Khaki;
this.cmboBoxSpecial.Items.AddRange(new object[]
    {"Whole Wheat", "Pumpernickel",
     "Seedless Rye", "Pita", "Sour Dough"});
this.cmboBoxSpecial.Location = new
    System.Drawing.Point(17, 154);
this.cmboBoxSpecial.Name = "cmboBoxSpecial";
this.cmboBoxSpecial.Size = new
    System.Drawing.Size(168, 24);
this.cmboBoxSpecial.TabIndex = 4;
this.cmboBoxSpecial.KeyPress += new
    System.Windows.Forms.KeyPressEventHandler
    (this.cmboBoxSpecial_KeyPress);
this.cmboBoxSpecial.SelectedIndexChanged += new
    System.EventHandler
    (this.cmboBoxSpecial_SelectedIndexChanged);

// label2
this.label2.Location = new
    System.Drawing.Point(45, 130);
this.label2.Name = "label2";
this.label2.Size = new
    System.Drawing.Size(112, 23);
this.label2.TabIndex = 5;
this.label2.Text = "Special Requests";

// ckBoxWater
this.ckBoxWater.Location = new
    System.Drawing.Point(69, 210);
this.ckBoxWater.Name = "ckBoxWater";
this.ckBoxWater.Size = new
    System.Drawing.Size(64, 24);
this.ckBoxWater.TabIndex = 6;
this.ckBoxWater.Text = "Water";
this.ckBoxWater.CheckedChanged += new
```

9

```
            System.EventHandler
            (this.ckBoxWater_CheckedChanged);

        // OrderGUI
        this.AutoScaleBaseSize = new
            System.Drawing.Size(6, 15);
        this.BackColor = System.Drawing.Color.Goldenrod;
        this.ClientSize = new
            System.Drawing.Size(342, 253);
        this.Controls.AddRange
            (new System.Windows.Forms.Control[]
                { this.ckBoxWater,
                  this.label2,
                  this.cmboBoxSpecial,
                  this.groupBox2,
                  this.label1,
                  this.lstBoxEntree} );
        this.Font = new
            System.Drawing.Font("Arial", 9.75F,
            System.Drawing.FontStyle.Regular,
            System.Drawing.GraphicsUnit.Point,
            ((System.Byte)(0)));
        this.ForeColor = System.Drawing.Color.Navy;
        this.Icon = ((System.Drawing.Icon)
            (resources.GetObject("$this.Icon")));
        this.Menu = this.mainMenu1;
        this.Name = "OrderGUI";
        this.Text = "Student Union   -" +
            "   Diner by the Valley";
        this.Load += new
            System.EventHandler(this.Form1_Load);
        this.groupBox2.ResumeLayout(false);
        this.ResumeLayout(false);

    }
    #endregion
    static void Main( )
    {
        Application.Run(new OrderGUI( ));
    }

    // Instantiates an object of the Order class when
    // the form is first loaded.
    private void Form1_Load(object sender,
                            System.EventArgs e)
    {
        newOrder = new Order ( );
```

```
        for(int i = 0;
              i < newOrder.menuEntree.Length; i++)
        {
              this.lstBoxEntree.Items.Add
                 (newOrder.menuEntree[i]);
        }

}

// Event handler that gets the entree from the
// ListBox and sets the entree price.

private void lstBoxEntree_SelectedIndexChanged
              (object sender,System.EventArgs e)
{
    newOrder.Entree = this.lstBoxEntree.Text;
}

// Event handler that gets the special request -
// if one is selected from the predefined list.
private void cmboBoxSpecial_SelectedIndexChanged
              (object sender, System.EventArgs e)
{
    newOrder.SpecialRequest =
        this.cmboBoxSpecial.Text;
}

// Menu item that displays the order.
private void menuDisplayOrder_Click(object sender,
                              System.EventArgs e)
{
    MessageBox.Show
        (newOrder.Entree + "\n"
              + newOrder.SpecialRequest
              + " \n"
              + newOrder.DrinkSelection
              +  "\n" +
              newOrder.GetWaterSelection( ),
        "Current Order");
}

// Event handler that gets the radio button
// selected and sets the drink selection
private void Drink_CheckedChanged(object sender,
                              System.EventArgs e)
{
    if (this.radTea.Checked)
```

9

```csharp
                newOrder.DrinkSelection = radTea.Text;
        else
            if (this.radCoffee.Checked)
                newOrder.DrinkSelection =
                        radCoffee.Text;
        else
            if (this.radSoda.Checked)
                newOrder.DrinkSelection = radSoda.Text;
        else
            if (this.radLemon.Checked)
                newOrder.DrinkSelection = radLemon.Text;
        else
            if (this.radJuice.Checked)
                newOrder.DrinkSelection = radJuice.Text;
        else
            if (this.radMilk.Checked)
                newOrder.DrinkSelection = radMilk.Text;
    }

    // Event handler that gets raised when the check box
    // for Water gets clicked.
    private void ckBoxWater_CheckedChanged
                (object sender, System.EventArgs e)
    {
        if (this.ckBoxWater.Checked)
            newOrder.WaterSelection = true;
        else
            newOrder.WaterSelection = false;
    }

    // Event handler that gets raised when the
    // user types values into the text area of
    // the combo box.
    private void cmboBoxSpecial_KeyPress
                (object sender,
            System.Windows.Forms.KeyPressEventArgs e)
    {
        newOrder.SpecialRequest =
            this.cmboBoxSpecial.Text;
    }

    // Event handler that gets raised when the Edit menu
    // is clicked to change the entree.
    private void menuEditEntree_Click
                (object sender, System.EventArgs e)
    {
        MessageBox.Show("Please select a new Entree");
```

```
        newOrder.Entree = "";
        this.lstBoxEntree.ClearSelected( );
}


// Event handler that gets raised when the Edit menu
// is clicked to change the drink.
private void menuEditDrink_Click
            (object sender, System.EventArgs e)
{
    MessageBox.Show("Please select a new Drink");
    newOrder.DrinkSelection = "";
    this.ClearDrinks( );
}


// Clears selections for all drink radio buttons.
public  void ClearDrinks( )
{
    this.radMilk.Checked = false;
    this.radJuice.Checked = false;
    this.radSoda.Checked = false;
    this.radLemon.Checked = false;
    this.radTea.Checked = false;
    this.radCoffee.Checked = false;
}


//  Clears all selections so that a new order
//  can be placed. Resets the Order object back
//  to its default values.
private void menuClearOrder_Click
            (object sender, System.EventArgs e)
{
    this.lstBoxEntree.ClearSelected( );
    this.ckBoxWater.Checked = false;
    this.cmboBoxSpecial.SelectedIndex = -1;
    this.cmboBoxSpecial.Text ="";
    this.ClearDrinks( );
    newOrder.DrinkSelection = "";
    newOrder.Entree = "";
    newOrder.SpecialRequest = "";
    newOrder.WaterSelection = false;
}


// Displays the values for the current instance of
// Order object members
private void menuPlaceOrder_Click
            (object sender, System.EventArgs e)
{
    MessageBox.Show(newOrder.Entree + "\n" +
```

9

```
                    newOrder.SpecialRequest + "\n" +
                    newOrder.DrinkSelection + "\n" +
                    newOrder.GetWaterSelection( ) +
                    "\n\n\n" + "Total: " +
                    newOrder.DetermineTotalCharges( ).ToString
                    ("C"), "Placed Order");
        }

        // Event handler that gets raised when the Edit menu
        // is clicked to change the special requests.
        private void menuEditSpecial_Click
                    (object sender, System.EventArgs e)
        {
            MessageBox.Show("Special Request cleared.");
            newOrder.SpecialRequest = "";
            this.cmboBoxSpecial.SelectedIndex = -1;
            this.cmboBoxSpecial.Text ="";
            newOrder.SpecialRequest = "";
        }

        // Event handler that gets raised when the Help
        // menu is clicked to show the About message.
        private void menuAbout_Click
                    (object sender, System.EventArgs e)
        {
            MessageBox.Show("Student Union -" +
                            " Diner by the Valley" +
                            "\n\n\nVersion 1.0");
        }

        // Event handler that gets raised when
        // Exit is clicked.
        private void menuExit_Click
                    (object sender, System.EventArgs e)
        {
            Application.Exit( );
        }
    }
}
```

Figure 9-28 shows the original user interface with the File menu selections. Notice that a new icon is used in the title bar. The icon was added by setting the **Icon** property for the **OrderGUI** form.

Figure 9-28 Interface showing menu selections

> **NOTE** Among the icons and images that come bundled with Visual Studio .NET, the red pen is named PEN04.ico. On most systems it is located in the Microsoft Visual Studio .NET\Common7\Graphics\Icons\Writing subdirectory. Depending on where Visual Studio .NET was installed on your system, the red pen may be in a different location on your system. Any file that ends with an .ico extension can be used. Many sources on the Internet contain free graphics. They are easily added to your Windows applications.

All that is required to add pictures to a form is to instantiate an **object** of the **PictureBox class**. If you are using Visual Studio .NET, drag the **PictureBox** control **object** to your form. Set the **Image** property to the desired picture.

> **NOTE** You can select graphic file types such as *.bmp, *.gif, *.jpeg, *.jpg, *.png, and *.ico or metafile types such as *.emf or *.wmf for the **Image** property. Store the image in the bin\debug subdirectory of the current project.

The **Form object** also has a **BackgroundImage** property that can be set to display a picture on the background. To have a picture in the background, using Visual Studio .NET select the form and then use the Properties window to select the **BackgroundImage** property. Browse to a location that contains a bitmap or metafile.

When the form is loaded, the **Form1_Load** event is raised. At that time an **object** of the **Order class** is instantiated. Using the entrée array of the **Order class**, the list box is filled. With each click on the form, a different event is fired. Figure 9-29 shows the message displayed after several options were selected including the Place Order menu option.

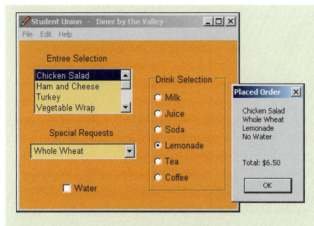

Figure 9-29   Message displayed from Place Order menu option

The `ComboBox` **object** allows special requests to be typed. Any new selections set new values for the instance of the `Order` **class**. When users type values in the text area of the `ComboBox` **object**, the `KeyPress( )` event is fired. Figure 9-30 illustrates a typed entry for the `ComboBox` **object**. The `MessageBox.Show( )` method is used to display messages from the menu options. Figure 9-30 is displayed from the File>Display Order option.

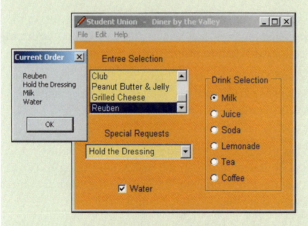

Figure 9-30   Message displayed from Current Order menu option

When events are raised from the Edit menu, the event-handler methods display a message indicating the selections are being cleared. Then the control on the form GUI is cleared and the **Order** instance data member is set back to its default value. Figure 9-31 shows the result of selecting the Edit>Special Requests menu option.

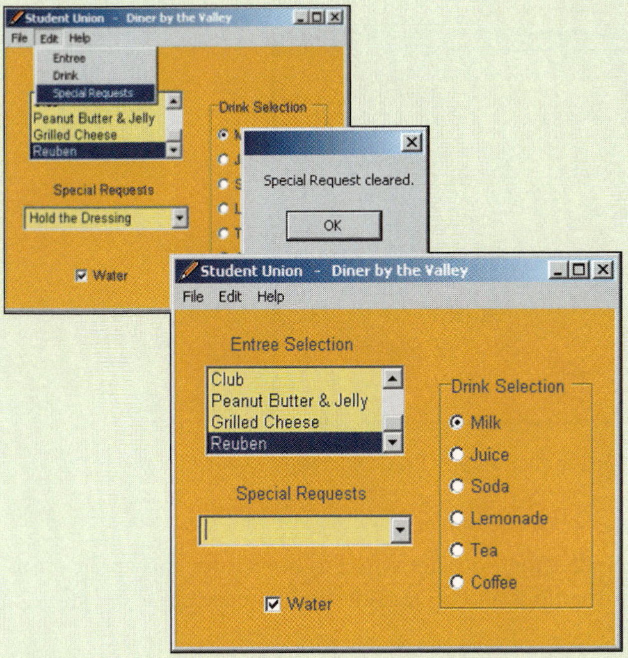

Figure 9-31   Special Requests click event fired

Firing the Clear Order menu option (shown in Figure 9-32) deselects all entries on the form and resets the **Order** instance data members to their default values. The Windows application is in a run state until the Exit menu option is fired or the close button is clicked.

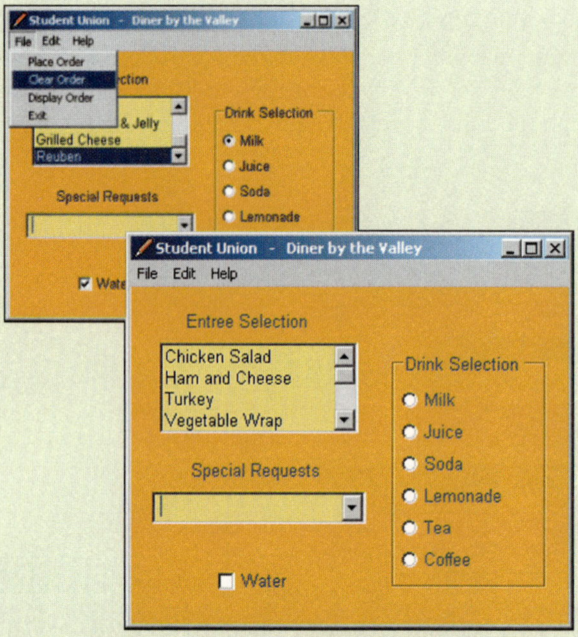

Figure 9-32 Clear Order click event fired

A number of event-handler methods are wired to objects for this application. Table 9-8 lists the event-handler methods and their associated objects. These are all instantiated in the `OrderGUI` class.

Table 9-8 DinerGUI events

Event-handler method	Class	Object
ckBoxWater_CheckedChanged	CheckBox	ckBoxWater
cmboBoxSpecial_KeyPress	ComboBox	cmboBoxSpecial
cmboBoxSpecial_SelectedIndexChanged	ComboBox	cmboBoxSpecial
Drink_CheckedChanged	RadioButton	radTea, radSoda, radLemon, radMilk, radCoffee, radJuice
Form1_Load	OrderGUI	this
lstBoxEntree_SelectedIndexChanged	ListBox	lstBoxEntree

Table 9-8 DinerGUI events (continued)

Event-handler method	Class	Object
menuAbout_Click	MenuItem	menuAbout
menuClearOrder_Click	MenuItem	menuClearOrder
menuDisplayOrder_Click	MenuItem	menuDisplayOrder
menuEditDrink_Click	MenuItem	menuEditDrink
menuEditEntree_Click	MenuItem	menuEditEntree
menuEditSpecial_Click	MenuItem	menuEditSpecial
menuExit_Click	MenuItem	menuExit
menuPlaceOrder_Click	MenuItem	menuPlaceOrder

QUICK REVIEW

9

1. Delegates are special types of .NET classes whose instances store references (addresses) to methods.

2. A declaration for a **delegate** looks more like a method declaration than a **class** definition. Every **delegate** type has a signature, which may include zero or more parameters. The signature indicates what method signatures must look like if they are to be referenced by the **delegate**.

3. Multicast delegates are wired to multiple methods, all of which are executed, one after the other, when an event is raised.

4. Events can be considered special forms of delegates in C# because they enable you to place a reference to event-handler methods inside a **delegate**. Once this reference is made, or the event is registered, the **delegate** is used to call the event-handler methods.

5. To respond to events in your program, two things must occur. First, you must register the event as being of interest, and second, an event-handler method must be generated. This process is called event wiring.

6. All event-handler methods normally have the same signature. They do not return anything; they have a **return** type of **void**. They have two parameters.

7. **ListBox** controls can be used to display a list of items from which the user can select. Single or multiple selections can be made. A scroll bar is automatically added to the control if the total number of items exceeds the number that can be displayed.

8. At design time or dynamically at runtime, you can add or remove items to and from the `ListBox` control.

9. The default event for the `ListBox` `object` is the `SelectedIndexChanged( )` event. It is raised or triggered when the selection changes for the `ListBox` `object`.

10. The `ListBox` `class` has a number of interesting properties including `Items`, which get the items of the list. `SelectedIndex` and `SelectedItem` properties get or set the selected item.

11. `ListBox` and `ComboBox` objects are zero-based structures. `SelectedIndex` and `SelectedIndices` properties access the `object` by its indexed location.

12. The `Text` property is the most often used property. It receives the text of the currently selected item.

13. `ListBox` controls and `ComboBox` objects share many of the same properties and methods. `ComboBox` objects contain their own text box field as part of the `object`. This makes it easy to add a new value at runtime.

14. A `KeyPress( )` event occurs when the user presses a key. Actually, the event is fired with each and every keystroke. This event-handler method is sometimes used with `ComboBox` objects.

15. The `SelectedIndexChanged( )` event-handler method is often wired to `ComboBox` and `ListBox` objects.

16. Using the Visual Studio .NET Toolbox Window and the `MainMenu` `class`, it is easy to drag and drop a `MainMenu` control `object` onto your form.

17. You can create shortcuts to menu options. Shortcuts using the Alt key are quickly and easily created. When you type the text that is to appear in the menu (using the `Text` property), preceding the character with an ampersand (&) enables the user to press the Alt key plus the key that follows the ampersand as a shortcut.

18. To have the menu be displayed on the `Form`, you set the `Menu` property on the `Form` to the name of the `MainMenu` `object`.

19. There are a number of preconfigured dialog boxes that can be added to menus. They include those that resemble the standard Windows File Open, File Save, File Print, File Print Preview, Format Font, and Format Color dialog boxes. These can be added to your application by dragging and dropping the control `object` onto your form.

20. Check boxes appear as small boxes that allow users to make a Yes/No or True/False selection. The default event-handler method for `CheckBox` objects is `CheckedChanged( )`. A `Click( )` event can also be wired to `CheckBox` objects. Double-clicking on one of the `CheckBox` objects registers a `CheckedChanged( )` event for that one `object`.

21. For visual appearances, `CheckBox` objects may be grouped together using the `GroupBox` control. The grouping also aids design because you can move all the objects as a group. However, grouping does not provide any additional functionality for `CheckBox` objects.

22. A `GroupBox` control should be placed on the form for radio buttons. Radio buttons give users a choice between two or more options. Remember that it is appropriate to select more than one `CheckBox object`. Not so with `RadioButton` objects.

23. Multiple radio buttons can be wired to the same event-handler method.

EXERCISES

1. Delegates store:

   a. the address for signatures of data

   b. data and methods about the events in a program

   c. events

   d. the address of methods

   e. all of the above

2. Given the following **delegate** declaration

```
delegate void PerformsSomeTask(int arg1, double arg2);
```

which of the following statements would appear to create a **delegate** instance of `PerformsSomeTask( )` with no syntax errors?

   a. `PerformsSomeTask task1 = new PerformsSomeTask`
     `(CalculateThis);`

   b. `PerformsSomeTask task1 = new PerformsSomeTask`
     `(CalculateThis( ));`

   c. `PerformsSomeTask( ) task1 = new PerformsSomeTask`
     `(CalculateThis( ));`

   d. `PerformsSomeTask( ) task1 = new PerformsSomeTask`
     `(CalculateThis(int, double));`

   e. `PerformsSomeTask task1 = new PerformsSomeTask(CalculateThis`
     `(int arg1, double arg2);`

3. Given the following **delegate** declaration

```
delegate void PerformsSomeTask(int arg1,
                double arg2);
```

which of the following represents a method heading that could be associated with the **delegate**?

   a. `int CalculateThis(int value1, double value2)`

   b. `double CalculateThis(int value1, double value2)`

   c. `void CalculateThis(int value1, double value2)`

   d. `int CalculateThis( )`

   e. all of the above

9

4. The signature for a method includes only the:

a. `return` type, method name, number of parameters, and the type of parameters

b. method name and `return` type

c. number of parameters and the type of parameters

d. method name, number of parameters, and the type of parameters

e. `return` type, number of parameters, and the type of parameters

5. A multicast `delegate` is one that:

a. has more than one method wrapped to it

b. has more than one parameter

c. has more than one instance of itself created in a program

d. has more than one `return` type

e. none of the above

6. The following statement best sums up a delegate's relationship to an event:

a. Delegates are instances of events.

b. Delegates are used to call event-handler methods.

c. Delegates must be registered with events.

d. The event maintains a list of delegates in the program.

e. all of the above

7. One distinguishing characteristic between a `ListBox` control `object` and a `ComboBox` control `object` is that:

a. Multiple selections are possible with `ListBox` objects.

b. `ComboBox` objects are used for output only.

c. A scroll bar can be seen with `ComboBox` objects.

d. It is easier to program the `ComboBox` `object` event-handler method(s).

e. none of the above

8. A default event-handler method for a `ListBox` `object` is:

a. `KeyPress( )`

b. `Click( )`

c. `SelectedItem( )`

d. `SelectedIndexChanged( )`

e. `Selected( )`

9. The property that returns a collection of the indexes selected for a `ListBox` `object` is:

a. `SelectedIndex`

b. `SelectedIndices`

c. `Text`

d. `Items`

e. `SelectedItems`

10. `ComboBox` objects offer the added functionality over a `ListBox` `object` of:

   a. allowing values to be removed at runtime

   b. allowing multiple selections to be made

   c. including a scrollbar for moving down the items

   d. containing a text box for values to be entered at runtime

   e. none of the above

11. Assuming `comboBoxData` is instantiated as a `ComboBox`, which of the following statements would retrieve its selection and place it in a `string` variable?

   a. `string` s = `ComboBox.Selection;`

   b. `string` s = `ComboBox.comboBoxData.Text;`

   c. `string` s = `comboBoxData.Text;`

   d. `string` s.Text = `comboBoxData.Text;`

   e. none of the above

12. After you type the text for a menu, what else must be done before the menu will be seen on the form?

   a. Set the `Menu` property on the form to the name of the menu.

   b. Set the `Form` property on the menu to the name of the form.

   c. Create `menuItems` subordinate to the menu.

   d. Program the event-handler methods for each `menuItem`.

   e. all of the above

13. When you type the text for the Help menu option, which of following creates a shortcut of Alt+P for the Help?

   a. Help(Alt p)

   b. &Help

   c. &Hel&p

   d. Hel&p

   e. Help(Alt &p)

9

14. If you want always to see all options on the screen, but allow only one of the options to be selected, which type of structure is normally selected?

a. check box

b. combo box

c. menu

d. radio button

e. text box

15. Which property is used with **CheckBox** and **RadioButton** objects to determine whether their option is selected?

a. **Selected**

b. **SelectedIndex**

c. **SelectedItem**

d. **Checked**

e. none of the above

16. Wiring an event handler to multiple objects involves:

a. using the same method to handle the events fired for more than one **object**

b. selecting the same Objects property for each event-handler method

c. creating multiple methods that do the same task

d. naming the object's Event property with an ampersand

e. none of the above

17. The **GroupBox object** provides more functionality for which type of objects?

a. **ComboBox**

b. **ListBox**

c. **CheckBox**

d. **RadioButton**

e. **TextBox**

18. **Click( )** events are the default event for which type of **object**?

a. **Button**

b. **RadioButton**

c. **MenuItem**

d. **CheckBox**

e. all of the above

19. Which statement could be used in C# to set a **ListBox** object's selection mode to MultiExtended if you did not have Visual Studio .NET's Properties window available? The name for the **ListBox** `object` is `lstBox1`.

    a. `lstBox1.SelectionMode = SelectionMode.MultiExtended;`

    b. `lstBox1 = MultiExtended;`

    c. `SelectionMode = MultiExtended;`

    d. `SelectionMode.MultiExtended;`

    e. all of the above

20. Which property can be set for a form to enable the Enter key to function like a mouse click for a selected **Button** `object`?

    a. `Enter`

    b. `Button_Click`

    c. `EnterKey`

    d. `AcceptButton`

    e. `AcceptKey`

21. Describe what is required to make a menu option clickable or a check box functional.

22. When is a **RadioButton** control preferred over a **CheckBox** control? When is a **ComboBox** control preferred over a **ListBox** control?

23. How is a `delegate` related to an event?

24. For the following table, identify which properties can be used to set the given values for the controls.

Desired action	Property
Get the selected item from a ComboBox `object`	
Change the label over a group box	
Arrange the items in a list box in ascending order	
Change the color of the text in a label	
Change the text that appears in the title bar of a form	
Associate a menu to a form	

25. From the following partial code listing, identify the name(s) of event-handler method(s) that would need to be written. To what object(s) are they wired?

```
public class Question : System.Windows.Forms.Form
    {
        private System.Windows.Forms.Label label1;
        private System.Windows.Forms.TextBox textBox1;
        private System.Windows.Forms.CheckBox ckBoxSwim;
        private System.Windows.Forms.CheckBox ckBoxSnorkel;
        private System.Windows.Forms.TextBox txtResult;
:    // Colon indicates items missing.
:
private void InitializeComponent()
        {
            this.label1 = new System.Windows.Forms.Label();
            this.ckBoxSwim = new System.Windows.Forms.CheckBox();
            this.ckBoxSnorkel = new System.Windows.Forms.
CheckBox();
            this.lstBoxEvents.SelectedIndexChanged += new
                System.EventHandler
(this.listBox1_SelectedIndexChanged);
:    // Colon indicates items missing.
:
            this.label2.Size = new
                System.Drawing.Size(120, 24);
            this.txtBoxResult.Location =
                new System.Drawing.Point(-2, 240);
            this.btnNew.Text = "Add New One";
            this.btnNew.Click +=
                new System.EventHandler(this.btnNew_Click);
            this.AutoScaleBaseSize = new
                System.Drawing.Size(8, 19);
            this.BackColor = System.Drawing.Color.FromArgb
                (((System.Byte)(128)), ((System.Byte)(128)),
                ((System.Byte)(255)));
            this.ClientSize = new
                System.Drawing.Size(292, 273);
            this.Controls.AddRange
                (new System.Windows.Forms.Control[]
                            { this.btnNew,
                                this.txtBoxNewAct,
                                this.label3,
                                this.label1,
                                this.txtBoxResult,
                                this.label2,
                                this.lstBoxEvents } );
:    // Colon indicates items missing.
:
```

PROGRAMMING EXERCISES

1. Create a graphical user interface that allows the users to enter their names, e-mail addresses, and phone numbers. Add a menu option that has two features. The first displays the information entered by the user in a message box. The other clears the entries so that new values can be entered.

2. Create a Message Displayer that has one **ComboBox** object with a list of four of your favorite sayings. In your design include the capability of letting users enter their own sayings. When a selection is made or a new entry is typed, display the selection on a **Label** object on your form.

3. Add a menu to the application in Exercise 2 that includes at least the menu options of Format and Help. Under the Format selection, include options of Font and Color. Wire the Font and Color options to the Windows predefined Font and Color dialog boxes so that when their values are changed, the text in the **Label** object displaying the saying is changed.

4. Create a graphical user interface that includes radio buttons with five different sport names. Only one of these should be selectable. Program your event-handler method so that a message is displayed with each selection of a different sport. For example, if one of the sports is skiing, the message might say, "Get warm clothes!" An enhancement would be to include a **PictureBox** object on the form to display pictures of the sporting event. When the particular sport is selected, make the **PictureBox** visible. You can find free graphics on the Internet to use in your application.

5. Create a Windows application that can be used as a sign-up sheet for ski equipment for the Flyers Sports Club. The club has ski equipment that it makes available to members at a minimal charge. In an attempt to determine what type of equipment members might need for an upcoming trip, they have asked you to design and implement an equipment-needs form. Include **CheckBox** objects that allow users to select the type of gear they will need to purchase for the trip. Include selections of snow gloves, skis, goggles, earmuffs, and other items, as you feel appropriate. After all selections are made, display a message indicating what items have been selected. You will probably want to include menu options to display the order and clear the order for the next user.

6. Create a Windows application for purchasing carpet. Allow the length and width of a room to be entered. Have a control that displays different prices of carpet. Include, for example, prices such as $21.95 per square yard. After the users enter their room dimensions and the price of the carpet, display the total cost to carpet the room.

7. Create an order form that allows bags to be purchased. There are six different types: full decorative, beaded, needlepoint design, fringed, fringed beaded, and plain. Create a **ListBox** object for the different styles. After the user makes a selection, display a message indicating which selection was made.

9

8. Add to the application in Exercise 7 by including a control that allows the user to enter the quantity desired. Include a set of radio buttons that contain shipping options of overnight, three day, and standard. The price for each bag is as follows: full decorative—$50.00; beaded—$45.00; needlepoint design—$40.00; fringed—$25.00; fringed beaded—$30.00; and plain—$20.00. The shipping charges are based on the total purchase. The following percentages are used: overnight—10%; three day—7%; and standard—5%. Display in a message box the shipping charge along with the selection, quantity, and total cost.

9. The computer club is selling T-shirts. Create an attractive user interface that allows users to select sizes (S, M, L, and XL) and quantity. Which controls would be most appropriate? Remember, the fewer keystrokes required of the user the better. Display the selections made by the user with the Process menu option.

10. Add to your solution in Exercise 9 by including two more sizes, XSmall and XXLarge. Add statements that process the order by calculating the total cost. Each shirt is $16 except the XSmall and XXLarge; their specialty prices are $20.00 each. Display the total cost of the selection. You can enhance your solution by allowing users to purchase different sizes on the same order.

10

Advanced Object-Oriented Programming Features

In this chapter, you extend your knowledge of programming by exploring advanced features of object-oriented design. You are introduced to component-based development and learn how to create your own `class` library files. You investigate new ways to write classes and new ways to use the more than 2000 classes that make up the Framework Class Library (FCL).

In addition, you learn more about inheritance and are introduced to interfaces and `abstract` classes. You explore the differences between extending a `class` through inheritance and implementing an `interface`. You learn how polymorphism relates to object-oriented design and learn how to do polymorphic programming using .NET-supported languages. Advanced features such as overriding, overloading, and the use of `virtual` methods are included in this chapter.

OBJECT-ORIENTED LANGUAGE FEATURES

For a language to be considered a true object-oriented programming (OOP) language, it must support the following four major concepts, which C# and the .NET platform embrace:

- **Abstraction**—The language must provide a way to manage complex problems by allowing you to abstract or identify the objects involved in the problem.

- **Encapsulation**—The language must provide support for packaging data attributes and behaviors into a single unit, thus hiding implementation details.

- **Inheritance**—The language must provide features that enable reuse of code through extending the functionality of the program units.

- **Polymorphism**—The language must enable multiple implementations of the same behaviors so that the appropriate implementation can be executed based on the situation.

These features form the foundation for object-oriented development. From your first introduction to C#, you have experienced abstraction in your design of applications. Through designing classes, you are able to abstract out common characteristics that all objects of that type possess, including both behavioral and data characteristics. You defined the data in terms of instance fields and the behaviors in terms of methods. You encapsulated or packaged these common characteristics into a single entity labeled a `class`. Through defining the data members as private, you protected the data and enabled access only through the object's methods and properties.

Through using read-only properties and methods, you hide the implementation details. You have experienced inheritance, especially when you designed your graphical user interfaces. You extended the `Form` `class` to add to the functionality that was already part of that `class`. In this chapter, you gain a deeper understanding of the power of inheritance and learn how to build your own polymorphic components that can be extended.

Object-oriented development focuses on designing classes that can be reused in many applications. One way to ensure this reuse is through designing and building components that can be stored in a library and called on when needed. The next section describes how to accomplish this through the .NET platform.

COMPONENT-BASED DEVELOPMENT

In the past, applications were developed mainly as single, self-contained, monolithic programs. Most new applications are large systems involving development efforts from teams of programmers. These applications often require the packaging together of many different components to respond to business functions. Instead of writing a program that includes all the features in a single file, development today is often geared toward writing multitier applications similar to that shown in Figure 10-1.

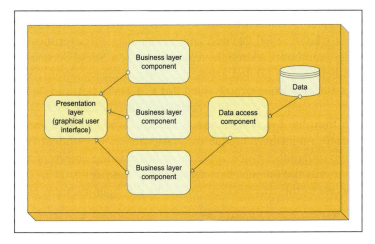

Figure 10-1   Component-based development

Components are implemented through classes in C#. In Chapters 8 and 9, you learned how to design graphical user interfaces, which enable creating a presentation tier. Chapter 12 introduces you to Web applications that facilitate creating another type of presentation tier, which can be viewed over a browser by different types of platforms. In the next chapter, Chapter 11, you learn how to add the data access tier by writing classes that access data from text files and databases such as those created using Microsoft Access. All the work you have accomplished with previous chapters in this book has prepared you to develop the business logic for the center tier of components.

Object-oriented development techniques work well for constructing multitier applications. As you review Figure 10-1, think of each of the components in the diagram as independent classes, separate from each other. Classes can be designed and new subclasses created that extend the functionality of the original **class**. Many different applications can reuse these classes through extending or combining them into new applications.

In C#, in addition to creating .EXE files, you can create **class** library files with a dynamic link library (DLL) extension. These files can become the components that are referenced from any number of applications. To take advantage of the features of object-oriented programming, one of the key concepts you must understand is inheritance.

INHERITANCE

Inheritance allows you to create a general **class** and then define specialized classes that have access to the members of the general **class**. These new specialized classes can extend functionality by adding their own new unique data and behaviors. Inheritance is associated with an "is a" relationship. A specialized **class** "is a" form of the general **class**. For example, you might create a **class** called **Person** and include data characteristics of identification number, name, age, and home address. In regions that use a Social Security number for identification such as here in the United States, the Social Security number would be the identification number. Behaviors or methods titled **Eat( )**, **Walk( )**, and **Talk( )** might be included. After these are defined, you could create specialized classes such as **Student** or **Faculty** that inherit from the **Person class**. **Student** "is a" **Person**, just as **Faculty** "is a" **Person**. **Student** might have unique data characteristics of student ID, major, and year in school. Through using inheritance, applications instantiating objects of the **Student class** would have not only the unique characteristics of the student (student ID, major, and year), but also have access to the characteristics of the Person (identification number, name, age, and address).

 Classes can also have a "has a" relationship in which a single **class** is defined to have instances of other **class** types. This is a concept called **containment** or **aggregation**. You experience containment in C# when you define classes that instantiate objects of the **string** or **int** classes. However, "has a" relationships are usually associated with user-defined classes. For example, a Person "has a" medicalRecord and "has a" dentalRecord.

Inheriting from the Object Class

You have been creating your own classes since you wrote your first program in Chapter 2. You learned that every **object** created in C# automatically inherits from a **base class** named **object** that is in the **System namespace**. Object has four methods that every

class written in C# inherits as long as it provides a reference to the **System namespace**. One of these, the **ToString( )** method, you have used in many of your programs. Figure 10-2 uses IntelliSense to show the signature for **Object.ToString( )** and the names of the other methods inherited from **object**.

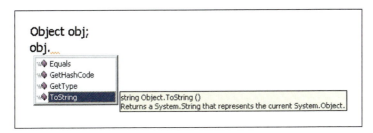

Figure 10-2   Methods inherited from an object

Inheriting from Other .NET FCL Classes

You also experienced inheritance when you developed Windows-based programs in Chapters 8 and 9. The Windows forms classes that you created inherited from the **System.Windows.Forms.Form class**. Extending that **class** enabled you to build on the functionality that was included as part of that .NET Framework **class**. Adding instantiated objects from classes such as **Button**, **Label**, **TextBox**, and **ListBox** enabled you to add functionality to your program with minimal programming. To inherit from the **System.Windows.Forms.Form class**, new entries were added to your **class** definition. Figure 10-3 illustrates what Visual Studio .NET adds when you decide to build a Windows application by choosing the Windows Application template from the Project Type menu.

10

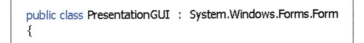

Figure 10-3   Derived class

In object-oriented terminology, the **class** listed after the colon in Figure 10-3 is the **base class**. The **class** to the left of the colon, **PresentationGUI**, is called the **derived class**. To inherit from a **base class**, a colon is used as a separator between the derived **class** and the **base class** as shown in Figure 10-3. **PresentationGUI** is the user-defined name. The **Form class** belongs to the **System.Windows.Forms namespace**. For this example, the user-defined **class** is inheriting from a predefined .NET **class**; however, the same concepts apply when a user-defined **class** is inheriting from another user-defined **class**. By using the colon, you indicate that the **PresentationGUI class** derives from the **Form class**.

Creating Base Classes for Inheritance

You can define your own classes from which other classes can inherit characteristics. Example 10-1 creates a **class** named **Person** with four data members. This **class** is used as a **base class** from which other classes can inherit characteristics. The **base class** is sometimes called the **super** or **parent class**.

Example 10-1

```
public class Person
{
        private string idNumber;
        private string lastName;
        private string firstName;
        private int age;

        public Person()             // Constructor with zero arguments
        {
            idNumber = "";
            lastName = "unknown";
            firstName = "unknown";
            age = 0;
        }
        public Person(string id, string lname, string fname,
                      int anAge) // Constructor with four arguments
        {
            idNumber = id;
            lastName = lname;
            firstName = fname;
            age = anAge;
        }
        public Person(string id, string lname, string fname)
        {                           // Constructor with three arguments
            idNumber = id;
            lastName = lname;
            firstName = fname;
            age = 0;
        }
        public Person(string id)
        {                           // Constructor with one argument
            idNumber = id;
            lastName = "unknown";
```

```
            firstName = "unknown";
            age = 0;
        }
}
```

Only data members and constructor methods are shown for the **Person class** in Example 10-1. Notice that the data members are defined with a **private** access modifier and constructors are defined with **public** access modifiers. The next section reviews why these choices were made.

Access Modifiers

Access to members that have been defined with the **private** access modifier is restricted to members of the current **class**. The **private** members are not accessible to other classes that derive from this **class** or that instantiate objects of this **class**. Using a **private** access modifier enables the **class** to protect its data and only allow access to the data through its methods or properties. This ensures the data-hiding characteristic of encapsulation.

Constructors Use Public Access   Constructors, named the same name as the **class** name, are defined with **public** access. It is important to note that if you do not use a **public** access modifier with constructors, no objects can be instantiated from the **class**. Constructors differ from other methods in that they cannot have a **return** type. Remember that you have an **overloaded method** when you have more than one method using the same identifier. The requirement for an overloaded method is that each of the methods must have a different number and/or type of parameter from the others. Thus, by definition, when you have two or more constructors for a class, you have overloaded methods.

10

Properties Offer Public Access to Data Fields   Before creating a specialized **class** to inherit the characteristics of the **Person class**, properties are added to the **Person class**. By including properties, there is less need to write accessor (getter) and mutator (setter) methods. The **private** member fields can be accessed through these properties.

 Properties are new to the C/C++/C# programming family line. They look like data fields, but are implemented as methods that can be used to get or set a **private** data field instance.

Example 10-2 shows some of the properties added to the **Person class**. Due to space constraints, only two of the four properties are shown. The first enables the data field, **firstName**, to be a read-only property; it does not contain a set property. Without defining an additional mutator method, **firstName** can never be changed after it is constructed.

If you were implementing this solution, you might consider some important design issues. First, one or more of the constructors allows an object to be instantiated by assigning "unknown" to `firstName`. But, no property is available to change that value for classes that instantiate objects from it. Thus, you would need to write a mutator (`set_firstName( )`) method; otherwise the name could never be changed from "unknown".

In Example 10-2, the `FirstName` property is shown as read-only to reinforce the idea that properties do not have to include both a get and set. You should probably define read-only properties only for fields that should not be changed, such as identification numbers.

Example 10-2

```
// Read-only property. First name cannot be changed.
public string FirstName
{
    get
    {
        return firstName;
    }
}

// Property for last name
public string LastName
{
    get
    {
        return lastName;
    }
    set
    {
        lastName = value;
    }
}
```

Once you add the `LastName` property to the `class`, you can retrieve the current contents of `lastName` using the `LastName` identifier. Notice you do not declare `value`. It can be used, almost like magic, to refer to the value that is sent in through an assignment statement.

Notice how `get`, `set`, and `value` appear in blue code. When you began reading this book, you were told that keywords would be shown in blue. Visual Studio follows this standard with a few exceptions. One exception is that `set`, `value`, and `get` are displayed, by default, in Visual Studio in blue, but they are not keywords. Since you see them in blue in the IDE, they are shown in blue in this book.

Properties are not included in all of the .NET languages. For example, J# does not support properties. Adding them to your solutions enables access to the **private** data using the property identifier, as opposed to writing additional methods.

Overriding Methods

Two additional methods are added to the **Person class** and shown in Example 10-3. The first overrides the **object ToString( )** method. When you override a method, you replace the method defined at a higher level. Notice that the keyword **override** is added onto the **ToString( )** method heading and **virtual** is added onto the **GetSleepAmt( )** method heading.

Example 10-3

```
public override string ToString( )   // Defined in Person
{
    return firstName + " " + lastName;
}
public virtual int GetSleepAmt( )
{
    return 8;
}
```

10

> **NOTE** Overriding a method differs from overloading a method. An overridden method must have exactly the same signature as the method it is overriding. New functionality is normally defined with overridden methods. Overloaded methods must have a different signature than others with the same name. Overloaded methods are usually defined to perform a similar behavior, but with different data types.

Using the Override Keyword

The **override** keyword allows a method to provide a new implementation of a method inherited from a **base class**. When you **override** a method, the signature of the methods must match. To **override** a **base** method, the **base** method must be defined as **virtual**, **abstract**, or **override**. Figure 10-4 shows the signature for the **ToString( )** method that belongs to the **object class**. This is taken from the online documentation in Visual Studio .NET.

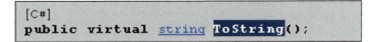

```
[C#]
public virtual string ToString();
```

Figure 10-4 ToString( ) signature

Virtual Methods

Because the developers of .NET included the **virtual** modifier as part of the **ToString( )** method signature, the method can be overridden by any C# **class**. Every **class** inherits methods from the **object class**. **ToString( )** does not have to be overridden. It returns a string representing the current object. It is often overridden to offer differing functionality based on which **object** is calling it.

> This is an example of polymorphism, meaning many forms. You read more about polymorphism later in this chapter. Think about the meaning of morphing—an object reshapes itself. In that context, the **ToString( )** method can have many different definitions. The definition that is used when you call on the method is determined by which **object** calls it.

In Example 10-3, the **GetSleepAmt( )** method also uses the **virtual** modifier, implying that any **class** that derives from **Person** can **override** that method. To **override** a method, the new method must have exactly the same parameters that are used in the method you plan to **override**.

Creating Derived Classes

Classes that inherit from a **base class** are called derived classes. They are also referred to as subclasses or child classes, because they inherit the characteristics of a parent **class**. Any number of classes can inherit from the **Person class** that was defined in the previous examples. **Person** is defined using a **public** access modifier.

Protected Access Modifiers

Although it is true that derived classes inherit all the characteristics of the **base class**, they do not have direct access to change their **private** members. In addition to **private** and **public** access, C# offers **internal** and **protected** access. Internal members are accessible only within files in the same assembly. Protected members are accessible to any **class** that is derived from them, but not to any other classes. So if you want methods in derived classes to have access to change data in the **base class**, define the data members using a **protected** access, instead of a **private** access. This way the data is still hidden from other classes, but available for use in derived classes.

To demonstrate inheritance, a new file is created in Visual Studio for a **Student class**. The **Student class** inherits all members of the **Person class** and adds two additional data field members. This is an "is a" relationship. **Student** "is a" **Person**. Example 10-4 shows some of the source code from the **Student class**.

Example 10-4

```
public class Student : Person
{
    private string major;
    private int studentId;
    // Default constructor
    public Student( )
        :base( )          // No arguments sent to base constructor
    {
        major = "unknown";
        studentId = 0;
    }
    // Constructor that sends three arguments to base class
    // constructor
    public Student(string  id, string fname, string lname,
                   string maj, int sId)
        :base (id, lname, fname) // base constructor arguments
    {
        major = maj;
        studentId = sId;
    }

    public override int GetSleepAmt( )
    {
        return 6;
    }
}
```

Example 10-4 includes a number of interesting features. First, the heading for the **class** indicates that **Student** is derived from **Person**. The **class** heading is repeated in Example 10-5.

Example 10-5

```
public class Student : Person    // Student is derived from Person
```

> **NOTE**   Base classes follow the colon. Derived classes appear to the left of the colon.

Calling the Base Constructor

To call the constructor for the **base class**, an extra entry is added between the constructor heading for the **Student** subclass and the opening curly brace as shown in Example 10-6.

Example 10-6

```
public Student( )
    :base( )                    // No arguments sent to base constructor
{  . . .
```

This calls the **default** constructor for **Person**. To send data to the **base** constructor, you must have a matching signature.

To send data to the **Person** constructor at the same time you instantiate an **object** of the **Student class**, the keyword **base** is followed by arguments that match one of Person's constructors as follows:

```
public Student(string   id, string fname, string lname,
               string maj, int sId)
    :base (id, lname, fname)  // base constructor arguments
{  . . .
```

The reserved word **base**, which is shown with a colon and set of parentheses (**: base( )**) in Example 10-6, is used to indicate which **base class** constructor should be used when an **object** of the derived **class** is created. Notice it is placed in the **class** heading before the opening curly brace. The first call to the **base** constructor uses the default constructor without any arguments for **Person**.

The call to the constructor, :base( ), could have been omitted on the second line. The default constructor would have been called automatically when an object of the derived class was instantiated. For readability purposes, it is best to include the call to the default constructor with no arguments.

The second constructor in Example 10-6 indicates that the **Person** constructor with three **string** arguments should be used when an **object** of the **Student class** is instantiated using that constructor. Notice that to instantiate an **object** of the **Student class** using that constructor, four **string** and one **int** arguments are expected. Three of the four **string** arguments are used by the **base class**. Thus, if an **object** of the **Student class** is constructed inside a **class** that, for example, is taking care of the presentation layer, the code might appear as in Example 10-7.

Example 10-7

```
// Student object might be instantiated in a different class
// such as a PresentationGUI class
Student aStudent = new
        Student ("123456789", "Maria", "Woo", "CS", 1111);
```

The first three arguments, "123456789", "Maria", and "Woo", are sent to the constructor for the **Person class**. Remember that this occurred because the **Student** constructor included as part of its constructor heading the following code:

```
:base (id, lname, fname)   // Appears in Student constructor heading
```

The last two arguments ("CS", 1111) are used by the **Student class constructor**.

The order of the arguments being sent to the base constructor is extremely important. Notice how **lname** is listed before **fname** in Example 10-7. The names selected for the identifier do not matter; however, their position does. There must be a constructor accepting three string arguments. The placement of the arguments in the parameter list for the constructor determines the order that must be used by derived classes. Review the constructors for the **Person class** in Example 10-1. Notice the three arguments the constructor expects. The constructor expects the first argument to be an identification number, the second argument to be the last name, and the last argument the first name.

Objects created using the **default** constructor do not send any arguments to the **Person** constructor. Both the **Person default** constructor and the **Student default** constructor with no parameters are called when a **Student** object is instantiated with no arguments, as follows:

```
Student anotherStudent = new Student( );
```

10

Using Members of the Base Class

After objects are instantiated from the **Student class**, any of the **public** methods or properties from both the **Person class** and the **Student class** can be used with a **Student object**. You do not have to do anything special to use the **public** access members of either **class**. If, in the **class** that instantiates the **anotherStudent object**, you want to set a value representing a last name, you can use the property for **LastName** defined in the **Person class** as follows:

```
anotherStudent.LastName = "Garcia";
```

Calling Overridden Methods of the Base Class   When you have a method that has the same name in both the **base** and the derived **class**, the keyword **base** can be used in the derived **class** to refer to methods in the **base class** that are overridden in the derived **class**. Example 10-8 shows a method defined in the **Student class** that calls an overridden method in the **Person class**. Notice that the method name was qualified with the **base** keyword. If **base** had been omitted, the **GetSleepAmt( )** method defined in the **Student class** would have been called.

Example 10-8

```
public int CallOverriddenGetSleepAmt( )
                                  // Defined in Student class
{                                 // (derived class)
      return base.GetSleepAmt( )  // Calls GetSleepAmt() in Person
}
```

It is useful to see how the classes are related. Figure 10-5 shows the inheritance relationship between the **Person** and **Student** classes. The **PresentationGUI class** is related through instantiating an object of the **Student class**. In class diagrams, arrows with empty arrowheads are used to show the inheritance relationship between the **Student** and **Person** and **PresentationGUI** and **Form** classes.

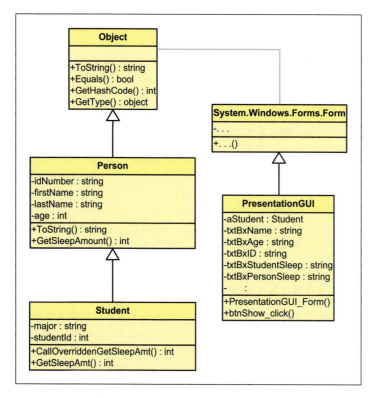

Figure 10-5   Inheritance class diagram

> The derived **class**, Student, has access to the **public** access members of the **base class**, Person. But, the **base class** does not have access to the members of the derived Student **class**. The **base class** has no knowledge of any of the derived classes.

As shown in Figure 10-5, **Student** is derived from **Person**; **PresentationGUI** is derived from the **Form class** in the **System.Windows.Forms namespace**. Open or unfilled arrows are used in the **class** diagram to point to the **base class**. Because **Object** is the **base class** of all classes, every **class** inherits the four methods shown previously in Figure 10-2. Example 10-9 lists the statements in the **Person class**.

Example 10-9

```
// Person.cs
using System;
namespace PersonNamespace
{
    public abstract class Person
    {
        private string idNumber;
        private string lastName;
        private string firstName;
        private int age;

        public Person()            // Constructor with zero arguments
        {
            idNumber = "";
            lastName = "unknown";
            firstName = "unknown";
            age = 0;
        }
        public Person(string id, string lname, string fname,
            int anAge)            // Constructor with four arguments
        {
            idNumber = id;
            lastName = lname;
            firstName = fname;
            age = anAge;
        }
        public Person(string id, string lname, string fname)
        {                          // Constructor with three arguments
            idNumber = id;
            lastName = lname;
            firstName = fname;
            age = 0;
        }
```

```csharp
public Person(string id)
{                              // Constructor with one argument
    idNumber = id;
    lastName ="unknown";
    firstName = "unknown";
    age = 0;
}

// Read-only property. ID can not be changed.
public string IdNumber
{
    get
    {
        return idNumber;
    }
}

// Property for last name
public string LastName
{
    get
    {
        return  lastName;
    }
    set
    {
        lastName = value;
    }
}

// Read-only property. First name can not be changed.
public string FirstName
{
    get
    {
        return firstName;
    }
}

public int Age
{
    get
    {
        return age;
    }
```

```
            set
            {
                age = value;
            }
        }

        // Overrides ToString( ) method from the Object class
        public override string ToString( )
        {
            return firstName + " " + lastName;
        }

        // Virtual method can be overridden by classes that
        // derive from the Person class.
        public virtual int GetSleepAmt( )
        {
            return 8;
        }
    }
}
```

The program statements that constitute the **Student class** are shown in Example 10-10. Note that a new **using** statement is added (**using PersonNamespace;**). This is typed manually and matches the name of the **namespace** in the **Person class**. Adding references to other classes is discussed in the next section.

Also, notice that the identifier for the **namespace** in the **Student class** is **StudentNamespace**. This identifier is different from the **namespace** identifier in the **Person class**, because two separate projects are developed to demonstrate use of components.

The **Student class** includes two additional data fields, properties for those fields, and a **GetSleepAmt( )** method that overrides the **GetSleepAmt( )** method of the **Person class**. A second method is included to illustrate how a **base** method that has been overridden can be called. The **Student class** appears in Example 10-10.

Example 10-10

```
// Student.cs
using System;
using PersonNamespace; // Added to avoid using fully qualified names

namespace StudentNamespace
{
```

```csharp
public class Student : Person
{
    private string major;
    private int studentId;

    public Student( ) : base ( )
    {
        major = "unknown";
        studentId = 0;
    }
    // Constructor that sends arguments to base class
    public Student(string id, string fname, string lname,
                                string maj, int sId)
        :base(id, lname, fname)
    {
        major = maj;
        studentId = sId;
    }
    // Read-only Property for studentID
    public int StudentId
    {
        get
        {
            return studentId;
        }
    }

    // Property for major data field
    public string Major
    {
        get
        {
            return major;
        }
        set
        {
            major = value;
        }
    }

    // Overrides GetSleepAmt( ) method of the Person class
    public override int GetSleepAmt( )
    {
        return 6;
    }
```

```
        // Using the base keyword, calls the overridden
        // GetSleepAmt( ) method of the Person class
        public int CallOverriddenGetSleepAmt( )
        {
            return base.GetSleepAmt( );
        }
    }
}
```

> **NOTE** Because the identification numbers have read-only properties, mutator methods would need to be defined if you wanted to enable their values to be changed.

Making Stand-Alone Components

The two classes, **Student** and **Person**, could be used with a third **class** that includes a **Main( )** method. They could then be compiled just as you have done previously to create a single assembly. By doing this, you associate the **Student** and **Person** with that one assembly.

> **NOTE** **Assemblies** are the units that are configured and deployed in .NET.

10

The byte code of an assembly can be reused in other applications, and doing so represents the component-based development approach. Figure 10-1, on the other hand, introduced another approach to enabling component-based development. Each of the classes can be compiled and then stored as a dynamic link library (DLL) file, and any number of applications can then reference the classes. That is the beauty of component-based development and object-oriented programming.

Dynamic Link Library (DLL)

C# and Visual Studio .NET offer several options for creating components. One option is to compile the source code files into a DLL file instead of into the EXE file type that you have been creating. After you have a DLL, any application that will use that component simply adds a reference to the DLL and that referenced file with the .dll extension becomes part of the application's private assembly. Visual Studio creates the DLL for you or you can compile the .cs files at the command line using the Visual Studio command prompt. To do this from the Visual Studio command prompt, you would type the following command:

```
csc /target:library /out:Person.dll Person.cs
csc /target:library /out:Student.dll Student.cs
```

When you type this command, you must either be in the directory that contains the .CS files or prefix the source code file name with the full path to the location of the files.

If you want to include both the **Person class** and the **Student class** in one DLL, you would type:

```
csc /target:library /out:Student.dll Student.cs Person.cs
```

The **/target:library** compiler option tells the compiler to output a DLL instead of an EXE file. The **/out:** compiler option followed by a file name is used to specify the name for the new DLL file. You can omit the **/out:** option, and the DLL takes on the name of the first file listed. For this example, omitting **/out:Student.dll** would still create a Student.dll file because Student.cs is listed first.

Using Visual Studio to Create DLL Files

A second option, and one you may find more appealing, is to do everything within Visual Studio. When you first start a new solution or a new project, one of the options is to create a **class** library using the Class Library template as shown in Figure 10-6.

![New Project dialog box. Project Types list on the left shows: Visual Basic Projects, Visual C# Projects (selected), Visual C++ Projects, Setup and Deployment Projects, Other Projects, Visual Studio Solutions. Templates list on the right shows: Windows Application, Class Library (selected), Windows Control Library, ASP.NET Web Application, ASP.NET Web Service, Web Control Library, Console Application, Windows Service, Empty Project. Description: "A project for creating classes to use in other applications". Name: Person. Location: C:\CSharpProjects\LibraryFiles. Options: Add to Solution, Close Solution (selected). "Project will be created at C:\CSharpProjects\LibraryFiles\Person." Buttons: More, OK, Cancel, Help.]

Figure 10-6   Creating a DLL component

You should create the **Person class** first, so that **Student** can be derived from it. Creating **Person** first enables you to use IntelliSense in Visual Studio .NET. After selecting the

Class Library template option and naming the file, you create the `class` in the same way you have created other files that produce an .exe extension when compiled.

> By default Visual Studio .NET assigns the `namespace` name the same name as the project name (`Person`). You should change the `namespace` name; otherwise, when you start adding a reference to a created DLL, it can become quite confusing.

The `namespace` name selected for this example for the `Person class` is `PersonNamespace`. To change the name, just highlight the old `namespace` name with your mouse and type a new name. No other changes, related to the `namespace`, need to be made.

Building Instead of Running the Project

After you finish typing the `class`, you do not run the application. The `Person class` does not have a `Main( )` method. If you press F5 or Ctrl+F5, an error message is generated similar to that shown in Figure 10-7.

Microsoft Development Environment   ⊠

⚠️   A project with an Output Type of Class Library cannot be started directly.

In order to debug this project, go to the Debugging tab under Configuration Settings in Project Properties, and set the Start Action to Start External Program or Start URL. Alternatively, you can add a non-library project to this solution that uses a reference to this project and set it as the startup project.

OK

10

Figure 10-7   Attempting to run a class library file

To compile and create the DLL, use one of the Build options under the Build menu bar. You can select **Build>Solution** or select **Build** followed by the project name. After you save your work, close the project. A completely new project should be created for the `Student class`. You create a `class` library for the `Student class` just as you did for the `Person class` by using the Class Library template from the Visual Studio .NET Start page.

>
> You learned in Chapter 1 that .NET supports having an application include code from multiple .NET languages. This is possible because all .NET-supported and NET-managed languages use the same common language runtime (CLR) and the same Framework Class Library (FCL). The `Person class` could be written in C#. The `Student class` could be written in J#. A graphical user interface presentation `class` instantiating the `Student class` that is deriving from the `Person class` could be written in Visual Basic .NET.

The only requirement for applications with multiple languages is that projects include source code files from only one language. Thus, if you had a solution file that had three projects, each project would contain source code files in one language.

Adding a Reference to the Base Class

Because you are deriving from the **Person** base class, one of the first things you should do is Add a Reference to Person.dll. By doing this first, you gain access to the members of the **Person** class inside this newly created **Student** class. This can be done several ways in Visual Studio .NET. One option is to use the Solution Explorer window. After selecting the Project name, click the right mouse button and select Add Reference as shown in Figure 10-8.

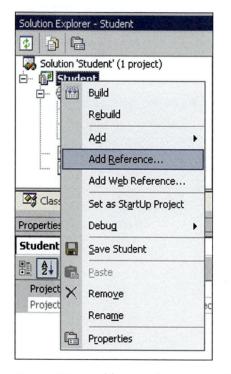

Figure 10-8   Adding a reference to a DLL

A window is displayed similar to that shown in Figure 10-9 that enables you to select the Browse button so that you can locate Person.dll.

Add Reference   [×]

.NET | COM | Projects

Browse...

Component Name	Version	Path
Accessibility.dll	1.0.3300.0	C:\WINDOWS\Microsoft.N
adodb	7.0.3300.0	C:\Program Files\Microsof
CRVsPackageLib	1.0.0.0	C:\Program Files\Common
CrystalDecisions.CrystalReports.Engine	9.1.3300.0	C:\Program Files\Common
CrystalDecisions.ReportSource	9.1.3300.0	C:\Program Files\Common
CrystalDecisions.Shared	9.1.3300.0	C:\Program Files\Common
CrystalDecisions.Web	9.1.3300.0	C:\Program Files\Common
CrystalDecisions.Windows.Forms	9.1.3300.0	C:\Program Files\Common
CrystalEnterpriseLib	1.0.0.0	C:\Program Files\Common
CrystalInfoStoreLib	1.0.0.0	C:\Program Files\Common
CrystalKeyCodeLib	1.0.0.0	C:\Program Files\Common

Select

Selected Components:

Component Name	Type	Source

Remove

OK   Cancel   Help

Figure 10-9   Adding a reference to Person.dll using the Browse button

Once you select the Browse button, navigate to the location where the project is located. The
DLL is stored in the Debug directory under the bin folder wherever you created your project.
For this example, the **Person** project was created in the C:\CSharpProjects\LibraryFiles
folder. Thus, it was necessary to navigate into that directory to locate Person.dll as shown in
Figure 10-10.

10

Figure 10-10   Locating the Person.dll component

After the reference is made, you can derive new classes from the **class** defined in the
component.

Adding a Using Statement

Now that you are back in the **Student class**, if you simply type:

```
public class Student : Person
```

you receive an error message as shown in Figure 10-11.

Figure 10-11   Namespace reference error

Just adding the reference is not enough—you need to accomplish one more step. You have to qualify **Person** by adding the **namespace** and a dot before the **class** name as shown in Example 10-11.

Example 10-11

```
public class Student : PersonNamespace.Person
```

An even better option is simply to add a **using** directive at the top of the source code file. The **using** statement should indicate the **namespace** identifier for the **Person class**. In the **Person class**, the name typed for this example was **PersonNamespace**; thus, by adding the **using** statement, you can avoid having to qualify all references to the **Person class**. Example 10-12 includes the **using** directive for **PersonNamespace**.

Example 10-12

```
using PersonNamespace;   // Use whatever name you typed for the
                         // namespace for Person
```

After adding the **using** statement, your **class** header can now read:

```
public class Student : Person    // No need to fully qualify now
```

After typing your program statements, build the DLL from the Build option under the Build menu bar. Save your work and close the project.

Creating a Client Application to Use the DLL

You now have two components that can be reused with many different applications. All that is necessary is to add a reference to the components in your program and include a **using** statement with the appropriate **namespace**. To illustrate how a client program could use the **Student** component, a Windows application is developed to instantiate an **object** of the **Student class**.

Using Visual Studio .NET, create a new project and select the Windows Application template as the project type. The **class** is named **PresentationGUI**.

Adding a Reference to the DLL

A reference must be added for both the **Person** and **Student** classes. Review Figures 10-8 through 10-10 if you need help adding the references. Both should be referenced in the **PresentationGUI** project as shown in Figure 10-12.

Figure 10-12   DLLs referenced in the PresentationGUI class

Adding a Using Statement for the Namespace

To avoid typing the fully qualified name, add a **using** directive for the **Student namespace**. In the previous example, the **namespace** used for the **Student** project was **StudentNamespace**. Thus, Example 10-13 shows how to add a **using** directive for the **StudentNamespace**.

Example 10-13

```
using StudentNamespace;
```

Because the **Student class** included a **using** statement for **PersonNamespace** and no **Person object** is being instantiated, it is not necessary to add a **using** statement for **PersonNamespace** here in the **PresentationGUI class**. No syntax error would be generated, however, if **using PersonNamespace;** is also added.

Declaring an Object of the Component Type

You must declare a `Student` object. This is done inside the `PresentationGUI` class as a `private` data member as shown in Example 10-14.

Example 10-14

```
public class PresentationGUI : System.Windows.Forms.Form
{
    Student aStudent;
```

The statement in Example 10-14 is declaring one Student object. Of course, you could define a collection of Student objects using an array.

Instantiating the Object

To create or instantiate an actual `object` of the `Student` `class`, one of the `Student` constructors must be used. Remember there are two constructors defined for the `Student` `class`. Thus, one way to instantiate the `class` is to write:

```
aStudent = new Student("123456789", "Maria", "Woo", "CS", 1111);
```

This instantiation is placed in the method that handles the form load event. It could have also been placed in the `InitializeComponent( )` method where the Windows Form Designer generated code is placed.

Using Members of the Derived and Base Classes

A number of control objects are added to the form. `TextBox` objects are dragged to the form for displaying name, age, student ID, the amount of sleep for the student, and the amount of sleep for others. A `Button` `object` is added for populating the `TextBox` objects. Example 10-15 shows the program statements for the PresentationGUI. Due to space constraints, the code generated by the Windows Form Designer is not included in the listing.

Example 10-15

```
using System;
using System.Drawing;
using System.Collections;
using System.ComponentModel;
```

```
using System.Windows.Forms;
using System.Data;
using StudentNamespace;          // Added for Student class

public class PresentationGUI : System.Windows.Forms.Form
{
    Student aStudent;
    private System.Windows.Forms.Label label1;
    private System.Windows.Forms.TextBox txtBxName;
    private System.Windows.Forms.Button btnShow;
    private System.Windows.Forms.Label label2;
    private System.Windows.Forms.Label label3;
    private System.Windows.Forms.TextBox txtBxAge;
    private System.Windows.Forms.TextBox txtBxID;
    private System.Windows.Forms.Label label4;
    private System.Windows.Forms.Label label5;
    private System.Windows.Forms.TextBox txtBxStudentSleep;
    private System.Windows.Forms.TextBox txtBxPersonSleep;
    private System.ComponentModel.Container components = null;

    public PresentationGUI( )
    {
        InitializeComponent( );
    }
    protected override void Dispose(bool disposing)
    {
        if(disposing)
        {
            if (components != null)
            {
                components.Dispose( );
            }
        }
        base.Dispose(disposing);
    }

    #region Windows Form Designer generated code
    private void InitializeComponent( )
    {
        // Due to space constraints
        // Windows Form Designer code omitted
    }
    #endregion
```

10

```csharp
static void Main( )
{
    Application.Run(new PresentationGUI( ));
}

private void PresentationGUI_Load
            (object sender, System.EventArgs e)
{
    aStudent =
        new Student("123456789", "Maria", "Woo", "CS", 1111);
}

private void btnShow_Click(object sender, System.EventArgs e)
{
    // uses Age property defined in the Person class
    aStudent.Age = 25;

    // Calls overridden ToString() defined in Person class
    this.txtBxName.Text = aStudent.ToString();

    // Calls ToString( ) defined in object class
    this.txtBxAge.Text = aStudent.Age.ToString( );

    // uses StudentID property defined in Student class
    this.txtBxID.Text =
        System.Convert.ToString(aStudent.StudentId);

    // Calls GetSleepAmt( ) defined in Student class
    this.txtBxStudentSleep.Text =
        System.Convert.ToString(aStudent.GetSleepAmt( ));

    // Calls method defined in Student class that
    // has calls to base.GetSleepAmt( ) in Person class
    this.txtBxPersonSleep.Text =
        System.Convert.ToString
                (aStudent.CallOverriddenGetSleepAmt( ));
}
}
```

Figure 10-13 shows the output generated from running the **PresentationGUI**. It references the two DLL components.

Figure 10-13   PresentationGUI output referencing two DLLs

Any number of classes can use the **Student** and **Person** components by instantiating objects of their type. All that is required is that new applications reference the files ending in .dll. A **using** statement can be added for the **namespace** to avoid typing the fully qualified names of the **class** and its members.

 Another option, of course, is to have the actual source code (.CS files) included within the application, as you have been doing with projects you developed in previous chapters. Inheritance does not require use of components.

10

Using ILDASM to View the Assembly

The DLL files cannot be modified or viewed as source code. Visual Studio .NET includes a number of developer tools. One, the **Intermediate Language Disassembler (ILDASM)** tool, is useful for working with files ending in .dll. The tool is used to view an assembly. ILDASM can be run from the command line or added as an external tool to Visual Studio .NET and run from within the IDE. The assembly shows the signatures of all methods, data fields, and properties. One of the ILDASM options is to display the source code as a comment in the assembly. Figure 10-14 shows the assembly for **Student.dll** generated using ILDASM.

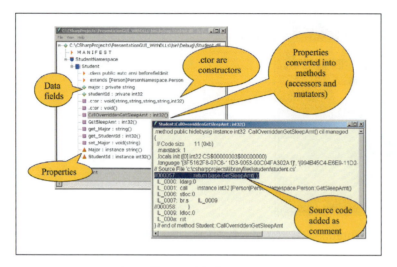

Figure 10-14   Student.dll assembly from ILDASM

> **NOTE** To add ILDASM as a menu option in Visual Studio .NET, select **External Tools** from the **Tools** menu. After selecting Add, you can browse to the location where Ildasm.exe is located. On most systems, it can be found in the C:\Program Files\Microsoft Visual Studio .NET\FrameworkSDK\bin subdirectory. If you do not locate it here, use the Search feature on your system to locate it. Once it is added, it appears as a regular option under your Tools menu.

Viewing the assembly helps you determine how to call or use methods. The ILDASM output includes the identifiers for the data fields and properties and their data types. As illustrated in Figure 10-14, any defined properties shown with a red triangle also appear as methods in the assembly. The identifiers for the property methods are prefixed with **get_** or **set_** depending on whether they are read-only or whether they provide both get and/or set as part of the property.

The assembly also shows the arguments needed for the constructors. **Student** defines two constructors (.ctor). Drilling down in the assembly by clicking on the method names shows the intermediate language (IL) for the method, as illustrated when the **CallOverriddenGetSleepAmt( )** method is selected.

Global Assembly Cache

To run applications that contain DLL components, the DLL files must be in the current directory, a child directory, or the Global Assembly Cache (GAC). The **Global Assembly Cache** is a machinewide code cache that is available on every machine that has the Common

Language Runtime installed. GAC stores assemblies designated to be shared by several applications and also stores some .NET components. Although you could put your assemblies in the GAC, it is best not to do this. Because it is a cache resource, space is limited. Keep your assembly dependencies private by placing them in the application directory.

ABSTRACT CLASSES

With the preceding examples, you can instantiate objects of the **Person class** in the same manner as you construct objects of the **Student class**. Most modern languages, including C#, allow you to add an **abstract** modifier to classes that prohibits other classes from instantiating objects of a **base class**. You can still inherit characteristics from this **base class** in subclasses, which enables you to ensure a certain amount of identical functionality from subclasses. This **base class** can have data and method members. To create an **abstract class** in C# you write:

```
[access modifier] abstract class ClassIdentifier { }  // Base class
```

When you use the **abstract modifier** keyword with a **class**, you mark it so that the **class** can be used only as the **base class** from which other classes can be derived. No objects can then be instantiated of the **base class** type. To indicate that the **Person class** is intended to be used only as a **base class** of other classes, you add the **abstract** keyword as shown in Example 10-16.

10

Example 10-16

```
public abstract class Person
{ . . . }
```

After the **abstract** modifier is added, any attempt to instantiate objects of the **Person class** results in the following syntax error: "Cannot create an instance of the abstract class or interface PersonNamespace.Person." Adding the **abstract** keyword, does not keep you from instantiating classes derived from the **Person class**, such as the Student class.

Abstract Methods

An **abstract class** may contain one or more abstract methods. Abstract methods are only permitted in **abstract** classes. An **abstract method** is one that does not include the implementation details for the method. The method has no body. The implementation details of the method are left up to the classes that are derived from the **base abstract class**. The syntax for creating an **abstract** method is as follows:

```
[access modifier] abstract returnType
               MethodIdentifier([parameter list]) ; // No { }
```

The declaration for an **abstract** method ends with a semicolon following the signature. No braces ({ }) are used with the method. Example 10-17 illustrates defining `Person` as an **abstract class** with an **abstract** method named `GetExerciseHabits( )`.

Example 10-17

```
public abstract class Person
{       :
        public abstract string GetExerciseHabits( ); // No { }
        :
```

Now any and every **class** that derives from the **Person class** must provide the implementation details for the `GetExerciseHabits( )` method. That is what adding the **abstract** keyword does. It is like signing a contract. If you derive from an **abstract base class**, you sign a contract that details how to implement its **abstract** methods.

 You receive a syntax error if you use the keyword **static** or **virtual** when defining an **abstract** method. There is an implicit assumption that the method will be overridden; thus, the keyword **virtual** is unnecessary.

If the **abstract class** includes more than one **abstract** method, derived classes must provide implementation details for every **abstract** method included in the **base class**. Abstract classes can include regular data field members, regular methods, and **virtual** methods in addition to **abstract** methods. Remember that a **virtual** method tags the method as being capable of being overridden in a derived **class**. This does not mean that all derived classes have to provide new implementation details for those tagged as **virtual**, just that they *can*. Other than the fact that the derived **class** must implement all **abstract** methods, no additional special keywords are used when a new **class** is defined to inherit from the **abstract base class**.

All .NET languages only support **single inheritance**, which means that a **class** can extend or derive from at most one **class**. One-way languages such as C# and Java work around this is by implementing multiple interfaces, which are the topic for the next section.

 C++ permits multiple inheritances. A **class** can extend from more than one **base class** in C++. This is not possible in C#, Java, J#, or any of the managed .NET languages.

INTERFACES

When you use the **abstract** modifier with a **class**, you are indicating it is intended to be used only as a **base class**. Normally that **class** is incomplete, in that one or more of its methods are declared as **abstract**. No objects can be constructed from an **abstract class**, but it can still perform a number of functions. In addition to having data members, an **abstract class** can have methods that have full implementation details (bodies).

You can think of an **interface** as a **class** that is totally **abstract**. Interfaces contain no implementation details for any of their members; all their members are considered **abstract**. Even more of a contract is required to use an **interface** than was required for the **abstract** method. By implementing the **interface**, the **class** agrees to define details for all of the interface's methods.

One advantage of using interfaces is the fact that a **class** can implement any number of interfaces. But, you can only inherit from one **class**, **abstract** or nonabstract. An **interface** may even implement multiple interfaces itself. The syntax for defining an **interface** is as follows:

```
[modifier] interface InterfaceIdentifier
{
        // members   -   no access modifiers are used
}
```

The members of an **interface** can be methods, properties, or events. No implementation details are provided by the **interface** for any of its members. The definition of the **interface** simply specifies a signature for the members that must be supplied by classes implementing it. Interfaces are usually named using an uppercase I as the first character, such as **IComparable**, **ISearchable**, or **IPayable**.

Interfaces are useful for forcing functionality in classes that implement them. If a **class** implements the **interface**, it must provide the details for all of the interface's members. Whereas **abstract** classes are used with classes that are closely related, interfaces are often best suited for providing some common functionality to unrelated classes. Because the **abstract class** is used as the **base class**, the "is a" relationship must exist.

Defining an Interface

Interfaces can be defined as members of a **namespace** or **class** or by compiling to a DLL. You do this in much the same way that you created the dynamic link library components for **Person** and **Student**.

An easy approach is to put the **interface** in a separate project. In Visual Studio .NET, use the Class Library template to start, and after you go into the Code Editor, replace the **class** definition with your **interface** definition. There is no separate template for interfaces.

You could also define the interface inside the file that implements it. However, you lose out on the advantages of component-based development.

Figure 10-15 shows an interface that is implemented by the Student class. It contains three abstract methods. Unlike an abstract class, it is not necessary to use the abstract keyword, probably because all methods are abstract. The ITraveler interface in Figure 10-15 includes three member methods. Notice the identifier for the namespace is different from the interface name.

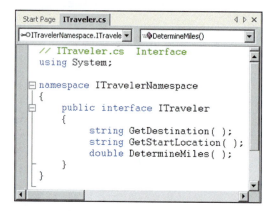

Figure 10-15 ITraveler interface

 Be sure to change the name of the namespace in the interface file also. Otherwise, you experience problems when you try to reference the file and add your using statement.

After you type the statements, build the interface DLL by using a **Build** option from the **Build** menu bar. You can either select **Build>Solution** or **Build** followed by the name of the project. Close the project and get ready to use the interface.

Implement the Interface

If you stored the interface as a separate project and created the DLL, to use the interface you follow the same steps as with the Person and Student DLLs. From the

Solutions Explorer window, add a reference to the file ending in .dll. Type a `using` statement identifying the `namespace` for the `interface`.

The heading for the `class` definition can specify not only a `base class` following the colon, but one or more interfaces as follows:

```
[modifier] class ClassIdentifier   :   identifier [, identifier]
```

To indicate that the `Student class` derives from the `base class` `Person` and implements the `ITraveler interface`, Example 10-18 shows that you add `ITraveler` to the `class` definition line.

Example 10-18

```
public class Student : Person, ITraveler   // Base class comes first
    { . . . }
```

If a `class` implements more than one `interface`, they all appear on the `class` definition line separated by commas. The `base class` is listed first if the `class` is inheriting from a `base class`.

Reviewing Figure 10-15, you see that `ITraveler` has three `abstract` methods as part of its definition. Because the `Student class` is implementing the `ITraveler interface`, it must define the implementation details for all three methods. Example 10-19 includes bodies for the methods. This satisfies the implementation requirements for the three methods.

Example 10-19

```
public string GetDestination( )
{
    return "Home";
}
public string GetStartLocation( )
{
    return "School";
}
public double DetermineMiles( )
{
    return 75.0;
}
```

No other changes need to be made to the **Student class**. Of course, the body of these methods could be as sophisticated as is needed to support the business function. That is all there is to implementing an **interface**. No special changes have to occur to the **Person** or **PresentationGUI** component. They are separate, stand-alone components.

The **Student class** now has access to three additional methods, which are called as if the members were defined in the **Student class**.

For testing purposes the **PresentationGUI class** is modified to include calls to the three methods defined in the **interface**. Figure 10-16 shows the output generated when the new methods are called. They return the travel details.

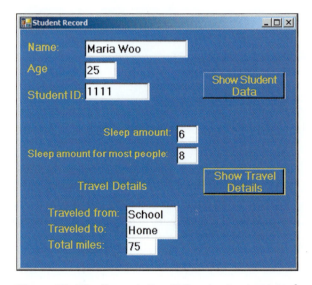

Figure 10-16 PresentationGUI output using interface methods

Additional Label and TextBox objects are added to the **PresentationGUI class**. The visibility property for each of these objects is initially set to **false**. When the Show Travel Details button is clicked, the text boxes are populated with data returned from the new **interface** methods that were implemented in the **Student class**. Then the **Visible** property for each of these new controls is set to **true**. The event-handler method for the button click event, where this code is placed, is shown in Example 10-20.

Example 10-20

```csharp
private void btnShowTravelDetails _Click
                    (object sender, System.EventArgs e)
{
    // GetStartLocation( ) defined as abstract method in ITraveler
    // GetStartLocation( ) implementation details in Student class
    this.txtBxFrom.Text = aStudent.GetStartLocation( );
    this.txtBxFrom.Visible = true;

    // GetDestination( ) defined as abstract method in ITraveler
    // GetDestination( ) implementation details in Student class
    this.txtBxTo.Text = aStudent.GetDestination( );
    this.txtBxTo.Visible = true;

    // As above, but DetermineMiles( ) returns a double, must
    // be converted to a string type
    this.txtBxDistance.Text =
                aStudent.DetermineMiles( ).ToString( );
    this.txtBxDistance.Visible = true;
    this.lblHeading.Visible = true;
    this.lblDistance.Visible = true;
    this.lblFrom.Visible = true;
    this.lblTo.Visible = true;
}
```

10

GetStartLocation( ), GetDestination( ), and DetermineMiles( ) are the members of the ITraveler interface. When the Student class implements this interface, the body of these methods has to be written. Notice that a call to these methods resembles any other call. The class instantiating objects of the Student class do not make a distinction between those methods, methods inherited from another class, or methods that are originally defined in the Student class.

.NET Framework Interfaces

Interfaces play an important role in the .NET Framework. Collection classes such as the Array class, ArrayList class, Hashtable class, Stack class, and Queue class implement a number of interfaces. .NET includes these classes to enable you to manage collection of data. Designing the classes to implement interfaces provides common functionality among them. The .NET Array class, for example, is an abstract class, used as a **base class** for language implementations that support arrays. If you explore the .NET documentation, you find that the signature for the **Array class** shows that it implements several interfaces (**ICloneable**, **IList**, **ICollection**, and **IEnumerable**).

C# and other .NET languages must extend this **base Array class** to add constructs for individual arrays in their languages. This includes a requirement for defining the implementation details for the **interface** methods. For a developer, such as you, all this is happening behind the scenes. But, this **base class**, **Array**, provides methods for manipulating arrays, such as iterating through the elements, searching, adding elements to the array, copying, cloning, clearing, removing elements from the array, reversing elements, and sorting. If you examine this functionality closely, you find that much of it is in place because of the contracts the interfaces are enforcing. The cloning functionality is contracted as part of implementing **ICloneable**. The **IList interface** requires implementation details for **Add( )**, **Clear( )**, **Remove( )**, **Insert( )**, plus other methods. The **ICollection interface** has a method for **CopyTo( )**. The **IEnumerable interface** has a method titled **GetEnumerator( )** that returns an enumerator that can iterate through a collection.

The signatures for some of the collection classes are shown in Example 10-21.

Example 10-21

```
public abstract class Array : ICloneable, IList, ICollection,
                                   IEnumerable
public class ArrayList : IList, ICollection, IEnumerable, ICloneable
public class Queue : ICollection, IEnumerable, ICloneable
public class Stack : ICollection, IEnumerable, ICloneable
public class Hashtable : IDictionary, ICollection, IEnumerable,
    ISerializable, IDeserializationCallback, ICloneable
```

Notice that each of the collection classes implements **ICloneable**. The **Array class** is the only one in the collection that is an **abstract class**. The **Hashtable class** is the only one that implements the **IDeserializationCallback interface**. You are encouraged to explore the documentation for these classes and interfaces. By doing so you can see some of the real power of object-oriented development. As you explore the documentation, you notice that it includes not only the members that must be implemented but also a list of the .NET classes that implement the **interface**. For example, the **IDeserializationCallback interface** has only one member method. Figure 10-17 shows the .NET classes that implement the **IDeserializationCallback interface**.

IDeserializatio...lback Interface   ◁ ▷ ×

☐ ☑ ☑ *.NET Framework Class Library*
IDeserializationCallback Interface

Classes that Implement IDeserializationCallback

Class	Description
AssemblyName	Describes an assembly's unique identity in full.
CompareInfo	Implements a set of methods for culture-sensitive string comparisons.
Hashtable	Represents a collection of key-and-value pairs that are organized based on the hash code of the key.
NameObjectCollectionBase	Provides the abstract (**MustInherit** in Visual Basic) base class for a collection of associated String keys and Object values that can be accessed either with the key or with the index.
PermissionSet	Represents a collection that can contain many different types of permissions.
TextInfo	Defines properties and behaviors, such as casing, that are specific to a writing system.
WindowsIdentity	Represents a Windows user.

Figure 10-17   Classes of .NET Framework that implement the IDeserializationCallback interface

10

Notice that only seven .NET Framework classes implement this **interface**. One of them is the **Hashtable class**. As the figure indicates, the documentation provides links to the classes so that you can drill down and uncover additional information.

 One of the most powerful features of the .NET Framework Class Library and Visual Studio .NET is the extensive library of documentation available. In addition to syntax grammar, it includes tutorials and examples of feature use.

The **Hashtable class** implements **Add( )** by adding an element with the specified key and value pair into a collection. The **ArrayList class** implements **Add( )** by adding an **object** to the end of a collection. Can **Add( )** mean something different based on what type of **object** it is being used with? That is the idea behind polymorphism, the topic of the next section.

POLYMORPHISM

Polymorphism is the ability for classes to provide different implementations of methods that are called by the same name. You already understand and use polymorphism in your everyday life when you determine what situation or **object** is being used with a verb to determine the verb's true behavior. For example, by itself the meaning of the verb "drive" is vague. Driving a car differs from driving a nail, driving a boat, or driving someone crazy. Only when you put "drive" in context do you know what behavior or activity is associated with it.

You have also experienced the use of polymorphism in your programs a number of times. One quick example is with the **ToString( )** method. Remember that this method is defined as one of the four methods of the **Object class**. This means that for every **class** in .NET, both user-defined and Framework classes have a **ToString( )** method. Based on what kind of **object** calls the **ToString ( )** method, it performs a different function. The end result is to convert some **object** to its **string** representation. Converting an **integer** to a **string** is a different activity than converting a single character to a **string**. You can think of it as having a number of different implementations, and the implementation is determined by the type of **object** that calls it. Example 10-22 shows two calls to the **ToString( )** method, which were included in the **PresentationGUI class**.

Example 10-22

```
// Calls overridden ToString( ) defined in Person class
// Returns the first name, a space, and the last name
   this.txtBxName.Text = aStudent.ToString( );

// Calls ToString( ) defined in object class
// Returns a number representing age in a string format
   this.txtBxAge.Text = aStudent.Age.ToString( );
```

As is noted in the comment, the first call to the **ToString( )** method calls the method defined in the **Person class**. Remember that the method overrides the object's **ToString( )**. This implementation of **ToString( )** (included in Example 10-9) was to concatenate the first and last name with a space between them. The CLR recognized that it should use this method because it was called with a **Student object**. **Student** did not contain an implementation of the **ToString( )** method; thus, the CLR looked next to the **class** from which it had been derived, the **Person class**.

The second call to the **ToString( )** method does not use the **Person** class's implementation. Notice that this call is made with an **int object**. The **Age** property returns an **int**. Thus, based on the **object** making the call, the **ToString( )** method from the **Object class** is called.

Polymorphism allows a method of a **class** to be called without regard to what specific implementation it provides. Thus, in .NET, polymorphism is implemented through interfaces, inheritance, and the use of **abstract** classes.

Polymorphic Programming in .NET

As you saw, multiple classes can implement the same `interface` or implement more than one `interface`. The `interface` describes the methods and the types of parameters each method member needs to receive and return, but it leaves the actual details of the body of the method up to the classes that implement the `interface`. Every `class` that implements the `interface` may have a completely different behavior. The method name is the same in all the classes implementing the `interface`, but the functionality can be much different from one `class` to another.

 The black box concept of object-oriented development comes into play here. You do not have to know how the method goes about doing its work. All you have to know is what arguments to send, if any, and what you expect to be accomplished when the object finishes it work. That may be a return value or just an indication that the method is complete.

Through inheritance, polymorphism is made possible by allowing classes to override **base class** members. This makes **dynamic binding** possible. The CLR determines which method to call at runtime based on which `object` calls the method. Marking the method with the `virtual` keyword enables derived classes to write their own functionality for the method.

 Remember that a `class` does not have to `override` a `virtual` method. The `class` can choose to use the `base` class's implementation.

10

Because an **abstract class** cannot be instantiated, the features of both interfaces and inheritance come into play with polymorphic programming. Through the use of **abstract** classes, classes that derive from them are forced to include implementation details for any **abstract** method. Unlike interfaces, which simply provide the heading for the methods that have to be implemented, some or all of the members of an **abstract class** can be implemented. Abstract classes can also include data members, properties, events, and methods. The methods can be marked as `virtual` or as `abstract`, or be completely implemented. The determination of which method to use is based on the `object` that makes the call.

Inheritance is very useful for adding to the functionality of an existing `class` without having to reinvent the wheel with each new application. With .NET you have to remember that you only have single inheritance. A `class` can implement multiple interfaces, but it must provide the implementation details for all of the interface's methods. Component programming is probably the way of the future for development. It is a powerful technique that enables you to implement the multiple interfaces of an `object` easily. The common goal of all these advanced object-oriented features is to enable polymorphic programming.

PROGRAMMING EXAMPLE: STUDENTGOV APPLICATION

This example demonstrates developing an application using a number of components. An **abstract base class** is created to include data members and properties. An **interface** is designed. Three classes are derived from the **base abstract class**; two of those classes implement the **interface**. After these components are stored in a **class** library, they are available for use by any number of applications. To test the design, a Windows application presentation **class** is created.

An application is written for the Student Government Association. The problem specification is shown in Figure 10-18.

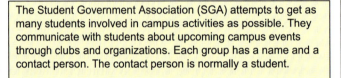

The Student Government Association (SGA) attempts to get as many students involved in campus activities as possible. They communicate with students about upcoming campus events through clubs and organizations. Each group has a name and a contact person. The contact person is normally a student.

During registration all students pay a small activity fee, which is transferred into an SGA account. SGA then disperses money from its budget to groups on campus. This enables a number of individual organizations to provide activities for their members. In order to receive funding, each group registers with the SGA at the end of the academic year for the upcoming year. A preset dollar amount is dispersed to groups based on their classification type. Groups funded include academic clubs at $600 per group and fraternity and sorority organizations at $500 per group. The SGA also keeps records on intramural groups for communication purposes; however, they do not receive any funding.

Design an application that displays on a Windows form the group name, contact person, and amount of funding, if any, the group receives. Other applications may be designed in the future to display a club's meeting location, date, and time, or the primary sporting event for an intramural group, and the address and status of a fraternity or sorority group.

Figure 10-18   Problem specification for StudentGov example

Analyze the Problem

You should review the problem specification in Figure 10-18 to ensure that you understand the problem definition. Objects should be able to be instantiated for the following types of groups:

- Club
- Fraternity and sorority
- Intramural

These groups share some common characteristics. Each has a unique name and a contact person. Two of the groups (clubs, and fraternities and sororities) may receive funding from the Student Government Association. Fraternities and sororities that are chartered receive funding; others cannot.

Unique information regarding clubs include the date, time, and place they hold their meetings. The type of sport associated with the intramural group is unique to the Intramural classification. Distinctive characteristics for the fraternity or sorority classification include whether the group is chartered or not and their house address. After you understand the problem definition, you can begin to abstract out the characteristics for each of the classes. Table 10-1 shows the data fields organized by group. The common data is included with the Organization category.

Data

10

Table 10-1   Data fields organized by class

Class	Identifier	Data type
Organization	orgName	string
Organization	primaryContact	string
Organization	fundedAmt	decimal
Club	meetingDay	string
Club	meetingTime	string
Club	meetingLocation	string
FratSorority	chartered	bool
FratSorority	houseAddress	string
Intramural	sportType	string

It should not be possible to create a group in this application unless it is associated with a club, fraternity, sorority, or intramural team.

Design a Solution

The desired output is to display data on a Windows form about the different organizations. An application is created using the Windows **Form** **class** to test the design. It should ensure that objects can be instantiated from the **Club**, **FratSorority**, and **Intramural** classes, but not from the **Organization** **class**. It should make sure that derived classes have access to **base class** members. Figure 10-19 shows a prototype for the form.

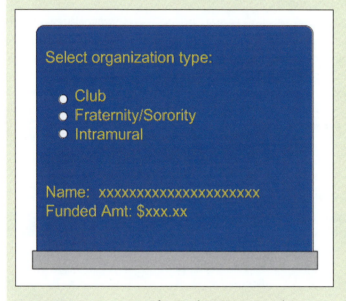

Figure 10-19   Prototype for StudentGov example

The business logic is separated into several classes to include an **Organization** **class** that serves as a **base class**. No objects should be instantiated from this **class**, so it is defined as an **abstract class**. Derived classes of **Club**, **Intramural**, and **FratSorority** are defined to inherit from the **Organization** **class**. The **IFunding** **interface** is defined to force functionality of setting the funding amount. **FratSorority** and **Club** both implement this **interface**.

Class diagrams are used to help design and document these characteristics. Figure 10-20 shows the **class** diagrams for the **StudentGov** example.

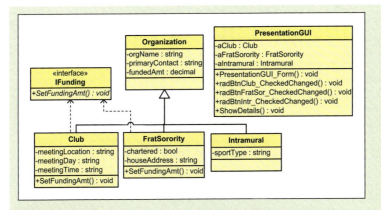

Figure 10-20 Class diagrams for StudentGov example

The dotted arrows in Figure 10-20 represent the **interface** link. Notice that the Unified Modeling Language (UML) notation for the interfaces includes the name of the methods in italics, indicating that implementation details must be defined.

 UML is the industry-standard modeling language for specifying and documenting both data and processes. Class diagrams are one of the modeling diagrams used with object-oriented applications. The standards for UML were released in November 1997. To find out more about UML visit *www.omg.org*, the Object Management Group's Web site responsible for the release.

The **interface object** cannot have member data, just methods. The **class** diagrams do not show the properties. No accessor or mutator methods are defined for accessing or changing the **private** data members of the classes. However, during design it is decided that properties are defined with get and set behaviors for most data members. Minimal business logic is needed for this application; thus, no pseudocode or additional design tool is constructed.

Code the Solution   After you complete the design, it is time to translate the design into source code. For this application, six projects are created inside one solution. It is not necessary to put the files under a single solution umbrella. This was done for ease of demonstration. All of the classes could be defined as stand-alone components. The **interface** and all classes except the **PresentationGUI** could be stored in your library with other DLL files. The PresentationGUI generates an EXE file; all other projects generate files ending with a .dll extension.

10

The Organization class is created first. The DLL is built so that other classes can reference it during their design. The source code for the Organization class is shown first:

```csharp
// Organization.cs
// Abstract class used a base class
using System;
namespace OrganizationNamespace
{
    public abstract class Organization
    {
        private string orgName;
        private string primaryContact;
        private decimal fundedAmt;

        public Organization(string name, string contact)
        {
            orgName = name;
            primaryContact = contact;
            fundedAmt = 0M;
        }

        public Organization ( )
        {
            orgName = "unknown";
            primaryContact = "unknown";
            fundedAmt = 0M;
        }
        // Properties for each private data member follows
        public decimal FundedAmt
        {
            set
            {
                fundedAmt = value;
            }
            get
            {
                return fundedAmt;
            }
        }

        public string OrgName
        {
            set
            {
                orgName = value;
            }
```

```
        get
        {
            return orgName;
        }
    }

    private string PrimaryContact
    {
        set
        {
            primaryContact = value;
        }
        get
        {
            return primaryContact;
        }
    }
  }
}
```

With the exception of the fact that the `Organization class` is defined as
`abstract`, nothing else differs in this `class` from previous exercises. A number of
properties are defined.

The file containing the `interface` is created next. Like the `Organization class`, it
is a stand-alone component. Using the Class Library template in Visual Studio, the following source code is added to the solution:

```
// IFunding.cs    interface
using System;
namespace IFundingNamespace
{
        public interface IFunding
        {
                // No implementation details for SetFundingAmt( )
                // Method must be defined by classes
                // that implement the interface
                void SetFundingAmt( );
        }
}
```

The `interface` includes one method. Classes that implement it must provide the body
for the method. After this DLL is built, the subclasses can reference it.

The `Intramural class` is defined next. Like the `IFunding interface`, a new
proj-ect is created after building and closing the `interface`. The Class Library template
is selected as the project type. The selection on the Visual Studio .NET Start page that
enables the source code to be added to the solution is selected.

10

When you create a new project with another project open, the New Project dialog box includes two radio buttons enabling you to add the new project to the solution or close the solution. The recommendation here for the `interface class` is to add the project to the solution. Review Figure 10-6 to see the two radio buttons.

`Intramural` inherits from the `Organization class`, but does not implement the `interface`. To use the `Organization` component in the `Intramural` project, a reference had to be made to that DLL before typing the program statements.

 Remember that one way to add the reference is to select the project in the Solution Explorer window, and then choose Add Reference from the Project menu bar. Because each of the components is stored as a separate project, be sure to browse the project subdirectory to locate the DLL in the bin\debug directory.

The `using OrganizationNamespace;` statement is also added to eliminate the need to fully qualify references to the `Organization class`. The source code for the `Intramural class` is shown next:

```
// Intramural.cs
using System;

// OrganizationNamespace added to avoid fully qualifying references
using OrganizationNamespace;

namespace IntramuralNamespace
{
    public class Intramural : Organization
    {
        private string sportType;

        public Intramural(string name, string pContact,
                          string sport)
            // Call to Organization (base) class constructor
            : base(name, pContact)

        {
            sportType = sport;
        }

        // Default constructor
        public Intramural( )

        {
            sportType = "unknown";
        }
```

```
        // Property for sportType
        public string SportType
        {
            get
            {
                return sportType;
            }
            set
            {
                sportType = value;
            }
        }
    }
}
```

A number of references were added during design to build the application. Figure 10-21 shows which references are needed for the six projects in the **StudentGov** solution. It is best to add the references when you first create the project.

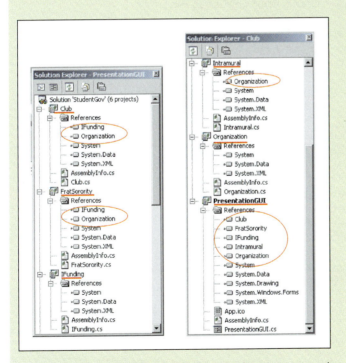

Figure 10-21   References added to StudentGov example

Notice that **IFunding** and **Organization** contain no additional references beyond those automatically added by Visual Studio .NET.

Both the **Club** and **FratSorority** classes must add references to **Organization** and **IFunding**. Remember that placing the **using** directive at the beginning of the file allows you to use the unqualified **class** names to reference methods during design. The source code for the **Club class** follows:

```
// Club.cs
using System;

// OrganizationNamespace added to avoid fully qualifying references
using OrganizationNamespace;
using IFundingNamespace;

namespace ClubNamespace
{
    public class Club : Organization, IFunding
    {
        private string meetingLocation;

        // Private member data
        private string meetingDay;
        private string meetingTime;

        public Club(string name, string pContact,
                    string mLoc, string mDay,
                    string mTime)
            // Call to base constructor
            : base(name, pContact)

        {
            meetingLocation = mLoc;
            meetingDay = mDay;
            meetingTime = mTime;
        }

        // Required method - because of interface
        public void SetFundingAmt()
        {
            FundedAmt = 600M;
        }
    }
}
```

As you review the code for the **Club**, **FratSorority**, and **Intramural** classes, notice that each one has one constructor that calls the **base** constructor in the

Organization class. They send values for the organization name (orgName) and the primary contact person for the group (primaryContact).

The SetFundingAmt( ) method from the IFunding interface is implemented in the Club and FratSorority classes. The source code for the FratSorority class follows:

```csharp
// FratSorority.cs
using System;
using OrganizationNamespace;
using IFundingNamespace;
namespace FratSororityNamespace
{
    public class FratSorority : Organization, IFunding
    {
        private bool chartered; // Private member data
        private string houseAddress;

        public FratSorority( )
        {
            houseAddress = "unknown";
            chartered = false;
        }

        public FratSorority(string name, string pContact,
            bool isChartered,
            string address)
            : base(name, pContact)
            // Call to base constructor
        {
            houseAddress = address;
            chartered = isChartered;
        }

        // Required method - because of interface
        public  void SetFundingAmt( )
        {
            if(chartered)
            {
                FundedAmt = 500M;
            }
            else
            {
                FundedAmt = 0M;
            }
        }
}
```

10

```csharp
        // Properties
        private bool Chartered
        {
            get
            {
                return chartered;
            }
            set
            {
                chartered = value;
            }
        }
        private string HouseAddress
        {
            get
            {
                return houseAddress;
            }
            set
            {
                houseAddress = value;
            }
        }
    }
}
```

The last **class**, **PresentationGUI**, is used to test the components. It is a GUI Windows application. Notice that Figure 10-21 shows that a reference is added to each of the components for the **PresentationGUI class**. In this **class**, objects are constructed of the **Club**, **FratSorority**, and **Intramural** classes. The **PresentationGUI class** includes three **RadioButton** objects inside a **GroupBox object**. The radio buttons correspond to the three different types of organization objects being constructed. The source listing for this **class** follows. Due to space constraints, some of the Windows form-generated code is omitted. Table 10-2 shows what properties are set for the **Form** and control objects, and extra comments are added to the source code to aid you in following the example.

Table 10-2 PresentationGUI property values

Name	Object type	Property	Value
PresentationGUI	Form	BackColor	Teal
PresentationGUI	Form	Font	12F
PresentationGUI	Form	ForeColor	Yellow

Table 10-2   PresentationGUI property values (continued)

Name	Object type	Property	Value
PresentationGUI	Form	Text	Student Government
groupBox1	GroupBox	Text	Select organization type
radBtnIntr	RadioButton	Text	Intramural team
radBtnFratSor	RadioButton	Text	Fraternity/Sorority
radBtnClub	RadioButton	Text	Club
label1	Label	Text	Name:
label1	Label	Visible	false
label2	Label	Text	Funding Amt:
label2	Label	Visible	false
txtBxName	TextBox	Text	" "
txtBxName	TextBox	Visible	false
txtBxFund	TextBox	Text	" "
txtBxFund	TextBox	Visible	false

The final project source code listing is shown next.

```
// PresentationGUI.cs
using System;
using System.Drawing;
using System.Collections;
using System.ComponentModel;
using System.Windows.Forms;
using System.Data;
using ClubNamespace;          // Namespace for Club class
using IntramuralNamespace;    // Namespace for Intramural class
using FratSororityNamespace;  // Namespace for FratSorority class

namespace PresentationGUI
{
    public class PresentationGUI :  System.Windows.Forms.Form
    {
        private Club aClub;       // Object of Club class
        private Intramural aTeam; // Object of Intramural class
        // Object of FratSorority class
        private FratSorority aFratSorority;
        private System.Windows.Forms.GroupBox groupBox1;
        private System.Windows.Forms.Label label1;
        private System.Windows.Forms.Label label2;
        private System.Windows.Forms.RadioButton radBtnIntr;
```

```csharp
private System.Windows.Forms.RadioButton radBtnFratSor;
private System.Windows.Forms.RadioButton radBtnClub;
private System.Windows.Forms.TextBox txtBxName;
private System.Windows.Forms.TextBox txtBxFund;
private System.ComponentModel.Container components = null;

public PresentationGUI( )
{
    InitializeComponent( );
}
// Windows Form Designer Code omitted. Code added controls
// to the Form object and set properties.

static void Main( )
{
    Application.Run(new PresentationGUI( ));
}

// Objects are instantiated when the form is loaded.
// Another GUI could be designed for entering data.
private void PresentationGUI_Load(object sender,
                    System.EventArgs e)
{
    aClub = new Club
        ("ACM", "Jones", "Davis 203",
            "Tues", "12:30");
    aFratSorority = new FratSorority
        ("Delta PI", "Brenda Wynn",
            true, "86 SmithField");
    aTeam = new Intramural
        ("Winners", "Joe Kitchen", "VolleyBall");

}

// Three CheckedChanged event-handler methods included.
// Double-clicking on the RadioButton adds the method
// heading and registers the event.
private void radBtnClub_CheckedChanged(object sender,
                    System.EventArgs e)
{
    this.txtBxName.Text = aClub.OrgName;
    this.aClub.SetFundingAmt( );
    this.txtBxFund.Text = aClub.FundedAmt.ToString("C");
    ShowDetails( );
 }
```

```
    private void radBtnFratSor_CheckedChanged(object sender,
                            System.EventArgs e)
{
    this.txtBxName.Text = aFratSorority.OrgName;
    this.aFratSorority.SetFundingAmt( );
    this.txtBxFund.Text =
        aFratSorority.FundedAmt.ToString("C");
    ShowDetails( );
}
    private void radBtnIntr_CheckedChanged(object sender,
                            System.EventArgs e)
{
    this.txtBxName.Text = aTeam.OrgName;
    this.txtBxFund.Text = aTeam.FundedAmt.ToString("C");
    ShowDetails( );
}

// Area at the bottom of the form initally set to
// Visible = false using the Properties Window.
// Since each of the RadioButton objects needed to reset
// the objects to Visible = true, a method is used.
public void ShowDetails( )
{
    this.txtBxName.Visible = true;
    this.label1.Visible = true;
    this.txtBxFund.Visible = true;
    this.label2.Visible = true;
}
    }
}
```

When you complete the `PresentationGUI`, it should be set as the startup project because it is the only project in the solution that contains a `Main( )` method. One way to do this, as illustrated in Figure 10-22, is to right-click the `PresentationGUI` project in the Solution Explorer window. When you right-click, you see the following option: Set as StartUp Project. This is necessary because you have multiple projects in a single solution.

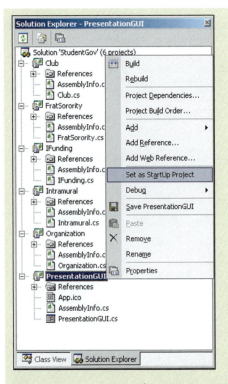

Figure 10-22 Setting the StartUp Project

The `PresentationGUI` is considered by many developers an example of a **client application**. It is considered a client because it is using the components that you created. Other client applications can make use of these same components. When you build the solution and run the application, Visual Studio copies the DLL from each of the references that were added into the application's private subdirectory. If you explore the files that are created, you notice you have multiple copies of the DLLs. Actually each project has its own copy of any referenced DLLs. Figure 10-23 shows the directory listing for the `PresentationGUI` folder. Notice that it contains copies of all of the .dlls and one .exe. This makes up the `PresentationGUI` assembly.

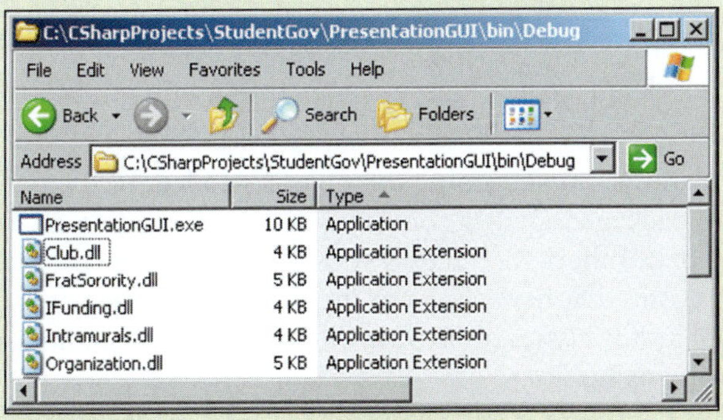

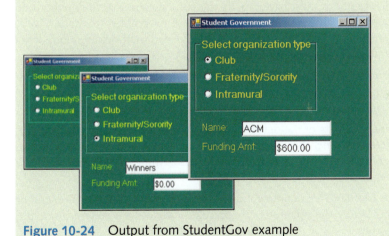

Figure 10-23   Part of the PresentationGUI assembly

The application can be run by double-clicking on the EXE file here in the folder containing the EXE file, or it can be run from within Visual Studio .NET as you have done with all the applications you have developed previously. The original user interface as it appears when the application is launched is shown in Figure 10-24. The figure contains overlapping windows produced by clicking the `RadioButton` objects.

10

Figure 10-24   Output from StudentGov example

QUICK REVIEW

1. For a language to be considered a true object-oriented programming (OOP) language, it must support abstraction, encapsulation, inheritance, and polymorphism.

2. Abstraction is used to identify and determine the objects needed for the design. Encapsulation is used to package together common characteristics into a **class** consisting of behaviors and data. Inheritance allows you to create a general **class** and then define specialized classes that have access to the members of the general **class**. Polymorphism is the ability for classes to provide different implementations of methods that are called by the same name.

3. Instead of writing a program that includes all the features in a single file, development today is often geared toward writing multitier applications consisting of a number of components.

4. Components are implemented through classes in C#.

5. A colon is used as a separator between the derived **class** and the **base class**. The **base class** is sometimes called the super or parent **class**. Classes that inherit from a **base class** are called derived classes or subclasses.

6. Constructors, named the same name as the **class** name, are defined with **public** access.

7. Overridden methods must have exactly the same signature as the methods they override. New functionality is normally defined with overridden methods. Overloaded methods must have a different signature. Overloaded methods are often defined to perform a similar behavior, but with different data types.

8. The **override** keyword allows a method to provide a new implementation of a method inherited from a **base class**. Base methods are normally defined as **virtual** if they are to be overridden.

9. If you want members of the derived classes to have access to members in the **base class**, define the members using **protected** access. Private restricts access to **class** members only. Public opens access to any **class**. Internal members are accessible only within files in the same assembly.

10. To call the **base class** constructor, **base( )**, precede it with a colon and place it in the heading before the opening curly brace. Arguments can be sent inside the parentheses if constructors other than the default are used.

11. Classes can be compiled and stored as a dynamic link library (DLL) file and then referenced by any other applications. To do this in Visual Studio .NET, select the Class Library template option from the Start page.

12. .NET enables multiple languages such as Visual Basic, J#, and C# to be used to create a single application. The only requirement for doing this is that a project must include source code files from only one language.

13. After you create your own DLL file, to use it in an application one of the first things you should do is add a reference to the DLL. Just adding the reference is not enough. You have either to add a `using` statement at the top of the source code file indicating which `namespace` is used, or to qualify the `class` and members by using the `namespace` and a dot before each use of the `class` and its members.

14. Add the `abstract` modifier to classes to prohibit other classes from instantiating objects of a `base class`.

15. Abstract classes can include regular data field members, regular methods, and `virtual` methods in addition to `abstract` methods. Derived classes must provide implementation details for every `abstract` method included in the `base class`.

16. Think of an `interface` as a `class` that is totally `abstract`. All of its members are considered `abstract`. No implementation details are provided by the `interface` for any of its members.

17. One advantage of using interfaces is the fact that a `class` can implement any number of interfaces. But, inheritance can only be from one `class`, `abstract` or nonabstract.

18. To create an `interface` in C#, you use the Class Library template from the Start page. Interfaces can be compiled to a DLL. Instead of using the keyword `class`, you use `interface` in the heading.

19. If a `class` implements more than one `interface`, they all appear on the `class` definition line separated by commas. The `base class` is listed first.

10

20. Interfaces play an important role in the .NET Framework. `Collection` classes like the `Array class`, `ArrayList class`, `Hashtable class`, `Stack class`, and `Queue class` implement a number of interfaces.

21. One of the most powerful features of the .NET Framework Class Library and Visual Studio .NET is the extensive library of documentation available. In addition to syntax and grammar, the library includes tutorials and examples of how features are used. You are strongly encouraged to explore this material.

22. Through inheritance and marking the method with the `virtual` keyword, polymorphism is made possible by allowing classes to override `base class` members.

23. Through the use of `abstract` classes, polymorphic programming is possible. Classes that derive from `abstract` classes are forced to include implementation details for any `abstract` method. Polymorphic programming is encouraged with interfaces, because interfaces provide the heading for the methods. Classes that implement the `interface` must provide implementation details.

24. ILDASM is a tool available in Visual Studio .NET that is used to view an assembly. The assembly shows the signatures of all methods, data fields, and properties.

Exercises

1. To be considered a true object-oriented language, designers of the language must provide support for:

    a. properties

    b. objects

    c. inheritance

    d. IDEs

    e. command-line tools

2. Packaging data attributes and behaviors into a single unit so that the implementation details can be hidden describes an object-oriented feature called:

    a. abstraction

    b. inheritance

    c. objects

    d. encapsulation

    e. polymorphism

3. Polymorphism is useful in languages because it facilitates _____ methods.

    a. overriding

    b. overloading

    c. overstriking

    d. interfacing

    e. inheriting

4. Components are normally compiled and stored with a file extension of:

    a. .exe

    b. .sno

    c. .proj

    d. .dll

    e. .csc

5. The "is a" relationship is associated with:

    a. inheritance

    b. interfaces

    c. polymorphism

    d. encapsulation

    e. all of the above

6. In C#, the super **class**, or **base class** of all others, is:

    a. super

    b. **base**

    c. value

    d. **class**

    e. **object**

7. Using the following declaration, which of the statements below is true?

    public class aClass : bClass, cClass

    a. **cClass** is an **interface**.

    b. **aClass** is the derived **class**.

    c. **bClass** is the **base class**.

    d. all of the above

    e. none of the above

8. If you want to keep classes that instantiate objects of a **class** from changing their data members, but enable derived classes to change **base class** data members, the data members in the **base class** should be defined with a/an _____ access modifier.

    a. **private**

    b. **public**

    c. **internal**

    d. **static**

    e. **protected**

9. Constructors are normally defined with a/an _____ access modifier; data members with a/an _____ access modifier; and properties with a/an _____ access modifier.

    a. **public, public, public**

    b. **private, private, private**

    c. **public, public, private**

    d. **public, private, public**

    e. **private, public, public**

10. To enable derived classes to override methods defined in a **base class**, methods should be defined using a(an) _____ keyword.

    a. **virtual**

    b. **override**

    c. **static**

    d. **public**

    e. none of the above

10

11. In .NET, applications are deployed in terms of:

    a. .dll's

    b. .exe's

    c. solutions

    d. assemblies

    e. applications

12. The one constraint for having a solution include code from more than one programming language is the requirement that:

    a. Each project must consist of code in one language only.

    b. Each project must reference all the other projects.

    c. A `using` directive must be placed in the source code files for each project.

    d. The solution can have no more than 10 projects.

    e. Both b and c are correct.

13. To avoid having to use fully qualify referenced classes, you could:

    a. Add a reference to the `class`.

    b. Add an import statement for the `class`.

    c. Add a `using` directive.

    d. Inherit from the `class`.

    e. Package the classes in the same solution.

14. A `class` from which an `object` cannot be instantiated could be a(n):

    a. `base class`

    b. derived `class`

    c. implemented `class`

    d. `virtual class`

    e. `abstract class`

15. Classes can extend or derive from _____ class(es) and implement _____ class(es).

    a. one, one

    b. many, one

    c. many, many

    d. one, many

    e. one, twelve

16. Abstract classes can include:

    a. data members

    b. `abstract` methods

   c. nonabstract methods

   d. properties

   e. all of the above

17. Interfaces can include:

   a. data members

   b. `abstract` methods

   c. nonabstract methods

   d. properties

   e. all of the above

18. _____ allows a method of a `class` to be called without regard to what specific implementation it provides.

   a. Polymorphism

   b. Abstraction

   c. Assemblies

   d. Versioning

   e. Class libraries

19. The feature that is included as part of C#, but not J#, that reduces the need for accessors and mutators is a(n):

   a. event

   b. `base class`

   c. dynamic link library

   d. property

   e. package

20. A multitier application would probably have:

   a. a `class` defined to interface with the user

   b. one or more classes defined to handle the business logic

   c. a `class` defined to deal with the data

   d. a client `class`

   e. all of the above

21. Explain the difference between an overloaded and an overridden method. Give an example of each.

22. How do `abstract` classes differ from `interface` classes?

10

23. Given the following program segment, answer questions a through g.

```
public class Employee
{
        private int empNumber;
        private decimal pay;
}
```

a. Define a read-only property for the **pay** data member.

b. Define a default constructor for **Employee**.

c. Define a more useful constructor that could be used to instantiate objects of the **class**.

d. Define a subclass named **HourlyEmployee** with additional members of **hours** and **payrate**.

e. Define a constructor for **HourlyEmployee** that sends the employee number to the **Employee class** when an **object** is instantiated. Are there any changes needed in the **Employee class**? If so, what?

f. Create a method in the **Employee class** to determine the pay amount. It should be capable of being overridden in subclasses.

g. Provide new implementation details in the **HourlyEmployee class** for the method you defined in the preceding question (f).

PROGRAMMING EXERCISES

1. Create a **base class** to hold information about sporting teams on campus. It should not be possible to instantiate the **class**. Include common characteristics such as primary coach and type of sport. Define a minimum of one **virtual** method.

2. Select two types of sporting teams and define subclasses for them. These classes should inherit from a **base** team **class** such as that created in Exercise 1. Include unique characteristics about the sport. For example, for a sporting team such as a tennis team, the field location and/or the person to contact to restring rackets may be of interest. Be sure to implement any **virtual** methods included in the base **class**.

3. Create a **class** to test your designs of the **base** team **class** and individual sporting team subclasses. Your **class** can be a console or Windows application. For an extra challenge, make DLL components out of the sporting classes and add a reference to them in the presentation **class**.

4. Define an **interface** for the sporting team called **ITraveler**. It should include a method that returns whether the next event is home or away. Modify your design for Exercises 1 through 3 to implement the **interface**.

5. Define an application to include classes for **Student**, **GraduateStudent**, and **UnderGraduate**. **GraduateStudent** should include a data field for the type of undergraduate degree awarded, such as B.A. or B.S., and the location of the institution that awarded the degree. **UnderGraduate** should include classification (for example, freshman, sophomore), and parent or guardian name and address. Create a presentation **class** to test your design.

6. Create a **base class** to store characteristics about a loan. Define subclasses of automobile loan and house loan. Include unique characteristics in the derived classes. Create a presentation **class** to test your design by displaying information about both types of loans.

7. Create a **base** banking account. Decide what characteristics are common for checking and saving accounts and include these characteristics in the **base class**. Define subclasses for checking and savings. In your design, do not allow the banking **base** account to be instantiated—only the checking and saving subclasses. Include a presentation **class** to test your design.

8. Create a **base class** titled **ReadingMaterial**. Include subclasses of **Book** and **Magazine**. Define an **interface** called **IPrintable** that has a method that returns the date of publication. Design your classes so that common characteristics are placed in the **ReadingMaterial class**. Include a presentation **class** to test your design.

9. Create a ticket reservation **class** for issuing tickets to on-campus events such as plays, musicals, and home basketball games. Design the ticket **class** to be **abstract**. Create subclasses for at least three different types of events. Determine unique characteristics for each of the events. Define a client application to test your **class** designs.

10. Create a housing application for a property manager. Include a **base class** named **Housing**. Include data characteristics such as address and year built. Include a **virtual** method that returns the total projected rental amount. Define an **interface** named **IUnits** that has a method that returns the number of units. Create subclasses of **MultiFamily** and **SingleFamily**. **SingleFamily** should include characteristics such as size in square feet and availability of garage. **MultiFamily** might include characteristics such as the number of units. Define a presentation **class** to test your design.

Handling Exceptions and Stored Data

In this chapter, you will:

- ○ Learn about exceptions, including how they are thrown and caught
- ○ Become aware of and use exception-handling techniques to include `try`...`catch`...`finally` clauses
- ○ Explore the many exception classes and learn how to write and order multiple `catch` clauses
- ○ Instantiate objects of the file stream classes and use their members to create and process text files
- ○ Be introduced to technologies used for accessing databases
- ○ Learn how to access and update databases using ADO.NET classes

This chapter introduces you to a special type of error, called an exception. **Exceptions**, as the name implies, are unexpected conditions that happen infrequently. They are usually associated with error conditions that cause abnormal terminations if they are not handled. The chapter introduces structured exception-handling techniques called `try...catch...finally`, which are available in C# and other languages. You also learn that not all program errors should be treated as exceptions. Exception-handling techniques should be reserved for error conditions from which your program cannot recover.

In this chapter you also discover how to use data from sources other than the keyboard for your applications. You write programs that access data stored in files and database tables. The file stream and ActiveX Data Objects (ADO.NET) classes are introduced. You use the stream classes to read and write records to text files and use ADO.NET to retrieve and update data in databases such as those created using Microsoft Access. You also work with data reader objects for read-only access to databases and use dataset objects to update data table values.

EXCEPTIONS

For most of the programs you have developed to this point, you have assumed nothing unusual would occur. Given perfect situations for running applications, your programs may perform beautifully. However, errors do occur. Some circumstances are beyond the control of the programmer, and unless provisions are made for handling exceptions, your program may crash or produce erroneous results. It is now time to take your programming skills to the next level and learn how to prevent abnormal terminations.

You have probably experienced unhandled exceptions being thrown while you browsed Web pages or during your development of C# programs. Were you ever asked if you wanted to debug some application while you were on the Internet? Or, have you seen a screen similar to Figure 11-1 or Figure 11-3 while you were developing your C# applications in Visual Studio .NET?

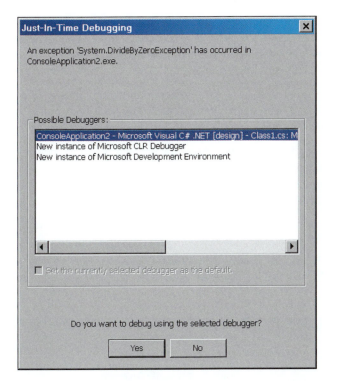

Figure 11-1 Exception thrown

When a Just-In-Time dialog window such as that in Figure 11-1 is displayed, you normally do not want to try to debug the application while it is running. Clicking the **No** button when you are creating a console application in Visual Studio .NET often causes a message to be displayed that is similar to that shown in Figure 11-2. This output indicates that an unhandled exception has occurred. It also identifies what caused the exception ("Attempted to divide by zero.").

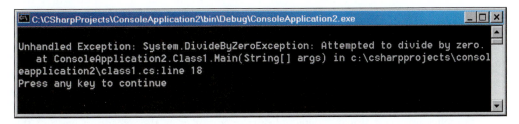

Figure 11-2 Unhandled exception in a console application

The messages displayed in Figures 11-1 and 11-2 were generated when a console application was run without debugging being started (**Debug >Start without Debugging**). The program, therefore, performed an illegal division by zero.

The messages from Figures 11-1 and 11-2 were generated during runtime, and the entire application halted. No error had been detected when the program was compiled. It was only when the application ran that the program crashed and the message was displayed.

 Remember that during the compilation stage, the only errors that are detected are those in which specific statements violate the syntax or grammar of the language, such as omission of a semicolon at the end of a statement.

Another type of message you may have seen is shown in Figure 11-3. You learned earlier that you can run applications in Visual Studio in two ways: using the same application you can select either **Debug>Start** or **Debug>Start Without Debugging**. Selecting **Debug>Start** generates a message similar to that shown in Figure 11-3.

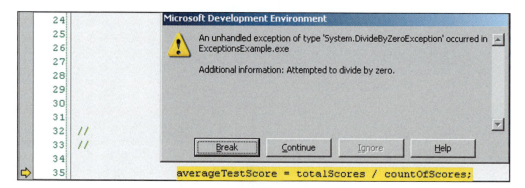

Figure 11-3   Unhandled exception thrown—dividing by zero

Notice in Figure 11-3 that a yellow arrow marks the line of the code where the error was found and the erroneous code itself is highlighted in yellow. These markings were placed by Visual Studio .NET. To stop debugging, click the **Continue** button.

The exact message from Figure 11-3 is also generated within a Windows application during runtime when an attempt to divide by zero is reached. The Windows application had a statement in a button event-handler method that tried to divide by zero. Like the console application that generated the messages for Figures 11-1 and 11-2, the divide by zero in the Windows application error was not detected during compilation; the exception was not thrown until the user selected the button wired to the event-handler method that included the division statement. If that button had never been pressed, the application would have run smoothly.

Raising an Exception

If a program encounters an error such as division by zero during runtime, and the program cannot recover from the error, it **raises** or **throws an exception**. When this happens, execution halts in the current method and the Common Language Runtime (CLR) attempts to locate an exception handler to handle the exception. An **exception handler** is a block of code that is executed when an exception occurs. You learn how to write exception handlers in the next section.

If the CLR finds an exception handler in the current method, control is transferred to that code. If the current method does not contain an exception handler, that method is halted, and the parent method that called the method that threw the exception attempts to handle the exception. The exception is said to be **thrown back** to the calling method. If more than two methods are used, the exception continues to be thrown backwards until it reaches the topmost method. If none of the methods includes code to handle the error, the CLR handles the exception—by halting the entire application. This can be very abrupt, as you saw with the messages displayed in Figure 11-1 through 11-3. Because data can be lost, you of course want to try to avoid such an experience with your programs. If the CLR handles the exception by halting your application, it is called an **unhandled exception**.

Bugs, Errors, and Exceptions

You learned that, in some instances, you can use selection statements, such as `if...else`, to programmatically prevent your programs from crashing. By checking for conditions that are likely to occur and writing statements to manage those situations, you prevent abnormal terminations. You could have avoided the problem presented for Figures 11-1 through 11-3. As you learned in Chapter 5, you can write program statements to test your divisors to make sure they are not zero before using them in division. Example 11-1 shows a statement that would have prevented those unhandled exceptions from being thrown.

11

Example 11-1

```
int countOfScores = 0;
if (countOfScores > 0)
{

    averageTestScore = (examScore1 + examScore2 + examScore3)
                        / countOfScores;
}
else
{
    messageLabel.Text = "Problem with scores-"
                        + "unable to compute average";
}
```

The previous example is easy enough to fix. The problem identified may even be more appropriately labeled a bug instead of an exception. **Bugs** differ from exceptions in that they are normally labeled "programmer mistakes" that should be caught and fixed before an application is released. The problem that created the exception generated for the Figure 11-3 was this: `countOfScores` was originally initialized to zero with no provisions made to change it from zero. This oversight caused an unhandled exception to be thrown.

In addition to bugs, programs may experience **errors** because of user actions. These actions may cause exceptions to be thrown. Entering the wrong type of data from the keyboard is an example of a common user mistake. When an application requests numeric data be entered as the program is running, C# initially stores the value entered in a `string` variable. But, as you are aware, to perform calculations with the value, it must be converted from the `string` to a number. If the user types nonnumeric characters when requested to enter numeric values, an exception is thrown. This happens as soon as the statement that has the call to the `Parse( )` method or methods in the `Convert class` is executed with the nonnumeric data. If no instructions are found in the application for handling the exception, an unhandled exception message similar to that shown in Figure 11-4 is generated.

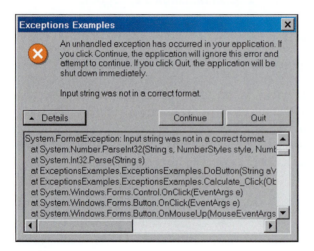

Figure 11-4   Unhandled exception raised by Parse( ) method

> **NOTE** Figures 11-1 through 11-4 are all examples of messages that are displayed when unhandled exceptions are thrown from a .NET application. They look different because of differences in the programs executed and the type of applications. The message displayed in Figure 11-4 was generated when a Windows application was run after the following choice was made: **Start without Debugging** from the **Debug** menu. Figures 11-1 and 11-2 were console applications launched the same way. Launching the application by selecting **Start** from the **Debug** menu produces the unhandled exception message shown in Figure 11-3 for both Windows and console applications.

When an unhandled exception message is displayed as shown in Figure 11-4, you click on the **Details** button in Visual Studio to view a stack trace of methods with the method that raised the exception listed first. A **stack trace** is a listing of all the methods that are in the execution chain when the exception is thrown.

As you are already aware, when a program first starts, it begins execution in the `Main( )` method. From `Main( )`, it calls on or executes other methods, which can also call on other methods, and so on. When execution reaches the bottom of a given method, control is returned to the method that called it. This continues until control eventually returns to the end of the `Main( )` method, where the program finishes its execution. A stack is used to keep up with the execution chain. Unlike other types of memory, a stack can hold multiple entries. The stack is used as follows: when a method calls on another method, the calling method's identifier is placed on a stack. If another method is called, that calling method's name is placed on the stack. Thus, the first one placed on the stack is always `Main( )`—as the calling method of other methods. This puts `Main( )` on the bottom of the stack execution chain. After a method finishes its execution, the top method name is used (popped off the stack) and control is returned to it. This is the method that previously called the method that just finished. The first one placed on the stack is `Main( )` and the last one that eventually gets popped off the stack is `Main( )`. The stack is used to determine to which method along the execution chain control returns after a method finishes.

 The stack used for the execution chain works exactly like the stack of trays at a food center. The top one comes off first. The first one added to the stack is on the bottom.

11

`ParseInt32( )` is the .NET equivalent to the C# `Parse( )` method. It is this method that threw the exception. Notice, `ParseInt32( )` is the first method listed in Figure 11-4. No exception-handler method was found there, so the exception then bubbled up to the parent method, `DoButton( )`. The CLR again looked for an exception handler in this `DoButton( )` method. Because none was found, it continued bubbling the exception up through the `Calculate_Click( )` method, the `Windows.Forms.Control.OnClick( )` method, and so on. The stack trace includes all the methods that are still active at the time the exception is raised. Since none of the methods listed in the stack trace included code to handle that type of exception, the unhandled exception message is displayed. So how do you handle the exception?

EXCEPTION-HANDLING TECHNIQUES

First remember there are bugs, errors, and exceptions. If an event that creates a problem happens frequently, it is best to write program statements, using conditional expressions, to check for the potential error and provide program instructions for what to do when that problem is encountered. This is what you saw listed in Example 11-1. If the CLR has to halt a method and find an appropriate event handler, execution is slowed down. Thus, if a situation that might crash your program occurs frequently, write program statements using conditional expressions to deal with that situation.

Exception-handling techniques are for serious errors that occur infrequently. As stated previously, exceptions are those events from which your program would not be able to recover, such as attempting to read from a data file that does not exist. Included as part of .NET are a number of classes that can be used with your applications to enable them to be less prone to crashing. These exception classes are part of the original design of .NET, and thus are integrated within the FCL. They facilitate managing exceptions in a consistent, efficient way. They are used with the **try**…**catch**…**finally** program constructs to handle unexpected types of conditions.

 Realizing the importance of handling exceptions using an object-oriented approach, the developers of C# included as part of the original design of the FCL provisions for handling exceptions. The classes were not just added on as an afterthought as in some languages.

Try…Catch…Finally Blocks

C#, like C++, Java, and other languages, handles exceptions through **try**…**catch**… **finally** blocks. The code that may create a problem is placed in the **try** block. The code to deal with the problem (the exception handler) is placed in **catch** blocks, which are also called **catch clauses**. The code that you want executed whether an exception is thrown or not is placed in the **finally** block. The syntax for a **try**…**catch**…**finally** block is as follows:

```
try
{
     // Statements
}
catch [(ExceptionClassName exceptionIdentifier)]
{
     // Exception handler statements
}
:    // [additional catch clauses]
[finally
{
     // Statements
}]
```

 The **:** is used in the examples in this book to indicate that additional statements may be added to the program listing. Here the colon would have to be replaced by additional **catch** clauses.

More than one `catch` clause may be included. One is required when you include a `try` block. Notice that a square bracket follows the keyword `catch` to indicate that the parentheses and the argument list are optional. Omitting the argument list makes the `catch` **generic**—meaning any exception that is thrown is handled by executing the code within that `catch` block. If you include an exception type as part of the argument list, only exceptions that match the type listed are handled by that `catch` clause. You will see examples using multiple `catch` clauses in this chapter.

The `finally` clause is also optional. It can be included if there is a segment of code that needs to be executed, no matter what. When code is included in all three blocks for the `try`...`catch`...`finally` construct, the statements inside the `try` block are attempted first. If no problem exists and the `try` block code is finished, the `catch` clause(s) is (are) skipped, and control transfers into the `finally` block where that code is executed.

If an unexpected error occurs in the `try` block that throws an exception, the code in the `try` block is halted at the line that caused the problem. The CLR tries to find a matching exception handler within the current method. If one is found, control transfers to the first listed `catch` clause that can handle the type of execution thrown. The `catch` clause statements are executed, and control transfers to the `finally` block where its code is executed. Notice with both situations (exception thrown and no exception thrown) that if a `finally` block is included, the statements in it are executed.

Another important point to make sure you understand is the fact that control is never returned into the `try` block after an exception is thrown. The statement that creates a problem in the `try` block is the last one tried in the `try` clause. Once control is transferred out of the `try`, no other statements inside the `try` block are ever executed.

11

Example 11-2 uses a `try`...`catch` block to keep the program from terminating abnormally. The example includes a generic `catch` clause—no specific exception type is listed.

Example 11-2

```csharp
// ExceptionApp.cs
// Uses a generic catch block to catch any
// type of exception that is thrown.
using System;
namespace ExceptionsExample
{
    class ExceptionApp
    {
        static void Main(string[] args)
        {
            int [ ] examScore;
            int totalScores = 0;
            int countOfScores = 0;
            string inValue;
```

```
            double averageTestScore;
            try
            {
                Console.Write("How many scores will you enter? ");
                inValue = Console.ReadLine();
                countOfScores = int.Parse(inValue);
                examScore = new int[countOfScores];

                for (int i = 0; i < countOfScores; i++)
                {
                    Console.Write("Enter score {0}: ", i+1);
                    inValue = Console.ReadLine();
                    examScore[i] = int.Parse(inValue);
                    totalScores += examScore[i];
                }

                averageTestScore = totalScores /
                                   countOfScores;
                Console.WriteLine("Average is {0}",
                                  averageTestScore);
            }
            catch
            {
                Console.WriteLine("Problem with scores - " +
                                  "Cannot compute average");
            }
        }
    }
}
```

If the application is run and the user types a nonnumeric character, such as the value 9U (shown entered for score 3 in Figure 11-5), the program does not crash. Instead the exception handler code found in the **catch** block is executed and alerts the user of the error.

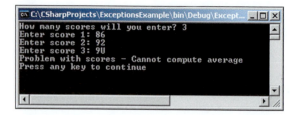

Figure 11-5 Generic catch block handles the exception

Generic Catches

The problem with using a generic `catch` to avoid abnormal termination is that because any type of exception is handled by the `catch` code, you are never quite sure what caused the exception to be thrown. Take for example the two output listings shown in Figure 11-6.

```
C:\CSharpProjects\ExceptionsExample\bin\Debug\Except...
How many scores will you enter? 0
Problem with scores - Cannot compute average
Press any key to continue
```

```
C:\CSharpProjects\ExceptionsExample\bin\Debug\Except...
How many scores will you enter? 3
Enter score 1: 86
Enter score 2: 92
Enter score 3: 99
Problem with scores - Cannot compute average
Press any key to continue
```

Figure 11-6   Exceptions thrown due to division by zero and programmer error

11

What caused these exceptions to be thrown? The first output in Figure 11-6 is generated due to an attempt to divide by zero. The second one threw an "Index outside the bounds of the array" exception. The message, "Index outside the bounds of the array" is displayed in response to a bug in the program. The exception was thrown when the statement that computes the average from Example 11-2 was changed to the statement shown in Example 11-3.

Example 11-3

```
averageTestScore = totalScores / examScore[10]; // Invalid
```

There is no `examScore[10]`. Example 11-2 had the correct arithmetic statement; the divisor should be `countOfScores`.

```
averageTestScore = totalScores / countOfScores;  // Correct
```

 The computation was modified to illustrate that programmer mistakes (bugs) can lead to exceptions being thrown.

Although you can keep the program from terminating abnormally by using a generic `catch` clause, you can debug more easily if you know what caused the exception to be thrown. Just displaying a message saying there is a problem does not help a lot.

Exception Object

When an exception is raised with .NET languages, an `object` is created to represent the exception. All exception objects inherit from the `base class` for exceptions, named `Exception`. It is part of the `System namespace`. An exception `object`, like other objects, has properties and behaviors (methods). The `catch` clause may list an exception `class` name, and an `object` identifier inside parentheses following the `catch` keyword. Actually to use any of the properties of the exception `object` that is created, you must have an `object` name. Using the `catch { }` without an exception type does not give you access to an `object`.

One of the properties of the `Exception base class` is `Message`. `Message` returns a `string` describing the exception. Since it is a property of the `base class`, it can be used with any exception `object`. Example 11-4 includes the `Exception class` in the argument list for the `catch` clause. The `object` identifier `e` is used to name an `object` of that `class`. The `object` `e` may now be used with any of the properties or methods of the `Exception class`. The `Message` property, associated with `object` `e`, is used inside the `catch` clause to display a message describing the exception.

 You cannot use the `Message` property or any of the other members of the `class` without an `object`. This is one reason the argument list (`System.Exception e`) needs to be included.

Example 11-4

```
catch (System.Exception e)
{       Console.Error.WriteLine("Problem with scores - " +
                        "Cannot compute average");
        Console.Error.WriteLine(e.Message);
}
```

 No filtering of exceptions occurs by adding the (`System.Exeception e`) for the argument list. Any exception that is thrown in this method is caught because all exceptions are derived from this `base System.Exception class`. The advantage of typing the argument list is that you have an `object` identifier to use with properties.

In Example 11-4, in addition to displaying the programmer-supplied message indicating there is a problem, an additional `string`, "Index was outside the bounds of the array," is displayed. That is the current value of the `Message` property for `object` `e`. Both of these strings are displayed on the Error output device. Now if the application is run again and it still contains the programmer error previously entered, the output window lists what caused the exception to be thrown as shown in Figure 11-7.

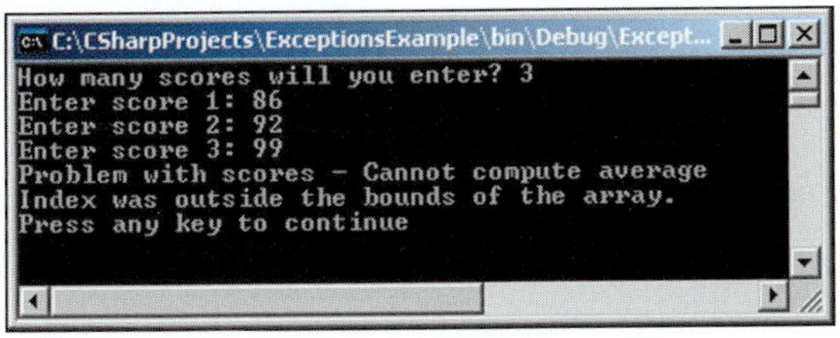

Figure 11-7   Use of Message property with the exception object

> **NOTE** Calls were made to the `System.Error.WriteLine( )` method to illustrate that it is probably more appropriate to display error messages to the Error output device. By default, its output goes to the console screen, just as it does for `Console class` output. However, the Error output device may be changed to display to a different device.

The argument list is normally included to filter the exceptions. By specifying more than one exception filter, you can write code in the **catch** clauses that is specific to the particular exception thrown. To do that you have to know more about the different exception classes that make up the .NET Framework Class Library, and the next section discusses some of them.

EXCEPTION CLASSES

When an error occurs, it is reported by creating and throwing an **object** that corresponds to the specific type of exception that is thrown. The **object** contains information about the error. There are a number of different types of exceptions that can be thrown.

Derived Classes of the Base Exception Class

Table 11-1 shows the derived classes of the **base** `Exception` `class`. The `ApplicationException` and `SystemException` classes form the basis for runtime exceptions and are discussed following Table 11-1.

Table 11-1 Derived classes of the base Exception class

Classes that inherit from Exception
`System.ApplicationException`
`System.IO.IsolatedStorage.IsolatedStorageException`
`System.Runtime.Remoting.MetadataServices.SUDSGeneratorException`
`System.Runtime.Remoting.MetadataServices.SUDSParserException`
`System.SystemException`
`System.Windows.Forms.AxHost.InvalidActiveXStateException`

From Table 11-1, the two exception classes of interest are the `ApplicationException` and `SystemException` classes. The other classes listed in the table are not discussed in this chapter; however, you are encouraged to explore the MSDN documentation to learn more about them.

ApplicationException Class

You can write your own exception classes or use one of the many supplied .NET exception classes. The `ApplicationException` exception was included by the designers of .NET to enable a distinction to be made between user-defined exceptions and exceptions defined by the system. If you write your own exceptions, they should derive from `ApplicationException`. The `ApplicationException` exception is thrown by a user program, not the CLR.

SystemException Class

The system-supplied exception classes for runtime exceptions derive mainly from the `SystemException` class. `SystemException` adds no functionality to classes. Except for its constructor, the `SystemException` class has no additional properties or methods other than those derived from the `Exception` and `Object` classes. The `Exception` class has several properties. You have already seen the results of two of them—`Message` and `StackTrace`. `StackTrace` returns a `string` that contains the called trace of methods. The `Message` property provides details about the cause of the exception. Another property of the `Exception` class, `HelpLink`, can contain a URL to a Help file that can provide additional information about the cause of the exception. The `Source` property gets or sets the name of the application or the `object` that caused the error, and the `TargetSite` property gets the method that threw the exception.

Over 70 classes derive from the `SystemException` class. Table 11-2 lists a few of the more common exceptions that are thrown. You may want to consider adding handlers to catch many of these.

Table 11-2 Derived classes of SystemException

Exception classes derived from the SystemException class	Description of circumstances causing an exception to be thrown
`System.ArgumentException`	One of the arguments provided to a method is invalid.
`System.ArithmeticException`	There are errors in an arithmetic, casting, or conversion operation. Has derived members of System.DivideByZeroException and System.OverflowException.
`System.ArrayTypeMismatchException`	An attempt is made to store an element of the wrong type within an array.
`System.FormatException`	The format of an argument does not meet the parameter specifications.
`System.IndexOutOfRangeException`	An attempt is made to access an element of an array with an index that is outside the bounds of the array.
`System.InvalidCastException`	There is invalid casting or explicit conversion.
`System.IO.IOException`	An I/O error occurs.
`System.NullReferenceException`	There is an attempt to dereference a null `object` reference.
`System.OutOfMemoryException`	There is not enough memory to continue the execution of a program.
`System.RankException`	An array with the wrong number of dimensions is passed to a method.

11

Many of the exception classes included in Table 11-2 have additional classes that are derived from them. You will want to explore the documentation to learn about those derived **class** members. As shown in Table 11-2, one derived **class** of the `System. ArithmeticException` **class** is the `System.DivideByZeroException` **class**. This is the exception thrown previously in this chapter.

You should be aware that division by zero involving floating-point operands does not throw an exception. Exceptions are only thrown for integral or integer data types. The result of division by zero is reported as either positive infinity, negative infinity, or Not-a-Number (NaN). This follows the rules from IEEE 754 arithmetic. .NET languages were designed to implement these rules.

> **NOTE** Since implicit type conversion occurs when you have a floating-point operand with an integer, if either operand is of type **double** or **float**, no exception is thrown when you divide by zero.

Filtering Multiple Exceptions

Following a single **try** block, you can include multiple **catch** clauses. This enables you to write code specific to the thrown exception. When you do this, the order of placement of these clauses is important. They should be placed from the most specific to the most generic. Because all exception classes derive from the **Exception class**, if you are including the **Exception class**, it should always be placed last. Because the **DivideByZeroException** exception derives from the **ArithmeticException class**, if both are included, **DivideByZeroException** should be listed first. Example 11-5 illustrates using several **catch** clauses to filter the exceptions. A **finally** clause is also included.

Example 11-5

```
// MultipleCatches.cs
// Demonstrates the use of multiple catch
// clauses and a finally clause.
using System;
namespace MultipleCatches
{
    class MultipleCatches
    {
        static void Main(string[] args)
        {
            int [ ] examScore;
            int totalScores = 0;
            int countOfScores = 0;
            string inValue;
            double averageTestScore;
            try
            {
                Console.Write("How many scores will you enter? ");
                inValue = Console.ReadLine();
                countOfScores = int.Parse(inValue);
                examScore = new int[countOfScores];

                for (int i = 0; i < countOfScores; i++)
                {
                    Console.Write("Enter score {0}: ", i+1);
                    inValue = Console.ReadLine();
                    examScore[i] = int.Parse(inValue);
                    totalScores += examScore[i];
                }

                averageTestScore = totalScores / countOfScores;
                Console.WriteLine("Average is {0}",
                                    averageTestScore);
            }
```

```
        catch (System.FormatException e)
        {
            Console.Error.WriteLine("Problem with one of " +
                "the operands - Cannot compute average!");
            Console.Error.WriteLine("Exception type: {0}",
                                            e.Message);
        }

        catch (System.DivideByZeroException e)
        {
            Console.Error.WriteLine("No scores were " +
                "entered - Cannot compute average!");
            Console.Error.WriteLine("Exception type: {0}",
                                            e.Message);
        }
        catch (System.ArithmeticException e)
        {
            Console.Error.WriteLine("Error in your " +
                "arithmetic or casting.");
            Console.Error.WriteLine("Exception type: {0}",
                                            e.Message);
        }
        catch (System.Exception e)
        {
            Console.Error.WriteLine("Any other problem" +
                "Cannot compute average!");
            Console.Error.WriteLine("Exception type: {0}",
                                            e.Message);
        }
        finally
        {
            Console.WriteLine("...\n...\n...\n" +
                "Terminated Normally!!!");
        }
    }
}
}
```

The application in Example 11-5 is poised to avoid terminating abnormally. Because `System.Exception` is the **base** exception **class**, the **catch** could have been written without the parenthesized arguments. It is acceptable in C# to write:

```
try
{
    // Statement(s)
}
```

```
catch
{
    // Statement(s)
}
```

In Example 11-5, you cannot just remove the (`System.Exception e`) from the last `catch`. If you do, a syntax error is generated. The error is not generated because of removal of the type; it is because the `catch` block uses the identifier `e` to display the exception type. If you remove "(`System.Exception e`)", be sure to modify the `catch` clause code so that it does not refer to the `e` `object`.

 You cannot write a `catch` unless you include it within a `try` block.

Now, when the user enters nonnumeric characters, such as the 9U entered during the running of the application shown in Figure 11-5, the output shown in Figure 11-8 is produced.

Figure 11-8 Number FormatException thrown

After the statements in the `catch` clause are executed, the `finally` clause is executed as shown in Figure 11-8. Figure 11-9 shows the output produced when no scores are entered.

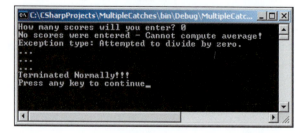

Figure 11-9 DivisionByZero exception thrown

When no scores are entered, a different exception is thrown; a different **catch** clause is executed. Normally division by zero in an application such as this should not be caught by an exception. Instead it should be dealt with programmatically by checking to ensure that scores are entered before the division occurs. If division by zero errors rarely occur in your programs, you can write an exception-handling technique to deal with those extreme cases.

Integer division was performed for the calculation of the average. No exception would have been thrown when no scores were entered if one of the operands had been cast to a **double** as follows:

```
averageTestScore = (double)totalScores / countOfScores;
```

The application terminates normally. The floating-point division by zero produced the result of NaN as shown in Figure 11-10.

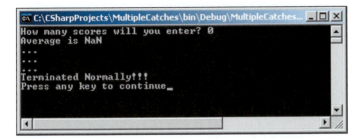

Figure 11-10　Floating-point division by zero

No control was transferred into any of the **catch** clauses for this run. The division occurred (division by zero), followed by execution of the last statement in the **try** block, which printed "Average is NaN". The NaN was the result of the floating-point division. From the **finally** clause, "Terminated Normally!!!" is printed.

The **catch** clauses for Example 11-5 simply displayed messages indicating what type of error occurred. You would expect that real-world applications would do much more. Corrective action to ensure that the program not only terminates normally, but also produces correct results every time the application is run should be your goal when you are writing programs. If an exception error is caught, you should fix the problem and keep the application running.

Custom Exceptions

There are many more exceptions in the **System.SystemException class** than you will ever use; however, you also have the opportunity to write your own exception classes. The only requirement is that custom exceptions must derive from the **ApplicationException class**.

When defining your own exception classes, it is a good idea to use the word "Exception" as part of the identifier. This adds to the readability and maintainability of the code.

Creating an exception **class** is no different from creating any other **class**. Example 11-6 shows a customized (programmer–defined) exception **class** that can be thrown when floating-point division by zero is attempted. Using the word "Exception" as part of its identifier name, it is named FloatingPtDivisionException.

Example 11-6

```
public class FloatingPtDivisionException :
                    System.ApplicationException
{
     public FloatingPtDivisionException(string exceptionType)
            : base (exceptionType)
     {
          // Empty body
     }
}
```

No additional functionality is added by the `FloatingPtDivisionException` **class**—beyond what is available from the parent classes. The constructor for the `FloatingPtDivisionException` **class** has one argument. It is sent to the **base** constructor using the keyword **base**. This argument is a **string** indicating the exception type. The `FloatingPtDivisionException` exception **class** could be saved as a DLL and referenced by numerous applications.

To test the exception, a new **class** is created to include a **try**...**catch** block. For simplicity both classes are included in the same file. `TestOfCustomException` is written as shown in Example 11-7.

Example 11-7

```
public class TestOfCustomException
{
        static void Main(string[] args)
        {
            double value1 = 0,
                    value2 = 0,
                    answer;
```

```
        try
        {
            // Could include code to enter new values
            answer = GetResults(value1, value2);
        }
        catch (FloatingPtDivisionException e)
        {
             Console.Error.WriteLine(e.Message);
        }
        catch
        {
            Console.Error.WriteLine("Something else happened!");
        }
    }

    static double GetResults(double value1, double value2)
    {
        if (value2 < .0000001) // Be careful comparing floating-
                               // point values for equality
        {
            FloatingPtDivisionException e = new
                FloatingPtDivisionException
                    ("Exception type: " +
                      "Floating-point division by zero");
            throw e;
        }
        return value1 / value2;
    }
}
```

11

The result of one test run of Example 11-7 is shown in Figure 11-11.

Figure 11-11   TestOfCustomException threw FloatingPtDivisionException exception

In the `GetResults( )` method of Example 11-7, the conditional expression of `(value2 < .0000001)` was used to determine when `value2` was zero. Notice that a relational test was performed, instead of using an equality expression such as `(value2 == 0)`. Using the equality operator with floating-point variables produces inconsistent results, because the value is not stored as a finite value.

 To learn more about the IEEE Standard for Binary Floating-Point Arithmetic, explore the Web site *www.ieee.org*.

In Example 11-7, two `catch` clauses are included. The first listed is the most specific. Listing the most specific to the most generic is a requirement when you include multiple catches; otherwise, the most specific would never be reached. As soon as one of the filters matches, its block of code is executed and then control either transfers to the bottom of the entire `try...catch` statements or to a `finally` statement if one is present.

 Also, had the last `catch` clause (`catch (System.Exception)`) been listed first, C# would issue a syntax error for the second `catch` clause indicating "A previous `catch` clause already catches all exceptions of this or a super type."

Remember that writing the `catch` clause without an argument list is the same as writing `catch (System.Exception)`, which is the `base` of all exceptions. The last `catch` clause catches all other exceptions. If any exceptions other than `FloatingPtDivisionException` are encountered, `System.Exception` is thrown.

Throwing an Exception

In the `GetResults( )` method that tested the programmer-defined custom exception, an exception `object` is instantiated when "an exceptional condition occurs." This exceptional condition is `(value2 < .0000001)`. It could be any condition, but it should be one that happens very infrequently. After an `object` (e) of the `FloatingPtDivisionException` `class` is instantiated with a `string` value of "Exception type: Floating-point division by zero", the e `object` is thrown. The `GetResults( )` method is presented again in Example 11-8 for your review.

Example 11-8

```
static double GetResults(double value1, double value2)
{
    if (value2 < .0000001) // Be careful comparing floating-
                           // point values for equality
    {
        FloatingPtDivisionException e = new
```

```
            FloatingPtDivisionException
                ("Exception type: " +
                    "Floating-point division by zero");
        throw e;
    }
    return value1 / value2;
}
```

Notice the CLR is not throwing the exception here. Instead the exception is thrown by the program using the **throw** keyword. When the **object** e is thrown in the **GetResults( )** method, the exception **object** propagates back up the call chain, first stopping at the method that called it to see if a **catch** is available to handle it. As you examine Example 11-7, notice that the **GetResults( )** method was called from within the **try** block in the **Main( )** method. When the **object** e is thrown in **GetResults( )**, it is thrown back to the **Main( )** method's **catch** clause because that is the position from which it was called.

From inside the **catch** clause, e.Message is printed. Observe that the value displayed in Figure 11-11 is exactly the same value as that used to instantiate the **object** in the **GetResults( )** method. The **string** argument, "Exception type: Floating-point division by zero", which is used to construct the **object** in this case, is sent to the **base** constructor. The heading for the **FloatingPtDivisionException class** defined in Example 11-6 is shown again as follows:

```
public FloatingPtDivisionException(string exceptionType)
            : base (exceptionType)
```

The argument **exceptionType** sets the **Message** property for the **base Exception class**. This is why "Exception type: Floating-point division by zero" is printed when e.Message is displayed in the **catch** clause found in the **Main( )** method.

When no exceptions are thrown in the **GetResults( )** method, the result of dividing value1 by value2 is returned back to **Main( )**.

Input Output (IO) Exceptions

Exceptions are extremely useful for applications that process or create stored data. Thus far your programs have processed only data that was interactively typed while the program was running. All of the output from your programs has been displayed on the console screen. In some situations, it is more appropriate to place the data in a file or use a file for input as opposed to having the user type entries. In other situations, it is best to store the output to a file, as when the input would overflow a single screen or when the output produced by one application is used as input for another application. Copious support is available in C# for dealing with files. The next section details how a file is created and processed. First examine the predefined exception classes available for dealing with files.

The primary exception **class** for files is **System.IO.IOException**. It derives from the **SystemException class** which, as you learned, is a direct descendent of **Exception**. An **IO.IOException** exception is thrown for the following types of unexpected errors: a specified file or directory is not found; your program attempts to read beyond the end of a file; or there are problems loading or accessing the contents of a file. Table 11-3 shows the classes derived from the **IO.IOException class** and briefly describes the reasons for throwing the exceptions.

Table 11-3   Derived classes of IO.IOException

Exception classes derived from the IO.IOException class	Description of circumstances causing an exception to be thrown
DirectoryNotFoundException	A directory cannot be found.
EndOfStreamException	You read past the end of the file.
FileNotFoundException	A disk fails or you try to access a file that does not exist.
FileLoadException	The file is found, but it cannot be loaded.
PathTooLongException	A pathname or filename is longer than the system-defined maximum length.

You experience writing **IO.IOException** exception handlers in the next section when you work with file streams.

> **NOTE**
> In C# there are none of the checked exceptions that you find in languages such as Java. Java distinguishes between checked and unchecked exceptions. A **checked exception** is one that must be included if you use a specific construct. If you do not include exception-handling techniques for that construct, a syntax error is generated. All file interactions in Java are treated as checked exceptions—meaning you must include your file processing inside **try…catch** blocks in Java. Although you are encouraged also to do this in C#, you do not receive a syntax error if you do not place your file-handling statements in a **try…catch** block. There are *no* checked exceptions in C#!

FILE STREAMS

C# uses file streams to deal with stored data. Several abstract classes, including **Stream**, **TextWriter**, and **TextReader**, are defined for dealing with files. These classes are defined in the **System.IO namespace**. The stream classes provide generic methods for dealing with input/output, and these methods reduce the need for providing specific details about how the operating system actually accesses data from particular devices. Figure 11-12 shows the hierarchy of many of the classes used for file processing in .NET. The boxes containing three dots indicate additional classes are derived.

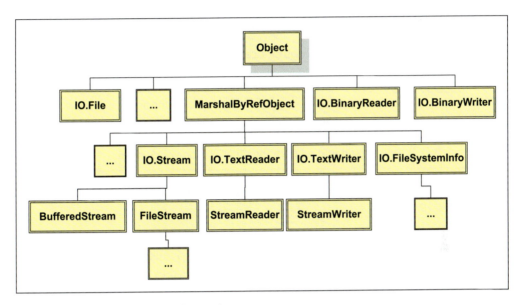

Figure 11-12 .NET file class hierarchy

11

The `IO.Stream` **class** and its subclasses are used for byte-level data. `IO.TextWriter` and `IO.TextReader` facilitate working with data in a text (readable) format. For the programs you develop in this chapter, you use `StreamReader` and `StreamWriter`, which are classes derived from the `TextReader` and `TextWriter` classes.

The `StreamWriter` and `StreamReader` classes make it easy to read or write data to and from text files in C#. The `StreamWriter` **class** has implementations for `Write( )` and `WriteLine( )` methods similar to the `Console` **class** methods. `StreamReader` includes implementations of `Read( )` and `ReadLine( )`. The simplest constructor for these classes includes a single argument for the name of the file. The name may include the full path indicating where the file is located.

 If you do not specify the full path for the filename, Visual Studio uses the bin\Debug subdirectory of the current project. To specify the full path, you must either use escape characters for the backslash or the verbatim `string character` (`@`). To specify that the file is stored at C:\CSharpProjects\Proj1, you would include as an argument either (`" c:\\CSharpProjects\\Proj1"`) using two backslashes for each backslash, or you would write (`@"C:\CSharpProjects\Proj1"`). When you place an @ in front of the `string`, it becomes a verbatim `string`.

The file name may be sent as a **string** literal or specified as a variable with a **string** value. The following statements construct objects of the **StreamWriter** and **StreamReader** classes:

```
StreamWriter outputFile = new StreamWriter("someOutputFileName");
StreamReader inputFile = new StreamReader("someInputFileName");
```

 The identifiers of `outputFile`, `someOutputFileName`, `inputFile`, and `someInputFileName` are all user-supplied identifiers. `outputFile` and `inputFile` represent the file stream objects. `someOutputFileName` and `someInputFileName` would be replaced by the actual filenames associated with the file—the names you see from MyComputer or Windows Explorer. If you are creating a data file, place a file extension such as .dat, .dta, or .txt onto the end of the file so that it can be distinguished from the other files on your system.

To avoid fully qualifying references to objects of these classes, include the **System.IO** **namespace**.

```
using System.IO;
```

When you use the **Write( )** or **WriteLine( )** methods with the instantiated stream **object**, the characters are written to the file specified by the filename. The values are stored in the file as text characters—**string** objects. **ReadLine( )** reads a line of characters and returns the data as a **string**. The following statements write and read a test message to and from files after an **object** of the **StreamWriter** **class** has been constructed:

```
outputFile.WriteLine("This is the first line in a text file");
string inValue = inputFile.ReadLine( );
```

Tables 11-4 and 11-5 show members of the **StreamWriter** and **StreamReader** classes.

Table 11-4 StreamWriter members

StreamWriter members	Description
`AutoFlush`	(Property) Gets or sets a value indicating whether the `StreamWriter` flushes its buffer to the underlying stream after calls to the `Write( )` or `WriteLine( )` methods
`Close( )`	Closes the current `StreamWriter`
`Dispose( )`	Releases the unmanaged resources used by the `StreamWriter`
`Flush( )`	Clears all buffers for the current writer and causes any buffered data to be written to the underlying stream
`NewLine`	(Property) Gets or sets the line terminator **string** used by the current `TextWriter`
`Write( )`	Writes the characters to the stream
`WriteLine( )`	Writes the characters to the stream, followed by a line terminator

Table 11-5 StreamReader members

StreamReader member	Description
Close( )	Closes the current `StreamReader`
DiscloseBufferedData( )	Allows the `StreamReader` to discard its current data
Dispose( )	Releases the unmanaged resources used by the `StreamReader`
Peek( )	Returns the next available character but does not consume it
Read( )	Reads the next character or next set of characters from the input stream
ReadBlock( )	Reads a specified number of characters from the current stream and writes the data to buffer, beginning at the index
ReadLine( )	Reads a line of characters from the current stream and returns the data as a `string`
ReadToEnd( )	Reads the stream from the current position to the end of the stream

The `IO.File class` shown in Figure 11-12 provides a number of `static` methods that aid in the creation and use of files. Some `static` members can be used to copy, delete, and move files. Table 11-6 lists some of the `static` members of the `IO.File class`.

11

Table 11-6 File members

Static file member	Description
Copy( )	Copies an existing file to a new file
Delete( )	Deletes the specified file
Exists( )	Determines whether the specified file exists
GetCreationTime( )	Returns the date and time the specified file was created
GetLastAccessTime( )	Gets the date and time the specified file was last accessed
GetLastWriteTime( )	Gets the date and time the specified file was last written to
Move( )	Moves a specified file to a new location

Every member of the `IO.File class` is `static`. Remember that a `static` method does not require that an `object` of the `class` be instantiated in order to use it. The method name is instead preceded by the `class` name. For example, to make a copy of sourceFile, naming the new file targetFile, you would write: `File.Copy("sourceFile", "targetFile");`, assuming the `using System.IO;` `namespace` was included.

Writing Text Files

All attempts to access text files can be enclosed inside **try**...**catch** blocks to check for exceptions. This is not required in C#, but is encouraged to avoid unhandled exceptions being thrown during runtime. The constructor for the **StreamWriter class** is overloaded, in that you can include additional arguments such as a Boolean variable indicating whether the file should be appended to or overwritten if it already exists. If you do not include an argument for the **Append** mode, a new file is created by default, overwriting any previously created versions. Using the **Append** mode enables you to add lines onto the end of an existing file.

 Constructing an **object** of the **StreamWriter class** using **true** as the second argument enables you to append values onto the end of a file. The following statement opens the file named info.txt, stored in the project subdirectory, so that records will be added onto the end of the file:

```
fileOut = new StreamWriter("../../info.txt", true);
```

Values are placed in the file in a sequential fashion. A pointer moves through the file, keeping up with the current location into which the next values are to be placed in the file. After the file is created, the **Close( )** method is used to finish storing the values. When the **Close( )** method is called, any values waiting in the buffer to be written are flushed to the file and the resources associated with the file are released. Example 11-9 creates a text file containing the user's favorite sayings. This example illustrates using exception-handling techniques with the **StreamWriter class**. For the sake of brevity, some of the Windows Form-generated code is not included in the listing.

The application includes a **Textbox object** for data entry and a **Label object** for displaying error messages. The label is originally set to **null** (an empty value) at design time. One **Button object** is included. Its event-handler method is used to save the entry to the text file.

Example 11-9

```csharp
// SayingGUI.cs
// Windows application that retrieves
// and stores values from a text box
// in a text file.
using System;
using System.Drawing;
using System.Collections;
using System.ComponentModel;
using System.Windows.Forms;
using System.Data;
using System.IO;      // Added for file access
```

```
namespace SayingsApp
{
    public class SayingGUI : System.Windows.Forms.Form
    {
        private System.Windows.Forms.TextBox txtBxSaying;
        private System.Windows.Forms.Button btnSaying;
        private System.ComponentModel.Container components = null;
        private System.Windows.Forms.Label lblMsg;
        private System.Windows.Forms.Label label1;
        private StreamWriter fil;  // Declares a file stream object

        public SayingGUI()
        {
            InitializeComponent();
        }

        protected override void Dispose( bool disposing )
        {
            if( disposing )
            {
                if (components != null)
                {
                    components.Dispose();
                }
            }
            base.Dispose( disposing );
        }

        #region Windows Form Designer generated code
            // Note: Windows Generated Code
            // Removed - Due to space constraints

        #endregion
        static void Main()
        {
            Application.Run(new SayingGUI());
        }

        // Form load event handler used to construct
        // object of the StreamWriter class, sending the
        // new file name as an argument. Enclosed in
        // try...catch block.
        private void SayingGUI_Load(object sender,
                        System.EventArgs e)
        {
            try
            {
                fil = new StreamWriter("saying.txt");
            }
```

11

```csharp
            catch (DirectoryNotFoundException exc)
            {
                lblMsg.Text = "InValid directory"
                        + exc.Message;
            }

            catch (System.IO.IOException exc)
            {
                lblMsg.Text = exc.Message;
            }
        }
        // When the button is clicked, write the characters
        // to the text file.
        private void btnSaying_Click(object sender,
                    System.EventArgs e)
        {
            try
            {
                fil.WriteLine(this.txtBxSaying.Text);
                this.txtBxSaying.Text = "";
            }

            catch (System.IO.IOException exc)
            {
                lblMsg.Text = exc.Message;
            }
        }

        // When the form is closing (default window x
        // box is clicked), close the file associated
        // with the StreamWriter object.
        private void SayingGUI_Closing(object sender,
            System.ComponentModel.CancelEventArgs e)
        {
            try
            {
                fil.Close();
            }
            catch
            {
            }
        }
    }
}
```

The application is run and three different sayings are entered by the user as shown in
Figure 11-13.

Figure 11-13   Data being stored in a text file

As you review the statements in Example 11-9, notice that three event–handler methods are included in the Windows application. In the form-loading event handler, an **object** of the **StreamWriter class** is instantiated. This is included in a **try…catch** clause. The button click event-handler method retrieves the **string** from the text box and writes the text to the file. It is also enclosed in a **try…catch** clause. The third event-handler method is an on form-closing event. In this event-handler method, the file is closed inside another **try…catch** block. Using the data input from Figure 11-13, the contents of the file created from this run of the application are shown in Figure 11-14.

11

```
saying.txt - Notepad
File  Edit  Format  View  Help
Today is the first day of the rest of your life.
Live life to the fullest.
You may not get a second chance...
```

Figure 11-14   Contents of text file created by SayingGUI application

In Visual Studio .NET when you create a file (or attempt to access one), if a path is not specified for the filename, the bin\Debug subdirectory for the current project is used. If an invalid path is listed in the constructor for the `StreamWriter` `object`, an `IOException` exception is thrown as soon as the application launches and the form is loaded. To demonstrate this, the call to the constructor was changed in Example 11-9. On the system on which this application is run, there is no C:\Bob subdirectory. Thus, replacing the `object` constructor in the `SayingGUI_Load( )` method from:

```
fil = new StreamWriter("saying.txt");
```

to:

```
fil = new StreamWriter(@"C:\Bob\saying.txt");
```

throws an exception as soon as the form is loaded. When the user interface was designed for Example 11-9, a label, initialized with `" "`(an empty `string`), was placed on the form to display error messages. Figure 11-15 shows the message displayed when the `DirectoryNotFoundException` exception is thrown.

Figure 11-15   DirectoryNotFoundException thrown

The `"InValid directory"` `string` literal was concatenated onto the `string` returned from the `Message` property of the `DirectoryNotFoundException` `object` `exc`. Example 11-10 reprints the `SayingGUI_Load( )` method that is executed when the form is loaded. This time it includes the invalid path argument used to construct the `object` when the exception was thrown as shown in Figure 11-15.

Example 11-10

```csharp
private void SayingGUI_Load(object sender,
                        System.EventArgs e)
    {
        try
        {
            fil = new StreamWriter
                (@"C:\Bob\saying.txt"); // invalid path
        }

        catch (DirectoryNotFoundException exc)
        {
            lblMsg.Text = "InValid directory"
                    + exc.Message;
        }

        catch (System.IO.IOException exc)
        {
            lblMsg.Text = exc.Message;
        }
    }
```

Without including the **try...catch** clause in the `SayingGUI_Closing(  )` method, the program would have crashed with an unhandled exception, because no file can be created when an invalid path is specified.

11

You also cannot close a file that does not exist or is not currently open. As you examine the **try...catch** clause in the `SayingGUI_Closing(  )` method, notice the body of this **catch** is empty. If an exception is thrown and caught when an attempt to close the file is made, the exception is passed back to the CLR to handle.

Reading Text Files

The **StreamReader class** was designed to enable lines of text to be read from a file. If you do not specify a different type of encoding (coding representation), the characters read are converted by default to strings of Unicode characters.

> **NOTE** By default the Unicode UTF-16 encoding schema is used. This represents characters as sequences of 16-bit integers. You could specify Unicode UTF-8, in which characters are represented as sequences of 8-bit bytes, or use ASCII encoding, which encodes characters as single 7-bit ASCII characters.

Using members of the **StreamReader class**, accessing the contents of a text file is as easy as creating it. As shown in Table 11-5, several methods, including the **ReadLine( )** method, are available to read characters from the file. As with the **StreamWriter** class, the constructor for **StreamReader** is overloaded. You may specify a different encoding schema or an initial buffer size for retrieval of data. If you specify a buffer size, it must be given in 16–bit increments.

With the **StreamReader** and **StreamWriter** objects, you can use members of parent or ancestor classes or **static** members of the **File class**. As shown in Table 11-6, **File.Exists( )** can be used to determine whether the file exists. You can send the filename as an argument to **Exists( )** before attempting to construct an **object**. This is a way programmatically to avoid having a **FileNotFoundException** or **DirectoryNotFoundException** exception thrown in your applications. This is illustrated in Example 11-11 that follows.

Values are read from text files in sequential fashion. Just as when you create a text file, a pointer moves through the file keeping track of the current location for the next read. Example 11-11 reads strings from a text file that contains a list of names. The text file uses those values to populate a list box for a Windows application. This application illustrates using exception-handling techniques with the **StreamReader class**. For the sake of brevity, some of the Windows Form-generated code is not included in the listing that follows. The application includes a **Listbox object** for data display and a **Label object** for displaying error messages. The label is originally set to a **null** empty value.

 Because you often want to read from one or more files and write the output to another file, you can have multiple files open at the same time.

Example 11-11

```csharp
// FileAccessApp.cs
// Windows application that retrieves
// and stores values from a text file
// to a list box.
using System;
using System.Drawing;
using System.Collections;
using System.ComponentModel;
using System.Windows.Forms;
using System.Data;
using System.IO;      // Added for file access
```

```csharp
namespace FileAccessApp
{
    public class FrmFileGUI : System.Windows.Forms.Form
    {
        private System.Windows.Forms.ListBox lstBoxNames;
        private System.Windows.Forms.Label lblMsg;
        private System.Windows.Forms.Label label1;
        private StreamReader inFile; // Declares a file stream object
        private System.ComponentModel.Container components = null;

        public FrmFileGUI()
        {
            InitializeComponent();
        }
        protected override void Dispose( bool disposing )
        {
            if( disposing )
            {
                if (components != null)
                {
                    components.Dispose();
                }
            }
            base.Dispose( disposing );
        }

        #region Windows Form Designer generated code
        // Note: Windows Generated Code
        // Removed - Due to space constraints
        #endregion
        static void Main()
        {
            Application.Run(new FrmFileGUI());
        }
        // Form load event handler used to construct
        // object of the StreamReader class, sending the
        // new file name as an argument. Enclosed in
        // try...catch block.
        private void FrmFileGUI_Load(object sender,
                    System.EventArgs e)
        {
            string inValue;
            if (File.Exists("name.txt"))
            {
                try
                {
                    inFile = new StreamReader("name.txt");
```

11

```
                    while ((inValue = inFile.ReadLine()) != null)
                    {
                         this.lstBoxNames.Items.Add(inValue);
                    }
             }
             catch (System.IO.IOException exc)
             {
                    lblMsg.Text = exc.Message;
             }
        }
        else
        {
             lblMsg.Text = "File unavailable";
        }
    }

    // When the close X is clicked, as the form is
    // closing, close the file associated with the
    // StreamReader object.
    private void FrmFileGUI_Closing(object sender,
                    System.ComponentModel.CancelEventArgs e)
    {
        try
        {
             inFile.Close();
        }
        catch
        {
        }
    }
}
}
```

 Be sure to close all files before you exit the application. This ensures that the data is usable for the next application. Close the file by calling the `Close( )` method as shown in Example 11-11. No arguments are sent to the method; however, it must be called with the file `object` (`inFile.Close( );`).

Figure 11-16 shows the contents of the file used for testing the application in Example 11-11.

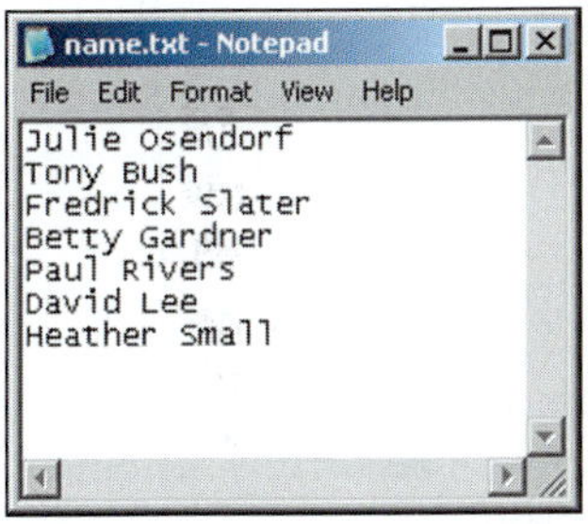

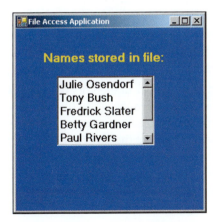

Figure 11-16   Contents of name.txt file

> **NOTE** The file is displayed using Notepad. However, it was created in Visual Studio using the Text File Template found under the **File>New>File>General** menu option. It is physically located in the project subdirectory under the bin\Debug folder. If you attempt to create it in a word-processing application, such as Word, be careful. It must be saved as a plain text file without any special formatting.

A sample run of the application is shown in Figure 11-17.

Figure 11-17   Output from the FileAccessApp application

> **NOTE** One of the properties of the `ListBox` objects is `Sorted`. By default it is set to `false`; however, you can change that and have the entries in the list box in sort order—even if they are not sorted in the file. For this application, because the values are entered by the first name, sorting is inappropriate.

In Example 11-11 the `try...catch` block was enclosed inside a selection statement. The `if` statement was used to check to see if the file existed. When an invalid path was specified, an exception was not thrown and the `try...catch` block was skipped. Examine the `while` statement that appears in Example 11-11.

```
while ((inValue = inFile.ReadLine()) != null)
```

The `ReadLine( )` method is used with the `infile` `object` to retrieve one line of text from the file. The line is stored in the `inValue` variable. The `while` statement tests each access from the file and continues looping until `inValue == null`, indicating all the lines have been read.

Streams are also used in C# for the following processes: reading and writing of data on the network; reading and writing binary files; and reading and writing to an area in memory. `NetworkStream` works with network connections. `MemoryStream` works directly with data in memory. `BinaryReader` and `BinaryWriter` read and write data in (nonreadable) binary format. `FileStream` supports randomly accessing data in a file. Instead of processing values sequentially from top to bottom, values can be processed in any order when random access is used. You may want to explore the documentation for these classes.

Objects of streams can be wrapped with an `object` of the `BufferedStream` `class`— enabling buffering of characters. This can improve the speed and performance of file-handling operations. By wrapping a `BufferedStream` `object` around a file stream `object`, you can bring chunks of characters (more than one record) into memory for retrieval. After the data is stored in memory, members of the `class` read the data from the buffer reducing the number of actual accesses to secondary storage devices, which slows down applications.

Buffering can also be used for creating files. Here instead of writing every record physically to the secondary storage device, the write stores data in a buffer in memory. After the buffer contains a specified number of characters, the buffer is written to the actual file. All that is required to use buffers is to instantiate an `object` of the `BufferedStream` `class` and send as an argument an `object` of one of the stream classes. Then use the `BufferedStream` `object` to access the data. You are encouraged to explore the MSDN documentation for examples.

DATABASE ACCESS

For small applications, you can use text files to store data for later processing. However, as the data needs increase, text files become less viable options. Database management systems (DBMSs) facilitate storage, retrieval, manipulation, and reporting of large amounts of data. DBMSs include programs such as SQL Server, Oracle, DB2, and Access. Many of these DBMSs store data in tabular format and are considered relational databases. The data in the tables are related through common data field keys. This enables a single database to consist of multiple tables. Because databases are such an important component to many applications, the rest of this chapter is devoted to the topic. Examples of how to retrieve and update data in a database are presented. This should enable you to incorporate stored data from databases into your applications.

Databases are a big topic for C# and for other programming languages. Complete books are written on this subject alone. Thus, it is beyond the scope of this book to provide a discussion on creating databases. An assumption is made that you know what a database is and can create a small relational database using a database management system such as Microsoft Access.

Access creates relational databases. As mentioned above, data is stored in tabular format for a relational database. Each row in the table represents a record, which consists of one or more data fields. Each data field is stored in a single column. For a Student database, one table might contain personal information. In that table, one row might include the student identification number, first name, last name, and local phone number for a single student. A second row in the same table would include exactly the same data fields for a different student. Look ahead several pages at Figure 11-18 to see a table from an Access database.

All DBMSs provide reporting capabilities; however, these capabilities can be limited, and there is often a need for processing the data beyond what the DBMS package enables. There is also often a need for a single application to process data from multiple vendors. For both of these scenarios, a programming language is required. Typically when you are programming for database access, you use a query language. One of the most commonly used query languages, structured query language (SQL), includes statements to access, manipulate, and update data in a database. Using SQL queries, you can access single rows, all rows that meet some criteria, or all rows from one or more tables. This retrieval can include one or more of the fields per row. SQL is very powerful, and again complete books are available on the topic. It is beyond the scope of this section to detail the writing of SQL statements. You are encouraged to explore and learn the syntax requirements for writing SQL statements. Simple queries are used in this book in the examples presented as program statements to retrieve specific data items. The language details of these queries are explained so that you can use and modify those statements for your applications.

The .NET Framework includes a data access technology called ActiveX Data Objects (ADO.NET) for accessing data in databases. It is discussed in the next section.

To experience accessing data from an Access database, you do not need the Microsoft Access program, only the table generated using that application. If you are new to databases or do not have Access, your instructor might provide the table for you. One is included with the electronic version of the examples in this chapter.

11

ADO.NET

Included as part of ADO.NET are a number of classes that can be used to retrieve, manipulate, and update data in databases. ADO.NET offers the capability of working with databases in a disconnect mode—meaning the entire database table(s) can be retrieved to a temporary file or to a local machine if the database is stored on the network. Once the database is retrieved, you no longer need to be connected to it. Processing can occur at the local level. If changes are made to the database, the connection can be remade and the changes posted. With multitier applications, the database can be stored on a different computer or across the Internet. With the growth of Web-centric applications, this disconnect feature is extremely important.

To retrieve data from a database programmatically several things are required. First you must connect to the database. Once connected you need a mechanism to retrieve the data. The connection can be constant so that as you retrieve one record, you process it, and then retrieve another record. Or, as noted previously you can work in disconnected mode. For disconnected modes, the data is stored so that your code can work with it. Whether you work in disconnected mode or stay connected to the database, at some point you should release the resources by closing the connection.

Classes that are part of ADO.NET can be used for each of these steps. In the sections that follow, you see how to incorporate these features into your program.

Data Providers

ADO.NET uses a feature called **data providers** to connect, execute commands, and retrieve results from a database. The ADO.NET architecture encapsulates the details of differing database structures such as Oracle, as opposed to Access, in the form of data providers. The four data providers currently included with .NET are:

- **Microsoft SQL Server**—Applications using SQL Server 7.0 or later.

- **Oracle**—Applications using Oracle data sources.

- **Object Linking and Embedding Database (OLE DB) technology**—Applications that use SQL Server 6.5 or earlier and other OLE DB providers, such as the Microsoft Access Jet.OLEDB.4.0 database.

- **Open Database Connectivity (ODBC) technology**—Applications supported by earlier versions of Visual Studio, Access Driver (*.mdb), and Microsoft ODBC for Oracle.

 The data provider classes for ODBC are not included in version 1.0 of the Framework. They are included as part of Visual Studio .NET 2003. At the time of writing they are able to be downloaded at *msdn.microsoft.com/downloads*. The `namespace` for the downloaded .NET Framework data provider for ODBC is `Microsoft.Data.Odbc`.

Each of the data provider classes is encapsulated into a different **namespace**. Provider classes include classes that allow you to connect to the data source, execute commands against the source, and read the results. The unique namespaces for each of the data providers follows:

- `System.Data.SqlClient`—These classes are used with SQL Server, which allows you to connect to SQL Server 7.0 and later versions. `System.Data.SqlTypes` provides classes for native data types within SQL Server.

- `System.Data.OracleClient`—These classes are used with Oracle data sources.

- `System.Data.OleDb`—These classes are used with OLE DB-compatible data sources.

- `System.Data.Odbc`—These classes are used with ODBC data sources.

A number of third-party vendors also provide ADO.NET data providers for their vendor-specific databases.

In addition to these specific data provider namespaces, two additional namespaces are used with ADO.NET classes to access databases. They include:

- `System.Data`—These classes represent the ADO.NET architecture, which enables you to build components that use data from multiple data sources.

- `System.Data.Common`—These classes are shared by all of the data providers.

Each data provider includes a collection of classes used to access a data source, such as a database. Four core classes make up each data provider. They include:

- **Connection**—Establishes a connection to a data source.

- **Command**—Executes a command against a data source. This is often in the form of a SQL statement that retrieves data from the data source.

- **DataReader**—Performs a forward-only (sequential) access of the data in the data source.

- **DataAdapter**—Populates a dataset and updates the database.

Each of these core classes is used in subsequent sections of this chapter to retrieve and update data stored in an Access database.

Connecting to the Database

To access a database created with Microsoft Access, use classes from the `System.Data.OleDb` namespace. To avoid fully qualifying references to classes in its **namespace**, the following `using` directive is needed:

```
using System.Data.OleDb;
```

A connection **object** is instantiated based on the type of database or type of database provider you are using. .NET includes within the **System.Data.OleDb namespace** the **OleDbConnection class** for connection. It represents an open connection to a database. To instantiate an **object** of this **class**, you specify a connection **string** that includes the actual database provider and the data source. The data source is the name of the database. You can include the full path to the database as part of the **string** argument, or the database can be placed in the bin\Debug subdirectory for the project.

 When specifying the full path as part of the **string**, the verbatim **string** is useful (the verbatim **string** uses the ' @ ' character). This eliminates the requirement of using the escape sequence character (' \ ') with the backslash character in the path.

Example 11-12 instantiates an **object** using a connection **string** for an **OleDb** data provider. The **"member.mdb"** database is stored in the current project's bin\Debug subdirectory. After an **object** of the **OleDbConnection class** is instantiated, the connection is opened using the **Open( )** method of the **OleDbConnection class**.

Example 11-12

```
string   sConnection;
sConnection = "Provider=Microsoft.Jet.OLEDB.4.0;" +
              "Data Source=member.mdb";

OleDbConnection   dbConn;
dbConn = new OleDbConnection(sConnection);
dbConn.Open();
```

Connection strings are vendor specific. The syntax for the **string** requires **"Provider=someValue"**. The value for later versions of Access is **"Microsoft.Jet.OLEDB.4.0"**. One of the more challenging portions of connecting to a database is identifying the connection **string** that should be included as the provider. At the time of writing, www.connectionstrings.com listed quite a few strings for different vendors. Another site, www.able-consulting.com/ADO_Conn.htm, also listed connection strings. If you do not find the specific connection string that you need listed at one of these two sites, you could use your favorite search engine and do a keyword search on .NET, "connection string", and the database vendor name.

Exceptions can be thrown when you are working with databases. You can enclose statements that establish the connection to the database within a **try** block and write program statements inside the **catch** clause for those exceptional times when the connection cannot be made.

Retrieving Data from the Database

Once connected to the database, one way to retrieve records programmatically from the database is to issue an SQL query. Another **class**, a command **class**, is available in each of the different data providers' namespaces. The **OleDbCommand class** is used to hold the

SQL statement or stored procedures for OleDb database management systems, such as the Microsoft Access Jet. Once an **object** of the **OleDbCommand class** is constructed, it has several properties that enable you to tie the command (SQL query) to the connection **string**. Example 11-13 instantiates an **object** of the **OleDbCommand class** and sets the **CommandText** and **Connection** properties of that **class**.

Example 11-13

```
string sql;
sql = "Select * From memberTable Order By LastName Asc, "
    + "FirstName Asc;";      // Note the two semicolons

OleDbCommand dbCmd = new OleDbCommand();
dbCmd.CommandText = sql;     // set the command to the SQL string
dbCmd.Connection = dbConn;   // dbConn is the connection object
                             // instantiated in Example 11-12
```

SQL Queries

Select * From memberTable Order By LastName Asc, FirstName Asc; is a simple SQL statement that retrieves every row and column in the **memberTable** table. The asterisk (*) used in the SQL query specifies the selection of all fields in the database table named **memberTable**. The **Asc** is an abbreviation for ascending—indicating that the result of the query is to be returned with the listing in ascending order by **LastName**. Because **FirstName** also includes **Asc**, any duplicate last names are ordered in ascending order by first name. Notice the SQL query ends with a semicolon and the entire query is placed inside double quotes, which end with another semicolon. The last semicolon is required to end the assignment statement that assigns the query to a **string** variable named **sql**.

Any valid SQL statement can be used to retrieve data once the connection is open. If you do not want to retrieve all fields, you replace the asterisk (*) with one or more data field names that are used as column headings in the database table. Figure 11-18 shows the Access database table used with this example.

11

memberTable : Table			
StudentID	FirstName	LastName	PhoneNumber
1234	Rebecca	Smith	2677720
1235	James	Tutle	2877790
1237	Sara	Winston	9047089
1257	Brenda	Bowers	5497876
1260	Gary	Jones	8867889
1276	Ralph	Abbott	3207965
1283	Linda	Bishop	8507654
1299	Colleen	Bennett	4568871
*			0

Figure 11-18   Access database table

The SQL statement that retrieves only the first name, last name, and phone number is:

```
Select FirstName, LastName, PhoneNumber From memberTable;
```

The SQL statement included in Example 11-13 retrieves all records from the table. To retrieve a single row or just some of the rows from the table, you add a `Where` clause to the SQL query. For example, to retrieve the phone number associated with Gary Jones, the SQL statement would read:

```
Select PhoneNumber From memberTable Where FirstName = 'Gary'
                AND LastName = 'Jones';
```

This returns only the phone number since that is the only field specified following the `Select` statement. It does not return the name. Notice that for SQL statements, `string` literal values ('Gary' and 'Jones') are enclosed in single quotation marks.

Processing the Data

Several classes are available to process the data once it is retrieved through the SQL query. You can retrieve one record at a time in memory and process that record before retrieving another, or store the entire result of the query in a temporary data structure similar to an array and disconnect from the database.

For simple read-only access to the database, ADO.NET includes a data reader `class` that can be used to read rows of data from a database. Like the connection and command classes, each data provider has a different data reader `class` defined in its `namespace`. The data reader `class` for accessing OleDb providers is the `OleDbDataReader class`.

Retrieving Data Using a Data Reader

The `OleDbDataReader class` allows read-only forward retrieval of data from the database. Results are returned as the query executes. Using a data reader, you can sequentially loop through the query results. This is an especially good choice for accessing data from the database when you need to retrieve a large amount of data. The data is not cached in memory. By default only one row is stored in memory at a time when the `OleDbDataReader class` is implemented.

To process the data using a data reader, you declare an `object` of the `OleDbDataReader class` and then call the `ExecuteReader( )` method. The `ExecuteReader( )` method of the `OleDbCommand class` is used to build the `OleDbDataReader object`. You saw in the previous section that the `OleDbCommand object` contains the SQL command and the connection `string` representing the data provider.

To position the `OleDbDataReader object` onto the row of the first retrieved query result, you use the `Read( )` method of the `OleDbDataReader class`. The `Read( )`

method is also used to advance to the next record after the previous one is processed. To understand the processing of data retrieved using the `Read( )` method, you can think about what is retrieved from a single access using a data reader **object** as a one-dimensional table consisting of the fields from that one row. The fields can be referenced using the actual ordinal index representing the physical location within the record in which the field is located, much as you index through a single dimensional array. Thus using the database table shown in Figure 11-18, the first call to the `Read( )` method with a data reader **object** named `dbReader` references the value "1234" when you write `dbReader[0]`. `dbReader[1]` refers to "Rebecca". `dbReader[2]` refers to "Smith".

You can also use the table's field names as indexers to the data reader **object**. If the table in the database consists of the fields named `StudentID`, `FirstName`, `LastName`, and `PhoneNumber`, as shown in Figure 11-18, `dbReader[1]` references the first name as does `dbReader["FirstName"]` when `dbReader` is instantiated as an **object** of the `OleDbDataReader` **class**. Thus, in addition to pulling out the values using their ordinal location, you can pull out the values using the individual database field names, such as `LastName`. This is sometimes more convenient and leads to more readable code.

 The first call to `dbReader.Read( )` refers to value 1234 when `dbReader` ["StudentID"] is written. `dbReader["FirstName"]` refers to "Rebecca"; and `dbReader["LastName"]` refers to "Smith". You should note that the field name must be enclosed in double quotes when you use the field name as an indexer.

In addition to accessing the data through indexes, the `OleDbDataReader` **class** includes a number of typed accessor method members. The argument sent to each of the methods is the ordinal location of the data field, or the column number with the first column being column 0. Each of these methods returns the value in the type specified by the method. If you do not use these methods, you must perform an additional step, that being to convert the returned **object** to its correct data type. Table 11-7 lists some of the typed accessor methods and other members of the `OleDbDataReader` **class**.

11

Table 11-7 OleDbDataReader class typed accessor members

OleDbDataReader methods	Description
`Close( )`	Closes an `OleDbDataReader` **object**
`FieldCount`	Property; gets the number of columns in the current row
`GetBoolean(int)`	Gets the value of the specified column as a Boolean
`GetChar(int)`	Gets the value of the specified column as a `char`
`GetDecimal(int)`	Gets the value of the specified column as a `decimal`
`GetDouble(int )`	Gets the value of the specified column as a `double`
`GetInt16(int), GetInt32(int), GetInt64(int)`	Gets the value of the specified column as an integer

Table 11-7 OleDbDataReader class typed accessor members (continued)

OleDbDataReader methods	Description
GetName(int)	Gets the name of the specified column as a Boolean
GetOrdinal(string)	Given the name of the column, gets the ordinal location
GetString(int)	Gets the value of the specified column as a string
GetType(int)	Gets the type of a specified column
Read( )	Advances the OleDbDataReader object to the next record

Example 11-14 illustrates using the data reader to process results retrieved using the SQL command. In this example the values are first stored in an **object**, aMember, of the **Member class**. The **Member object** is then used to populate a list box **object** for a Windows application.

Example 11-14

```
Member aMember;
OleDbDataReader dbReader;
dbReader = dbCmd.ExecuteReader();   // dbCmd is the OleDbCommand
                                    // object instantiated in Example 11-13
while (dbReader.Read( ))
{    // retrieve records 1-by-1...
     aMember = new Member(dbReader["FirstName"].ToString(),
               dbReader["LastName"].ToString());
     this.listBox1.Items.Add(aMember);
}
```

Example 11-15 shows the statements that make up the **Member class**. Notice that one of the constructors of the **Member class** accepts two **string** arguments. In Example 11-14, a **Member object**, aMember, is instantiated using two of the retrieved **dbReader** objects. The database field names (from Figure 11-18) are used as indexers with the retrieved **dbReader object**. Notice how the **ToString( )** method is called with the **dbReader object** in Example 11-14. This is because the **dbReader** returns each data field as an **object**. You have to do the type conversion before sending it to the **Member** constructor; otherwise, an exception is thrown. For the sake of brevity, the **Member class** shown in Example 11-15 contains only the read-only properties, a **ToString( )** method, and two constructors.

Example 11-15

```csharp
// Member.cs
// This class includes private members of
// identification number, first and last
// names, and local phone number. Read-only
// properties are included. The ToString( )
// method is overridden to return a formatted
// full name.
using System;
namespace DBExample
{
    public class Member
    {
        private string id;
        private string firstName;
        private string lastName;
        private string phoneNumber;

        public Member()
        {
        }

        // Constructor
        public Member(string fname, string lname)
        {
            firstName = fname;
            lastName = lname;
        }

        public string FName
        {
            get
            {
                return firstName;
            }
        }

        public string LName
        {
            get
            {
                return lastName;
            }
        }
```

```
        public string ID
        {
            get
            {
                return id;
            }
        }

        public string PhoneNumber
        {
            get
            {
                return phoneNumber;
            }
        }

        public override string  ToString( )
        {
            return firstName + " " + lastName;
        }
    }
}
```

One last thing should be added to your program statements for the **class** that is accessing the database. You should always close the connections before exiting the application.

Closing the Connection

This is one of the easiest things to do, but is often overlooked. You need to close the reader **object** and the connection **object**. By doing this you unlock the database so that other applications can access it. Example 11-16 includes calls to the **Close( )** method to close the connection and data reader objects instantiated in the previous examples.

Example 11-16

```
dbReader.Close();
dbConn.Close();
```

An exception can be thrown when you attempt to close connections as well as when you are trying to access data. You can also enclose the close connection statements in a **try...catch** block, alerting the user if problems arise so that corrective action can be taken.

A special `using` statement can be added to surround the entire block of code accessing a database. When this is added, it is no longer necessary to call the `Close( )` methods. All objects are disposed of when the statements included in the `using` block (surrounded by curly braces) go out of scope.

Example 11-17 pulls together the statements from Examples 11-12, 11-13, 11-14, and 11-16 enclosing them in a `try...catch` block. For the sake of brevity, some of the Windows Form-generated code is not included in the listing. The application includes a `Listbox object` for data display and a `Label object` for displaying error messages. The label is originally set to a `null` value.

Example 11-17

```
// DBExample.cs
// A Windows application is used as the
// front end to display records retrieved
// from an Access database.
using System;
using System.Drawing;
using System.Collections;
using System.ComponentModel;
using System.Windows.Forms;
using System.Data;
using System.Data.OleDb;

namespace DBExample
{
    public class DbGUI : System.Windows.Forms.Form
    {
        private System.Windows.Forms.ListBox listBox1;
        private System.Windows.Forms.Label label2;
        private System.Windows.Forms.Label lblErrorMsg;
        private System.Windows.Forms.Button btnLoad;
        private System.ComponentModel.Container
                components = null;
        private OleDbConnection  dbConn; // Connection object
        private OleDbCommand  dbCmd;     // Command object
        private OleDbDataReader dbReader;// Data Reader object
        private Member aMember;
        private string  sConnection;
        private string sql;

        public DbGUI()
        {
            InitializeComponent();
        }
```

```csharp
// Dispose( ) method removed from listing
#region Windows Form Designer generated code
// Note: Windows Generated Code
// removed - Due to space constraints
#endregion
static void Main()
{
    Application.Run(new DbGUI());
}
private void btnLoad_Click(object sender,
        System.EventArgs e)
{
    try
    {
        // Construct an object of the OleDbConnection
        // class to store the connection string
        // representing the type of data provider
        // (database) and the source (actual db).
        sConnection =
            "Provider=Microsoft.Jet.OLEDB.4.0;" +
            "Data Source=member.mdb";
        dbConn = new OleDbConnection(sConnection);
        dbConn.Open();

        // Construct an object of the OleDbCommand
        // class to hold the SQL query. Tie the
        // OleDbCommand object to the OleDbConnection
        // object.
        sql = "Select * From memberTable Order " +
                "By LastName Asc, FirstName Asc;";
        dbCmd = new OleDbCommand();
        dbCmd.CommandText = sql;
        dbCmd.Connection = dbConn;

        // Create a dbReader object
        dbReader = dbCmd.ExecuteReader();

        while (dbReader.Read())
        {   aMember = new Member
                    (dbReader["FirstName"].ToString(),
                        dbReader["LastName"].ToString());
            this.listBox1.Items.Add(aMember);
        }
        dbReader.Close();
        dbConn.Close();
    }
```

```
            catch (System.Exception exc)
            {
                this.lblErrorMsg.Text = exc.Message;
            }
        }
    }
}
```

 Special note: If you do not override the `ToString( )` method in the `Member` `class`, when you add an `object` of that `class` to the list box, you will get a list box full of the member type names.

The output generated from the program listing in Example 11-17, which uses the `Member` `class` (illustrated in Example 11-15), is shown in Figure 11-19. Remember that the database was previously displayed in Figure 11-18.

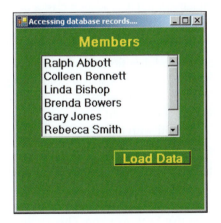

Figure 11-19   Accessing the member.mdb database using the database reader object

The data reader `class` enables read-only access to the database. There are situations that require you to change or update the data in the database. This can be accomplished several ways. You can write SQL statements that include Insert, Delete, and Update statements and then execute those queries by calling the `OleDbCommand.ExecuteNonQuery( )` method. Another easier approach is to instantiate objects of the dataset and data adapter classes. You use the data adapter `object` to populate the dataset `object`. The data adapter `class` has methods such as `Fill( )` and `Update( )` that can eliminate the need to write SQL updates. The sections that follow explain how this can be accomplished.

11

Updating Database Data

ADO.NET does not require that you keep a continuous live connection to the database and process one retrieved record at a time. Additional classes are available that enable you to connect to the database long enough to retrieve records into memory. The data can then be changed and you can reconnect to the database to update the data. This can improve the performance of your applications and allow other applications to access the database while you are working in a disconnected mode. When you do this, you create a temporary copy in memory of the records retrieved from the database and then work with the temporary data as opposed to the live data stored in the database. This is accomplished in .NET using a dataset. A **dataset** is a cache of records retrieved from some data source that may contain one or more tables from the data source. The interaction between the dataset and the actual database is controlled through a data adapter.

Using Datasets to Process Database Records

As with the data reader objects, you use different dataset and data adapter classes in each of the different data provider namespaces depending on the type of database you are accessing. For an Access database provider **class**, you would still add: **using** `System.Data.OleDb;`

Up to the point where you are processing the retrieved data from the SQL query, you need to include the same program statements that you used with the database reader **object**. You still instantiate a connection **object** using the connection **string** for the OleDb data provider and still specify the database name. You read about this in a later section in this chapter, but it is not necessary to call the `Open( )` method with the connection **object** when you use a data adapter **object**. This is handled automatically for you.

You still select the records (and fields) from the database by executing a SQL Select statement. As you saw in Example 11-13, the SQL statement is packaged in a data command **object**. Thus, you still need an **object** of the `OleDbCommand` **class** instantiated and the `CommandText` property for the **class** set to that SQL **string**. These statements from Example 11-13 are repeated for you here in Example 11-18. The only difference between using the database reader **class** and the dataset and data adapter classes, thus far, is that `dbConn.Open( )` is omitted. Connection and command objects are needed.

Example 11-18

```
private OleDbConnection  dbConn;
private OleDbCommand  dbCmd;
private string  sConnection;
private string sql;
            :
            :
// Construct an object of the OleDbConnection
// class to store the connection string
```

```
// representing the type of data provider
// (database) and the source (actual db).
sConnection =
        "Provider=Microsoft.Jet.OLEDB.4.0;" +
            "Data Source=member.mdb";
dbConn = new OleDbConnection(sConnection);

// Construct an object of the OleDbCommand
// class to hold the SQL query. Tie the
// OleDbCommand object to the OleDbConnection
// object.
sql = "Select * From memberTable Order " +
        "By LastName Asc, FirstName Asc;";
dbCmd = new OleDbCommand();
dbCmd.CommandText = sql;
dbCmd.Connection = dbConn;
```

Dataset Object

The data reader **object** held one record of the query result at a time. The dataset **object** stores an entire relational tablelike structure. More than one table, plus relationships and constraints on the database, can be stored with the dataset **object**. The dataset is considered a memory-resident representation of the data. An **object** of the **DataSet class** can be instantiated as follows:

11

```
DataSet memberDS = new DataSet();
```

Data Adapter Object

An easy way to use a **DataSet object** is to instantiate an **object** of the **DataAdapter class**. Adapters are used to exchange data between a database source and a dataset **object**. The adapter also makes it easier to update the database if changes are made. An **object** of the **DataAdapter class** for an **OleDb** provider can be instantiated as follows:

```
OleDbDataAdapter memberDataAdap = new OleDbDataAdapter();
```

Command Builder Object

One additional **class** can be used to generate SQL statements automatically so that you do not have to do additional SQL programming beyond the initial Select statement used to retrieve the records. This is the **OleDbCommandBuilder class**. An **OleDbCommandBuilder object** automatically generates SQL statements for updates once you set the **SelectCommand** property of the **OleDbDataAdapter class**. This property is set to the SQL statement that retrieves the data from the database. Instantiation of the **class** and setting the property are shown in the following code segment:

```
private OleDbCommandBuilder cBuilder;
:
cBuilder = new OleDbCommandBuilder(memberDataAdap);
memberDataAdap.SelectCommand = dbCmd;
```

 The CommandBuilder **object** can only be used for datasets that map to a single database table. The SQL statement used to set the SelectCommand property must also return at least one primary key or unique column. A primary key is a value that uniquely identifies the row. For example, every student has a unique student ID. It makes a good primary key. If none are present, an InvalidOperation exception is generated, and the commands are not generated.

Filling the Dataset Using the Data Adapter

After you have objects instantiated of the data adapter, dataset, and command builder classes, you are ready to go. You fill the dataset using the data adapter by specifying the name of the table to use as the data source, as follows:

```
memberDataAdap.Fill(memberDS, "memberTable");
```

The **Fill( )** method can be used without writing additional SQL statements because you instantiated an **object** of the command builder **class**. The command builder automatically generates SQL statements for the **InsertCommand, UpdateCommand,** and **DeleteCommand** properties of the **DataAdapter class**. You could set the value for each of these properties in exactly the same manner you set the **SelectCommand** property—using a **string** containing a SQL statement.

 If your application requires that the dataset contain values from two or more tables, you cannot have the command builder **class** automatically generate the SQL statements for you. In this case, you have to set the InsertCommand, UpdateCommand, and DeleteCommand properties of the DataAdapter **class**. You do this by setting the DataAdapter object's InsertCommand property with a SQL Insert statement, DeleteCommand property with a SQL Delete statement, and UpdateCommand property with a SQL Delete statement.

That is all that is required to retrieve records from a database. To show the contents of the table and enable the user to make changes, a presentation user interface layer is needed. The table values could be displayed on the console screen or on a control in a Windows application. The grid control is especially well suited to dataset objects. The next section explains how to bind a dataset **object** to a data grid on a Windows application.

Adding a DataGrid Control to Hold the Dataset   To see the data from the database, the records can be placed in a `DataGrid` control `object` on a Windows Form. The `DataGrid` control creates a structure that is divided into rows and columns much like the structure you associate with a relational database table. In addition to being able to navigate around in the data grid, you can make changes by editing current records as well as inserting and deleting new records. To tie the `DataGrid` `object` to the dataset, the `SetDataBinding(  )` method is used as follows:

```
this.dataGrid1.SetDataBinding(memberDS, "memberTable");
```

 Using Visual Studio, a `DataGrid` `object` can be selected from the ToolBox. You can drag and drop the control onto a Windows Form `object`. It contains properties similar to other controls you added to Windows forms such as `Font`, `AutoScroll`, `BackColor`, `ForeColor`, and `Text`.

Updating the Database

Any additional SQL statements needed are generated automatically for you if you instantiated an `object` of the command builder `class`. If you load the database into a `DataGrid` `object` and make changes such as adding records or changing the value of one or more fields, you can flush the changes back up to the live database using the `Update(  )` method of the `DataAdapter` `class`. There are no additional requirements to write Insert, Delete, or Update SQL statements. All you do is write a single statement as follows:

```
memberDataAdap.Update(memberDS, "memberTable");
```

11

This statement is issued after the database table (`"memberTable"`) is tied to the `DataGrid` `object` using the `SetDataBinding(  )` method.

Example 11-19 contains the statements that create a Windows application with a `DataGrid` control `object` populated from the `Member.mdb` database used previously. The application includes statements that enable the database to be updated with changes made in the `DataGrid` `object`. For the sake of brevity, some of the Windows Form-generated code is not included in the listing for Example 11-19.

Example 11-19

```
// DataSetExample.cs
// A Windows application is used as the
// front end to display records retrieved
// from an Access database.
// Values can be changed and the
// database is updated using these changes.
using System;
using System.Drawing;
```

```csharp
using System.Collections;
using System.ComponentModel;
using System.Windows.Forms;
using System.Data;
using System.Data.OleDb;

namespace DataSetExample
{
    public class frmUpdate : System.Windows.Forms.Form
    {
        private System.Windows.Forms.DataGrid dataGrid1;
        private System.Windows.Forms.Label label1;
        private OleDbDataAdapter memberDataAdap;
        private DataSet memberDS;
        private OleDbCommandBuilder cBuilder;
        private OleDbConnection  dbConn;
        private OleDbCommand  dbCmd;
        private string  sConnection;
        private string sql;
        private System.Windows.Forms.Button btnLoad;
        private System.Windows.Forms.Button btnUpdate;
        private System.Windows.Forms.Label lblErrorMsg;
        private System.ComponentModel.Container components = null;

        public frmUpdate()
        {
            InitializeComponent();
        }
        // Dispose( ) method removed from listing
        #region Windows Form Designer generated code
        // Note: Windows Generated Code
        // removed - Due to space constraints
        #endregion
        static void Main()
        {
            Application.Run(new frmUpdate());
        }

        private void btnUpdate_Click(object sender,
                            System.EventArgs e)
        {
            try
            {
                cBuilder = new OleDbCommandBuilder(memberDataAdap);
                memberDataAdap.Update(memberDS, "memberTable");
            }
```

```csharp
            catch (System.Exception exc)
            {
                this.lblErrorMsg.Text = exc.Message;
            }
        }

        private void btnLoad_Click_1(object sender,
                    System.EventArgs e)
        {
            try
            {
                sConnection =
                    "Provider=Microsoft.Jet.OLEDB.4.0;" +
                    "Data Source=member.mdb";
                dbConn = new OleDbConnection(sConnection);

                sql = "Select * From memberTable Order " +
                    "By LastName Asc, FirstName Asc;";
                dbCmd = new OleDbCommand();
                dbCmd.CommandText = sql;
                dbCmd.Connection = dbConn;

                memberDataAdap = new OleDbDataAdapter();
                memberDataAdap.SelectCommand = dbCmd;
                memberDS = new DataSet();
                memberDataAdap.Fill(memberDS, "memberTable");
                this.dataGrid1.SetDataBinding
                    (memberDS, "memberTable");
            }
            catch (System.Exception exc)
            {
                this.lblErrorMsg.Text = exc.Message;
            }
        }
    }
}
```

11

Exception-handling techniques were included in Example 11-19. As with previous examples presented in this chapter, a blank label **object** was placed on the form to display error messages.

Notice how there are no calls to the Open( ) or Close( ) methods. When needed, the Fill( ) and Update( ) methods implicitly open the connection that the DataAdapter is using. These methods also close the connection when they are finished. This simplifies your code.

Figure 11-20 illustrates the application running. The image in the background of Figure 11-20 shows what the form looks like before the Load Data button is clicked. Its event-handler method populates the **DataGrid object** from the **member.mdb** database by first calling the **Fill( )** method of the **OleDbDataAdapter class**. Notice that two arguments to the **Fill( )** method are the **DataSet object** and the database table. These are the same two arguments used to call the **DataGrid** object's **SetDataBinding( )** method to set its **DataSource** and the **DataMember** properties.

Figure 11-20   Output from DataSetExample after the database is loaded

One of the powerful features of the **DataGrid object** is that it enables you to delete or insert new records (rows) into the data grid. You can also change the values of individual fields (columns) in the data grid. However, the changes are to the local copy of the database. To update the live database, those changes must be posted back to the **DataMember** database table. This is done in Example 11-19 when the Update Data button is pressed.

This **btnUpdate_Click( )** event-handler method included a call to the **Update( )** method of the **OleDbDataAdapter class**. The live database connection is reopened, and the current contents of the dataset (bound to the data grid) are written to the database table specified by the **DataMember** property listed as the second argument.

As shown in Figure 11-21, several changes were made to the local database to illustrate that records could be inserted (Charlene Boswick), or deleted (Gary Jones and Colleen Bennett), and values in fields could be changed (Ralph Abbott changed to Roger Adams). The back image in Figure 11-21 shows the updated database table. The image in the foreground in Figure 11-21 shows the changed values in the **DataGrid object**.

Figure 11-21   Updated database records

QUICK REVIEW

1. Exceptions are unexpected conditions that happen very infrequently. They are usually associated with some type of error condition that causes an abnormal termination if they are not handled.

2. If a program encounters an error during runtime from which it is unable to recover, such as division by zero, it raises or throws an exception.

3. If none of the methods along the call chain include code to handle the error, the CLR handles the exception by halting the entire application.

4. "Bugs" are programmer mistakes that should be caught and fixed before an application is released.

5. In addition to bugs, programs may experience errors because of user actions. These actions may cause exceptions to be thrown.

6. A stack trace is a listing of all the methods that are executing when an exception is thrown.

7. Exception-handling techniques are for serious errors that occur infrequently. Exceptions are those events from which a program is not able to recover, such as attempting to read from a data file that does not exist.

8. For exception handling in C#, **try...catch** blocks are used. Code that may be a problem is placed in a **try** block. The code to deal with the problem, the exception handler, is placed in **catch** blocks, which are also called **catch** clauses. The code found in the **finally** block is executed whether an exception is thrown or not.

11

9. When an exception is raised, an **object** is created to represent the exception. All exception objects inherit from the **base class** named **Exception**, which is part of the **System** **namespace**.

10. If you create your own exception classes, they should derive from the **ApplicationException** **class**. Other system exception classes derive from the **SystemException** **class**. It is a good idea to use the word "Exception" as part of the identifier.

11. When you include filters for multiple exceptions in your **class**, the order of placement of these clauses is very important. They should be placed from most specific to most generic.

12. The **StreamReader** and **StreamWriter** classes make it easy to read or write text files in C#. The **StreamReader** **class** was designed to enable lines of information to be read from a text file. The **StreamWriter** **class** implements methods for **Write( )** and **WriteLine( )** similar to those you learned for the **Console** **class**.

13. To terminate normally, the **Close( )** method is used with the stream classes. It is called without arguments, but does require that an **object** be used with the call.

14. .NET includes a number of ActiveX Data Object (ADO.NET) classes that can be used to retrieve, manipulate, and update data in databases.

15. One of the most significant advancements of ADO.NET is the ease with which it is able to work in a disconnect manner—that is, the database table(s) can be retrieved to a client or local machine.

16. To retrieve data from a database programmatically, you must first connect to the database and then use a mechanism to retrieve the data.

17. Four data providers are included with .NET. To connect to an Access database, use the **OleDb** data provider.

18. Connection strings are vendor specific. The syntax for the **string** requires **"Provider=someValue"**.

19. Once connected, one way to retrieve records programmatically from the database is to issue a SQL query. The **OleDbCommand** **class** is used to hold the SQL statement.

20. For simple read-only access to the database, .NET includes a data reader **class** that can be used to read rows of data from a database.

21. The **OleDbDataReader** **class** allows read-only forward retrieval of data from the database. The data is not cached in memory. By default only one row is stored in memory at a time when the **OleDbDataReader** **class** is implemented.

22. To process the data using a data reader, you declare an **object** of the **OleDbDataReader** **class** and then call the **ExecuteReader( )** method of the **OleDbCommand** **class** to build the **OleDbDataReader** **object**.

23. To position the **OleDbDataReader** **object** onto the row of the first record retrieved, you use the **Read( )** method of the **OleDbDataReader** **class**. The **Read( )** method is also used to advance to the next record once the previous one is processed.

24. To understand the processing of the data retrieved using the `Read( )` method, you can think about what is retrieved from a single access attempt using a data reader **object** as a one dimensional table consisting of the fields from that one row.

25. You need to close the reader **object** and the connection **object** to unlock the database so that others can access it.

26. ADO.NET does not require that you keep a continuous live connection to the database. This is accomplished in .NET using a dataset. A dataset is a cache of records retrieved from some data source that may contain one or more tables from the data source.

27. Using the `DataAdapter` **object** with the `Fill( )` and/or `Update( )` methods eliminates the need to open and close the connections. Connections are opened and closed automatically when the `Fill( )` or `Update( )` methods are called.

28. Adapters are used to exchange data between a database source and a dataset **object**.

29. The `OleDbCommandBuilder` **object** automatically generates SQL statements for updates to the database. It is usable for queries involving one table.

30. The `DataGrid` control **object** is a structure that is divided into rows and columns and can be used to store dataset objects. The `DataGrid` control **object** allows you to change values, or delete or insert new records.

31. To tie the `DataGrid` **object** to the dataset, the `SetDataBinding( )` method of the `DataGrid` **class** is used.

EXERCISES

11

1. _____ are unexpected conditions that happen very infrequently.
    a. Bugs
    b. Conditions
    c. Exceptions
    d. Streams
    e. Objects

2. A Just-In-Time debugging window is displayed when a(an):
    a. application is executed
    b. unhandled exception is thrown
    c. handled exception is thrown
    d. unhandled exception is caught
    e. handled exception is caught

3. Raising an exception is the same as:

   a. catching an exception

   b. trying a block of code that might create an exception

   c. throwing an exception

   d. defining a new exception `class`

   e. rolling back an exception

4. The segment of code that might create an unexpected problem should be:

   a. placed in a `try` block

   b. placed in a `catch` block

   c. placed in a `finally` block

   d. placed on the outside of the `try...catch...finally` block

   e. included in the `Main( )` method

5. What type of exception would be thrown if the user enters the wrong type of data when requested from the keyboard?

   a. `System.FormatException`

   b. `System.Invalid.CastException`

   c. `System.NullReferenceException`

   d. `System.IndexOutOfRangeException`

   e. `System.ArithmeticException`

6. What type of exception would be thrown if a program statement attempted to access location 0 in an array defined to hold 20 elements?

   a. `System.FormatException`

   b. `System.Invalid.CastException`

   c. `System.NullReferenceException`

   d. `System.IndexOutOfRangeException`

   e. none of the above

7. What type of exception would be thrown if the following arithmetic were performed?

   ```
   double aValue = 0,
              bValue = 0;
   int result = (int) aValue / (int) bValue;
   ```

   a. `System.FormatException`

   b. `System.Invalid.CastException`

   c. `System.ArgumentException`

   d. `System.DivideByZeroException`

   e. none of the above

8. If an application is written to filter several exceptions including `System.Exception`, `System.DivideByZeroException`, and `System.ArithmeticException`, in what order should they be listed?

   a. `System.Exception`, `System.DivideByZeroException`, then `System.ArithmeticException`

   b. `System.Exception`, `System.ArithmeticException`, then `System.DivideByZeroException`

   c. `System.DivideByZeroException`, `System.Exception`, then `System.ArithmeticException`

   d. `System.DivideByZeroException`, `System.ArithmeticException`, then `System.Exception`

   e. It does not matter.

9. To avoid an `IOException` exception with files, you can either use a **try...catch** block or make sure there is a file before attempting to read characters from it. This can be done by:

   a. calling the `File.Exists( )` method

   b. using a loop to cycle through the file structure

   c. throwing an exception

   d. including statements in a **finally** block

   e. placing a test loop in the `Main( )` method

10. Writing a **catch** clause without including the parentheses and an argument list such as **catch { }**:

    a. generates a syntax error

    b. requires a **finally** clause

    c. has the same effect as **catch** (`System.Exception`) { }

    d. throws an exception

    e. none of the above

11. Which of the following is an **abstract class**?

    a. `TextReader`

    b. `Stream`

    c. `StreamReader`

    d. all of the above

    e. none of the above

11

12. In Visual Studio, if you do not specify the full path of a file or database, what directory is used?

    a. C:\

    b. the project directory

    c. C:\Bob

    d. C:\bin\Debug

    e. C:\WorkDirectory

13. Using the verbatim `string`, you could write the full path of C:\CSharpProjects\Ch10\WorkDirectory as:

    a. `@"C:\CSharpProjects\Ch10\WorkDirectory"@`

    b. `@"C:\\CSharpProjects\\Ch10\\WorkDirectory"`

    c. `@"C:\CSharpProjects\Ch10\WorkDirectory"`

    d. `"@C:\CSharpProjects\Ch10\WorkDirectory"`

    e. none of the above

14. What method in the `StreamReader` `class` retrieves a full line of text—up until the newline character is encountered?

    a. `Flush( )`

    b. `ReadBlock( )`

    c. `Retrieve( )`

    d. `ReadLine( )`

    e. `Peek( )`

15. To make a duplicate copy of a file, you could use a `static` method in the _____ `class`.

    a. `File`

    b. `StreamWriter`

    c. `Stream`

    d. `TextWriter`

    e. `BinaryWriter`

16. Streams can be used in C# for writing data to:

    a. text files

    b. networks

    c. memory

    d. binary files

    e. all of the above

17. To retrieve specific records from a database programmatically, use a(n):

    a. SQL statement

    b. data provider

    c. `OleDbConnection`

    d. `try...catch...finally` block

    e. Command statement

18. A connection `string` contains:

    a. a `using` directive

    b. the name of the data source

    c. the version number of database management system

    d. the list of fields in the database

    e. a SQL statement

19. The core classes available with each data provider include all of the following except:

    a. connection

    b. data adapter

    c. command

    d. dataset

    e. data reader

11

20. The following namespaces (`System.Data.OleDB`, `System.Data.SqlClient`, `System.Data.Odbc`, `System.Data.OracleClient`) include classes for different:

    a. data providers

    b. file streams

    c. ADO.NET applications

    d. databases

    e. data readers

21. For read-only access to databases, use the _____ `class`.

    a. dataset

    b. data adapter

    c. command builder

    d. connection

    e. data reader

22. To provide access to an Access Jet database management system, the _____ data provider is used.

    a. `System.Data.OleDb`

    b. `System.Data.SqlClient`

    c. `System.Data.Odbc`

    d. `System.Data.OracleClient`

    e. `Microsoft.Jet.OLEDB.4.0`

23. You can create a disconnected database using the _____ `class` with the dataset `class`.

    a. `DataAdapter`

    b. `DataReader`

    c. `Command`

    d. `OleDbConnection`

    e. `Fill`

24. To avoid writing additional SQL statements to update a live database, instantiate an `object` of the _____ `class`.

    a. `DataAdapter`

    b. `DataReader`

    c. `DataSet`

    d. `CommandBuilder`

    e. `DataGrid`

25. To release the database so that it can be used by other applications, call the _____ method.

    a. `ReleaseDb( )`

    b. `Release( )`

    c. `StopAccess( )`

    d. `Close( )`

    e. none of the above

26. The result of division by zero is undefined for both integral and floating-point values. Describe how avoiding floating-point division by zero differs from integral division by zero.

27. Give one example of what would cause each of the following exceptions to be thrown:

    a. `System.ArithmeticException`

    b. `System.FormatException`

    c. `System.IndexOutOfRangeException`

    d. `System.IO.IOException`

    e. `FileNotFoundException`

28. Write a file declaration for a file that holds text characters and can be stored in C:\CSharpProjects\WorkDirectory. The file will be used to store data.

29. For the file declared in Exercise 28, write a method that stores the numbers 10 through 50 in the text file. Include a **try** block and at least two appropriate **catch** clauses inside the method.

30. Explain how dataset, data adapter, data grid, and command builder objects are used to update a database.

PROGRAMMING EXERCISES

1. Write an application that includes **catch** clauses for `System.ArithmeticException`, `System.FormatException`, `System.IndexOutOfRangeException`, and `System.Exception`. Write a **try** block to throw each of the exceptions. As you test the application, comment out each problem as you add additional errors for testing purposes. Your final solution should include at least one statement per exception that throws each exception. The statements should all be commented out by the time you finish testing. Be sure to include documenting comments with each statement.

2. Design an application that includes three arrays of type **int**. Allow the user to enter values into the first two. Write a method to store the product of the two arrays in the third array. Produce a display that shows the contents of all three arrays using a single line per indexed value. Your solution should include exception-handling techniques with a minimum of three **catch** clauses.

3. Given any number of inputted scores, write a program that calculates an average. After values are entered and the average calculated, test the result to determine whether an A, B, C, D, or F should be recorded. The scoring rubric is as follows: A—90–100; B—80–89; C—70–79; D—60–69; F < 60. Your solution should include exception-handling techniques with a minimum of three **catch** clauses.

11

4. Write a program that stores your name, address, and local phone number in a text file. Surround your phone number with asterisks. Include appropriate exception-handling techniques in your solution.

5. Place the following values in a text file: 86, 97, 144, 26. To simplify the problem, the values can each be placed on separate lines. Write a C# program to retrieve the values from the text file and print the average of the values formatted with two decimal places.

6. Write an application that retrieves a student name and three scores per line from a text file. Process the values by calculating the average of the scores per student. Write the name and average to a different text file. Test your application with a minimum of eight records in the original file.

7. Modify your solution to Exercise 10 of Chapter 7 so that it includes exception-handling techniques. The modified problem definition is as follows: write a program that determines the number of students who can still enroll in a given class. Design your solution using parallel arrays. Do a compile-time initialization using the following values:

Class name	Current enrollment	Maximum enrollment
CS150	18	20
CS250	11	20
CS270	32	25
CS300	04	20
CS350	20	20

Define a custom exception **class** for this problem so that an exception is thrown if the current enrollment exceeds the maximum enrollment by more than three. When this unexpected condition occurs, halt the report and display a message indicating which course is over-enrolled.

8. Create a small Access database to include customer numbers, customer names, and customer areas. Place eight records in the database. For the customer area field, use the designations of N for North, S for South, and so on. Write a C# program to display only the names of all customers.

9. Using the database created in Exercise 8, write a C# program to display the customer number and name in a data grid. Allow the user to add records to the database. If your designed solution involves the use of a disconnected database, post the changes back to the live database.

10. Using the database created in Exercise 8, write a C# program that retrieves records from the customer table and displays the customer number and name in a data grid. Allow the user to select an entry from the data grid. Display the corresponding customer area for the one selected. It should be displayed on a different control on the Windows application, such as a label or text box.

Web-Based Applications

Web Forms, Web Services, and Mobile Device Applications

In this chapter, you will:

- O Discover how Web-based applications differ from Windows applications
- O Use ASP.NET to create Web applications
- O Develop and configure Web Forms pages
- O Learn about the different types of controls that can be added to Web applications
- O Add HTML and Web Forms server controls to Web applications
- O Add validation, custom, and composite controls to verify user input, display calendars, and connect to database tables
- O Become aware of Web Services and their implications for distributed applications
- O Learn how mobile applications are developed using the Compact Framework (optional)

In previous chapters, you learned how easy it is to develop graphical user interfaces for Windows applications using C# and the drag-and-drop construction approach of Visual Studio .NET. In this chapter, you discover that this same approach can be used to develop applications for the Web. You learn how the design of Web-based applications differs from Windows applications. You discover the differences between HTML and Web server controls. You learn what a Web Service is and how to write one. This chapter also includes an introduction to mobile applications that can be viewed with small personal devices such as a personal digital assistant (PDA).

Web-based applications are often data driven. In Chapter 11, you learned about the rich set of classes that are used to access and update data stored in database tables. You learned about data providers, and the connection, command, data reader, and data adapter core classes included within each data provider. You will use these ADO.NET classes with the Web applications you develop. You will learn how to use validation controls to check a user's input values. You will learn how to add calendar controls to your Web pages. By the time you complete this chapter, you will be creating very sophisticated, highly interactive, data-driven Web applications.

WEB-BASED APPLICATIONS

A Web-based application runs within an Internet browser—which means it is designed to be accessible to multiple users, run over different platforms, and deliver the same content to every user. A **Web application** is simply a collection of one or more related files or components stored on a Web server. Web applications are also called **Web sites**. A **Web server** is software that hosts or delivers the Web application. The hardware on which the Web server software is loaded is often called a Web server, but it is the software that makes the equipment special and thus enables the computer to be called a server.

Web Programming Model

The programming model for Web pages is somewhat different from Windows applications, especially in terms of the interaction with users. For example, `MessageBox` dialog boxes, commonly used with Windows applications, are not used with Web applications. Their output is displayed on the server computer instead of at the client computer requesting the page. Messages to users accessing a Web page are normally displayed through the `Label object` or other objects on the page.

Each request to view a Web page requires a **round trip to the server** on which the page is stored. This simply means that the user requests the page via Hypertext Transfer Protocol (HTTP) by typing the Web address, the **universal resource locator** (**URL**), into a Web browser. That request is forwarded to the Web server on which the page is stored. The page is then sent back as a Hypertext Markup Language (HTML) document where it is **rendered** (converted from HTML) to a formatted page on the client computer that requested the page.

Second and subsequent requests for the page require a postback to the server. But, not all events are automatically posted back to the server when an event is triggered. Some events such as the `SelectedIndexChanged` or `CheckedChanged` events for `ListBox` and `RadioButton` objects are queued, and their event-handler methods not executed until an event that causes a postback to the server is fired. `ButtonClick` events are one of the few events that cause an automatic postback.

Every postback trip to the server creates a **new object**. This causes Web pages to be **stateless**—meaning they do not retain their values from one trip to the Web server to the next. Values that you type into `TextBox` objects, for example, are not automatically saved and redisplayed when a page is sent back to a client computer. Second and subsequent requests for the page may require programmatically retrieving and storing inputted values and then sending them back to the control when the page is sent back for redisplay on the client computer. Thus, the Web programming model requires some important additional considerations. In the sections that follow, you learn how this model is implemented using C# and ASP.NET.

Static Pages

The files that make up a Web application end with file extensions such as .htm, .html, .asp, .aspx, .asmx, or the files may be image, video, music, or data files. Web application pages are commonly categorized as either static or dynamic. **Static Web pages** do not require any processing on the client computer or by a Web server. They are precreated, reside on the server's hard drive, and basically are delivered as HTML documents. An HTML file contains formatting markup tags that are converted (rendered) to their displayed images by browser software such as Internet Explorer. Figure 12-1 shows a static HTML document opened within Internet Explorer. As shown in the Address bar of the browser software, the file ends with a .htm extension as part of its name.

12

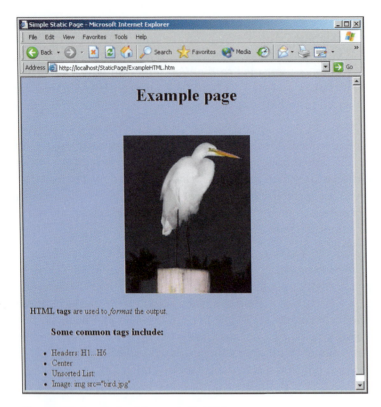

Figure 12-1 Output from static Web page

Example 12-1 shows the HTML file used to display the static Web page for Figure 12-1.

Example 12-1

```
<html>                              <!-- ExampleHTML.htm   -->
  <head>                            <!-- Creates caption   -->
    <title>
    Simple Static Page
    </title>
  </head>                           <!--    Comments       -->
    'v bgColor="#aabbff">           <!--  blue background -->
        nter>
            xample page </p> </H1>
              ->                    <!--Break to next line-->
                ="bird.jpg" >
                 >
```

```
<br>
<Strong>HTML tags</Strong>       <!--Strong - bold    -->
are used to <EM>format</EM>      <!--EM - italic       -->
the output.
<UL>                             <!--Unsorted list     -->
    <H3>
        Some common tags include:
    </H3>
    <LI>                         <!--Element in list   -->
        Headers: H1...H6         <!--H1 is the largest -->
    </LI>                        <!--H6 is the smallest-->
    <LI>
        Center                   <!--text shown on page-->
    </LI>
    <LI>
        Unsorted List:          <!-- UL    and LI      -->
    </LI>
    <LI>
        Image: img src="bird.jpg"<!--Image             -->
    </LI>                        <!--End list element  -->
    </UI>                        <!--End unsorted list -->
</body>
</html>
```

 Unlike C#, in HTML you can mix and match case with your tags. In addition, HTML is not case sensitive.

12

The Web server does not have to process any of the statements in Example 12-1. Static pages are client-side applications and, as the name implies, they involve no interaction with the user. The pages are simply displayed as static material on the client's Web browser. Rendering of the pages can occur at the client (local workstation) where the pages are displayed. The Web server simply delivers the requested page as an HTML document.

Some Web applications require processing before pages are displayed. One common way to add functionality to a page is to include code written in a scripting language as part of the HTML file. This creates **dynamic Web sites**—pages that enable the user to interact and see the result of their interaction. Dynamic Web sites are discussed next.

Dynamic Pages

Dynamic Web pages involve processing in addition to rendering the formatting HTML tags. One programming model for creating dynamic Web pages is to use traditional or classic **Active Server Pages (ASP)**. The **ASP** model extends the HTML file by including script code in the same file. The file may still be able to be executed on the client machine, without additional processing at the server level. In this case, the code that is embedded in the HTML document is called a **client-side script**, and it involves only **client-side processing**. **Server-side scripts** require the processing to be done at the server level before the page is delivered. A number of scripting languages are used to write this code for the HTML document. Two of the most common scripting languages are VBScript and JavaScript. **VBScript**, a subset of Microsoft Visual Basic 6.0, has been very popular. The only Web browser, however, with built-in support for VBScript is Microsoft Internet Explorer (IE). Thus, for the VBScript scripts to be executed on the client computer, the pages must be viewed using IE.

 With the introduction of Visual Basic .NET, no update was included for VBScript as part of .NET.

JavaScript is also a very popular scripting language. **JavaScript** is not a subset of Java. There are some syntax similarities to Java, but it is not a full-featured programming language like Java. **JScript** is Microsoft's implementation of JavaScript. Using these scripting languages, developers are able to take static pages and add functionality—creating dynamic Web pages.

 Scripting languages are interpreted, instead of compiled, and the code is embedded directly into the HTML page.

JavaScript, JScript, VBScript, or any one of the other scripting languages could be used to write the embedded code for the HTML document. This code provides functionality beyond the formatting that the HTML tags provide. User input for Web applications is often validated using scripting code. When a request is sent to the server to display a page that contains server-side scripting, the page is interpreted (converted to binary form) and then the scripted code is run to get the output results. The output of the script code is merged with the static HTML output found in the page before sending the output back to the client ┐mputer that requested the page. Figure 12-2 illustrates this scenario. The client system ⌐s a page using Hypertext Transfer Protocol—sending the URL as part of the HTTP ┐ind the scenes, the script is executed on the server. The client receives a response ┐f a displayed HTML document.

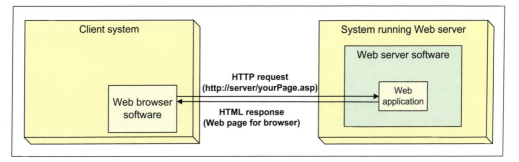

Figure 12-2 Server-side processing of a dynamic Web page

Figure 12-2 illustrates a **client–server** type of relationship. The client requests a page; the server gets it ready by executing the scripts inside the HTML document; and lastly, the client sees the result in the form of an HTML document. This is the way traditional ASP is used to enable dynamic Web pages to be viewed on client computers. A newer model for Web development is included as part of .NET. That model is called ASP.NET. It is discussed in the next section.

ASP.NET

ASP.NET is different from classic ASP. You do not have to write code in a separate scripting language with ASP.NET, as you do with ASP applications. ASP is interpreted; ASP.NET is compiled. **ASP.NET** is a completely new programming model that includes a number of classes as part of the .NET Framework. These classes allow you to take full advantage of the features of the Common Language Runtime and inheritance. You can use ADO.NET with ASP.NET applications to develop data-driven Web sites. Using Visual Studio .NET and ASP.NET, you can design the user interface for the Web application using a drag-and-drop approach.

12

> NOTE
>
> One way to identify an ASP Web application from an ASP.NET Web application is by looking at their file extensions. An ASP Web page, which contains the HTML tags and the program logic written in a scripting language, ends with an .asp file extension. The ASP.NET Web page file that contains the HTML tags ends with an .aspx file extension and includes no scripting language code for the program logic. This logic is stored in a separate file.

You can use Visual Basic .NET, J#, and C# to develop ASP.NET Web applications, and th[...] applications you create run on the computer functioning as the Web server. To develop [...] ASP.NET application, Microsoft Internet Information Services (IIS) must be installed [...] provides the software tools for managing the Web server. You do not have to work [...]

with IIS. Most everything dealing with IIS happens behind the scenes. However, to develop Web applications in Visual Studio .NET, IIS must be loaded.

IIS

The Web server software can be running locally on the same machine on which the Web application is developed or it can be running at a remote location, but it is needed for the development of ASP.NET applications. IIS requires a server-like operating system. The Home editions of the following operating systems do not support IIS: Windows 98, Windows ME, and Windows XP. Thus, you cannot develop ASP.NET Web applications on these platforms. IIS is part of Windows 2000, Windows XP Pro, Windows Server 2003, and later operating system versions.

To use Visual Studio .NET's IDE to develop ASP.NET Web applications, the IIS component should be installed *before* loading the .NET Framework. On your home system, where you have administrative rights, you can verify that IIS is installed (or install it) using the Add/Remove Programs option from the Control Panel. Clicking Add/Remove Windows Components launches the Components Wizard as shown in Figure 12-3.

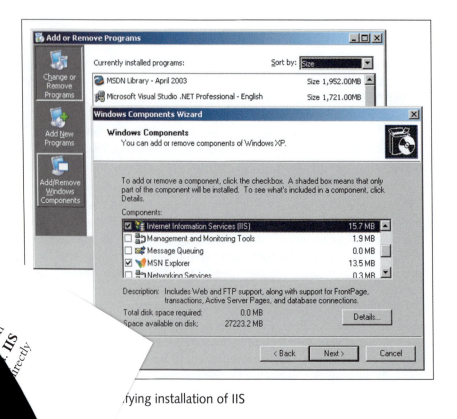

...fying installation of IIS

If you have installed Visual Studio with ASP.NET and the .NET Framework on a computer that does not have IIS installed, ASP.NET does not work correctly. An error message is generated when you try to create your first ASP.NET Web application. You can repair ASP.NET after you load the IIS component using the ASP.NET IIS Registration tool (Aspnet_regiis.exe). This program must be executed from the command line.

 To repair ASP.NET (after loading IIS), move into the directory containing the Aspnet_regiis.exe file. For example, you might type: cd:\windows\microsoft.NET\ framework\v1.1.4322 (replacing v1.1.4322 by the version you have installed). Use search to find the file; the version number is shown as the last subdirectory name. Once you are in the directory, type Aspnet_regiis.exe –i followed by the Enter key. When that is finished, type iisreset.exe.

To develop Web applications using Visual Studio .NET, you must also have administrative debugging privileges. This was not an issue for developing Windows applications. It is a requirement for creating Web applications. Working on your own home system this should not be a problem; however, for campus intranet environments, it requires administrative privileges.

 The terms Web applications and Web sites are used interchangeably.

Requests to display pages managed by IIS are classified as requests for static or dynamic pages—based on the file extension associated with the Web site. When IIS gets a request to display a file that ends with an extension of .htm or .html, no additional processing is required. IIS simply returns the HTML document. Dynamic ASP.NET files end with an extension of .aspx. Requests for these pages require processing on the server.

12

Requests come from a browser in the form of Hypertext Transfer Protocol (http://...). Responses take the form of a returned Hypertext Markup Language (HTML) document.

Virtual Directories

IIS assigns a virtual name to the directory storing your Web applications. This virtual name becomes part of the Web site's address. It is virtual because there is not a one-to-one correspondence between this virtual name and the actual physical location of the files. IIS manages the mapping of the virtual name to its actual physical location. Using Visual Studio .NET, you do not have to work directly with IIS. However, you can manually create virtual directories and access Web applications within a Web browser using the virtual name. You manually create virtual directories using the Administrative Tools option in Control Panel. After selecting Internet Information Services within the Administrative Tools window, expanding Web Sites (clicking the "+") reveals the Default Web Site icon. By right-the Default Web Site icon, you can bring up the option to create a new Virtual Directory as illustrated in Figure 12-4. The Administrative Tools window is displayed by selecting **Start>Control Panel>Administrative Tools**.

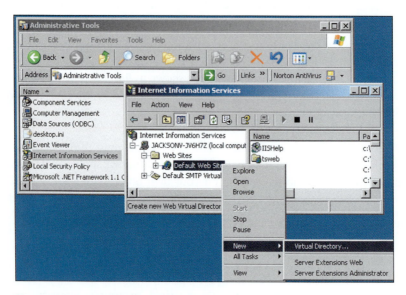

Figure 12-4   Manually creating a virtual directory

The Virtual Directory Creation Wizard walks you through the creation of the directory. You are asked to enter an alias name for the location and identify the physical location on the hard drive where the Web site files should be stored. The name you select as the alias becomes the virtual name—the name of the Web site. Then, when you want to access the Web site from the computer where it is developed, you can use a browser to do so. Request that the page be displayed using http:// followed by the Web site's name (which is the alias name) using your Web browser. The alias name is preceded by the default home directory name, which is **localhost** on most computers. Thus, you would type http://localhost/NameYouSelectedAsTheAlias in the Address bar of the Web browser to retrieve the page.

Every Web site has a home directory where the files are physically located. The default home directory is C:\Inetpub\wwwroot. By default, typing http://localhost maps to ___etpub\wwwroot.

_____eated for the file shown in Example 12-1. Remember that this file was _____ntained only HTML tags. The virtual directory alias name selected is _____physical location of the files is shown in Figure 12-5. Using MyComputer, _____ows that the file is physically stored deep within the hard drive.

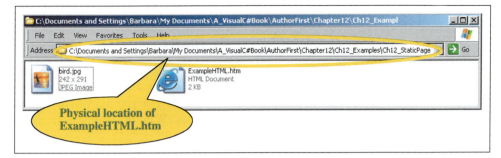

Physical location of
ExampleHTML.htm

Figure 12-5   Location of ExampleHTML.htm

Figure 12-6 illustrates how the file is accessed using its virtual directory name. It is not necessary to type the long filename path shown in Figure 12-5. You simply type the virtual name for that path. The file to be displayed is ExampleHTML.htm.

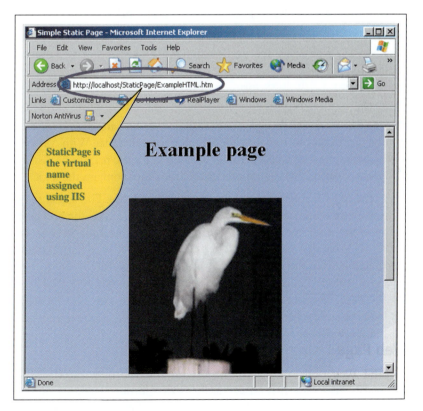

StaticPage is
the virtual
name
assigned
using IIS

12

Figure 12-6   File accessed using a virtual filename

If you are using Visual Studio .NET, you do not have to create virtual directories manually for the Web sites you build. You still have the benefit of accessing them using http://localhost followed by the Web application or site name. However, Visual Studio automatically creates the virtual directory for you.

Using Visual Studio .NET, you have access to all of the Framework Class Library (FCL) classes and can drag and drop controls in the same manner you did when you created Windows applications. Instead of placing the controls on a Windows forms page, the controls are dropped onto a Web Forms page.

WEB FORMS PAGE

The `System.Web.UI namespace` organizes the classes that are used to create .NET Web applications. This `namespace` includes a `Control class`, inherited by the `HTMLControl` and `WebControl` classes. Like the `Control class` in the `System.Windows.Forms namespace`, `Control` provides some common functionality for all classes that are derived from it. The `System.Web.UI namespace` also includes a `Page class`, which is instantiated when you create a Web application using Visual Studio .NET.

Building ASP.NET Web applications involves many of the same concepts you learned when you built Windows applications. They are designed with the event-driven model, but there are fewer events. Web sites are created using a Web Forms page. As opposed to dragging and dropping controls onto a Windows form, controls are dropped onto a Web Forms Page. There are, however, some significant differences between a Windows and Web application.

When you build an ASP.NET Web application, two separate files are created for the user interface. With Windows applications, only one file is built for the interface. With ASP.NET applications, both of these files must be available to the Web server for the page to be displayed. One of the files contains the visual HTML components, and the other contains the logic.

The file storing the logic is referred to as the **code-behind file**. The actual file storing the visual elements is the one referred to as the Web Forms page. This is the container file from which the controls are displayed. The Web Forms page contains static HTML tags and any ASP.NET server controls that have been added to the application. The programming logic resides in a separate file from the file containing the HTML tags. All the event-handler methods are stored in this code-behind file. This file contains the code that enables the user to ⌐ct with the page. The next section examines how these two files function when an ⌐ is built using Visual Studio .NET.

⌐ge Using Visual Studio .NET

⌐ Application template to create a Web user interface. By default, as ⌐, the project is created at http://localhost. Whatever name you type for ⌐llowing "localhost" becomes the virtual directory name for the Web site. ⌐cally stored at the default home directory for the Web application. Unless **default home directory**, the files are stored at C:\Inetpub\wwwroot.

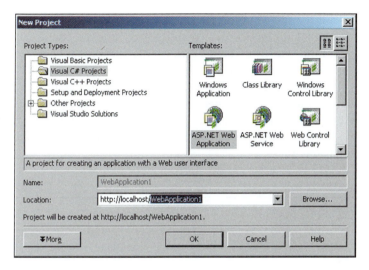

Figure 12-7   Web application template for ASP.NET

Changing `WebApplication1` (shown in Figure 12-7) to `DynamicPage` creates a Web site named `DynamicPage`. This also becomes the virtual directory name. All files for the Web site application, except two solution files, are stored in the C:\Inetpub\wwwroot\ DynamicPage directory as shown in Figure 12-8.

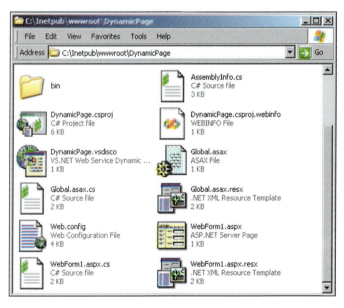

Figure 12-8   Virtual directory for DynamicPage

12

Visual Studio .NET places the two solution files at a different location. A directory is created using the name you typed for the project, and the directory is placed (along with the two solution files) at the location you configured Visual Studio to store all your Visual Studio projects. The two solution files have the same name as the Web application (Visual Studio project); they end with file extensions of .sln and .suo. As shown in Figure 12-9, using the **Tools>Options** menu option, you can change the Settings for the storage location of your projects. Because C:\CSharpProjects was entered as the location for projects for this book, DynamicPage.suo and DynamicPage.sln are stored under the DynamicPage subdirectory at C:\CSharpProjects\DynamicPage.

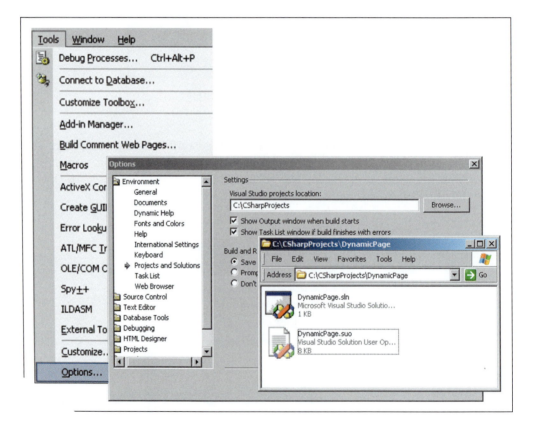

Physical location of DynamicPage solution files

...plication is created, saved, and closed, it can be reopened differently
...vs application. To reopen a Web application, select **File>Open>Project**
...istead of **File>Open>Project**. By doing this, you are shown the list of all
...cations (sites) stored at localhost (C:\Inetpub\wwwroot).

Web Forms Page

When you first create the Web application project, a blank page is displayed with a message indicating that grid layout mode will be used. When you add controls to a Web page, several page layout modes are available. As shown in Figure 12-10, grid layout is the default. As with Windows applications, the page container **class** has a number of properties that can be set. `pageLayout` is one of the page's properties. It can be changed to `FlowLayout`, which has traditionally been the default layout mode used for creating Web applications. However, using Visual Studio .NET, you will probably find the grid layout easier to use for development.

 With `FlowLayout`, you cannot drag elements across the Design view surface or use the positioning grid. You can with `GridLayout`, which also supports the Snap to Grid feature. With `FlowLayout`, the Web browsers arrange elements in the order that they occur on the page, from top to bottom.

Figure 12-10 shows the Web Forms page displayed when the DynamicPage project is created.

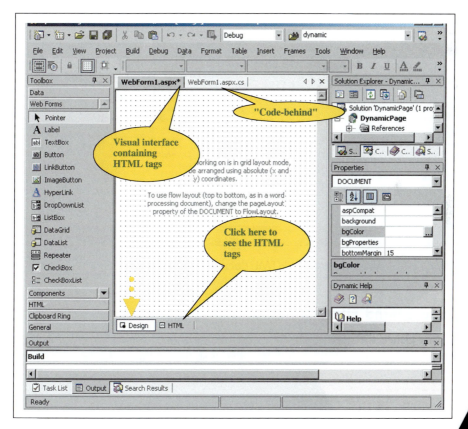

Figure 12-10 Work area of the original DynamicPage

12

In Figure 12-10, DynamicPage.aspx is shown in Design mode. This file (ending in .aspx) holds the HTML tags. Selecting the HTML tab shown at the bottom of Figure 12-10 displays the file's HTML tags. Figure 12-11 shows the contents of this file without any changes made. As you examine the file, notice that tags identify the language used for the application and the name of the code-behind file. The document includes the standard tags associated with an HTML file. While you can change the tags by typing new values, this is not the preferred method. You will probably prefer to drag and drop the controls onto the form, and let Visual Studio generate the tags for you.

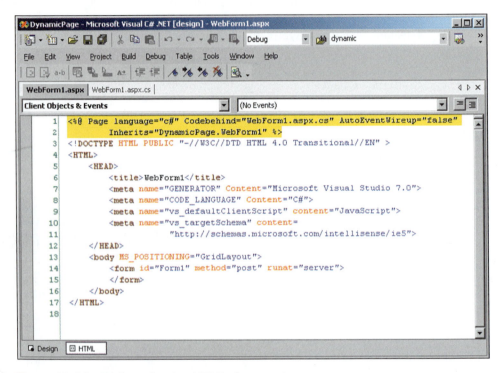

Figure 12-11   Web application HTML document

...hind File

...aspx.cs code-behind file looks very similar to a Windows application. ...umber of differences, as shown in Figure 12-12.

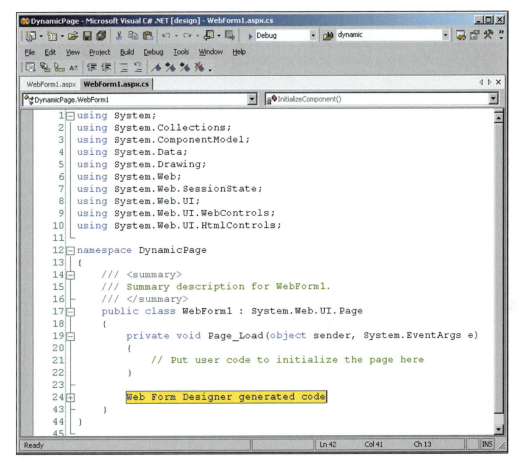

Figure 12-12   Code-behind file

As you examine Figure 12-12, notice that there is no **Main( )** method. Instead there is a **Page_Load( )** event handler. It is added automatically when the project is created. Highlighted in yellow is a collapsed region containing the code generated by the Web Form Designer, which is similar to the code generated by the Windows Form Designer. Note the many namespaces imported automatically when the ASP.NET Web application template is selected.

As with a Windows application, you can debug and execute a Web application from within the IDE. It is a fully functioning application from the beginning. When you run the application, the default Web browser is launched and the file is opened inside the browser.

HTML Document File

The `Page` `object` has a number of properties. In the Properties window, you have access to the HTML `Document` properties as well as much of the same functionality that was available for setting a Windows application form. Differences exist. There are fewer properties available, and they go by different identifiers. Table 12-1 shows some of the page (HTML document) properties that can be set. The table was adapted from the Visual Studio MSDN documentation.

Table 12-1 HTML document properties

Property name	Description
aLink	Color of the active links on the page
Background	Background picture used behind the text
bgColor	Background color for the page
bottomMargin, leftMargin, rightMargin, topMargin	Margins for the page
Description	Description of the page
enableSessionState	Session state mode
enableViewState	Function to maintain view state across page requests
errorPage	URL of the page to be displayed for unhandled errors
Lcid	Locale identifier
Link	Color of unvisited links
pageLayout	Page layout model
Text	Color for the foreground text on the page
Title	Caption for the title bar
vLink	Color of links in the document that have already been visited

As with Windows applications, you can set the properties during design using the Properties window by selecting the individual property and either typing a new value or selecting a value from a pull-down list when available. Doing so adds code to the visual interface file containing the HTML tags (.aspx extension). Table 12-2 shows the properties set for the document.

Table 12-2 Properties set for the document

Property	Actions performed
aLink	Selected pink color (#aff99ff)
bgColor	Selected green color (#ccff99)
Text	Selected yellow color (#ffff66)
Title	Typed "Dynamic Web Pages Example"
vLink	Selected navy color (#330066)

Example 12-2 includes the HTML statements modified as a result of the changes in the property values.

Example 12-2

```
<! --      WebForm1.aspx     -- >
<! --    Statements removed   -- >
<title>Dynamic Web Pages Example</title>
<! --    Statements removed   -- >
<body MS_POSITIONING="GridLayout" text="#ffff66"
          bgColor="#ccff99" ALINK="#ff99ff"
          VLINK="#330066">
```

As shown in Example 12-2, these property changes are all made to the .aspx file, which is the file containing the HTML tags.

12

CONTROLS

The following types of controls can be added to a Web Forms page:

- HTML
- HTML server
- Web Forms
- Validation, custom, and composite

Working in Design mode in Visual Studio .NET, you can display from the Toolbox two types of controls. They are grouped under HTML and Web Forms. HTML controls are discussed first.

HTML Controls

HTML controls are also called client-side controls. When added to a Web page, they map straight to HTML. They can be added to your page using a **WYSIWYG** (what you see is what you get) drag-and-drop approach. You have all the IDE support for aligning and placing the items on the page. The properties, however, associated with the HTML controls are different from those you saw previously with Windows applications. For example, when you add a `Label` object, you do not select a `Text` property and type a value into the Properties windows. Instead, you type the value directly onto the label located on the form. To change font type or size, select the control you want to change and choose Style in the Properties windows. This brings up a Style Builder dialog box where you can define cascading style sheet (CSS) style attributes for these HTML controls. These settings are made by selecting from a group of options. Thus, you can still change these formatting features from within Visual Studio; it is just done a little differently than with Windows applications.

Adding HTML Controls

As shown in Figure 12-13, there are a limited number of HTML controls included in the IDE. Figure 12-13 lists them all.

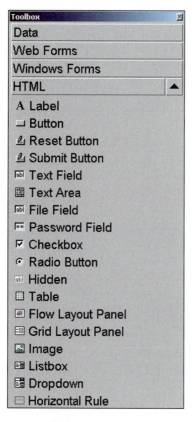

Figure 12-13   HTML controls

To illustrate their usage, `Label`, `Submit Button`, and `Image` objects were added to the DynamicPage Web application. Like a Windows application, the application can be executed from within Visual Studio. Or, once built, the page can be opened within a Web browser using the application name—because Visual Studio created a virtual directory for it. Figure 12-14 shows the Web application after values are entered and the Submit button is clicked.

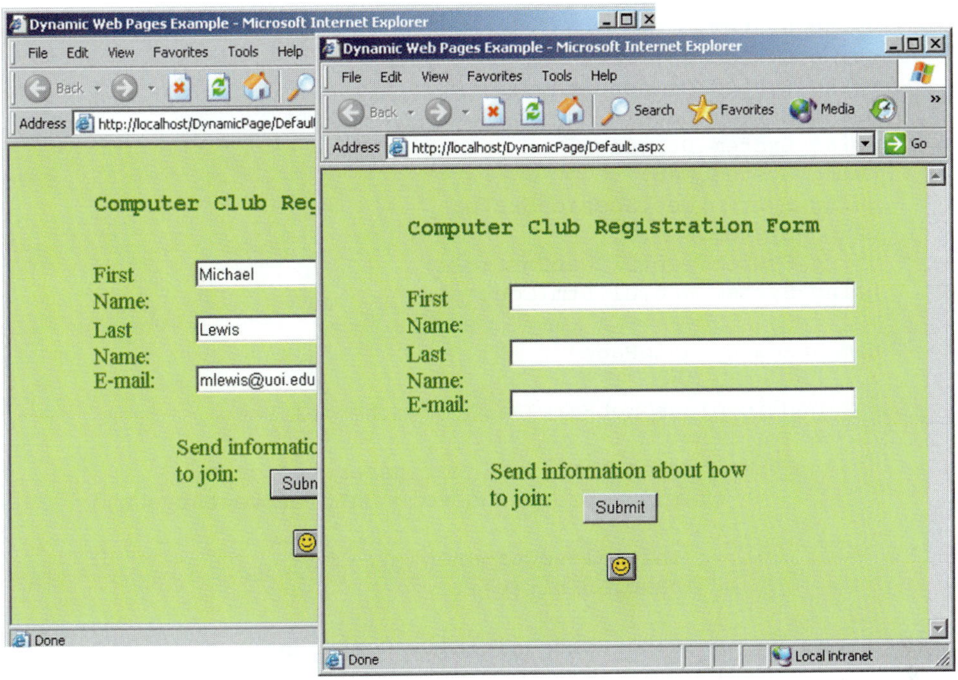

Figure 12-14   Submit button clicked

> **NOTE**
> You might think the illustrations in Figure 12-14 are layered incorrectly. They are not. As noted previously, Web pages are stateless. When the Submit button is clicked, a postback to the Web server occurs. When the page is redisplayed upon return from the round trip to the server, the values in the text box are lost and not available for redisplay.

Adding the label, text box, button, and image controls to the form alters the code in the file containing the HTML (.aspx). It does not add any statements to the file ending in .aspx.cs (the code-behind file). The only statements that appear in the .aspx.cs file are those originally placed when the page was created. Example 12-3 shows the contents. Notice the number of namespaces imported automatically. Both `System.Web.UI.WebControls` and `System.Web.UI.HtmlControls` are among them. These two namespaces enable the traditional HTML controls and the new Web Server controls to be added, which you read about in a later section.

Example 12-3

```csharp
// Default.aspx.cs
using System;
using System.Collections;
using System.ComponentModel;
using System.Data;
using System.Drawing;
using System.Web;
using System.Web.SessionState;
using System.Web.UI;
using System.Web.UI.WebControls;
using System.Web.UI.HtmlControls;

namespace DynamicPage
{
    public class WebForm1 : System.Web.UI.Page
    {
        #region Web Form Designer generated code
            override protected void OnInit(EventArgs e)
            {
                InitializeComponent();
                base.OnInit(e);
            }
            private void InitializeComponent()
            {
            }
            #endregion
    }
}
```

Because all the controls that were added are HTML controls, the code-behind file, Default.aspx.cs, for the DynamicPage application is not changed. Additional HTML tags are added to the Default.aspx file. As you review the Default.aspx file in Example 12-4, take note that the entries that appear in bold were added when the HTML controls were placed on the page. `Label` objects are converted to `<div>` elements; The Submit Button and Text Field objects are converted to `<input>` elements. Example 12-4 shows the matching file that goes with Example 12-3 for the Web application named DynamicPage.

The HTML counterpart for the Windows **TextBox object** for single line entry is a text field. Text area is the counterpart for multiple line entry.

Example 12-4

```
<%@ Page language="c#" Codebehind="Default.aspx.cs"
     AutoEventWireup="false"
          Inherits= "DynamicPage.WebForm1" %>
          <!DOCTYPE HTML PUBLIC
              "-//W3C//DTD HTML 4.0 Transitional//EN" >
<HTML>
    <HEAD>
        <title>Dynamic Web Pages Example</title>
        <meta name="GENERATOR" Content=
                    "Microsoft Visual Studio 7.0">
        <meta name="CODE_LANGUAGE" Content="C#">
        <meta name="vs_defaultClientScript"
                content="JavaScript">
        <meta name="vs_targetSchema"
          content=
        "http://schemas.microsoft.com/intellisense/ie5">
    </HEAD>
    <body MS_POSITIONING="GridLayout"
        text="#006600" bgColor="#ccff99"
        ALINK="#ff99ff" VLINK="#330066">
        <form id="Form1" method="post"
                runat="server">
            <DIV style="DISPLAY: inline;
                FONT-WEIGHT: bold;
                FONT-SIZE: 14pt; Z-INDEX: 101;
                LEFT: 70px;
                WIDTH: 355px; FONT-FAMILY:
                    'Courier New'; POSITION: absolute;
                TOP: 36px; HEIGHT:
                44px" ms_positioning="FlowLayout">
            Computer Club Registration Form
            </DIV>
            <INPUT style="Z-INDEX: 102; LEFT: 216px;
                POSITION: absolute; TOP: 319px"
            type="submit" value="Submit">
            <DIV style="DISPLAY: inline; Z-INDEX: 103;
                LEFT: 58px; WIDTH: 81px;
                POSITION: absolute;
                TOP: 93px; HEIGHT: 25px"
                ms_positioning="FlowLayout">
```

12

```
First Name:
</DIV>
<DIV style="DISPLAY: inline; Z-INDEX: 104;
    LEFT: 133px; WIDTH: 229px;
    POSITION: absolute;
    TOP: 291px; HEIGHT: 21px"
    ms_positioning="FlowLayout">
Send information about how to join:
</DIV>
<INPUT style="Z-INDEX: 105; LEFT: 154px;
    WIDTH: 288px; POSITION: absolute;
    TOP: 92px; HEIGHT: 22px"
type="text" size="42">
<DIV style="DISPLAY: inline; Z-INDEX: 106;
    LEFT: 60px; WIDTH: 78px;
    POSITION: absolute;
    TOP: 137px; HEIGHT: 20px"
    ms_positioning="FlowLayout">
    Last Name:</DIV>
<INPUT style="Z-INDEX: 107; LEFT: 154px;
    WIDTH: 288px; POSITION: absolute;
    TOP: 136px; HEIGHT: 22px"
    type="text" size="42">
<DIV style="DISPLAY: inline; Z-INDEX: 108;
    LEFT: 61px; WIDTH: 70px;
    POSITION: absolute;
    TOP: 177px; HEIGHT: 15px"
    ms_positioning="FlowLayout">
E-mail:</DIV>
<INPUT style="Z-INDEX: 109; LEFT: 154px;
    WIDTH: 288px; POSITION: absolute;
    TOP: 176px; HEIGHT: 22px"
type="text" size="42">
<IMG style="Z-INDEX: 110; LEFT: 235px;
    POSITION: absolute; TOP: 367px"
alt="Thanks for the inquiry!" src=
"file:///C:\Inetpub\wwwroot\DynamicPage\HAPPY.BMP">
    </form>
  </body>
</HTML>
```

HTML controls do not maintain state. When the page is requested from a Web browser, its static contents—formatted using the HTML tags—are displayed. HTTP is considered a stateless protocol. The property values that are set have a very short lifetime. As you look at

Figure 12-14, note that once the Submit button is pressed, the text boxes are cleared. This is actually happening: when the Submit button is clicked, the page is posted to the Web server. The Web server does not have access to what is typed into the HTML controls. This is because the HTML controls do not maintain their state during the round trip from the Web server. So, when the Web server sends back the results as a new HTML document, the original values in the text boxes disappear. The Web server has access only to the contents of the HTML tags. The biggest advantage HTML controls offer is that the page is rendered as is to the browser. No processing is necessary by the Web server.

But, if you want to retrieve the values entered by the user, you can programmatically analyze the HTTP request. This has been the traditional method; however, it requires more coding. A better approach is to make the controls available to the Web server, as described in the next section.

HTML Server Controls

To add functionality at runtime, you can give the server access to the values entered by the user. One way to do this is to add scripting statements within the HTML file using a scripting language such as JavaScript or VBScript. This was discussed previously in conjunction with classic ASP. When using JavaScript or VBScript, however, you miss out on many of the benefits of object-oriented development and the large collection of predefined classes available within .NET. Another approach is to use the new Web Forms server controls included within Visual Studio .NET. You read about them in the next section. Web Forms server controls are more powerful and closely akin to Windows Forms control objects. However, a third approach exists. You can take the HTML controls that you learned about in the previous section and convert them to server controls. Once converted, they are called **HTML server controls**.

12

 If you are developing an application from scratch, you will probably simply use Web Forms server controls. Having the capability of converting the HTML controls into server controls was probably included as part of Visual Studio .NET for developers using classic or traditional ASP who were accustomed to writing scripts to handle events such as button clicks.

.aspx and .aspx.cs Files

As you examined the code-behind file in Example 12-3 and the file containing the HTML tags in Example 12-4 against the page displayed in Figure 12-14, you should have realized that no code was written for processing the data entered by the user. No event-handler method for the button click was included. When the user clicked the Submit button, the page was refreshed from the Web server, which caused the **TextBox** objects to be cleared.

During design, if you were thinking that you would add an event handler to be executed when the user clicked the Submit button and you double-clicked on the Submit button to register the event, the message shown in Figure 12-15 would have been displayed.

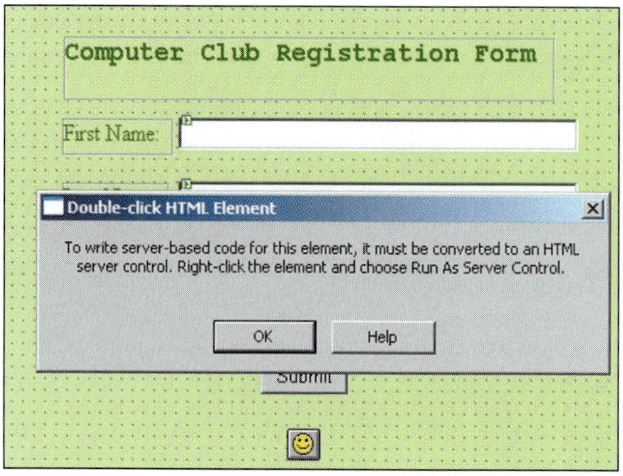

Figure 12-15   Trying to register a click event

Running HTML Controls as Server Controls   With HTML controls, you cannot add a button click event handler. However, right-clicking on an HTML control permits you convert it to a server control as illustrated in Figure 12-16.

Figure 12-16   Converting an HTML control to an HTML server control

Selecting **Run As Server Control** accomplishes important things. First, it declares a corresponding .NET **object** of that control type. This code is added to the code-behind file. Once the code is added, when the page is requested, the Web server has access to both the .aspx file with the HTML tags and also the .aspx.cs file with code referencing the Web server controls. These controls can now be treated as objects complete with their own data and behaviors, which means the Web server now has access to the entered values referenced by the objects.

 Any of the controls that are converted to server controls can be referenced in the code-behind (.aspx.cs) file.

Selecting **Run As Server Control** also appends the `<runat="server">` attribute to the HTML tag of the control you change. Example 12-5 illustrates the addition of the Submit button.

Example 12-5

```
<INPUT id="btnSubmit" style="Z-INDEX: 102; LEFT: 214px;
       POSITION: absolute; TOP: 259px" type="submit"
       value="Submit" name="Submit1"
runat="server">
```

To add functionality to the **Submit Button object**, each of the **Text Field** objects was converted to server controls and a new label added. The **Label object** is also converted to a Web server control. This makes the HTML controls visible or accessible to the Web server—meaning they become programmable. The **Label object** is used by the Web server to store a message containing the retrieved name and e-mail values from the HTML **Text Field** objects. Right-clicking on each of these controls and selecting Run As Server Control added the statements to the code-behind **class** shown in Example 12-6.

12

Example 12-6

```
public class WebForm1 : System.Web.UI.Page
{
   protected
      System.Web.UI.HtmlControls.HtmlInputText txtFirst;
   protected
      System.Web.UI.HtmlControls.HtmlInputText txtLast;
   protected
      System.Web.UI.HtmlControls.HtmlInputText txtEmail;
```

```
protected
    System.Web.UI.HtmlControls.HtmlGenericControl lblResult;
protected
    System.Web.UI.HtmlControls.HtmlInputButton btnSubmit;
```

Notice how the `Text Field` objects are converted to `HtmlInputText` objects. The server uses `HtmlInputText` controls to allow for the entry of a single line of text. For multiple lines of input, the HTML `Text Area object` is dragged to the page. If you convert it to an HTML server control, an `object` of `HtmlTextArea` is instantiated.

 The `id` property for each of the controls was set to an appropriate identifier. The `id` property is similar to the Windows application `Name` property. Identifiers of `txtLast`, `txtFirst`, `txtEmail`, `lblResult`, and `btnSubmit` were used. If you do not give each control an `id`, you cannot use it in program statements.

Server Control Events

Once you select Run As Server Control for the button, an `object` is instantiated of the `HtmlInputButton class`. You get an `object` complete with `object` characteristics. You can register events such as a button click event for the `object`. Now when you double-click the Submit button, you do not receive the error message shown in Figure 12-15. Instead, the following statement is added:

```
this.btnSubmit.ServerClick += new
    System.EventHandler(this.Submit1_ServerClick);
```

Double-clicking registers the button click event exactly as it was done when you created button click events for Windows applications. An empty button click event-handler method is added. This code is inserted into the code-behind (.aspx.cs) file. Now when the page is requested using HTTP, the Web server has access to these controls and can retrieve and process the data entered by the user. To demonstrate how the application functions now that the server has access to the controls, the statements shown in Example 12-7 were added to the event-handler method.

Example 12-7

```
private void Submit1_ServerClick(object sender,
                                        System.EventArgs e)
{
    this.lblResult.InnerText = "Thanks!! " +
        this.txtFirst.Value + " " +
        this.txtLast.Value +
        " Information will be forwarded to: " +
        this.txtEmail.Value;
}
```

Properties of HTML Server Controls   As noted previously, the properties of HTML controls are different from those you became accustomed to using Windows applications. This is because they are mapped to HTML elements. Notice that the **Text** property is not used to get or set values in the label or text fields. The **InnerText** property is used with **Label** objects to get and set values. The **Value** property is used with **Text Field** objects to get and set values. **Value** is also used to set the caption for the various button types (**Button**, **Submit Button**, and **Reset Button**). Figure 12-17 shows the page after it is posted back from the Web server. It is no longer blank after the round trip to the Web server.

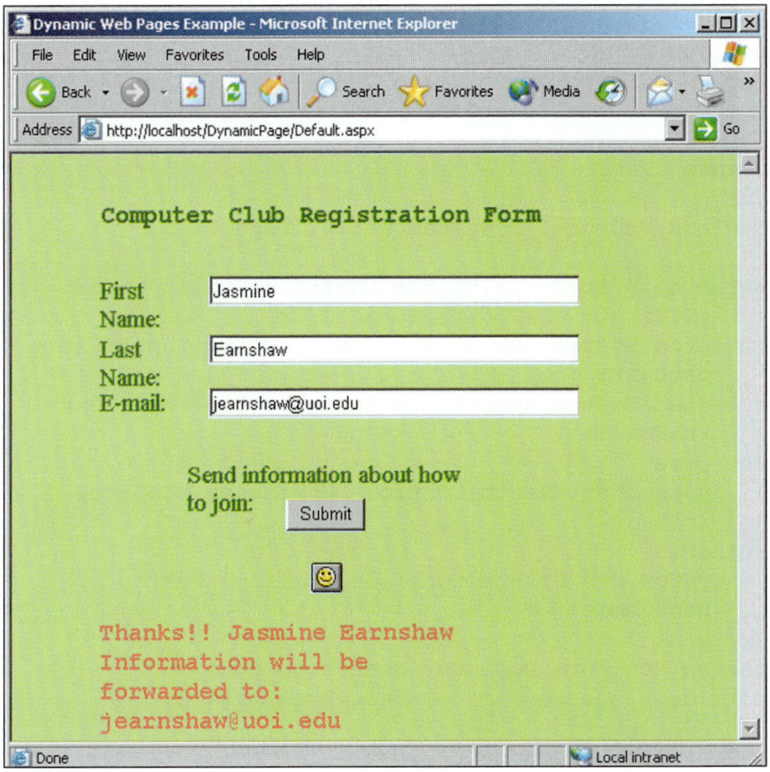

Figure 12-17   Web page after postback

Notice in Figure 12-17, that upon return from the server the text box-like objects (**HtmlInputText**) contain the typed values—unlike the illustration shown in Figure 12-14. This is because these HTML controls are now HTML server controls. Program statements are added to retrieve the inputted values and display their contents in a **Label object**. Example 12-8 shows the program statements that make up the code-behind file.

Example 12-8

```
// http://localhost/DynamicPage/default.aspx
// Default.aspx.cs
// code-behind file
using System;
using System.Collections;
using System.ComponentModel;
using System.Data;
using System.Drawing;
using System.Web;
using System.Web.SessionState;
using System.Web.UI;
using System.Web.UI.WebControls;
using System.Web.UI.HtmlControls;

namespace DynamicPage
{
    public class WebForm1 : System.Web.UI.Page
    {
        protected System.Web.UI.HtmlControls.HtmlInputText
            txtFirst;
        protected System.Web.UI.HtmlControls.HtmlInputText
            txtLast;
        protected System.Web.UI.HtmlControls.HtmlInputText
            txtEmail;
        protected
            System.Web.UI.HtmlControls.HtmlGenericControl
            lblResult;
        protected
            System.Web.UI.HtmlControls.HtmlInputButton
            btnSubmit;

        #region Web Form Designer generated code
        override protected void OnInit(EventArgs e)
        {
            InitializeComponent();
            base.OnInit(e);
        }
        private void InitializeComponent()
        {
            this.btnSubmit.ServerClick += new
                System.EventHandler(this.Submit1_ServerClick);
        }
    #endregion
        private void Submit1_ServerClick
                (object sender, System.EventArgs e)
        {
```

```
        this.lblResult.InnerText = "Thanks!!   " +
                this.txtFirst.Value + " " +
                this.txtLast.Value +
                " Information will be forwarded to: " +
                this.txtEmail.Value;
        }
    }
}
```

Using the Solution Explorer in Visual Studio .NET, the name of the .aspx file was changed to default.aspx. This enables you to surf to the Web site by typing http://localhost/ DynamicPage without a filename. Visual Studio automatically changed the name of the code-behind file (Default.aspx.cs) to match, once the .aspx filename was changed.

As you experienced with this example, you can convert traditional HTML controls to server controls. However, there are other options for server-side processing. As part of Visual Studio .NET, you have a whole group of other controls called Web Forms controls. They are the topic of the next section.

WEB FORMS SERVER CONTROLS

Referred to as **Server controls**, **Web controls**, **Web Forms server controls**, **ASP server controls**, or simply **Web Forms controls**, these controls have more built-in features than the HTML controls. They are the controls you want to use in Visual Studio .NET—especially if you need to have the Web server process the data on the page. The Web Forms server controls are designed to look and act like their Windows counterparts. The programming model used for these controls is more closely aligned to the object-oriented model you have used throughout this book. There are fewer of these controls than there are Windows Form controls, but their functionality and many of their properties are similar.

12

With simple Web Forms controls, you have a `Text` property such as `Label` and do not have to learn new identifiers such as `InnerText`, which was used with the HTML control `Label`.

Server controls slow applications down because the Web page containing them is sent back to the server for processing. Because of this, fewer events can be programmed for server controls.

Available Web Forms Controls

Figure 12-18 shows some of the Web Forms server controls available in Visual Studio .NET. Notice how the drop-down tabs shown in Figure 12-18 include tabs for Web Forms and HTML. The controls discussed in this section refer to the Web Forms controls available from the Toolbox.

If you do not see the Toolbox, it can be viewed by selecting **View>Toolbox** or by using the Ctrl+Alt+X shortcut. Other controls can be added to the Toolbox. Right-click within the Web Forms Toolbar, and select Customize to add or remove controls.

Figure 12-18   Web Forms server controls

 You can mix and match HTML controls, HTML server controls, and Web Forms controls. A single Web application can contain all three.

Web Forms controls do not map straight to HTML. Often it may take several HTML tags to represent one Web Forms control. When you drag and drop a Web Forms control onto the page, an HTML tag is placed in the .aspx file representing the control. This tag contains an extra attribute, which is not found on HTML controls, as follows:

```
<asp:control> attributes runat="server"
</asp:control>
```

To indicate that the control is a Web Forms control, Visual Studio prefixes the control name with `<asp:control>` and ends the tag with `</asp:control>`. You saw `runat="server"` previously. This was added when you converted an HTML control to an HTML server control. It is also added for Web Forms controls.

Other attributes are included with the HTML tags. This is also true for HTML controls. When you set the control's property using the Properties window in Visual Studio, the settings are stored in the HTML document—the file ending with the .aspx extension. Remember that this differs from the operation of Windows applications. For one thing, Windows projects do not generate two files for each application. With Windows applications, the property settings are placed in the Windows Form Designer Generated Code region. ASP.NET Web applications also have a Form Designer Generated Code region; however, it is primarily used to store and register events to which the server must respond. Property settings are not stored in the Web Form Designer Generated Code region for Web applications. They are stored in the file containing the HTML tags. All the visual interface settings are stored in this .aspx file.

Web Forms Controls of the Common Form Type

As you examine Figure 12-18, notice several identifiers that you have seen previously: `Button`, `Label`, `TextBox`, `ListBox`, `DataGrid`, `CheckBox`, `Image`, and `RadioButton`. These common controls function similarly to their Windows counterpart objects. There are differences, however, between the controls and how their properties are added to an application. First, examine the HTML visual interface file.

HTML (.aspx) File

Dragging a Web Forms `Button` object onto a form, setting its `id` (name) to `btnSubmit`, and changing its text value, style, and color properties produces the HTML statement shown in Example 12-9.

Example 12-9

```
<asp:Button id="btnSubmit" style="Z-INDEX: 114;
    LEFT: 359px; POSITION: absolute; TOP: 183px"
    runat="server" Text="Submit Info"
    BorderStyle="Groove" ForeColor="DarkGreen"
    Font-Bold="True">
</asp:Button>
```

12

As you can see from Example 12-9, the settings for the properties are not placed in the code-behind file. These attributes are added to the .aspx file—the file that contains all the HTML tags. The entries added to the code-behind file (.aspx.cs file) include only the declaration of objects and the registration of event handlers along with their methods.

Changing Properties Within Visual Studio .NET

It is valuable to examine the properties that can be set for the buttons, labels, text boxes, radio buttons, check boxes, and other form type controls. As shown in Figure 12-18, there are fewer properties found with Web Forms types of controls than you find with their Windows

Forms counterparts. In addition, a few differences exist between the properties. One obvious difference is in naming the **object**. With Windows Forms controls, the **Name** property is used. With Web Forms controls, the **id** property is used. The following list shows the number of events and properties that can be registered for different types of control buttons:

- Windows Forms button—48 events

- Web Forms button control—8 events

- Windows Forms button control—32 properties

- Web Forms button control—20 properties

This comparison is representative of all of the other controls.

Take a look at Figure 12-19 to see the properties for the Web Forms **Label** control.

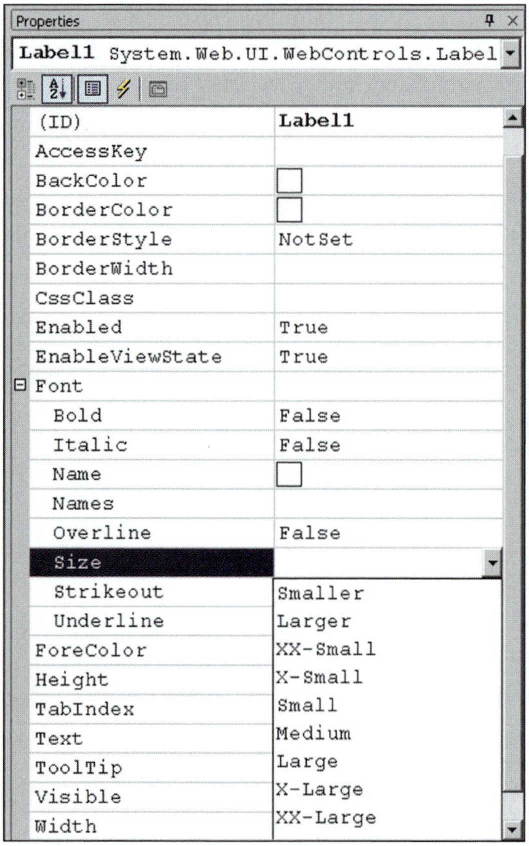

Figure 12-19   Properties for the Label control object

Figure 12-19 expands the properties for `Font`, revealing the options for `Size`. Instead of typing a point value, `Size` is set with relative values. This same `Font` property is found with most Web Forms controls.

Events

The events for Web applications are both raised and handled on the server. The response is sent back through HTML to the client browser. To the user, this event handling appears to be like events with Windows applications. However, by default only a few events trigger a post-back to the server. Common user interface events such as mouse moves and key presses are not automatically posted to the server. The click events fired by buttons automatically trigger a postback. Changes in selections to `ListBox`, `RadioButton`, `RadioButtonList`, `CheckBox`, `CheckBoxList`, and `DropDownList` do not cause an automatic postback to the server by default.

Automatic PostBack   Each of the controls listed in the previous paragraph (`ListBox`, `RadioButton`, `RadioButtonList`, `CheckBox`, `CheckBoxList`, and `DropDownList`) has a property called `AutoPostBack` that can be set to `true` to trigger a postback to the server automatically. When a control's `AutoPostBack` property is set to `true`, the control's events trigger an HTTP request to the server when the control's registered event is fired. You will notice that the `TextBox` `object` also has an `AutoPostBack` property. It is also set to `false` by default. Normally when you design a form, you do not want the page to be posted back after each change on the form. Not only is this an expensive activity involving the server, but it is also more difficult to program. It is expensive because every postback to the server involves an HTTP request with the page's URL. The server determines if additional processing is necessary, and if so, it performs the processing. Then the server sends the page back as an HTML document. You can imagine that if every click or mouse move on the form required a round trip back to the server, you would not only be using more resources than necessary, but also slowing down your application and requiring more work than necessary. Thus, you should be judicious with your changes to this `AutoPostBack` property.

12

The server loads an ASP.NET Web page every time it is requested by a client browser and then unloads it back to the browser after it processes the server-side code to render the HTML. Even though this communication is actually disconnected, a feeling of continuity is needed at the client side. When a second postback of the page is sent to the server, the client should experience the postback merely as the next step in the progression of dealing with the page. The client should not know that the page is being reloaded or seen for the first time. One way ASP.NET pages accomplish this transition—so that it seems like a seamless interaction with the Web site—is through state management. You can write code to store page information between round-trips to the server. State management can occur at the client or server side.

You are encouraged to explore the MSDN documentation to learn more about maintaining state at the client side using the `ViewState` property and cookies. Explore the documentation using the Help>Search option within Visual Studio .NET. The `HttpApplicationState class` has members for maintaining state for the entire application across many users. For example, you may wish to include a counter on a Web page to track the number of hits an application (Web page) gets. The `HttpSessionState class` provides access to individual user session state values.

Adding Common Form-Type Controls

To illustrate some of the Web Forms controls that can be added to a Web form, Figure 12-20 shows a Web site containing some of the controls discussed previously and controls that are added to the Computer Club Inquiry Form in the sections that follow.

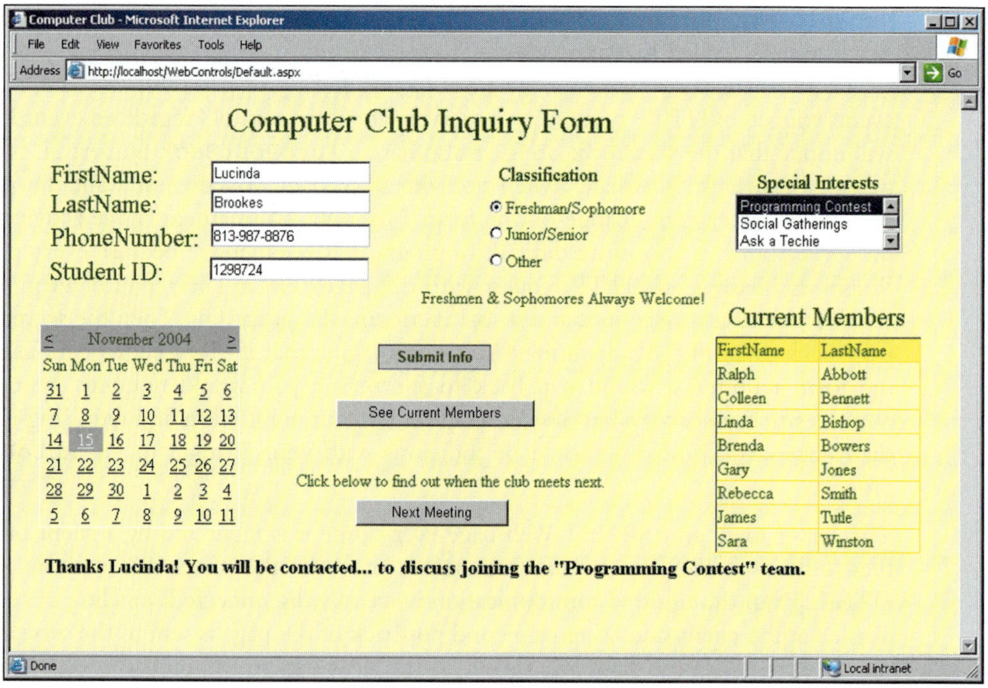

Figure 12-20   Web site after adding server controls

Label, Button, RadioButton, and ListBox Objects

As shown in Figure 12-20, `Label`, `Button`, `RadioButton`, and `ListBox` objects were added. You should be able to identify those controls on the form from your work with Windows applications. Event-handler methods for button clicks were written for the three buttons in the center of the form. Other than naming the `TextBox` controls using the `id` property, setting their `Text` properties to `""`, and sizing them, no other properties were set. Their `AutoPostBack` property was left unchanged (set as `false`).

The four `TextBox` objects appear in white in Figure 12-20. They are currently storing values for first name, last name, phone, and student ID.

Setting the Properties of the Controls   The `id` properties and the individual `Text` properties were set for the `RadioButton` objects. The `GroupName` property is set for all three `RadioButton` objects. It is set to the same identifier (`Classif`) for all three objects. Adding the three objects to a group creates a **mutually exclusive set of controls** (only one can be selected at a time). If they did not belong to a group, all three could be checked. When one of the buttons is selected, a message is displayed in the label below the radio button. So that the message is displayed as soon as the user clicks the radio button `object`, the `AutoPostBack` property is set to `true`. Without changing its default value, the message would not display until one of the `Button` objects triggered the postback event.

Remember, by default `Button` objects automatically trigger a postback.

12

The only property set for the `ListBox object` in the upper-right corner of the page is the ID. `SelectionMode` was left unchanged (set as `Single`). Thus, only one selection from the list box could be made. Changing the property to `Multiple` enables multiple selections. The program logic for determining which items were selected would also have to be modified. The `AutoPostBack` property was left unchanged (set as `false`). It is not necessary to post the page back to the server as soon as a selection is made from this control.

Wiring Event-Handler Methods

All three radio buttons were wired to the same event-handler method. This can be done by selecting all three buttons before selecting the method name in the Events Properties window as shown in Figure 12-21.

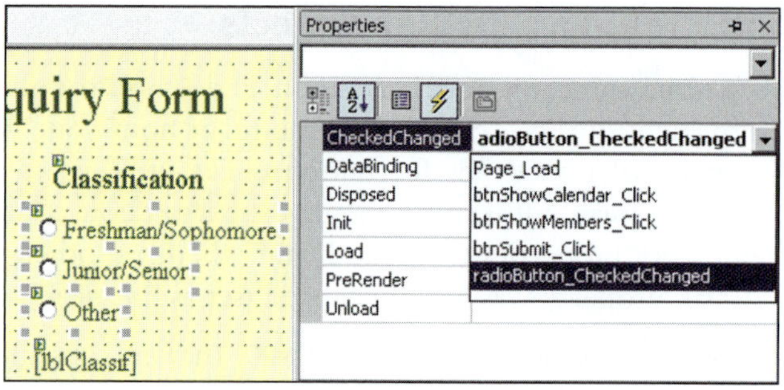

Figure 12-21   Wiring the same event to three RadioButton objects

Example 12-10 shows the event-handler method for the RadioButton CheckedChanged( ) event.

Example 12-10

```csharp
private void radioButton_CheckedChanged(object sender,
                        System.EventArgs e)
{
    if (this.radBtnFresSop.Checked)
    {
        this.lblClassif.Text =
                "Freshmen & Sophomores ";
    }
    else if (this.radBtnJrSr.Checked)
    {
        this.lblClassif.Text = "Junior & Seniors ";
    }
    else if (this.radBtnOther.Checked)
    {
        this.lblClassif.Text = "Special Students ";
    }
    this.lblClassif.Text += " Always Welcome!";
}
```

The event-handler method for the Submit button is used to retrieve the values entered into the **TextBox** fields and the selections made from the **ListBox object** by the user. These values are used to populate the **Label** controls that are to be displayed when the page is reloaded for the client. Example 12-11 shows the **btnSubmit** event-handler method.

Example 12-11

```
private void btnSubmit_Click(object sender, System.EventArgs e)
{
    this.lblSubmit.Text = "Thanks " + this.txtBxFname.Text +
            "!    You will be contacted... ";
    if (lstBxInterests.SelectedIndex > -1)
    {
        this.lblSubmit.Text +=  " to discuss joining" +
            " the \"" + this.lstBxInterests.SelectedItem.Text +
            "\" team.";
    }
}
```

In Figure 12-20 you can see that two other controls were added to the Web application shown: `Calendar` and `DataGrid`. In addition, a validation control was added to the form. These special controls are discussed in the next section.

VALIDATION, CUSTOM, AND COMPOSITE CONTROLS

As shown in Figure 12-20, a `Calendar` control is added to the lower-left corner and a `DataGrid` control is added to the bottom right for data retrieved from an Access database. These are special types of controls that will be discussed in this section. In addition, you did not see it, but another type of control, a validation control, is added to the form. Validation controls are discussed first.

12

Validation Controls

Review Figure 12-18. Notice there are several different types of **validation controls** listed in the Toolbox under the Web Forms tab. These controls enable input to be validated or checked by the server. Table 12-3 lists and describes the various predefined validation controls available for Web Forms in .NET.

Table 12-3 Controls of .NET validation

Type of control	Description
CompareValidator	Compares an input value against a preset constant value using comparison operators
CustomValidator	Checks the input value using program statements you write yourself

Table 12-3   Controls of .NET validation (continued)

Type of control	Description
`RangeValidator`	Compares an input value to see if it is between specified lower and upper boundaries (can check ranges of dates, numbers, or alphabetic characters)
`RegularExpressionValidator`	Matches an input value to a pattern defined as a regular expression (used for entries such as e-mail, telephone numbers, and Social Security numbers to see if the values match a predictable sequence)
`RequiredFieldValidator`	Checks that the entry has a value

Validation Control Properties

To use one of these controls, drag the control to the Web Forms page and place it beside the control you want to validate. You can then treat the validation control **object** like any other control. It has properties that can be set. Using the `ControlToValidate` property, you tie the validation control to a specific form control **object** such as a `TextBox` **object**. The `ErrorMessage` property can be set to the message you want to display when the input control does not pass the validation test. The default color for the error message is set to **red**, but of course, the color can be changed.

Adding a RequiredFieldValidator Control

Figure 12-22 illustrates adding a `RequiredFieldValidator` control for the first name.

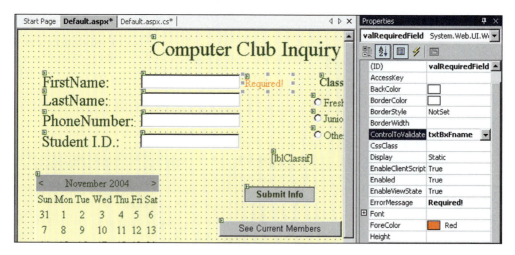

Figure 12-22   Adding a RequiredFieldValidator control

Notice that in Figure 12-22, `txtBxFname` is set as the value for the `ControlToValidate` property. The `RequiredFieldValidator` control is physically placed beside (not on top of) the `TextBox object` that it is validating.

 Place the validation control in the location where you want the error message to be displayed; it does not have to be placed beside the control. Sometimes due to space constraints the validation control cannot be placed beside the control it is validating. As with other controls, to get it on the form, drag and drop it from the Toolbox window.

Once you add the `RequiredFieldValidator` control and tie it to the `txtBxFname object`, `"Required!"` is displayed in red if the form loads and is submitted to the server with no value entered into the `txtBxFname` control. `"Required!"` is displayed because the `ErrorMessage` property value is set to `"Required!"`. This was just a typed value entered during design.

Using the `Text` property available with validation controls, you can also customize the error information displayed to users. A common practice is to set the `Text` property of the validation control to a red star (asterisk) and place it next to the input box to be validated. If you do this, an asterisk is displayed at runtime if the control fails validation.

 Notice that the `Text` property and the `ErrorMessage` property are both used to set the message that prints when validation fails. If you set both, the `Text` property overrides the `ErrorMessage` property.

Page Validation

By default, **page validation** occurs when *any* button on the form is clicked. It is called page validation because every control field on the page that has an associated validation control is checked to see if it passes the validation rules. If you do not want one or more of the `Button` objects to cause page validation, you can set a property on the `Button` called `CausesValidation`. By default, every `Button` object's `CausesValidation` property is set to `true`.

As you design your solutions, give careful thought to which of your buttons should cause page validation of the input controls. Set `CausesValidation` to `false` for all other `Button` objects.

Clicking the Submit Info button before typing values into the first name text box causes the validation error message "Required!" to be displayed in red, as shown in Figure 12-23.

12

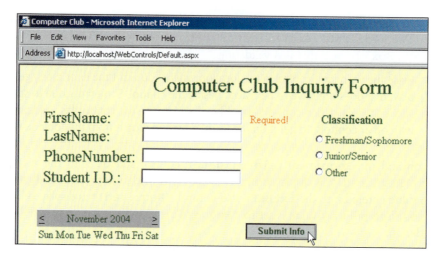

Figure 12-23   Error message from the RequiredFieldValidator control

Review the list of predefined validation controls in Table 12-3. Another one of the validation controls listed is `RangeValidator`. Using `RangeValidator`, you can make sure that the value entered by the user falls between a predetermined set of values. This control can be used to test for valid dates to ensure that the dates entered fall within a specific range, or to test numeric values to ensure that they fall within a range specified during design. You can do pattern matching with the `RegularExpressionValidator` control. Checks of e-mail addresses to ensure that the @ symbol is included are performed using the `RegularExpressionValidator` control. More than one validation control can be associated with an input **object**. You are encouraged to experiment and review the MSDN documentation.

 At runtime, you can use the `Page.IsValid` property to check whether all validation controls on a page are currently valid. The property can be placed in a selection statement and actions performed based on its Boolean result.

Calendar Control

A `Calendar` control is used to display calendar months on a Web page. Once placed on the page, the calendar is live and users can use the calendar to view and select dates. For the application displayed in Figure 12-20, which is being used to demonstrate the server controls, a `Calendar` control is dragged and dropped onto the Web page from the Web Forms Toolbox. Doing so adds the following line to the code-behind file:

```
protected System.Web.UI.WebControls.Calendar Calendar1;
```

At the same time that it instantiates an **object** of the `Calendar` **class**, it adds the lines shown in Example 12-12 to the HTML (.aspx) file.

Example 12-12

```
<asp:Calendar id="Calendar1" style="Z-INDEX: 105;
      LEFT: 28px; POSITION: absolute;
      TOP: 216px" runat="server"
      Width="179px" Height="180px">
</asp: Calendar>
```

Remember, you use the tabs above the page to switch between viewing the .aspx file and .aspx.cs file. To switch between HTML and Design view, use the tabs at the bottom of the page as shown in Figure 12-24. Use the View menu options, if you have trouble locating any of these tabs.

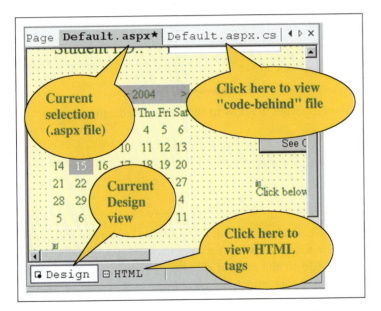

12

Figure 12-24 Switching between .aspx and .aspx.cs files

The `Calendar` control has a number of properties including the `SelectedDate` property. `SelectedDate` is used to pick the month, day, and year for display. The `SelectedDate` property is initially set to the current date. This is done when the page is loaded. But, you can also set the date programmatically or during design using the `SelectedDate` property found in the Properties window. Setting the date during design enables you to use the built-in `Calendar` control on the Properties window as shown in Figure 12-25.

Figure 12-25 Using the Properties window to set the SelectedDate property

> If you are going to set the date programmatically, use the `Page_Load( )` event-handler method.

The **Calendar** control is based on the .NET **DateTime class**, which enables you to work with dates in different formats. Program statements were added to the **Page_Load( )** event handler to set the date to the current day the application is run. This is shown in Example 12-13. Notice that the statements are placed in a **try...catch** exception block.

Example 12-13

```
private void Page_Load(object sender, System.EventArgs e)
{
        try
        {
                Calendar1.SelectedDate = DateTime.Today;
        }
```

```
        catch (System.Exception exc)
        {
            this.lblMsg.Text = exc.Message;
        }
}
```

DateTime Class

To work with the calendar for the WebControls application programmatically, an **object** of the `DateTime` **class** is declared. Its declaration is placed in the code-behind file, where Visual Studio placed the declaration for the `Calendar` control **object**. The **object** declaration statement is as follows:

protected DateTime meetingDate;

The `DateTime` **class** has a large number of useful members that can be used with `Calendar` control objects. Table 12-4 shows some of the more interesting members of this **class**.

Table 12-4 Members of the DateTime class

DateTime members	Description
AddDays( ), AddHours( ), AddMinutes( ), AddMonths( ), AddYears( )	Adds a specified number of days, hours, minutes, months, or years
Compare( )	Compares two instances of `DateTime`
Date	Gets the date
Day	Gets the day of the month
DayOfWeek	Gets the day of the week (0 for Sunday; 6 for Saturday)
DayOfYear	Gets the day of the year
DaysInMonth( )	Returns the number of days in the specified month
Hour	Gets the hour of the date
Minute	Gets the minute of the date
Month	Gets the month of the date
Parse( )	Converts a `string` to the `DateTime` format
Subtract( )	Subtracts a specified time from an instance
Now	Gets the current date and time

12

Table 12-4 Members of the DateTime class (continued)

DateTime members	Description
`Today [Static]`	Gets the current date
`Year`	Gets the current year
`+, -, =, ==, <, >, >=, <=`	Operators defined to work with `DateTime` instances

NOTE Properties are shown in Table 12-4 without ( ).

Using a Calendar Control in Applications

To continue creating the `WebControls` application, a button labeled Next Meeting is added to the form. Remember, the final result of the application was shown in Figure 12-20. When the button labeled Next Meeting is clicked, the calendar changes to show the date of the next computer club meeting. Programmatically, this is set as exactly seven days from the current date. A selection statement is then used to test the meeting date to make sure the date does not fall on Sunday. If it does, the meeting date is set for the following Monday. Example 12-14 shows the event-handler method for this button.

Example 12-14

```csharp
private void btnShowCalendar_Click(object sender,
                                   System.EventArgs e)
{
    Calendar1.SelectedDates.Clear();
    meetingDate = new DateTime(DateTime.Today.Year,
                   DateTime.Today.Month,
                   DateTime.Today.Day, 8,0,0);
    // Meeting is schedule for one week from today!
    meetingDate = meetingDate.AddDays(7);
    // Unless, of course it's Sunday - if so
    // meet on Monday.
    if (meetingDate.DayOfWeek.ToString() == "Sunday")
    {
        meetingDate = meetingDate.AddDays(1);
    }
    Calendar1.SelectedDate = meetingDate;
```

```
this.lblMsg.Text = ("Meeting next week: " +
                    meetingDate.DayOfWeek + ", " +
                    meetingDate.Month + "/" +
                    meetingDate.Day +  " at " +
                    meetingDate.Hour + " P.M.");
}
```

Figure 12-26 shows the Web page before and after the user clicks the Next Meeting button.

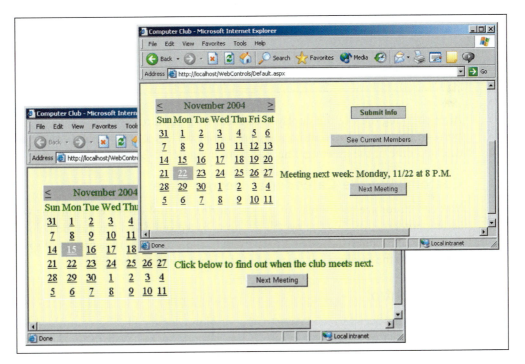

Figure 12-26   Calendar showing different dates selected

The SelectedDate property of the Calendar control is set in the btnShowCalendar_Click( ) method. This method instantiates the **object** of the DateTime **class** declared previously (meetingDate), initializing it using the current year (Today.Year), current month (Today.Month), and current day (Today.Day). As shown in Table 12-4, Today is a static member of the DateTime **class**; thus, it must be referenced with the **class** name, as opposed to an **object**. When the meetingDate `object` is instantiated, the constructor for six arguments is used. The last three arguments (`8, 0, 0`) set the `Hour`, `Minute`, and `Second` properties. It displays P.M. because that `string` literal is concatenated onto the end of the value returned from the `Hour` property, as shown in the last line for Example 12-14.

The date of the next Computer Club meeting is seven days from today's date—unless that date falls on a Sunday. If it does, the meeting date is the following Monday. This is what the code in Example 12-14 accomplishes. In the example, the `AddDays( )` method is used to set the `meetingDate` object's new `Day`, `Month`, and `Year` if necessary. The value of 7 is sent as an argument to the method. The selection statement, shown in Example 12-15, checks to see if the date falls on Sunday.

Example 12-15

```
if (meetingDate.DayOfWeek.ToString() == "Sunday")
{
    meetingDate = meetingDate.AddDays(1);
}
```

After checking the day, the displayed calendar is changed to reflect the value stored with the `meetingDate` `object` and a message is displayed on a `Label` `object`. It contains the date and time of the meeting. This is shown in Figure 12-26.

Customizing the Calendar at Design Time

You can customize the display of the `Calendar` control `object` by turning on gridlines, adding borders, changing the overall size, font, background and foreground colors, or by setting the cell padding and spacing properties. Cell padding sets the amount of space between the cells and the border. Cell spacing sets the space between the cells.

DataGrid Control

You were introduced to the `DataGrid` control in Chapter 11. This control is very useful for displaying data in a tabular format on both Windows and Web forms. As you learned in Chapter 11, to use the `DataGrid` control, you must bind the control to a data source.

Data Binding

At design time, you can bind the data by setting properties in the Properties window, such as the `DataSource` property, or by writing program statements to do this. Two common data source classes used to bind `DataGrid` objects to the actual data are the `DataReader` and `DataSet` classes. The actual data used to populate these controls can come from sources such as arrays or database tables. You experienced using both the `DataReader` `object` and the `DataSet` `object` in conjunction with the `DataAdapter` `object` in Chapter 11.

You are encouraged to review the sections in Chapter 11 that relate to accessing data from database tables.

Using a DataGrid Control in Applications

The WebControls application that is being developed in this chapter includes a DataGrid control, which displays data from an Access database. To add this control to a Web form, you should follow the same design guidelines presented previously. You may want to review Example 11-19 in Chapter 11. It displayed data from an Access database on a standard Windows form. Example 11-19 instantiated objects from the DataSet and DataAdapter classes. These same classes are used to retrieve data for display on a Web form in this example.

OleDB Data Provider   You learned in Chapter 11 that .NET organizes ADO.NET classes into different provider namespaces. This enables you to work with data from different databases such as Oracle and Access using a consistent object-oriented approach. Each of these namespaces has its own classes prefixed with the provider type, one of which is OleDB for working with Access databases. Objects of the OleDbDataAdapter, DataSet, OleDbConnection, and OleDbCommand classes are declared for the WebControls example in this chapter. This declaration occurs at the top of the code-behind file in the location where other objects are declared.

 Visual Studio has a Data tab as part of the Toolbox. All of these controls (DataSet, OleDbDataAdapter, OleDbConnection, OleDbCommandBuilder, and OleDbCommand) can be dragged to your form to add their declaration to the source listing. You drag and drop them onto the form in exactly the same manner you drag other control objects, such as buttons.

12

Connecting to the Database   A button labeled See Current Members is added to the WebControls application. When the user clicks the button, a Connection object is instantiated. The same connection string that you saw in Chapter 11 is used as an argument to the constructor. The connection string identifies the provider as an Access database. It also specifies the name of the database—including the full path to the database location. The example that follows, Example 12-16, shows the statements that make up the btnShowMembers_ Click( ) method. As you review the code, notice the comment that appears in the method. A minor modification is needed to the code presented in Chapter 11 (only one line of code). The DataBind( ) method call is different for Web applications. To display the data using the DataGrid, objects of the DataAdapter and DataSet classes are used for both Web and Windows applications.

> **NOTE** Note that the path of the database is listed as
> "C:\\CSharpProjects\\WebControls\\ member.mdb". In order to have the backslash rec-
> ognized as part of the path, two backslashes were typed. The first is the escape character.

Example 12-16

```csharp
private void btnShowMembers_Click(object sender,
                        System.EventArgs e)
{
    lblMembers.Visible = true;
    try
    {
      sConnection =
          "Provider=Microsoft.Jet.OLEDB.4.0;" +
          "Data Source=" +
            "C:\\CSharpProjects\\WebControls\\member.mdb";
            dbConn = new OleDbConnection(sConnection);
            sql =
          "Select FirstName, LastName From memberTable " +
                  " Order By LastName Asc, FirstName Asc;";
          dbCmd = new OleDbCommand();
          dbCmd.CommandText = sql;
          dbCmd.Connection = dbConn;
          memberDataAdap = new OleDbDataAdapter();
          memberDataAdap.SelectCommand = dbCmd;
          memberDS = new DataSet();
          memberDataAdap.Fill(memberDS, "memberTable");
          // Binding is only change needed from the Windows app
          this.dataGrid1.DataBind();
    }
    catch (System.Exception exc)
    {
          this.lblMsg.Text = exc.Message;
    }
}
```

> **NOTE** The members.mdb database should be placed in C:\CSharpProjects\WebControls. The
> database is available with this chapter's example files. You can place it in another location
> on your hard drive. However, you must change the Data Source string for Example 12-16
> and 12-17 if it is not stored at C:\CSharpProjects\WebControls to the new path.

Retrieving Data from the Database   As with Example 11-19, a SQL statement stored in the **string** identifier, **sql**, is used to select the records. In this example, the data fields of **FirstName** and **LastName** from **memberTable** are retrieved. The SQL statement arranges the result by **LastName**. When there are duplicate records with the same last name, the records are arranged in ascending order by **FirstName**. The **sql string object** is set as the `CommandText` property value. The connection **string**, `dbConn`, is set as the `Connection` property as follows:

```
dbCmd.CommandText = sql;
dbCmd.Connection = dbConn;
```

To use the `Fill( )` method with the `DataSet` **object**, an **object** of the `DataAdapter` **class** is instantiated. Notice that each of these classes is part of the OleDb **namespace**, thus **class** names are prefixed with `OleDb`. The `SelectCommand` property of the `DataAdapter` **class** is set to the `CommandText` **object** holding the SQL statement. Using the DataAdapter's `Fill( )` method, the table from the actual Access database (`memberTable`) is used to populate the `DataSet` **object** (`memberDS`). The last statement in the try block for Example 12-16 binds the `DataGrid` **object** to the `DataSet`. Recall that this is the only statement that changed from the Windows application.

 Remember, Figure 12-20 shows this application running after all the controls are added to the page and event-handler methods wired.

The complete program listing for the code-behind file for the `WebControls` project is shown in Example 12-17.

Example 12-17

```
// WebControls
using System;
using System.Collections;
using System.ComponentModel;
using System.Data;
using System.Drawing;
using System.Web;
using System.Web.SessionState;
using System.Web.UI;
using System.Web.UI.WebControls;
using System.Web.UI.HtmlControls;
using System.Data.OleDb;
namespace WebControls
{
    public class WebForm1 : System.Web.UI.Page
    {
        protected OleDbDataAdapter memberDataAdap;
        protected DataSet memberDS;
        protected OleDbConnection  dbConn;
        protected OleDbCommand  dbCmd;
        protected string  sConnection;
        protected System.Web.UI.WebControls.DataGrid
            dataGrid1;
```

12

```
protected System.Web.UI.WebControls.Label Label2;
protected System.Web.UI.WebControls.Calendar
    Calendar1;
protected System.Web.UI.WebControls.Label lblMsg;
protected DateTime meetingDate;
protected System.Web.UI.WebControls.Label Label3;
protected System.Web.UI.WebControls.Label Label4;
protected System.Web.UI.WebControls.Label Label5;
protected System.Web.UI.WebControls.Label Label7;
protected System.Web.UI.WebControls.Label Label6;
protected System.Web.UI.WebControls.Label Label8;
protected System.Web.UI.WebControls.Button
    btnMembers;
protected System.Web.UI.WebControls.Label
    lblMembers;
protected System.Web.UI.WebControls.Button
    btnSubmit;
protected System.Web.UI.WebControls.Label
    lblSubmit;
protected System.Web.UI.WebControls.Button
    btnNextMeet;
protected System.Web.UI.WebControls.TextBox
    txtBxFname;
protected System.Web.UI.WebControls.TextBox
    txtBxLname;
protected System.Web.UI.WebControls.TextBox
    txtBxPhone;
protected System.Web.UI.WebControls.TextBox
    txtBxID;
protected System.Web.UI.WebControls.RadioButton
    radBtnFresSop;
protected System.Web.UI.WebControls.RadioButton
    radBtnJrSr;
protected System.Web.UI.WebControls.RadioButton
    radBtnOther;
protected System.Web.UI.WebControls.ListBox
    lstBxInterests;
protected System.Web.UI.WebControls.Label
    lblClassif;
protected
    System.Web.UI.WebControls.RequiredFieldValidator
    valRequiredField;
protected System.Web.UI.WebControls.Button Button1;
protected string sql;
```

```csharp
private void Page_Load(object sender,
                        System.EventArgs e)
{
    try
    {
        Calendar1.SelectedDate = DateTime.Today;
    }
    catch (System.Exception exc)
    {
        this.lblMsg.Text = exc.Message;
    }
}

#region Web Form Designer generated code
override protected void OnInit(EventArgs e)
{
    InitializeComponent();
        base.OnInit(e);
}
private void InitializeComponent()
{
    this.btnSubmit.Click += new
        System.EventHandler(this.btnSubmit_Click);
    this.btnMembers.Click += new
        System.EventHandler
            (this.btnShowMembers_Click);
    this.radBtnFresSop.CheckedChanged += new
        System.EventHandler
            (this.radioButton_CheckedChanged);
    this.radBtnJrSr.CheckedChanged += new
        System.EventHandler
            (this.radioButton_CheckedChanged);
    this.radBtnOther.CheckedChanged += new
        System.EventHandler
            (this.radioButton_CheckedChanged);
    this.Button1.Click += new
        System.EventHandler
            (this.btnShowCalendar_Click);
    this.Load += new System.EventHandler
            (this.Page_Load);
}
#endregion

private void btnShowCalendar_Click
        (object sender, System.EventArgs e)
{
    Calendar1.SelectedDates.Clear();
    meetingDate = new
        DateTime(DateTime.Today.Year,
```

```csharp
                              DateTime.Today.Month,
                              DateTime.Today.Day, 8,0,0);
            // Meeting is schedule
            // for one week from today!
            meetingDate = meetingDate.AddDays(7);
            // Unless, of course it's Sunday - if so
            // meet on Monday.
            if (meetingDate.DayOfWeek.ToString() ==
                              "Sunday")
            {
                meetingDate = meetingDate.AddDays(1);

            }
            Calendar1.SelectedDate = meetingDate;
            this.lblMsg.Text =
                ("Meeting next week: " +
                 meetingDate.DayOfWeek +
                 ", " + meetingDate.Month +
                 "/" + meetingDate.Day +
                 " at " + meetingDate.Hour +
                 " P.M.");
        }

        private void btnShowMembers_Click
                (object sender, System.EventArgs e)
        {
            lblMembers.Visible = true;
            try
            {
                sConnection =
                 "Provider=Microsoft.Jet.OLEDB.4.0;" +
                 "Data Source=" +
                 "C:\\CSharpProjects\\WebControls\\member.mdb";
                dbConn = new OleDbConnection(sConnection);

                sql = "Select FirstName, LastName From "
                        + "memberTable Order " +
                        "By LastName Asc, FirstName Asc;";
                dbCmd = new OleDbCommand();
                dbCmd.CommandText = sql;
                dbCmd.Connection = dbConn;

                memberDataAdap = new OleDbDataAdapter();
                memberDataAdap.SelectCommand = dbCmd;
                memberDS = new DataSet();
                memberDataAdap.Fill(memberDS, "memberTable");
                // Binding is only change needed
                // from the Windows application in
                // Example 11-19
```

```csharp
                this.dataGrid1.DataBind();
            }
            catch (System.Exception exc)
            {
                this.lblMsg.Text = exc.Message;
            }
        }

        private void btnSubmit_Click(object sender,
                System.EventArgs e)
        {
            this.lblSubmit.Text = "Thanks " +
                this.txtBxFname.Text +
                "!    You will be contacted... ";
            if (lstBxInterests.SelectedIndex > -1)
            {
                this.lblSubmit.Text +=
                    " to discuss joining" +
                    " the \"" +
                    this.lstBxInterests.SelectedItem.Text +
                    "\" team.";
            }
        }

        private void radioButton_CheckedChanged(object sender,
                System.EventArgs e)
        {

            if (this.radBtnFresSop.Checked)
            {
                this.lblClassif.Text = "Freshmen & Sophomores ";
            }
            else if (this.radBtnJrSr.Checked)
            {
                this.lblClassif.Text = "Junior & Seniors ";
            }
            else if (this.radBtnOther.Checked)
            {
                this.lblClassif.Text = "Special Students ";
            }

            this.lblClassif.Text += " Always Welcome!";
        }
    }
}
```

12

Modifying the Data   By default, the `DataGrid` control displays data on a Web form in a read-only format. To allow users to edit data stored in the `DataGrid` object, you can use the Property Builder Wizard, which is accessible at the bottom of the Properties window. You must select the `DataGrid` control to see the Property Builder. Using the Property Builder, you create additional columns for the table for use in editing and add code to the `EditCommand`, `UpdateCommand`, and `CancelCommand` events of the `DataGrid object`. When the application is run, the column displays a button labeled Edit. Clicking the button causes that row of data to be displayed in an editable format. The Edit button is replaced with Update and Cancel buttons. After you change the data, and click the Update button, the `UpdateCommand` event is raised or triggered, and the code written to change the data in the database table is executed.

Other Controls

You are encouraged to review Figure 12-18. It shows the different Web Forms controls that can be added to a Web Forms page from the Toolbox using a drag-and-drop approach. A number of other Web Forms server controls are available to you. Explore the `System.Web.UI.WebControls` namespace to find others. By default, not all of the Web Server controls are included in the Toolbox.

Due to space constraints, this chapter uses only a small subset of the classes available to you for creating ASP.NET applications. Entire books are written on ADO.NET and ASP.NET. The intent is to give you a foundation and introduce you to what is available, so that you can continue learning after finishing this chapter. You may want to do that by exploring some of the classes listed in Table 12-5. The table was adapted from the Visual Studio .NET's MSDN documentation—retrievable using the **Help>Search** menu option.

Table 12-5   Additional Web Forms control classes

Class identifier	Description
AdRotator	Displays an advertisement banner on a Web page
HyperLink	Displays a link to another Web page
Image	Displays an image on a Web page
ImageButton	Displays an image and responds to mouse clicks on the image
LinkButton	Displays a hyperlink style button control on a Web page
Panel	Represents a control that acts as a container for other controls
Table	Displays a table on a Web page
ValidationSummary	Displays a summary of all validation errors on a Web page, in a message box, or both
Xml	Displays an XML document

One way to transport a Visual Studio ASP.NET application from one computer's Web server to another for development is to perform the following steps:

1. On the destination computer that also has IIS installed, create a Visual Studio ASP.NET project. Use exactly the same name as the original project name.

2. Close Visual Studio. Notice you are not developing anything new. You are just creating the project and then closing the application. This sets up the structure and creates a solution and project file for that application.

3. Using MyComputer or Windows Explorer, copy all the original files from the original target folder into the C:\Inetpub\wwwroot\projectName subdirectory. Notice that projectName would be replaced by the name of your Web application.

4. During the copy, when prompted about replacing existing files, answer Yes to all prompts.

5. After completing Steps 1 through 5, you can open the project on the new system by selecting the **File>Open>Project** From Web menu option.

6. Using the Solution Explorer, right mouse click on the file that ends with the .aspx extension and select **Set as Start Page**. You should now be able to modify and/or run the application.

Other IDEs

As you learned in this section, Web applications use a different programming model than Windows applications. To use Visual Studio .NET for the development, you must have IIS installed and have administrative debugging rights on the computer used for development. Other integrated development environments exist. WebMatrix, for example, is a free IDE that can be used to develop ASP.NET Web-based applications. It includes a personal Web server so that IIS need not be installed. At the time of writing, WebMatrix can be downloaded at *www.asp.net/WebMatrix/*.

SharpDevelop (#develop) is another IDE option for developing Windows-based applications. At the time of writing, it could not be used for developing ASP.NET applications. SharpDevelop is a free download available at *www.icsharpcode.net/OpenSource/SD/default.asp*. You are again encouraged to use a search engine and see what other IDEs might be available for you at the current time.

WEB SERVICES

Imagine including a link on your Web page to enable users to search the Web for a keyword. You could, of course, link to another page that has a search engine. But doing so takes the user away from your page. What if you want to keep the user at your page, but offer the same functionality as the large search engine sites? Or, what if you want to allow the user to learn the

12

temperature for any city from your page? What if you want the user to obtain driving directions from his location to your location? If you do not want users to link to another site, but instead stay on your page and receive this data, you should explore adding a reference to a site that offers a Web Service method to do one or more of the previously described functions.

This is an age in which data is readily available but is often in different formats, so computers need to be able to share and use data from many different sources. In the simplest case, **Web services** enable you to exchange data from one computer to another over the Internet or an intranet. This exchange can involve the data being processed or manipulated before being sent. **Web services** are applications that return data. They actually constitute a unit of managed code that can be remotely executed using HTTP. Web services involve neither the presentation layer nor how the data is displayed once it is delivered to another computer. Web services are designed to transfer data in a usable format to another computer.

The concept of **distributed computing**, in which applications are spread over more than one computer system, has been around for many years. Using Web services to communicate is not new with .NET. A number of technologies have been available for some time that enable heterogeneous applications to share data. Included as part of the .NET FCL are a number of classes that support using existing Web services and creating new services.

Web Services Protocols

.NET includes classes in the `System.Web.Services` `namespace` that enable you to exchange messages (data) using the standard protocols of HTTP, Extensible Markup Language (XML), Simple Object Access Protocol (SOAP), and Web Services Description Language (WSDL). These are the keys to .NET's success with Web services. Each protocol is briefly discussed in the sections that follow.

Messages in XML

Messages are sent from one method to another, and these methods may be stored hundreds of miles from each other. Because the methods follow the same object-oriented model you have used with all other applications, they belong to a `class`. When called, the methods have a return value of a specific type, such as `int` or `string`, which is physically returned as part of an XML message.

Extensible Markup Language (XML) stores structured data in readable text files. XML and HTML are both languages that use tags to mark up their contents. HTML tags tell the browser how to display data in different formats, for example, in bold or italics or in different fonts or font sizes. XML, on the other hand, uses tags as a format for describing data. Like HTML, XML is a standard that enables applications to communicate using XML-based messages over the Web, regardless of what operating system or language is being used.

Examples of readable XML statements are presented in the sections that follow. XML is at the core of many features of the .NET Framework. Using XML, cross-platform application development is possible because data is passed back and forth between applications as XML.

HTTP and SOAP

To consume or use the data returned from a Web service, HTTP and SOAP protocols are used. First, as with other requests for pages on the Web, the request for the Web service is transmitted across the Web as an HTTP request. Since the request is transferred using the HTTP protocol, it can normally reach any computer on the Internet. **SOAP** is an XML-based protocol used to encapsulate method calls (and return results) into XML statements so they can be sent via HTTP.

The SOAP message that includes a request for the service is called a **SOAP request**. When the Web server that hosts the Web service receives the message, it translates the SOAP method call into its own language, performs any processing needed, generates a return value, and produces a SOAP message (called a **SOAP response**). This is sent back to the client, which receives and translates the message to its own data type.

To use the Web service, you must know where it is and what methods it has available. WSDLs and UDDIs provide this information.

WSDL

Web Services Description Language (WSDL) is a language formatted in XML that is used to describe the capabilities of a Web service and is itself part of that service. WSDL includes details about the method in terms of what type of data it can receive and what type of results it will return. Think about the signature and return type of a typical method. To use or call on the method, you must know what arguments it receives and what, if anything, it returns. To use a Web service, client applications must know the method name, the number and type of parameters the method is expecting, and what is expected upon return from the method. A Web service that offers keyword search functionality would expect to receive a data item in a string format. The Web service would return a string containing a list of Web addresses in which the keyword is located. The WSDL would provide the details in XML format.

A number of Web services are already available that you can add to your application, and the list is growing daily. Typically, a Web service defines a business object that executes a unit of work. You use the WSDL to determine how to call the Web service. But, for clients to use a Web service, they have to know that the Web service is available. For this, UDDIs are helpful. **UDDI** stands for **Universal Description, Discovery, and Integration**.

UDDI, like WSDL, uses an XML grammar. Web services publish information in a standardized format about their location and functionality in a UDDI registry. In the sections that follow, you learn how Visual Studio can aid you in discovering new Web services using a **UDDI registry**.

 Do you want to know what Web services are already available? Check out a UDDI registry. A number of Web sites maintain these registries, which include a collection of documents about Web services companies. Microsoft (*http://uddi.microsoft.com*) and IBM (*http://uddi.ibm.com*) maintain large UDDI registries.

Building a Web Service

You can also use Visual Studio .NET to create and publish your own Web services. You begin a project exactly as you have been doing by selecting **File>New>Project**. As shown in Figure 12-27, the Web service template stores the project in the same location (localhost) as other Web applications. The ASP.NET Web Service template is selected when you want to build a Web service.

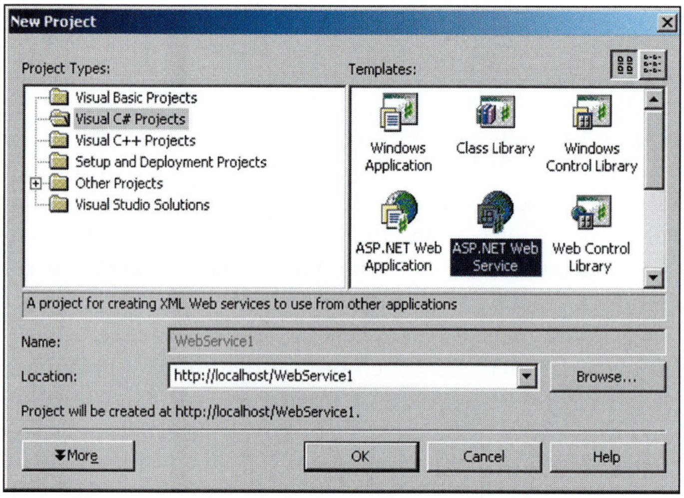

Figure 12-27   Building a Web service application

It is easy to create a Web service in Visual Studio .NET, which includes a number of predefined features as well as a special Web interface for testing your Web service. After you select the ASP.NET Web Service from the New Project window, a blank form appears with a link enabling you to view the code. When you view the code, you see a large area commented out. Notice the lines that appear in green in Figure 12-28.

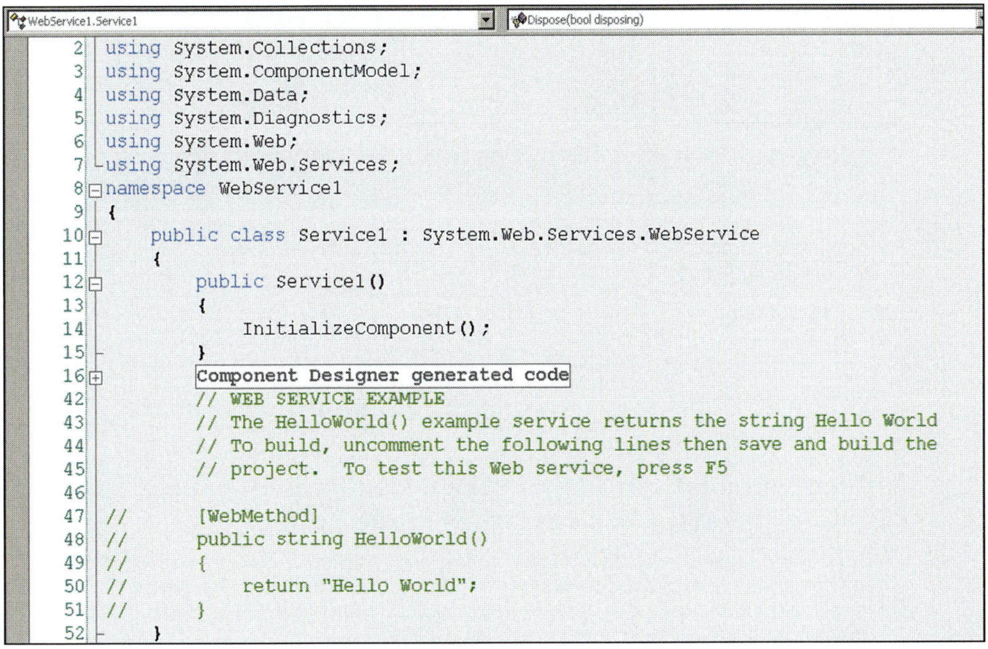

```
  WebService1.Service1                              Dispose(bool disposing)
   2  using System.Collections;
   3  using System.ComponentModel;
   4  using System.Data;
   5  using System.Diagnostics;
   6  using System.Web;
   7  using System.Web.Services;
   8  namespace WebService1
   9  {
  10      public class Service1 : System.Web.Services.WebService
  11      {
  12          public Service1()
  13          {
  14              InitializeComponent();
  15          }
  16          Component Designer generated code
  42          // WEB SERVICE EXAMPLE
  43          // The HelloWorld() example service returns the string Hello World
  44          // To build, uncomment the following lines then save and build the
  45          // project.  To test this Web service, press F5
  46
  47  //      [WebMethod]
  48  //      public string HelloWorld()
  49  //      {
  50  //          return "Hello World";
  51  //      }
  52      }
```

Figure 12-28   Predefined WebMethod

As indicated on lines 43 through 45 in Figure 12-28, this example Web service returns **"Hello World"**. When you uncomment the method that begins on line 47, you have a functioning Web service.

Line 47, which is required for Web services, is as follows:

`[WebMethod]`

WebMethod is an attribute that indicates that you want the method exposed as part of a Web service. The **class** name, by default, is **Service1**. Visual Studio associates a .asmx file extension with Web services.

Running the application produces the output shown in Figure 12-29.

12

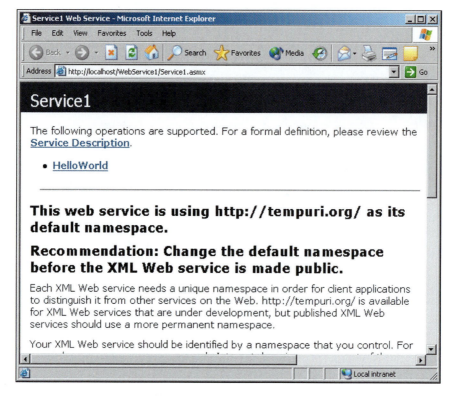

Figure 12-29   User interface for testing the Web service

This interface is automatically created for you within Visual Studio. It lists the methods included as part of the Web service. For this example, the only method included is `HelloWorld`.

Clicking the Service Description link shows the XML tags generated for the WSDL service agreement. These XML statements are shown in Figure 12-30. Notice that the Address bar now ends in WSDL.

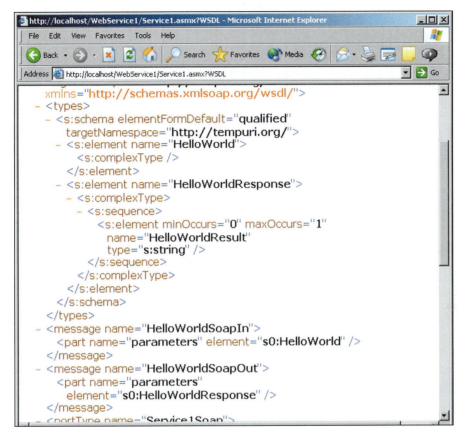

Figure 12-30 WSDL service description

If you click the method name, **HelloWorld**, shown in Figure 12-29, another Web page is displayed, which gives you an opportunity to call up and test the Web service. This file also shows a sample SOAP request and response as displayed in Figure 12-31.

12

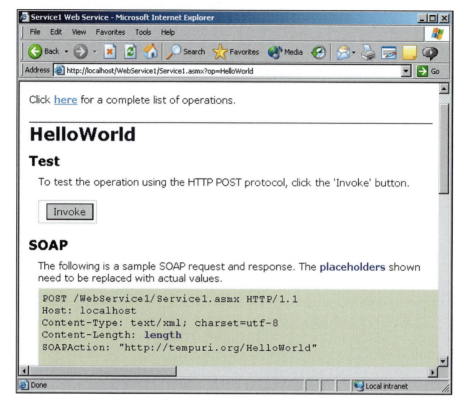

Figure 12-31   Test of Web service HelloWorld method operation

Figure 12-32 shows what happens when the `HelloWorld` Web service method is executed. The `string` `"Hello World"` embedded within XML tags is produced.

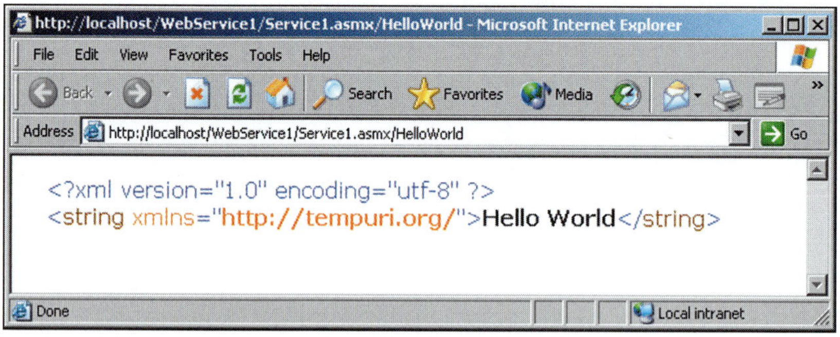

Figure 12-32   XML produced from Web service call

The previous figures illustrated creating the Web service that returned a **string** value. This is very simple output. You are only limited by your imagination now. To create useful Web services, add the **[WebMethod]** attribute to your methods and have your **class** be derived from the **System.Web.Services.WebService namespace**. Example 12-18 includes the complete program listing used for the Web service.

Example 12-18

```
// WebService1      Author: Doyle
using System;
using System.Collections;
using System.ComponentModel;
using System.Data;
using System.Diagnostics;
using System.Web;
using System.Web.Services;
namespace WebService1
{
    public class Service1 : System.Web.Services.WebService
    {
        public Service1()
        {
          InitializeComponent();
        }
        #region Component Designer generated code

        private IContainer components = null;

        private void InitializeComponent()
        {
        }
        protected override void Dispose( bool disposing )
        {
            if(disposing && components != null)
            {
                components.Dispose();
            }
            base.Dispose(disposing);
        }

        #endregion
        // WEB SERVICE EXAMPLE
        // The HelloWorld() example service returns the
        // string Hello World
        // To build, uncomment the following lines then
        // save and build the project.
        // To test this Web service, press F5
```

12

```
        [WebMethod]
        public string HelloWorld()
        {
            return "Hello World";
        }
    }
}
```

Using or Consuming Web Services

Once the Web service is created, applications can use it by adding a reference to the component. To illustrate this, a separate Web application is created to display the returned value. The Web application is populated with three **Label** objects and one **Button object**. To add the reference to the Web service, right-click References in the Solutions Explorer window. Select Add Web Reference. As shown in Figure 12-33, a browser window is displayed. This can be used to locate available Web services on the Internet.

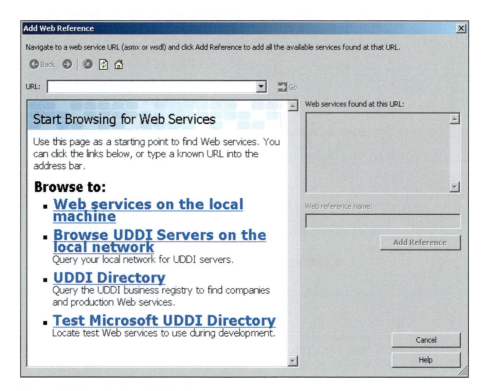

Figure 12-33   Adding Web reference

Navigating the UDDI Registry

If you click the UDDI Directory or Test Microsoft UDDI Directory link shown in Figure 12-33, two text boxes appear enabling you to search by the service or provider name. Or, you can navigate through the registered Web services by categories. Figure 12-34 shows the level of categories displayed in the registry after "Test Microsoft UDDI Directory\ VS Web Service Search Categorization" is selected.

 An error message may be displayed in the right column indicating "The proxy settings on this computer are not configured correctly for Web discovery." Visual Studio states, "This error appears in the Add Web Reference dialog box if you are developing on a machine that is behind a firewall and a proxy server has not been explicitly specified for Internet Explorer connections." Getting this message does not mean you cannot add references to Web service methods; you can still add references. You just cannot use Visual Studio's Web Discovery tool. You need the WSDL to determine how to call the Web service. Explore some of the UDDI registries to get this information.

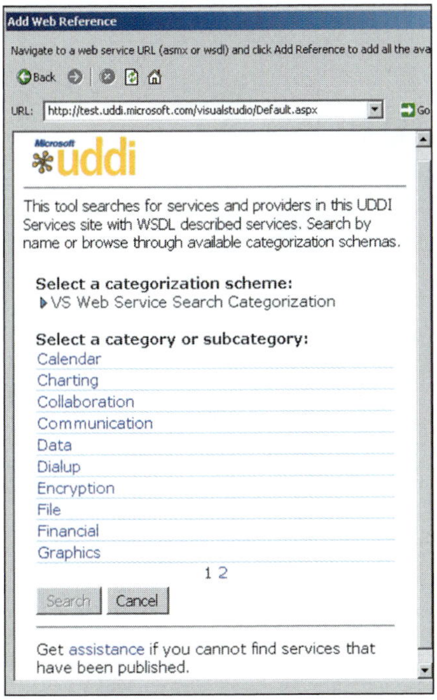

Figure 12-34 Categories of UDDI registry Web services

Continuing to traverse down the list of categories leads you to the actual listing of available services. Then this message appears: "To add references, click on the service you would like, then click on that service's corresponding interface definition, and then click the 'Add Reference' button below." A Web service that generates graphics and data charts is shown in Figure 12-35. The Graphics category was searched and a Web service from BeatWear Inc. called LiveAssetsWS was found (at the time of writing this book). Its service description is shown in Figure 12-35. When you explore the UDDI registries you may find different services and many more. New Web services are added every day to the UDDI registries.

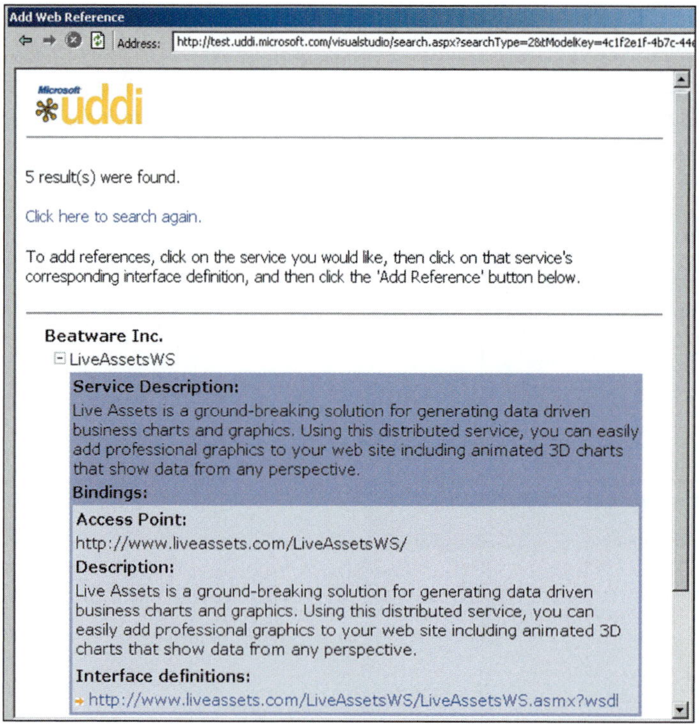

Figure 12-35 Date and time Web service

Typing the URL

Another option is to type the URL for the Web service. To add the reference to the Web service created previously, the URL is typed in the Address bar. The value typed is:

http://localhost/WebService1/Service1.asmx

Notice how Web services files end with a .asmx extension.

When a valid address is referenced, the methods available for the Web service are displayed in Visual Studio .NET as shown in Figure 12-36.

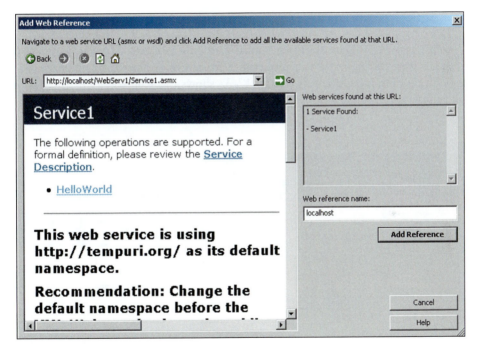

Figure 12-36   Referencing Service1 Web service

The images shown in Figures 12-33 through 12-36 were taken from Visual Studio .NET 2003. If you are using a different version, your images may look slightly different.

Calling the Web Service Method

The `UseWebService` application, which was created to illustrate using the Web service, contains a button that calls the Web service method. To call the method, the `Button` click event instantiates an **object** of the Web service **class**, which was created previously. Using that **object**, it calls on the `HelloWorld( )` method. The statements that make up the `Button` click event are shown in Example 12-19.

Example 12-19

```
private void Button1_Click(object sender, System.EventArgs e)
{
    localhost.Service1 obj = new localhost.Service1( );
    this.Label1.Text = obj.HelloWorld( );
}
```

This is the only program statement added to the `UseWebService` project. The only other changes were setting the `Text` properties for each of the controls and changing the background and foreground colors. Figure 12-37 shows the Web page when it was first loaded and after a round-trip to the server.

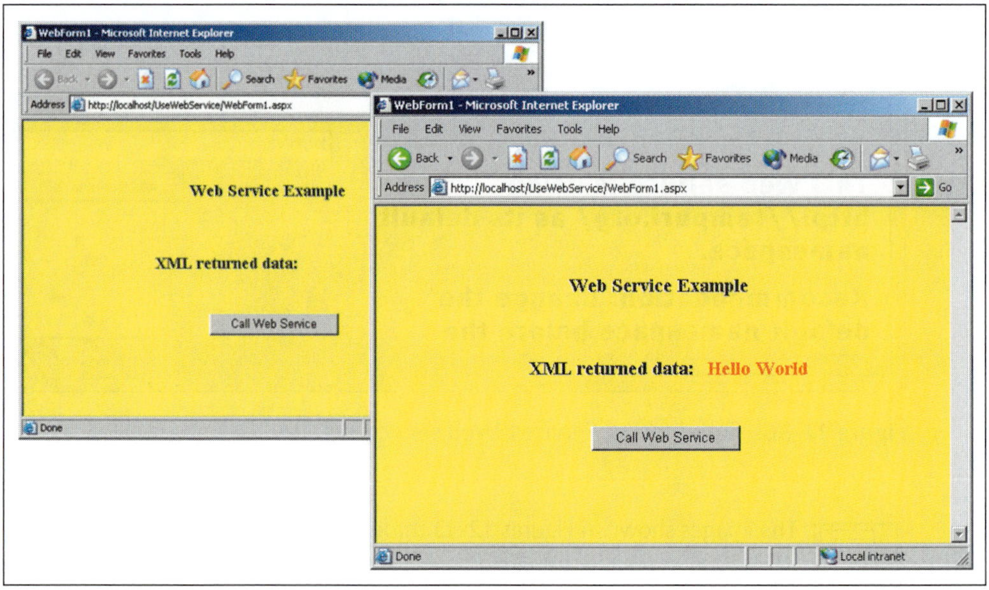

Figure 12-37   Web service called

When the **object** was instantiated, localhost prefixed the **class** name. If the Web service were on a remote computer, localhost would be replaced by the address of the server hosting the Web service.

There is a large amount of information on the Web about Web services. You are encouraged to explore. At the time of writing, one site that contained substantial amounts of information was: *http://msdn.microsoft.com/webservices.*

SMART DEVICE APPLICATIONS (OPTIONAL)

Visual Studio .NET 2003 includes a template for developing applications for smart devices, such as the Pocket PC. Using the .NET Compact Framework, which is a subset of the .NET Framework, you can design, develop, debug, and deploy applications that run on personal digital assistants (PDAs), mobile phones, tablet PCs, and other resource-restricted devices. These applications can be created even if you do not own a PDA. An emulator that simulates the device is included as part of the IDE. The **emulator** has many of the same features you find on PDAs. It enables you to see what the output would look like displayed on the real device.

Since there has been and continues to be such an explosive growth in wireless devices, this section is included to illustrate the ease of development for these types of applications. You are encouraged to continue exploring beyond what is presented in this limited example. You use the same programming development model that you have been using to develop complete smart device applications using C#.

Currently all mobile devices are significantly less powerful than desktop computers. They run more slowly, have less memory available, and their display capability restricts their functionality. Keep in mind that for development purposes, the typical Pocket PC display screen is only about 6x8 centimeters. Thus, the user interface should be kept simpler than traditional applications.

Smart device development is not available in stand-alone editions such as the Visual C# .NET 2003 Standard Edition CD-ROMs supplied with this book.

The .NET Compact Framework

As part of Visual Studio .NET 2003, a new smaller Framework Class Library is included called the **Compact FCL**. The Compact Framework is about 1.5 megabytes. The fact that the .NET Compact Framework uses the same programming model across a number of devices makes it easy to develop applications that run on multiple devices. You still have access to the core methods and classes so that the business logic, data access, and XML Web service layer can be used. Your graphical user interfaces are less sophisticated. Like Web applications, you have fewer controls to drag and drop and fewer events to program. You can use or consume Web services in smart device applications, but you cannot create new Web services. In the sections that follow you create a small application.

12

Creating a Smart Device Application

After selecting **File>New>Project** and choosing C# as the Project type, select the Smart Device Application. You name the Project as you have done with previous applications. A wizard walks you through the creation, first asking for platform and project type. The options are Pocket PC and Windows CE. Select Pocket PC and Windows Application for the Project Type and click OK. A blank miniature form is displayed with a main Menu control automatically included.

Using the WYSIWYG approach, you can drag and drop controls to the form. To illustrate developing an application for a smart device, a multiplier is designed as an example. As shown in Figure 12-38, two text boxes, one button, and four labels are added to the form.

Figure 12-38 Adding controls to the smart device application

A number of properties were set. The **Text** property for the form was set for the title bar. **Text** properties were set for each of the controls. For the **TextBox** objects, **Text** was set to **""**. **BackColor** was set for the form; **Font** and **ForeColor** were set for each of the labels. The controls that are used in the program statements were named using the **Name** property.

You have the same formatting tools under the Format menu available for creating these small smart device applications as you had with Windows and Web applications. The Align option from the Format menu is used to arrange the controls. Vertical and horizontal spacing options are also used in this example.

Menus on a Pocket PC are displayed differently than with Windows or Web applications. They are displayed from the lower-left corner of the interface. To add text for the menu option, before selecting the main menu, scroll down to the bottom of the form. After selecting the `mainMenu1` control (which is the default name assigned to the menu when it is dragged onto the form), click in the lower-left corner of the form to type the text. Once the text is added, you register event-handler methods in the same manner you do with Windows and Web applications. Figure 12-39 illustrates adding **File>Exit** options.

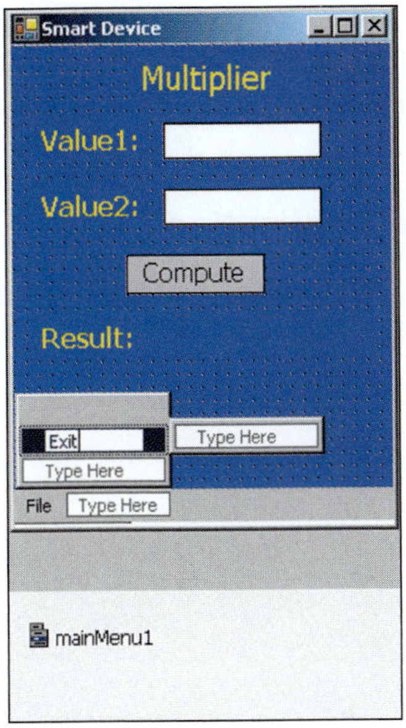

Figure 12-39   Adding a menu to a smart device application

The only programming statements added were those included in the event-handler methods. The other changes were to the properties in the Properties window. Those statements are shown in Example 12-20.

Example 12-20

```
private void btnCompute_Click(object sender,
                System.EventArgs e)
{
    this.lblResult.Text +=
            (double.Parse(this.txtBxV1.Text) *
                double.Parse(this.txtBxV2.Text)).ToString();
}
```

```
private void menuExit_Click(object sender,
                System.EventArgs e)
{
        this.Close( );
}
```

The `btnCompute_Click( )` event handler retrieves the values from the `TextBox` objects, converts them to integers, multiplies their values, and then concatenates the result to the text already stored in the `lblResult` object. The `menuExit_Click( )` event handler closes the entire application.

Building and Running the Smart Device Application

Clicking Start Without Debugging on the Debug menu displays the message shown in Figure 12-40 asking for the type of device to target for the deployment.

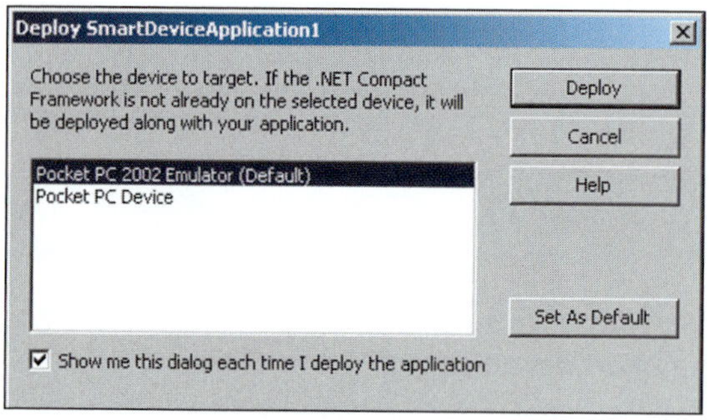

Figure 12-40   Choosing a device as a target for deployment

Select Pocket PC 2002 Emulator as the device type. The first time the application is deployed, it takes a couple of minutes to load the emulator. It copies the .NET Compact Framework files as shown in Figure 12-41.

> **NOTE** To use the emulator in Visual Studio .NET, you need a network connection on the system you are developing. You do not have to be connected to the network, but must have the card installed. This is normally not a concern, because your development is usually on machines that are Internet ready. However, for machines without a network card, you can install the loopback network adapter from Microsoft to simulate a network connection.

Figure 12-41   .NET Compact Framework being installed

12

After a couple of minutes, a fully functioning Pocket PC is displayed complete with the operating system. As shown in Figure 12-42, you can use it like a PDA. A keyboard and mouse are available as well as a number of applications such as Excel and Word.

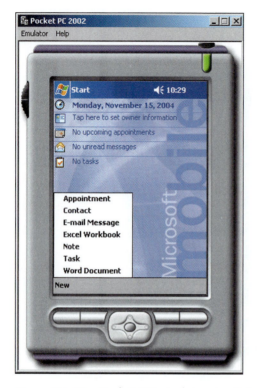

Figure 12-42   Pocket PC emulator created

After another minute or so, the application is downloaded to the device and the interface displayed. Figure 12-43 shows the smart device application after the user enters values and presses the Compute button.

Figure 12-43　Smart device application output

Due to space constraints the source listing is not included; however, the only program statements added to the smart device application were the bodies for the `btnCompute_Click( )` and the `menuExit_Click( )` event-handler methods shown in Example 12-20. Property values were set as indicated previously using the Properties window. These values affect the visible appearance of the interface.

You can easily reuse existing code with smart devices. A new interface must be designed for these types of applications. However, the business logic, data tiers, Web service XML connectivity, and event-driven programming model can all be extended to work with smart device applications. The market for mobile devices is growing by leaps and bounds. You are encouraged to take advantage of the opportunities and continue your exploration of programming these devices using .NET.

There are rich resources on the Web for developing in the .NET environment. Here are a few to add to your bookmarks:

www.gotdotnet.com

www.asp.net

www.microsoft.com/mobile

QUICK REVIEW

1. A Web application, also called a Web site, is simply a collection of one or more related files or components stored on a Web server. Web servers are software that is responsible for hosting or delivering the Web application.

2. When a page is requested using HTTP protocol, the request goes to the Web server, which sends back the document in an HTML format. This is considered a round-trip to the server. Another round-trip is required when changes are made on a dynamic Web page.

3. Every trip to the server creates a new **object** because Web pages are considered stateless. They do not retain their values from one trip to the Web server to the next.

4. Static pages do not require any processing by a Web server. They are precreated and reside on the server's hard drive. Dynamic Web sites involve processing in addition to rendering the formatting HTML.

5. To develop ASP.NET applications, you must have Microsoft Internet Information Services (IIS) installed.

6. ASP.NET Web application projects are created at http://localhost. Physically the files are stored in the home directory, C:\Inetpub\wwwroot. This is the default for the home directory. A directory is also created with the name you typed for the project, and it is placed (along with the two solution files) at the location you configured Visual Studio to store all of your Visual Studio projects.

7. The Web Forms page **object** has a number of properties, many with the same functionality that was available for setting a Windows application form.

8. Two files are created for Web applications. Code for the visual interface file is placed in the file containing the HTML tags (.aspx extension). The other file, the code-behind file, contains the logic for the application.

9. HTML controls are also called client-side controls. The biggest advantage HTML controls offer is that the page is rendered "as is" to the browser. Client-side controls require no processing by the Web server.

10. Converting HTML controls into HTML server controls requires right-clicking the HTML controls and selecting Run As Server Control. The code-behind file receives the declaration of the HTML **object** and the program statements for the event-handler methods.

11. HTML controls' properties differ from Windows and Web Forms controls' properties. `InnerText` is required for HTML controls instead of `Text` to set the text on controls, and `id` is used instead of `Name` to identify the control.

12. Server controls are referred to as Web controls, Web Forms server controls, ASP server controls, or simply Web Forms controls. Visual Studio prefixes the control name with `<asp:control>` and ends the tag with `</asp:control>`.

13. Only a few events trigger a postback to the server. `ListBox`, `RadioButton`, `RadioButtonList`, `CheckBox`, `CheckBoxList`, and `DropDownList` have a property called `AutoPostBack` that can be set to `true` to trigger a postback automatically.

14. Validation controls enable input to be validated or checked by the server. You can check to make sure that values have been entered, that values fall between a range of values, or you can create custom validation checks.

15. You tie the validation control to a specific control such as a `TextBox` `object`, using the `ControlToValidate` property. The `ErrorMessage` property can be set to the message you want to display when the input control does not pass the validation test.

16. By default, page validation occurs when any button on the form is clicked.

17. A `Calendar` control is used to display a monthly calendar on a Web page. Once placed on the page, the calendar is live and users can employ it to view and select dates. To work programmatically with the calendar for the `WebControls` application, you declare an `object` of the `DateTime` `class`.

18. The `DataGrid` control is very useful for displaying data in a tabular format. To populate these controls, the actual data can come from sources such as arrays or database tables.

19. Web services are applications that return data. Web services do not involve the presentation layer or the method for displaying data once it is delivered to another computer.

20. The key to the success of .NET with Web services is that the services enable the exchange of messages (data) using the standard protocols of HTTP, Extensible Markup Language (XML), Simple Object Access Protocol (SOAP), and Web Services Description Language (WSDL).

21. XML is a markup language that uses tags to provide a format for describing data. Data is passed back and forth between applications as XML.

12

22. SOAP is an XML-based protocol used to encapsulate method calls (and return results) into XML statements so they can be sent via HTTP.

23. The Web Service Definition Language (WSDL) describes a Web service. It includes details about what messages it can receive and what results it returns.

24. For clients to use a Web service, they have to know that the Web service is available. Universal Description, Discovery, and Integration (UDDI) registries include cataloged listings of Web services available.

25. `WebMethod` is an attribute that indicates that you want the method exposed as part of a Web service. Web services files end with .asmx extensions.

26. Using the .NET Compact Framework, which is a smaller subset of the .NET Framework, you can design, develop, debug, and deploy applications that run on personal digital assistants (PDAs), mobile phones, and other resource-restricted devices. The Compact Framework is included with the Visual Studio .NET 2003 version, not version 1.0.

EXERCISES

1. .NET Web applications differ from Windows applications in that Web applications must take the following into consideration:

   a. Multiple users need to be able to access the application at the same time.

   b. An application must be viewable by multiple types of platforms including Linux and Windows.

   c. Fewer graphical user interface controls are available for Web applications.

   d. IIS must be loaded for development of Web applications.

   e. all of the above

2. The term "Web application" is synonymous with:

   a. Web server

   b. IIS

   c. Web form

   d. Web page

   e. Web site

3. Interaction with users on Web applications cannot include the use of:

   a. `MessageBox`

   b. `Label`

   c. `TextBox`

   d. `ListBox`

   e. `Button`

4. The term used to reference converting an HTML document to a viewable format for display purposes is:

   a. request

   b. host

   c. illustrate

   d. viewState

   e. render

5. Web pages do not require any processing by the server when they include which of the following?

   a. HTML controls

   b. HTML server controls

   c. Web Forms controls

    d. HTML controls or HTML server controls

    e. HTML controls, HTML server controls, or Web Forms controls

6. To convert an HTML control to an HTML server control:

    a. Drag HTML server controls onto the form.

    b. Right-click the HTML control and choose Run As Server Control.

    c. Select Convert to HTML control from the Format menu.

    d. Use Web Forms control for the control.

    e. none of the above

7. Classic ASP applications are characterized by which of the following?

    a. Program statements written in languages such as Java are included inside the HTML file.

    b. A code-behind file is created.

    c. Only formatting HTML tags can be used with the application.

    d. Only static pages can be developed.

    e. Script is embedded in the HTML document.

8. ASP.NET applications are characterized by which of the following?

    a. Program statements written in languages such as Java are included inside the HTML file.

    b. A code-behind file is created.

    c. Only formatting HTML tags can be used with the application.

    d. Only static pages can be developed.

    e. Script is embedded in the HTML document.

9. The HTML control property used to set the text on a label is:

    a. `Text`

    b. `Name`

    c. `InnerText`

    d. `id`

    e. none of the above

10. When you set property values for Web Forms controls, the program statements referencing the settings are:

    a. placed in the code-behind file

    b. placed in the .aspx.cs file

    c. stored in the .aspm file

    d. stored in the file containing the HTML tags

    e. none of the above

12

11. The default home directory for storing C# Web applications is:

    a. C:\CSharpProjects

    b. C:\localhost

    c. C:\Inetpub\wwwroot

    d. C:\WebApps

    e. none of the above

12. Events associated with which of the following trigger a postback to the Web server?

    a. `ListBox`

    b. `TextBox`

    c. `DropDownList`

    d. `Button`

    e. all of the above

13. Which control is often used to display data from a database table?

    a. `DataGrid`

    b. `DataTable`

    c. `Table`

    d. `DataList`

    e. none of the above

14. A file ending with the extension of .asmx is associated with which type of application?

    a. ASP.NET Web page

    b. smart device

    c. Web service

    d. Windows

    e. classic ASP

15. The validation control used to make sure values have been entered into a field is:

    a. `RangeValidator`

    b. `FieldRequiredValidator`

    c. `CompareValidator`

    d. `RequiredFieldValidator`

    e. `Required`

16. To work programmatically with the `Calendar` control, instantiate an **object** of the _____ `class`.

    a. `Calendar`

    b. `DateTime`

   c. `Date`

   d. `CalendarDate`

   e. none of the above

17. Web services are applications that return:

   a. data

   b. program statements with value-added logic

   c. graphical user interfaces

   d. fully functioning Web applications

   e. none of the above

18. The protocol used to encapsulate method calls (and return results) into XML statements is:

   a. HTTP

   b. HTML

   c. SOAP

   d. SXML

   e. WSDL

19. To create Web services, what must be added to the program?

   a. `WebService` directive

   b. `WebClass` attribute

   c. `WebMethod` attribute

   d. `using System.Web.Service` directive

   e. all of the above

20. An XML protocol that is used to locate Web services is:

   a. SXML

   b. SOAP

   c. WSDL

   d. UDDI

   e. none of the above

21. Describe how the classic or traditional ASP programming model differs from the ASP.NET programming model for creating Web pages.

22. How do dynamic pages differ from static pages?

23. Compare and contrast HTML controls with Web Forms controls in terms of the code generated for each type and the property values that can be set.

12

24. What is a Web service? Give three examples of services that you might find useful to include on a school Web site.

25. Identify and describe three types of validation controls that can be added to a Web application.

PROGRAMMING EXERCISES

1. The computer club has decided to take a field trip to the hometown of one of the members during spring vacation. To determine the destination, each member has been charged with creating a Web page to highlight the features of his hometown. Create a static Web application that contains details about your hometown. If you would prefer that the members visit another location, you may choose a different locale. Set the properties on the form for the controls so the form is aesthetically pleasing. Be sure to change both background and foreground colors, font size, and type.

2. Modify the Web application developed for Exercise 1 to include an HTML server control that causes a message to be displayed (on a **Label object**) when the user clicks a button. The message should include additional details about the locale.

3. Using Web Forms controls, create a Web application to include a **TextBox object**, a **Button object**, and a **ListBox object**. Allow the user to input values into the **TextBox**. Use those values to populate the **ListBox object**. Fill the **ListBox** with names, shopping items, types of secondary storage, or some other items of your choosing. Allow the user to make a selection from the **ListBox** and display the selection on a **Label object**.

4. Create a dynamic Web site that functions like a calculator. Add features for addition, subtraction, multiplication, division, modulation, and so on. For simplicity you can use two **TextBox** objects to accept data input and a **Button object** to trigger the event.

5. Create a Web application that enables the user to enter first name, last name, and e-mail address. Accept those values and store them in a text file. Add validation controls to all three controls to ensure each has a value before loading it to the file. Confirm that the values are written to the file.

6. Create a Web application that enables users to select from a **Calendar** control **object** the date of their next exams. Using program statements, retrieve their selections and then display the date along with an appropriate message.

7. Create a Web service that returns your favorite saying to the requesting client.

8. Write a client application to use the Web service created in Exercise 7. Have the message displayed on a Web application in a **Label object**.

9. Create and consume a Web service that accepts a number between 0 and 10 and returns the **string** equivalent for the entered value.

10. Create a smart device application that allows users to input their names and student IDs. Create and display a new identification number. The new ID should consist of the first initial of their names followed by the original identification numbers. Append onto the end of those values the total number of characters in their names. For example, if the name Sofyia ElKomaria and the ID 12467 is entered, the new identification number would be S1246716.

12

Appendix A

Compiling and Running an Application from the Command Line

This appendix describes how to run applications at the command line without using the Integrated Development Environment of Visual Studio .NET. To begin, you can download Microsoft's **.NET Framework Software Development Kit (SDK)** from the Microsoft Web site as a free download. At the time of writing, the URL for the download was *www.microsoft.com/downloads*. The size of the download is approximately 100 MB. It can be used on Windows 2000, Windows XP, and later versions of Windows operating systems. The SDK includes the extensive library of .NET classes, C# compiler, Common Language Runtime, and everything you need to build, test, and deploy applications.

COMMAND-LINE EXECUTION

You can type your source code statements into a simple editor, such as Notepad. To start, navigate to the directory where you store your programming work. In the editor, select the Save As option from the File menu when you are ready to save the source code file. When you save the file, use the same name as the class name for the file name identifier. In addition, add a dot following the file identifier name and an extension of cs onto the end of the filename. Figure A-1 illustrates saving your work from within Notepad.

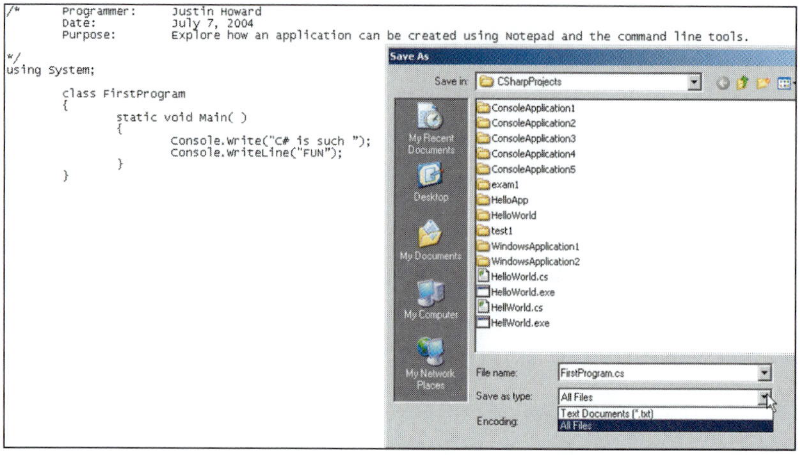

```
/*      Programmer:     Justin Howard
        Date:           July 7, 2004
        Purpose:        Explore how an application can be created using Notepad and the command line tools.
*/
using System;

        class FirstProgram
        {
                static void Main( )
                {
                        Console.write("C# is such ");
                        Console.writeLine("FUN");
                }
        }
```

Figure A-1   Saving the Notepad file with a .cs extension

Notice in Figure A-1 that the name of the class is `FirstProgram`; thus, the name of the file should be FirstProgram.cs.

When you save the text file, do not use .txt extension as part of the filename. To avoid having the .txt extension automatically added by the editor, you can either enclose the entire name, including extension, in double quotes (" "), as `"FirstProgram.cs"` or select All Files from the Save as type selection as illustrated in Figure A-1.

Compiling the Source Code from the DOS Command Prompt

Open a command window to compile and execute your application by selecting: **Start>Run**.

Type cmd as shown in Figure A-2. This opens a DOS window with a command prompt.

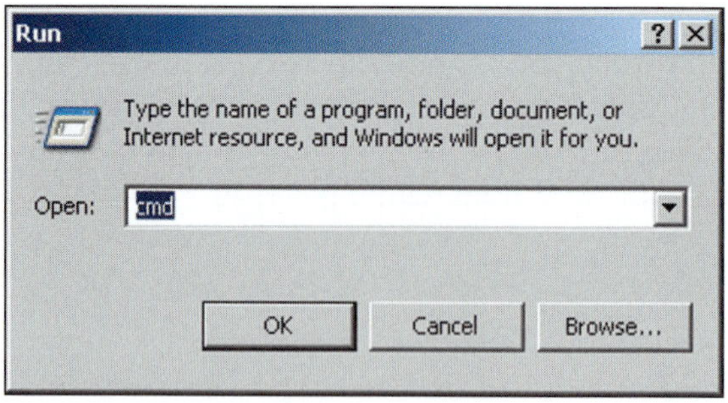

Figure A-2   Opening a cmd window

A command window can also be opened by typing the word "command." However, issues related to long filenames are easier to deal with if you open the command window with cmd instead of command.

A

At the cmd prompt, you move into the directory in which you stored your source code file by typing cd (change directory) followed by the full path of the directory. If you created a directory named CSharpProjects on your local hard drive and placed it at the root level, you would type cd C:\ CSharpProjects as shown in Figure A-3.

Figure A-3 Moving into the folder used to store your projects

Start the compiler from the cmd line by entering the compiler's program name: csc.

Submit the source code file to the compiler by entering its filename on the command line, as in the following:

```
csc fileName.cs
```

To compile the source code file named FirstProgram, type the following:

```
csc FirstProgram.cs
```

 Be sure to type the .cs extension. Otherwise you receive a "source file not found error".

Receiving the error message shown in Figure A-4 indicates that csc is not recognized as an internal or external command, operable program, or batch file, and the operating system is not able to locate the csc.exe file. You need to indicate where the operating system can find the csc.exe file. When you loaded the .NET SDK or Visual Studio .NET, the environment variables for the path may not have been set.

Figure A-4   Error message indicating compiler cannot be found

If you have Visual Studio .NET loaded, but want to run your application from the command prompt, you can skip the next few paragraphs and continue your reading in the section entitled, Compiling the Program Statements from the Visual Studio .NET Command Prompt.

Setting the Path to the Compiler (csc)

First you need to locate the compilation program, csc.exe, on your system. This can be done using the Search feature on your computer (either from the Start menu, My Computer Icon, or Windows Explorer). Search for the file named csc.exe. Be sure to include System Folders in the search. If you are using Windows XP, you can select the Search System Folders option under the Advanced Search tab. On the system used to write this book, two versions are loaded. csc.exe, version 1.1 is located at: C:\WINDOWS\Microsoft.NET\Framework\ v1.1.4322 and csc.exe Version 1.0 is located at C:\WINDOWS\Microsoft.NET\ Framework\v1.0.3705.

After you locate the csc.exe, you compile from the cmd prompt by typing the full path to the csc.exe file (C:\WINDOWS\Microsoft.NET\Framework\v1.1.4322\ csc.exe). What a pain! Obviously, you don't want to type the full path to compile your code. Another approach is to issue a path command. To do this at the cmd prompt, type path = followed by the full path beginning at C:\ . For example, on the system used for this book, since csc.exe was found at C:\WINDOWS\Microsoft.NET\Framework\v1.1.4322, you would type:

path = C:\WINDOWS\Microsoft.NET\Framework\v1.1.4322

This sets the path for this cmd session only. If you close the cmd prompt window, you have to reissue the path command the next time you run the compiler (and each time you want to run csc).

Changing the System Path Settings

A better approach for setting the path is to use System Properties to make a one-time change to the path. This establishes the path from then on. These changes can be made only when using an Administrator login. If you are using a classroom or lab computer, have an instructor help you with this change. For your home systems, the path can be changed by selecting the following:

A

Start>Control Panel>System>Advanced tab>Environmental Variables> System Variables>Path>Edit

 These steps are specific to the Windows XP operating system. If you are running Windows 2000, you must click Settings before clicking Control Panel.

You should add the path to csc.exe onto the end of the list. Do not simply replace the values found in the Path variable. If you do, some of your other programs may not function properly. Begin by typing a semicolon (;) and follow that with the full path starting at C:\. Figure A-5 illustrates typing a new path string onto the end of the list. Notice the figure shows the semicolon being typed as the separator between what was previously stored in the path's variable value and the new entry that is being typed. The full path string to be typed is shown here.

```
;c:\Windows\Microsoft.Net\Framework\v1.1.4322
```

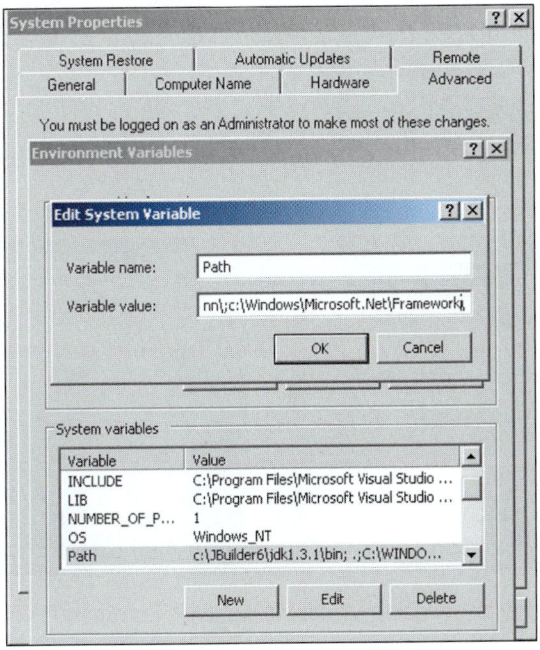

Figure A-5 Adding the path to the environment variables

> On your personal computer system, the path string you add onto the end of the list may be slightly different from that shown in Figure A-5. The typed value must match the location where csc.exe is stored on your system. Remember the path can be found using the Search feature of the operating system.

After you add this path to the existing environment variables, you do not have to type the path command again. If you do not have Visual Studio .NET installed, this setting is saved and is definitely the preferred method for setting up your system to use the SDK.

Compiling Program Statements from the Visual Studio .NET Command Prompt

If you have Visual Studio .NET installed, but decide not to use the Integrated Development Environment, a better alternative for command-line compilation and execution is to use the Visual Studio .NET command-line tools. You could still create the source code using a simple editor such as Notepad. When you are ready to compile, do not open a DOS command window from the **Start>RUN** option. Instead, use one of the Visual Studio .NET tools. This approach offers the advantage of not having to deal with setting any path commands. When you install Visual Studio .NET, the installation includes a tool, which enables you to open a command window with the correct environment variables already set. As shown in Figure A-6, you can open the Visual Studio .NET 2003 command prompt by selecting the following menu items in this order:

Start>All Programs>Microsoft Visual Studio .NET>
Visual Studio .NET Tools>Visual Studio .NET 2003 Command Prompt

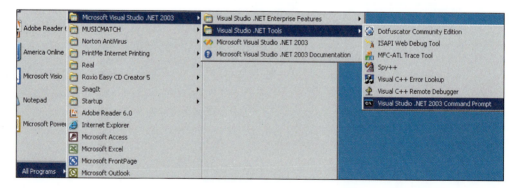

Figure A-6   Opening a command window using Visual Studio .NET Command Prompt Tool

Navigate to the directory in which you stored the source code file. If you created a directory named CSharpProjects, you type cd C:\ CsharpProjects, as shown in Figure A-4. You start the compiler from the command line just as previously presented. Type the program name for the compiler—csc. Then pass in your source code file by entering the filename on the command line, as in the following:

```
csc FirstProgram.cs
```

As noted before, be sure to include the .cs file extension. If you get syntax error messages, go back to the simple editor and modify the source code. After you save the source code, you can try compiling again. When you receive no errors, you are ready to move to the next step.

Executing the Application from the Command Prompt

When there are no syntax errors, a new file is created. This file has the same name as the source code file with one exception: instead of having the source code extension of .cs extension, the object file has an .exe extension.

After you create the object file, you might want to use MyComputer or Windows Explorer to confirm that you actually created the new file.

Move to the directory containing the file, just as you do when compiling, and type the name of the file. It is not necessary to type the .exe extension. Simply type the filename identifier without any file extension as follows:

```
fileName
```

For example, to see the results of the FirstProgram application from the command line, execute the application by typing at the command prompt the name of the file, without any file extension. To run the FirstProgram application, you type:

```
FirstProgram
```

Compiler Options

There are several options that can be used when compiling with a command line. Some programmers use the command line because of the flexibility of its options. Table A-1 includes some of the more commonly used compiler options.

Table A-1   C# command-line compiler options

Compiler Option	Description
/?	Lists all compiler options with a brief description of each one
/doc	Produces an XML document containing the XML comments
/help	Displays a listing of all compiler options with a brief description of each one
/main	Specifies the name of the file (and location) containing the main method
/out	Specifies the name of the output (.exe) file when it should differ from the original source name
/target:exe	Causes the output to be an executable console application
/target:library	Causes the output to be a library file (.dll)
/target:winexe	Causes the output to be an executable Windows application

Each of the above options would be added to the command-line compilation statement. To compile, you type csc followed by the source code file name. Thus to compile a file named testFile.cs and produce a .dll named testFile.dll, you would type the following at the command line:

```
csc /target:library testFile.cs
```

Other Platforms

There are a number of third-party vendors creating C# compilers. Some do not even have to be run on a Windows-based platform. If you develop on a Linux platform, you might consider downloading Mono (*www.go-mono.com/c-sharp.html*). You are encouraged to search the Internet to locate new compilers that may be developed after this book is printed.

Appendix B
Visual Studio Configuration

To increase productivity, you may want to configure the appearance and behavior of the Integrated Development Environment (IDE) for Visual Studio .NET. This appendix presents suggestions for possible settings.

CUSTOMIZING THE DEVELOPMENT ENVIRONMENT

You can use the Options from the toolbar as shown in Figure B-1 to make most useful changes.

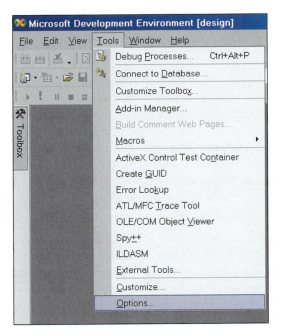

Figure B-1 Using Tools>Options to configure Visual Studio .NET

Environment

After you select **Options**, the first tab shown is Environment. When you select the **Environment** tab, a dialog box is displayed, as shown in Figure B-2.

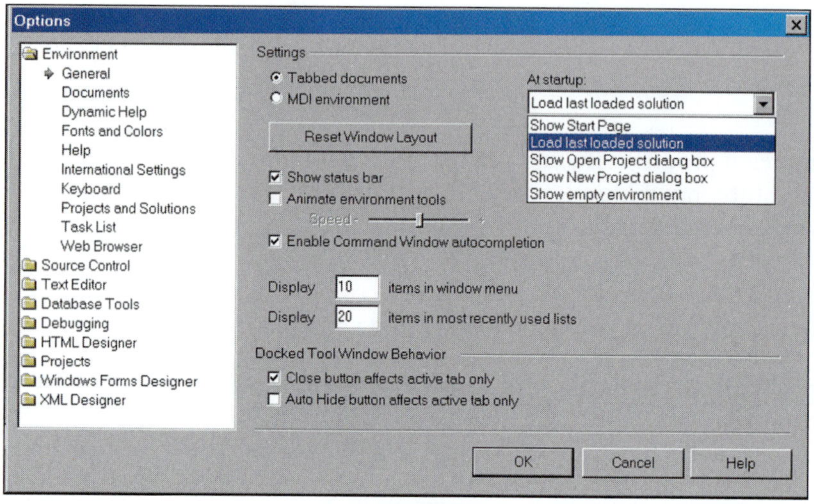

Figure B-2   Environment general options

The first selection you may want to consider is called **Settings**, as shown in Figure B-2. Selecting **Tabbed documents** in the Settings section enables you to see tabs in the workspace window where your code or forms are displayed. This setting is useful for allowing you to switch between multiple open documents—or between Design and Code view. The **MDI** (multiple document interface) **environment** offers the advantage of freeing up the space that the tabs consume. However, if you select the MDI setting, to switch between documents you must either use the menu options or press Ctrl+Tab. Thus, if you create a Windows or Web application in which you might want to move between the Design and Code view, select Tabbed documents.

As shown in Figure B-2, the **General** tab also enables you to identify what to display when you start Visual Studio .NET. Selecting the **Load last loaded solution** option automatically loads the project you were working on the last time you started Visual Studio. This can save you time locating the last application. Another useful option, **Show Open Project dialog box**, displays a dialog box every time you start Visual Studio that prompts you to select the project to open. It displays the list of projects stored in the folder that has been identified as the location where you want to store Visual Studio projects. You identify this location using the **Projects and Solutions** tab as shown in Figure B-3.

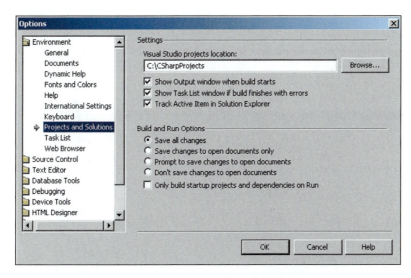

B

Figure B-3   Setting the location for Visual Studio projects

Whether you choose the Show Open Project dialog box or another option from the drop-down list box entitled **At startup**, you should definitely configure the **Visual Studio projects location** setting as shown in Figure B-3.

You are encouraged to review and explore the other settings available under the **Environment** tab. You can change, for example, the size and type of the font for the text editor and dialog boxes. This is useful if you are performing pair programming (working as a team of two) at a computer station.

The **Help** tab enables you to specify whether you use the Help from within Visual Studio, the MSDN quarterly updated documentation, or both. You also have the option within Help of selecting specific External help. When you use one of the options under the Help menu such as Search, selecting the **External help** option automatically opens a separate window. If you select **Internal help**, as opposed to External help, the dialog box for Help is integrated into the current window.

The Documents tab under Environment allows you to select **Auto-load changes** and/or **Allow editing of read-only files**. When you select the Allow editing of read-only files option, you receive a warning when you attempt to save the document. From this same tab (Documents), you can set the **Find and Replace** feature to **Initialize the Find text from the editor**. By checking this feature, the IDE automatically populates the Find what textbox with the string of characters that are highlighted prior to your selecting the Find and Replace option from the Edit menu.

Text Editor

If you do not like the auto-completion IntelliSense feature of Visual Studio, you can turn the feature off under the General Tab for C# at the Text Editor option.

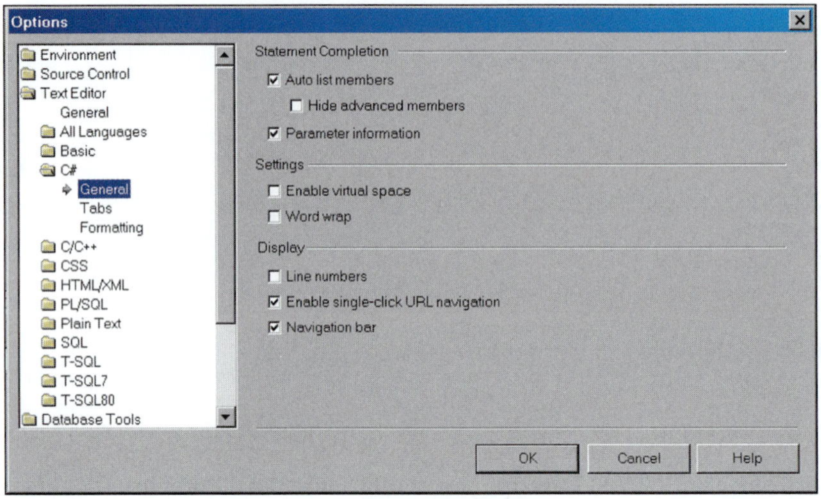

Figure B-4   Text Editor General settings for C#

On the dialog box shown in Figure B-4, you can also set the display to show line numbers and specify whether parameter information is displayed from IntelliSense. When you select **Display Line numbers**, the line numbers are displayed to the left of the source code in the IDE.

The **Tabs** option, which is immediately below the **General** option, enables you to specify the amount of space inserted when a tab or indent is set and whether tabs or spaces are inserted for tabs. This is shown in Figure B-5.

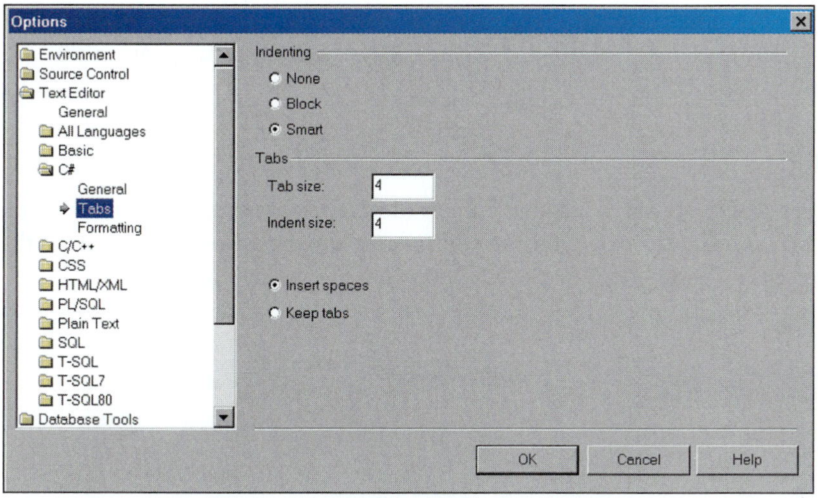

Figure B-5   C# Text Editor Tabs options

As shown in Figure B-5, you can also set **Smart indenting** so that it automatically indents the next line, if a statement doesn't fit on a single line.

Smart indenting does not always work the way you think it should. As the name implies, it tries to be smart and sometimes you have to override it.

As shown in Figure B-6, you can deselect **Leave open braces on the same line as construct**, if you prefer to align your braces in the same column. This is how braces have been displayed in this book.

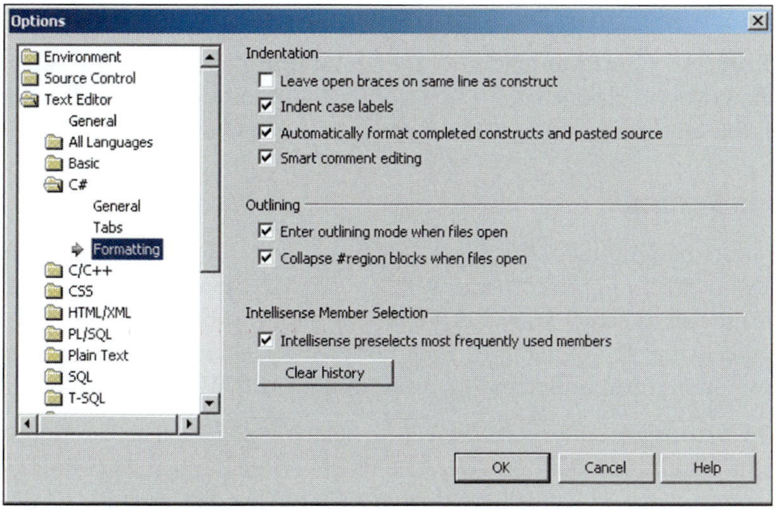

Figure B-6   Formatting settings for C# Text Editing

The other options shown in Figure B-6 are selected to increase productivity in the IDE. Selecting **Indent case labels** and **Smart comment editing** causes the indention to occur automatically.

Debugging

A number of settings can be changed under the **Debugging** option. You will probably want to select the **Color text of current statement and breakpoints** option so that the currently executing code line is displayed when you run the debugger.

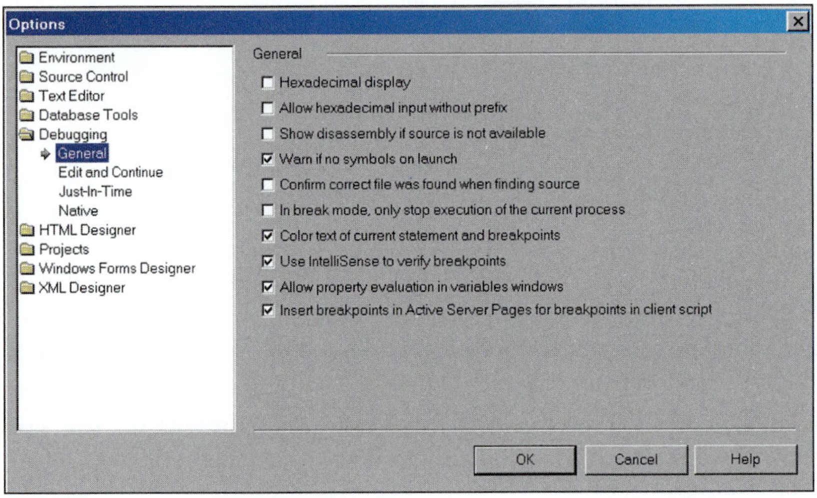

Figure B-7   Debugging settings

Under the **Edit and Continue** option of the **Debugging** tab, selecting **Enable edit and continue** allows you to change your source code while your program is still running, but in break mode. You can edit the code without ending the debug session.

Other Options Settings

Explore the other options under the **Tools>Options** menu. The **HTML Designer** enables you to specify whether you prefer to start Web and HTML pages in Design or HTML Code view. You also specify whether you want to see the grids or not from the HTML Designer tab. You can specify the size of the grids, both horizontally and vertically. You also see both of these last two options (grid or not and size of grid) under the Windows Forms Designer tab.

The **Tools>Customize** option enables you to select which toolbars are displayed in the IDE. Using this option, you not only select the names of the toolbars, but you can also specify which commands are to be included within each toolbar. For example if you choose to display the Standard toolbar, you see icons including Save, Open file, Cut, Copy, and Paste. To add icons to a toolbar, select the button icon and drag it to the location on the desktop where you want it to appear as shown in Figure B-8.

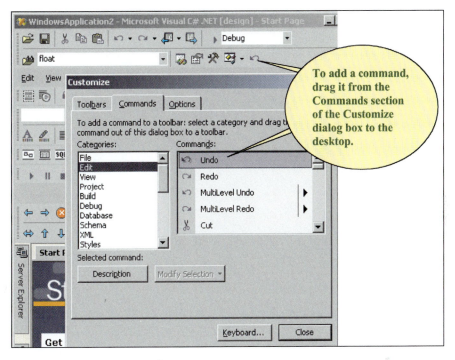

Figure B-8   Customizing the IDE

You remove icons in the same manner. Open the **Tools>Customize** dialog box and drag the icon from the desktop back down to the dialog box.

 Of course, you would not customize the desktop for classroom computer stations since other users may have different preferences. These changes should be reserved for your personal system.

Appendix C
Character Sets

The Unicode standard is a universal character encoding scheme that assigns a unique numeric value, called a code point, to each character used in many of the written languages of the world. Over 65,000 characters can be represented. This appendix shows a subset of the characters commonly used with the English language. The ASCII (American Standard Code for Information Exchange) character set corresponds to the first 128 characters of the Unicode character set. Thus, the table that follows shows many of the ASCII and Unicode representations. C# and other .NET-supported languages use the Unicode standard.

Table C-1

	0	1	2	3	4	5	6	7	8	9
0	Null							Bell	Backspace	Horizontal tab
1	Line feed	Vertical tab	Form feed	Carriage return						
2					Cancel			Escape		
3			(space)	!	"	#	$	%	&	'
4	(	)	*	+	,	-	.	/	0	1
5	2	3	4	5	6	7	8	9	:	;
6	<	=	>	?	@	A	B	C	D	E
7	F	G	H	I	J	K	L	M	N	O
8	P	Q	R	S	T	U	V	W	X	Y
9	Z	[	\	]	^	_	'	a	b	c
10	d	e	f	g	h	i	j	k	l	m
11	n	o	p	q	r	s	t	u	v	w
12	x	y	z	{			}	~	Del		

The numbers in the first column represent the first digit for the decimal value. That value is concatenated to the numbers found in row 1 to form the decimal equivalent for that symbol in ASCII and Unicode. For example, the lowercase "s" is located in the row labeled 11 and in the column labeled 5. Its code value is 115. A subset of the characters is shown in the table.

The Unicode standard makes it easier to develop applications that can be implemented worldwide. Developers do not have to keep up with which coding schema is used—because it is a worldwide standard. For additional information, see "The Unicode Standard" at *www.unicode.org*.

Operator Precedence

When an expression has multiple operations to be evaluated, the order of evaluation of the operators is determined by the precedence and associativity of the operators used in the expression. Most operators are left-associative—meaning the operations are performed from left to right. All binary operators are left-associative. The assignment operators and conditional operators are right-associative. The following table shows the C# operators by category of precedence. The operators are shown from highest to lowest precedence.

Table D-1

Category	Example Operators
Primary	[] () x++ x-- new typeof
Unary	+ - ! ++x --x (cast)
Multiplicative	* / %
Additive	+ -
Shift	<< >>
Relational and type testing	< > <= >= is as
Equality	== =!
Logical AND	&
Logical XOR	^
Logical OR	|
Conditional AND	&&
Conditional OR	||
Conditional	?:
Assignment	= *= /= %= += -= <<= >>= &= ^= |=

Operators have equal precedence within the category. Thus in the expression `answer = anumber + val1 * val2 / 7`, the order of operations would be *, /, +, and =.

C# Keywords

This appendix lists the reserved words of C#. Each has a special meaning associated to it. Notice that all keywords begin with a lowercase letter.

abstract	as	base	bool	break	byte
case	catch	char	checked	class	const
continue	decimal	default	delegate	do	double
else	enum	event	explicit	extern	false
finally	fixed	float	for	foreach	goto
if	implicit	in	int	interface	internal
is	lock	long	namespace	new	null
object	operator	out	override	params	private
protected	public	readonly	ref	return	sbyte
sealed	short	sizeof	stackalloc	static	string
struct	switch	this	throw	true	try
typeof	uint	ulong	unchecked	unsafe	ushort
using	virtual	volatile	void	while	

Glossary

abstract method — A method that includes no implementation details (no method body) in the declaration. Abstract method declarations are only permitted in abstract classes.

abstract modifier keyword — When used with a class, the class can only be used as the base class from which other classes are derived. No objects can be instantiated of an abstract class. Also see abstract method.

abstraction — The act of generalizing or thinking about an object in general terms. Through abstraction, data members and behaviors of a class are identified.

accumulation — An operation commonly found in applications that need to add together the values that a single variable holds. A variable initialized to zero is used to hold the running total. For example, to determine the average of a set of values, the values are normally added to an accumulator variable and divided by the number of entries.

Active Server Pages (ASP) — A Microsoft programming model for creating dynamic Web pages. Using the traditional or classic Active Server Pages (ASP) model, code written in a scripting language, such as JavaScript or VBScript, is added to the HTML file.

actual arguments — The actual data that is sent to a method. Actual argument refers to the variable or literal that is placed inside the parenthesis in the method call. Sometimes referred to as actual parameters.

aggregation — See containment.

algorithm — A clear, unambiguous, step-by-step process for solving a problem. These steps are expressed completely and precisely so that all details are included.

American Standard Code for Information Interchange (ASCII) — A subset of Unicode, in which the first 128 characters correspond to the Unicode character set. ASCII consists of the alphabet for the English language, plus numbers and symbols.

application software — Programs developed to perform a specific task. A word processor, such as Microsoft Word, is an example of application software.

argument — The data included inside the parenthesis during a method call. Parameter often refers to items appearing in the heading of the method; argument refers to the data appearing in the call to the method.

array — A data structure that allows multiple values to be stored under a single identifier.

array of array — See ragged array.

ASCII — See American Standard Code for Information Interchange.

ASP — See Active Server Pages.

ASP server controls — See server controls.

ASP.NET — The Microsoft programming framework that enables the creation of applications that run on a Web server and delivers functionality through a browser, such as Internet Explorer.

assembler — Software that converts the assembly programming language, which is a low-level programming language, into machine code.

assignment operator — The equals symbol (=) is used to perform a compile-time initialization or make an assignment. The value of the expression on the right side of the assignment operator (=) is determined, and then that value is assigned to the variable on the left side of the assignment operator (=).

attribute — The data member or field of the class. For example, one attribute of a Student class is studentNumber.

auxiliary storage — Nonvolatile, permanent memory that can hold data for long periods, even when there is no power to the system. Also called secondary storage.

base class — A class from which other classes can inherit characteristics. The base class is sometimes called the super or parent class. The ultimate base class of all classes in C# is Object.

base type — The data type of the object. The type can be one of the predefined types such as int or string, a user-defined class that you create, or some other .NET class. All data values placed in an array must be of the same base type.

basic programming constructs — General-purpose programming languages provide three categories of programming statements (simple sequence, iteration, and selection). These categories are referred to as the basic programming constructs.

behavior — A process data goes through. The class definition uses methods to define the behavior of the data.

beta version — A working version of an application that has not been fully tested and may still contain bugs or errors.

binary operator — An operator in C# that requires two operands such as for the operators * or /. There must be divisor and dividend operands with the / operator.

block comment — See multi-line comment.

bug — An error in a software program that is usually caused by a programmer mistake.

call by value — The value of an argument that appears in the method call is copied and stored in a separate, different, memory location.

Camel case — A naming convention used for variable and object identifiers in C#. The first letter of the identifier is lowercase and the first letter of each subsequent concatenated word is capitalized (i.e., amountDue). Also called Hungarian notation.

case statement — See switch statement.

casting — Casting makes a variable temporarily behave as if it were a different type.

catch block — Code that deals with a problem (the exception handler) is placed in a catch block, which is also called a catch clause.

catch clause — See catch block.

central processing unit (CPU) — The brain of the computer. Housed inside the system unit on a silicon chip, it is the most important hardware element.

checked exception — In some languages, in order to use certain constructs, they must be enclosed inside a try…catch block—checking for a specific type of exception to be thrown. All file interactions in Java are treated as checked exceptions. Thus, file interactions in Java must be surrounded by a try…catch block. C# does not have any checked exceptions.

class — A term denoting the encapsulation of data and behaviors into a single package or unit. Class is the template from which many objects are instantiated.

client application — A client application instantiates objects of classes defined elsewhere or uses components that were previously defined and stored as .dlls. Many client applications can make use of these same classes and components.

client-server relationship — In a client-server relationship, the client requests a Web page; the server gets it ready by executing the scripts inside the HTML document; and then the client sees the result in the form of an HTML document.

client-side controls — See HTML controls.

client-side scripts — Code that is embedded in the HTML document. It is executed on the client computer normally in a Web browser.

CLR — See Common Language Runtime.

code-behind file — When you build an ASP.NET Web application, two separate files are created for the user interface. The file storing the logic is referred to as the code-behind file.

Common Language Runtime (CLR) — The .NET run-time environment that enables the code to be compiled and executed. The CLR is also responsible for loading predefined .NET classes into a program and performing just-in-time (JIT) compilation.

Compact Framework Class Library (FCL) — A new smaller Framework class library that is included as part of Visual Studio .NET 2003 for use with mobile and smart devices such as PDAs, tablets, and cell phones.

compiler — Software that examines an entire program and translates the source code statements written in a programming language such as C# into machine-readable format.

compile-time initialization — Compile time initialization occurs when a variable is declared or created and at the same time initialized to a value.

conditional expression — An expression that produces a Boolean result. Also known as the test condition or simply the test.

conditional logical operators — C# uses two ampersands (&&) and two pipes (||) to represent AND and OR respectively. These two operators are called the conditional logical operators.

conditional operator — See ternary operator.

constant — A data item defined and initialized to keep the same value throughout the life of the program.

containment — Classes can have a "has a" relationship in which a single class is defined to have instances of other class types. This is a concept called containment or aggregation.

controls — Controls are objects that can display and respond to user interactions, such as button clicks.

counter-controlled loop — Used when the loop should be executed a specified number of times. With a counter-controlled loop, a variable simulating a counter is used as the loop control variable to keep track of the number of iterations.

data — The raw facts or the basic numbers and characters that are manipulated to produce useful information.

data provider — Data providers are used for connecting to a database, executing commands, and retrieving results. Each data provider includes a collection of classes. .NET includes data providers for SQL server, OLE DB (Access), ODBC, and Oracle.

decimal value type — A value type appropriate for storing monetary data items because it allows both integral (whole) numbers and a fractional portion.

declare a variable — The act of allocating memory for a data item in a program. To declare a variable you select an identifier and determine what type of data will appear in the memory cell.

definition — The definition of a method includes the heading and the body of the method, which are enclosed in curly braces.

delegates — Delegates are special types of .NET classes whose instances store references (addresses) to methods as opposed to storing actual data.

derived — When a class is derived from another class, the new class inherits all the functionality of the base class.

design method — An approach used by programmers to plan and structure computer programs. Procedural and object-oriented design methodologies are the two most commonly used design methods.

desk check — The use of sample data to verify programming algorithms by mimicking or walking through each step the computer will take to solve the algorithm.

dimension an array — To instantiate an array by indicating how many elements to allocate.

distributed computing — Computing that takes place when applications are spread over more than one computer system.

divide and conquer design — See top-down design.

domain — A range of the values that a data item can store. For example, the domain of letterGrades awarded in most college courses is 'A' through 'D', and 'F'.

dynamic binding — The determination of which method to call is done at execution time or runtime, not during the compile phase. The decision about which method to call is based on what type of data is sent as the argument.

dynamic Web pages — Web pages that involve processing in addition to rendering the formatting of HTML tags.

dynamic Web site — Web pages that enable users to interact and see the results of their interactions.

element — An individual variable in an array is called an element of the array and is accessed through an index. Elements in an array are sometimes referred to as indexed or subscripted variables.

empty bodied loop — A loop that has no statements to be performed. Placing the semicolon at the end of a conditional expression produces a loop that has no body, or an empty bodied loop.

emulator — A device that simulates the operation of some type of hardware, such as a personal digital assistant (PDA).

encapsulate — Used in object-oriented programming, the act of combining the attributes and behaviors (characteristics and actions) of data to form a class.

encapsulation — One of the four major concepts that form the basis of an object-oriented programming language. With encapsulation, the language provides support for packaging data attributes and behaviors into a single unit, thus hiding implementation details.

entity — Classes define entities. An entity is usually associated with a person, place, or thing; it is normally a noun. Through defining a class, the entity is described in terms of its current state and behaviors.

equality operator — Two equal symbol characters (==) used as part of a conditional expression for comparing operands. Char and `string` operands are compared using the dictionary order. No space is inserted between the two equal symbols.

error — Programs may experience an error caused by a user action that may cause an exception to be thrown. Entering the wrong type of data from the keyboard is an example of a common error.

event — An event is a notification from the operating system that an action, such as the user clicking the mouse or pressing a key, has occurred.

event firing — When a user clicks a button, an event is fired that causes the operating system to send a message to a program indicating that a registered event has occurred.

event handler — Event handlers are methods that define what should happen when an event such as a mouse click on a button or a click on the keyboard occurs.

event wiring — Associating a method in a program to an event, such as the user clicking a button. The method is automatically called when the event occurs.

event-driven model — The model used by Windows and Web applications wherein, once the program is executed, it sits in a process loop waiting for an event, such as mouse clicks, to occur.

exception — An unexpected condition in a computer program that occurs infrequently and is usually associated with error conditions that cause abnormal terminations if they are not handled.

exception handler — A block of code that is executed when an exception occurs.

explicit type coercion — Forcing a variable to be a different type. Explicit type coercion is performed using casting in C#. For example to store only the integer portion of the following value, an explicit coercion would take the form: int answer = (int) 53.77;

Extensible Markup Language (XML) — A markup language that provides a format for describing data using tags similar to HTML tags.

fall through — A feature associated with switch statements in which the break statement(s) are optional. This feature is found in many programming languages—but not in C#. C# enforces a "no fall through" rule with switch statements. You are not allowed to leave off a break and fall through executing code from more than one case. C# requires the break for any case that has an executable statement(s).

flag-controlled loop — A loop that uses a Boolean variable in the conditional expression to control the loop. The variable is initialized to a value before entering the loop. When a condition changes, the variable is changed. The next test of the conditional expression causes the loop to terminate.

floating-point value — One of the types of numbers in C#. A floating-point value can contain a fractional portion. C# supports two types of floating-point values: `float` and `double`.

formal parameter — The paired group(s) of identifier and type that appears in the heading of a method.

general-purpose computer systems — Electronic devices that process data under the control of a program.

generic catch — Omitting an argument list following the catch keyword creates a generic catch clause. With no specific exception type listed, any exception that is thrown is handled by executing the code within that catch block.

graphical user interface (GUI) — A graphical user interface (GUI) includes the menus, buttons, pictures, and text that enable users to interact with applications.

GUI — See graphical user interface.

hardware — The physical devices of a computer system that you can touch.

HCI — See human-computer interaction.

heading — The first line of a method is called the heading of the method. It includes the visibility modifier, return type, and the identifier with the parameter list enclosed in parentheses.

hexadecimal numbering system — The Base 16 system uses powers of 16 and the symbols 0-9 and A-F.

high-level programming language — A modern programming language that is designed to be easy to read and write because it is written in English-like statements. High level programming languages include C#, Visual Basic, FORTRAN, Pascal, C++, Java, and J#.

HTML — See Hypertext Markup Language.

HTML controls — Controls added to a Web page that are rendered by the browser when the page is displayed. When added to a Web page, they map straight to HTML formatting tags. HTML controls are also called client-side controls.

HTML server controls — Pure HTML controls that are converted to server controls so that the server has access to the code. The attribute runat = "server" is added to the element when it is converted. This is done in Visual Studio by right-mouse clicking on the HTML control while in the Web Forms Designer.

human–computer interaction (HCI) — A field of research that concentrates on the design and implementation of interactive computing systems for human use.

Hungarian notation — See Camel case.

Hypertext Markup Language (HTML) — HTML tags tell the browser how to display data in different formats, for example in bold or italics or in different fonts or font sizes.

IDE — See Integrated Development Environment.

identifiers — The names of elements that appear in a program, such as the names of data items, variables, objects, classes or methods. Some identifiers are predefined; others are user defined.

if statement — The selection statement, classified as one-way, two-way, or nested, that is used in combination with a conditional expression to facilitate specifying alternate paths based on the result of the conditional expression.

IL — See Intermediate Language.

ILDASM — See Intermediate Language Disassembler.

immutable — Objects of the string class store an immutable series of characters. They are considered immutable because the value given to a string cannot be modified.

implicit type coercion — Automatic conversion, without using casting, from one type to another. C# includes a number of built-in implicit conversions. Normally conversion occurs from less precise to more precise data types. For example, if a binary operation involves a double and an int, implicit type coercion is performed so that both operands are treated as double.

increment/decrement operator — The operator used for the common arithmetic operation of adding or subtracting the number one (1) to or from a memory location. To add or subtract one from an operand, place either two plus (++) or two minus symbols (—) before or after the identifier. Both are considered binary operators.

indefinite loop — See sentinel-controlled loop.

index — The index, also called the subscript of an array, references the location of the variable relative to the first element in the array. In C#, the index of the first element is always 0.

indexed variable — See element.

infinite loop — A loop that has no provisions for termination. Placing a semicolon at the end of the conditional expression can create an infinite loop situation.

inheritance — The concept of defining subclasses of data objects that share some or all of the parent's class characteristics.

instance — An object is an instance of a class.

instantiate — To create an instance of a class. If you define a template (blueprint) for a class (house), you instantiate the class when you create an object (construct the building).

integer (int) — One of the types of numbers in C#. A whole number, between a certain range of values that contains no decimal point and can be positive or negative.

Integrated Development Environment (IDE) — A program environment, such as Visual Studio .NET, in which you type your source code statements, debug, compile and run your application. IDEs include a number of useful development tools: IntelliSense (pop-up windows with completion options); color coding of different program sections; and online help and documentation.

IntelliSense — A feature of the Integrated Development Environment (IDE) that attempts to sense what you are going to type before you type it. When the IntelliSense window pops up, you can quickly select from the pull-down menu without having to complete the typing.

interface — The interface is the front end of a program. It is the visual image you see when you run a program, and it allows users to interact with programs.

interface class — An interface class is totally abstract. Interfaces contain no implementation details for any of their members; all their members are considered abstract. Classes that implement the interface must define details for all of the interface's methods.

Intermediate Language (IL) — When no syntax errors are found during compilation, .NET source code is converted into the Intermediate Language (IL). All languages targeting the .NET platform compile into an IL. IL code must be compiled a second time before results are seen.

Intermediate Language Disassembler (ILDASM) — Intermediate Language Disassembler (ILDASM) is a developer tool used for parsing machine-readable .exe and .dll files into human-readable format.

interpreter — Software that checks computer programs line-by-line for rule violations before translating them into machine-readable format.

iteration structure — A looping structure in C#. Iteration enables you to identify and block together one or more statements to be repeated based on a predetermined condition. Also called repetition.

iterative approach — An approach used by programmers, which calls for frequent return to the design and/or analysis phases to make modifications as a program is being developed.

jagged array — See ragged array.

JavaScript — A scripting language that Web developers use to create interactive Web sites. The script is embedded in the file that contains the HTML tags.

JIT — See just-in-time.

JITer — The Common Language Runtime tool used for a just-in-time compilation, which converts the IL code to CPU specific code.

JScript — The Microsoft implementation of JavaScript.

jump statement — A statement that changes the sequential order of statement execution by transferring control to a different point in the program. The break statement is one jump statement. When encountered inside a switch statement, control is redirected to the statement on the outside of the switch block.

just-in-time (JIT) — The second compilation. JIT converts the intermediate language code into the platform's native code.

keywords — In C# keywords are predefined reserved identifiers that have specially defined meanings for the compiler.

left-associative — Left-associative actions in an expression are performed from left to right. All binary operators, except the equality operators and the conditional operator (?:) are left-associative.

length of an array — The number of elements of an array is called the length or size of the array.

lining up — When programming a nested if…else statement, it is important to know which else matches which if statement. The rule for lining up, or matching else is that an else goes with the closest previous if that does not have its own else.

literal — The numbers, characters, and combinations of characters used in a program. They can be assigned to a variable or used in an expression and their values stay constant. For example, 5 is a numeric literal, 'A' is a character literal, and "Bob" is a string literal.

logic error — An error in programs that causes an abnormal termination of a program or produces incorrect results.

logical negation operator — The exclamation symbol (!) is a logical negation operator. It is a unary operator that negates its operand and is called the NOT operator. It returns true when operand1 is false. It returns false when operand1 is true.

logical operators — The logical operators in C# are (&),(&&),(|),(||), and (!).

loop condition — The conditional expression or the logical condition to be tested. A loop condition is enclosed in parentheses and is similar to the expressions used for selection statements.

loop control variable — Used with a counter-controlled loop. A loop control variable is a variable that simulates a counter.

looping — See iteration.

machine language — Code that can be read by a computer. Also called native code.

main memory — See random-access memory.

matching — See lining up.

methodology — A plan or approach for solving computer-related problems.

methods — How behaviors are implemented in C#. Similar to functions found in other languages.

mixed mode expression — When an expression has operands of different types, the statement is considered a mixed mode expression.

multicast delegate — A delegate is wired to more than one method. When the multicast delegate is used, multiple methods are called automatically, one after the other. The (+=) and (−=) operators are used to add or remove methods to and from the delegate chain or invocation list. One requirement for multicast delegates is that the return type be void.

multi-line comment — A remark in code that explains its function. A forward slash followed by an asterisk (/*) marks the beginning of a multi-line comment, and the opposite pattern (*/) marks the end. Also called a block comment.

mutator — A special method used to change the current state or value of an object member's data. A mutator normally is written to include one parameter that represents the new value a data member should have. Also known as a setter. In C#, having properties, reduces the need for mutators.

mutually exclusive set of controls — A set of controls of which only one can be selected at a time. Radio buttons are often included in this category.

native code — See machine language.

nested if statement — See nested if...else statement.

nested if...else statement — When you place an if statement as the statement to be executed within an if statement, you create a nested if...else statement. If no else is included the construct is referred to as a nested if statement.

not equal operator — An exclamation point followed by a single equal symbol (!=) represents not equal. No space is embedded between the exclamation point and equal symbol.

NOT operator — See logical negation operator.

null (empty) statement body — When you place a semicolon at the end of a parenthesized expression, such as the expression used with a loop or selection statement, you are creating a null (empty) statement body.

object-oriented analysis, design, and programming — A programming methodology that focuses on determining the objects to be manipulated rather than the processes or logic required to manipulate the data.

object-oriented approach — An approach to programming that focuses on determining the data characteristics and the methods or behaviors that operate on the data.

object-oriented programming (OOP) language — For a language to be considered a true object-oriented programming (OOP) language, it must support the following four major concepts, which C# and the .NET platform embrace: abstraction, encapsulation, inheritance, and polymorphism.

Octal numbering system — The Base 8 system that uses powers of eight with symbols 0 through 7.

off-by-one error — A common programmer error in which a loop body is performed one too many or one too few times.

one-way selection statement — A one-way selection statement is used when a single expression needs to be tested. When the result of the expression is true, additional processing is performed.

OOP — See object-oriented programming.

operating system — The system software that is loaded when a computer is powered on and that oversees and coordinates the resources on a computer. Examples of operating systems include Windows XP, Windows NT, and UNIX.

order of operations — The order in which calculations are performed.

overloaded methods — Multiple methods with the same name, but each method has a different number or type of parameter.

overloaded operator — The following are overloaded operators: (+), (==), and (!=) They behave differently based on the type of operands they receive.

override keyword — A keyword that can be added to the method heading to allow a method to provide a new implementation (method body) of a method inherited from a base class.

page validation — Every control field on the page that has a validation control is checked when page validation occurs to determine whether it passes the validation rules. By default page validation occurs when Click events are fired.

parameter — The paired data type and identifier that appears in the heading of the method.

parameter array — When a method uses the `params` modifier, the parameter is considered a parameter array. It is used to indicate that the number of arguments to the method may vary.

parent class — See base class.

Pascal case — A naming convention used for class, method, namespace, and property identifiers. With Pascal case, the first letter in the identifier and the first letters of each subsequent concatenated word are capitalized.

peripheral devices — The input (keyboard, mouse, disk drive) and output devices (monitor, printer, disk drive) of a computer system.

polymorphism — The ability of classes to provide different implementations of methods based on what type of argument is used for the call. Polymorphism is one of the four major concepts that form the basis of an object-oriented programming language.

precedence of the operators — The order in which the individual operators are evaluated when an expression contains multiple operators.

preprocessor directive — Indicates that an action should be taken before processing. Preprocessor directives are often associated with conditionally skipping sections of source files or reporting certain types of errors. C# does not actually perform a pre-process.

pretest loop — A conditional expression is tested before any of the statements in the body of the loop are performed. If the conditional expression evaluates to false, the statement(s) in the body of the loop is (are) never performed. The while and for statements are both pretest types of loops.

primary storage — The internal or main memory of a computer system.

prime the read — The act of inputting a value before going into the body of the loop.

primitive — The basic set of built-in data types. The built-in data types in C# are implemented as classes.

procedural programming — A programming approach that is process oriented and focuses on the processes that data undergoes from input until meaningful output. This approach is effective for small, stand-alone applications.

program — A set of instructions that tells the computer exactly what to do. Also referred to as software.

programming language — A set of syntactical and semantic rules for how to write computer instructions.

prototype — A mock-up of screens depicting the look of the final output of a program.

pseudocode — A tool used during the programming design stage to develop an algorithm. As the name implies, with pseudocode, steps are written in "pseudo" or approximate code format, which looks like English statements.

ragged array — A multi-dimensional array that has a different number of columns in one or more rows. Jagged, or ragged arrays, differ from rectangular arrays in that rectangular arrays always have a rectangular shape, like a table. Jagged arrays are called "arrays of arrays." One row might have five columns; another row 50 columns.

raise an exception — To throw an exception. When a program encounters an error such as division by zero during runtime, and the program cannot recover from the error, it raises or throws an exception.

RAM — See random-access memory.

random-access memory (RAM) — The device that holds a computer's instructions and data. Also commonly called main memory.

rectangular two-dimensional array — A two-dimensional array visualized as a table divided into rows and columns. Much like a spreadsheet in which the rows and columns intersect, data is stored in individual cells.

relational operators — Relational operators allow you to test variables to see if one is greater or less than another variable or value. The symbols used for relational operators are >, <, >= and <=.

render — To convert a Web page from HTML to a formatted page on the client computer that requested the page.

repetition — See iteration structure.

right-associative — Actions in an expression that are performed from right to left. The assignment operators (such as =, +=, *=) and conditional operator (?:) are right-associative. All other binary operators are left-associative.

round trip to the server — Each request to view a Web page requires a round trip to the server on which the page is stored. The user requests the page via Hypertext Transfer Protocol by typing the Web address into a Web browser. That request is forwarded to the Web server on which the page is stored. The page is then sent back as a Hypertext Markup Language document where it is rendered (converted from HTML) to a formatted page on the client computer that requested the page.

row major language — Languages that store data from two-dimensional arrays by row in contiguous memory locations. All elements from row 0 are placed in memory first followed by all elements from row 1, and so on.

scope — Scope refers to the region in the program in which a variable exists. For example, if a variable is declared in a method, it can be used in that method only. It is out of scope in other methods.

secondary storage — See auxiliary storage.

selection statement — A statement used for decision making that allows you to deviate from the sequential path laid out by a simple sequence and perform instead different statements based on the value of an expression.

selector — With the `switch` statement, this is the expression enclosed inside the parenthesis. It follows the word "switch." Its value determines, or selects, which of the cases is executed.

semantic meaning — The meaning of a programming instruction statement rather than the rules for how it should be written.

sentinel value — A value used to terminate a loop. It should be an extreme or dummy value that should not be processed, such as a negative value when only positive scores are to be processed.

sentinel-controlled loop — A type of loop that is terminated by entering or encountering a sentinel value. Sentinel-controlled loops are often used for inputting data when you do not know the exact number of values to be entered.

server controls — Controls that are treated as objects, complete with data, behaviors, and properties. The Web server has access to these controls. Also referred to as Web controls, Web Forms server controls, ASP server controls, or simply Web Forms controls.

server-side scripts — Code that requires processing to be performed at the server level before a Web page can be delivered.

setter — See mutator.

short-circuit evaluation — With short-circuit evaluation, evaluation of second and subsequent expressions is performed only when necessary. As soon as the value of the entire expression is known, evaluation stops. For example, in a conditional expression combined using (&&), when the first expression evaluates to false, there is no need to evaluate the second expression.

short-circuiting logical operators — Operators that enable the minimal execution of code to produce the final result. The logical and (&&) and or (||) operators are the short-circuiting logical operators in C#.

signature — The name of the method, modifiers, and the types of its formal parameters. Differs from the method heading in that the heading also includes the return type for the method and identifiers for the data type.

Simple Object Access Protocol (SOAP) — Used for communicating with XML Web services. An XML-based protocol that encapsulates method calls (and return results) into XML statements so they can be sent via HTTP.

simple sequence — One of the three basic programming constructs that causes sequential execution of programming statements. Execution begins with the first statement and continues until the end of the method or until another type of construct (loop or selection) is encountered.

single entry and single exit guideline — Guidelines for providing only one way to enter and exit loops, selection statements, and methods. You violate the single entry and single exit guideline when you use break and continue statements within the loop body or when you write a method that has more than one return statement inside the method body.

single-line comment — A remark in code that explains its function. Two forward slashes (//) are used to mark the beginning of a single-line comment; the comment is terminated at the end of the current line when the Enter key is pressed.

size of an array — See length of an array.

SOAP — See Simple Object Access Protocol.

SOAP request — A request for a Web service method.

SOAP response — When a Web server that hosts a Web service receives a SOAP message, it translates the SOAP method call into its own language, performs the processing needed, and generates a return value. The return value is a SOAP message (called a SOAP response).

software — Computer programs or instructions that perform a task or manage the functions of a computer.

source code — Program statements written using a programming language, such as C#.

stack trace — A listing of all the methods that are in an execution chain when an exception is thrown.

state-controlled loop — A variable is initialized to some value before entering the loop. When a condition changes, the variable is changed. The next test of the conditional expression causes the loop to terminate. A state-controlled loop is similar to a sentinel-controlled loop, and is sometimes called flag-controlled loop.

stateless — A stateless Web page does not retain its values from one trip to the Web server to the next.

static Web page — A Web pages that does not require any processing on the client computer or by a Web server. It is precreated, resides on the server's hard drive, and basically is delivered as an HTML document.

stepwise refinement — See top-down design.

Structured English — A tool used during the programming design stage to develop an algorithm using a mixture of English and code statements.

subscript — See index.

subscripted variable — See element.

super class — See base class.

switch statement — The `switch` statement is considered a multiple selection structure. The `switch` statement allows you to perform a large number of alternatives based on the value of a single variable. This variable or expression must evaluate to an integral or `string` value. It cannot be used with a `double`, `decimal`, or `float` variables. But is appropriate for `short`, `int`, `long`, `char`, and `string` data types. Also called a `case` statement.

syntax — Rules for writing programs.

ternary operator — A ternary operator consists of a question mark and a colon (? :) and provides a way to express a simple `if...else` selection statement. Also called the conditional operator.

test condition — See conditional expression.

test plan — The strategy devised to test code. Usually includes plans for testing extreme values, identifying possible problem cases, and ensuring that these cases are tested.

the test — See conditional expression.

throw an exception — See raise an exception.

throw back — To send an exception backwards through the call chain until a method is found that can handle the exception or until it reaches the operating system, which halts the program execution.

top-down design — A design methodology that divides a problem into a number of sub-problems. Each sub-problem is then further subdivided into smaller units until the method is manageable. Also called divide and conquer approach or step-wise refinement.

truncate — To chop off the fractional part of a number. For example, if the number 3.87 is placed in an integer variable, the integer can only hold the whole number portion; thus, .87 is truncated and 3 is stored in the variable.

two-way if statement — An `if` statement with the `else` portion included. With a two-way `if` statement, either the true statement(s) following the `if` is (are) executed or the false statement(s) following the `else`, but not both.

UDDI — See Universal Description, Discovery and Integration.

unary operator — An operator that requires a single operand. Examples in C# are the (++) and (−−) operators that increment and decrement by one.

unhandled exception — When a computer program runs and encounters an error it cannot handle, it raises an exception. If none of the methods includes code to handle the error, the common language runtime handles the exception by halting the entire application. This type of exception is called an unhandled exception.

Unicode — The character set used by programmers of C#. The Unicode character set uses 16 bits to represent a character; thus, 2^{16} or 65,536 unique characters can be represented.

Universal Description, Discovery and Integration (UDDI) — A directory listing of Web services. The UDDI uses XML grammar to publish information about the Web services including the URL location and the functionality of the Web service in terms of what methods it has available.

universal resource locator (URL) — An address on the Internet.

uppercase — One of three .NET conventions for naming identifiers. All uppercase characters are used for the names of constant literals and for identifiers that consist of two or fewer letters.

URL — See universal resource locator.

validation controls — Controls that can be added to a Web page that enable user input to be validated or checked by the server to ensure that the information entered is valid or is in the right format.

value type — A fundamental data type of the C# language that is copied when passed as an argument to a method. Can include built-in floating and integral types or user-defined types.

variable — The representation of an area in the computer memory in which a value of a particular data type can be stored.

VBScript — A scripting language used to add additional functionality to Web pages beyond what HTML formatting tags do. Used with traditional ASP applications. VBScript is a subset of Microsoft Visual Basic 6.0.

verbatim string literal — By preceding a string literal with the at symbol (@), the characters are interpreted exactly as they are typed. Using @-quoted string literals eliminates the need of including an extra backslash before the backslash when it is part of the string.

Visual Studio .NET — A suite of products that includes several programming languages, including C# along with a large collection of development and debugging tools.

Web application — A collection of one or more related files or components stored on a Web server. Web applications are also called Web sites.

Web controls — See server controls.

Web Forms — A tool of ASP.NET technology that enables the building of programmable Web pages that serve as a user interface for Web applications.

Web Forms controls — See server controls.

Web Forms server controls — See server controls.

Web server — Software that hosts or delivers a Web application. The hardware on which the Web server software is loaded is often called a Web server, but it is the software that makes the equipment special and thus enables the computer to be called a server.

Web Service Definition Language (WSDL) — A language written in XML grammar that describes a Web service. It defines how an XML Web service behaves and details how client applications can interact with the service.

Web services — Applications that enable you to exchange data that may be different formats from one computer to another over the Internet or an intranet.

Web site — See Web application.

wrap — Associating a delegate to one or more methods, so that when a delegate is used, the method(s) are automatically called.

WSDL — See Web Service Definition Language.

WYSIWYG — What you see is what you get.

XML — See Extensible Markup Language.

Index